About Business and Computers

Richard D. Jones, Ph.D.
New York State Department of Education

Barbara W. Williams
Elizabeth, New Jersey, Public Schools

In Collaboration With
Benedict Kruse

West Publishing Company
St. Paul   New York   Los Angeles   San Francisco

Production: i/e, inc.
Composition: Freedmen's Organization
Text Design: John Banner
Cover Art: Jack Takeshita

Printed in the United States of America
96 95 94 93 92 91 90 89   8 7 6 5 4 3 2 1 0

Library of Congress Cataloging-in-Publication Data

Jones, Richard D., 1947–
  About business and computers.

  Includes index.
  1. Business—Data processing—Vocational guidance. 2. Business
education. 3. Vocational qualifications.
I. Williams, Barbara W. II. Title.
HF5548.2.J565 1990   650′.028′5   89-5298
ISBN 0-314-51368-X

Contents

COURTESY OF TRANSWORLD AIRLINES

PART II

Preface

WELCOME TO TRANSACTIONLAND!

Transactionland is where people do business. Transaction-land is where there are shortages of qualified workers. Transactionland is where employers offer challenging careers and rewarding pay rates.

How do you get to Transactionland? What are the costs of admission?

This book addresses those questions. Transaction-land, of course, is imaginary. It is a place that takes in the world of business and its opportunities. Success in the world of business is not automatic. To gain admission, people have to prepare themselves.

Certain skills and knowledge are necessary. These skill and knowledge requirements change as the society served by businesspeople develops. Dramatic examples abound:

- There were times and places that required adults to be able to ride a horse or drive a buggy.

- The ability to use a pick and shovel was regarded as a job qualification just a few generations ago.

- Sweeping streets or hoeing weeds once were saleable job skills.

No longer! These skills would not get you very far today. Over the years, new requirements have emerged. People had to learn to use a telephone. Many people had to learn to use typewriters. Driving a car became a near-universal requirement. Now, society is moving into a situation that demands basic capabilities for use of computers and the information they generate.

Businesses have organized themselves to meet the de-mands of an information society. **What does this mean?**

It means that the world has become more complicated than it used to be. Human activities are based on the use and exchange of information.

Consider: A customer goes to a store and buys an item of clothing. The item is given to a cashier along with a little plastic card. The cashier processes the garment tag and the plastic card through a cash register. No money changes hands. No paperwork is needed. The information machines take over. Money is transferred from the cus-tomer's bank account to the store's account. The store's computer includes information about the sale in an inven-tory file that may be used to order a garment to replace the one that was sold.

Transactionland is a place where people generate and act upon information. Businesses have organized them-selves accordingly. Transactionland is a place where people have to appreciate and understand the demands of an information-driven world. This book is a passport to Transactionland.

A REALISTIC LOOK AT THE WORLD OF BUSINESS

Buggy whips are gone. So are green eyeshades, arm garters, and high stools as office work stations. Business runs on information. In turn, the information that drives business stems from transactions. In effect, the customer who makes a purchase is casting a ballot. The act of do-ing business, the transaction, generates a chain reaction that carries through to the processes of management. Managers, as is well known, follow a cycle: They plan, organize, and control. Today, all of these functions are based on the use of information.

In the past, textbooks on business have led students into a kind of vacuum. Students have been expected to grasp and apply theories for which there was no practical basis. This book covers the basic requirements of virtually all high school business introduction curricula. A big difference is that this book presents information from the student's perspective.

For high school students, the transaction is the logical place to begin building an understanding of business. All students understand transactions. Someone buys something to fulfill a need or want. Some value changes hands. If the value is in money, the customer has less money. The business has more money but less merchandise. Eventually, the business has to replenish its inventories. Chains of events that drive the operation and management of business stem from information generated by the basic act of business, the transaction.

This book starts the student at a universal point of understanding, the simple, straightforward, everyday transaction. In the first half of the book, the impact and effects of transactions are traced to provide a general introduction to the world of business. In the second half, the book demonstrates how computers serve as tools that respond to information needs. The point bears repeating: **Computers are tools!** This book helps students to master the value and use of tools. The process is essentially the same as procedures for dealing with other technologies. For example, a person has to learn to drive before the automobile can provide transportation.

By starting from a point of familiarity, this book takes the complexity and the mystique out of business organizations and the computers they use as tools.

SPECIAL FEATURES

This text is the framework for developing a full, satisfying experience for students who are being introduced to the world of business. Special features designed into the text to ease the learning process and provide a pleasing experience include the following:

- Each chapter opens with a learning challenge entitled *The Think Tank.* These are learning objectives stated as a series of questions that provide a framework to challenge the student. This approach follows the learning model of the proven SQ3R technique. Under this approach, each learning assignment starts with a series of questions. (The learning objectives are stated in declarative terms in the accompanying Teacher's Resource Guide.)

- The textual portion of each chapter opens with a scenario presented under the heading *DOING BUSINESS.* This is a realistic (but fictitious) recounting of a transaction-based situation that highlights the theme or content of the chapter. The characters in the "Doing Business" scenarios are devised so that students can relate to them and to the lessons they learn. To drive home the lessons, each opening scenario is followed by a text section entitled *MEANING.* This draws upon and emphasizes the lessons that unfold in the dramatized opening incident.

- The vocabulary of business is reinforced immediately. At the bottom-right of each two-page "spread" in the book, the key terms used within the text are defined. Thus, students have a kind of running glossary. Even though the same terms are included in the glossary at the end of the book, these definitions are there for immediate reference and reinforcement.

- Intermittently, at three or four points within each chapter, there are *Review* segments that contain factual questions on the topics covered. The intermittent reviews help students to reinforce their learning in small segments, or "chewable bites."

- For further reinforcement, each chapter ends with a *Chapter Summary* designed as a study review and information refresher. Following the summary, there are three review/reinforcement exercises. The first is an exercise in *Definitions.* Students are given a list of key terms from the chapter and are asked to define each term in one or more **complete sentences.** The requirement to write definitions can help to build student comprehension and communication capabilities.

- Next, students face a series of *Questions to Think About.* This assignment provides yet another solid reinforcement opportunity. A series of between eight and 12 questions is presented. These can be assigned as written homework or can be used as the basis for class discussions. In either instance, the effect is that the answers provide a full recap of the key learning points within the chapter.

- Also at the end of each chapter is a group of *Projects* that can be assigned for advanced or enhanced learning experiences. Each project requires additional reading and/or logical interpretation of the information presented in the chapter.

ORGANIZATION OF THIS BOOK

The book is organized in two parts. The parts are modular. Each can provide the basis for a full semester's work. However, the continuity of the book as a whole is such that students may be able to deal with the content of the entire text in a single term.

- **Part I** is about businesses, how they developed, why they exist, what they do, and how they have become dependent upon information. The content of this portion of the book could stand alone as possibly the most modern business-introduction text available at the high school level. In particular, the vocabulary level and the experience-based presentation technique make these materials relevant to teen-aged students.

- **Part II** continues the emphasis on information sources and resources. The added dimension is that the chapters in this portion of the book demonstrate the role of computers as tools for managers and for increasing numbers of "information workers."

Part I Content

Chapter 1 is a developmental survey of why and how business practices and organizations evolved to meet increasingly complex societal needs. The entire perspective of the discussions is structured to show how information has become increasingly important. Stress is placed on the evolution of methods to capture, store, retrieve, and use information.

Chapter 2 answers the question: *What Are Businesses and What Do They Do?* The answers provided in the chapter are transaction-based. The idea: Businesses are formed by motivated entrepreneurs. To be successful, a business must start with a defined mission. Each successful business has a *strategy* that establishes the types of transactions to be conducted and the markets to be served. The strategy, in turn, provides a basis for establishing the organization that will carry out the mission. Also, the monitoring functions that lead to operational controls stem from the strategy. The idea of transaction-based

strategies leads to universal understanding of the goals and purposes of business organizations. This approach helps students to understand the importance of getting and serving customers.

Chapter 3 covers the effects of a strategy on a business and its employees. Specific examples are used to demonstrate how strategies differentiate competing businesses. The point is made that every business has a strategy. If managers do not set strategies, they come into being by default, through common practices that evolve. The differences between strategies and strategic plans are described. A strategy identifies the purposes and goals of the business. Strategy is timeless. Strategic plans, however, are long-range in nature. Strategic plans are developmental targets.

Chapter 4 helps students to understand, first, how strategies become frameworks for business plans. Next, the chapter reviews the planning process and presents plans as expectations. Expectations are desired results. Meeting expectations is the way businesses measure their success. Three levels of plans are covered: strategic, tactical, and operational.

Chapter 5 leads students through the transitions from plans to organization structures. Organization charts and organizational hierarchies are described. Also covered are the legal forms of business organizations: proprietorship, partnership, corporation, and cooperative. Special forms, such as franchises, also are discussed.

Chapter 6 is about business operations. Stress is placed on the value of customers as a business asset. A successful business must understand and provide for customer needs or wants. Relationships between customers and employees of a business are shown to be critically important. Operations personnel are identified as both sources and users of highly detailed information.

Chapter 7 leads students into the concepts that apply to management responsibilities in the area of operational control. Specifically, students learn how information becomes a tool for monitoring the results of operations. The basis for this understanding becomes the role and function of budgets—followed by the development of information that compares actual performance with budgets. The concept that information resources model a business is introduced and emphasized.

Chapter 8 is about success. Information models and reports form the scoreboards that measure success. The specific measure discussed in this chapter is profitability. However, stress also is put on the fact that the attitudes and actions of employees are important ways of evaluating the success of a business. Still another aspect of success deals with the role and performance of a business as a citizen of its community.

Chapter 9 deals with industries—what they are and what role they play. Topics include competition within industries, differentiation among companies in the same basic business, and dependencies between industries. Also covered are identification of horizontal and vertical industries and their characteristics.

Chapter 10 covers information sources. This chapter reinforces the concepts presented in earlier chapters about information as a model and as an essential management tool. The basic information hierarchy is covered from a bottom-up view. That is, discussions start with the generation of information as transactions take place. Then there are explanations about transformations that convert raw data into useful information. The potential for external information sources is covered. The chapter ends with the steps involved in building and testing an information model.

Chapter 11 covers the uses of information in business operations and management. Descriptions deal with the accumulation of transaction information into detailed files by operations personnel. The process of summarization is covered to explain how information is organized according to user needs at different organizational levels. Students learn about the differences in information usage at operational, tactical, and strategic management levels.

Chapter 12 begins a two-chapter sequence that deals with the principles of integration and differentiation among companies. This chapter covers the features and factors common to many organizations. Factors that promote standardization include government laws and regulations, accounting and auditing principles, educational standards at colleges and universities, standard computer application packages, and overall similarities in information systems.

Chapter 13 covers the differences and unique characteristics of companies. Differences lie in strategies followed, even though a given company may be one of several serving the same market. Examples cited include hamburger chains that precook food as a basis for fast service in comparison with others that make their burgers to order. Differences are facilitated and supported by the special features of information systems that match the orientation of each company. The chapter concludes with a description of the value to a job seeker of an understanding of company differences.

Chapter 14 is about trends that can be expected to affect the world of business. Changes will respond to two major pressures—technology and societal demands. Some obvious trends and prospective changes are identified and discussed. This chapter also covers the characteristics of command and market economies and the potential growth that can be expected through the continuing trend toward worldwide markets.

Chapter 15 is about the potential for business careers. It is pointed out that business has become the most popular major for college students. Business has grown rapidly through the 1980s, creating about 1.3 million new jobs each year. Shortages of qualified personnel already are developing. This could mean opportunity for the future. Specific opportunity areas are cited.

Part II Content

Chapter 16 provides a background aimed at building an understanding of the "paperwork avalanche" that contributed to the development of computers. The growing volume of paperwork is related to events surrounding the Industrial Revolution. Key events that led to increased needs for data processing capabilities are described. These include the 1890 Census, Social Security legislation, and the administrative buildup in the Armed Forces during World War II. The characteristics and capabilities of computers are described.

Chapter 17 describes the ways in which data items are organized for computer processing. Students learn about the binary system for coding data. Then the relationships among bits, bytes, fields, records, and files are covered. Data storage methods are described, with emphasis on the role of disk files in supporting random access capabilities. The ability of random access systems to support user information needs is covered.

Chapter 18 is about computer information systems. The chapter covers the equipment that forms a CIS and the principles of data processing. Students learn that data are transformed during processing to generate useful information. These explanations are presented within the context of the basic information processing cycle: input, processing, output, and storage.

Chapter 19 covers the basic principles of system development and operation. That is, each business computer application is built upon a series of standard elements and/or requirements. These include the creation of master files, the collection of transaction data, and the use of transaction records to update master files. Students learn about the organization of files for sequential or random processing, including the sorting and collating operations that can be important in the creation and handling of files. The chapter also contains an overview of standard applications for which off-the-shelf programs and procedures are available. Overviews are provided for five applications: word processing, database management, spreadsheet preparation, graphics, and data communications.

Chapter 20 previews the experience of working at a computer. The operations described and understandings established deal with microcomputer applications. Students learn about the role of system software, particularly operating systems, in making the capabilities of computers available to them. Related to the software functions are explanations about the interactions between main memory and secondary storage. Students "walk through" the procedures for booting a microcomputer and loading its operating system.

Chapter 21 is about word processing applications with microcomputers. The chapter begins with an explanation of interactive processing in which users and computers respond to one another. Application package loading is described. Then there is in-depth coverage of both generic features of word processing software and examples based on a specific, popular word processing product. Stress is placed upon an understanding of the major functions found in virtually all word processing packages.

Chapter 22 is about computer files and databases. The idea is to relate the principles of the organization of data to the solution of business problems. In this chapter, students learn the rudiments of database organization plans and functions. (Specific operations are covered in the chapter that follows.) Students begin by learning about files and how they support computer applications. Then, the need for access to multiple files is established and students are led through the organization structure of a relational database. The chapter also reviews the principles of hierarchical and network databases. These reviews are made relevant by the fact that they are covered within descriptions of typical applications.

Chapter 23 walks students through a series of realistic examples of database services. A practical application is described and its implementation through use of popular database management system (DBMS) software is presented. Students review procedures for creating and loading files. The principles of file access and use of query languages are covered. The development of reports from databases is described in terms of both query languages and host-language programs.

Chapter 24 is about the use of electronic spreadsheet software and the need for spreadsheet reports in business. The creation of spreadsheet formats is described. Students then walk through the procedures for entering headings, labels, and data values in cells. The creation of formulas and the application of spreadsheets to "What if...?" simulations is described. The chapter concludes with descriptions of the capabilities of graphics software modules in spreadsheet programs. The formats and values of bar charts, pie charts, and line graphs are covered.

Chapter 25 is about implementation of graphics and desktop publishing capabilities on microcomputers. This chapter picks up where Chapter 24 leaves off with the coverage of graphics. Chapter 24 describes the generation of graphics by spreadsheet software. Chapter 25 deals with creation of graphics through the use of drawing and painting software packages. The principles of bit mapping and vector graphics are covered. There also is a description of how graphics techniques are applied in desktop publishing.

Chapter 26 is about data communications and the use of integrated software capabilities. The purpose and use of modems is described. Network architectures and functions also are discussed. Windowing and other methods for integrating content from multiple software packages are covered as well.

Chapter 27 is the first of a series of three chapters that deal with application of computers to operations and management in specific industries. This chapter deals with manufacturing requirements and supporting computer applications. Special manufacturing-support capabilities include computer-assisted design (CAD) and computer-assisted manufacturing (CAM). Other, production-related applications include computer-integrated manufacturing (CIM) and robotics. In addition, traditional information system applications also are required by manufacturing companies. These are used for such applications as order entry, shipping, invoicing, accounts receivable, inventory management, and others.

Chapter 28 deals with the special role of computers in distribution organizations. It is pointed out that costs of distribution represent a major portion of the prices consumers pay for the products they purchase. The contributions of computers are described in the distribution industry functions of direct delivery of products from factories, en-route transfers of products to other vehicles, and warehousing. Other industry-related topics include computer control of materials handling systems (including conveyors), container shipment operations, and automated rail freight yards. The role of decision support systems and the generation of special documents and reports for the distribution industry also are covered.

Chapter 29 covers the application of computers to retail and service businesses. Since retail and service organizations are labor-intensive, it is stressed that payroll processing applications are vital. The special value of point-of-sale transaction processing terminals also is highlighted. Other presentations cover reservation systems, computer-assisted instruction, law enforcement, legislation, real estate operations, and automated customer services.

Chapter 30 deals with the future of computers and with the future impact of computers on the working careers of today's students. A range of topics reviewed in this chapter includes major technological trends. Discussions encompass data communications networks, advanced microchips, reduced instruction set computers, parallel processing, audio input and output, devices that process light-based signals, and use of superconducting materials. Also discussed are the ways in which computers are expected to restructure jobs, including flexible hours, satellite offices, and offices at home. Key issues involving computers are reviewed. These include privacy, security, and protection for information resources.

Appendix Content

Four appendices enrich and add practical value to the text.

Appendix A is a brief, practical tutorial in touch keyboarding. A series of 10 lessons guides students to familiarity in keystroking techniques for the full alphabetic and numeric keyboard. The lessons can be implemented through use of any word processing program.

Appendix B provides an extensive review of the basic applications for microcomputers: word processing, database, spreadsheet, graphics, and integration of files from other programs into word processing reports. In addition, there are instructions on use of operating systems and techniques for booting a microcomputer. The presentation is organized for completion of the exercises in either of two ways. First, the work can be done on IBM PC or compatible systems through use of STARTware, a special pedagogical software package made available to teachers. Second, the same exercises are structured for completion on Apple II systems with support of AppleWorks software. For Apple users, a special data disk is provided as a basis for student exercises. Twelve assignments are included. Appendix B includes enough assignments to support computer lab activities offered in conjunction with courses in business or in computer information systems.

Appendix C reviews computer-related occupations. Careers for users and computer professionals are covered.

Appendix D presents and demonstrates use of a methodology for problem solving and decision making in computer-related situations.

COMPLETE PEDAGOGICAL PACKAGE

The text described above is the main segment of a set of materials that provides a complete pedagogical package to support courses that introduce students to business and to business applications of computers. In addition, three extensive study supplements are available for students and two complete volumes of material are provided for the teacher. These ancillary materials include:

- *About Business and Computers: Workbook and Keyboarding Tutor* is a student workbook designed to reinforce learning of text content. For each chapter in the text, the workbook contains a summary of major content. Also, there are written reviews designed to help students interpret and apply the information they have acquired. As a special enhancement for the course in which these materials are used, this workbook also provides a complete course in touch keyboarding. The workbook is supported by a comprehensive software tutorial package, *TYPEware*, special software that tracks the accuracy and speed of student performance. TYPEware diskettes are provided for teachers who adopt these text materials. Versions are available for both IBM PC (or compatible) and Apple II computers.

- *Doing Business: A Computer Lab Manual* is a computer-based practice/study program. It comes with a dedicated software package, TRANSware. The software is coordinated with realistic work assignments. Students perform basic business applications on IBM PC or compatible systems. The students generate invoices, accounts receivable records, inventory status information, and operating reports that replicate realistic business operations. The source information they need—as well as specific instructions—are provided in this manual. The operating support comes from a diskette provided to teachers which includes working files and the formats needed to input transaction data that drives the system.

- *Computer Applications in Business: A Computer Lab Manual* imparts skills in the use of standard microcomputer applications. Coverage encompasses word processing, database, spreadsheet, graphics, and integrated applications. All of these applications are presented within the context of realistic case experiences. The assignments can be implemented on IBM PC (or compatible) equipment through the use of STARTware, special pedagogical software that resembles commercial programs. The exercises also can be carried out on Apple II systems through use of AppleWorks software. For the AppleWorks version of the program, a special data disk is provided to the teacher for student use.

- A complete *Teacher's Resource Guide* provides extensive support for classroom presentations. To correspond with each chapter of the text, the Guide provides a set of learning objectives and a lecture outline. In addition, complete sets of answers to all questions and problems presented in the text and in the accompanying workbooks and lab manuals are provided. The Resource Guide also has an extensive set of transparency masters. These are reproductions of art elements from the text that can be converted to overhead transparencies for class presentation.

- An extensive *Test Bank* is provided. This includes sets of multiple choice, true/false, and essay questions for each chapter. There also are complete examinations for each Part of the text.

ACKNOWLEDGMENTS

The authors express special thanks to their editor, Carole Grumney of West Publishing, for her willingness to support this project and for her tireless efforts that made it possible to meet tight deadlines and production schedules. Lynda Kessler, an associate editor at West, and John Orr, the production editor responsible for this project at West, made contributions without which this book could not have been developed.

The staff of i/e, inc., Arleta, CA, provided the editorial and production services that made it possible for this book to respond promptly to market needs. Benedict Kruse and Ron Pronk of i/e, made direct contributions to the development and editing of manuscripts. Bettijune Kruse supervised editorial and production operations. Vivian McDougal served as production editor. John Banner was art director.

To assure relevance and market responsiveness for this text, a group of reviewers read the manuscript while it was under development. Their suggestions for changes and additions have added to the quality of the final materials. For these contributions, the authors are pleased to recognize:

Madeline Alessi, Longwood Senior High School, New York
Sharon Anderson, Apple Valley High School, California
Kay Baker, State Department of Education, Arkansas
Maggie Cervantes, Edinburg High School, Texas

xx   PREFACE

Emadene Davidson, Caprock High School, Texas
Linda Friedel, Blue Springs High School, Missouri
Judy Griggers, Halston High School, Texas
Linda A. Hardman, Judson High School, Texas
Robert N. Lohse, Chesterton High School, Indiana
Robert Luby, Barrington High School, Illinois
Stephen M. O'Neil, Binghamton High School, New York

Ellen Pitrelli, Longwood Senior High School, New York
Murry Schwab, Norman Thomas High School, New York
Stanley Shalkop, Ramapo High School, New York
Richard D. Walters, Connetquot High School, New York
Carol White, Cottonwood High School, Utah

COPYRIGHT/TRADEMARK NOTICE

The following names, printed in bold face, are subject to copyright and/or trademark protection of the identified companies.

dBASE	Ashton-Tate
dBASE III+	Ashton-Tate
WordPerfect	WordPerfect Corporation
dBXL	WordTech Systems, Inc.
Lotus	Lotus Development Corporation
1-2-3	Lotus Development Corporation
MS-DOS	Microsoft Corporation
IBM	IBM Corporation
IBM PC	IBM Corporation
MultiMate Professional Word Processor	Ashton-Tate
Applesoft	Apple Computer, Inc.
ProDOS	Apple Computer, Inc.
AppleWorks	Apple Computer, Inc.
Apple	Apple Computer, Inc.
STARTware	i/e, inc.

I
Doing Business

COURTESY OF CHICAGO CONVENTION AND VISITORS BUREAU, RON SCHRAMM PHOTOGRAPHY

The pages that follow contain 15 chapters that cover business basics. Information in these chapters explains what businesses are, how they developed, why they exist, and what they do. A special point of emphasis deals with information and its use within business organizations. In today's society, every person and each business depends on information. That's why it is said that you live in an Information Society and that most people in this society are "information workers." That is, the majority of workers require information as a basis for doing their jobs. The chapters that follow should help you to understand where information comes from, why it is valuable, and what role information will play in your future.

CHAPTER 1

How Did Today's Business Situation Develop?

A *think tank* is an organization that solves problems and answers questions. The Think Tank at the beginning of each chapter of this book presents questions for you to think about. When you finish reading this chapter and complete your work assignments, you should be able to answer the following questions:

- ❑ Why was it simpler to do business when the United States was a nation primarily of farmers?
- ❑ When did the Industrial Revolution occur in the United States and what impact did it have on businesses?
- ❑ What is a service economy and how does it differ from an industrial economy?
- ❑ What is the Information Age and what does that term mean?
- ❑ What is an information worker and what knowledge and skills should an information worker have?

DOING BUSINESS

"This job is like a course in geography," said Maria. "I just finished entering an order from a place called Truth or Consequences, New Mexico. When I go on break, I want to look it up on a map."

"You'll get used to it," replied Tom. "The whole world is at the other end of the 'answer' button on your computer terminal. You never know who will be on the line or where the call is from. That's the idea of having a central order processing department."

"What was it like before?" Maria asked. Maria was new in the order department of National Medical Supply Company. Tom, her supervisor, had been with the company almost eight years. Tom, Maria, and others handled calls from all over the United States. They also took calls from parts of Mexico and Canada. They wore telephone headsets and worked at computer terminals. Customers called a toll-free number and were connected to a telephone salesperson.

To Maria, it still seemed like a miracle. All she did was ask for the customer's name or identification number. When she entered either item into her keyboard, the computer displayed the complete name and address. There also was a code to let her know if the customer's credit was okay. As the customer gave her information on items to be ordered and quantities, Maria entered those. The computer responded by displaying a description of the product and its price. Maria checked to be sure she had the right customer. She did this by reading the information from her computer screen to the customer. This verified that there was no mixup on the numbers.

"It wasn't always like this," Tom recalled. "We used to have a small office that served just this area. When customers called, we kept them on the line. Then we called the warehouse. Someone had to look at the shelves to see if we had the product in stock. There were 18 small warehouses and sales offices all over the country. But we never seemed to have everything a customer wanted all in one place. It was a complicated mess. Now the computer takes care of the complications and we can concentrate on taking care of customers.

"Isn't it more expensive this way?" Maria asked. "The company must have tremendous long-distance phone bills. Also, we ship everything out of here by overnight air express. Doesn't that cost more than local service?"

"Actually," Tom said, "it costs millions of dollars less. It's cheaper to use long distance phone service and air shipment than to run small operations all over the country.

"You could say," Tom concluded, "that you and I are working in a shrinking world. Whoops, here's another call."

"I wonder where it's from," Maria said as she turned to her computer.

Geographic limits *are eliminated for businesses that use telephones and computers effectively. An entire world of opportunity can be set up at any location where technology is applied with skill and imagination.*
PHOTO BY LIANE ENKELIS

MEANING

Management at National Medical Supply Company had solved modern-day problems with modern-day business tools. First, company managers had recognized that the entire country could be regarded as a single market. The company had set up a series of customer service points in multiple regions. Overnight, nationwide air delivery introduced a major change. Today, air express companies provide overnight delivery all over the country. A package can be picked up from any location, on any afternoon. The next morning, delivery is made to locations thousands of miles away.

National Medical Supply managers recognized an opportunity: They noted that it would cost less to ship by air from a single point than to operate 18 separate distribution centers. Overnight air delivery was combined with two other technology-based services.

One was free long distance calling for customers through an 800 number. This is called Wide Area Telephone Service (WATS).

People power was the main source of energy on farms in the early days of United States history. So much manual labor was needed that 90 percent of the people were farmers.

The other technology was supplied by computers. Sales representatives like Maria and Tom were given magic windows. Through their computers, they could find information on customers and on thousands of separate products. The information was reliable. This meant that the sales representatives could provide complete information on availability and delivery of products—immediately.

The point: Alert managers are flexible. They are aware of changing opportunities. They accept and use new tools that make it possible to build and/or improve business operations. The business environment is *dynamic,* or constantly in a state of change. Change results partly from the introduction of new technologies that lead to improved products and services.

In today's business situation, change is said to be the only *constant,* or unchanging factor. Of course, change always has been a factor. However, the pace of change has quickened in recent years. Today's business conditions have developed gradually through a series of critical periods. These developments go back to the earliest days of the nation. These key periods are identified and described in the discussions that follow.

WHAT WAS BUSINESS LIKE WHEN AMERICA WAS A NATION OF FARMERS?

The American Colonies were established specifically to provide farm products. The original settlers were

Business Terms

dynamic
In a state of constant change.

constant
Unchanging, steady.

farmers. When the Colonies were set up, England needed farm products. Cotton, tobacco, and food crops were needed by factories and growing populations in England. Some of the colonists came to America specifically for the free land available for farming. Even the colonists who left England seeking religious freedom had to support themselves when they got here. Most of them became farmers.

At the time of the American Revolution, more than 90 percent of the population lived on farms. The nature of farms as businesses varied in different Colonies. Up North, in New England, the farms were small and were worked by individual families. In the South, the main crops—cotton and tobacco—required large land areas. The Southern Colonies set up farming operations on large plantations. For labor, the Southern farmers turned to slavery. This action eventually threatened the very existence of the United States as a nation.

In both North and South, business was transacted locally and on small scales. Farmers sold their crops to and bought the supplies they needed from local merchants. Separate companies handled the importing of manufactured products from and the shipment of raw materials to Europe. The crude nature of transportation and communication facilities limited business opportunities. Transportation was by water or by horse and wagon. Ocean voyages to Europe could take months. The same was true about transportation in canoes or rafts on America's lakes and rivers.

Once they settled in the colonies, Americans were quick to identify markets and opportunities. Example: Tobacco and corn were products that were unknown in Europe before America was settled. Early explorers were introduced to these products by Indians. Very quickly, these crops became key products that supported Americans and their growing business community. Early businesspeople also recognized that New England was laced with rivers that could provide power for factories. New England businesses were closer than the English factories to American sources of cotton. So, weaving of cotton became an early, major American industry.

Business opportunities, however, were limited. Farming was the main business. Other businesses supported farms or handled the products grown on farms. These other businesses were small. They had to be small. Transportation and communication were limited and did not enable them to grow. Almost all businesses were operated by their owners. At the most, a typical business in a farming community would employ just a few workers.

Businesspeople of this *agrarian period,* or agricultural period, were independent. They had no choice. Through their independence, they established a heritage of entrepreneurship. An *entrepreneur* is a person who innovates and takes risks to conduct business and to earn a livelihood. In communities served chiefly by small businesses, the traditions of entrepreneurship sank some deep roots. These traditions served as a basis for growth in the years and centuries that followed.

Review 1.1

1. What percentage of settlers in the American colonies were farmers? 90

2. What conditions blocked the growth of business during the colonial period in America? TRANSPORTATIO & COMMUNICATIN

3. What is an entrepreneur? INOVATES & TAKES RISKS BUSINES

HOW DID THE INDUSTRIAL REVOLUTION AFFECT BUSINESS DEVELOPMENT?

During the nineteenth century, the *Industrial Revolution* transformed the United States from a nation of farmers to a society of factory workers. The Industrial Revolution is a major historic period during which large-scale production in factories replaced hand labor in small shops.

Mass production methods were applied in factories that employed many workers. The workers, in turn, had to move into the towns and cities where the factories were located. They no longer could grow their own food or make their own clothing. Instead, the workers became customers for manufacturers and

The Industrial Revolution *changed the way people worked and lived. There was a mass movement of workers from farms to factories like this early steel mill. Also, many immigrants went into industrial jobs.*
COURTESY OF CARNEGIE LIBRARY OF PITTSBURGH

merchants. The scale of business operations grew rapidly.

The Industrial Revolution led to movement of a continuing stream of people from farms to towns and cities for factory jobs. Immigrants who came to America by the tens of millions found jobs that involved building cities or working in factories.

In part, the growth of industry resulted from America's vast gifts of natural resources. As settlers moved West, they discovered treasures in coal, iron, oil, and, eventually, gold and silver. Another important resource proved to be the inventive genius of key American people. The dreams that built America to greatness were introduced at a fast and furious rate by people like those identifed below.

Eli Whitney is most famous for invention of the "cotton gin." Gin is short for "engine." Whitney's engine made a major difference in the processing of cotton. Cotton grows in "bolls," or small puffs. The seeds are nestled in the fluffy cotton. The seeds must be removed before cotton can be spun into thread and used to make cloth. Those seeds must be saved. They are squeezed to produce an oil that is a valuable part of the cotton crop. Before Whitney invented the gin, seeds were separated by hand. This slow process limited the harvesting of cotton. Whitney's gin separated seeds by machine. The cotton gin became a major factor in the growth of the United States as a leading producer of cotton.

Whitney didn't make much money from the cotton gin. It was a simple machine that was copied

Business Terms

agrarian
Related to farming.

entrepreneur
A person who innovates and takes risks in business.

Industrial Revolution
Period of rapid development of manufacturing and introduction of work-performing machinery.

The cotton gin was one of the major contributors toward growth of the United States economy. The photo above shows Eli Whitney's original cotton gin. Below, a worker feeds cotton into a more modern gin for rapid processing.
BOTH PHOTOS COURTESY OF THE NATIONAL COTTON COUNCIL OF AMERICA

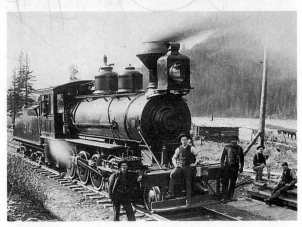

Steam power contributed to improved transportation by river boat (above) and railroad.
TOP PHOTO COURTESY OF PROVINCIAL ARCHIVES OF BRITISH COLUMBIA;
BOTTOM PHOTO COURTESY OF WHYTE MUSEUM OF THE CANADIAN ROCKIES

widely. However, he made his fortune on an earlier development. This wasn't so much an invention as a technique that was a forerunner for mass production methods that followed. Shortly after his graduation from college, Whitney set up a factory that built rifles. He was awarded a contract to build 10,000 rifles for the recently formed United States Army.

Until that time, rifles had been built from scratch, one at a time, by skilled craftsmen. When any part of a rifle broke, the gun was useless—and the soldier could be defenseless. Whitney designed a rifle that was assembled from a series of standard, *interchangeable parts*. This meant the same parts would fit any rifle. The rifles were manufactured quickly and were of superior quality. Whitney's rifles

became a major factor in the United States' victory in the War of 1812.

The point: The seeds of industrial development were planted at the very beginning of the nineteenth century.

James Watt invented the steam engine. With this device, power for transportation and production was brought under control of people. Previously, ocean transportation had depended on the winds. Manfacturing locations had been limited to the banks of rivers and streams, where water power was available. With steam engines, factories could be built wherever their production was needed. Also, the railroads that unified the country became possible

Samuel F. B. Morse was an artist whose imagination led to invention of the telegraph, and to greatly improved communication over distances.
COURTESY OF NATIONAL ARCHIVES

Urgent information was communicated by telegraph during the Civil War and for many years later.
COURTESY OF NATIONAL ARCHIVES

Thomas A. Edison helped light the way toward geatly increased industrial and business growth with the invention of the electric light.
COURTESY OF NATIONAL ARCHIVES

when Watt's invention was harnessed to build steam locomotives.

Samuel F. B. Morse was an artist who became interested in the then-new field of electricity. He devised a way to use electromagnets to send clicking sounds over wires. His telegraph provided a communication capability that made it possible for businesses to send information to distant points. Commerce and the newspaper business boomed as telegraph wires spread across the country.

Thomas Edison enabled people to work whenever or wherever there was no natual light. His light bulb brightened streets, homes, and factories. With his invention, factories and offices could grow in size. This was because it no longer was necessary for everyone to be near a window to have workable visibility. Edison also gave America the phonograph and the motion picture.

Business Terms

interchangeable part
A part of a product that will fit any device of the same make and model.

Alexander Graham Bell expanded communication horizons by inventing the telephone. The photo below shows an early telephone exchange. Operators at switchboards had to connect every call by hand.
BOTH PHOTOS COURTESY OF NATIONAL ARCHIVES

Alexander Graham Bell developed a way to carry voices over electric lines. With Bell's telephone, the ability to do business—and to keep up with family and friends—was expanded greatly. To appreciate Bell's contribution, think of what your own life would be like without the telephone. Suppose you had to write letters whenever you wanted to say something to a person across town or in another city.

Cyrus McCormick invented and built machines that could harvest, cultivate, and plant crops automatically. The backbreaking burdens were lifted from farm workers. As farms became more productive, increasing numbers of people drifted into towns and cities to become industrial workers.

Elisha Graves Otis invented the passenger elevator. Buildings no longer were limited in height by the ability of people to climb stairs. Modern cities began to surround Otis' elevators.

These and other inventors helped to reshape the economy and the very lifestyle of the United States. At the beginning of the nineteenth century, the country was a nation of farmers. By the end of the century, America was a world-class industrial power. Around the inventions of these and other leaders, the country built its industrial machine. Factories, towns, and cities seemed to grow right out of the country's vast landscape. One result: People no longer worked primarily on farms. They were grouped in growing factories, offices, and in crowded towns and cities.

How Did the Industrial Age Shape American Business?

Success in industry led to major changes in the way people lived and conducted business. Some key developments that changed the shape and scope of business organizations and operations included:

- **Markets grew larger** as railroad lines expanded across the country. Mass shipment of products (goods) could be handled quickly and inexpensively. Between the railroads and the telegraph lines that ran alongside them, transportation and communication improved greatly. It became possible for businesses to expand to regional, then national, scope. The railroads carried the goods for business operations. The telegraph lines carried the information needed to manage distribution and marketing.

Agricultural production *was multiplied with the invention of the McCormick reaper. This machine was an example of industry serving agriculture, and freeing up workers to move from farms to factories.*
COURTESY OF CARNEGIE LIBRARY OF PITTSBURGH

- **Ownership and operation of businesses were separated.** Owners invested in businesses, but did not participate in running them. *Absentee owners* were interested primarily in the profits that businesses could make. It became possible for workers to have unseen employers. Factory employees were treated as instruments of production. The workplace was largely dehumanized during the nineteenth century. Later, employer abuses helped to promote the formation and growth of labor unions.

- **Management became a full-time profession.** People ran businesses without actually participating in production or operation. Managers were given responsibility for achieving the goals set for the business. They developed plans, then directed operations aimed at achieving the results called for in the plans.

- **Major business support functions** grew around banking and other financial services, such as credit. Lending and management of money became an occupation on its own. Money became a necessity. Commercial banks grew and people accepted check-writing services in preference to the danger of carrying cash.

- **Workers who flocked to the United States by the millions also became consumers.** The United States grew rapidly as a market for products and services.

Business Terms
absentee owner
A person who invests in, but does not operate, a business.

What Caused the United States To Become the World's Largest Industrial Nation?

During the Industrial Age in the United States, growth followed discovery. As the early settlers moved inland to explore the continent, they kept uncovering treasures in natural resources. Some of the key resources and the developments they supported are described below. In considering these natural resources, bear in mind that the labor and the drive of American workers also represented vital ingredients for success.

Iron ore and coal.   Deposits of iron ore and coal led to formation of a steelmaking industry. Steel supported construction of factories, office buildings, and railroads. Coal became a major source of fuel for power.

Oil helped fuel business growth.   When oil was discovered in Pennsylvania, the United States gained a vital resource. Oil helped to fuel the country's growth into a position of world leadership. Oil resources led to many changes in the business structure and lifestyle within the United States. During the early 1800s, daring sailors from New England became the main suppliers of fuel for the lamps of Americans. These were the New England whalers who sailed the world. Whales were processed to produce oil for lamps.

The discovery of petroleum in the late 1850s led to the setting up of an industry to derive kerosene and lubricating oil from crude oil. Quickly, kerosene replaced whale oil as fuel for lamps. However, the heritage of the whalers has remained to this day. Whaling led the United States to establish its claims for the Hawaiian Islands and a number of other islands in the Pacific.

Another interesting point about the petroleum industry centers upon a fortune established by John D. Rockefeller. Rockefeller was one of the early entrepreneurs who recognized the potential of the oil deposits in Pennsylvania. His activities in refining and marketing oil made him one of the richest men in the world. An interesting sidelight on the Rockefeller fortune: Rockefeller accumulated his vast wealth and went into retirement before the first automobile took to the American roads. His money came chiefly from kerosene and lubricating oil sold to factories and railroads. The automobile then multiplied the value of the holdings that he left for his family.

The North American continent as a growth factor. The size of the North American continent, in itself, helped to promote business growth during the nineteenth century. During much of the century, vast amounts of land were made available to adventuresome people just for the taking.

Some people rushed West to use land for ranching and farming. Railroads were given land holdings the size of some European countries. These gifts were intended to promote the laying of tracks that would join the 3,000-mile expanse of the country. The railroads did, in fact, expand the business horizons. They opened frontiers that were to grow into some of the world's largest consumer markets.

Later, the size of the country and the growth of its cities created a need for still better transportation. This led to the rapid acceptance and use of automobiles for personal transportation. The automobile is an example of a business dream come true: the right idea and product at exactly the right time.

Before automobiles came into general use, people depended on horses for local transportation. As cities grew, horses became something of a nuisance. City dwellers didn't appreciate the need to have stables alongside their homes. In New York City alone, street sweepers were picking up about eight tons of horse manure each day in 1912. The auto was seen as the answer to the need for clean transportation. Also, the passenger car provided a way to put people in command of their own transportation.

Still another industry that prospered partly as a result of America's size was aviation. The first powered flight took place in 1902. By 1936, it became possible to fly across the country in a passenger

The discovery of oil provided light for homes and power for industry. Eventually, the automobile depended on oil supplies for its development. The entrepreneur who did much to build the oil industry was John D. Rockefeller (below).

airliner. The trip by plane took two days. But it cut almost five days off the travel time by train. During the 1950s, aviation became the dominant form of passenger transportation in the world. Airliners overtook and passed both trains and steamships as passenger carriers.

Key events. Challenges and opportunities of history also contributed to the growth and eventual worldwide dominance of American industry. In particular, a succession of wars created emergencies that required rapid industrial growth. Earlier in this chapter, there is a description of how Eli Whitney devised manufacturing techniques for the production of rifles. Whitney's rifles helped to defeat the British in the War of 1812.

Later, the Civil War led the North to harness its steel industry to build cannons. Also, the Union

Navy commissioned construction of the first steel-sided ship. The United States emerged from the Civil War well on its way toward independence from Europe as an industrial nation.

By the time of the Spanish-American War (1898), the United States had put a world-class Navy to sea.

Support of the Allies during World War I stimulated the steel, automotive, and aviation industries in the United States. America pioneered development of trucks and tanks for battlefield use. Also, World War I provided an important proving ground for the then-new field of aviation.

By the conclusion of World War II, the United States was the most powerful industrial nation in the world. Out of World War II came products and concepts that changed the world. Included were large passenger aircraft adapted from planes supplied to the military. Also, the electronics technologies that led to the building of the television and computer industries were developed. During the War, innovations in electronics helped to meet the needs of the military for weapons and communications systems. Atomic energy, the source of almost 20 percent of the world's electric power, also had its inception at the end of World War II.

Some further notes: One factor that contributed to business growth was the production efficiency brought to farms during the Industrial Revolution. The workers who moved from farms to cities helped make possible the growth of America's industrial might.

A factor in business growth that should not be overlooked is the political climate that made it all possible. The government of the United States is a democratic republic that permits unsurpassed freedoms for its citizens, including its businesspeople. Inventors had the freedom to innovate. Entrepreneurs were encouraged to take risks. In this political climate, small companies grew large. In time, bigness itself became a problem. Eventually, businesspeople had to devise special tools and develop special skills to deal with the size of business organizations.

Automobile and airplane *transportation developed in parallel through much of the twentieth century. In this photo, entitled "The Great Race," the car is a 1908 Stanley Steamer and the plane is a 1912 Curtiss Pusher.*
COURTESY OF OWLS HEAD TRANSPORTATION MUSEUM

Review 1.2

1. How did the Industrial Revolution change the kind of jobs held by Americans?

2. How did the discovery of oil contribute to America's growth?

3. What industry grew through use of coal and iron resources?

4. How did the size of the continent contribute to America's growth?

5. What effect did the political system in America have on the country's business growth?

WHAT IS A SERVICE ECONOMY AND HOW DOES IT AFFECT BUSINESS?

Business growth of the kind experienced in the United States doesn't just happen. Business needs special support. Government agencies must build roads to connect towns and cities. Airports must be available. Lighting, telephone, water, sewage, and traffic control systems are needed. Additional ser-

Commercial aviation owed much of its early success to the Ford Trimotor, a three-engine cargo and passenger plane. The Trimotor body was made of corrugated aluminum for strength. This early metal plane became known as the "Tin Goose."
COURTESY OF OWLS HEAD TRANSPORTATION MUSEUM

vices are required from such agencies as law enforcement, the courts, and the military. Education, health care, and housing also are counted among the services needed to support a modern society.

In addition, working people need a variety of services to support the lifestyles they maintain. Services considered necessary in a modern society include entertainment, dining facilities, fixing cars and appliances, transportation, parking, and many others. Other service-type requirements include banking and insurance. Care for elderly people is becoming a major service industry. These needed services are provided both by government agencies and private businesses.

As business activity increases, the need for services rises as well. Recall the example of agriculture. It used to require the efforts of 90 percent of the people to operate farms in the United States. This figure has been reduced to about 3 percent today. And, this small minority of workers now provides food for a large part of the world's population.

Similar developments have occurred in industry. Automatic machinery, some of it controlled by computers, has made manufacturing more efficient. At one time, the majority of workers in the United States held industrial jobs. Developments in automation and computer control following World War II made it possible for fewer people to produce more products.

At the same time, the number of people required for service functions increased. Currently, about one-quarter of all workers are employed by government agencies, including the military services. In addition, millions of other workers hold jobs in nongovernment service businesses.

These combined needs led to a situation that was noted widely during the late 1960s and early 1970s. The majority of workers held service jobs. It was estimated then that some 60 to 70 percent of the people were service providers.

HOW IS INFORMATION USED IN BUSINESS AND WHY IS IT IMPORTANT?

Service jobs are extremely diverse (different from each other). For this reason, the idea of a service economy is hard to define and understand. There are few common denominators: A soldier or sailor has little in common with a telephone operator or a person who maintains a city's street lighting. Also, many so-called services involve products. Does a cook or counterperson who sells hamburgers provide a product or service? Is a checker in a supermarket in a product or service business?

Specialists who study business trends have proposed a common denominator. Information is the glue that holds a modern *economy* together. An economy takes in all of the buying and selling activities, or exchanges of value, within a region or country. The United States is said to have become an *information society.* A society, in this sense, consists of all of the people and organizations that make up

Business Terms
economy All buying and selling activities, or exchanges of value, within a region or country.
information society A condition in which most workers in an area deal with information on their jobs.

a region or country. The current time period is being called an *information age.*

WHAT IS THE INFORMATION AGE AND HOW WILL IT AFFECT YOUR FUTURE?

The information age, it is believed, represents a time when most workers—and virtually all business managers—create or use information. An *information worker* is a person who creates or requires information to do his or her job. Some 70 percent of all workers now are said to fit into this category.

Think back to the scenario at the beginning of the chapter about the handling of orders from hospitals. This story is based on a combination of experiences in real companies. Customer service and product distribution have been centralized. The people who answer the phones and work at computer terminals clearly are information workers. They never actually see the customers they serve or the products they sell. Instead, they enter information into and access information from a computer. The collections of information represent the resources and status of the company's customers and products. These workers, the customers they serve, and the co-workers who receive the orders all are part of an information network.

The same is true of modern business managers. The president of a modern bank doesn't actually handle money. It is true that hundreds of millions—possibly billions—of dollars worth of operations may occur on any given day. But the bank president and employees use computer terminals. They process information that represents the money that is handled.

Managers of manufacturing plants used to spend at least some time on a factory floor. Today, there may be no people at all on a factory floor. Many production plants are operated by computer-controlled robots, often in darkness because the machines don't need light. People receive the products at the end of a production line and also perform a number of maintenance functions. The rest is done with information.

The point: Modern business runs on information. The challenge for information workers is to understand the processes for collecting and using information. Also, it is important to recognize that information has become a necessary tool for planning and decision making. The chapter that follows describes the basic patterns for doing business. Also covered are the ways in which businesses generate and use information to achieve their basic operating goals.

Review 1.3

1. What is the main difference between an industrial economy and a service economy?

2. What is the information age?

3. Who are information workers?

Chapter Summary

❑ During its early years, the United States was a nation of farmers. More than 90 percent of the people lived and worked on farms.

❑ Businesses in early America tended to be small. This was largely because crude transportation and communications facilities limited opportunities.

❑ Entrepreneurship was a major factor in business development during America's early years. The tradition of entrepreneurship was one of the factors that led to business growth.

❑ The Industrial Revolution came to the United States during the nineteenth century. This period saw the country evolve from a nation of farmers to a world-class industrial power.

❏ The size of the country itself contributed to business growth.

❏ The political freedom available to businesspeople in the United States helped to promote business expansion.

❏ A service economy is one in which a major portion of workers provide services rather than make products.

❏ The information age is seen as a time when the majority of workers create or use information in performing their jobs.

Definitions

Write a complete sentence that defines each of the terms below.

absentee owner	dynamic
entrepreneur	economy
Industrial Revolution	information

Questions to Think About

Based on what you have learned to date about business, answer the following questions in one or more complete sentences.

1. Why might air express shipments of orders from a single location be more efficient that many regional shipping centers?

2. At one time, 90 percent of American workers were farmers. Today, only about 3 percent work on farms. Explain this change.

3. How did Eli Whitney help to introduce mass production methods?

4. How did invention of the steam engine affect the location of factories in America?

5. How did the Morse telegraph promote the expansion of business in America?

6. How did the electric light affect the design of factories and offices?

7. What contribution did the telephone make to business development?

8. How did the elevator contribute to the growth of cities?

9. How did natural resources and geographic size figure in the development of business in the United States?

10. What is a service economy?

11. What is meant by the term "information age"?

12. What are the key elements of the job of an information worker?

Projects

The purpose of the assignments below is to encourage you to increase your learning through outside reading or work assignments.

1. Pick one of the inventors identified in this chapter. Go to your library to get more information about him. Describe the experiences that led to his invention. Also describe the contribution to business and the economy by his invention.

2. Identify one business in your community with which you are familiar. Describe its products and/or services. Identify the customers that the business tries to serve.

3. Through library research, identify one major technology that was developed during World War II. Describe the contribution of that product to the economy and to American business. Suggestions: radar, atomic energy, and the jet airplane.

Business Terms

information age
Name given to the current period, in which most people work with and depend on information.

information worker
A person who creates or requires information on the job.

CHAPTER 2

What Are Businesses and What Do They Do?

When you finish reading this chapter and complete your work assignments, you should be able to answer the following questions.

❑ What is a business?

❑ What is the basic act of doing business?

❑ What is the role of customers in shaping a business?

❑ What is a business strategy?

❑ How does the strategy of a business affect the way it is organized?

❑ How do customers and strategies for customer service affect the average worker?

DOING BUSINESS

"What do you feel like eating?" Juanita asked. She and Harry had agreed to stop off after practice for a snack. Harry was a defensive back on the football team. Juanita was on the drill team.

"You pick," Harry answered. "I'll go for anything. After a practice like we had today, I'm starved. I'll eat anything, as long as there's a lot of it."

"It's not easy," Juanita said. "Most of the fast-food places serve just one kind of meal. If we both wanted hamburgers, chicken, pizza, or fried fish, it would be no problem. But we have two different tastes. You could eat a side of a cow. And all I want is a salad. That limits us. At Rick's, I can get the kind

of salad I enjoy and you can get fried chicken and mashed potatoes with gravy. Oh, yes, then you can top it off with a superthick shake. It's a good thing the coach runs you guys so hard. Now that we've decided, get in and drive."

As he swung the car into traffic, Harry became serious. "It's interesting what you just said about different places having different kinds of menus," Harry said. "It fits in with the stuff on marketing in my business class. A restaurant chain that operates on a large scale usually picks one thing and tries to do it well. Remember when the Pickin' Chicken chain tried to add ribs to their menu? They bombed—and they deserved it. Did you ever taste their ribs? Yuk!"

"I guess that's why those places specialize," Juanita commented. "It's an interesting situation. A

Businesses serve identified markets and customers with specific products or services. Shopping malls like the one shown provide opportunities for consumers to select among products offered by many different businesses.
PHOTO BY ROBERT KOCH

chain can train people to make hamburgers, or chicken, or pizza. But you rarely see a chain operation with a mixed menu. It seems to work better if they keep things simple for the help. And I guess they also want to avoid having to stock foods and trimmings for a whole bunch of different menu items.''

"What you say is true from the company's viewpoint," Harry said. "Another way to look at it is from the customer's viewpoint. Customers like a change now and then. Very few people eat at the same restaurant every time they go out. The chains are willing to go after the people who have a taste for hamburgers at any one time—or chicken, or pizza, or whatever. But," Harry concluded as he pulled into the parking lot, "that's enough theory about the food business. Let's eat."

MEANING

Juanita and Harry are thoughtful **consumers.** A consumer is a person or organization that buys products or services of a business. As consumers, Juanita and Harry have recognized that businesses try to attract them (and their money) in different ways. In this situation, their interest was in food. They recognized that restaurants appeal to consumers by offering specialized menus. The fact that they thought only about fast-food chains also means

that their choices were based on price ranges. Most fast-food restaurants have low-cost menus.

This scene also makes another point: Just about everyone relies on the products or services provided by business organizations to meet everyday needs and wants. Putting it another way, businesses exist to satisfy the needs and wants of consumers.

WHAT IS A BUSINESS?

A *business* is a person or an organization that sells products or services to other organizations or to individual people.

The price at which goods and services are sold to consumers is higher than the costs paid by the business. The difference between cost and selling price

Business Terms
consumer   A person or organization that buys products or services from a business.   **business**   A person or an organization that sells products or services to other organizations or to individual people.

The horizon is crowded with business organizations, particularly in large cities. Each of the millions of businesses in the United States is set up to serve identified markets with specific products or services.
COURTESY OF NEW YORK CONVENTION & VISITORS BUREAU

is used for many purposes, such as rent, supplies, and pay for employees. Anything left over after costs are covered represents money earned by a business—*profit.*

How About Some Basic Business Definitions?

Describing businesses and their operations calls for use of a number of special terms. These need to be identified so that meanings used in this book are clear. Any special words used in this book—technical, business, or money-related terms—are defined as they are used. Part of your understanding of business depends on understanding these terms.

To help, any special terms used in this book are defined in the lower-right corner of each right-hand page. In addition, there is a *glossary* at the end of this book. The glossary is a kind of dictionary that relates specifically to the meaning of the words used here. To start things off, the section that follows includes definitions of some of the terms used above. In addition, some related terms also are defined.

An *organization,* in a business sense, consists of people, places at which they work, equipment they

use, and the instructions they follow. Also included, of course, is the money needed to set up and operate a business.

Remember these elements of a business:

- People
- Places or business locations
- Equipment
- Job instructions
- Investments, the money needed to start and operate a business.

A business is organized to serve an identified group of consumers with specific products or services. For example, a fast-food chain might be an organization set up specifically to serve consumers who enjoy pizza. The people in the organization are expected to work together as a team. The teamwork idea is much the same as the cooperation expected of members of a sports team. The business team cooperates to provide products and services to consumers, or *customers.* Success of a business team occurs when customers are satisfied.

A *product* is a physical object that can be used by people. A product also is called a *good.* Most products or goods can be moved or controlled by their users. This means, for example, that an office building or factory is not a product. Rather, a structure in which people work or live is a *facility.* By comparison, the sizes of products range from microscopic to cars or trucks.

The term, product, also means that a product is *manufactured,* or put together from a series of parts. The products you use personally include the food you eat and the clothing you wear. The games with which you play and the vehicles in which you ride also are products. In a business sense, products are objects that are bought and sold.

A *service* is an act performed by a *supplier* that has value to a customer. Note the term, supplier. A supplier, or *provider,* is a business or person that delivers a product or service to a customer. Examples of services include medical treatments, auto repair, and feeding of consumers in restaurants. Notice that services can be related to products. For example, the doctor who examines you may use a product such as an x-ray machine. The auto mechanic installs parts in your car. And the restaurant serves food products.

The key to identifying a service is that the consumer receives attention or actions that go beyond delivery of a product. For example, you buy products in a supermarket but receive food service in a restaurant. Similarly, you buy clothes in a store but receive services when you take a dress or suit to a tailor to be altered.

A *selling price* is the value of a product or service on which the seller and buyer agree. For example, when you pay $1.69 for a hamburger, you have agreed that the item is worth that price. Also, the restaurant owner has agreed to accept that amount. So, you and the restaurant agree on the value of the product.

The selling and buying of a product in this way completes a *transaction,* or a basic act of doing business. Transactions do not have to be based on money. *Barter* also can be the basis for a transaction. People who swap sports cards or other items engage in barter.

Business Terms

profit
The money earned by a business, the difference between income and expenses.

glossary
A set of definitions of terms used in a publication such as a textbook.

organization
In business, a combination of the people, places at which they work, equipment they use, and the instructions they follow.

customer
A person or organization that purchases goods or services.

product
A physical object that can be used by people.

good
See product.

facility
A structure in which people work or live.

manufacture
To put together from a series of parts.

service
An act performed by a **supplier** that has value to a customer.

supplier
A business or person that delivers a product or service to a customer.

provider
See supplier.

selling price
The value of a product or service on which the seller and buyer agree.

transaction
A basic act of doing business; usually involves delivery of goods or services in exchange for something of equal value.

barter
A transaction based on the exchange of goods or services of equal value.

Transactions involve *exchanges of value. Usually, money is exchanged for products or services.*

In barter, the ***exchange of value*** involves a swapping of goods or services. Most of the time, however, money is the ***medium of exchange,*** or an element of value involved in a transaction. In modern society, most transactions involve the exchange of products or services for money.

The ***cost*** of a product or service is the price paid by its buyer. The cost of a hamburger at a restaurant may be $1.69. At the other end of the transaction, the cost of a hamburger patty may be 27 cents and the cost of a roll might be 19 cents.

For the restaurant, the cost of the parts of a product or service are part of the ***expense*** of doing business. Note the word expense. In business, expenses include all costs of operations or items that are sold. For example, a store might buy a sweater for $7 and sell it to you for $11.95. The $7 is the purchase cost, which is lower than the selling price. In addition, there will be expenses connected with selling you the sweater. The store will have to pay the shipping cost of having the sweater delivered from the manufacturer. Expenses will be involved in putting a price tag on the sweater and placing the

sweater on the shelf where you find it. The person who sells you the sweater will be paid for services as part of the value you buy—the selling price.

Profit is the difference between the ***income*** received and the expense of running a business. Income is the total of all the money received from selling products or services. Suppose the cost of materials and the expense of preparing and delivering a $1.69 hamburger is $1.37. The profit to the restaurant is 32 cents for each hamburger. Profits consist of the money earned by a business for providing products and services to consumers. Profits often are the main reason that a business exists.

Review 2.1

1. What is a business?
2. What is a business organization and what are its parts?
3. What is the basic act of doing business and what is required to complete that act?
4. What is the profit of a business and how is profit determined?

WHO ARE CUSTOMERS AND WHAT DO THEY DO?

Customers are people and organizations that need or want products or services. All people require certain necessities. These are ***needs.*** As you know, the basic necessities of life include food, clothing, and shelter. In ancient times, each person or family group took care of supplying its own necessities. Shelter might have been a cave, a hut made from mud and sticks, or a log cabin. Food came from hunting, later from farming. Clothing came from animal hides, later from the weaving of cloth.

Wants are the things a person likes to have but does not actually need. You need to eat. But a candy bar would be a want rather than a need. You need

Customers demand choices *from a wide range of products or services. The modern supermarket was developed to meet demands of customers who wanted to pick and choose from offerings of many products.*

clothing for warmth. But a necklace or necktie are not needs. You need a certain amount of exercise. But a racing bicycle is a want, not a need. Customers must provide for their needs. Wants are purchased with any money that is left over. Businesses exist to meet the needs and wants of customers.

How Did the Barter System Work?

In the ancient days, there were no customers and no money or other standard medium of exchange. Because there was no standard medium of exchange, barter was based on the needs of the buyer and the work involved in creating a product. A wool garment that took two days to make might be bartered for a sack of flour that took two days to grind. People's needs were simple. Barter represented a simple solution.

Some modern-day practices are holdovers from the barter system. A good example occurs when a consumer trades an old car against a new one. The value in the old car is, in effect, bartered against the value of the new one.

Business Terms

exchange of value
The basis for a transaction; the seller and buyer each receive satisfactory value to cover a purchase.

medium of exchange
One of the values exchanged during a transaction; money is the most common medium of exchange.

cost
The price paid to secure a product or service.

expense
In business, the total cost of operations or for delivery of a good or service sold to a customer.

income
The money received from selling products or services, or from other sources.

need
Necessities required by consumers.

want
A product or service a person likes to have but does not actually need.

How Did Money Come Into Use?

As communities grew larger, life became more complicated. People who moved to towns or cities did not have time to create their own food, clothing, and shelter. Instead, they worked in factories or other businesses and received money for their efforts and skills. The money was exchanged for the basic needs. Money became the basis of value, a medium of exchange.

One advantage of money was that it did not spoil or lose its value quickly. When a baker bartered bread for other products, the medium of exchange lost value as bread got stale. This didn't happen with money. Money could be saved and spent at any time.

With money as a medium of exchange, people could go beyond buying just the necessities of life. They could spend money to meet wants, as well as needs. Over the years, many consumers collected enough money so that they could buy products and services for enjoyment, as well as to meet necessities. They could spend their remaining money on *luxuries,* products purchased for enjoyment rather than for necessity. Consumer spending was divided. One part of consumer purchases was for necessities or needs, the other for luxuries or wants. Once consumers had more money than they needed for necessities, they could afford luxuries.

Who Decides What Products Are Available?

Individuals began to work together to produce far more goods than they needed for their own use. These groups became businesses that could provide goods to others. People met most of their own needs and wants as customers of businesses. In time, more businesses were formed to provide the products and services that people were willing to buy. Multiple businesses offered the same or similar products to consumers. *Competition* occurred. Competition develops when two or more people or organizations attempt to supply products or services to the same consumers. Competition also can exist among customers who want to buy the same products or services.

The products or services that are offered for sale are known as *supply.* The amount of those products or services that customers are willing to buy is known as *demand.*

If sellers offer more products or services than customers want, the supply is greater than the demand. To sell their products, suppliers generally must reduce the price. As prices come down, consumers generally will buy more.

On the other hand, if demand is greater than supply, a *shortage* occurs. A shortage is a condition in which there is not enough of a product or service to meet total consumer demand. When shortages occur, people are willing to pay more for the items they need or want. Prices rise.

Remember that a selling price is a value agreed upon by a seller and a buyer. Supply and demand help establish these values. If demand is greater than supply, the selling price will rise. If demand is lower than supply, the price will come down. This is known as the *law of supply and demand.*

Consumers form markets. A *market* consists of all of the demand by all of the consumers who might need or want a given product or service. *Market segments* are portions of a market that can be identified separately as targets for business transactions.

Consider an example: The total market for hamburgers is everyone who eats. However, the people most likely to purchase hamburgers form only a portion of the total market. This group represents the prime market for hamburgers and may consist of persons under 25, workers in large cities who have short lunch breaks, families with young children, and persons in the general population with limited budgets.

Businesses identify markets in which they want to operate. Products and services then are designed to appeal to consumers that form this market segment. The idea is to create products or services on which people will want to spend their money. Each

Customers determine the products that are offered for sale. In modern retail stores such as this supermarket, information on customer purchases is entered into computers. Computer-maintained information then determines the products that store managers will order and stock.

business is in general competition with every other business that appeals to the same group of consumers. For example, the fast-food hamburger chain is in competition with the fast-food fried chicken chain.

There also is direct competition. Many businesses compete to make their hamburgers more appealing than those offered by other businesses. One hamburger chain, for example, appeals to families with small children by adding playgrounds to its restaurants. Another chain appeals to suburban residents by comparing its hamburgers with those made on backyard grills. Still another appeals to people who prefer to think that each hamburger is made to order for individual tastes.

The point: Each business is set up to appeal to a given market or market segment. For example, all people are prospective customers for hamburgers. But teenagers make up a specific segment of that market. Competition centers around the development of products or services designed for specific appeal to the target market. Putting it another way, **each business determines the types of transactions it wants to conduct and the customers with whom it wants to deal.** The types of transactions and customers are the goals that the business is out to achieve. Once the goals are set, each business must be organized and operated to support achievement of those goals.

Business Terms

luxury
A product or service purchased for enjoyment rather than for necessity.

competition
A situation in which two or more people or organizations attempt to supply products or services to the same consumers.

supply
The total amount of a product or service that is available.

demand
The total amount of a product or service that consumers are willing to buy.

shortage
A condition in which demand for a product or service exceeds supply.

law of supply and demand
A set of principles indicating that prices and supplies of products or services adjust to the willingness of consumers to pay for them.

market
All of the demand by all of the consumers who might need or want a given product or service.

market segment
A portion of a market that can be identified separately as a target for business transactions.

Teamwork is a key to success for a business, just as it is for a team on an athletic field.
COURTESY OF CALIFORNIA STATE UNIVERSITY AT NORTHRIDGE, PHOTO BY JAMES E. SEFTON

Review 2.2

1. What is barter and how does it work?

2. What is a medium of exchange? What is the main example of a medium of exchange?

3. Who are customers and what goals do they try to achieve?

4. What is competition?

5. What is the main goal that most businesses have in common?

HOW IS A BUSINESS ORGANIZATION LIKE A TEAM?

The job of a business as a whole is to serve identified customers by providing specific products or services. To do this overall job, a business must employ a group of people. Each person who works for a company must contribute to making or delivering the products or services that the customer receives. You may hear it said that the purpose of a business is to earn a profit. It is necessary to realize, however, that there can be no profit without satisfied customers.

A business is like a team in that the efforts of all employees, like those of teammates, must be coordinated. Employees must work together to achieve company goals in the same way that members of a football team, for example, have assignments that involve blocking, tackling, or carrying the ball. Assignments in companies and on teams are based on shared information. Teamwork involves action based on common information sources.

Think back to the basic transaction of buying a hamburger. Suppose you are a customer ready to spend money. You deal with a counterperson who takes your order and enters it into a *computer terminal*. A computer terminal is a device that communicates with a computer. In a fast-food restaurant, the cash register at the counter often is attached to a computer. The counterperson is responsible for the service you receive. It is up to the counterperson to be courteous and friendly because these kinds of actions help to satisfy paying customers.

The team of employees at the fast-food restaurant backs up the counterperson. In effect, the counterperson becomes a customer for the cooks. If the restaurant provides good service, the counterperson is trained to be sure you get the items you order. If you are not satisfied, it is the job of the

Identity and image are important in helping a business establish itself in a market. This photo shows the headquarters building of Capitol Records, located along the ''Walk of Stars'' in Hollywood.

COURTESY OF THE GREATER LOS ANGELES VISITORS AND CONVENTION BUREAU

egy is a set of guidelines that establish the identity, or *image,* of a company. For a company, its image is the way it is seen by its employees, its customers, and others.

A strategy determines the products or services a company sells. It also identifies the markets served. Finally, a strategy establishes the results to be delivered as profits and the *resources* to be used. Resources include money to be made available and facilities to be developed. In other words, a strategy describes what a business is, as well as what owners and managers want it to be.

Many elements go into forming the strategy of a business. Usually, an individual or small group starts with a key idea. In some instances, this key idea is more of a dream—a vision of a special kind of success. The results of this vision establish *goals,* or results to be achieved. Determination to reach these goals must be backed by commitments of people and resources. In effect, the goals and commitments form a company's strategy. Every strategy is different, as is every company.

counterperson to make sure you are satisfied, no matter what it takes.

In turn, the cook is the customer for people who make sure that hamburger patties, rolls, and other needed items are available. To round out this team, the *manager* of the restaurant is the coach who oversees everybody's performance. The manager is responsible for developing work assignments and plans for running that single operation. Instructions from the manager serve the same purpose as the play book followed by a football team.

HOW ARE BUSINESS OPERATIONS DIRECTED AND CONTROLLED?

In business, team spirit, particularly the will to win, goes by a special name: *strategy.* A business strat-

Business Terms

computer terminal
A device that communicates with a computer.

manager
A person responsible for operation of and/or decision making about a business.

strategy
A set of guidelines that establish the identity, or image, of a company.

image
In business, the way an organization is seen by its employees, its customers, and others.

resources
In business, the money to be made available and facilities to be developed for the operation of a company.

A new strategy *for building auto-mobiles was established in this factory. This was the first assembly line in the United States, the site where Model T Fords were built.*
FROM THE COLLECTIONS OF HENRY FORD MUSEUM & GREENFIELD VILLAGE

America has grown partly as a result of the strategies that have carried out the dreams of its business leaders. As one dramatic example, consider the dreams and strategies of Henry Ford. Ford started as a tinkerer, a person who liked to build things. He became interested in a new invention, the automobile. Like others, he started with a small garage and hired people to build cars one or a few at a time.

Progress was slow, partly because cars were expensive, too expensive for the average person to afford. Ford recognized that, if prices could be reduced, the size of the market could increase because working people would be able to buy cars. He dreamed up the assembly line, a factory in which cars would move to workers who would perform only one operation each. Ford's idea led to mass production—and to the idea of the automobile as personal and family transportation. Ford identified a market and developed a product that the market would buy. This was the first step toward his success—and remains the first step toward success for almost any business.

Review 2.3

1. How does a business organization resemble a team in sports?

2. What is a business strategy?

3. What does a strategy do for a business team?

HOW IS A STRATEGY USED IN RUNNING A BUSINESS?

A company's strategy can be formal or informal. If the strategy is formal, the top people in a company meet from time to time specifically to work on strategy. They discuss the company and where they want to lead it. Then they prepare a written statement that defines the strategy. This statement serves as a set of guidelines for continuing operation of the company.

Even if there is no formal statement, every company has a strategy. An informal strategy is based

Entrepreneurship led to success for Henry Ford, shown here with a Model T. For many years, half of all cars produced were Model T Fords, a result of the headstart gained from the invention of the assembly line.

FROM THE COLLECTIONS OF HENRY FORD MUSEUM & GREENFIELD VILLAGE

upon the history of the organization and upon the experiences and beliefs of its managers. Whenever people work together regularly, they develop a sense of purpose, or an understanding of "the way we do things around here."

Whether it is formal or informal, strategy becomes a framework within which a business is built and operated. With the strategy as a starting point, the coaches—the managers of a business—make plans to build the company to match its strategy. The team wins when the goals of the strategy are achieved.

How Are Strategies Carried Out?

A lot of work has to be completed between formation of a strategy and a company's success in achieving its goals. The strategy becomes a basis for creating plans that direct the actual activities of workers. At the highest level in the company, managers or owners make *long-range plans.* These plans generally extend for a period of perhaps five to seven years. They attempt to establish a picture of what the

company should look like in that time frame. For example, a company that does business on the East Coast may have a long-range plan that calls for opening new operations in the Midwest, South, and possibly on the West Coast.

Other managers, who oversee the continuing operations of parts of a company, prepare *intermediate-range plans.* These follow the guidelines set by the long-range plans. Intermediate-range plans generally cover a time span of one to four years into the future.

Business Terms

goals
In business, targets, or plans to be achieved by an organization.

long-range plans
Plans intended for implementation over extended time periods, such as five to seven years.

intermediate-range plans
Plans intended for implementation in time frames such as one to four years.

To illustrate, suppose a company based in Philadelphia decided to expand into the Memphis market as part of its long-range plans. Other managers would begin by studying the Memphis market to identify the best locations for future operations. Once areas were targeted, the managers would begin to look for buildings to rent. Then, they would plan to hire and train people to run the new operation. With approval of top managers, arrangements would be made to provide the money and other resources needed.

There is a lot of work to be done in following through on that kind of plan. That's why a time span of a few years is allowed for intermediate-range planning. Note a characteristic that intermediate-range plans share with long-range plans: The managers are looking toward the future. Their planning activities are not involved in the day-to-day operations of the business. Rather, they concentrate on things that have not yet happened.

The current operations of the business are covered by *short-range plans.* Responsibility for this planning generally is handled by operating managers. Short-range plans concentrate on making sure the business has the facilities and materials needed for operations. These basic business needs include the people, the supplies, and the facilities in which to make its products and/or provide its services.

As an example of short-range planning, think about the situation of a manager of a local outlet for a fast-food chain. Long-range plans picked the area in which the company wanted to open restaurants. Intermediate-range planners made arrangements to find the land and construct the building—subject to approval of top managers. Now, short-range plans are concerned with providing the people, supplies, and materials needed to run individual restaurants. Consider: Every time a hamburger is sold, another meat patty and roll must be ordered to replace it. These become the supplies used to prepare food for future customers.

The different sets of plans must be coordinated. The plans must fit together to direct the development and operation of the company. A strategy might have to be changed or delayed if the company does not have the people or the money to expand into a new market. As another example, suppose prices change for the supplies that are used to run a business. If the price of hamburger meat doubles, the chain's plans could be upset. Strategies would have to be adjusted to deal with the effects of this change. Then, plans would have to be adjusted to the new strategies.

The point: Plans shape the organization. Plans determine the way people work together within the organization and the products or services provided to customers.

HOW IS INFORMATION USED IN RUNNING A BUSINESS?

Plans are one thing. Experience is different. Things don't always go according to plan. Sometimes results are better than plans. In other cases, there are disappointments. Managers of a business need a way to review what is happening and to compare results with plans. The tool they use for this purpose is information.

A sports example can help to demonstrate the value of information in business. At a ball game, the scoreboard lets you know how things are going. The scoreboard is an information tool for the sports fan. For the business manager, information about operations is provided on reports that usually are prepared on computers.

To illustrate the use and value of information in business, return to the situation of the fast-food chain. As a local restaurant serves customers, opportunities and problems arise. If the restaurant does not have enough workers to take care of customers, the customers become angry. Some may leave. If there are too many workers, costs are high and profits are affected. If the manager doesn't order enough food, the restaurant could run out of hamburger patties or rolls. Customers would be disappointed. If too many supplies are ordered, the food may become stale or spoil.

Keeping track of one restaurant can be a challenge. However, it might be possible to manage one location just by noticing what is going on. The problem changes in size and becomes more critical as a business grows. The manager who must keep track of several hundred restaurants can't be in all of them to observe what's happening. Instead, as part of routine operations, the business collects information that presents a meaningful scoreboard to its managers.

In the case of the fast-food chain, the scoreboard is developed by computers. These computers handle information on transactions and communicate results to people who must make decisions. The information usually is collected and processed by computers. Computer-maintained information can be referenced or reports can be issued to let managers know what is happening. If there are problems, the computer-produced information identifies them.

The information-collection process starts with you and other customers. You create information about the business when you order a hamburger. The counterperson enters your order, usually by pressing a button on a special cash register. The computer processes information by making electrical connections. The key that represents a hamburger is linked to an "electronic memory" that contains information on products sold. The computer responds to an order for an item by causing a device in the kitchen to print an order. In the kitchen, the hamburger is prepared and delivered to the counterperson, who collects your money.

The same information sent to the kitchen also is recorded for use in reports to managers. The signals from the cash registers represent food items that are sold. These information items are collected and used to report sales totals, by menu items. Information on the number of hamburgers sold tells the manager how many new patties and rolls to ship to each restaurant. In this way, use of information helps the chain to be ready for new business. The same information helps tell managers how many employees are needed in each restaurant.

Information guides all business operations, including construction projects like the one shown here. Information directs the workers who erect the building and also guides the managers who monitor progress and costs.
PHOTO BY LIANE ENKELIS

The combination of information from all of the restaurants in the chain provides a super scoreboard. Operations are controlled and plans are monitored through use of information. Information is a business necessity. In turn, the ability to use information is a vital skill necessary to business success. The use of information as a basis for building a business strategy is covered in the chapter that follows.

Review 2.4

1. What role does strategy play in business planning?

2. What kinds of plans are developed in business and what time frames do they cover?

3. How do plans help in controlling day-to-day operations of a business?

Business Terms

short-range plans
Plans to be followed during a current operating time frame, such as one year.

Chapter Summary

4 ❑ A business exists to provide products or services to specific groups of customers.

5 ❑ When a product is sold and bought, an exchange of value takes place. When the exchange is completed, this is known as a transaction, the basic act of doing business.

6 ❑ The difference between expense and income is profit. Profits are the monies earned by a business.

7 ❑ Customers are the reasons why businesses exist. Each business is formed and operated to serve a specific group of customers.

8 ❑ Businesses compete to get specific groups of customers to buy their products or services.

9 ❑ A business organization is like a team because workers depend upon each other in the same way as teammates in sports.

❑ The goal of a business team is to serve customers by providing specific products or services.

❑ The efforts of employees to serve customers are guided by a view of what a company is and what it does, a strategy.

❑ A strategy identifies opportunities and establishes targets that should be met.

❑ A strategy provides a framework within which a business is built and operated.

❑ To make strategies usable in guiding actions and operations, business managers develop plans.

Definitions

Write a complete sentence that defines each of the terms below.

consumer	business
profit	product
service	transaction
competition	demand
supply	market

Questions to Think About

Based on what you have learned to date about business, answer the following questions in one or more complete sentences.

1. What is a business?

2. What are customers and why are they important to a business?

3. What are profits and why are they important?

4. What happens when demand for a product or service is greater than the available supply?

5. In what ways is a business organization like a team in sports?

6. What is a business strategy and what is its value?

7. What are plans and how do plans relate to strategies?

8. Why do different plans cover different time frames?

9. What is the role of information in business?

10. How are customers involved in creating information that helps to run business organizations?

Projects

The purpose of the assignments below is to encourage you to increase your learning through outside reading or work assignments.

1. One purpose of a strategy is to provide a framework for success. Think of your own career as a student. Develop and write down the elements of a strategy to guide you through the remainder of your education.

2. Visit and observe operations of two different stores or restaurants. Pay particular attention to the transaction patterns between customers and employees. Notice the kinds of customers attracted to each business and the differences in the service provided, including differences in the products that are sold. For example, are prices in one of the businesses higher than in the other? On the basis of your observations, describe what you believe to be the strategies of the businesses.

CHAPTER 3

What Is a Business Strategy?

The Think Tank

When you finish reading this chapter and complete your work assignments, you should be able to answer the following questions.

❑ What is a business strategy?

❑ What should a strategy mean for employees of a business?

❑ How does a strategy separate a business from its competitors or from other businesses?

❑ Does every business have a strategy?

❑ What are the differences between strategies and strategic plans?

DOING BUSINESS

On July 4, 1956, Walter Elias Disney fulfilled a dream he had been developing for many years. Disneyland, his Magic Kingdom, was opened to the public. Since then, hundreds of millions of people have learned about and visited Disneyland and other Disney theme parks.

The design and building of Disneyland created many pressures for Walt Disney and his business associates. In considering all offers and opportunities, Walt Disney insisted on remaining true to his image for Disneyland. His business strategy was to appeal to children and to the child that remains in each adult. Walt Disney wanted Disneyland to be a place for families. He went to extremes to assure that his theme park would be clean and safe—as well as enjoyable.

One of the offers presented to the Disney organization as the theme park was being built was a sure moneymaker. Everybody agreed on that. The proposal: Serve beer at selected restaurants and refreshment stands in Disneyland. Given the hot Southern California weather, nobody doubted that sales would be brisk—and profitable.

The idea was reviewed many times. Each time, Walt Disney responded that he felt it was more important to be true to the commitment he had made to his public. Walt's strategy—and the image he projected—was as a producer of family entertainment. He felt this commitment was more important than the additional profits to be realized from the sale of beer.

A strategy for family service led Walt Disney to reject the idea of serving beer in Disneyland. A clear image of services to be provided and markets to be served has led to a solid, successful business operation.
PHOTO BY BENEDICT KRUSE

MEANING

A strategy provides guidelines that link a business with its markets and identify its products or services. Carrying out a strategy establishes the requirements for organization and operation of the company. The strategy determines the kind of people who should be hired and how their efforts are to be organized. Strategies also define the facilities that will be needed by a business and how much they should cost.

In other words, a strategy is an image. The job of managers is to build a business that fits the image formed by its strategy.

WHAT ARE THE ELEMENTS OF A STRATEGY?

Through the image it helps to create, a strategy is a challenge to managers: Build a company that matches the image formed by the strategy. The image to be built consists of a number of separate elements:

- Markets
- Products or services
- People/organization structure
- Facilities
- Finance.

How Are Markets Defined?

A market for a company's products or services is any identifiable group of customers or potential customers. This group of customers is the sales target at which a business aims. In many situations, customers are the reason a business exists.

To qualify as the target of a strategy, a market must be well known to a company's managers. People tend to set up businesses to serve markets they know. For example, Henry Ford spent years building cars one or a few at a time. Then, he built a strategy around a new idea: Ford felt that a mass market could be created for cars if prices could be reduced. Price reductions, in turn, were to be made possible by mass production on Ford's assembly lines. In other words, the idea of the assembly line was the basis of Ford's strategy.

Think of a marketing technique you experience regularly—the self-service store. At one time, all

Self-service provides *a good illustration of how customers help to define business strategies. This photo illustrates a special strategy: A plastic curtain around refrigerated displays conserves energy.*
COURTESY OF BATTELLE MEMORIAL INSTITUTE

service, in all retail stores, required that sales clerks wait on customers. Consider what it was like to shop in a food store of the 1930s. People waited in front of a counter and told a sales clerk what items they wanted. The salesperson walked around to find the items and to bring them to the customer. When all items were ordered, the prices were written on a paper bag. Then the sales clerk added the amounts by hand, with a pencil. After the sale was totaled and checked, the groceries were stuffed into the same paper bag. The cash register was used only to ring up the total amount of the sale.

In the mid-1930s, a few experienced retailers recognized that most customers would prefer to pick their own products. The supermarket was born—and was an immediate success. After that, self-service techniques were introduced into virtually every type of retail operation. Clothing, hardware, auto parts, and department stores all converted to self-service layouts. The wishes of the market, clearly, had been understood. Businesses responded.

To develop a strategy, businesspeople should understand the total expectations of prospective customers. For many companies, market definition is the start of strategy development. For any successful business, market definition must be part of its strategy.

How Are Products and Services Developed?

One type of strategy for a product or service is demonstrated by the example of Disneyland, cited earlier. Walt Disney had a new idea, one that had not been tried before. There had been many amusement parks that offered thrill-type rides. But Disneyland introduced the idea of a "theme park." The theme was a visit with the characters and experiences that millions of people enjoyed in Disney movies. Tens of millions of visitors have proved that Disneyland had a new, different marketing and product strategy. As described below, this is one of two basic approaches to business strategy.

Innovation. Disneyland represents one type of product or service strategy: *innovation.* Innovation introduces something new or different. Innovators want to be leaders in their fields. Innovation can pay off extremely well, as happened in the case of Disneyland.

But innovation involves risks. There always is the chance that the market will not accept a new idea. If this happens, loss of money—as well as disappointment and frustration—can occur. As just one of countless examples, consider the food processing company that introduced a round, flat hot dog that matched the shape of a hamburger. Frankfurter meat was packed into a round casing. The product was designed for ballparks and fast-food restaurants. The idea: Food-service companies would not have to buy

Business Terms

innovation
A type of strategy that stresses development of new or different products or services.

two kinds of rolls. Both hot dogs and hamburgers could be served on hamburger buns.

The idea was logical from the viewpoint of food-service organizations. But the food processing company misjudged its market. That portion of the public who ate hot dogs wanted them to be long and narrow, not round. The round hot dog disappeared from the market quickly.

Imitation.   Not all products and services are innovations. Some are *imitations*. That is, some companies wait until a new product or service has been introduced and accepted. Then, they develop and introduce, as quickly as possible, items that are the same as or similar to the successful items. Imitators frequently sell their products for lower prices. Sometimes imitators are able to capture a good share of a market.

As one example of the innovation-imitation cycle, consider the ball point pen. When this product was introduced in 1946, there was only one innovative supplier. Ball point pens became popular because of their convenience, and because they eliminated liquid ink. The first pens sold for $15 each. Within a short time, imitators had dropped the price to $1.98. Imitators eventually took over the market. Today, ball point pens sell for pennies. Also, millions are given away as advertising or promotional items.

Forming a strategy.   In forming strategy, managers must decide whether they want their products or services to be innovators or imitators. This decision has far-reaching effects on the entire company. This strategy determines the level of commitment a company may have to make in research and development of new products or services. Product or service strategy also affects the kinds of people a company must hire. There is room for both kinds of strategies —innovation and imitation. There even may be room for a company to innovate in some areas and imitate in others. The only requirement is that a company's employees should have a clear idea of what is expected.

How Does Strategy Affect A Company's Organization?

A business organization is a lineup of people whose efforts are coordinated to deliver specific products or services to identified customers. Organizational design and development are important elements of strategy. The organization begins with people. But a business has to do more than hire people and give them a place to work. Elements of organization include the relationships among people for direction and communication. Also, organization includes the instructions or procedures that people follow to build products or serve markets.

A strategy for failure.   If the organization doesn't serve its markets effectively, the business can decline or die. One of the major national retail chains in America failed because its organization lost touch with its markets. The company was W. T. Grant. At one time, hundreds of its stores transacted hundreds of millions of dollars worth of business annually.

The chain grew by providing clothing and a range of household products in neighborhood stores. Managers structured the organization for efficiency in ordering merchandise for the stores. Detailed records were collected on sales. As products were sold, replacement items were shipped under orders from a central office staff. Emphasis was on replacement of products sold.

By the time top managers recognized that sales of items in stock were slowing down, it was too late. The store's operating system had been built to deal with history, with products purchased in the past. Managers had lost track of consumers and their tastes for new and different merchandise. The chains that studied changing trends in consumer tastes took customers away from W. T. Grant.

A strategy for success.   Now contrast this story with an operation like McDonald's. The chain employs a large staff that checks each outlet in detail, frequently. The purpose: to assure quality of food,

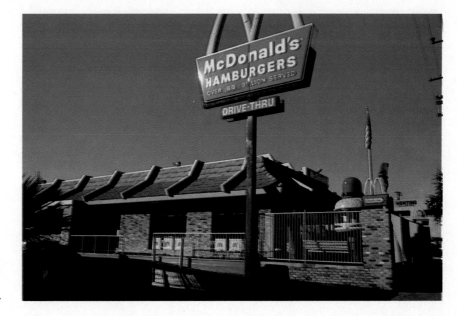

A successful strategy can be observed by visiting any McDonald's fast food outlet. McDonald's strategy is based on the idea that customers want prompt service and a clean place to eat.

PHOTO BY BENEDICT KRUSE

excellence of service, and even cleanliness of rest rooms. Also, the central office conducts continuing research to develop and market new products that will appeal to a wider range of customers.

McDonald's started with emphasis on hamburgers. It has retained this image. But the chain also has carried out successful introductions of other products. The new-product strategy was to get extra use, and income, from facilities that already existed. One example was the introduction of chicken nuggets. This new item was added to the menu to increase sales without increasing expenses. Chicken nuggets are cooked in the same kitchen equipment used for french fries. Thus, business could be increased without requiring extra money for facilities or equipment.

Even more growth was contributed by the idea of adding a breakfast menu. This idea increased the number of hours per day in which a McDonald's restaurant could earn money. Clearly, the McDonald's organization is sensitive to what its customers want. Also, the organization structure is set up to promote quality service and to deliver known, dependable products. Management also is on the lookout for ways to increase business without adding to costs of facilities or equipment.

The outstanding characteristic of McDonald's as an organization is the commitment of its staff. Everyone in the organization is schooled on the importance of customer satisfaction. Counterpeople monitor customer demand continuously. Food is ordered from the kitchen in anticipation of what customers will be wanting in the next few minutes. Then, if a hamburger is not sold in 10 minutes, the counterperson is responsible for throwing it out.

Counterpersons and cooks are teammates. Managers are coaches who check performance continuously. Just to be sure that quality is monitored, supervisors who work for the marketing organization travel the country continuously. The jobs of these

Business Terms

imitation
A type of strategy that waits until products are introduced and proven; then develops copies.

Facilities can be vital to a successful strategy. Auto assembly plants like this one are essential to the mass marketing of quality automobiles.
COURTESY OF FORD MOTOR COMPANY

people focus entirely on assuring the quality of products delivered and the service provided.

The company's organization, made up of people, implements strategy. As far as customers are concerned, each employee IS the company. An effective strategy cannot be carried out without quality people.

What Role Do Facilities Play?

Facilities often are places where customers are served. In addition, facilities always support people. Part of a company's strategy should be to provide places where customers want to be and employees want to work. Location can be critical to success of any business. A retail or service business must find a location that is convenient for its customers. A distribution or manufacturing business must find a location that is close to transportation routes or facilities. A well-known businessman once said that there are three critical factors in the success of a hotel. These are location, location, and location.

How Do Finances Fit Into Strategy?

Every business strategy should plan for a profit. Therefore, one of the elements of strategy lies in commitments for use of profits. Some money may be earmarked for development of new products. Some money may be committed to increasing the stocks of goods that are offered for sale. Funds also may be needed to build new facilities.

Products, materials, facilities, and money to pay employees all are included within the resources needed to run a business. Strategies should establish how much money and what facilities should be available. Then strategies should indicate where the money and other resources will come from. Also, some money should be left over for profits. These are goals of the business that should be understood as part of strategy.

Profits have to be earned. Earnings don't happen until a business has operated for some time. A business that is new or expanding may require that money be invested before profits are earned. Owners or managers may have to invest this money personally and/or arrange to borrow some from a bank. Sources and investments of money are important elements of strategy.

All of the elements covered here are parts of an overall strategy for any business. The importance of some individual elements as compared with others can vary according to the type of business and the values established by managers. The discussion that follows covers the need to establish priorities among these strategic elements.

Review 3.1

1. What elements make up a company's strategy?

2. What management policies can be expected in a company with a strategy for innovation?

3. What effect would a policy for imitation have on a company's operations?

WHICH ELEMENT OF A COMPANY'S STRATEGY IS MOST IMPORTANT?

To be effective, a strategy needs a focus. Usually, this focus is achieved by selecting one element of strategy for emphasis above the rest. The element selected plays an important part in establishing the image that a company presents for its audiences. These audiences include customers, employees, other businesses, and the community at large.

The strategic element selected as most important can be thought of as the company's *driving force*. The driving force, in turn, determines the products or services to be offered, the markets served, and the resources to be used.

The driving force should be selected consciously by the managers who establish the company's strategy or image. However, a driving force will be in place even if a specific selection is not made. Without guidance, the driving force will become the area of operations in which the top managers of a company are most interested. If the president of a company is

an accountant, financial concerns may drive decisions that shape the organization. If the head of the company is a marketing person, customer service and product development will receive the most attention.

In any case, one of the five elements of strategy identified above will become a driving force. The effects of different elements of strategy as driving forces are covered in the discussions below.

What Effects Do Different Driving Forces Have on Strategy?

As indicated, any of the elements of strategy may guide the company and be represented most heavily in its image.

Markets as driving force. In a company that is marketing oriented, managers will tend to concentrate on sales efforts. Also, top people in the company will watch their competitors closely. They may use such slogans as: ''Let's give the customers what they want.'' Another possibility: ''Let the market tell us what it wants. We'll provide it.''

Do you recognize the attitude behind such statements? These are words that are likely to come from imitators. That is, if the market is the driving force, managers probably will want proof of success for a product or service. Then, they will want to move quickly to meet proven demands.

Products or services as driving force. Managers of a product-oriented company usually will place great importance on market service. As a matter of fact, managers of a product-oriented company might well insist that the market is their driving force. The actual difference between markets and products

Business Terms

driving force
The element of strategy that is most important in determining the products or services developed and the markets served.

Products can be critical *in implementing a company's strategy. This photo of a Kroger outlet demonstrates that, with product selection, a supermarket can become much more than a food store.*

COURTESY OF THE KROGER COMPANY

as driving force may seem slight. But they are significant.

A product-oriented company concentrates on its production. The strategy may be to reduce costs, as was the case with Ford. Product-oriented strategies may seek advanced designs or new appearances. The fashion industry is an example. Companies have product strategies aimed at creating new fashions or imitating fashions that are popular.

Product-oriented companies often are innovators. In such companies, there will be a willingness to take risks. Managers are apt to talk about ''playing hunches.'' They will think of themselves and their companies as entrepreneurs. Walt Disney was a product-oriented entrepreneur.

A successful product often creates its own market. However, if companies do not continue to innovate, market success may suffer. Ford's Model T car was a good example. For some years after the assembly line was introduced, 50 percent of cars sold in the United States were Model T Fords. Production concerns remained Ford's driving force for some 15 years. As an example, Ford felt it was most efficient to paint all of his cars the same color. He was

quoted as saying that customers could have any color they wanted, as long as it was black. Eventually, other car makers began to offer other colors. Ford's market share slipped. Had Ford's driving force shifted to a market orientation, the company would have offered choices of color much sooner than it did.

Organization as driving force. In a strategic sense, a company's organization includes both people and the practices or procedures they normally follow. Traditions may be more important to managers than product opportunities or market trends.

Organization can be either a strength or a weakness as a driving force. For example, it might be argued that the training and dedication of its people is a driving force for McDonald's. The markets served and the products are similar to those of other fast-food operators. A major difference is that McDonald's people have the pride to keep their facilities clean and to work together for success. You've undoubtedly heard many commentators remark that teamwork separates champions from losers. Team spirit can be as important in business as it is on an athletic field.

A classic example of how organizational factors can drive a company to destruction can be seen in the history of the Packard Motor Car Company. Up until Word War II, Packard was a prestige car. Many believed it to be the best car on the road. During World War II, production of automobiles stopped. Packard made engines for tanks used by the U. S. Army and its allies.

After the war, Packard and other manufacturers rushed back into production to take advantage of the demand brought on by the wartime shortage. During the war, wages and prices of parts needed to make cars had increased sharply. Before the war, cars had sold for perhaps $600 to $1,000 or slightly more. The Packard had been at the top end of the price range.

Post-war studies showed that a car built to the standards of the pre-war Packard would have to sell for more than $4,000. Accountants and others in the Packard organization concluded that consumers would never pay that much for a car. Accordingly, the existing strategy of quality was discarded. Cheaper parts and methods were used so that Packard could bring out a car that sold for about $2,800. Customers became dissatisfied. Within a few years, the organization at Packard had put itself out of business.

Facilities as driving force. Some organizations seem to exist just to keep their factories busy. Many of these organizations are headed by engineers or scientists. They seem to believe that all they have to do is to produce products in given quantities. Once these products are shipped, managers seem to believe that the sales force can move anything that is delivered.

Manufacturing capacity can be a valid driving force for companies that make products that are standard and undergo little change. Examples include screws, nuts, bolts, and other fasteners. There is little or no way to distinguish one company's product from another's. The company with the most efficient machinery should be in the best competitive position.

On the other hand, emphasis on production as the driving force can lead to problems. An example can be seen in the manufacturing systems of large American car makers. Until the 1970s, emphasis was on tooling up for efficient production. Major investments in tooling led to situations in which major model changes occurred only every six or seven years. With this driving force in place, a number of companies were unable to respond to the oil shortages of the mid-1970s. Suddenly, customers needed small cars that were fuel efficient. The major car manufacturers were locked into big gas guzzlers.

Finance as a driving force. Some companies go into businesses chiefly as investments. Managers measure success according to the ***return on investment (ROI).*** Return on investment is a measure of earnings from money put into a company. ROI usually is measured as a percentage. That is, the profits are a percentage of the investment.

When financial return is the driving force of a company, managers typically set targets for their expected ROI. Companies and/or products that fail to deliver the targeted ROI are treated as problems. In some instances, managers may be fired and others appointed. In other cases, the decision may be to sell or discontinue the business or product.

Some companies that use financial return as their driving force are known as ***conglomerates.*** A conglomerate, in effect, is a group of companies managed primarily for the profits they can deliver. In a

---

Business Terms

return on investment (ROI)
Earnings that result from the money and other resources put into a company; usually stated as a percentage.

conglomerate
A company that controls a number of smaller companies and tends to judge results on the basis of financial returns.

typical conglomerate, each company is permitted to operate separately in its own field. Results are judged primarily by ROI reports.

Under this type of strategy, it can be difficult to plan for long-term growth. For example, a new product may take years to develop and require large investments. If ROI is the main measure of success, a company of this type could look bad. Managers look better if they concentrate on cutting costs and getting as much short-term profit as possible.

Changes in strategy or in driving force can make big differences in determining whether a company is successful. Magazines and newspapers carry stories about many companies that are "turned around" by changes in management. In many instances, the turn-around is achieved largely through a new strategy or driving-force emphasis. A strategy is the identity of a company. If managers and employees see their company as a winner, the chances are great that they will become winners.

1. What is a driving force?
2. How does driving force relate to a company's strategy?
3. How did a false assumption about driving force contribute to the downfall of the Packard Motor Car Company?

WHERE DO STRATEGIES COME FROM?

Every company has a strategy, or an image that establishes its identity. The strategy may result from a conscious effort by managers. However, if managers don't make the effort, a strategy will exist anyway. An unplanned strategy will be formed by decisions and actions of managers. These actions are given meaning by interpretations of employees, customers, and other businesspeople. In other words, the strategy consists of what others think about the company.

If managers think about and prepare a statement that describes strategy, the company has a *formal strategy.* A strategy created by actions and decisions of managers without being recorded in writing is an *informal strategy.*

There is no right way or wrong way to establish a strategy. It's just that managers, other businesspeople, or future job applicants should be aware that a strategy will exist. Success in a business career can be aided—may even depend—on an understanding of strategy. When you go to work for a company, your actions and decisions become part of its strategy. If your actions don't match the understood strategy of the company, you may be unhappy at work. You also may find you are out of a job.

As indicated, without special effort, strategy is formed as something of an accident. If managers recognize the importance of strategy, they may hold special work sessions at which they develop strategy statements. The managers consider—and often argue over—a series of questions that may seem simple but often require serious thought. Examples:

*   Who are we?
*   What do we stand for?
*   Do others—the community, our customers, and other businesspeople—see us the way we see ourselves? If there are differences, how can we adjust our image?
*   What do our customers expect from us? What do we expect from them? How do we define the relationships we seek?
*   How do our employees see the company? Do employees share management's view of the organization? If not, why not?
*   What is the main reason that our business exists?
*   Are we satisfied with the condition and status of the business? If not, what do we want to change?

One value that can result from development of a formal strategy is that the people involved become part of the strategy. Strategy establishes teamwork. A team that shares goals and ideas has a good chance of becoming a winner.

Strategies can be developed at special meetings. The purpose of strategy sessions is to establish the position of the company in terms of markets to be served and products or services to be offered.

HOW DO STRATEGIES GUIDE MANAGERS?

A strategy becomes a framework, or a set of guidelines, within which a business is organized and operated. Some managers regard strategy as a mirror that hangs on the wall. Each major decision is placed in front of this mirror and its reflection is studied. Decisions that don't match the strategy should be challenged. If an idea that seems good violates strategy, the strategy itself may be challenged—and possibly altered.

For a dramatic example, consider the situation of Chrysler Corporation. In 1979, Chrysler was on the verge of bankruptcy, or business failure. The problems were extensive and complicated. In terms of strategy, however, it can be said that the driving force of the company probably was organizational, with facilities playing an important role. Chrysler had a large staff of people who had done things the same way for a long time. The company had factories that had turned out large cars in the same way for many years. As one result, Chrysler's cost of making cars was higher than that of other auto makers. The de-

signs of Chrysler cars were out of favor in the marketplace. As a result of these combined factors, Chrysler lost money. The company was threatened with a need to go out of business.

When new management took over, the initial focus was simply on survival. One effort consisted of seeking loan guarantees from the U. S. Government. These guarantees were given largely to preserve the jobs of tens of thousands of workers. These jobs would have been lost if Chrysler were allowed to fail. Another driving force was to sell almost any part of the business that could be converted to cash. The money was needed for investment in Chrysler's basic business, making cars. The company sold its European and Mexican operations

Business Terms
formal strategy A stated strategy developed through a special effort by managers.
informal strategy A strategy that develops without planning, through the beliefs and actions of managers.

To carry out strategies the ideas and principles that determine a company's identity must be communicated to its employees and to its marketplace. One effective method of communication to widespread audiences is through video conferencing sessions like the one shown here.
COURTESY OF AMERICAN VIDEO TELECONFERENCE CORP.

and also sold its profitable consumer credit division. During this brief period, finance obviously was the driving force.

Once the financial driving force of cash in hand had been achieved, strategy changed. The driving force shifted to emphasis on product design and development. Company officials told the car-buying world, and stressed for their own employees, that quality was vital. To emphasize its drive for product quality, Chrysler announced warranties for its cars that were far ahead of those offered by other car makers. Chrysler turned around.

The point: Strategy guides a company. But strategies are not fixed or unchangeable. Strategies can be adjusted to the company's situation or to the dreams and goals of its managers. Under any circumstances, managers can benefit by using strategy as a basis for their decisions and commitments.

HOW IS STRATEGY COMMUNICATED?

To be of value, a strategy has to be known and used. The point: The people who set strategy have a responsibility to communicate that strategy to those who are expected to follow it. As with the setting of strategy, communication of its content can be organized or accidental. People who have to understand a company will make their own interpretations if they are not informed. If there is a formal program to set strategy, therefore, there also should be a formal program to make it known.

A first step in communicating strategy is to identify those who have to be informed. Then, programs can be devised for reaching those people. Communication channels can include the full range of media—from face-to-face meetings, to memos, to bulletins or newsletters, to audio or video tapes. These media can be used individually; or communication programs can combine any or all of these channels.

The main requirement for communication regarding strategy is that people must be convinced of management support. To build respect and understanding for strategy, the top managers of the company must support it—personally. This can be done through meetings with as many employees as possible. Other communication media can be added to this effort. But, if strategy is to succeed, the people who establish it must take part in communicating information to those who need to know where the company is going. Additional communication efforts should be aimed at helping people make strategy part of their normal thought processes and actions.

HOW DOES STRATEGY GUIDE PLANNING?

Strategy is carried out by the formation of plans and commitments. Strategy covers the overall organization. Plans cover different aspects of a company and apply to different people, according to their job responsibilities. Recall that strategy provides a framework for planning. Plans, as indicated briefly in Chapter 2, cover long-, intermediate-, and short-range time frames. Now that you know more about strategy, the chapter that follows describes how business plans are formed within the framework of strategy.

Review 3.3

1. What are formal and informal strategies and what are the differences between them?

2. Why is it important for employees to understand and follow a company's strategy?

3. How does the Chrysler turnaround illustrate that strategy changes can be effective?

Chapter Summary

❑ A strategy is an image that reflects the way managers want a company to be seen by its customers, employees, and other markets.

❑ Elements of strategy include markets, products or services, organization, facilities, and financial resources.

❑ One of the elements of strategy will be the driving force for the company. The driving force is that element of strategy that is most important in determining the products or services sold and the markets served. Any of the strategic elements may be the driving force. Each alternative driving force has a different effect on the company.

❑ Strategies originate with the view of what owners or managers want a company to be.

❑ Everyone who works for or does business with a company should understand its strategy, whether the strategy is formal or informal.

❑ A strategy can be identified by questioning what a company is, what market it serves, and what its driving force is.

❑ If strategy is to be of value in guiding a company's operations, managers should take time to communicate the strategy to those who are expected to carry it out.

Definitions

Write a complete sentence that defines each of the terms below.

imitation	innovation
driving force	formal strategy
conglomerate	return on investment

Questions to Think About

Based on what you have learned to date, answer the following questions in one or more complete sentences.

1. In what ways does a strategy form an image of a company?

2. What are the elements of strategy?

3. How are a company's markets defined?

4. How does a company determine the products and services it should sell?

5. How does a company's organization structure fit into its overall strategy?

6. What is the relationship between a company's facilities and its strategy?

7. How do money and other resources fit into a company's strategy?

8. What is a company's driving force?

9. How are company strategies formed?

10. What can you do to help understand the strategy of a company?

11. What should be done to communicate information on strategy to people who are expected to carry out that strategy?

Projects

The purpose of the assignments below is to encourage you to increase your learning through outside reading or work assignments.

1. Find two or more advertisements for competing products. Explain how the advertisements show likely differences in the strategies of the companies that prepared the advertisements.

2. Visit two or more competing stores. They can be supermarkets, department stores, or others. Notice how each store displays its merchandise. In particular, notice differences in placement of displays. For example, what locations are given to meats, vegetables, canned goods, nonfood items and other kinds of merchandise in a supermarket? From your observations, explain how you think the strategies of the businesses are similar and how they are different.

CHAPTER 4

What Are Business Plans and Where Do They Come From?

The Think Tank

When you finish reading this chapter and complete your work assignments, you should be able to answer the following questions.

❑ What guidelines are used in the development of business plans?

❑ What is a strategic plan and what does it do?

❑ What is a tactical plan and what does it do?

❑ What is an operational plan and what does it do?

❑ What are the job responsibilities of the people who develop and follow each type of plan?

DOING BUSINESS

"It won't be so bad," George said. "I'll get used to it. The extra pay will help."

George had just informed his friend, Sarah, that he had been transferred to the night shift at the warehouse of National Medical Supply Company. His new working hours were to be from 11 P.M. until 7 A.M. He was to receive bonus pay of eight percent for working the overnight, or "graveyard," shift.

George continued: "I'll still have weekends off to see the gang. And it will be only for a short time, until the new hospitals are built."

Sarah commented: "It was pretty clever for the company to figure out that a temporary night shift could handle this special business. It's certainly better than having everybody work overtime for two months."

"It also was smart the way they explained what was happening," George said. "The company got this big chunk of new business. We are equipping two whole new hospitals. It just happens that both are opening at the same time. The extra business would have overloaded us normally. But, since the orders are received in advance and don't have to go through the computer system item by item, somebody figured out that we could turn the work over to a special crew.

"Everybody wins," George concluded. "The two regular shifts will be able to handle our normal business. The customers who call for service will not suffer at all. The temporary night shift will be able to pack and ship the stuff for the new hospitals

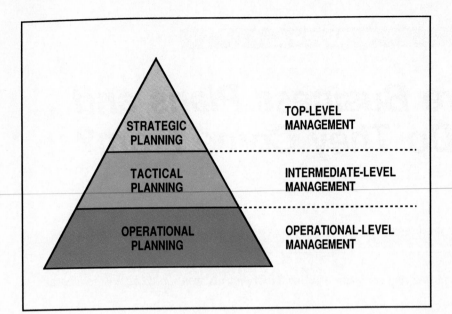

STRATEGIC PLANNING — TOP-LEVEL MANAGEMENT

TACTICAL PLANNING — INTERMEDIATE-LEVEL MANAGEMENT

OPERATIONAL PLANNING — OPERATIONAL-LEVEL MANAGEMENT

Different types of planning occur at different levels within an organization. The pyramid diagram indicates that higher levels of an organization have fewer people and also use smaller volumes of information. The information that supports planning is selected to match the needs of responsible managers.

without getting in anybody's way. By the time the day shift arrives, the packages put up by the night shift will be loaded into special trucks. The stuff will be out of here without interfering with other work.''

''I hope you do get used to the crazy hours,'' Sarah said.

''With the holidays coming up, the extra money will help me to adjust,'' George commented.

MEANING

Imaginative planning has paid off at National Medical Supply. Managers had an opportunity. Two major orders were received at the same time. There also was a problem: This new business could interfere with the quality of service for existing customers.

Management recognized that regular customers are valuable to a business. The company would not risk the quality of service to regular customers, even for really big, special orders. The solution was a working arrangement that could give everybody quality. A special night shift was created

to handle the orders for the new hospitals. In that way, service to regular customers who called during the daytime hours would not be disturbed.

The point: Management recognized a potential problem. Rather than wait until the staff was swamped with work, the company planned its way around the situation. That's the main idea of planning—to look ahead and to deal in advance with opportunities and/or problems.

WHERE DO PLANS COME FROM AND WHAT TYPES OF PLANS DO COMPANIES MAKE?

A strategy establishes the directions in which managers want to lead the business. A strategy represents a big picture. For example, a strategy might say that a food chain wants to open 2,000 new restaurants. That's a big picture. A lot of plans, and a lot of work, will be needed to build, equip, and start operating those restaurants.

Goals are the achievements targeted for an organization. Goals are reached in a series of specific steps. These steps establish what has to be done to realize success, as defined by the strategy. The series of steps to be taken in the future are *plans.*

Plans define future actions to be taken and the resources to be used. These plans, as indicated in Chapter 1, cover different time frames—long-, intermediate-, and short-range.

- *Strategic plans* deal with long-range time frames—perhaps five to seven years.
- *Tactical plans* deal with the intermediate time frame, one to four years.
- *Operational plans* cover the short range, the current year.

Within most companies, the three types of planning are handled by managers who operate at different levels.

Review 4.1

1. What is the relationship between a company's strategy and its plans?

2. What are strategic plans and what time frames do they cover?

3. What are tactical plans and what time frames do they cover?

4. What are operational plans and what time frames do they cover?

WHO DOES STRATEGIC PLANNING?

Strategic planning is the responsibility of top-level executives. Some directors of the company may be involved. Executives with direct responsibility for strategic plans generally are the chairman and president. In addition, some specialized staff members may support the formation of strategic plans. The challenge to strategic planners is to use their imaginations and experience to predict future developments. Their job is to be sure the company is prepared for future problems and opportunities.

Strategic plans are like strategy in that they deal with the position and image of the company. However, strategy differs from strategic plans in some important ways. First, strategy calls for results but does not indicate specific programs or actions to be followed. Second, strategy is timeless. A strategy guides all of the company's people and commitments, over all time frames.

Consider the situation of a fast-food chain. There might be 3,000 or more individual restaurants operating under the same name and serving the same menu items. Top-level people cannot—and are not expected to—keep up with what's happening at individual outlets. They use information to look at overall results. Top managers identify opportunities for growth and development. For example, they might decide to open restaurants in new areas, or even in foreign countries. Also, decisions such as major menu changes or addition of breakfast to the working day would start as strategic plans.

Thus, strategic planning reflects more than long-range trends, although trends are included. For example, suppose a chain has been opening 400 new restaurants a year and has 3,000 units today. The strategic plan may call for 5,000 restaurants in five

Business Terms

plan
A projection for future conditions and steps to be taken in the future to deal with expected situations.

strategic plan
A plan that foresees the condition of a company in the long-range future, perhaps five to seven years.

tactical plan
A plan that deals with the intermediate time frame, one to four years.

operational plan
A plan that covers the short range, the current year.

years. This type of forecast is based on extensions of historic information. However, plans to move into foreign countries or to add to the menu come from the research of the company and the imaginations of its managers.

WHO DOES TACTICAL PLANNING?

Tactical planning is done by middle-level managers, including vice presidents and department heads. To get the idea of the job and responsibilities of a middle-level manager, consider the fast-food chain identified above in the description of strategic planning. Each of the 3,000 facilities around the country has a manager responsible for day-to-day operations. At the central office is a top-level executive group that plans for and supports the entire operation.

It is not possible for the central office executives to deal with operations in each of 3,000 outlets. That's the job of regional managers. Each regional manager might be in charge of an area that contains 100 restaurants. The operations manager at the central office would use information and advice from the regional managers in building tactical plans.

At the operations manager level, it is impossible to be on top of operating details for each outlet. However, operations and regional managers can look at information that describes the condition and status of individual restaurants. When information indicates that an outlet is not doing as well as expected—or is doing better—the regional manager reacts. If there are problems, the regional manager tries to work with the individual restaurant manager to fix them. If things are going better than expected, congratulations are extended. Also, the regional manager will want to see if there are lessons in the success of one restaurant that can help the operation of others.

The point: Regional managers use information as tools. Obviously, a regional manager could not personally be in each of 100 or more restaurants every day. So, information represents, or ''models,''

the actual operations. From looking at information, the regional manager knows how each outlet is doing. If a restaurant is producing the results that are expected or is doing better, there are no problems that require immediate attention. If results are worse than expected, the regional manager can take action. He or she can be confident that it is okay to concentrate on the problems because things are okay elsewhere. The observations and recommendations of regional managers become a basis for the building of tactical plans.

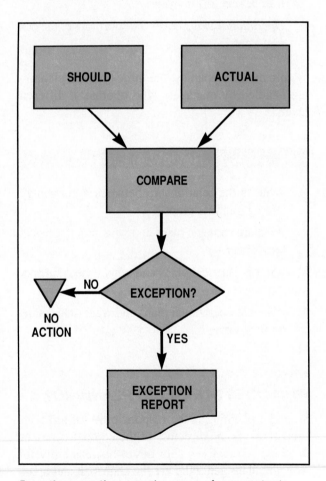

Exception reporting uses the power of a computer to compare values. This flowchart shows how exception reports are developed for inventories. The computer compares values for the minimum level of a product that ''should'' be in stock. If the inventory level is within the ''should'' range, no action is taken. If stock is below the required level, an exception item is included in a report.

Plans are the foundations for operation and growth of a company. Plans hold the future of a company just as a foundation is the base upon which a building is constructed.

PHOTO BY BENEDICT KRUSE

What Are Exceptions?

The situations identified as problems are called *exceptions*. This term means that the results reported are different than they should be. A system in which information identifies problems and directs management attention where it is needed is called *management by exception (MBE)*.

WHO DOES OPERATIONAL PLANNING?

Operational plans cover day-to-day functions. They deal with making products in a factory or delivering services to customers. In other words, operational plans deal with the *details* of running an organization. In business terms, detail means small. The information entry to record the selling of a hamburger is a detail information item.

By comparison, the information on the selling of more than 1,000 hamburgers in a day's business represents a *summary,* or recap. As another example, the fact that Julio Lopez got a hit in the third inning of today's game is a detail. His season batting average is a summary of how he has performed at the plate. The combined batting average of the entire team is a higher-level summary.

Business Terms

exception
An information item that identifies a condition that is outside the normal limits set by managers.

management by exception (MBE)
A system in which information identifies and directs management attention to problems.

detail
In the information field, a reference to information source items that are generated in great quantities and cannot be analyzed without special processing.

summary
A total or recap that reduces the volume of information items and helps managers to analyze conditions or situations.

Operational managers deal with details and with some summaries of information. For example, a manager at an individual fast-food restaurant would supervise the delivery of services to customers. He or she would oversee the counterpeople and cooks. Totals on sales registers would be checked against stocks of hamburger patties and buns in the kitchen.

These details would have to be summarized for meaning in terms of operations of the individual restaurant. For example, the manager would have to know about the numbers of customers served at breakfast, lunch, and other key times. In the manager's mind, numbers of customers can be related to the number of employees needed to serve them. So, through summaries of transaction information, the manager determines the size of the staff needed to run the restaurant.

Summaries also may be developed on a seasonal basis. For example, some businesses require extra help over the summer or during the pre-Christmas rush in December. These are operational decisions that require a detailed knowledge of the business involved. An operational manager needs detailed knowledge and also the ability to determine the meaning of summary information. On the basis of this detailed knowledge, operational managers provide information that describes present situations and future needs.

This information is used in a joint effort involving operational and regional managers. The regional managers develop operational plans and review them with managers of individual restaurants. The regional manager, then, is in a middle position. He or she is responsible for operational plans and also is a contributor to tactical plans.

Review 4.2

1. Who develops strategic plans and what inputs are used?
2. Who develops tactical plans and what inputs are used?
3. Who develops operational plans and what inputs are used?

HOW ARE PLANS COORDINATED?

Strategic, tactical, and operational plans cover three different time frames and levels of working detail. Managers responsible for each type of plan use information differently. However, all three levels of plans take place within the same framework, strategy. It also is true that the three levels of plans form frameworks for each other: Strategic plans are the overall framework and cover the longest time frames. Tactical plans carry out strategic plans. And operational plans carry out tactical plans.

Why Are Plans Originated Under a Top-Down Structure?

These relationships form a *top-down* structure for business planning. That is, planning starts at the top of an organization. Top managers set strategic plans. These plans, then, are made known to the people who are to work on tactical plans. The middle managers work out the tactical plans and submit them to top managers, who make sure that the two levels of plans fit together. If necessary, adjustments are made in either set of plans to be sure they support each other.

To illustrate, strategic plans for a fast-food chain might select a specific year for opening of operations in Minneapolis. On examining the strategic plans, mid-level managers might find a problem. For example, suppose the chain has its headquarters in Los Angeles. Top managers may have overlooked the fact that Minneapolis, because of severe winters, has a short building season. Mid-level managers may find that the facilities can't be built within the schedules that top managers would like. Or, if they can be built, the costs of winter construction may be so great that costs will be out of line.

The middle managers may decide to submit a plan that they consider realistic. Top managers, then, are faced with a need to make at least some change in the strategic plan. As one option, they can re-

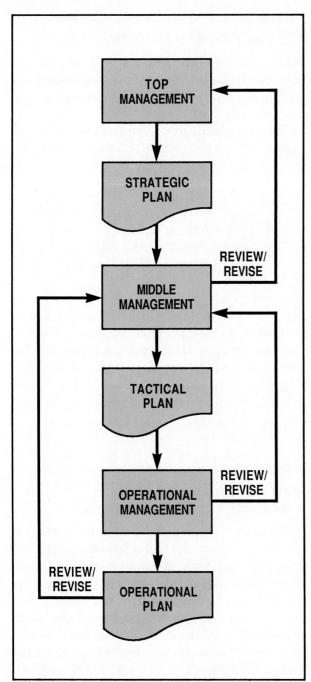

```
        ┌──────────────┐
        │     TOP      │◄──────┐
        │  MANAGEMENT  │       │
        └──────┬───────┘       │
               │               │
               ▼               │
        ┌──────────────┐       │
        │  STRATEGIC   │       │
        │    PLAN      │       │
        └──────┬───────┘       │
               │        REVIEW/│
               │        REVISE │
               ▼               │
        ┌──────────────┐       │
   ┌───►│   MIDDLE     │◄──────┤
   │    │ MANAGEMENT   │       │
   │    └──────┬───────┘       │
   │           │               │
   │           ▼               │
   │    ┌──────────────┐       │
   │    │   TACTICAL   │       │
   │    │     PLAN     │       │
   │    └──────┬───────┘       │
   │           │       REVIEW/ │
   │           │       REVISE  │
   │           ▼               │
   │    ┌──────────────┐       │
   │    │ OPERATIONAL  │───────┘
   │    │ MANAGEMENT   │
   │    └──────┬───────┘
   │           │
   │REVIEW/    ▼
   │REVISE ┌──────────────┐
   └───────│ OPERATIONAL  │
           │    PLAN      │
           └──────────────┘
```

The planning process follows a pattern like the one shown in this flowchart. Top managers generate strategic plans, which provide the framework for tactical planning by middle managers. Tactical plans, then, become the framework for operational plans. As plans are made at each level of an organization, they are reviewed at the next higher level. Adjustments are made as necessary.

schedule construction and make the strategic plan match the tactical plan. Another option would be to hold the original schedule and set aside more money to cover the expense of winter construction.

The same kind of relationship must exist between tactical and operational plans. That is, tactical plans provide a framework for operational plans. In turn, if it is impossible for operational plans to carry out tactical plans, changes will be necessary. Suppose, for example, that a tactical plan called for installing equipment and hiring people to serve breakfast in a fast-food restaurant. Previously, the restaurant had opened in late morning and served lunch and dinner. Under the new system, some employees will have to begin reporting for work at 6 A.M.

Suppose one specific restaurant is staffed largely with students who are released from school in time to serve lunch. Students get time off in the afternoon for school work, then they return to help with the dinner rush. The manager of the restaurant does not have a source of qualified help to serve breakfast. Part of the problem is that the area is enjoying full employment. There are plenty of jobs available. People simply won't work for the amount paid by the restaurant.

The manager of the restaurant thinks about the problem and finds a potential solution: He may be able to hire college students who will come in and work the breakfast shift before school begins. However, the tactical plan calls for starting breakfast service over the summer, when college students will be away on vacation. The restaurant manager feels there will be a better chance of success if breakfast service were to begin in late September.

Business Terms

top-down planning structure
A system under which plans originate at the highest level in an organization, then are carried forward by managers at lower levels.

The regional manager will note a difference between the operational plan for the restaurant and the tactical plan for the area. Some adjustment will be necessary if the tactical and operational plans are to fit together.

Why Are Plans Reviewed and Revised on a Bottom-Up Basis?

There's an old saying that plans are made to be changed. Actually, the planning process in most companies includes procedures for review and change. As described above, planning generally begins at the top level of an organization. The strategic plan then is passed down to mid-level managers, who develop tactical plans. These are reviewed in comparison with the strategic plans. Changes are made to assure that the strategic and tactical plans will work together.

After that, operational plans are developed. As described above, the operational plans often show some differences from the tactical plans. Another round of reviews seeks to bring all of the plans into coordination. This process may be repeated several times before plans are accepted and the organization is committed to them.

The point: Planning starts from the top down. Changes to plans often start from the bottom up. The result of the series of plans and changes to plans should be a *commitment* by managers at all levels. Commitment means that the people involved feel that the plans can be achieved. Further, the people involved promise (commit) to do their best to meet the goals presented in the plans.

Review 4.3

1. What is meant by the statement that formation of plans occurs on a top-down basis?
2. Why are plans reviewed and revised on a bottom-up basis?
3. What action is required by employees at all levels before plans can be carried out?

HOW ARE PLANS MONITORED?

Plans are *predictions,* guesses about what is going to happen in the future. However, the future has a way of differing from people's predictions. Actual business operations often differ, at least in some way, from business plans. When actual results differ from plans:

- It is important to know about and to identify the differences as soon as possible.
- Managers should be prepared to take action. Available actions are few: Plans can be changed. Operational changes can be made that may help to achieve planned results.

Information that compares actual results with plans is called *feedback.* Information feedback is a kind of scoreboard. In business terms, *variances,* or differences between plans and results, are exceptions. The idea of information reporting, remember, is to call exceptions to the attention of managers. Information doesn't adjust plans or change operations. These decisions and actions come from people.

How Does Information Relate Plans and Actual Experiences?

To illustrate, consider a possible reaction to feedback at a local restaurant within a fast-food chain. The restaurant has been growing regularly since it opened. The regional manager and the manager of the restaurant have agreed on a plan for a five percent increase during the current year. There are no exceptions during the first four months. Then, in May, reports show that business is down by 18 percent. In June, the results are 14 percent below plans.

When the regional manager checks, she learns that a competing chain has opened a restaurant across the street. Obviously, some customers are taking their business to the new restaurant. The regional manager discusses the problem with the restaurant manager. The local manager feels that the area is

Competition may change plans.
Actions of competitors in a market situation can affect the results a business realizes. Plans have to be adjusted to show the effects of actual experiences.

growing. He believes that his restaurant eventually will get back to the sales level it had before the competitor opened.

The regional manager doesn't want to wait for the neighborhood to grow. She wants business increases now. So, the managers think about and review a series of actions. One reason the competition is getting some of the business, the local manager reports, is that the new restaurant is cutting prices on a number of products. Some business would come back if the price cuts were matched. Another possibility would be a special promotion. To promote business, glasses or mugs that tied in with a TV cartoon show could be sold at cost. If any of these ideas are tried, the managers will watch their information feedback closely to see how the new plans work.

The point: Management doesn't end with plans. Actual operations have to be monitored through use of feedback information. The reasons for problems have to be identified. Then, new plans or actions have to be considered to deal with the problems.

How Does Information Support Management by Exception?

Exceptions, remember, are conditions that require management attention. Generally, an exception is something that is going wrong, or is producing results that are worse than expected.

Business Terms

commitment
In business planning, a firm agreement among planners that their goals can be achieved.

prediction
A forecast covering future developments.

feedback
Information that compares actual results with plans.

variance
A difference between a planned and an actual result.

Managers must deal with exceptions. However, before anything can be done, exceptions must be identified and management attention must be focused on the real problem. In the example above, the problem that led to a lower volume of sales than planned was the opening of a competitor. However, the same kind of problem could result from many other causes. For example, the local manager may not be watching the housekeeping in the restaurant as closely as he should. The bathrooms may be dirty. Counterpeople may be wearing dirty uniforms. Maybe the trash cans are full and are not being emptied regularly.

Any or all of these problems could lead to a loss of business. Also, problems that reflect poor management are more serious than losses due to competition. A manager can't control what competitors do. But he or she certainly had better control the quality of products and services received by customers.

The point: A variety of problems may lie behind an exception. It takes a trained manager to spot the problem and to figure out what to do. Further, the manager must understand how to use available information.

What Kind of Information Is Needed?

Information doesn't just happen. Detailed planning is needed to identify the information that will model an organization. Then, instructions must be delivered on how and when to develop the identified information. Managing the preparation of management information isn't easy. The business may be suffering from information overload. It takes special knowledge and skills to be able to set procedures and instruct computers to select information that identifies exceptions.

To be useful, feedback information must have real meaning. A lot of information generated by business organizations is of only limited value. As a matter of fact, most of the information within an or-

ganization is not useful for planning or decision making. Some examples:

- A supermarket may cash 400 to 500 customer checks each business day. The manager of the store doesn't have to know about each check. If the bank accepts a check, information about the check is not necessary. The manager needs to know about the one percent or fewer checks that are rejected by the bank.

- If you drive a car, you aren't worried about the 10 or 15 days in which you have enough gas in the tank. The information that is important to you results when the gas tank is low and needs to be refilled.

- A supermarket has 50,000 items on its shelves. No manager can deal with stock levels for all 50,000 items on any given day. Instead, information must identify the items for which stocks are low. These are the items that need to be ordered. To illustrate, suppose a store sells an average of eight boxes a day of Apex Corn Flakes. The supermarket chain can replace this product in two days after it is ordered. At a sales rate of eight boxes a day, this means that the store should have at least 16 boxes in stock to avoid running out. (This is two days of sales at eight boxes a day.) However, a stock level of 16 boxes would be cutting it close. If sales run only one or a few units above average, stocks will run out. Therefore, managers generally plan for a *safety stock,* or an extra supply to protect against running out. In the case of the corn flakes, a safety stock of eight boxes may be planned. Instructions within the computer would be to report this item to the manager when stock levels hit 24 or lower. As long as there are more than 24 boxes on the shelves, the manager doesn't have to know about this item.

Within every business, decisions have to be made about what information is important and what managers need to know. The job isn't simple. One reason: The great majority of information is not needed by managers at any given time. The rule that

Information feedback to managers is the basis for evaluating a company's progress and for making any necessary adjustments to plans.

COURTESY OF APPLE COMPUTERS, INC.

applies to most information is that 80 percent of the information items in a system have 10 to 20 percent of the value. More important, 20 percent of the information has 80 to 90 percent of the value. People who work professionally with information know this as the *rule of 80-20.*

The people who design and operate computer systems are aware that this kind of selection will be necessary. The value for managers lies in the ability of a system to identify the 20 percent of the information that points to exceptions. The rules for identifying exceptions come from business plans. Plans define the results that managers expect—at all levels. Feedback systems then must be designed, in effect, to ignore success and recognize failure. This is a special requirement for information reporting. As long as results match or are close to expectations, there is no need for action. The information can be ignored. However, as soon as information varies from expectations, the manager in charge should know about it.

The point: For businesses to be successful, realistic plans must be in place. Then, there must be feedback that produces information to monitor actual operations in comparison with plans. Exceptions must be recognized and reported.

HOW AND UNDER WHAT CONDITIONS SHOULD PLANS BE UPDATED OR CHANGED?

Plans are changed all the time—whenever necessary. But changes in plans should not be made lightly. Managers should be convinced that there is a reason for each change. The reason should be identified and analyzed. Managers should attempt to understand

Business Terms

safety stock
Extra supply of an inventory item to protect against running out.

rule of 80-20
A principle governing the value of information: 20 percent of the information items have 80 percent of the value, and 80 percent of the items have 20 percent of the value.

why there are differences between plans and results. This understanding, in turn, can help lead both to better plans and to fewer exceptions in operating results. Realistic information also helps a company to organize for service to its customers. Use of information within organizations is covered in the chapter that follows.

1. How are a company's operations monitored for comparison with plans?
2. What is information feedback?
3. How do managers use exception information?

Chapter Summary

❏ Plans carry out a company's strategy.

❏ Strategic plans are long-range plans that cover a time frame of five to seven years.

❏ Tactical plans cover an intermediate time frame of one to four years.

❏ Operational plans cover the current year.

❏ Strategic plans are developed by top-level managers, possibly with participation by company directors.

❏ Tactical plans are developed by people at the vice president and department head level, with information and advice provided by regional managers.

❏ Operational plans are formed by the people who actually supervise delivery of a company's products or services. Managers of individual business units, such as fast-food outlets, contribute information and advice used in developing tactical plans.

❏ Development of plans begins at the top of an organization and is passed down to lower levels. Each higher-level plan becomes a framework for developing lower-level plans.

❏ After each set of plans is developed, it is reviewed—and revised if necessary—on a bottom-up basis.

❏ Actual operating results realized by a company must be compared with plans.

❏ Operating results are monitored through use of feedback information. The actual results are compared with the plans. Exceptions are reported and acted upon.

❏ Exception reporting focuses management attention on problems. Exceptions are identified by comparing information with definitions of normal conditions that are provided by managers.

Definitions

Write a complete sentence that defines each of the terms below.

plan	strategic plan
tactical plan	operational plan
exception	detail
summary	commitment

Questions to Think About

Based on what you have learned to date, answer the following questions in one or more complete sentences.

1. What time frames and types of projections are covered in strategic plans?

2. What time frames and operations are covered in tactical plans?

3. What are the purpose and time frames of operational plans?

4. How are strategies and strategic plans related?

5. At what levels of an organization do strategic, tactical, and operational planning take place?

6. How are strategic, tactical, and operational plans coordinated?

7. How and when are plans revised?

8. How are plans monitored in comparison with actual operations?

9. What is the rule of 80-20 and to what does the rule apply?

10. How is information used to make management by exception possible?

Projects

The purpose of the assignments below is to encourage you to increase your learning through outside reading or work assignments.

1. For a student, a strategic plan might be identification of a career to be pursued. If you have chosen a career target, identify your goals and explain your reasons for choosing them.

2. If you have not yet selected a career to follow, identify some choices you think you may consider and explain how these represent projections of your existing knowledge and experience.

3. Develop a tactical plan that covers the remainder of your education. Be sure to include the resources you will have to use. Be aware that education is a personal investment. Cover the return you expect on this investment.

4. Develop an operational plan that covers your activities for the remainder of the current year.

CHAPTER 5

How Are Businesses Organized?

The Think Tank

When you finish reading this chapter and complete your work assignments, you should be able to answer the following questions.

❏ What is an organization chart and what is its purpose?

❏ Why is a business organization plan called a hierarchy?

❏ What is a proprietorship and what are its advantages and limitations?

❏ What is a partnership and what are its advantages and limitations?

❏ What is a corporation and how is a corporation formed and managed?

❏ What is a cooperative and what are its special features?

DOING BUSINESS

"Who are all these guys?" Maria asked as she and Tom entered the conference room. Seated around a large table were a number of people Maria had never seen before. "This is weird," she said. "We're supposed to be meeting with fellow employees to help the company. How can we do that with a bunch of strangers?"

"You'll be introduced pretty quickly," Tom promised. "Nobody's going to bite you. The first thing you have to do is listen. You can't solve any problems if you don't take time to learn what they are."

Tom was escorting Maria to her first meeting of a "quality circle group." The people were strangers to Maria because they all worked for different departments within National Medical Supply Company. The purpose of the quality circle program was to bring together people from every area of the company. The groups discussed their jobs and working situations. The idea was to solve common problems or to work out better operating methods. Tom and Maria were from the telephone sales department.

As the meeting got started, the man at the head of the table introduced himself as Filipe, from the shipping department. Each person gave his or her name and department. There were employees from computer systems, the warehouse, manufacturing, accounting, purchasing, and credit. When Tom introduced himself and explained that Maria was a new employee, everyone welcomed her.

Delivery of products and ser-
vices is the end result of team-
work throughout an organization.
In this photo, an employee who
controls product shipments is
sharing information with other
company employees through use
of a computer system.
COURTESY OF TELEVIDEO SYSTEMS, INC.

After everyone was introduced, Filipe announced: "Chin, who works in the warehouse, has an idea to present."

Chin seemed nervous. "It's not entirely my idea," he started. "It came up the other day during a break. We were just sitting around talking. We all had the same problem. We all fill orders. When an order comes in, we try to figure out where the items are on our shelves. We organize the work so we can pick the items in order, starting from one end of the warehouse and going to the other. We all have experienced the same problem. We always seem to slip up on one item and have to go way out of our way to go back for it. We were wondering if the computer could print orders according to shelf location."

After Chin was finished, Florence asked to be recognized and Filipe told her to go ahead. Florence explained that she was a systems analyst in the computer services department. "That suggestion makes a lot of sense," she said. "It would be real easy to change the system so that items on invoices were in bin-location order. You would have to give us a floor plan of the warehouse and show where every item is stored."

"What about new items?" Chin asked. "Also, would that mean we couldn't move things in the warehouse?"

"Not at all," Florence replied. "Someone in the warehouse would have to be assigned to change the computer records if you stocked new products or moved locations for old ones. It would mean people in different departments would have to work together—closely."

"Isn't that what we're here for?" Tom asked.

MEANING

Each business must be organized to deliver its products or services to customers. A business organization is a group of people with different jobs to be done. An organization should be set up so that the people help each other. Each worker should make some contribution toward meeting company goals.

Employees in an organization are like a team. On a team, each player has his or her own position. In an organization, positions are held by small groups of people, usually called **departments.** A

Business Terms

department
A part of an' organization that performs a single, special job.

department performs a single, special job. Examples in the scenario above include telephone sales, warehouse, computer services, credit, accounting, and others. Each department is responsible for a **function** that helps to support the production or delivery of products and services.

Some organizations arrange for meetings of representatives from different departments. The idea is to improve the operation of the overall organization through cooperation among departments.

HOW IS A BUSINESS ORGANIZATION SET UP?

For a business to succeed, all of its parts have to work together smoothly. Each business should have an *organization plan.* This identifies the jobs that have to be done and shows how those jobs relate to one another. The organization plan usually includes an *organization structure.* An organization structure positions departments within an organization— something like the lineup for a team.

Each company will have its own, individual organization plan and structure. Recall that this is because a company must organize to carry out its strategy and plans. Since strategies and plans are individual, the organization of each company also will be different. One thing you know for sure is that an organization plan will involve three levels of responsibility. These correspond with the levels at which strategies are set and planning is done. These are top management, mid-level management, and operational management.

A company's organization plan also should correspond with the *segments* or functions of its individual business. A segment or function is any basic part of a business that requires special skill or experience. For example, functions of a fast-food chain might include one group that specializes in managing restaurant operations. Other groups would be responsible for planning menus and for testing new food recipes. Still others would be a real-estate function that buys land for new outlets and a construction group in charge of building restaurants.

At a company like National Medical Supply, there would be a distribution function to run the warehouse and ship customer orders. Other organizational units could include a marketing group to handle sales, a manufacturing segment, and possibly an engineering function.

All of the managers responsible for these functions would operate at the tactical, or second, organizational level. Operational managers *report to,* or work for, those at the tactical level. Thus, the managers at the functional level of an organization are right in the middle of the planning process: They work with top-level managers to create and get approval of tactical plans. Also, second-level managers work with lower-level managers to develop operational plans.

The second level of the organization establishes the functions performed in running a company. Therefore, the functional level of an organization gives a company its unique image. That is, organizational differences between companies are established at the functional level. These functions also give the organization its ability to carry out strategies and plans.

Review 5.1

1. What is an organization plan?
2. What is an organization structure?
3. What is a business function?

WHAT DOES AN ORGANIZATION STRUCTURE LOOK LIKE?

The structure of an organization often is represented in a diagram called an *organization chart.* An organization chart for a company is something like a lineup diagram for a football team. The lineup shows the position of each player in relation to the others. In the same way, an organization chart shows the positions of the functions that must work together to run a company.

Different viewpoints should be represented among managers to establish operating procedures for an organization. Managers from multiple departments or groups will view shared information differently. Positions and procedures must be developed that accommodate everyone.

PHOTO BY LIANE ENKELIS

To demonstrate, an organization chart for a typical large company is shown in Figure 5-1. One thing to notice about this organization chart is the levels of the people responsible for different types of plans and operations. Start at the top.

Who Are the Top Managers?

At the very top of the organization chart is a box that identifies the position of *stockholders.* A stock certificate represents a share of ownership. Stockholders, therefore, are the owners of a company. They are at the top of the organization chart because the company belongs to them.

In a large company, stockholders rarely are involved in running the business. Instead, the stockholders elect a *board of directors* who set the guidelines for strategy, plans, and operations. Directors, who are elected by stockholders, play a role similar to government legislatures. That is, the directors set up rules on how the company is to be operated.

Responsibility for running the company then is turned over to top-level executives. These company executives can be compared with the executive branch of government. That is, the executives run the company. In turn, the executives are responsible to

Business Terms

function
A required business operation or responsibility that is assigned to a specific person or department.

organization plan
A set of assignments that identifies the jobs that have to be done and shows how those jobs relate to one another.

organization structure
A document or understanding that positions departments within an organization.

segment
A basic part of a business that requires special skill or experience.

report to
To be responsible to or to work for a person.

organization chart
A diagram that shows a company's organization structure.

stockholder
A person who holds a certificate that represents ownership of a company.

board of directors
The group whose members oversee planning for and operation of a company; the board delegates responsibilities for company operations to top managers.

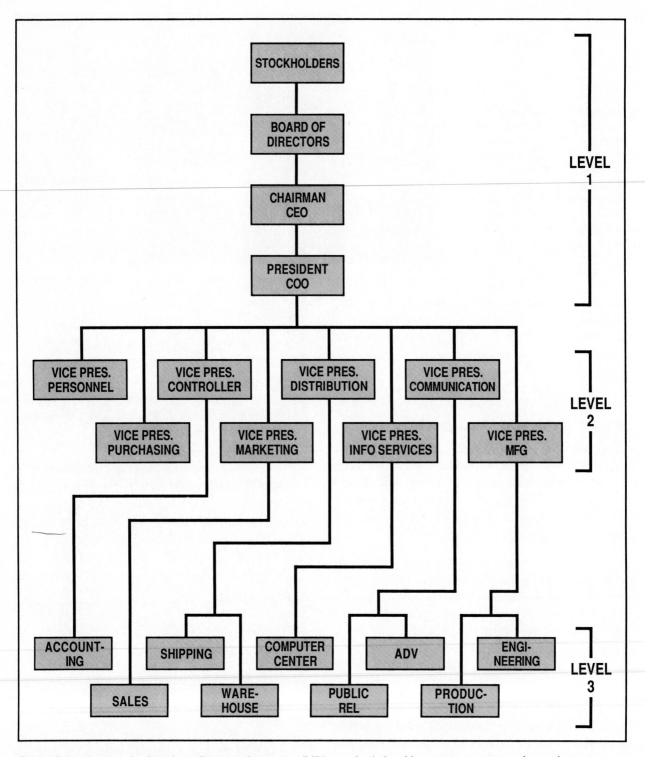

Figure 5-1.   *An organization chart diagrams the responsibilities and relationships among a company's employees. This organization chart represents a large company.*

the directors, who watch over the best interests of the stockholders.

The titles and responsibilities of the two top-level executives identified in the chart are typical. Just below the board of directors is a position entitled *Chairman of the Board* and *Chief Executive Officer.* The person who holds this job serves as chairman of the board of directors. In this capacity, he or she coordinates the work of the board and is responsible for carrying out board decisions. The job of carrying out the decisions means that the individual acts as chief executive as well as board chairman.

The final position at the top level of the company is *President* and *Chief Operating Officer.* The president runs the company and is responsible for its status and condition. The framework for the president's job comes from directions provided by the board and the chairman.

Together, this group makes up the top-level management of a company. These are the people who establish strategy and strategic plans. In a large company, top managers work with information that models the company. There just is not time for a manager at this level to be aware of details about the operations.

This is why it is possible for top-level executives to serve on boards of directors of a number of companies. These people are expert in analysis and decision making. They manage the company by getting information and suggestions from people at lower levels. Top-level managers base their decisions on the information and recommendations from lower positions on the organization chart.

Top-level management tends to have similar responsibilities in most companies. Also, top-level managers tend to have similar qualifications. In many instances, board chairpersons or presidents have been able to transfer successfully between companies in different fields or industries. People at the top are not required to be expert in operating details. Instead, top-level managers typically work with information models that help them to spot problems or opportunities. Also, top-level managers deal with stockholders, bankers, and others who provide resources that a company needs.

To illustrate, many company chairpersons and presidents have moved between organizations of entirely different types. Bank presidents have moved over to run manufacturing companies. Specialists in computer information systems have been able to hold top positions with companies in fields for which they had no functional or operating experience.

The idea: Each level of management must have its own qualifications. At the top level, people have skills needed to analyze information and set strategies. At the second level, managers must have extensive experience in the field in which the company operates. Specific experience also is important at the operational level.

Notice particularly that control and power within a company start at the top of the organization chart and work down. For this reason, organization charts sometimes are called *hierarchy charts.* A hierarchy simply is a set of top-down relationships within an organization.

Business Terms

chairman of the board
The person elected by a board of directors to carry out its instructions in the operation of a company.

chief executive officer
The highest executive in a company; often serves as chairman of the board of directors.

president
The person responsible for operations of a company; the president is responsible to the chairperson and to the board of directors.

chief operating officer
The person responsible for operations of a company; usually the president.

hierarchy chart
A diagram, such as an organization chart, that represents a set of top-down relationships.

Who Are the Second-Level Managers?

Below the top level are boxes lined up in a row. The positions at this level may carry titles of *vice president* or *director*. Regardless of title, each company will have a group of managers who are in charge of the important functions that must be coordinated to operate a business. These are the people who develop the tactical plans that guide a company toward its intermediate-range goals.

The positions identified in the accompanying chart are typical of those that exist in many companies. The exact responsibilities and titles of these jobs, and the number of jobs that exist at this level, will vary with types of companies. For example, a company in the retail or distribution business would not need a manufacturing function. In some companies, purchasing might be done by a lower-level (operating) manager who reports to a manufacturing vice president. In Figure 5-1, there is an Information Services function responsible for developing and operating computer systems. In some companies, the person responsible for information resources is at a lower level. This individual might report to a controller or financial vice president.

If you liken an organization chart to a sports team, the top-level executives make decisions in the front office. They may watch the action from the owner's box. The functional positions of second-level, or middle-level, managers can be compared with the coaching staff. They may be on the sidelines, but they are in direct touch with what is happening on the field. These are the people who call the plays. The players themselves are represented at the next level.

Who Are the Operations Managers?

Operations managers are the people responsible for face-to-face contact with a company's customers. They are the people who hire and manage the workers who actually run the company on a day-to-day basis.

For instance, in a fast-food chain, operations managers might be the regional or district managers who supervise groups of restaurants. In some companies, individual restaurant managers also might be considered operations managers.

In a department store, operations managers might include the people who run individual stores and/or those who buy and set prices for merchandise. In large banks, branch managers might be operations-level managers. Within a manufacturing company, the production manager would have operations responsibility. So would a warehouse or shipping manager.

Staff and line responsibilities. Operations management jobs have a special characteristic. They are considered to be *line* functions of the business. This means that operations managers have direct responsibility for producing products or delivering services to customers.

People who do not have line responsibilities hold *staff* jobs. A staff position is not directly involved in producing products or serving customers. Instead, a staff person deals in information or resources needed by line people. Examples of staff jobs include accounting, finance, computer information services, and personnel.

Planning responsibilities of staff people generally involve support of the managers who develop tactical plans. For example, the accounts receivable department that collects amounts due from customers performs a staff function. This department head would provide information for inclusion in the controller's tactical plan. Accounts receivable might not be asked for an operational plan. The controller, incidentally, would be responsible for administration. All office and support workers would come under the controller's supervision.

What Happens in Smaller Organizations?

The descriptions above cover a relatively large organization. A smaller company could not support as

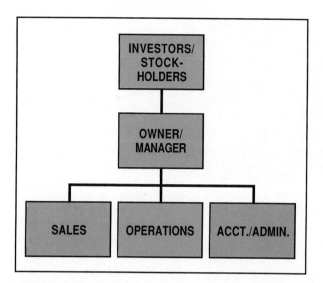

Figure 5-2. *This organization chart for a mid-size company applies the same principles as for a large company, except that there are fewer levels of management. Middle managers assume wider responsibilities.*

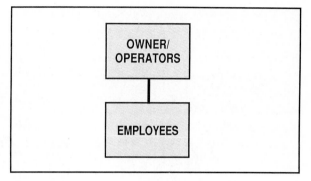

Figure 5-3. *The organization structure of a small company places a wide range of responsibilities with an owner or manager.*

much management as is described above. The principle that applies: The organization structure must be tailored to the needs of each individual company. To illustrate, Figure 5-2 presents a typical organization chart for a mid-size company. Figure 5-3 depicts the organization of a small company.

In these examples, the mid-sized company has fewer levels of management than the large company described above. The chief executive and chief operating officer responsibilities rest with a single manager, who also may be a stockholder or owner. The second-level positions are occupied by a few people who have both tactical and operational responsibilities. The principles of management are the same. The differences are based upon the size of the company. The volume of work does not require additional levels of supervision. With fewer workers to direct and fewer customers to serve, fewer managers are needed.

In a really small company, a single person may be owner, manager, and operator. As diagrammed, any employees are supervised directly by this owner-manager.

The point: The size of a company determines its organizational needs.

Review 5.2

1. What is an organization chart?
2. Why is an organization chart also called a hierarchy chart?
3. What are line and staff positions?

Business Terms

vice president
A person who reports to the president and is responsible for oversight of a portion of a company's operations.

director
A member of a board of directors.

line function
A person, department or group that holds direct responsibility for producing products or delivering services to customers.

staff job
A position that is not directly involved in producing products or serving customers; provides support to line personnel.

Even with automated equipment, people are key to the smooth functioning of an organization. People supply the understanding and judgment needed to apply teamwork to operation of an organization.
COURTESY OF HEWLETT-PACKARD CO.

HOW DO PEOPLE IN AN ORGANIZATION KNOW WHAT THEY ARE SUPPOSED TO DO?

The lines that link positions and functions on an organization chart also represent the contacts among people. The general idea: Plans and directions flow downward along the lines of an organization chart. Feedback on results from operations flows from the bottom of the organization upward. The top people react to feedback and may change plans or instructions.

In other words, there is a continuing cycle of direction and feedback. Directions are said to follow a top-down pattern. Reporting of results moves in a bottom-up direction.

The lines on the chart, in effect, are links between parts of an organization. That's why they are called lines of reporting. The organization chart also outlines *responsibility* and provides the basis for defining *authority* of managers. Responsibilities are

job assignments that a person is required to complete. Authority is the right, or power, to take actions to meet responsibilities.

In large organizations, responsibilities generally are outlined on documents that are distributed along with organization charts. For each box on the chart, the job of the individual or group is described. Also identified are any specific responsibilities that are not assigned to a given function. Definitions of responsibilities should include descriptions of the way positions within an organization relate to one another. For example, the responsibilities of a purchasing department would be to provide the parts needed by manufacturing.

Along with responsibility, there must be definitions of authority. Authority describes the directions that may be given and the commitments that can be made by any person or group. For example, the controller has authority over the accounting department and may define the work that this group does. The controller also may have definitions of authority that deal with commitments that can be made. For example, a controller of a large company may be authorized to approve purchasing requests by other managers of up to $25,000. Any larger requests might need approval from the controller and the president.

In addition, there should be specific instructions on how to perform individual jobs. These may be called *procedures,* or *procedures manuals.* These are performance guides. They contain step-by-step instructions on how a specific job is to be done.

In effect, the organization chart is the playing field. Actions of managers require the preparation of job descriptions that act as a kind of rule book. If any organization is to function as a team, each member must know what the others will and will not do.

1. What are business responsibilities?
2. What is authority?
3. How are responsibilities and authority of employees defined on organization charts?

WHAT OPTIONS DO BUSINESSES HAVE FOR LEGAL ORGANIZATION STRUCTURES?

As an individual and a consumer, you operate within a series of laws. For example, laws say that you can't attack fellow citizens or make false statements about them. Laws also say that you must pay for the things you buy.

Businesses also must obey sets of laws that cover their behavior as members of a society. In effect, a business has the same responsibilities that you do as an individual. However, a business is not an individual person. It is harder to define legal behavior for a company that might have thousands of owners and employees. However, it is necessary that businesses be set up to assure their responsibilities as suppliers, customers, and citizens. For this purpose,

laws have been established that create legal organization choices under which businesses must operate.

People who start or own businesses may choose the form of legal organization under which they wish to operate. The main choices include:

- Proprietorship
- Partnership
- Corporation
- Cooperative.

What's in a Business Name?

Each form of business shares one important, common feature: It is identified by a *fictitious name.* This term means simply that the owners have a right to give each business an individual name and identity. Even if the business is owned by one person, the owner can assign any name he or she wishes.

A name is established by registering the business with a local government agency. Registration can be at the state or county level, depending on the type of business. Once this is done, the business can open bank accounts and can transact business under its fictitious name. Even if an owner wants the business to be known under his or her name, this still becomes

Business Terms

responsibility
An assigned job that a person is required to complete.

authority
The right, or power, to take actions to meet responsibilities.

procedure
A set of instructions for job performance.

procedures manual
A document that presents instructions for job performance.

fictitious name
A name taken as an identity of a business.

a fictitious name. That is, the person's name becomes a fictitious business name for the purpose of banking and other transactions.

What Is a Proprietorship And How Does It Work?

The term, proprietor, describes a person who owns and operates a business. Therefore, a *proprietorship,* or *sole proprietorship,* is a business that is owned and operated by an individual. This is the simplest form of business organization and the easiest to set up. To run a proprietorship, a person simply registers the fictitious name and starts to do business. The procedure is so simple that many persons who hold full-time jobs start proprietorships as part-time activities.

In some situations, a proprietor may have to take out a business license with local city government. If products or services are sold to the public, it also may be necessary to collect sales taxes. Sales taxes, then, must be paid to the state or local government.

A major advantage of the proprietorship is that there are no special income-tax-reporting requirements. The business becomes an extension of the owner's income reporting. Income received in the business is personal income to the proprietor. Expenses are deducted from income and the results are covered in the personal tax return of the owner.

A proprietorship does not have to report its operating results to any federal or state agencies. The idea, simply, is that a person is in business for himself or herself. Eliminating the need to report to taxing and other government agencies can be a big factor in favor of the proprietorship form of business.

Many services and small retail stores are proprietorships. In numbers alone, most businesses are proprietorships. It is common for people to develop ideas about businesses they would like to start. A proprietorship, then, becomes the easiest and least expensive way to start a business.

What Is a Partnership And How Does It Work?

The term, partner, means that a person is part owner of a business or property. For a business to be a *partnership,* at least two or more people must share ownership. Not all partners have to be involved actively in running the business. Some partners may invest in a business in which they do not work. A person who invests money without working in a business may be called a *silent partner* or a *limited partner.*

To form a partnership, the partners must create a legal contract, called a *partnership agreement,* that sets up the terms of ownership. Often, a partnership agreement also determines how income from the business will be shared among the partners. A partnership must file a special income tax return with federal and state agencies. Profits must be distributed to the partners at the end of each year. These profits must be included in earnings reports filed by the individual partners. By comparison, a corporation, described below, may retain a part of its earnings for use in building the business.

In most cases, a partnership is a larger—and often a more complex—business than a proprietorship. Many partnerships, particularly those in some professions, have thousands of employees. Some of these organizations have business volumes that run into hundreds of millions of dollars a year. These firms retain the partnership form because of legal requirements. Partners are responsible for the actions taken or damages caused by a business. This is called *liability.*

In some fields, such as public accounting and some branches of law, partnerships are the main form of business organization. This is because of laws that require accountability for professionals who deal with certain government agencies. For example, large companies owned by stockholders must file business statements with the federal Securities and Exchange Commission. Only proprietorships and partnerships, organizations in which the owners are

Large corporations *seek symbols that identify them in their marketplace. This building is a distinctive symbol that identifies Transamerica Corporation.*
COURTESY OF TRANSAMERICA CORPORATION

liable for actions of their companies, may prepare these reports. The reason: Partner/owners are responsible for the transactions and commitments of their business. This situation changes when a corporation is formed.

What Is a Corporation And How Does It Work?

A *corporation* is an organization in which the functions of ownership and management are separated. It is possible for people who own corporations to work for their companies. But, if they do, they play two separate roles. A corporation, legally, is known as a *fictitious person.* That is, the corporation has an identity of its own. It is registered as a taxpayer. A corporation also may take part in legal actions in the same way as an individual person.

Ownership of a corporation is represented by a stock certificate. The owners are stockholders. Employees of a business may be stockholders. Under one popular plan, employee groups purchase stock

Business Terms

proprietorship
A business that is owned and operated by an individual.

sole proprietorship
See proprietorship.

partnership
A business owned by two or more persons who may but need not be involved in management.

silent partner
A part owner of a partnership business who is not active in management.

limited partner
An investor in a partnership who is not active in management and assumes only limited, defined responsibilities to the organization.

partnership agreement
A legal contract that presents terms for formation and operation of a partnership.

liability
Legal responsibility for individual or business actions.

corporation
An organization in which the functions of ownership and management are separated, with ownership represented by stock certificates.

fictitious person
The legal status of a corporation; a corporation has an identity of its own and the same responsibilities as any citizen.

in companies as part of their retirement income program. Part of the idea of such plans is to give employees a greater interest in the success of their company.

Regardless of whether they are employees or outsiders, stockholders have a special interest. They invest to receive income from the business or in the hope that the value of their shares will increase. Shares can be purchased or sold at any time.

As you know, management is through a board of directors. An important factor linked to the corporate form of business deals with liability. As you know, proprietors or partners can be held responsible personally for actions of businesses they own. A corporation is responsible for acts of its managers. Owners, or stockholders, are not liable; the fictitious person assumes legal responsibilities. Therefore, for legal purposes, a *corporate shield* is formed that protects owners from effects of business activities. In many instances, this is one of the major purposes for forming a corporation.

The corporate form of business can lead to special, costly tax situations. Owners of a corporation receive a portion of profits as income. These payments are called *dividends.* Dividends are paid according to the number of shares of stock owned. The tax problem comes from the fact that the corporation itself pays taxes on its earnings. The money used for dividends represents income after the business has paid its taxes. Then the stockholders must declare the dividend income and pay personal taxes on the amount received. In effect, then, dividend income is taxed twice.

In some instances, small corporations are formed by people who seek liability protection as the main advantage of this form of organization. In these instances, arrangements can be made to distribute all income to owners or managers, leaving the business with no taxable income. However, the corporate form of business often requires careful study and trade-offs between considerations over liability protection and tax exposures.

Until recently, people who provided professional services—including doctors, lawyers, and accountants—were not permitted to incorporate. Laws required that these people remain liable for their actions. Recently, a special form, the *professional corporation,* has been authorized. This makes it possible for professional people to enjoy some of the financial benefits of corporations. Included are the ability to set up pension and retirement programs and to make investments through the business. However, owners of professional corporations remain liable for the services they render. For example, a doctor still is liable if a patient is mistreated or injured in the course of medical care.

What Is a Cooperative And How Does It Work?

A *cooperative,* in effect, is a special form of business that is owned by its customers or suppliers. The owners of a cooperative are called *members.* There are two forms of cooperative, or *co-op.* One is a *consumer co-op,* the other a *producer co-op.*

A consumer co-op is owned by customers. For example, a number of food stores or other retail operations are owned by consumers. The members pay fees to join the co-op. Professional managers run the business. Since the co-op does not have to make a profit, it generally can sell products at prices lower than those of profit-making retailers. At the end of the year, any surplus money left in a co-op is distributed to members, often in proportion to the amount of their purchases.

Producer co-ops are most popular in agriculture. Two well-known producer co-ops are the distributors of Sunkist oranges and Land o' Lakes butter and other dairy products. The growers, dairy farmers, or other suppliers who deliver products to the co-op also pay membership fees. The co-op, run by professional managers, strives for a profit. Profits then are distributed to members as income.

Many supplier cooperatives process and market well-known products, such as California raisins. Popular promotions, such as the TV commercials that use clay animation techniques, help to promote the products of all grower members of the co-op.
COURTESY OF CALIFORNIA RAISIN ADVISORY BOARD

The cooperative form of business has some of the features of a corporation. These include liability protection because a co-op is a fictitious person and employs professional managers who are not owners. However, a co-op also is like a partnership because all profits are distributed to members.

Can Organization Options Be Combined?

The legal organization forms described above are basic structures provided for under laws in individual states. In addition, companies or individuals can set up structures that modify or combine these basic options. Some examples:

- A *franchise* is a right, or assignment, that permits one business to use the name of another. For example, a fast-food chain may sell rights for private businesses to use its name. Usually, the company that grants the franchise provides identifying signs and sales literature. Also, the company that grants the franchise requires that the franchise holder perform in certain ways. As an

Business Terms

corporate shield
The legal protection against liability afforded to owners or employees of a corporation, which is legally responsible for acts of its owners or managers.

dividend
Corporate profits distributed to shareholders.

professional corporation
A special form of business organization available to professional persons.

cooperative (co-op)
A form of business organization that is owned by its customers or suppliers.

member
Term for an owner-participant in a cooperative.

consumer co-op
A cooperative owned by its customers.

producer co-op
A cooperative owned by its suppliers.

franchise
A right, or assignment, that permits one business to use the name of another.

example, almost all auto dealers hold franchises from manufacturers. A franchise operator can use any business form—proprietorship, partnership, or corporation. However, most franchise operators are incorporated.

- A *limited partnership* is one in which one partner takes primary responsibility for running a business. This person or organization is the *general partner.* The other partners, whose responsibilities are limited by the terms of partnership agreements, are limited partners. This organization form is used frequently for real estate investments.

- A *joint venture* is an organization formed to do just one job or to operate in a special, limited area. The joint venture generally is formed through an agreement of two or more companies.

Organization is a vital factor that can determine success or failure of a business. The organization operates the business to carry out its strategies and plans. In this and earlier chapters, you have looked at factors connected with forming, planning for, and organizing a business. Starting with the next chapter, you will be ready to take a close-up look at the work involved in running a business. You will begin this experience from the bottom up; the next chapter deals with business operations.

Review 5.4

1. What is a fictitious name?

2. What are the main characteristics of a proprietorship?

3. What are the main characteristics of a partnership?

4. What are the main characteristics of a corporation?

5. What are the main characteristics of a cooperative?

Business Terms

limited partnership
A form of organization that assigns limited roles and responsibilities to some partners and gives other partners the right to run the organization.

general partner
The partner who undertakes management duties and is responsible for the operation of a limited partnership.

joint venture
An organization formed by two or more persons or businesses to do just one job or to operate in a special, limited area.

Chapter Summary

- Each company needs an organization plan that identifies the jobs that must be done to deliver its products and services.

- The organization of a business often is described with a diagram called an organization chart.

- Top-level positions in an organization chart may be assigned to stockholders (owners), directors, a chairperson, and a president.

- Second-level positions in an organization chart generally are used to establish the functions necessary to run the company.

- Operations managers are responsible for day-to-day delivery of products or services.

- The lines on an organization chart define the links among a company's workers.

- Responsibilities and authority should be defined in documents that accompany an organization chart.

- Responsibilities are the things a person is assigned to do.

❑ Authority is permission to take specific actions to get a job done.

❑ Individual jobs should be described, step by step, in procedures manuals.

❑ A business has the same legal and financial responsibilities as a person.

❑ The name by which a business is known is called a fictitious name. This name must be registered with a local government agency.

❑ A proprietorship, or sole proprietorship, is a business owned by an individual. The individual is responsible for the business and its taxes as an extension of personal activities.

❑ A partnership is owned by two or more people. Partners may or may not be active in running the business. Partnership income is distributed to the partners before the close of each year.

❑ A corporation is a fictitious person that has an identity of its own. A corporation is liable for its acts and shields owners from responsibility for actions taken by the business. Corporations pay taxes on their own income. Then, shareholders who receive dividends as income also pay taxes.

❑ A cooperative is a business owned by its customers or suppliers. Two types of cooperatives are consumer cooperatives and producer cooperatives.

Questions to Think About

Based on what you have learned to date, answer the following questions in one or more complete sentences.

1. What are the titles of top-management positions and what do top-level executives do?

2. What are the functions and responsibilities of second-level managers?

3. What are the functions and responsibilities of operations managers?

4. What do the terms responsibility and authority mean and what are the differences between them?

5. What is a fictitious name and how is it created?

6. What is a proprietorship and what are its advantages and disadvantages?

7. What is a partnership and what are its advantages and disadvantages?

8. What is a corporation and what are its advantages and disadvantages?

9. Why is a corporation sometimes called a fictitious person?

10. How is it possible that earnings of a corporation are taxed twice?

Definitions

Write a complete sentence that defines each of the terms below.

department	function
organization plan	organization structure
stockholder	board of directors
proprietorship	partnership
corporation	fictitious person
chief executive officer	chief operating officer
chairman of the board	director

Projects

The purpose of the assignments below is to encourage you to increase your learning through outside reading or work assignments.

1. Draw an organization chart for your school. Ask your teacher about positions and lines of responsibility with which you are not familiar.

2. Through readings in a library or in a textbook on government, develop an organization chart for the federal government. Show the related positions of the voters, the judicial system, the two houses of the legislature, and the executive branch.

CHAPTER 6

What Operations Do Businesses Perform?

The Think Tank

When you finish reading this chapter and complete your work assignments, you should be able to answer the following questions.

❑ What is the role of the operations function of a business?

❑ What are the relationships between operations personnel and the customers of a business?

❑ What resources are needed by the operations function?

❑ What are the main organizational groups within the operations function?

❑ How is information reported among the organizational groups within the operations function?

❑ How are results of operations measured?

DOING BUSINESS

"That's not the way to do it!" Tom was tense. It showed in his appearance as he gave Maria a sharp look.

Tom had been called upon to handle a complaint from a customer who had insisted on talking to Maria's supervisor.

"Let's go over this and make sure that this kind of thing doesn't happen again," Tom said. "Tell me what happened."

"That creep wouldn't listen," Maria started, still angry. Tom cut her off.

"We won't get anywhere calling customers names," Tom said. "Our goal now is to understand what happened and to figure out what should be done if you get the same kind of call again. Start over. Give me information. He may truly be a creep. But he has a right to be. He's a customer."

"Okay," Maria said. She took a deep breath and continued. "Mr. Johnston started screaming the minute I picked up the phone. He said he had been promised a shipment of gauze and hypodermic needles by overnight express. The order didn't arrive for three days. Then, he got the wrong shipment. The stuff he got was supposed to go to another hospital. He was almost out of the supplies, an emergency.

"What did you say?" Tom asked.

"I told him not to yell at me. I didn't ship his order. It wasn't my mistake."

"Okay," Tom said. He seemed relieved at the explanation. "There's our problem. The customer

74

Smooth operations require cooperation from employees who perform different jobs. In this photo, a production worker is receiving needed parts from an inventory stock room.

PHOTO BY LISA SCHWABER-BARZILEY

didn't want to know whose fault it was or wasn't. He wanted something done. Also, he wanted to be told that we would take care of the problem and get him the items he needs.''

Tom continued: ''When anyone from National Medical Supply picks up the phone and talks to the customer, we are the company. We are responsible for the services our customers get. If there's been a mistake, it's up to us to fix it. It doesn't matter who made the mistake. Mistakes do happen. Anybody can understand that. Our job is to understand what happened and to correct the situation. We're here to satisfy customers. We can't satisfy anyone with arguments about who's right or wrong.''

''What did you do?'' Maria asked.

''I told him that I would contact the warehouse personally and make sure that his order got out immediately. I invited him to wait on the line a moment while I contacted the warehouse. Then I called Chin and explained what had happened. I got his promise that he would take care of the order personally, right away. After that, I got back to the customer and said everything was taken care of. That satisfied him.''

''I see what you mean,'' Maria said. ''That's a lot better than trying to argue with someone who has a legitimate complaint. I'll keep my cool from

now on, even with people who get nasty on the phone.''

MEANING

Tom made an important point: As far as a company's customers are concerned, the operations people who serve them **are** the company. If one operations person makes a customer unhappy, the whole company suffers. On the other hand, satisfied customers **make** a business.

In any business, nothing happens until a customer buys something. It is the job of operations people to provide products and services that lead to satisfied customers. Without satisfied customers, there might not be a business.

WHAT DOES THE OPERATIONS FUNCTION DO?

The operations function actually runs a business. The term, run, refers to day-to-day, routine actions without which there could be no business. Included are service to customers, manufacturing products, warehousing, shipping, issuing bills, collecting money due, and ordering needed supplies.

Recall that operations people and departments are "line" functions. In a typical company, the operations function produces all of the *revenue,* or money received. In addition, 70 to 90 percent of the employees of a company usually work in operations jobs. The majority of company expenses generally go to salaries and supplies for operations. Possibly most important of all, operations people serve the company's customers.

The remaining staff and executive jobs, though they are vital, are small in number. Top- and second-level managers plan for and monitor the work of operations.

Although the following list is not complete, it covers many of the jobs and services within operations. Each of these areas is described in the discussions that follow:

- Sales
- Engineering
- Manufacturing
- Distribution.

As these operations areas are reviewed, think about the links between them. Keep in mind that a company's organization structure should be like the lineup for a sports team. The company functions should support one another. Working relationships should be smooth.

WHAT DO SALESPEOPLE DO?

The *sales,* or *marketing,* function is responsible for customer service. The marketing group's most critical job is to complete transactions with customers. A transaction, remember, is a basic act of doing business. The most typical transaction occurs when a customer buys and a seller delivers a product or service. At that time, an exchange of value takes place.

How Are Sales Transactions Handled?

Usually, a sales transaction involves an exchange of money for a specific product or service. At that time, the transaction is *documented.* Sales documents can include *invoices,* or *bills.* An invoice, also called a bill, is a document prepared by a seller. The invoice contains information that describes, or documents, the sale. This information includes the identification of the buyer and descriptions of items sold. The descriptions of products or services include quantities delivered and the prices for each. Other information on an invoice includes entries for taxes collected and a total amount of the sale. An invoice is shown in Figure 6-1.

For some types of transactions, the customer pays the seller at the time products or services are delivered. In these cases, an entry is made on the invoice to note that payment was received. The invoice then serves as a proof of payment, or *receipt,* for the buyer.

Credit transactions. The invoice also can be a demand for a future payment. That is, the products or services are delivered and the customer agrees to pay the seller later. Payment can be made under a number of different plans. One arrangement is typical for sales between businesses. This requires complete payment of the invoice at a given time. Payment typically is due 30 days after delivery of products or services.

Under another arrangement, payment can be made over time. That is, the buyer makes a series of payments, perhaps once a month for 12, 24, or 36 months. This means the buyer receives *credit.* Credit is a sales plan in which the buyer is given an extended time to pay for purchased items.

In exchange for the ability to pay over time, the buyer pays special, additional charges. These may be called *interest* or *carrying charges.* Interest is a charge for the use of money. In effect, the buyer borrows money for the purchase and repays with interest. The interest represents a charge for the

Banner Manufacturing Company

187 Hudson Street   Troy, NY 14302

INVOICE No.   16-3077

Invoice Date   04/02/89

CUST. #:   78-4324

Sold To: Kent Company
                10 Green Avenue
                Pasadena, CA 91106

ITEM NO.	QTY	DESCRIPTION	UNIT PRICE	TOTAL
0640	15	Ratchet sets	$ 38.00	$ 525.00
0321	150	5mm Allen Wren	0.50	75.00
			TOTAL DUE	600.00

Figure 6-1. Invoices like the one shown document transactions. Invoices also are the basis for producing the income on which a business depends.

convenience of paying in a series of small payments, or **installments**. A carrying charge is a fee paid for the services and costs of extending credit. Some sales involve both interest and carrying charges.

Depending upon your viewpoint, credit can be either very costly or very profitable. Consider a home loan of $50,000 for 30 years at 10.5 percent interest. The purchaser of the home will make payments that total approximately $5,400 per year for 30 years. Total payments on a $50,000 loan come to $162,000. For the business that lends the money, a loan of this type will produce a $112,000 profit on an investment of $50,000. For many businesses, interest and carrying charges are major sources of profit.

Receipts for cash sales. In some types of selling situations, transaction documents are receipts, rather than invoices. This is the case when cash registers are involved. The salesperson enters information on your purchases. The register lists the items bought and totals the amount due. When money is presented to the salesperson, the register records the payment and calculates your change. Following payment, a printed tape is removed from the register and given to the customer. This printed tape lists and totals the purchases for the transaction. The transaction is complete when money is presented in exchange for the register tape and the merchandise.

Business Terms

revenue
The money received by a business.

sales
The function of a business that is responsible for completing transactions with customers.

marketing
See sales.

documented
Completion of a transaction through the recording of information, often on a special business form.

invoice
A document that records information on a sales transaction.

bill
See invoice.

receipt
A document that records delivery of money or goods.

credit
A sales plan in which the buyer is given an extended time to pay for purchased items.

interest
A charge (or payment) for the use of money.

carrying charge
A service fee related to a credit purchase.

Credit card transactions. In other situations, products are exchanged for a credit card charge slip. The principle remains the same: A transaction is an exchange of value. On the seller's side, the value is in products or services. On the buyer's side, the value generally is money or a promise for future payment. From the standpoint of business operations, these different forms of sales transactions represent procedures that operations people have to master.

Review 6.1

1. Are operations people considered to be line or staff employees?

2. What are the main duties of sales personnel?

3. What forms can sales transactions take?

How Do Salespeople Deal With Customers?

Salespeople contact and deal with customers in a number of different ways. Some of the most common arrangements, or transaction patterns, include:

- Outside sales
- Inside sales
- Telephone sales
- Direct-mail sales.

Outside sales. *Outside sales* transactions are conducted in the customer's place of business. That is, the salesperson visits the customer's office or store and attempts to sell products or services. This pattern is typical for sales transactions among businesses. Salespeople visit stores to attempt to sell products to be displayed for sale to consumers. Salespeople from steel mills or machinery companies visit factories to sell tools or materials.

Many sales of this type are classified as *wholesale.* This means that buyers are not the consumers of the product. For example, a wholesale transaction might involve sale of two dozen jump suits to a department store. The department store then will offer these garments to consumers at *retail.* In general, a wholesale transaction delivers products to a business that will, in turn, sell them to consumers. Retail sales are made to consumers, usually in a place of business operated by a retailer.

However, some retail sales are made by outside salespeople who visit the homes of consumers. This applies to some services, such as insurance policies. Also, some companies specialize in selling items such as laundry products and cosmetics through outside sales forces. These salespersons travel to customer homes or offices.

The point: One method of selling requires that sales representatives travel to meet their customers. The transactions take place in customers' homes, offices, or factories.

Inside sales. *Inside sales* take place at the stores, offices, or factories of selling companies. The people who serve you in retail stores are inside salespeople. A requirement for inside selling is that customers must take the action of visiting the store or other place of business. The seller must have an attractive place of business. Generally, location is important. The store must be in a location that attracts people. Sometimes, the seller must provide large parking areas for customers. Often, special advertising is needed to attract customers.

Companies that conduct inside sales face the expense of setting up and operating customer-service facilities. By contrast, outside sales operations do not have to set up special stores or showrooms. However, outside sales expenses do include the costs of operating cars. The time it takes salespeople to travel to customer locations also builds operating costs.

Inside sales transactions are different in nature from outside sales. When a customer comes to a seller's place of business, this is an expression of interest. The salesperson can assume that the customer is interested in buying the products displayed. In some instances, such as supermarkets and some department stores, the customers sell themselves.

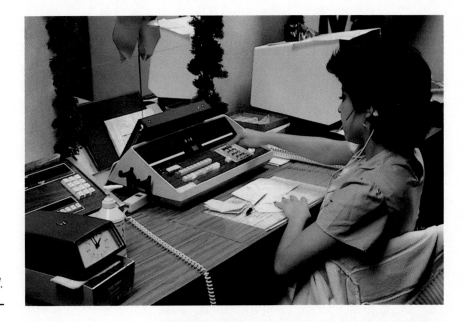

Salespeople are responsible for service to customers. The satisfaction of customers, in turn, is essential to the success of any business. This photo shows a telephone salesperson accepting calls on an electronic switchboard.

These are self-service outlets. The customer selects merchandise and brings it to a cashier. Transactions require only minimum service and support. Sales personnel simply take money from buyers.

Telephone sales.   *Telephone sales* are conducted by people who do not see their customers. In some situations, customers call the seller to place orders. Telephone sales are a common technique for wholesalers of business or manufacturing supplies. For example, many automotive service garages place orders for parts by calling distributors.

In addition, many companies market their products or services by calling prospective customers by phone. The salesperson describes the offering. If the customer wishes to buy, the exchange of value can be a credit invoice or a charge against a credit card number provided by the buyer.

This method of selling became possible with introduction of special telephone services. The service is known as *WATS,* for Wide Area Telephone Service. Companies pay a flat fee to the telephone company for special lines that support customer contact. Some lines provide "in-WATS" service that permits customers to make toll-free calls. "Out-WATS"

Business Terms

installment
A time payment against a credit purchase.

outside sales
Transactions conducted in the customer's place of business by a sales representative who travels to deliver products or services.

wholesale
Sales transactions conducted with companies or people who are not consumers, but are purchasing and stocking products for sale to consumers.

retail
Description of an operation that sells products directly to consumers.

inside sales
Transactions that take place at the stores, offices, or factories of selling companies.

telephone sales
Transactions in which the buyer calls the seller or the seller calls the buyer to offer products.

WATS (Wide Area Telephone Service)
A plan that permits extended, sometimes unlimited, telephone calling privileges under special, volume-discount fees.

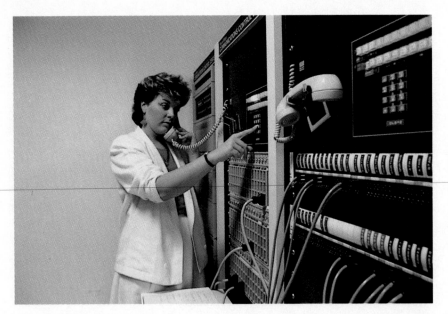

Communication networks that process both voice and data transmissions have become essential for supporting business operations. This communications center is in the headquarters of a large bank. The communications facilities connect computer terminals at multiple branches to a central computer.

PHOTO BY LISA SCHWABER-BARZILEY

lines permit company salespeople to make unlimited calls for fixed service charges.

Direct-mail sales.   *Direct-mail sales,* as the name suggests, is a technique for offering products or services through the mail. The U. S. Postal Service and other organizations have special rates for volume customers. These customers offer products or services through mailings to lists of people. Compiling and selling mailing lists is a big business in itself. Each direct-mail offering includes some method for the prospective customer to respond. This may be a WATS number with an 800 area code. Or it may be a coupon that the customer returns to place an order.

How Are Transactions Processed?

Regardless of how customers are contacted, all salespeople are responsible for *recording* and documenting transactions. The term "recording" indicates that information on the transaction is entered into an accounting and/or computer system. This means that the transaction is included in the information on the condition or status of the company.

If the recorded transaction is a credit sale, the information system will show that money is owed to the company. The item becomes an *account receivable,* which means the money is due from a customer. If the salesperson receives cash or a check, the money becomes part of a bank deposit. All sales, cash or credit, generate information that guides manufacturing or distribution people. Sales transactions reduce the number of products in stock, *inventory.* In turn, the inventory reduction means that the items that were sold have to be replaced. This is done by manufacturing new items or buying them from a wholesale supplier.

The point: Processing a sales transaction is a starting point for the communication of information that supports the entire company.

What Are the Internal Relationships Between Sales and Other Groups?

In addition to serving customers, salespeople must establish relationships within their own organization. Salespeople support the manufacturing and distribution functions. Sales creates the outlets that make it possible to deliver products or services at profitable prices. Possibly most important of all, sales generates the income that supports the entire company.

Salespeople are the ones who generate orders for a company's products or services. These products or services, in turn, come through a long chain of support and contacts. The sales function is supported by all departments and employees within an organization. These other functions, in effect, are selling their services and support to the sales department.

If a company is well organized, everyone has a customer. That's the purpose of lines of responsibility and authority. Lines of responsibility define customers. In any business organization, customer satisfaction is everybody's business. The final responsibility for customer service rests with the president or chief operating officer. In many organizations, the president can't know and serve every customer. So, responsibility for customer service is *delegated,* or assigned to, persons at lower levels in the organization.

Through lines of responsibility, the whole organization contributes to the quality of products and services delivered. Only comparatively few employees of a company actually deal with customers. However, the rest should be aware of customer-service responsibilities within the organization. Everyone has customers. Those who don't serve customers outside the company should recognize that they have "inside customers." Inside customers are the users of services or information provided. Customer service results from a chain of relationships among inside suppliers and customers.

Tom's actions in the incident at the beginning of this chapter are an example. Tom recognized that it was his job to find out what would satisfy the customer. When he knew what was expected, he turned inward within the National Medical Supply organization. Tom recognized that, within the organization structure, he was a customer. He recognized that Chin was responsible to help him satisfy customers. That's the way it should be. The end result of a company's operations should be satisfied customers.

The point: Everyone who works for and collects a paycheck from a company has a responsibility for serving its customers. Every job in a company can and should contribute toward customer satisfaction.

What Qualifications Are Needed for Sales Jobs?

To work successfully in sales, a person must like people. A salesperson must enjoy meeting and satisfying customers. Most successful salespeople have an outgoing, or *extroverted,* personality. An extrovert is a person who enjoys the company of others.

Sales work carries risks. If a salesperson is successful, everyone in the company benefits from the income generated. If sales are not as high as expected, the salesperson must be able to endure blame for failure. Many salespeople are paid on a *commission* basis. This means their earnings are based on

Business Terms

direct-mail sales
A technique for offering products or services through the mail.

recording
The entry of transaction information on a business or into a computer for inclusion in the company's information processing and/or accounting systems.

account receivable
A charge-sale item for which payment is due.

inventory
Items that are being held in storage for sale or use in a manufacturing operation.

delegate
To assign responsibility to another person.

extrovert
A person who is "outgoing" and enjoys the company of others.

commission
A plan under which people are paid a percentage of the value of products they sell.

a percentage of the value of the sales they transact. This, in itself, is risky. If sales are high, so are earnings. If sales fall off, the saleperson's income also declines.

Many people prefer jobs in which they are not required to be nice to customers. The risky nature of sales income bothers many people. Also, not everyone enjoys meeting and interacting with other people. People who prefer to be by themselves or with a limited number of friends usually don't belong in sales. People with inward-looking personalities, *introverts,* probably will do better in other occupations. Some other operational functions and their opportunities are covered below.

Review 6.2

1. What are outside sales and inside sales and what are the differences between these activities?

2. What is the starting point for developing sales information?

3. What are lines of responsibility?

4. What is meant by the term "internal customer"?

WHAT CONTRIBUTION IS MADE BY ENGINEERING?

An *engineer* is a person who applies technology to designing and building products. An engineer also selects the tools and materials to be used in production. These jobs are part of the engineering function. But other responsibilities also are included.

The engineering function, in effect, is the planning, monitoring, and operating management for production of a company's products. Engineers design the products. Then, they determine how the products are to be made and from what materials. In addition, engineers determine the time that will be required to build products. Engineers also may be involved in setting up production methods and schedules. Specifications for products and work to be done also come from engineers.

In effect, engineers manage technology. Technology itself is not a topic to be covered in this book. However, the engineering function also has a business aspect. Within this function are the people who purchase and provide materials for production. Responsibilities also include recommendations about what production machinery is needed, how large a factory should be, and how many workers are required. Engineers determine how much a product will cost to make. This information is used by the marketing function to determine if the product can be sold profitably—and at what price.

Engineering as a specialty represents a marriage between technology and management. Engineers, for example, react to marketing information to help develop the products that customers appear to want. Engineering then works with manufacturing to set up facilities and procedures to build the products.

The background and qualifications of an engineer are highly specialized. An engineer generally is a college graduate trained in mathematics and science, as well as in materials and production methods. Some engineers interact with customers and require marketing skills. Others may work in laboratories and in shops where production methods are developed.

WHAT ROLE DOES MANUFACTURING PLAY?

A *manufacturing function* makes a company's products. Manufacturing operations are positioned in a middle ground between engineering and marketing. Engineers or production planners place orders to be filled by manufacturing. Often, the products are turned over to distribution specialists who receive sales orders and make deliveries.

Manufacturing has its highly technical aspects, which are not covered in this book. However, manufacturing also applies business principles. A factory is a resource that has to be used properly. The factory must produce enough products to assure that the business operates profitably. Production management requires expertise in *shop loading.* Shop load-

Manufacturing people create the products that represent a company in its marketplace. People within the manufacturing function need technical expertise and also should enjoy building things.

COURTESY OF MCDONNELL DOUGLAS, CORP., ST. LOUIS

ing is a scheduling and work assignment process. Production jobs are assigned to specific work centers in a factory. Scheduling of jobs also is part of shop loading. So is problem solving. For example, if demand for products is high, manufacturing managers must schedule overtime or start extra shifts. If demand falls, manufacturing managers have the unpleasant job of laying people off.

Manufacturing people must enjoy building things. They also must be the kind of people who enjoy the security of working in one place day after day. A manufacturing employee may have to do the same job repeatedly. Therefore, manufacturing people must be able to handle routine.

Finally, there is the matter of product quality. This is strictly a manufacturing opportunity. Manufacturing people must have pride in doing something well, in turning out quality. There is an old saying among production people: Quality cannot be inspected into a product, it must be built in. Quality and productivity are the challenges faced by manufacturing. Marketing and others in the organization depend on manufacturing to meet these challenges.

WHAT DOES THE DISTRIBUTION GROUP DO?

Most sales are made—and customers are served—from stocks of products that exist and are ready to deliver, inventory. Management of inventory is a key

Business Terms

introvert
A person who tends to be quiet and who generally prefers to avoid meeting or working with strangers.

engineer
A person who applies technology to design and build products.

manufacturing function
The operating unit or department that makes a company's products.

shop loading
A scheduling and work assignment process for a manufacturing facility.

to both quality of service and profits. Managing inventories and deliveries of products is, therefore, a vital operations function.

A major challenge in distribution management is to monitor sales and to match inventories to customer needs. Sales information provides a measure of customer demand for a product. Predictions about product demand are used to determine how much inventory to stock. For example, suppose customer demand for a product is averaging 100 units per week. A distribution manager must determine how long it will take to receive new stocks from a supplier.

Assume the time required for ordering, delivery, and restocking the warehouse is three weeks. If sales average 100 a week, the warehouse needs at least 300 units as a minimum stock. However, if only 300 units are ordered, there is a chance the company might run out of the item. Thus, a manager might decide to keep 450 units in stock. When information indicates stocks are lower than 450, a new order is placed. If demand for the product rises or falls, inventory levels must be adjusted.

Thus, distribution management depends upon information provided by other functions within the business. Distribution managers, in turn, must be able to react to constant change in supply and demand. They also require skills for collecting and analyzing information.

Review 6.3

1. What responsibilities do engineers assume?

2. What is shop loading and why is this job important?

3. What is inventory and why are inventory levels important?

WHAT RESOURCES ARE NEEDED FOR SUPPORT OF OPERATIONS?

Operationally, each company is a *system*. In a business sense, a system is a set of related parts that function together to produce a planned result. Each system is made up of a basic set of resources. These include:

- People
- Procedures
- Information
- Tools
- Machines
- Capital
- Energy
- Time.

People are the key. They develop the ideas around which businesses are built. People identify markets and develop products or services. They make the plans for delivering products or services to identified markets.

Procedures are the guides that direct the people who operate the business. Following procedures, people perform the operations needed to serve customers.

Information models the operations of a company and provides the basis for identifying and dealing with exceptions.

Tools are devices used by individual people for specific jobs.

Machines are units of equipment that actually manufacture or handle products.

Capital includes the money, the buildings, and the land that supports business operations.

Energy, in the modern world, includes electricity, oil, natural gas, and other forces that power and provide light and transportation needed for doing business.

Time provides the framework for doing business. Time is when products have to be delivered. Time provides the opportunity to build and operate business organizations.

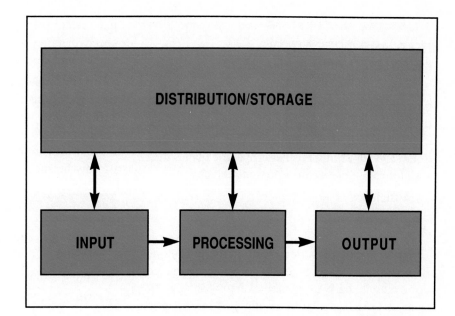

Figure 6-2. *The steps in an operational system, diagrammed here, include input, processing, output, and distribution/storage.*

HOW DO OPERATIONAL SYSTEMS WORK?

A business is a system. A system, in turn, consists of a series of steps that are followed to deliver planned results. The basic parts of an operational system are:

- Input
- Processing
- Output
- Distribution and storage.

A diagram showing the sequence and relationships of these steps is presented in Figure 6-2. The elements of a business operations systems are identified and discussed briefly in the paragraphs that follow.

Input takes in all of the resources needed to conduct business transactions. These include customer orders, materials, and money needed to create and deliver products and services.

Processing includes the procedures for running the company and for producing the products and services it sells.

Output is the actual completion of manufacturing or the preparations needed to provide services. For example, output might occur at the end of an assembly line. In an auto plant, the cars have been manufactured and are parked in a lot waiting for delivery.

Distribution and storage is the function that gets products to the points where they can be turned over to customers. Storage often is necessary as a means for holding products in inventories that support sales.

These elements exist within any business system. The descriptions above apply to actual product development and delivery. Similar processing cycles apply to the capture, processing, and delivery of information to users. The process steps are similar. But the processing of information can be different from the manufacture and distribution of products.

Business Terms

system
A set of related parts that function together to produce a planned result.

HOW ARE OPERATIONS MEASURED AND MANAGED?

As indicated, business operations are measured through use of information. Information represents, or models, the company. This information describes events and generates summaries that show the condition and status of a business. Specific values measured through use of information include:

- Efficiency
- Effectiveness.

Efficiency measures how well a thing is done. *Effectiveness* measures results, or values produced. For example, early computers were extremely efficient at processing large amounts of information. However, these computers were not highly effective as business tools. One problem was that early computers did not have the capacity to print business documents at high speeds. Another problem was that information storage capabilities were limited. Because of the way information was stored and accessed, computers could not be used for direct processing of business transactions. Computers did not realize their potential effectiveness until high-speed printing and disk storage devices were invented and developed.

At this point, the thing to remember is how business operations are evaluated. Operations are measured by how well a job is done and how useful its results prove to be. The chapter that follows provides more information in this area. It deals with the topic of how business operations are monitored.

Review 6.4

1. Why are company operations described as a system?

2. What is the meaning of efficiency?

3. What is effectiveness in company operations?

Business Terms

efficiency
A measure of how well a job or function is performed.

effectiveness
A measure of results, or values produced.

Chapter Summary

- ❏ The operations function in most businesses is divided into a series of working groups.

- ❏ The groups that make up an operations function can include sales, engineering, manufacturing, and distribution.

- ❏ The main job of salespeople is to conduct transactions with customers.

- ❏ Transactions are documented with invoices, cash register receipts, or credit card sales tickets.

- ❏ A transaction is complete when an exchange of value occurs. The exchange generally involves delivery of products or services and receipt of money or a promise to pay.

- ❏ Sales transactions are conducted in a number of different ways. Customer contacts may be made by outside salespeople in customer offices. Inside salespeople deal with customers in stores or other facilities. Sales also are made over the telephone and by mail.

- ❏ Salespeople generate sales information. Processing of information about sales begins with the capture of information on items sold and customers. This is the starting point for the handling of information necessary to run any company.

- ❏ In addition to serving external customers, salespeople must establish internal relationships with all operating functions within the organization.

❑ Because of the nature of their work, most salespeople are extroverts who enjoy meeting and dealing with others.

❑ Engineers apply technology to design and build products. The engineering function determines the equipment and materials to be used for each product. Also, standards and schedules often are developed in engineering.

❑ Manufacturing actually produces the products a company sells. A special challenge for manufacturing is to assure product quality.

❑ The distribution function stocks inventories of materials and products to support manufacturing and customer deliveries.

❑ Each company operates as a system. A system is a set of related parts that include people, procedures, information, tools, machines, capital, energy, and time.

❑ An operational system is made up of a sequence of functions: input, processing, output, and distribution and storage.

Definitions

Write a complete sentence that defines each of the terms below.

documented	invoice
receipt	credit
interest	carrying charge
installment	wholesale
retail	account receivable
inventory	delegate

Questions to Think About

Based on what you have learned to date, answer the following questions in one or more complete sentences.

1. What is meant by the saying: "The customer is always right"?

2. What portion of a typical company is devoted to the operations function?

3. What are the parts of a sales transaction?

4. What is credit and how are credit transactions completed?

5. What are the advantages and disadvantages of selling through an outside sales force?

6. What are the advantages and disadvantages of selling through an inside sales force?

7. How should employees in a sales department interact with other workers within the operations function of a business?

8. What are the roles and responsibilities of the engineering function?

9. What are the roles and responsibilities of the manufacturing function?

10. What are the roles and responsibilities of the distribution function?

11. What are the resources needed for any system?

12. What are the working parts, or operational steps, of any system?

13. How are operations evaluated and/or measured?

Projects

The purpose of the assignments below is to encourage you to increase your learning through outside reading or work assignments.

1. Describe how you use the operational system parts—input, processing, output, and distribution and storage—in your work as a student?

2. Describe one good sales experience and one bad sales experience that you have had. Describe what was wrong in the bad experience and tell what you liked about the good experience.

3. Many companies offer warranties—or guaranties of useful service—for their products. Tell how a company's warranty depends upon the manufacturing function to produce quality products.

CHAPTER 7

How Are Business Operations Monitored?

The Think Tank

When you finish reading this chapter and complete your work assignments, you should be able to answer the following questions.

❑ What are budgets and how are they used?

❑ What is data collection and what role does it play in management?

❑ What are information summaries and why are they important?

❑ What is management by exception and how is it used?

❑ How is an information model used to monitor operations?

DOING BUSINESS

"I thought I was making good money," Jaime said. "Then I found out how much it costs to live on your own. Now I realize what a break I've had being able to live with my folks. Even with the raise I just got, it would be rough to try to set up my own apartment. To be able to live on my own, I'll need a roommate to share expenses."

"It's the same with me," Paul responded. "I've been working longer than you have. And I don't have parents who live near work. Even though I earn more than you do, I still can't make it without someone to share the rent."

"My father is pretty good with money," Jaime continued. "We talked it over. My folks agree that it's time for me to move out on my own. But it's rough.

"When I began to talk to my father," Jaime said, "I thought I was in pretty good shape. With the new raise, my gross pay comes to more than $900 per month. But my first paycheck was a shock. Between income taxes, health care, and other deductions, I take home less than $700 a month. There's no way I could rent an apartment on my own. The place we're looking at rents for $530. Unless we split the rent, I can't afford anything I've looked at."

"That's why I'm glad we met," Paul responded. "We get along okay. We work together. I know you have a regular job. You do good work, so you should have no trouble keeping up your income. And you know I've been on the job even longer than you have."

"It should work out fine," Jaime said. "You've been on your own longer than I have. So, you should be a better cook."

Information represents and guides company operations. Computer-developed information schedules and directs operations such as the shipping of products. Entries into computer systems update information files that model the status of a company.
COURTESY OF HEWLETT-PACKARD CO.

MEANING

Jaime and Paul have recognized the importance of planning for use of their income. The two young men have done this by figuring out how much money they can expect to have—their take-home pay. Then they have figured their major living expense, housing. In the process, they have recognized that they have a common goal: Each needs an affordable place to live. By getting together, they have come up with a plan for sharing expenses. Each can afford half the rent. But neither could pay the entire cost of the apartment.

The same general principle applies in business operations. Managers have to predict how much money a company will earn. Then they have to plan for how the money will be spent. In business, the idea is to spend less than you earn. The amount left over is profit, a major goal for business operations. In business, just as in personal life, it takes information to manage the use of money. Jaime's information involved expected earnings and costs for rent

and other expenses. In business, the process is more complicated. But the idea is the same.

HOW ARE PLANS USED TO GUIDE OPERATIONS?

Jaime's personal strategy was to be able to live on his own, to take control of his own life. He translated his strategy to action by developing information about what it would take to carry out his strategy. Once he had information, he used it to make decisions.

Running a company calls for following the same basic steps. But there is more information to deal with. And the commitments involved in the use of money are on a larger scale.

Recall that a business operates within a strategy that is aimed at delivering specific products or services to identified markets. The strategy is carried out by planning for future time periods. Separate plans are set up for the current year, and for intermediate- and long-range time frames.

WHAT ARE BUDGETS AND WHAT VALUE DO THEY HAVE?

In business, day-to-day control is established by monitoring operations through use of information. As Jaime discovered, it is necessary to compare actual information with some kind of standard, or target. In business, the short-term plan that guides current operations is a *budget.*

A budget is a plan for receiving and spending money. In business, budgets generally cover current-year operations. Usually, the one-year planning period is broken into smaller parts. Some organizations budget on a quarterly (three-month) basis. Others break down annual budgets on a monthly basis.

The budget represents *expectations* from business operations. An expectation is something you think will happen in the future. To prepare a budget, managers predict the sales and other income they expect. Then they identify the portions of this expected income for expenses that will be required to run the business.

As operations go forward on a day-to-day basis, information is collected on actual operating results. If actual results match the budget, there are no major problems. However, if there are *variances,* or differences between planned and actual results, action is required. Managers have to figure out how to bridge the difference between the reality of operations and the projections used for budgets.

The name of this game is survival. A business must cover its expenses and generally must produce a profit for its owners or investors. Unless income is greater than expenses, there may not be a business. So, the ultimate success of a business lies in the ability of managers to:

1. Prepare realistic income and expense budgets.

2. Monitor operating results closely.

3. Make adjustments on the basis of experience.

HOW ARE BUDGETS DEVELOPED?

Most managers today use computers to help prepare budgets. The computer is an excellent tool for budgeting because of its ability to handle arithmetic operations in fractions of a second. However, the computer is just a tool. To use a computer effectively, it is necessary to understand the basic principles for developing and using information.

For example, suppose a manager is told that the economy will expand by five percent next year. It is a simple matter to take the figures for the current year's operations and tell the computer to add five percent to all items. This would be a slow, difficult job with pencil-and-paper methods. With a computer, a person who understands the principles involved can complete the figurework in seconds.

Because of such benefits, budgeting is credited with being the main reason for convincing executives to use computers personally. A typical budget for a small company is shown in a series of accompanying illustrations. The discussions that follow describe the way a budget is developed and used.

How About an Illustration of Budget Development Methods?

As an example, suppose Eunice Heinle is considering buying a small retail store called Rockin' Records. The store sells albums, compact discs, music videos, posters, and other items. There also is some business in video cassette rentals. Heinle knows the business. She has worked for record stores for more than six years. She was offered an opportunity to buy Rockin' Records when the owner, Jim Rounder, decided to retire. To help her determine whether to buy the store, Heinle decides to prepare a budget for a year's operation.

Her first step is simply to identify the items of income and expense for which plans will be necessary. This is done in Figure 7-1. Heinle has used her knowledge of the business to set up a framework for measuring its potential success. Notice that there are separate listings for INCOME and EXPENSE items. Each set of items will be totaled separately. Then expenses will be deducted from income. The resulting figures will be the NET INCOME, or profits before payment of taxes.

The resulting figures will be a measure of the potential profit for the business. Notice there are more expense items than income items. Heinle recognizes that success depends on her ability to control operating costs. She knows, for example, that the merchandise sold in the store has a good *markup*. In retailing, markup is the difference between the cost and selling price of an item. In the record business, markup typically is 100 percent. That is, an item that costs $5 would sell for at least $10. For a prospective owner or manager, the question is: Can the store sell enough merchandise so that the markup will be greater than the expenses for doing business?

To demonstrate Heinle's knowledge of the business, note the expense item for "shrinkage." This refers to a cost for merchandise that is worn out, broken, or possibly stolen. In the record business, it

Business Terms

budget
A plan for receiving and spending money.

expectation
Something you think will happen in the future.

variance
The difference between planned and actual results.

markup
The difference between the cost and selling price of an item.

```
              ROCKIN' RECORDS - ONE YEAR BUDGET
           ANNUAL   1ST QTR   2ND QTR   3RD QTR   4TH QTR   ACTUAL
INCOME
    Albums
    CDs
    Videos
    Posters
    Misc.

TOTAL INCOME

EXPENSES
    Rent
    Utilities
    Telephone
    Salaries
    Loan Paymt
    Shrinkage
    Advertising
    Owner Pay
    Albums
    CDs
    Videos
    Posters
    Misc.

TOTAL EXPENSES

NET INCOME
```

Figure 7-1. Budgeting begins with identification of key income and expense items. This preliminary spreadsheet contains the items to be reported for Rockin' Records.

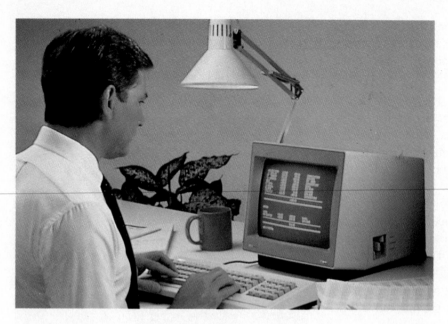

The need for budgeting is so widespread that special computer tools have been developed to help managers prepare spreadsheets electronically.
COURTESY OF RCA DATA COMMUNICATIONS PRODUCTS

is necessary to provide samples, or demonstrators. Prospective customers play these records to decide if they want to buy them. Merchandise handled in this way usually can't be sold. Therefore, the cost of these items represents an expense to the business.

As indicated, this form is a framework within which Heinle will enter information that gives her a meaningful look at the business. Heinle begins by determining the *fixed costs* that represent regular expenses of the business. As her fixed costs, she identifies rent, utilities, telephone, salaries, and the payment on the loan she will need if she buys the business. By listing the fixed costs first, Heinle can tell what her sales volumes must be to have a successful business. The sales will have to be large enough so that the markup on the merchandise sold is greater than the fixed costs.

In her study of the business, Heinle identifies the fixed costs on a monthly basis. She recognizes, of course, that there will be differences each month in costs for telephone and utility services. For these expenses, Heinle uses average costs. The following are the monthly fixed costs she anticipates:

Rent	$ 800
Utilities	70
Telephone	80
Salaries	1,700
Loan Payment	675
Total fixed costs	$3,325

Just by developing this information, Heinle can tell what the sales of her store would have to be. She knows that her markup will be 100 percent. She knows also that she will have to allow some money for advertising and shrinkage—and for her own earnings. She allows $200 per month for shrinkage, $1,000 for advertising, and a minimum of $1,500 per month for her salary from the business. This brings the expense total to about $6,000 per month. Heinle now knows that she must sell at least $12,000 per month worth of merchandise. This is the amount it will take to cover the costs of the merchandise and the average expenses, including her earnings.

By looking at past information on store operations, Heinle determines that sales have averaged between $15,000 and $16,000 per month. On the basis of this information, she decides she is interested in

```
                    ROCKIN' RECORDS - ONE YEAR BUDGET

               ANNUAL    1ST QTR   2ND QTR   3RD QTR   4TH QTR   ACTUAL
    INCOME
      Albums      92,000
      CDs         72,000
      Videos      15,200
      Posters      8,800
      Misc.        6,200

    TOTAL INCOME 194,200

    EXPENSES
      Rent         9,600
      Utilities      840
      Telephone      960
      Salaries    20,400
      Loan Payment 8,100
      Shrinkage    2,400
      Advertising 12,000
      Owner Salary 18,000
      Albums      44,000
      CDs         32,000
      Videos      26,400
      Posters      4,200
      Misc.        2,100

    TOTAL EXPENSES 181,000

    NET INCOME     13,200
```

Figure 7-2. *This spreadsheet includes the figures for an annual budget for Rockin' Records.*

buying the business. So she proceeds to do a complete operating budget for the first year, as shown in Figure 7-2.

To prepare the budgets in the accompanying illustration, Heinle uses a desktop computer with a *spreadsheet* program. A spreadsheet is a form or report with multiple columns and rows for entry of financial information. The desktop computer has become the primary tool for preparing budgets of the type shown. Also, the same computers and programs can be used to prepare operating reports that monitor actual business conditions. These "actual" figures can be compared with the budget amounts to measure how well a business is doing. Chapter 24 of this book provides more information on computer-generated spreadsheets. Also, this future chapter contains instructions that will qualify you to produce spreadsheet reports on desktop computers.

Review 7.1

1. What is a budget?

2. What time frame usually is covered by a budget?

3. What categories of financial items are shown in a budget?

4. What is the final amount shown on the bottom line of a spreadsheet that presents budget figures?

Business Terms

fixed costs
The regular, recurring expenses of the business.

spreadsheet
A form or report with multiple columns and rows for entry of financial information.

HOW ARE BUDGETS USED?

A budget is a target, an expectation of results from business operations. Most businesses use budgets as a basis for managing current operations. In large organizations, budgets generally are developed for individual operating units. For example, in a fast-food chain, each restaurant would have a budget. There also would be budgets for each region and for the company as a whole. Staff functions also would be budgeted. To illustrate, an advertising budget typically is set up to promote sales of company products.

Each manager whose operations are covered by a budget is expected to collect information on current operations. The information on actual operations is compared with the budget. Variances are analyzed and, if necessary, corrective actions are taken. Variances can occur if results are either better or worse than planned.

If actual performance is better than the budget, operations may be expanded. New people may be hired. In a fast-food chain, regional managers might suggest opening new restaurants near those that are showing high profits. If actual performance is lower than the budget, adjustments may be considered. The regional manager might consider additional billboard advertising to call attention to certain restaurants. Also, the work force may be reduced at restaurants where sales are lower than expected.

HOW DO BUDGETS RELATE TO FINANCIAL PLANNING?

As the above examples demonstrate, budgets generally cover short periods of time. Typically, a budget will be for a maximum of one year. In some businesses, budgets are reviewed and changed each three or six months. From information in earlier chapters, it is obvious that budgets support operational plans. There will be more information in an operational plan than in a budget. For example, a plan would identify new locations to be opened. Operational plans also would include descriptions of how they supported the company's tactical plans and strategy. The budget covers the financial portion of the operational plan.

The same is true for tactical and strategic plans. A portion of each plan typically includes a financial forecast of results to be achieved. A document that projects future income/expense results of operations is called a *pro forma* financial statement. To illustrate, a five-year pro forma forecast for Rockin' Records is shown in Figure 7-3. Generally, a pro forma statement is prepared to support tactical and strategic plans. These statements look much like the budgets reviewed above. The difference is that they cover a number of years.

In the continuous planning process of business management, pro forma statements often are used as tools for preparation of current-year budgets. All financial projections—budgets and pro forma statements—are used by managers to measure results of continuing operations. The idea: Compare information on actual results with the same figures used in pro forma statements and budgets.

Review 7.2

1. How are budgets used to control operation of a business?

2. A budget is a one-year forecast. What is a longer-range forecast called?

3. What role do current financial statements play in measuring the condition of a business?

WHERE DOES MANAGEMENT INFORMATION COME FROM?

Management information comes from the business that is being managed. Business transactions are information sources. Data items produced by transactions are accumulated and processed to develop information that describes, or models, a company.

```
                   ROCKIN' RECORDS - PRO FORMA STATEMENT
                 YEAR 1        YEAR 2        YEAR 3        YEAR 4        YEAR 5
INCOME
   Albums         92,000        96,600       101,430       106,501       111,827
   CDs            72,000        75,600        79,380        83,349        87,516
   Videos         15,200        15,960        16,758        17,596        18,476
   Posters         8,800         9,240         9,702        10,187        10,696
   Misc.           6,200         6,510         6,835         7,177         7,536

TOTAL INCOME      194,200       203,910       214,105       224,810       236,051

EXPENSES
   Rent            9,600         9,984        10,383        10,799        11,231
   Utilities         840           873           909           945           983
   Telephone         960           998         1,038         1,080         1,123
   Salaries       20,400        21,216        22,065        22,947        23,865
   Loan Payment    8,100         8,424         8,761         9,111         9,476
   Shrinkage       2,400         2,496         2,596         2,700         2,808
   Advertising    12,000        12,480        12,979        13,498        14,038
   Owner Salary   18,000        18,720        19,469        20,248        21,057
   Albums         44,000        45,760        47,590        49,494        51,474
   CDs            32,000        33,280        34,611        35,996        37,436
   Videos         26,400        27,456        28,554        29,696        30,884
   Posters         4,200         4,368         4,543         4,724         4,913
   Misc.           2,100         2,184         2,271         2,362         2,457

TOTAL EXPENSES    181,000       188,239       195,769       203,600       211,739

NET INCOME         13,200        15,621        18,336        21,210        24,312
```

Figure 7-3. *The computation capabilities of electronic spreadsheet programs have been used to develop this five-year "pro forma" financial statement for Rockin' Records.*

To be valuable, information has to be processed. Consider a supermarket. Transactions serve to capture basic, simple facts about an operation. For example, the checker moves a quart container of milk across a reading window of a checkout counter. The coded label on the container is read by a light beam and sent to a computer.

The code number for the product becomes the source item from which information is built. The computer uses its electronic files to provide a description of the item and its price. This type of information is processed and recorded for each item sold. The purchases of a single customer may lead to recording of 50 to 100 transaction items.

HOW IS MANAGEMENT INFORMATION USED?

For managers, each item of information becomes part of a bigger picture. For example, 10 checkstands in one market might record more than 100,000 items

Business Terms

pro forma financial statement
A document with information that predicts income, expense, and profits of an organization for a future time period.

during the course of a single day. Individually, these items are important source materials. But the individual items tell little about the condition of the business. To develop meaning for managers, the information must be *consolidated,* or *summarized.* Both consolidation and summarization mean that information items are combined and totaled.

In the case of a supermarket, automatic cash registers could produce a list of 100,000 items sold during a day. For a full week, the list might contain almost 1 million items. The ability to generate these lists might be impressive. But, as management tools, the lists would be useless. Managers trying to use this information would be buried under detail. Instead, they want the computer to consolidate the information according to product. It is helpful, for example, to learn that a supermarket sold 174 cans of peas or 398 chocolate bars. These figures have meaning. They can be used to study operations and make decisions.

For example, the manager who receives a consolidated report showing sales according to product can use this information to make decisions. The manager can ask the computer to report on how many chocolate bars are in stock. If stocks are low and sales are 398 per week, the information leads to a decision: Order more chocolate bars. The same type of comparison and decision making can be applied to the many thousands of items in a store.

The point: Management information stems from raw facts. These facts pour into an operating company. The process is like an avalanche that starts with a small pebble rolling down a hill. If the buildup is not checked, the avalanche can destroy whole forests, or even cities. However, if the snow on a mountain is kept in place, it melts in the spring. The water from the melting snow flows into a river. The river's water, in turn, can be used for transportation, irrigation, drinking, and bathing.

Businesses need systems that control the flow of information. These systems use resources that include people, procedures, equipment, facilities, time, and, of course, information. A system that provides information designed to support management of a business generally is called a *management information system (MIS).*

Each MIS consolidates detailed information that originates in transactions. The resulting information summaries represent, or model, the condition of the business. For example, the total of all sales for a day, week, or month model the situation of a store. An MIS then may report this information along with the same figures for the previous day, week, or month. Also, reports may compare actual figures with budget forecasts for the same period. By comparing actual results with past results and with expectations in budgets, managers measure business condition.

The starting point for an MIS, then, is to record, or capture, information generated by transactions. This information is combined to show the total results of transactions. Then, the transaction information is used again to build the files that show a total operating picture.

One of the major values of information, as you know, lies in the ability to call management attention to "exception" situations. The computers used to process information can compare operating figures with expected conditions. Consider how a budget might be used as a management tool. The budget indicates what managers expect of a business. A computer might be programmed to compare actual results with budgeted amounts. The computer could report each actual item that is 10 percent lower or higher than the budgeted amount. These are the items that managers examine. As long as things are going as planned within a budget, there is no need for management concern or attention.

HOW IS INFORMATION USED TO CARRY OUT MANAGEMENT BY EXCEPTION?

Recall that the idea of management by exception is to identify problems. A problem, in this sense, is any condition that is not normal. Exceptions can occur at almost any point within an information system that

Data capture occurs as part of transaction processing through use of the equipment shown here. The customer uses a plastic card to operate a gasoline pump. The information is entered into a computer system that withdraws money from the customer's bank account and deposits it in the oil company's account.
COURTESY OF FIGGIE INTERNATIONAL, INC.

handles transactions and provides summary reports. To illustrate, consider the flow of information that comes from sales transactions.

You already have looked in on a typical wholesale business: National Medical Supply Company. This situation is fictitious, of course. But, the situation described could exist in a real business. The flow of information is diagrammed in Figure 7-4.

When customers call National Medical Supply, they are connected to the order department. There, sales personnel ask the purpose of the call. When a customer indicates that an order is to be placed, the salesperson asks for an identification. The customer may give an identification number or the name of a company. When this information is entered, the computer calls up full customer information and displays it for the salesperson.

At this point, the first exception control is applied. The salesperson asks for the name of the caller. This is entered into the computer. The computer then checks a separate "authorization file" to be sure the name has been recorded. For each customer, National Medical Supply tells the computer which people are authorized to place orders. These names are provided by customers to be sure that only authorized people place orders. If an entered name doesn't

match, the customer is advised. An authorized person must confirm the order before it can be processed.

Once authorization is cleared, the salesperson enters numbers or names for each item ordered. The computer looks up each item in its files and provides descriptions and prices to be used on the invoice. When the salesperson enters the quantity of the item ordered, the computer multiplies the price by the quantity. This produces the sales price for each ordered item.

Business Terms

consolidate
To combine information for ease of use.

summarize
To develop totals for multiple information items to derive meaning from large volumes of data items.

management information system (MIS)
A system that provides information designed to support management analysis and decision making. An MIS is created by summarizing transaction information and applying management by exception principles.

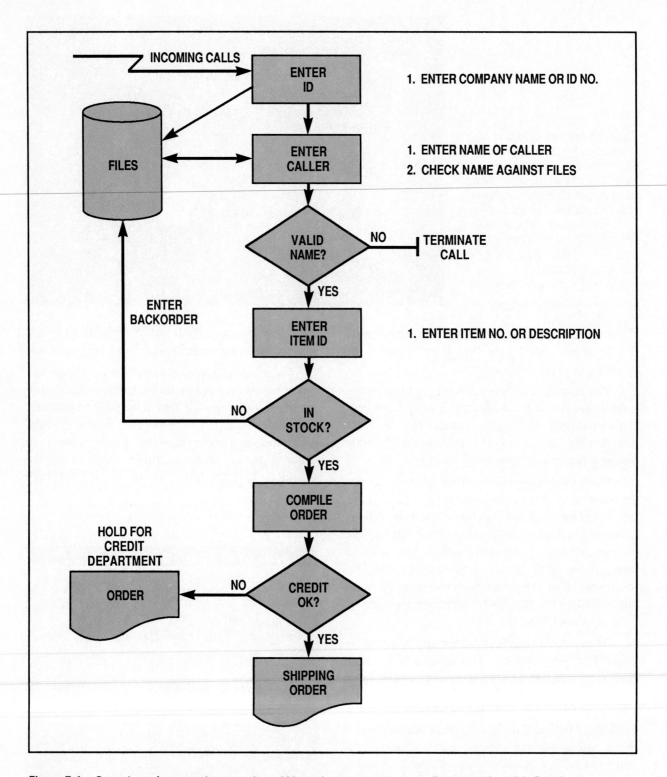

Figure 7-4. *Procedures for exception reporting within an inventory system are diagrammed on this flowchart.*

At the same time, the computer checks its product files to be sure that the purchased items are in stock. If the item cannot be shipped, the computer signals the salesperson, who advises the customer. The customer then has a choice of canceling the order or having it *backordered.* A backorder is an order for an item that is not in stock. The selling company keeps track of backorders and ships them as soon as new stocks are received.

After all items are ordered, the computer figures any taxes due and determines the total for the invoice. At this point, another exception check is performed: The computer adds the total for the present invoice to the amount a customer currently owes to National Medical Supply. Then, the new total is compared with a *credit limit* that also is included in each customer record.

A credit limit is the greatest amount that a customer is allowed to owe. If the new total is greater than the credit limit, the computer will report to the salesperson. The order cannot be processed unless a special authorizing code is entered into the computer. When the customer is informed that the credit limit is exceeded, several things can happen. One is that the customer can assure the salesperson that a check to pay outstanding bills is in the mail. Before the order can be processed, someone from the credit department must authorize the extra credit.

As indicated, several exception checks are made as routine procedures during transaction processing. First, when a customer identification is input, the computer checks to see that there is a record in the master file. The presence of the record means that the customer is set up to do business with National Medical Supply.

Next, the caller's name is checked for authorization to accept the order. For each item ordered, the computer checks to be sure the products are in stock. Finally, before an order is cleared for processing, the customer's credit status is checked. The diamond-shaped symbols on the system diagram indicate points at which decisions are made. At each of these points, the processing flow depends on the content of information.

Management by exception establishes, at each point, that the information presented either is normal or is reported as an exception. Normal means simply that the people who designed the system have told the computer to expect certain information or conditions. Any information that cannot be identified as normal is reported as an exception. If the order information matches the information in the computer files, there are no exceptions.

The principles of management by exception continue after the computer processes the order. For every item in the company's product file, managers establish a *reorder level.* As each ordered item is processed, the computer subtracts the quantity sold from information items that show current stock levels. When a deduction for a sale brings the current inventory level below the reorder point, an exception exists. This is reported to the responsible manager. Managers receive reports or special computer messages when inventory levels are below minimum amounts. Orders are placed as necessary to bring the stock levels back to normal.

Monitoring of reorder levels for inventory represents an important benefit of a management information system. Most companies have to stock materials or products to support their operations. The idea is to keep inventories at the minimum level needed to support efficient operations. This means the company doesn't want to run out of needed items. At the same time, however, overstocking can tie up

Business Terms

backorder
An order for an item that is not in stock, recorded so that delivery can be made as soon as goods are available.

credit limit
The greatest amount a customer is allowed to owe.

reorder level
The inventory level at which new supplies of an item are ordered.

money needlessly and can reduce profits. So, care is taken in setting the reorder levels for inventory items. There should be enough stock on hand at the reorder point to permit the company to order and receive new supplies. Exception reporting assures that managers will know about inventory problems as soon as they occur. At the same time, managers do not have to waste time on items with normal stock levels.

Note that, throughout this cycle, managers are working with information. There is no need actually to see or touch any warehouse items. The information is collected and analyzed as part of the routine transaction processing cycle. The purpose of this chapter is to answer the question: "How are business operations monitored?" The answer: Business operations are monitored by gathering and processing information on transactions. Then, information is consolidated and summarized to represent the condition of the business. Managers judge the condition of the business and make any necessary operating changes by evaluating information.

WHAT HAPPENS WHEN PLANS NEED TO BE CHANGED?

When plans, budgets, or schedules must be changed, the need shows up in information received by managers. In turn, the management information system becomes the vehicle for making needed changes. Managers enter instructions for changes into a computer that is part of the management information system. The computer generates information—instructions, budgets, or schedules—that direct people to make the needed changes.

The point: Operationally, a business runs on and through use of information.

1. What is the main source for management information?

2. Why is detailed source information of little use to managers?

3. How are exception controls used in processing sales transactions?

Chapter Summary

❏ Business operations are planned in advance. Then, to operate successfully, businesses need techniques to compare actual results of operations with plans.

❏ Operations functions within a business generally are controlled by budgets, or plans for receiving and spending money. Budgets generally cover the current year's operations.

❏ Budget development begins with an analysis of the business to determine the income and expense items to be included. Estimates are made about the expected results for each item. Then the amounts are totaled. The finished budget should show that income can be greater than expenses, leaving a profit.

❏ Completed budgets can be compared with actual results to measure the results of operations.

❏ Budgets and other financial forecasts are related to and often are part of operational, tactical, and strategic plans. Budgets are based on operational plans.

❏ Financial forecasts that support tactical and strategic plans are known as pro forma financial statements.

❏ Financial statements become the basis for measuring actual results of business operations.

❏ Management information comes from the business being managed. Information development begins with the processing of transactions. Data items on sales transactions are accumulated and summarized to represent information on the status of the business.

❏ Accumulated information is compared with data items that represent normal conditions. Examples of controls include credit limits for customers and reorder points for inventory items. Any time a current condition exceeds normal limits, an exception exists. Each exception is reported to the responsible manager for action.

❏ In effect, information models the operation of the company.

Definitions

Write a complete sentence that defines each of the terms below.

budget	variance
markup	fixed cost
spreadsheet	backorder
credit limit	reorder level

Questions to Think About

Based on what you have learned to date, answer the following questions in one or more complete sentences.

1. What is a budget?
2. How are budgets related to business plans?

3. How is a budget used in management of actual company operations?

4. Why is a budget set up in what is known as a spreadsheet format?

5. What kinds of financial statements are prepared to support tactical and strategic plans?

6. What is a management information system?

7. What is the basic source of data for a management information system?

8. Why is it necessary to consolidate or summarize data to produce useful information?

9. Within a management information system, what is an exception?

10. To whom are exception conditions reported and what is done with them?

11. What happens when actual results of operations differ widely from plans?

Projects

The purpose of the assignments below is to encourage you to increase your learning through outside reading or work assignments.

1. Prepare a personal budget. Cover a typical one-month period in your activities. List the money you expect to receive. Then enter items for the expenses you expect. Enter your necessary expenses first. Deduct these from your expected income. The remaining money will be available for entertainment or other optional items.

2. Think about the operation of your school. If possible, arrange for an interview with a school administrator. Find out how information is generated and used to manage the school. As an alternative, think about the information you have gathered as a student. Describe the normal transactions that generate information. Identify exception situations that should be monitored. Describe the limits or conditions that would lead to reporting of these exceptions.

CHAPTER 8

What Makes a Business Successful?

When you finish reading this chapter and complete your work assignments, you should be able to answer the following questions.

❏ What measures are used to determine the success of a business?

❏ What are assets and where do they come from?

❏ How does performance of employees help to determine the success of a business?

❏ What is meant by wealth and how do businesses create wealth?

❏ Why is it important for a business to be considered as a responsible citizen of its community?

DOING BUSINESS

"The program we are discussing is an investment in people, an investment that my company makes willingly," explained Monica Rodriguez. "People are a key asset for any business. A business needs the ability to bring in a continuing stream of motivated people who can contribute to its success.

"Even if you people don't spend your whole working careers at National Medical Supply, this program is worthwhile. The entire business community benefits when quality people seek business careers. And," she continued, "it goes even further. If business benefits, all of society gains. A successful business creates jobs. The money a business spends also helps the entire community in which it operates."

Ms. Rodriguez was on one of her regular visits to Central High School. She worked as Director of

Human Resources for National Medical Supply. On each visit, Ms. Rodriguez met with a small group of students who wanted to talk about careers in business. She usually began by explaining that business generally, and her company particularly, were committed to developing people. As an example, she often used her own job situation. Ms. Rodriguez had started at National Medical Supply in the Personnel Department. Recently, after she had been promoted to head the department, the title was changed. The title, Human Resources, gives a better description of what her department does, she would explain.

On this day, Ms. Rodriguez was talking with a group of eight students. All were in their second or third years at Central High. "Success begins with motivation," she stated. "And motivation begins with you. A motivated person wants something badly enough to work for it. Motivation leads to achievement of goals. All businesses want moti-

Success starts with commitment. *Henry Ford committed himself to the future of the automotive industry by setting up the manufacturing operation shown here. This photo shows a recreation of Ford's 1908 factory at the Henry Ford Museum.*
COURTESY OF HENRY FORD MUSEUM & GREENFIELD VILLAGE

vated people as employees. A business becomes successful by motivating people to work toward company goals. At National Medical Supply, we are willing to invest in the opportunity to hire motivated people. That's why I'm here.''

Ms. Rodriguez went on to explain that she was recruiting students for her company's marketing education program. The idea was to provide opportunities for students and also to identify future motivated employees. Students accepted into the program received course credit in high school for their on-the-job work experience. During the school year, students worked part time at National Medical Supply. During the summer, selected students were offered full-time jobs.

Some students would be offered full-time jobs following high school graduation. Others would be invited to participate in a college scholarship program. For these students, National Medical Supply would pay part of college tuition and would assure students of vacation jobs. In return, students would agree to work for National Medical Supply for two years after college. There also was another alternative: If students decided to take other jobs after college, they would pay back part of the tuition they received. These payments would go into funds to be used for scholarships for other deserving students.

"If you join this program," Ms. Rodriguez said, "we will expect a lot of you. First of all, you must keep up your school grades. Also, at work, you must show that you understand the purpose of the business and its commitments to customer service. You must work as part of a team. You must recognize that you share in both the successes and the problems faced by the company."

MEANING

A business—any business—is made up of a group of people. A successful business is one in which people work together to achieve common strategies and goals.

As you know, the success of a business is based on the strategy and goals set by owners or managers. Strategies, goals, and plans determine what a business is and what management wants it to become. These strategies, goals, and plans are used to measure results produced by a business. That is, success lies in the degree to which goals and plans are achieved.

One requirement for business success is committed people. The narrative above is based on actual programs supported by real businesses.

Another example of a commitment to people by a business was made by Henry Ford. At the time, Ford had introduced production-line methods for building cars. In those days, workers were being paid as little as a dollar a day. Ford announced that all workers in his factory would receive a minimum of $5 per day. His reason: A person who earned $5 a day during those years could afford to drive a Ford car. Further, potential car owners would appreciate the quality of work by committed employees.

Bear in mind that relationships with people represent just one measure of success for a company. This measure can be most vital to people who want to find jobs and build careers. However, to have good relationships with employees, a company needs to measure up in a number of other ways. Some of the main ingredients of business success are covered in the rest of this chapter.

WHAT MEASURES BUSINESS SUCCESS?

For a business, success lies in the achievement of goals and plans. Each business, as you know, has individual sets of goals and plans. Therefore, success for each business is measured differently. Success begins with the targets established by goals and plans. Even though goals and plans are individual, all businesses share some common goals by which success can be measured. These include:

- The most frequently mentioned goal of a successful business is profit.

- The quality of services to customers is vital. Satisfied customers are necessary to success. This is true even if a business does not seek a profit. Some business organizations are formed as not-for-profit corporations. Their strategy is to provide needed services. Public television stations are good examples. Other organizations are cooperatives. They do not realize profits as a business. Rather, their goal is to provide quality service and minimum costs for members.

- A major goal might lie in achievement of business growth.

- A measure related to growth lies in the *assets* of a business. Assets are the things a business owns, including buildings, equipment, and money.

- As it grows and builds its assets, a business creates *wealth.* In this sense, wealth includes the money and facilities that, in turn, create jobs and produce incomes for employees and owners.

- Market acceptance and/or entry into new markets are goals for many business organizations.

- As described above, development of human resources also can be a major goal.

- Many modern businesses measure success in terms of performance as citizens of the communities in which they operate.

Some of these measures of success are worth further exploration. The goals of profits, growth, assets, market development, wealth, and citizenship are discussed further in the sections that follow.

HOW DO PROFITS MEASURE SUCCESS?

Profits are necessities for most businesses. Profits, of course, are the earnings of a business. In general, the profit of a business is the difference between the money it receives and the money it spends, or expenses. That's the simple explanation. The key to the importance of profits to businesses lies in understanding why they are necessary.

Profits are a measure of how well—or how poorly—a business performs. The level of profits, then, is a kind of report card. A company's profits indicate how well managers are running the business. As an indicator of the degree of success for a business, profits are measured in different ways:

- Profits can be reported as a percentage in comparison with the investment made by owners of a business. This figure is known as return on investment. In turn, investors frequently compare returns on investments in business with other opportunities for use of money. The idea is that business investments involve a risk. Therefore,

Information measures success in business operations. Large companies need massive information processing capabilities like the one shown here at McDonnell Douglas in St. Louis.
PHOTO BY LIANE ENKELIS

investors expect to earn more than they would from interest on a bank deposit.

- Profits can be reported as a percentage of the sales made by a business. This is a common measure used in retailing and/or service businesses. Also, many businesses award special pay, or *bonuses,* to managers on the basis of the ratio of profits to sales.

- Profits almost always are compared with management plans or budgets. In setting operating plans and budgets, managers consider many factors. These include the need to invest in new products or operations. Sometimes, a decision is made to lower profits so that money can be invested in building the business. No matter what the case may be, managers are responsible for predicting business profits in plans and budgets. If actual profits vary from plans, managers are judged accordingly.

How Large Do Profits Have to Be?

For investors, a profit record over a number of years establishes the value of a company. For example, say

a company reports earnings of $10 per share of its stock. Assume that the company is in a field that is expected to support future growth. Investors probably would be willing to spend in the range of 10 to 15 times earnings-per-share to buy the stock. That is, the stock could be expected to sell for between $100 and $150 per share. The higher the stock price, the greater the success and future prospects of a company are judged to be.

Business Terms

assets
The things a business owns, including buildings, equipment, and money.

wealth
Money, facilities, and other resources used to create jobs and produce incomes for employees and owners.

bonus
Payment made to managers and possibly other employees on the basis of operating results delivered by a business.

Because profits help to establish the value of a company, there is pressure upon most managers to show high profits. However, there also are other factors that affect profits. For example, new companies or companies in high-technology fields may show small profits for many years. This is because large amounts of money must be invested in research or in development of new markets.

To illustrate, a company in the health-care field may make large investments to buy or build new hospitals. Large sums also are needed to attract skilled doctors and scientists. A company of this type may grow in revenues while profits remain low for some years. Investors who are convinced that future potential is good may invest anyway.

The point: The value of a business is reflected in more than simply year-to-year profits. If managers plan only to show large profits in current operations, this kind of policy could hurt the business. For example, if a company that owns a number of buildings cuts back on upkeep of its facilities, profits could be increased in the current year. But the business would suffer in the long run as tenants moved out of buildings that become dirty and run down. Managers must decide between short-term profits and long-term abilities of the business to serve customers. Earnings must be reinvested to maintain and build a business. Profits should reflect sound use of investments and income.

How Are Profit Levels Monitored?

To illustrate how owners or managers keep track of profits, recall the case of Eunice Heinle and Rockin' Records. This situation is covered in Chapter 7. As described, Heinle prepared a budget and a "pro forma" income statement before she bought the business. These financial reports helped her decide to make the purchase.

Once she took over and started running the business, the budget became a basis for monitoring operations. The budget showed income and expense items according to a quarterly breakdown. As actual figures accumulated, Heinle prepared a report like the one shown in Figure 8-1. This report contains an added column alongside the figures for the first quarter budget amounts. The new column shows actual figures for the same period.

Note that income figures for album sales during the first quarter are slightly higher than the budget amount. However, the expense figures for album purchases are much higher. The budget has helped Heinle make an important management decision. Right after she began operating the store, a number of hit albums were released. She found that there was potential for expanding record sales far beyond the levels realized by the previous owner. So, Heinle decided to increase her investment in record inventory. She believed that this extra stock would help to increase sales still further. This is an example of how monitoring of actual results leads to changes in strategies, plans, and budgets.

Review 8.1

1. Why is the success of each business measured differently?

2. How do a company's employees contribute to its success?

3. How is profit measured on the basis of return on investment?

4. Why is it not possible for companies to distribute all of their profits to shareholders?

HOW DOES GROWTH REPRESENT SUCCESS?

The size of a business can be a big factor in determining how efficiently it can operate and how well it can serve its customers.

Most businesses start small. A major restaurant chain, for example, started with a single hamburger stand with one counter and eight stools. The owner-operator featured extra-large hamburger patties.

ROCKIN' RECORDS — BUDGET AND OPERATING STATEMENT						
	ANNUAL	1ST QTR	ACTUAL	2ND QTR	3RD QTR	4TH QTR
INCOME						
Albums	92,000	23,000	23,690			
CDs	72,000	18,000	18,720			
Videos	15,200	3,800	4,066			
Posters	8,800	2,200	2,090			
Misc.	6,200	1,550	1,503			
TOTAL INCOME	194,200	48,550	50,069			
EXPENSES						
Rent	9,600	2,400	2,472			
Utilities	840	210	216			
Telephone	960	240	247			
Salaries	20,400	5,100	5,253			
Loan Payment	8,100	2,025	2,086			
Shrinkage	2,400	600	618			
Advertising	12,000	3,000	3,090			
Owner Salary	18,000	4,500	4,635			
Albums	44,000	11,000	14,850			
CDs	32,000	8,000	8,480			
Videos	26,400	6,600	6,270			
Posters	4,200	1,050	1,071			
Misc.	2,100	525	541			
TOTAL EXPENSES	181,000	45,250	49,829			
NET INCOME	13,200	3,300	240			

Figure 8-1. Budget reports like the one shown here are used to monitor actual results in comparison with planned figures for income and expenses.

Prices were good and service was excellent. The profit percentage also was high because the owner was the main employee of the business. At first, he needed just one other person, who washed dishes and kept the place spotless.

Before long, the owner had generated enough profits to replace the small hamburger stand with a large coffee shop. Along with building the larger restaurant, the owner made an important management decision: As he grew, he would hire and train people who could maintain the quality of service that he had provided.

The owner recognized that people are essential to the growth of a business. He recognized also that it was important that the new people maintain the products and quality of service that customers expected. To achieve this, he prepared detailed menus and instructions for preparing all menu items. These instructions included color photographs to show the appearance of all dishes. When he couldn't be in the restaurant, the owner hired "shoppers." These people acted as customers and checked out the quality of food and service.

What Are Some Advantages And Problems of Growth?

As employees demonstrated their ability in the first restaurant, the owner opened other outlets. Word got around. People who performed well were promoted.

With growth, the chain was able to realize *economies of scale.* This term means simply that big organizations buy and produce in volume. Volume purchases and production usually lead to lower unit costs. Reduced costs contributed directly to improving profits. Eventually, the business that started with an eight-stool hamburger stand became a national chain.

As the company grew, its size also proved to be a competitive advantage. Its name and its menu items became known. Consumers had confidence in the quality of food and service they would receive. As long as the menu remained popular and quality was maintained, size was a competitive advantage.

The owner followed the same proven method for training and promoting employees. Growth continued until change caught up with the company. All of the managers of the hundreds of restaurants had been trained to provide food items developed by a central office. But the public developed new and different tastes in fast food. The chain had grown to a size and had followed a management style that was not flexible enough to keep up with its markets. Eventually, the chain was purchased by another business organization that had the flexibility to innovate and to respond to public tastes.

The point: Growth can be a factor in success. Prospects of growth attract investors to a business. At the same time, growth can get out of hand. Managers should be careful not to lose the flexibility necessary to serve markets.

WHAT ROLE DO ASSETS PLAY?

Assets are the things a business owns. Assets have value. So, the amount of assets that a business has is one measure of its success. Assets also can be important to a company's market position and its ability to serve customers.

For one good example, consider the petroleum business. The success of an oil company depends largely on the assets it has available. One major asset lies in the amount of crude oil reserves a company

holds. Oil companies spend billions of dollars exploring for oil. When oil deposits are discovered, estimates are made about how much oil lies in the underground pools. These oil "reserves" are extremely valuable. Also, companies depend on these reserves for the ability to continue to make and market gasoline and other products.

Other assets include the refineries that produce petroleum products and the service stations that sell them. The volumes of products that can be produced and the ability to deliver products to customers are essentials of success. Therefore, assets are both a basis for and a measure of success.

Other businesses use different kinds of assets. To illustrate, important assets of an insurance company lie in the policies that are in force. People who buy insurance pay the companies to maintain these policies. The amount of income a company can expect depends on the policies it sells and maintains.

What Different Types of Assets Do Companies Own?

Money is an important asset for almost any business. Money is known as a *liquid asset* because it can be used easily and immediately. Companies use money to buy the supplies they need and to pay their employees. The availability of enough money to run a business is, therefore, a vital measure of its success. Assets that can be converted easily into cash also are considered to be liquid. Examples include stock certificates or bonds that can be sold easily.

Other assets are considered to be *fixed* or *nonliquid.* Examples include the oil refineries and service stations cited above. In other situations, office buildings, factories, or production machinery might be fixed assets. These items have value and are essential to company operations. But they are not available to be spent immediately. Before fixed assets can become liquid, they must be sold or must be used to secure loans of money.

In some situations, it may be hard to determine what a fixed asset is worth. For instance, a service

Wealth is generated by business activities like this construction project. The signs at the right indicate that other businesses are profiting from this activity through subcontracts. Also, the money earned by workers on a project like this is spent in transactions at other businesses within the community.

PHOTO BY BENEDICT KRUSE

station on a busy corner in a large city may have great value. The land occupied by the service station may be worth tens of thousands of dollars. In contrast, a service station on a lonely country road may have far less value than the amount paid for its equipment and buildings.

The types of assets a business accumulates and the present value of those assets represent important measures of success.

How Do Assets Relate to Wealth?

A company's assets are part of the wealth that it develops and uses. One of the measures of business success lies in the rate at which it creates wealth. In this sense, wealth includes all those resources that enrich the economy and put people to work.

Consider the man who started with one hamburger stand and built a chain of restaurants. When the chain was sold, it was worth hundreds of millions of dollars. This wealth was created by the business, since the owner started with an investment of just a few hundred dollars. Wealth of each business provides many potential benefits. For example, many people were employed in building and running the restaurants. These people earned and spent money in their communities. As people purchased homes, food, and clothing, other citizens of their community were supported as employees of local businesses. Also, the restaurants and their suppliers paid taxes used for schools and other community services.

Wealth is a source of support for both businesses and individual citizens within any community. The founding and growth of businesses is a major source of wealth, and of growth for the economy and the jobs it provides.

Business Terms

economies of scale
The savings or efficiencies that can be realized in purchases or production as volumes of items increase.

liquid asset
Cash or items that can be converted easily to cash.

fixed asset or **nonliquid asset**
Facilities, equipment, inventories, or other items that have value but are not easily converted to cash.

Review 8.2

1. What are the advantages of growth for a company?

2. What disadvantages can result from growth?

3. What are business assets?

4. What is wealth and how do businesses develop wealth for the economy?

HOW DOES A COMPANY'S MARKET POSITION MEASURE ITS SUCCESS?

You can observe the importance of market acceptance each time an election is held. Today, most candidates and officeholders use public opinion polls to find out what voters think about them. In today's political situation, candidates and officeholders are products. Like all products, candidates are packaged and presented to the consuming public. The package that has the greatest appeal can be expected to win the election. If polls show negative results, the "image" of the candidate may be adjusted to try to increase market appeal.

Consumer acceptance of the products and services of companies is measured in a similar manner. People are asked their feelings about the company and its products. The results of these surveys should provide managers with an idea of why people buy specific products and what they expect from those products.

How Is Market Appeal Developed?

Note that market analysis is different from advertising and sales programs. In most situations, the market analysis will come before major advertising programs. The idea is to find out exactly what people want to buy. Take toothpaste as an example. The basic idea of brushing teeth is to keep them from rotting—to have a healthy mouth. But this isn't how toothpaste is sold. People know there are many brands of toothpaste that do essentially the same

thing. So, purchasing decisions are based on other factors. These factors aren't always logical. But they do affect a company's sales. For example, people buy toothpaste for its taste. In effect, they are buying flavor rather than health protection.

In other words, customers tend to buy results or appearances rather than products. As another example, people tend to buy a total dining or entertainment experience rather than food products such as hamburgers. Thus, playgrounds for children have been a big attraction for a hamburger chain. Managers of this chain have recognized that they are selling an experience. The food products themselves are only one part of the experience.

To gain and/or protect market acceptance, a business must invest continually in developing new products. A company with management that knows its markets also should know what customers want and will buy.

Market appeal as an element of business value. An important measure of business success lies in the way a company is regarded by its customers. When businesses are bought and sold, one of the ingredients of the price is known as "goodwill." This means that familiarity of business products and customer loyalty to those products are important parts of the value of a business. Customer approval and respect have potential values. These values are separate from such factors as the assets a company owns or the immediate profits it realizes.

HOW DOES EMPLOYEE PERFORMANCE MEASURE A COMPANY'S SUCCESS?

Employees interact with customers to deliver a company's products or services. As far as customers are concerned, employees **are** the company they work for. Therefore, the success of the entire company is related directly to the quality of attention and service that employees provide to customers.

One way to measure this element of success is described above: "Shoppers" are hired to act as cus-

Employee performance develops and sells the products or services that support a company. Teamwork among personnel like the engineering professionals in this photo lead to creation of new products.

tomers. The shoppers report on the quality of service they receive. Management reacts accordingly.

How Can Performance of Employees Be Reviewed?

One example of how management can review employee performance was used some years ago by a major bank. An outside consultant appeared at the bank one day to open a new account. The man was dressed in a business suit. He presented a check drawn on a bank in another city as his opening deposit. The well-dressed customer was treated with courtesy. His account was welcomed by the employees he contacted.

A few days later, the same man appeared in work clothes. He had not shaved since his previous visit. In place of a belt, his pants were held up by a piece of rope. His opening deposit was for the same amount as it was when he was well dressed. However, this time the money was in the form of cash—small bills and coins carried in a shoebox. Employees treated this new depositor differently. Their behavior was rude.

Relationships between management and employees at this bank were changed by this experience. Managers recognized that the company's reputation and its operating success depended upon how employees dealt with customers. Employee jobs were redefined.

How Does Employee Satisfaction Affect Operations of a Business?

An operational business is a system in which employees carry out a cycle that involves input, processing, output, distribution, and storage. Within this overall system, employees are responsible for a number of *subsystems.* A subsystem is a set of procedures that fits within a larger system. The system has its

Business Terms

subsystem
A set of procedures that fits within a larger system.

own input, processing, output, distribution, and storage functions. A company's subsystems represent the operations necessary to create products and services and, eventually, to deliver them to customers. As shown in Figure 8-2, business subsystems can include research and development, engineering, manufacturing, marketing, and customer service. To carry out all the steps within the system, employees must function as a team. This is because what happens in one subsystem affects the whole organization.

The importance of employee performance to company success is highlighted by a point made in the opening narrative for this chapter: Many companies now use the term *human resources* to describe the department responsible for hiring and developing employees. This term recognizes that the knowledge, experience, and performance of people are important to the operating success of a company.

As Henry Ford discovered, one important factor in employee relationships is adequate pay. However, wages, in themselves, do not guarantee quality performance. People have to be challenged. They should understand what they do on the job and why they do it. Each employee should have a customer to satisfy, whether the customer is another employee or an outsider. Relationships must exist that make it possible for each employee to measure personal performance. Also, relationships must be set up to permit each employee to realize satisfaction from work that is done. When employees consider themselves to be part of a team, each becomes a potential winner. Winning, in any field, can be a solid source of satisfaction.

Review 8.3

1. What role do customers play in the success of a business?

2. What usually is the basis for overall customer buying decisions?

3. What contributions does employee performance make to the success of a business?

HOW DOES CORPORATE CITIZENSHIP RELATE TO BUSINESS SUCCESS?

Legally, a business is a fictitious person. In practice, businesses have the same rights and responsibilities as people. Each business is a citizen of the community in which it operates. Each business draws upon the resources of the community to support itself. Businesses use electricity, water, sewage and disposal services, streets and roads, and other community resources. Because businesses consist of groups of people, they play special roles and should assume special responsibilities.

A successful business should become a resource of its community. Its wealth should contribute to the community as a whole and to individuals who benefit from its presence. Success should be measured in terms of contributions made by a business. Contributions should be both economic and social.

How Does a Business Contribute To the Economy of Its Area?

Each business, by its very existence, helps to create wealth. In this sense, wealth includes anything of value that adds to an area's economy. One way a business can create wealth is to build or rent property. The stores, factories, and offices occupied by business become part of the wealth of the local community. The community collects taxes on the facilities used by business. The income from these taxes supports local services. Providing these services creates jobs.

The economic contribution of businesses to a community leads to the *circular flow of money*. This term describes what happens to money introduced into a community by a business. Each business spends money to buy supplies and services from other businesses. In turn, these businesses employ people who introduce more money into the local economy.

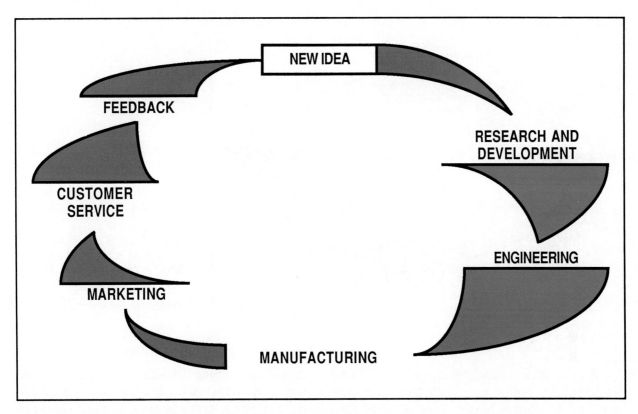

Figure 8-2. *Smooth business operations result from interactions among subsystems, as diagrammed.*

For all businesses, employees who earn wages spend most of that money within the community. This money goes to purchases of food, clothing, shelter, and entertainment. All of these purchases, in turn, help to create more jobs and to circulate more money. It is estimated that money spent by a business circulates within the community between three and five times. This circular flow of money is illustrated in Figure 8-3. The circular flow of money is part of the way in which businesses build wealth within the economy.

What Social Contributions Does A Business Make to Its Community?

Like people, businesses help to support the societies within which they exist. Almost all businesses make sizable charitable contributions within their communities. Many businesses help to build and maintain cultural and entertainment facilities. Included are museums, theaters, orchestras, opera companies, dance companies, and other activities. Public television programming depends heavily on business support. Many thousands of college scholarships are funded by businesses.

Business Terms
human resources
Name of the business function responsible for recruiting, hiring, and training personnel.
circular flow of money
Description of the way money spent by a business circulates through the economy of the community in which the business is located.

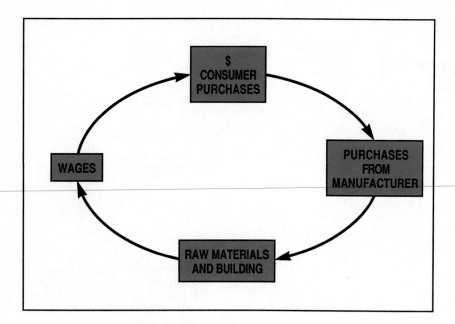

Figure 8-3. *Money flows through an economy in a continuous, circular pattern, as diagrammed here.*

Remember: Businesses are groups of people who work together. Businesses also are citizens of communities. As citizens, businesses must assume special roles and responsibilities. In many ways, the enjoyment and satisfaction of all citizens is a measure of the success of a community's businesses.

HOW DOES EXPERIENCE AFFECT A COMPANY'S STRATEGY AND PLANS?

A business is operated to achieve a strategy established by its owners and managers. Strategy establishes what a business is and what it should become. Specific goals and actions to carry out a strategy are included in business plans.

Strategies and plans should not be either fixed or permanent. Businesses live and must deal with continuing change. Some of the changes that affect a business also serve to outdate plans and strategies. A strategy and plans developed under one set of conditions doesn't work when the conditions change.

Therefore, one of the measures of business success lies in the way managers recognize and deal with

the effects of change. To illustrate, consider a situation based on actual occurrences. The ninth largest bank in a large metropolitan area had a young, innovative management group. In this position, the bank had a strategy for slow growth through use of limited resources. One day, the bank was offered an opportunity to buy a larger competitor, the fifth largest bank in the region. Once the merger was concluded, the new bank was third largest. Assets had increased by billions of dollars. Management had to move quickly to establish a big-bank strategy to replace the strategy of a ninth-place bank.

Changes of this type affect strategies and plans. In some situations, as described earlier, changes to strategy may be informal. Realities of the business world require a company and its people to do things differently. They respond. Reality can cause changes in strategy. Managers must recognize the need for change. Then they must act accordingly. One measure of success, then, lies in the changes needed to help a company take advantage of opportunities.

Strategies and plans also may have to change because of negative developments. The economy of any country or area tends to run in cycles. When the

Quality-control measures should be a regular part of a company's operations, as illustrated in this photo.

PHOTO BY LIANE ENKELIS

economy takes a downturn, business strategies and plans must reflect these realities. Goals may have to be reduced. It even may be necessary to discontinue some operations. Changes can be positive or negative. Businesses must adjust accordingly. Success may lie in the ability of managers to change plans to react to changing business conditions.

HOW DOES INFORMATION REPORTING CONTRIBUTE TO BUSINESS SUCCESS?

Judgments about how successful or unsuccessful a business is are based on information. Each business generates information as it conducts transactions. Transaction information is processed and summarized to model the business. The information model is what indicates the degree of success a business is realizing.

Therefore, one vital measure of the success for any business lies in how well its information system represents its condition. To be useful, an information system must meet certain standards. Information must be accurate, reliable, and timely.

What Does It Take to Assure Quality of Information?

Accuracy is vital because mistakes in input or processing of information can present a faulty picture of a company's condition. Simple mistakes can have major effects. For example, if a computer operator enters figures in the wrong positions, information is distorted. There have been dramatic examples. Mistakes by bank personnel have wiped out customer accounts or have added millions of dollars that weren't deposited.

Reliability means simply that the content of the information can be trusted. One way in which information can become unreliable is if it is incomplete. Another occurs when people use bad judgment. For example, if sales forecasts are wrong, a company may spend too much money making or buying products that customers don't want.

Timeliness is critical for managers who deal with constant change. Outdated information leads to bad decisions. Information must be current within the time frame required for decisions and commitments.

In some cases, information must be available instantly.

For example, an oil refinery processes millions of gallons of crude oil in a single batch. Managers of the refinery have to decide, quickly, about what products to produce from the crude oil. To do this, they need to know, immediately, about market demands and about the chemical makeup of the raw materials. In other situations, information is needed on a next-day basis. Other managers work on different cycles, which may be weekly, monthly, or quarterly.

Timeliness means that the information must match the use to which it will be put.

In summary, measurement of success for a business is individual. Success is measured in terms of achievement of strategy and plans. Also, success depends on the way managers handle information and use information to respond to change. The measurement factors covered in this chapter tend to be individual for separate businesses. In addition, however, there are factors that are common to a number of businesses. Businesses are grouped according to the types of products or services they provide. Organizations with similar products and services are said to be part of an industry. Grouping and classification of businesses by industry are explained in the chapter that follows.

Review 8.4

1. In what ways is a company a citizen of a community in which it operates?

2. What is the circular flow of money and what is its effect on an area's economy?

3. How do actual developments faced by a business affect its strategy?

Chapter Summary

❏ Management performance is measured by the level of success in meeting the goals of a business.

❏ Business success is measured through use of a number of factors. These include profits, quality of customer service, growth, assets owned, market coverage, development of human resources, and citizenship in the community.

❏ Profits can be reported and measured in a number of ways. Included are return on investment, percentage of total sales, and performance in comparison with plans and budgets.

❏ Growth can contribute to company success by creating a competitive advantage through economies of scale.

❏ Growth can be a disadvantage if it causes a company to lose flexibility or the quality of customer service diminishes.

❏ Assets are the things a company owns.

❏ Assets also are the buildings, equipment, and money needed to run a business. The size of a company's assets, therefore, can be a measure of wealth.

❏ Wealth is the combination of assets and jobs that supports an economy. Wealth leads to spending that circulates through a community. Other businesses and local governments are supported. Wealth is a basis for employment.

❏ Market acceptance depends upon how customers view a company's products or services.

❏ Customers buy overall experiences rather than specific products.

❏ Employee performance bears directly upon customer satisfaction.

❏ Effective performance by employees adds to the "goodwill" value of a business.

❏ A company is a citizen of its community. A successful company contributes to the well-being of other citizens, personal and business.

❏ One way in which a company helps its community is through the circular flow of money through the local economy. Money spent by a business is cycled through the economy to benefit many individuals and businesses.

❏ Businesses also benefit communities by supporting charitable and cultural activities.

❏ Managers should be responsive to results of operations and should be ready to modify strategies and plans to reflect experience.

❏ Information that models a business must be accurate, reliable, and timely.

Definitions

Write a complete sentence that defines each of the terms below.

assets	wealth
economies of scale	liquid asset
fixed asset	subsystem
human resources	circular flow of money

Questions to Think About

Based on what you have learned to date, answer the following questions in one or more complete sentences.

1. Why do many businesses use the term ''human resources'' in place of the older ''personnel department''?

2. Why are profits important in measuring the success of a business?

3. Is it necessary that each business show as much profit as possible on every status report? If not, why not?

4. What is meant by return on investment?

5. How does company growth represent a measure of management success?

6. What are assets and how do they reflect the level of success of a company?

7. How does customer response to a company and its products provide a measure of management success?

8. How do employee attitudes show the relative success of a company?

9. What contributions should a company make as a citizen of its community?

10. How should managers respond when actual performance of a company differs from strategies or plans?

11. What factors determine the quality of information needed for use in business management?

Projects

The purpose of the assignments below is to encourage you to increase your learning through outside reading or work assignments.

1. Find an article in a magazine or the business section of your local newspaper that describes a company. These publications usually analyze businesses as potential investments. For one company about which you find an article, explain whether you feel it is a good investment. Give reasons.

2. Visit or call a securities dealer (stock broker). Ask for a research report on a company that is recommended as a good investment. From this report, prepare a report of your own on how companies are evaluated as investments. Identify information about the company that is considered to be favorable or unfavorable.

CHAPTER 9

How Are Businesses Classified?

The Think Tank

When you finish reading this chapter and complete your work assignments, you should be able to answer the following questions.

❑ What is an industry?

❑ Why are businesses classified according to industry?

❑ What is meant by a vertical industry?

❑ What is meant by a horizontal industry?

❑ How can a knowledge of industry characteristics help you to select careers and apply for jobs?

DOING BUSINESS

"You spoil your customers," said Sally.

"What do you mean?" Horacio asked.

"Well," Sally explained, "I work at a service station. In gasoline retailing, self-service is the big thing. A customer drives up to a pump, parks, and comes to the cashier's window to pay in advance. Then the customer pumps the gas. My job is just to sit and collect money. On your job, you do all the work. The customer does nothing. And you don't get paid until after the customer is all through."

"It is funny," Horacio remarked. "You call your business a service station. But you don't give any service."

They both laughed. Then Horacio continued. "Seriously, though. The differences between businesses involve more than what you do for cus-tomers. As I understand it, the gasoline retailing industry has high product costs. A service station operator makes only a few cents per gallon. Any new or extra services you do for a customer would have to increase prices. Look at the stations that give full service at the pumps. Gas can cost 20 to 40 cents a gallon more than for self-service. In that business, with a high cost for the products you sell, self-service makes sense.

"Things are different in a restaurant," Horacio explained. "For one thing, our product costs are different. The actual food we serve represents only 25 to 30 percent of the selling price. Labor can represent 40 to 50 percent of the costs of operat-ing a restaurant. In gasoline retailing, the figure must be under 10 percent.

"In any business," Horacio went on, "you sell customers what they expect to receive. When cus-tomers come to a restaurant like this one, they ex-

Competition among businesses *takes many forms. This photo shows two fast-food restaurants located next door to each other. One specializes in fried chicken, the other in hamburgers and some specialty items. Consumers who want a quick meal make their choices according to food tastes.*

PHOTO BY BENEDICT KRUSE

pect service. We have what the restaurant industry calls a 'white tablecloth' house. This refers to the fact that we use cloth tablecloths and napkins. It also means that we cook food to order—and that we serve it with class.''

Sally's expression indicated she was trying to understand. ''What you are saying, I think, is that each business charges customers for the services they deliver. People may think they are buying a product only. But they are also paying for the cost of delivering the product to them. Some gas stations still provide service. But experience has shown that most people would rather pump their own gas than to pay for having their tanks filled.''

''It's the same in other fields as well,'' Horacio said. ''Look at the choices you have when you buy clothing. You can go to a store where the clothing is on racks and you help yourself, then go through a checkout. You also can go to stores where you can tell a salesperson what you want. You are waited on until you find the right garment. You pay for the service. The question is not so much the cost as what you are willing to pay to get what you want.

''People who expect service have to be willing to pay for it,'' Horacio continued. ''That's true in the restaurant business and in every other field. For ex-

ample, the people who come to this restaurant can eat for less money if they go to a fast-food stand. When they come here, they have decided to pay for the service they expect. That's part of doing business. You have to know what you want and be ready to pay for what you get.''

MEANING

Businesses operate in different ways and attract customers who expect different services. The conversation between Sally and Horacio makes this clear. Their observations also show that businesses tend to be grouped. Some service stations actually do provide service. Others are set up for customers who wait on themselves.

The same is true in restaurants. Some customers choose to wait in line to be served at a counter. They are willing to carry their own food to tables. Many customers even are willing to dispose of their own dirty dishes. In other restaurants, customers prefer to choose from individually cooked items listed on a menu. Servers bring the food to their tables, which may be set with tablecloths and napkins.

The point: In purchasing any product or service, customers have choices. These choices result, in part, from the fact that businesses divide themselves naturally into a series of categories, or classifications. This separation and classification of businesses helps customers to know what to expect. A system of classifications also helps managers to plan for and organize operations around customer expectations.

WHAT IS AN INDUSTRY AND HOW ARE INDUSTRIES FORMED?

The categories into which businesses are organized are called *industries*. An industry consists of a group of companies. Each company in the same industry provides a similar type of product or service to an identified market. Among professional organizations, special skills and services usually are called *disciplines*.

All organizations in the same industry or discipline compete with one another. Thus, the grouping of companies in this way serves to provide guidelines for consumers. If you need a given product or service, industry identification can help you find a supplier. Telephone and other directories are organized according to industry breakdowns. Thus, classification by industry helps to organize efforts of both businesses and customers.

An understanding of how and why industries are formed can be valuable. This information will make you a wiser consumer. Also, understanding industries and the nature of their customer relationships can help in selecting a career and/or in looking for a job.

What Is the Basis for Industry Identification?

Industries are formed according to common business features that apply to a number of companies. Thus, some industries are old and established. Others were formed in recent times as competing companies were attracted to new markets. Still others are considered to be new and growing industries that are still being formed.

Historically, the formation of industries stems from the days when the barter system was replaced by specialized crafts. When money became the medium of exchange, an organized system for identifying products and their values was needed. Early industries followed the established crafts of their age. Farmers became the basis for the agriculture industry. Other industries built up around grain milling, textile weaving, and construction of buildings. Today, these industries still exist and form part of the basis for the economies of regions and countries.

During the late nineteenth and early twentieth centuries, a number of industries formed around inventions that came into use. As the economy grew, banking became a major industry. The automobile, then the airplane, led to development of new industries. The same was true for the companies formed to supply electric power. Other new companies built a communications industry around the telephone and radio.

In recent times, inventions in the electronics field, including television, have led to the formation of new industries. The same is true for computers and for information services.

WHAT ARE THE BASIC INDUSTRY CATEGORIES?

Some industries are specialized. Companies in these fields deal only with specific kinds of products and services. These are known as *vertical industries*. The term means simply that companies within each industry qualify on a select, or "narrow," basis according to specific products and markets. Examples include agriculture, automotive, aerospace, and construction.

Other industries are general in nature. Their products or services apply to most businesses and

New industries are formed to respond to public acceptance of advanced products. Specialty stores that sell microcomputers and accessories provide a good, current example of the formation of a new industry.

PHOTO BY LIANE ENKELIS

categories of consumers. These are known as *horizontal industries* because use of their products or services applies across many fields. Examples include banking, insurance, entertainment, and information.

How Does Information Qualify as an Industry?

Information services is an excellent example of a horizontal industry that is involved in virtually all business activities. Some information needs tend to apply to specific companies or industries. But many information systems are the same or similar for most industries.

Possibly the most common example is payroll. All companies must pay employees. Also all payrolls must comply with certain government rules. Therefore, payroll processing and reporting has become a widespread, common information processing job. The same is true for preparation of tax reports, financial statements, and many other common business information requirements.

What Factors Identify Industries?

Differences among industries tend to relate to typical strategies followed by companies in the same field. In any given field, a number of companies will be formed to sell similar products or services. Also,

Business Terms

industry
A group of companies that provides similar products or services to the same market.

discipline
A group of professional firms that provides similar services to the same market.

vertical industry
A group of companies that use the same raw materials or resources to serve a select, specialized group of customers.

horizontal industry
A group of companies that provides similar services that can be used by companies in diverse fields.

these companies will compete for the same markets and groups of customers.

Within the same industry, there may be specific differences. For example, one retailer might offer customer service while the other operates on a self-service basis. However, these tend to be ways to identify and serve different segments of the same market. Within a given industry, there will be many characteristics that are common to most companies. These common features generally involve markets served and products or services delivered.

Generally, a person who is trained to work within one company in a given industry can move to another company in the same field. However, it can be more difficult to move to a company in a different industry.

Review 9.1

1. What qualifies a company to be part of an industry?

2. What is the main difference between an industry and a discipline?

3. What are vertical and horizontal industries and what are the differences between them?

WHY IS IT IMPORTANT TO CLASSIFY COMPANIES INTO INDUSTRY GROUPS?

Grouping companies according to type of business is a natural way to organize and monitor an economy. An economy, of course, takes in all of the transactions that make up the financial status of an area or country.

Recall that each business is formed to serve a specific market. That market is an industry, or a specific part of an industry. Therefore, it is correct to say that an industry is a defined market. All of the industries in an area or country make up its economy.

The basis for establishing an identity for an industry is that companies in certain fields have common needs. Natural supply patterns are formed. As

an illustration, consider automotive manufacturing. Companies that make cars need certain supplies. Examples include tires, headlight lamps, batteries, electric wire, steel, plastics, and thousands of other items. In turn, a company that makes tires needs to identify its prospective customers.

Typically, companies in the same industry will form an industry group, often called an *association*. An association is a group of companies and/or people with common interests. An association of automotive manufacturers can serve many common needs of its members. It works well, for example, for all automobiles to use 12 volt batteries. It would not work as well if each make or model of car used a different kind of battery. In turn, each kind of car would require a different kind of alternator, different headlights, etc.

How Are Industry Categories Used?

The government uses common requirements of industries to help meet its responsibilities to all the people. Among these responsibilities, for example, are the protection of natural resources and the environment. To illustrate, forests can be destroyed by companies that cut trees. The main users of forest resources are lumber companies and paper companies.

Working with companies in these fields, the government has acted to control use of timber resources. Some areas have been set aside as national forests or forest preserves. Trees in these areas are not cut for commercial use. In addition, laws have been established that make lumber and paper companies responsible for planting trees to replace those that are cut.

As another example, states that have coal and iron resources have passed laws that control mining operations. When coal or iron have been extracted, companies now are responsible to return the land to usable condition. Companies don't always like to be regulated. But the existence of known, identifiable industries has created a basis for coordinating efforts to protect the environment.

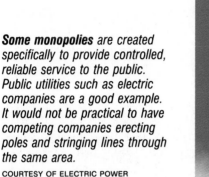

Some monopolies are created specifically to provide controlled, reliable service to the public. Public utilities such as electric companies are a good example. It would not be practical to have competing companies erecting poles and stringing lines through the same area.

COURTESY OF ELECTRIC POWER RESEARCH INSTITUTE

How Do Industry Categories Help to Preserve Competition?

Identification of industries also helps the government to protect consumers. As you may know, the laws of the United States make *monopolies* illegal. A monopoly is a condition in which one company controls business in one industry to a degree that lessens or eliminates competition. Under these laws, competition is seen as a protection for the consumer. When free competition exists, lawmakers have felt, the consumer has a choice. Competition helps to assure quality and fair pricing for products. The existence of industries makes such protective laws workable.

In the past, monopolies have caused problems. Individual companies gained control over supplies or services in their industry. Without competition, the companies were able to raise prices to unfair levels. These early abuses by some businesses led the United States to pass laws that make monopolies illegal.

But there are exceptions. In some industries, controlled service is believed to be an advantage. Examples include telephone, electric, and gas utilities. Also, radio and TV stations are given exclusive rights to broadcast channels. When the government authorizes a monopoly, a government agency is formed to monitor the interests of the people. These are known as *regulatory agencies*. Their job is to monitor the delivery of services, to review costs, and to approve rates that are charged.

Decisions about monopoly regulation can change with business and market conditions. For example, the interstate trucking industry was regulated for

Business Terms

association
An organization of companies and/or people with common interests.

monopoly
A condition in which one company controls business in one industry to a degree that lessens or eliminates competition.

regulatory agency
A government agency that monitors compliance with laws that control delivery of services, profits, and prices in specific industries.

several decades. The idea of regulation was to pre-vent a few big companies from taking over com-petitors and charging unreasonable prices. During the 1980s, with the economic picture changed by the growth of air freight and other factors, interstate trucking was deregulated. Deregulation has increased competition and has led to lower prices for shippers.

The point: Recognition of industry groupings helps government agencies to perform their mission of protecting the public interest.

Why Should You Know About Industry Groupings?

For the individual person, knowledge about indus-tries can play an important role in planning a career and/or finding a job. Companies within a given in-dustry or field are organized and operated similarly. Thus, you can learn about the products, services, markets, and operations within an industry as a whole.

When you do this, you are finding out about job and career potential in an entire area of the economy. You can match your own skills and job goals against the working conditions in a large number of com-panies. As you do, you can take stock of what it would be like to work in a field. You also can learn what lifestyle you can expect and how much you might earn.

WHAT ARE SOME VERTICAL INDUSTRY CLASSIFICATIONS?

More than 200 separate industries are identified by the U. S. Department of Labor. Identifying indus-tries, in turn, helps to recognize existing jobs. One example can be seen in the *Dictionary of Occupa-tional Titles (DOT),* a directory put out by the Bureau of Labor Statistics of the U. S. Department of Labor. The DOT lists and describes some 20,000 different jobs, classified by industry. The publication contains more than 1,300 pages.

Obviously, the average person doesn't need all this information to find a job. However, everyone can benefit from a general knowledge of industry structures and how companies in different fields re-late to one another. In particular, industry informa-tion can be valuable to students who are planning careers and workers who are seeking jobs. The descriptions below cover selected vertical industries.

Agriculture

The industry classified as agriculture specializes in growing foods and other useful plants. Although many crops are involved, the industry is vertical in nature. This is because of the concentration on use of land to grow crops. These crops result mostly in the production of food. However, many important nonfood crops also are produced by farmers. An ex-ample is cotton. Farming also takes in the area of livestock. Livestock includes the production of poultry, beef, pork, and other meats. Wool from sheep and hides from cattle are among the products of the agriculture industry.

Strategies and management challenges in agricul-ture center on planning for productive use of land. This field is known as *crop management.* Land is the critical resource in agriculture. Productive use of land is vital to success. Special concerns center on what crops to grow and when to rotate crops. Many farm crops tend to use up the supply of certain miner-als in the soil. If the same crop is grown for too many years on the same piece if land, the land eventually will produce less.

Skilled agricultural managers must decide when to let land lie idle to rebuild its mineral content. Also, crops can be rotated. The idea is to plant crops that rebuild mineral content of the soil. As one example, cotton farmers often rotate crops. They plant alfalfa to add nitrogen that has been used up by cotton grow-ing. The alfalfa, in turn, can be used as cattle feed. To carry out this type of planning, farmers need detailed knowledge about the markets and demands for different crops. As is true for any business, farm-

Food processing *generally requires mass-production techniques. This is because crops are ready for harvest at specific seasons and have to be processed in short time periods. This photo illustrates the mass-production processing of raisins, which have to be dried and packed in large volumes.*

COURTESY OF CALIFORNIA RAISIN
ADVISORY BOARD, PHOTO BY HANS
HALBERSTADT

ers must target specific markets for delivery of needed products.

Within the agriculture industry, farm jobs are not increasing. Technology keeps automating crop-related work. However, the business side of agriculture is offering new opportunities. These are largely in staff-type jobs such as financial management and marketing.

Food Processing

Food processors buy raw crops from farmers. They process the food so that it will be usable by consumers. They also package the food for delivery to consumers. The end products of food processing are cans, jars, bags, or other packages that contain food.

Food processing companies follow strategies aimed at serving such specific markets as food stores, restaurants, hospitals, or others. The challenge lies in knowing how much raw food to buy and process. Also, decisions have to be made about how big processing plants should be and how many people

should be employed. Note that processors are logical customers of farmers. In turn, processors serve customers that include food distributors and retailers.

Food Distribution and Retailing

Note that companies in this industry are part of a chain of supply and demand that includes farmers and food processors. Food distributors and retailers buy products to meet demands of their identified markets.

Business Terms

Dictionary of Occupational Titles (DOT)
A directory issued by the Bureau of Labor Statistics of the U. S. Department of Labor; lists and describes some 20,000 different jobs, classified by industry.

crop management
A management specialty in the agriculture industry; involves decision making about the use of land and other resources.

These markets can vary. They can include supermarkets. But other distributors sell to institutions such as hotels, hospitals, and restaurants. Demands of distributors and retailers help to determine the products that processors pack. In turn, processor requirements determine what crops are grown and what prices are paid for those crops.

Mining

Mining starts another chain of supply and demand. Companies in the mining industry meet demands for basic materials. They do this by extracting a wide range of minerals from the earth. These materials, in turn, are converted to many of the basic products and structures required by a modern society.

Mining companies extract such basic minerals as coal and iron ore from the ground. These materials are converted into steel beams used for bridges and buildings. Other uses include steel for automobiles and appliances and generation of electric energy in plants that burn coal.

In addition to coal and iron ore, miners also produce many other raw materials. Included are gold, silver, platinum, nickel, and even salt. Customers that create demands for these materials include the basic metals industry and the manufacturing field, described below.

The point: Industries form a structure of linked markets. Transaction chains tend to follow sets of industries.

Basic Metals

Companies in the basic metals industry process ores to develop raw materials for manufacturers. For example, iron ore is processed to create what is known as ''pig iron.'' These are basic masses of iron that can be processed further into steel. Some basic metals companies create steel products as well as pig iron. Others sell the pig iron to steelmakers. Similar arrangements exist in other fields.

Basic metals processors are part of a transaction chain that begins with mining and carries through to manufacturing of finished products. The position of basic metals companies within this chain pretty well establishes their potential markets and products.

Manufacturing

There are a number of manufacturing industries. These include automotive, appliance, furniture, and many others. There also are manufacturing companies with general capabilities. These organizations manufacture products for other companies.

A common trait of manufacturers is that they buy raw materials and parts from other companies and deliver finished products. In some instances, manufacturing companies make only parts that are sold to other companies.

Again, note the transaction chain that runs from mining to basic metals and then to manufacturing. Manufacturers are at the end of the chain. This position gives them a wide range of options in targeting markets and products. Manufacturers may plan to sell directly to consumers, to other businesses, or to distributors who market their products. They also have a wide range of choices in the types of products they make and the suppliers they choose.

Traditionally, a larger percentage of manufacturing jobs have involved straightforward assembly work. That is, people along assembly lines simply added items to products as they came past. During the 1980s, many of these jobs have been automated. Therefore, the number of assembly-type jobs has been reduced greatly. However, there are shortages of workers in skilled areas such as machining and welding. Although the total number of jobs has declined, there still are opportunities for skilled people.

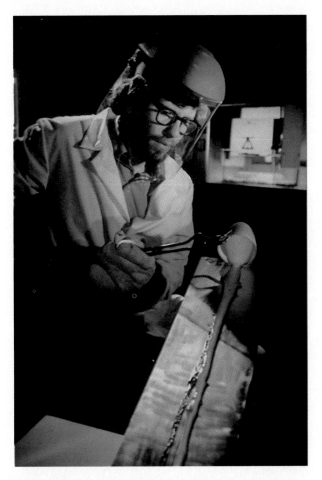

Basic metal production relies on critical natural resources. Researchers search continuously for better methods or new formulations that will deliver improved end products.
COURTESY OF BATTELLE MEMORIAL INSTITUTE

The Petrochemical Cycle

Transaction chains similar to those for metals stem from other kinds of raw materials. For example, a separate chain has been built around petroleum. Some companies specialize in *exploration*. These organizations search for oil and drill wells. The crude oil is sold to *refiners,* or processing companies that create gasoline, chemicals, plastics, and other products. Still other companies specialize in distribut-

ing and marketing petroleum-based products. Again, the organization of industries helps to define the kinds of transactions a company will seek. The kinds of products produced also tend to be defined by the properties of the raw materials.

Textile-Based Industries

The transaction chains for this set of industries start with producers of raw materials. These include farmers who provide cotton, wool, flax, and other agricultural products. Also included are producers of *synthetic* fibers. Synthetic means imitation or artificial. Most synthetic fibers are developed from petroleum-based chemical processes. Examples include nylon, Dacron, and many others.

Within the textile transaction chain, raw materials are sold to *converters,* companies that produce thread or cloth from raw materials. Cloth is created through such processes as weaving and knitting. Finished cloth is sold to companies that make clothing, furniture, linens, draperies, and other end products. Other suppliers to textile companies make buttons, zippers, and other items, known as "findings."

Business Terms

exploration
In the petroleum industry, the function of searching for oil deposits and drilling wells.

refiner
A company that inputs crude oil and produces finished petroleum products, such as gasoline or lubricating oil.

synthetic
Imitation or artificial; in the textile industry, description of fibers developed from chemical processes.

converter
In the textile field, a company that produces thread or cloth from raw materials.

The textile industries also have their own distribution channels and outlets that sell to consumers.

Forest Products

The forest products industry can be considered as related to agriculture. Raising trees uses land and depends upon the weather. However, lumber products become raw materials for production and construction industries. The customer base for forest products, therefore, is far different from the food and textile companies that buy agricultural products.

A major characteristic of the forest products industry lies in the long growth cycles involved. Once trees are cut, it can take 20 years or more to grow replacements. Therefore, forest products companies use vast amounts of land on a rotational basis to allow for the long growing cycles.

Within this industry, *vertical integration* is common. Vertical integration means that the same company performs several functions in connection with developing and marketing products. In the forest products field, most companies are growers of tress and product manufacturers. Companies that cut trees also may produce lumber or paper.

Like agriculture, the forest products field offers limited job potential. This is because the industry is highly automated.

Construction

The construction industry takes in all of the companies that build *infrastructure* and facilities. Infrastructure includes all of the support capabilities required by a region. Included are roads, airports, harbors, utilities, public buildings, and other requirements. Facilities, of course, include housing, offices, factories, and warehouses.

Construction industry organizations use raw materials from the forest products, mining, and manufacturing fields. Construction is a major industry that is subject to changes in demand that match trends in the economy. When money is tight, construction projects tend to be put off. When the economy turns upward, building booms usually follow.

A characteristic of the construction industry is that it is seasonal in some areas. That is, construction stops during heavy rains and snowstorms. Certain functions cannot be carried out satisfactorily during cold weather.

In the past, construction has been a highly labor-intensive industry. However, some changes are occurring with a trend toward *prefabrication.* Prefabrication techniques build sections of buildings in factories. These sections are assembled at construction sites in less time and with less labor than under traditional techniques.

Companies that operate within vertical industries are said to be narrow in their focus. That is, they target specific markets and create specialized products. A wider range of options, and some differences in focus, are available to companies that serve horizontal markets. Some examples of horizontal industries and their operations are covered below.

Review 9.2

1. What is meant by the term "transaction chain"?
2. Why do government agencies help to identify and monitor industries?
3. How can a knowledge of industry structures help the individual job seeker?
4. Describe the petrochemical transaction chain.

WHY ARE SOME INDUSTRIES CLASSIFIED AS HORIZONTAL?

Some industries are not part of a fixed transaction chain. Instead, companies in these fields provide

Forest products *are vital to construction of housing. In this plant, timber is processed into doors and windows for use in houses. A common denominator that links the forest products and construction industries is the use of wood, a key natural resource.*

COURTESY OF MORGAN PRODUCTS LTD.

services to all—or most—businesses or consumers. Managers in these fields have a wider range of choices in identifying markets. However, as with all industries, products or services tend to be specialized. That is, a company may provide a specialized service to a wide range of customers.

A special feature of horizontal industries is that most companies within this category deal in services, rather than products. As one of many examples, consider the banking industry. Banks provide financial services centered around the handling and lending of money. The services are well defined, specialized. But potential customers can be in any field. Also customers can be either companies or individuals.

Some horizontal industries and their structures are described below.

Transportation

As the name implies, companies in the transportation industry transport, or carry, people, products, or materials. Services include pickup of people or goods at shipping points, places where trips originate. Transportation companies then load, carry, and deliver people or products to destinations. Transportation companies tend to specialize in one type of service. Examples include *carriers* who transport by train, ship, airplane, truck, bus, or automobile. A carrier is an industry term for any company that provides transportation services.

Success story: Federal Express. In the transportation field, success can result from innovation. Better methods can lead quickly to market advantage. As

Business Terms

vertical integration
A company that performs several functions in connection with developing and marketing products.

infrastructure
All of the support capabilities required by a region.

prefabrication
Techniques for building sections of structures in factories for erection on building sites.

carrier
A company that transports people or goods by train, ship, airplane, truck, bus, or automobile.

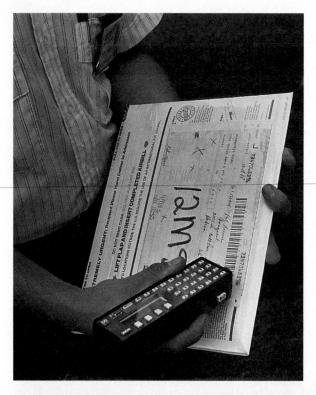

A real success story has resulted from the original idea that led to the founding of Federal Express, the overnight package delivery service. The idea: Send all packages by air to a single, central distribution point, then forward them to their destinations within hours. These photos illustrate the Federal Express operation. At left, package identification information is read through use of a portable computer input device carried by Federal Express couriers. The photo below shows part of the Federal Express fleet at the company's operating hub in Memphis, Tennessee. At right, on the facing page, is a photo of the package sorting operation in Memphis.

ALL PHOTOS COURTESY OF FEDERAL EXPRESS COMPANY

one dramatic example, consider the situation of Federal Express. This company provides overnight package delivery by air throughout the United States and to some foreign countries. The service is based on a new idea in transportation that was pioneered by Federal Express. The method is known as a "spoke and hub" operation.

As the service is provided by Federal Express, planes from more than 100 cities around the country fly to a hub in Memphis, Tennessee, every night. In Memphis, the incoming parcels are sorted and dispatched to destination cities on the return flights of the planes. This means that even parcels from cities close to one another are routed through Memphis. For example, consider a shipment from San Francisco to Los Angeles, California. The cities are about 400 miles apart. But a package routed from one city to the other would travel some 2,000 miles to Memphis. There, it would be routed to another 2,000 mile flight to its destination. It can be difficult to understand how this idea represents a major breakthrough. But it does.

Previously, most transportation companies used a "point-to-point" system. That is, packages were shipped directly from originating cities to destinations, often on commercial airplanes. To illustrate, an office in Los Angeles would have to break down shipments to all destination cities. Then, it would be necessary to place packages in containers for destinations. In some cases, the containers had to be transferred at in-between points. For example, to reach Columbus, Ohio, a container might be shipped to Chicago on one flight and transferred there.

The sorting and transferring operations actually slowed things down. Under the Federal Express method, all packages are shipped to one central location, Memphis. There, all packages are sorted once, when they are loaded into planes headed for the destination cities. Because Memphis is located centrally, deliveries can be made from Memphis to any other city in less than four hours.

The success of Federal Express has led to major changes in the transportation industry. Other parcel companies have adopted spoke-and-hub operations. Also, many airlines have found that they can offer lower fares by offering spoke-and-hub services to passengers.

This case example helps to illustrate the fact that imagination and innovation can help to reshape entire industries. It also works the other way. That is, an industry structure provides a framework within which people can innovate to deliver improvements. Success results from the ability to devise better services for identified markets.

Distribution

The distribution industry is related to transportation. However, distributors have a special role. They provide storage and product handling capabilities. These capabilities often make possible more efficient use of transportation services.

Consider a company in New England that receives orders from thousands of customers in California. If orders were shipped individually, there would be separate charges for each package. Instead, the New England company ships entire carloads of products to a *warehouse* in California. A warehouse is a building that stores and handles goods. It is far less expensive to ship a rail car full of goods to a single location in California than to pack and deliver thousands of parcels individually. When carload shipments are received in California, the local distributor fills orders. Local shipments are less expensive than cross-country deliveries.

Distribution also is a horizontal business. A distribution company can serve makers of almost any type of products. Some companies in this business function as wholesalers. That is, they purchase the goods they distribute, then resell them to retailers.

Retailing

A retail business is one that sells directly to consumers. Individual retailers can be either vertical or horizontal. You undoubtedly know of stores that specialize in such products as sporting goods, women's clothing, books, and so on. There also are stores that carry a wide range of products. Depart-

ment stores are an obvious example. Their name comes from the fact that they sell many different types of products in different departments.

In thinking about the overall business situation in an area, retailing serves a horizontal purpose. Retailers have the option to select their markets and to choose the products they sell. In this sense, retailing is horizontal. You undoubtedly have seen examples of horizontal trends in vertically organized stores. For example, many supermarkets offer clothing and some hardware products.

Finance and Banking

The horizontal nature of banking services is described earlier in this chapter. This industry is horizontal because its services support just about any industry. Also, banking can be a retail service because it serves consumers.

Insurance

Insurance companies protect customers against risks. Types of *insurance policies* are developed to cover specific kinds of risk. An insurance policy is a document that describes the risk protection to be provided. Types of policies offered include fire, theft, flood, earthquake, and many others. For individuals, life insurance also is available. All policies have stated benefits that are paid if the described condition occurs. Thus, a life insurance policy pays benefits when the insured person dies. Fire insurance pays for fire damages, and so on.

Insurance is a universal need for companies or people exposed to risks. Therefore, insurance is a horizontal industry that can serve virtually all businesses and consumers.

Health Care

The term ''health care'' generally is taken to mean that services are provided to people who become ill.

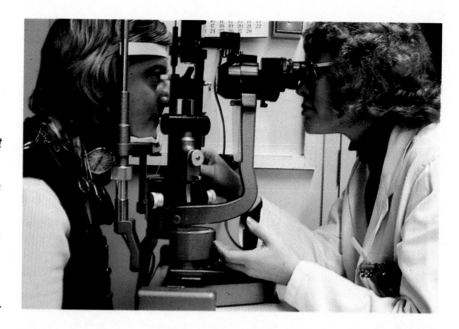

Health care professionals provide a wide range of services that protect the health of citizens and also care for those who become ill. The examination shown in this photo is providing a preventive medicine service: The patient's eyes are being tested for glaucoma, a disease that can lead to blindness.
COURTESY OF NATIONAL INSTITUTES OF HEALTH

Health care providers include hospitals, doctors, and clinics. There are many specialties in the health-care field, of course. Doctors specialize in caring for certain parts of the body or treating specific kinds of illnesses. There also are doctors who care only for children, women, athletes, and so on.

However, the overall market for health care takes in everyone. Businesses are specialized customers for health-care services. Many businesses arrange for health-care insurance for employees. Some of these policies are handled by insurance companies. In other cases, health care is provided by hospitals or health maintenance organizations (HMOs).

The point: health care is a multibillion dollar activity. Therefore, it is natural for an industry structure to build up to deal with common needs and problems.

Personal Grooming

Consumers spend hundreds of millions of dollars in beauty and barber shops. The personal grooming industry also has many specialties, including nail care, sun tanning, body building, and weight loss.

Entertainment

This field is both horizontal and specialized. Entertainment is horizontal because everyone has some leisure-time and recreational needs. However, there also are specialized groupings within the overall industry. Examples include motion pictures, live theater, television, radio, and special events such as rock concerts.

The entertainment field is a good example of a horizontal industry with its own transaction chain. Motion picture companies, for example, require

Business Terms

warehouse
A building that stores and handles goods.

insurance policy
A document that describes the risk protection to be provided to an insured person or organization.

health care provider
A person or organization that provides medical services, including patient care.

costumes, lighting equipment, cameras, film, laboratory services for developing film, sound recording, and theaters in which pictures are shown. The people and the companies that fall within this kind of industry are specialized. Each has a role within a transaction chain that contributes to the making of movies, the operation of theme parks, or other services. Because of the broad markets served, companies that contribute to entertainment activities are part of a horizontal industry.

Hospitality

The hospitality industry takes in hotels and restaurants. Companies in this industry provide housing and feeding services for millions of people. Hospitality companies are horizontal in nature. But they are served by many specialized functions, such as laundries, food processors, and makers of cooking utensils.

Information Services

It already has been established that information is a universal need. Information volumes and processing requirements have grown rapidly in recent years. Computers came into widespread use. In turn, the ability of computers to accumulate and provide access to information helped to create an important new management discipline. Today, most managers require computerized information support. Therefore,

even though databases model individual companies, information management also has become a horizontal industry.

All of these examples indicate that industry organization patterns create frameworks within which most companies exist. Industry organization patterns provide the basis for selection of markets, products, and transaction patterns. Industry structures also provide the basis for most interaction between businesses and government agencies.

A common denominator that applies in all industries—vertical and horizontal—is the need for and use of information. Information management through use of computers has become a vital requirement for all businesses. You will be learning more about computers and their uses in business as you continue your training. At this point, it is important to recognize that successful information workers must understand the structure of the industries in which they work. This knowledge makes it possible to collect and manage information to meet the needs of individual companies. The chapter that follows identifies information sources and explains the value of information as a business tool.

Review 9.3

1. Why are horizontal industries made up mostly of service companies.

2. Can you give examples of how innovation can play an important role in the success of a company in a horizontal industry?

Chapter Summary

❏ An industry consists of a group of companies that offer similar products or services to the same market.

❏ Professional organizations that offer similar products or services are called disciplines.

❏ Industries can be divided into two broad categories: vertical and horizontal. Vertical industries serve specialized markets. Horizontal industries provide general services that apply to many industries.

❏ Companies tend to organize themselves into natural transaction chains that cut across related industries.

❏ Industry structures are the basis for government activities in monitoring the economy. Government agencies look at industries to be sure that no one company controls all supplies or production. Such structures, known as monopolies, are illegal, except in situations where control is awarded to selected companies. In such cases, the government monitors operations and sets prices.

❏ A knowledge of industry structures can be valuable in selecting and planning for careers.

❏ Vertical industries serve narrow markets. Transaction chains tend to form among companies in different vertical industries. One example is the chain that runs from mining, to basic metals, to manufacturing. Other transaction chains exist in such fields as food, petroleum, textiles, and construction.

❏ Horizontal industries are composed almost entirely of service companies.

❏ Examples of horizontal industries include transportation, distribution, retailing, finance and banking, insurance, health care, personal grooming, entertainment, hospitality, and information services.

Definitions

Write a complete sentence that defines each of the terms below.

industry	discipline
vertical industry	horizontal industry
association	monopoly
regulatory agency	crop management

Questions to Think About

Based on what you have learned to date, answer the following questions in one or more complete sentences.

1. What is an industry?

2. How do government agencies use information on industry classifications?

3. How can knowledge about industry structures be useful in planning your future career?

4. What are vertical industries?

5. What are horizontal industries?

6. How do transaction chains establish links among companies in different industries?

7. Why is petroleum refining considered to be a vertical industry?

8. Describe the transaction chain that links companies involved in finding, processing, and delivering petroleum products?

9. Why is health care considered to be a horizontal industry?

10. Is information services a vertical or horizontal activity? Why?

Projects

The purpose of the assignments below is to encourage you to increase your learning through outside reading or work assignments.

1. Identify one industry that interests you as a possible career area. Find articles or information in reference books about this industry. Describe the transaction chain within which companies in your selected industry operate. Finally, describe the challenge or opportunities open to workers in this field.

2. Pick a product that you use, such as an article of clothing, a TV set, or other common item. Identify the place where you bought the item. Then, through reading or on the basis of what you already know, describe the transaction chain that caused the product to be created and delivered to you.

CHAPTER 10

What Are the Sources of Business Information?

The Think Tank

When you finish reading this chapter and complete your work assignments, you should be able to answer the following questions.

❑ What role does transaction processing play in building a database that models a business?

❑ What has to be done to transform transaction data into useful management information?

❑ What information resources can be used for managing a company?

❑ How can managers test an information model to be sure it is reliable?

DOING BUSINESS

"I'm glad I have someone I can trust to do business with," Roger said. "Buying your first car is a major experience."

Roger was in a small office off the showroom of a car dealership. He was addressing, Jeffrey Slocum, his uncle and owner of the agency. Roger continued: "It's a good thing you suggested that I shop with some other dealers before coming here. The experience has been an education. My work history covers less than a year. When you ask for credit, people laugh at you. As you know, Dad is willing to co-sign for my loan. But that doesn't cut much weight with most people. I couldn't believe how much information they wanted about Dad's financial condition. I really don't want to know that stuff myself."

Uncle Jeff laughed. "Now you know why I told you to shop elsewhere first," he said. "Your Dad and I can make things easier for you. But the experience you have had will help you to understand how serious a credit commitment can be.

"Also," he added, "you don't want to be too hard on the car dealers. Understand their position. It may seem that they are asking for a lot of information. It may seem like a hassle to have to fill out all the forms. But the car dealer has to work to get the money you are borrowing. The trail of information goes beyond the dealer. The dealer has to do business with a credit company or bank. These people may be in a different city. They won't have any idea who you are. They don't care. All they want is to be sure that they can count on being repaid for the money they lend."

"Do you mean the car dealer isn't giving me credit to buy the car?" Roger asked.

Prices for cars or other consumer products are set through use of information on costs and operating expenses. The money to buy and show new cars in showrooms comes from banks. The car dealer and the bank exchange information about products and loans through computers. Financial transactions are based largely on exchanges of information.

PHOTO BY LIANE ENKELIS

"No way," answered Uncle Jeff. "A car dealer is in the equipment business. Lending the kind of money needed to run a car dealership is a banking operation. A bank is in the money handling business. They take deposits from their customers and lend it to car buyers, home buyers, or credit card customers. Insurance companies do the same thing. They set aside money to be used if customers present claims for losses they have suffered. The money being held for claims can be invested to earn a profit. Both banks and insurance companies can be tough lenders. I know, I deal with them every day."

"You mean you have to apply for credit too?" Roger asked.

"You better believe it!" Uncle Jeff said forcefully. "A business like this runs on credit. A car dealer does well just to keep up with down payments."

"How does it work?" Roger wanted to know.

"The way it works," said Uncle Jeff, "is that the bank owns the business and I run it. Well, maybe it's not quite that bad. But that's the way it seems some days. When I sell you a car—and I certainly expect that I will—I will sell the loan to my bank.

Your payments will be made to the bank, not to me. In our case, that's better. I don't want to be your creditor—or your father's.

"I have to discount your loan to the bank to get my money," he continued. 'For instance, if I handle a loan for $10,000, the bank buys it from me for less than that amount. I may receive between $9,800 and $9,900. That means I have to add $100 to $200 to the price of a car to cover the cost of money.

"And that's not all," said Uncle Jeff. "The bank actually owns all of the cars that you see in the showroom and out on the lot. There's a special kind of financing. It's called 'flooring.' The bank lends me money to buy the cars from the factory. Then, when I sell a car, the bank lends money to the buyer. I wind up with the difference between the loans, less the discount. Now, did you ask if I understand how credit works?"

"Does the bank send somebody around to see the cars you have here?" Roger asked.

"That's not necessary," Uncle Jeff explained. "We are like other businesses. The whole thing runs on information. The bank uses information we get from the factory about the cars that are delivered.

The bank also gets information when we sell cars. That's why I have the computer you just looked at. Our computer talks to the bank's computer. We all live through the use of information.''

MEANING

You already know that transactions form a chain that helps determine the markets and products of a company. The collection and use of information also takes place in a continuous chain. The scenario above helps to dramatize the information relationships among organizations, industries, and the overall economy of an area.

As a young person, Roger finds that car dealers want to tie his credit standing to his father's. Putting it another way, there wasn't enough personal financial information about Roger for him to get credit. Car dealers wanted to combine information about his father with what they knew about Roger himself.

In talking with Uncle Jeff, Roger learned that the chain of information about consumers extends beyond car dealers. The car dealers have to get credit from banks before they can sell cars. Car dealers continually borrow money to buy and sell cars. Their earnings come from the differences between the sizes of loans. The loans to consumers should be bigger than the loans used to purchase cars from manufacturers.

Roger learned also that business transactions are based almost entirely on information. Banks do not have to see the cars against which they lend money. The lenders see information about cars. Information represents the values that are exchanged in business transactions. This chapter is designed to help you to understand where needed business information comes from. Also, you should understand how information is accumulated, processed, and used.

Usefulness of information is a key. Remember what it takes for information to be useful: Information delivered to users must be accurate, reliable, and timely.

WHERE DOES BUSINESS INFORMATION COME FROM?

This information can come from hundreds of *sources* and can undergo complex *processing*. A source is a point or person from which information originates. Processing includes the calculations and recording operations applied to information to make it useful.

In business, a common source of information is the transaction. Each transaction produces information about customers, products or services sold, the price, and many other items. Information items on transactions are considered to be source data. Data items, remember, consist of raw facts and figures.

Processing, then, accepts data items and combines them with existing information. Processing also applies calculations to the data. The functions applied during processing are said to *transform,* or change, data into information. Transformation occurs when data items are combined or when new items are created through computation. When transformed information is accumulated, the result is an information resource that models the condition of the company. An information resource, or a database, can consist of millions of items of information.

What Happens During Transaction Processing?

To illustrate, when you make a purchase with a credit card, this transaction is listed in your account record maintained at the bank or credit card company. The new purchase is added to a list of other purchases you may have made. In effect, a new item is added to the file record for your account. This new information item transforms your account. In addition, computation also takes place. The amount of the new sale is added to the total of what you owe. Arithmetic leads to transformation.

Transactions that a company conducts represent one kind of information source: internal. Information also can come from external sources. An example of

Information for processing *generally is provided from tapes or disks mounted on drives. In large computer systems, user programs can access files with many billions of characters of information. Mounting tapes or disks represents full-time work for many thousands of people.*

an external source of information would be the credit application received at a bank. The application comes from a car dealer and provides information on a borrower.

What Are Some Sources of External Information?

There are many other sources of external information. Among these sources are information provided by other businesses and the government. For example, the car dealer needs information from banks on interest rates. For the dealer, interest rates represent the cost of money to be borrowed.

The car dealer also receives reports on total car sales during each 10-day period. This information helps the dealer determine whether to expect sales to go up, go down, or remain the same. External information for a car dealer also comes from car manufacturers. Included are information on parts, service instructions, and prices of cars or parts.

The point: A business gathers a lot of the information based on day-to-day transactions. This information is essential for continuing operations. But each business also depends on outside sources of information. The processing and use of information

Business Terms
source A position or person from which information originates.
processing Operations within a computer that handle and/or transform data, including calculations, comparisons, or combinations among data elements.
transform To change or add to data items to generate information; transformation occurs when data items are combined or when new items are created through computation.

from internal and external sources are described in the discussions that follow.

HOW DO INTERNAL BUSINESS OPERATIONS GENERATE USEFUL MANAGEMENT INFORMATION?

Transactions are just as basic to information systems as they are to the operation of the business itself. Recall the earlier quotation that nothing happens until somebody sells something. It also is true that nothing is known about the status or condition of a business without transaction data. Collection and processing of internal information begins with source data.

How Do Transactions Generate Data?

Think about what happens when you buy your lunch at a fast-food restaurant. There are differences between the way transaction information is handled at different chains. But the general outlines can be summarized. You step up to be greeted by a smiling counterperson who wants to help you. After returning the smile, you recite your order, one item at a time.

As you state each item, the counterperson punches one key on a special electronic cash register. No amounts need to be entered. Instead, the counterperson touches a key with the name, or possibly a picture, of the item you want. The computer uses the key entry as a signal. From its electronic files, it draws a description and a price for the item you want.

If your food is to be cooked to order, the item name is printed in the kitchen. The cook then works from this computer printout. In other restaurants, food is precooked and left in a warming area. If this method is used, your order information is displayed at the register. The counterperson then gets the items from the warming area.

Accumulating source data. Through the day at perhaps thousands of restaurants, computers accumulate totals on ordered items. This can come to millions of items each day. The next day, supplies must be delivered to the restaurants to replace the items sold. This is the beginning of a need to process data to deliver information. The restaurants need new supplies so they can continue to serve customers. But it would be impossible for people to review lists showing millions of sales items—not on a daily basis anyway.

Instead, the computers do the *tallying.* A tally is a list of items with a total provided. A fast-food tally would contain totals for all units sold for each menu item, such as hamburgers or french fries. Tallies are developed for each restaurant, for geographic areas, and for the chain as a whole.

The results of this processing represent the beginning of management information. From the tallies, managers know how many hamburger patties, slices of cheese, tomatoes, rolls, and other ingredients will be needed. The information system develops these figures for regions as well as for restaurants. The processing plants of the chain use this information to set up production and delivery schedules for supplies. The information tells the plant managers, in total, how much food to prepare. The information also helps distribution people to break down shipments to meet the needs of each restaurant.

Generating management information. In a business situation, this is only one of several types of processing and analysis steps in the handling of information. For example, the same information used to total items sold also can be tallied differently. The computer presents information on how many customers are served in each restaurant during every hour of the day. The computerized registers also record the time that each order is entered. When the customer pays after receiving the food, another time entry is recorded.

The computer can process this information to figure out how many customers are served each hour. The computer also figures out how long it takes to

Transaction information should be captured for computer processing as close as possible to the point at which transactions take place. In this photo, a server is entering a food order in a restaurant. The computer terminal is located at the serving station within the restaurant. The server touches points on the computer screen to enter orders that are printed in the kitchen.

PHOTO BY BENEDICT KRUSE

serve each customer. From this information, the managers can determine how many employees are needed in each restaurant—hour by hour.

As processing continues, the computer can develop information that tells how much money each restaurant takes in, every day. The computer also can tally costs to run the restaurant. Then, costs are subtracted from income. With the results produced by computers, managers know the profit level for each restaurant—on a daily basis.

HOW IS INFORMATION HANDLED TO PRODUCE THESE RESULTS?

Consider what happens from an information management view: Cash register entries produce data items. These data items are recorded in files according to hamburgers, fries, and other menu items. This is the first transformation from data to information. The totals from each of the menu-item files become part of a database. Other database records reflect the processing of payrolls, the rent for restaurants, utility bills, and so on.

Special computer software then is used to control additional processing and information transformations. The software programs are used by managers to search the database to develop needed information. Individual managers receive information they need to do their own jobs. The operations manager is worried about delivering meat patties and other supplies. But the marketing manager wants to figure out whether each city can support more restaurants.

The point: Processing and transformation of data and information can go on endlessly. Today, managers must be able to define the information that will model their businesses. Managers work with information that represents the business. They don't have to go to each store to see what's happening. Information resources tell them.

Business Terms

tally
The operation that develops totals for a group or list of data items.

What Steps Are Included in the Information Processing Cycle?

From source data through to management information, computers are applied in a series of steps that is known as an *information processing cycle*. This cycle also is identified by the initials of the basic steps involved. The name *IPOS cycle* stands for the basic steps of input, processing, output, and storage. A diagram of the cycle is presented in Figure 10-1. As shown in this diagram, each of the basic steps includes a number of operations, as described below.

Input.   The first requirement is to bring data into the system. This can be done through operation of keyboards in a "capture" procedure. Another approach is to receive data transmitted from outside sources. These sources can be adjacent to the computer itself. They can be cash registers that are connected through communication lines. Or the sources can be across the country and can communicate over telecommunications circuits.

In any case, a vital part of input is to verify the accuracy of data. This can be done automatically, as happens when the computer verifies the value of purchases by checking with a cash register. Verification also can be done by people. This happens when people proofread and correct letters or financial statements.

Processing.   The processing function, as indicated, can involve calculation, comparison, combination, or transformation. Calculation involves use of arithmetic functions. Comparison is used to sort items into specific sequences. For example, a fast food chain might compare restaurant numbers to organize data for operating reports. Combination of numbers occurs when transactions change files, as occurs when your credit card purchase changes the balance of your account. Transformation is the overall process that converts data into useful information.

Output.   Output includes all of the operations needed to deliver information to users. Outputs can

be printed, stored on file devices, or transmitted over communication lines. Output distributes information to people who are authorized to receive it and who need it to perform their jobs.

Storage.   Storage is the banking center for information resources. Information is recorded in files and retrieved as necessary for delivery to authorized users. Transmission of data is an important part of the functions of recording and retrieving information in storage devices.

WHAT OUTSIDE INFORMATION SOURCES CAN HELP MANAGERS?

The narrative above covers information that is developed internally. As indicated, most companies also gather and process information that comes from outside sources. One example combines internal and external information sources. A company cannot process a payroll without mixing information from internal and external sources.

Internal information includes identification of employees and data items on pay rate, number of hours worked, and deductions. External information includes a table of tax deduction information. This information is provided by the government. Reference to tax deduction records would be incorporated in payroll processing procedures.

Another example includes information on sales taxes that must be charged in completing transactions. Thus, everyday information processing functions rely on both internal and external information sources.

How Can External Information Help to Identify Opportunities?

Many external information sources are used by businesses. To illustrate, consider the information you might want if you were a regional manager for a fast-food chain. Part of your job is to decide where to

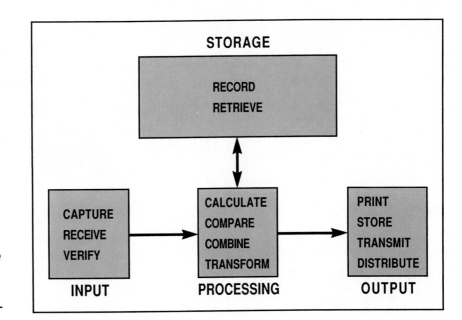

Figure 10-1. *The basic processing cycle followed by all computer information systems involves input, processing, output, and storage. Note, in the accompanying diagram, that stored files can support any of the other functions within the processing cycle. Stored data are the assets created by computer processing.*

build new restaurants. Another part of your job is to keep an eye on competition.

The two responsibilities are related. For example, you probably would want lists of building permits issued in cities in your territory. Building permits would tell you where new development is planned in a city. For example, if a new factory is to be built, you might be interested in opening a restaurant across the street. Also, the information on building permits would tell you about what your competitors are planning. Before another chain can build a restaurant, a permit would have to be issued.

Many other external sources must be consulted. As just one example, you would want information on zoning applications to the city council. Before a building permit is requested, the land must be zoned for specific use. Local governments pass laws that control land use for the benefit of citizens. Special areas are set aside for residential, commercial, manufacturing, or general business use. Often, it is necessary to get special ''variances,'' or changes in zoning laws, to authorize use of land for business. For example, a fast-food restaurant may require a change from residential to commercial zoning. You

might look at these zoning applications to spot locations for proposed new shopping centers. This information would identify potential future restaurant locations.

Return now to the situation of an automobile dealer. People in this business regularly ask state agencies for car registration information. For example, Jeff Slocum might buy a computer-generated list of registrations for cars that are four years old or older. His idea: People who own cars in these model years are logical prospects to buy new cars. Jeff then might arrange special mailings or telephone sales calls for prospective buyers in his market area.

These are just a few examples. But they do illustrate that external information sources can provide valuable business information.

Business Terms

information processing (IPOS) cycle
A sequence of operations followed in processing or transforming data into information; consists of the basic steps of input, processing, output, and storage.

Review 10.1

1. What is the main source of management information?

2. What happens when data items are transformed during processing?

3. What steps are included in the information processing cycle?

4. Why is it necessary for companies to gather information from both internal and external sources?

Video displays *are the main methods for presenting information for temporary reference by users.*
PHOTO BY LISA SCHWABER-BARZILEY

HOW IS INFORMATION DELIVERED TO USERS?

Most computer-produced information is delivered to users in one of two forms:

- Displays
- Printouts.

How Are Displays Used?

A *display* is a temporary view of information records. These records are retrieved from computer files especially for review by a user. The most common type of display is the video display terminal (VDT) or cathode ray tube (CRT) that is part of a computer configuration. Other types of displays include large lighted screens for meeting rooms or scoreboards at arenas or stadiums.

To see a display, a user has to enter an instruction into a computer. Generally, this is done through use of a keyboard. The user enters commands that instruct the computer to retrieve specific records. Sometimes computers provide menus that can be used to choose display options that provide specific, selected information. For example, it may be possible to enter a single instruction or choose a single menu item to present a financial status report.

In other cases, the user can enter commands that tell the computer what to do. To illustrate, suppose a fast-food manager has arranged to have information on building permits entered into a computer. The manager wants to know if competitors have applied for permits to build new restaurants. The manager would ask the system to search for records bearing the name of a competitor. The system would display all records containing the competitor's name. After reviewing information found in this search, a new name could be entered.

Each time a new command is entered, the display disappears. This is the nature of displays. They are temporary. When the computer terminal is used for another operation, the existing display disappears. To have a permanent record of the information, printouts must be requested.

How Are Printouts Used?

A *printout* or a *hard copy* consists of information imprinted on paper. Paper records, of course, are permanent. They can be packed in briefcases, marked with pencils, and copied for sharing with others.

Information can be retrieved from a computer in much the same way as for a display. The same kinds of menus or commands are used. However, a command entered by a user causes the information to be printed on paper.

When information is delivered specifically to meet a request of a single user, the printout is called a *custom report.* That is, the document contains information that was requested specifically.

Most companies that use computers also issue *scheduled reports.* These are printouts that are produced at regular times. Scheduled reports also have the same information items each time they are issued. An example of a scheduled report would be a summary of sales by menu item. The report could be organized according to individual restaurants, regions, and for the entire chain. Scheduled printouts also include payrolls.

When a report is scheduled, it is produced regularly, whether or not it is requested by users. In many companies, the practice of producing reports on regular schedules has led to problems. The needs of users change. But the content of scheduled reports does not change. After some time, the report loses its usefulness. However, unless a specific order is given to discontinue the report, it may be issued regularly without being used. This can lead to serious waste. One of the responsibilities of managers should be to monitor information reporting to be sure that printouts still are needed. Unneeded reports should be discontinued.

HOW ARE INFORMATION RESOURCES MANAGED?

To be of value, information resources should be organized for ease of use. In a large company, information accumulates at rates of millions of items per day. If managers fail to plan for the organization of and reference to data, needed information can become hard to find.

Consider a simple example: Customer records are used in many transactions. For example, in writing bills (invoices), the customer name and address are required. Customer information also is needed for credit files and for following up to collect bills. Salespeople need information about their customers.

Computer printouts provide permanent copies of information for user reference.

PHOTO BY LISA SCHWABER-BARZILEY

In organizing information, it would be tempting to include customer data in all files that relate to customers and/or sales. This could mean that the same information about the same customer might appear in a company's database six or more times. One obvious problem is that this takes up a lot of valuable space within a database.

But there is an even greater difficulty: Suppose a customer moves or changes a telephone number. Suppose a credit limit is changed. Each change would have to be made to every record about the customer. This is a lot of work. Also, if one change to one record is not made, the information no longer is accurate or reliable.

Business Terms

display
Information presented on a VDT screen.

printout
A computer output printed on paper.

hard copy
See printout.

custom report
A printout that contains information requested specifically by a user.

scheduled report
A printout with specified information content that is printed at regular intervals.

Massive computer files are accumulated to support the information needs of many businesses. Consider that each of the thousands of tapes stored in this facility holds billions of characters of information. Processing selects information needed by information users at different levels in the organization.
PHOTO BY LIANE ENKELIS

If enough incorrect records exist, the whole database becomes unreliable. This means the information can't be trusted. It also means that decisions based on the information may be incorrect.

How Are Data Redundancies Avoided?

Repetition of data items within a database is known as *redundancy,* another word for duplicated content. To avoid data redundancies and related problems, a database usually is organized to contain each master record only once. For example, a database typically would have a master file of customer records. When customer information is needed for an invoice, it is picked up from the master file. A computer user enters a reference code, such as customer name or number. The computer finds the proper record and inserts it in the invoice. In this way, when information is changed, there is only one correction to make.

It also is important to decide the form and level of detail in which information is to be saved. For example, fast-food chains record data items for each hamburger sold. There would be no point in including all of these items, in this level of detail, in a database. Instead, an information system might set up files that accumulate menu items sold in each restaurant for an entire day. These files could be accumulated at the end of the week and the daily information could be dropped. Managers have to think about the plans and decisions they make. Information must be organized to support these decisions.

Data structures. The organization of information to model businesses has become a major specialty within the information field. The plan for storing and using data is called a *data structure.* Development of data structures is one of the keys to successful management of information resources.

This and other specialized skills illustrate a point about the gathering and use of information: Information management is a service. The service is performed by technicians and other computer professionals. The technical aspects of information handling can get really complex. However, the principle is basic: Information must be organized to support ease of use. Users are the customers.

Information ownership and custody. Another factor is that users are *information owners.* Users identify information to be entered into and processed by computers. Users retrieve and apply information to solve problems and make business decisions.

As owners, users entrust their information to computer professionals. The job of the computer professionals is *information custody.* To have custody, means to be entrusted with something, to take care of it. A good comparsion: Users deposit information with computer professionals in the same way as financial managers deposit money in banks. Banks, too, are custodians of business resources.

Part of the custody responsibilities of computer professionals is to assure the security and protection of data. Security means that only authorized users can have access to information resources. Protection means that information files are protected against destruction. To do this, most large computer centers prepare duplicate copies of the disk and tape files every day. Copies of the files are sent to remote locations for protective storage. If information resources are lost, plans are in place to use the backup copies of files for *recovery* programs. Recovery, in this sense, means that the computer center can recover its information assets to the position that existed before the originals were destroyed.

Satisfying information users is the key to the success of any information system. The chapter that follows deals with users, their needs, and ways to satisfy those needs.

Review 10.2

1. What are the main differences between displays and printouts?
2. What is data redundancy and what should be done about it?
3. What is information ownership and who are information owners?
4. What is information custody and who performs this responsibility?

Business Terms

redundancy
In a database, the duplicated use of the same data item in multiple files.

data structure
A design for the organization and storage of data items within a database.

information owner
Users who generate information or for whom information resources are created and maintained. Information is said to belong to its users.

information custody
An assigned responsibility to maintain and protect data resources to assure their continued accessibility by users.

recovery
A plan for re-creating and making available data resources that are destroyed through use or accidental event.

Chapter Summary

❑ The source for much of the information needed to manage a company originates from transaction processing.

❑ During processing, source information is transformed to develop information.

❑ Transaction information is accumulated and tallied to provide information on current operations and needs.

❑ Information is developed by following a processing cycle that includes steps for input, processing, output, and storage. These steps include operations that communicate and deliver information as needed by the system and its users.

❏ To develop some outputs, information from external and internal sources must be combined. As an example, payroll processing requires that information on employees and hours worked be combined with data on tax rates.

❏ The main methods for delivering information to users are through displays or printouts.

❏ Displays are temporary. Most displays are presented on VDT screens at user work stations.

❏ Printouts are paper documents that can be stored, marked, and shared with other users.

❏ Information resources are managed by analyzing data content and designing plans of organization called data structures. A key idea of a data structure is to eliminate duplicate, or redundant, occurrences of data items.

❏ Information management is a service. Users own the information content of the system. Computer professionals assume custody for the resources.

Definitions

Write a complete sentence that defines each of the terms below.

source	processing
transform	tally
printout	scheduled report
redundancy	data structure
data structure	information custody

Questions to Think About

Based on what you have learned to date, answer the following questions in one or more complete sentences.

1. What are internal and external information sources and how are they similar and different?

2. What is data transformation and what are its results?

3. What is the main source of internal information?

4. Give examples of some sources of external information that are required for operations and decision making.

5. How and in what forms is information delivered to users?

6. What are data structures and what is their purpose?

7. What is data redundancy and what problems does it present?

8. What is meant by information ownership and who are information owners?

9. What is meant by information custody and who are information custodians?

Projects

The purpose of the assignments below is to encourage you to increase your learning through outside reading or work assignments.

1. As a student you are an information user. The information you accumulate in class and by reading this book comes from internal sources that are part of your normal course activity. In addition, many external sources of information are available to students of business. Identify and describe at least two external information sources that you have used or that are available for your use. It is okay to consider information sources available through a computer lab in your school.

2. As a customer, you play a role in restocking the products or supplies in places where you do business. Think about this statement. The idea carries information in this chapter one step further. The chapter explains that transaction information is used to order and deliver supplies to fast-food restaurants. It also could be said that customers cause the system to restock business outlets automatically. Explain the role of the customer in generating management information.

CHAPTER 11

How Do Businesses Use Information?

When you finish reading this chapter and complete your work assignments, you should be able to answer the following questions.

❏ Why is the accumulation, processing, and use of information described as a "bottom-up" process?

❏ Why is more detailed information provided to managers at lower organizational levels than at higher levels?

❏ What kind of information is required at the operational level of an organization?

❏ What kind of information is required at the tactical level of an organization?

❏ What kind of information is required at the strategic level of an organization?

DOING BUSINESS

"You've got the whole world in that box," said Tina.

Tina and her parents were at Global Travel making plans for a vacation trip. Homer, a travel agent, was seated at a computer terminal connected to an airline computer system. He explained to the family that his terminal was part of a worldwide computer network. A network is a group of communication devices that are connected to one another.

"Our agency is tied into a travel information network," Homer explained. "We work through one airline, Trans-Global. Once we are into the network, we can get information on flights and reservations for any commercial airline in the world. We also can get you special rail tickets in Europe. And—this is the good part—we also can book reservations into

hotels. All told, we have reservation information for more than a half million hotel rooms available. It's all right here, on this screen. I sometimes think of it as a kind of magic window."

To start their vacation planning, Tina's parents had given Homer a list of cities they wanted to visit. He called them "destinations." The overall plan was to make a first stop in Los Angeles. Tina was looking forward to seeing Disneyland and Universal City. Homer delighted her when he assured her he could make reservations through his computer. They would have their tickets in hand before they left home. After Los Angeles, the family was planning to fly to Honolulu. Then, on the return trip, they planned a stop in San Francisco.

At the start of the conference, Homer had entered destination information. Then, he checked the fares for several different airlines to come up with

Airlines fly on information.
Airline reservations are made through use of computer systems. Computers generate many tickets and the majority of boarding passes that confirm passenger seat assignments. In addition, many tickets are sold through use of credit cards that generate source documents for computer processing.

the lowest travel costs. In each case, Homer explained the costs and restrictions for each fare. On some fares, there was no refund if the trip was cancelled. On others, there was a penalty if reservations were changed. Still others could be changed without cost penalties. In general, the more options a passenger had, the more the ticket would cost.

"Here's what I can do to help you," Homer said. "I can put the reservations into the computer now. That will protect you to be sure you have your airplane seats. We can then wait up to a week before the tickets are issued. You don't have to pay anything now. The reservation system has that flexibility. It checks itself every day. If you don't buy your tickets by the final date, your reservations are cancelled."

Tina's father was impressed. He asked: "Do you mean the system checks the status of each reservation every day? There must be millions of reservations in that system. You have a full year of flights for maybe 20 major airlines. Then there are millions of nights for hotel room bookings."

"You've got it," Homer replied. "The system even goes further. If a cancelled reservation has been booked by a travel agent, the agent gets a cancellation notice."

Homer liked to explain the features of the computer reservation system to his customers. Experience had shown him that customers who understood what he was doing would have more confidence in his services. Homer realized that paying for a vacation was a big expense for a family. The family he was working with would spend more than $3,000 for the reservations he booked. Homer recognized that this was a serious investment. His job was to help assure that his customers enjoyed their vacations.

Homer turned to Tina's parents. "Now," he said, "pretend you're in Los Angeles. Let's decide what location and accommodations you want in hotels. You can stay in one place and drive. Or you can book different hotels that are close to the places you want to see."

MEANING

Computers and their information services are everywhere. Just about everyone relies on computers to meet some needs for information and services. To keep up with the vast needs of an information society, it has become necessary to interconnect computer systems. In effect, multiple computers talk to one another to find and deliver the information needed by users.

The travel agency situation described above provides a good illustration. Each of perhaps 20 airlines and more than a dozen hotel chains has its own reservation system. Separate reservation systems cover attractions such as theme parks, baseball stadiums, and theaters. A central index is maintained by computers. This permits users at terminals connected with any system to call for information from all of the interconnected computers.

Some observers try to compare today's information-based operations with the way things were done before computers were available. This approach is futile—useless. The truth is that people could not have had many of today's services without computers. Airlines could not have controlled reservations for thousands of flights on a seat-by-seat basis. Hotel chains could not have booked reservations for tens of thousands of rooms for a year or more in advance. For that matter, companies could not have grown large enough to operate more than a thousand hotels or hundreds of jet aircraft without computers.

The point: It does no good to imagine what things would have been like without computers. Computers are here. They are part of your life today. As you build a career, computers will affect you more and more. As a worker in an information society, you will need to know what computers can do for you. The rest of this chapter is designed to help you understand what is expected of computers. Note that computer services are different for different kinds of users. Some types of users and their needs are covered in the discussions that follow.

HOW ARE INFORMATION NEEDS OF MANAGERS DETERMINED?

The travel-planning example establishes that computers can tailor their services. Information can be provided to meet specific needs or interests of users. This principle applies to the design and operation of all information systems. That is, the starting point in

planning for and building an information system is to learn about information needs.

What information is desired and how will that information be used?

This question has different meanings—and different answers—for individual information users. A business manager might visualize needed information in terms of facts and figures displayed on a screen. A computer professional develops different images. He or she will think in terms of data and file structures.

Why Is Information Viewed Differently by Managers and Computer Professionals?

For example, to a department store manager, a code entry represents a product to be sold. For a computer professional, the product is not important. The systems analyst might see a data item that contains both alphabetic and numeric information. Each data item might be eight characters long.

The systems analyst also would need to know the size of the data items that contain descriptions, pricing, and other information about the product. In other words, the systems analyst is visualizing a record that has to be handled by the computer. The store manager doesn't need to see any of this. He or she should visualize use of the information to analyze sales and to decide when to order more merchandise.

The point: Data and information are viewed in different ways. In designing an information system, it must be remembered that the user is the customer. Any analysis of needs and services begins with the user's job and the role of information in that job.

How Does Management Level Affect Information Planning?

Recall that management jobs are defined according to level of responsibility. Managers operate at three levels—operational, tactical, and strategic. The operational level is lowest in the organization; the strategic level is highest.

Different kinds of planning and decision making take place at each level. To develop plans, the process starts at the top level, where managers create long-range, or strategic, plans. Planning then proceeds to the tactical and operational levels. That is, tactical and operational plans fit within and support strategic plans.

Why Do Managers at Lower Levels Need Greater Information Volumes?

The planning and organization of information systems moves in the opposite direction. You already know the logic for this: One of the major data sources for an information system comes from transactions. Transactions, of course, take place at a company's operational level. Transaction data items provide information building blocks. Therefore, information systems are built from the bottom up. The discussions that follow describe needs at each level and the methods used to meet those needs.

WHAT INFORMATION IS USED AT THE OPERATIONAL LEVEL?

The lower the organizational level, the closer a manager is to day-to-day operating detail. However, the areas of responsibility are narrower at lower levels. This means, for example, that the manager of a single fast-food restaurant needs to know about all transactions at one location. At higher levels, information on multiple locations is summarized. At the top, the restaurant may become just a mark on a map.

How Does Accountability Affect Management Information Needs?

Management assignments—and information needs—are based on accountability. That is, a manager is accountable for the results delivered by the operations

under his or her supervision. Accountability involves a number of different items. For example, an operational manager at a single fast-food restaurant would be accountable for human, physical, and financial results.

Human accountability would include hiring of staff, training, and *turnover,* or the rate at which employees quit their jobs. Physical accountability would be for the maintenance of equipment and the cleanliness of the restaurant and parking lot. These parts of accountability can be handled, at least partly, by inspection. A supervisor can look at the cleanliness of a restaurant and parking lot. Also, a supervisor must visit a restaurant and observe the quality of service delivered by employees. In-person review is needed to tell how well a manager is measuring up in the human and physical accountability areas. To monitor financial accountability, information is necessary.

How Does Information Determine Levels of Financial Performance?

The financial results delivered by managers are measured entirely through information, with one major exception. When financial operations are checked, cash is counted and other liquid assets are examined physically. Otherwise information is used to compare actual results with plans. Remember, financial planning generally is for a one-year period. The financial plan is a budget. For each operational unit, the budget lists income and expense items. The listings are for accountability periods, which can be weeks, months, or quarters.

To measure financial accountability, budget figures generally are set up in a computer file. Then, the information system develops actual operating figures that match the budget amounts. For example, one department in a store might have budget items for sales, payroll, and cost of goods sold. If this is the case, computer programs would accumulate transaction information in the same categories. The transaction information then would be tallied and

```
         OPERATING STATUS REPORT - ABC COMPANY
                        JANUARY

       ITEM              BUDGET      ACTUAL     VARIANCE
     INCOME
       Sales Income      92,000      89,000      -3,000
       Fees              52,000      54,720       2,720
       Interest Income   15,200      15,200           0
       Other Income       8,800       9,110       1,110

     TOTAL INCOME       168,000     168,030          30

     EXPENSES
       Rent              19,600      19,760         160
       Utilities          1,840       1,798         -42
       Telephone          2,960       2,820        -140
       Salaries          80,400      82,100       1,700
       Misc.             12,100      11,830         270

     TOTAL EXPENSES     116,900     118,308       1,408

     NET INCOME          51,100      49,722      -1,378
```

Figure 11-1. *Electronic spreadsheets can help managers to identify exception situations that require attention or that identify problems to be solved. In this example, the key to management evaluation is the column of items that show differences between planned and actual results.*

reported for the same periods as shown on the budget. The computer output for this information might have a column that showed the difference between budget and actual results for each item.

For example, for the month of January, the report might show budgeted sales, payroll, etc., in one column, as shown in Figure 11-1. In a second column, the actual figures for the same items would be listed. Then, in a third column, the computer would calculate and list the difference between budgeted and actual amounts. If results are less than budgeted, the computer would place a minus sign (−) in front of the amount for the difference.

Compare this report with what you know about management by exception. Each minus sign is an exception. These items would be inspected closely by the responsible manager and by his or her superior. Small items might be ignored. Major differences would attract serious investigation and, as necessary, corrective actions.

If you were a manager, which items in Figure 11-1 would you regard as exceptions?

The point: Financial performance at the operational level is measured by comparing expected with actual results. The information system must be set up

to report on actual operating results in a format that matches the budget. Evaluations consist of comparisons between budgeted and actual figures. The size of the difference between budgeted and actual results focuses management attention on a need for review and possible corrective action.

Review 11.1

1. Why is it useless to consider how businesses would operate if computers had not been invented?

2. In what ways might information needs of users and computer professionals differ?

3. Which group of people determines and controls the information that a computer system provides?

4. At which level in an organization do managers receive the greatest amount of information detail?

Business Terms

turnover
In terms of human resources, the rate at which employees quit their jobs.

Tactical information often is delivered in the form of displays that indicate inventory status for products or for parts needed in manufacturing. Tactical managers use this information as a basis for purchasing or production decisions.

PHOTO BY LIANE ENKELIS

WHAT INFORMATION IS USED AT THE TACTICAL LEVEL?

The tactical level of an information system serves middle managers. A middle manager's job takes in more area—or greater scope—than that of an operational manager. The principle, remember, is to report information to meet user needs. As an information user, a middle manager wants to be able to check status of operations in multiple areas.

A number of operational managers will report to one tactical-level manager. The tactical manager does not have the time or the need to review detailed information on all of the operations supervised. Instead, the tactical manager needs summary information that covers status only, not operating details.

manager who might be responsible for several departments or an entire store. If a store contains 50 or 75 cash registers, the store manager will not have the time or the need to review transaction details. A tactical manager will not even have time to check the sales status for each product offered for sale.

The tactical manager needs a management by exception (MBE) capability. The reported exceptions help to focus the manager's attention on current problems. A typical middle manager in a department store is known as a "buyer." As the title implies, a buyer purchases products to be offered for sale. Buyers usually specialize in specific product areas. Examples include women's clothing, men's clothing, housewares, linens, sporting goods, major appliances, and so on.

What Is the Value of Exception Reporting?

To illustrate, consider the department store in which an operational manager is responsible for one department. This operational manager reports to a tactical

How Does Exception Reporting Work?

Exception reporting is a way of tailoring information outputs to user needs. In the situation of a department store buyer, reporting *parameters* are set up when a system is designed. Then, these parameters are applied to monitor information status as transactions take place. A parameter is a boundary or limit.

For example, a buyer might order 400 boxes of computer disks for a store. The plan would be to sell 100 boxes per week. It takes a week to order and receive a new supply of disks. So, to allow for safety stock, the buyer sets up a reorder parameter at 200 boxes.

The computer record for these disks would show the current number of boxes in stock. This is the *inventory level.* Each time a box of disks is sold, the inventory level data item is reduced by one. When the inventory total for the disks reaches 200 or less, the item is included in an ''open-to-buy'' file that the computer sets up automatically. In some stores, the buyer may be able to look at the open-to-buy file on a display. As an alternative, a printed report may be delivered.

Regardless of reporting method, the computer disks become an exception when the inventory level falls below 200. Another type of exception condition may be set for the same item. In any large retail store, *turnover* of stock is an important measure of success. For example, a store may have a target that compares sales levels with the value of inventory in stock. Typically, management might expect the number of product items sold during a six-week period to equal the number of items in inventory. This means that each item in inventory should reach its reorder point in six weeks or less.

To check on this performance, an exception data item could be set up according to date. Each time a product is ordered, the date is changed. The date entered might be 60 days from the order date. This would allow two weeks to receive the products and six weeks to sell down to the reorder point. If no order is placed for the product in 60 days, it is reported as an exception. Then, managers can decide what to do about the product. One option might be to lower the price to try to increase sales. Another option would be to close out the item. That is, the product would not be reordered after stocks were sold out.

A large department store may have exception levels established for more than 100,000 products. This is another example of how computers have become necessities. A store just couldn't operate at this scale without computers.

For tactical-level managers, exception reporting meets one of the major requirements for information use. The accountability of tactical-level managers lies in monitoring a segment of a business. Their job is to spot and correct problems. Exception reporting does the spotting, eliminating the need to sift through detailed information. Correcting problems is a human task. Use of information systems allows managers to concentrate on solving problems because exceptions are identified by computers.

WHAT INFORMATION IS USED AT THE STRATEGIC LEVEL?

A review of the bottom-up handling of information also provides an insight into the way the *chain of command* works within a business. Operational

---

Business Terms

parameter
A boundary or limit; an information value that is used as a checkpoint for reporting items as exceptions.

inventory level
The number of units of a given stock item in inventory at any given moment.

turnover
In terms of inventory, the time period in which a given number of items should be sold. Turnover also is measured in terms of the number of ''turns'' per year of a store's total stock.

chain of command
A term that describes the top-down structure of authority and responsibility within an organization.

managers handle day-to-day transactions. Tactical-level managers monitor operations and make adjustments as necessary to guide a company toward its goals. Thus, operational and tactical managers, handle current business operations.

It is worth noting that most companies have far more operational managers than tactical managers. In general, there will be perhaps 10 or 12 operational managers for each manager at the tactical level. Then, at the strategic level, there will be far fewer managers than at the tactical level. A typical large company might have 15 or 20 tactical managers for each person at the strategic level.

Why Do Top-Level Managers Need Smaller Volumes of Information?

Just as fewer people are needed at higher levels, so is less information required. The operational manager needs the most detail and the greatest volume of information. At the tactical level, information volumes are reduced so that only operating summaries and exceptions are reported. However, tactical managers still are interested in unit-by-unit results. In a fast-food chain, for example, middle managers would need to know conditions at each restaurant.

As indicated, two levels of managers are concerned with controlling and monitoring operations. This means that people at the top level generally are not involved with operations at all. They look at overall results. Then, most of their attention is focused on overall status and future goals and plans.

Top-level managers generally will call for tactical-level information on operations only for special reasons. For example, if strategic planners are considering service to a new market, tactical information may be used. The planners would want to see operating summaries for markets similar to the new target areas. Aside from special requirements, however, top-level managers generally look at overall company summaries only. They concentrate on reporting status to stockholders and government agencies and on future products and markets. To do this,

Top-level managers *use limited amounts of information that model the organizations for which they are responsible, and for the decisions they make.*
PHOTO BY LIANE ENKELIS

they require information from many special sources, both internal and external.

What Are Some Sources of Strategic Information?

Operational and tactical information models the current condition of a company. Therefore, most operational and tactical information results from gathering and processing information based upon the company's transactions. At the strategic level, it often is necessary to develop new outputs from tactical information and also to gather information from external sources.

However, the principle is the same. Information should model the situation that management wants to create. This is true for companies of all sizes. Large-scale information systems simply are a way of assembling images that show company status to managers who can't take in all operations themselves. In a smaller business, the manager would be on the scene and would develop the same understanding through personal observation. To illustrate the value of information-processing tools for large organizations, consider some major decisions that have affected the fast-food field.

Increasing revenue without adding outlets. A major fast-food chain wanted to expand the number of items on the menu. The idea was to increase income from existing restaurants. This always is a desirable goal. Opening new restaurants requires large investments to buy land and construct buildings. Even if the chain doesn't own the buildings, there are rents to pay. It is far more profitable to figure out ways to bring more money into restaurants you already have.

Think about what you might do if you were a top-level manager in a chain with more than 2,000 restaurants. One thing you would do would be to ask for information on how much use existing equipment gets in present restaurants. You might find that the grills used to make hamburgers and cheeseburgers already are operating at capacity during busy lunch periods. However, you might learn that food preparation areas and the fryer are used at less than 50 percent of capacity. This is because most food preparation must be done before the busy lunch period. Also, you might learn that the fryers are used only for french fries. Making fries is a quick operation. So, fryers are used perhaps 25 percent of the time. However, you still need two fryers in each restaurant because they have to be cleaned and serviced frequently.

This information focuses your thinking. The idea: Figure out how you can generate more saleable food by increasing use of the food preparation area and the fryers. Notice that you started this process with an overall goal: Develop more revenue from existing restaurants—through use of existing equipment. You have developed special operational information that identifies your opportunities: If you are going to increase income from existing restaurants, it is going to have to be through use of the food preparation areas and the fryers.

New products during regular hours. You think hard to identify products that can be prepared in these available areas. You put food preparation experts to work and conduct some tests in a few restaurants or small markets. Your answer: Introduce fried chicken snacks through use of the fryers. Also introduce salads that can be handled in the food preparation areas.

Add hours to the business day. As you continue to think about opportunities, you are struck by the idea that your restaurants currently are open from about 11 A.M. until perhaps 8 or 9 P.M. The restaurants produce no income at all from 9 P.M. until 11 A.M. You recognize an opportunity and ask for studies about how your restaurants might be set up to serve breakfast.

Both internal and external information are needed. As you know, actual fast-food restaurants have benefited from this type of strategic planning. This type of management effort requires both internal and external information. Internal information leads to the finding that restaurants are available at breakfast and that the fryers represent added potential.

However, other information is needed before programs can be implemented. In this example, the fast-food chain had never bought or handled either chicken or breakfast previously. Source information had to be gathered about the costs of these food items. In addition, studies had to be run to determine how long it took to cook these items. Other information had to be developed on how many people would have to be hired to serve the new items on existing menus.

The point: Strategic planners often have to develop information models of situations that do not yet exist.

Review 11.2

1. Why is an allowance for "safety stock" made when inventory reorder levels are set?

2. Which levels of management are involved in directing the continuing operations of a business?

3. Under what circumstances might strategic managers require tactical information?

HOW ARE TOTAL MANAGEMENT NEEDS MET BY AN INFORMATION SYSTEM?

When businesses first started to use computers to handle information, all processing was centered on applications. Applications, of course, are single jobs. Each application had to be run separately. Every application needed its own files, which could not be shared with any other application. This led to duplication of information, such as customer and product records, in files that supported separate applications. Under these conditions, it was impossible to generate the information needed for exception reports.

Information became a planning and management tool with the introduction of database software. Database software keeps track of information at the data item level. That is, each item of data is identified and can be used independently. This is different from older methods that related entire files of information to individual applications. Database processing makes possible advanced exception reporting. A database also can be used to analyze operations to

help managers identify problems or opportunities. The study of fast-food operations for new-product opportunities is a good example.

In summary, the ability to provide managers at all levels with needed information centers around some key capabilities:

- An information system should have the ability to store and retrieve individual items of information.

- It should be possible for multiple users and applications to share information.

- It should be possible to create special data files to meet individual user needs. This can be done if an information system has sets of instructions that permit users to examine the content of and build special outputs from information resources.

In summary, a system must treat information as a resource that belongs to users. Computer professionals must understand and be prepared to meet user needs. The user is the customer. Managers and executives, in turn, must learn to appreciate the value of information in performing their own jobs.

In the building of information systems, some methods and principles apply to many businesses. Others are for individual industries. The chapter that follows demonstrates how common needs have been identified to provide information tools usable for multiple industries.

Review 11.3

1. What contribution did database software make to the value of information for management use?

2. What is the main difference between a database and a series of files that support individual applications?

Chapter Summary

❑ To get all the information needed, a business may have to use an information network.

❑ Business has grown to a level at which today's operations could not exist without support from computers.

❑ Computer systems are built to meet user needs.

❑ Management is a top-down process. Information systems that model organizations are structured on a bottom-up basis.

❑ The lower the management level of the user, the greater the volume of information that will be required.

❑ Tactical managers are served through management by exception systems.

❑ At the strategic level, managers have little need for operational data. Their concerns are for reporting to stockholders and the government and for setting strategies and plans.

❑ Some strategic information comes from internal sources.

❑ To support management of the entire company, information resources must be organized under database concepts. A database permits sharing of information among many applications, for a wide range of users.

❑ It should be possible to produce special information reports that combine internal and external items.

Definitions

Write a complete sentence that defines each of the terms below.

parameter	turnover (staff)
turnover (inventory)	inventory level
chain of command	

Questions to Think About

Based on what you have learned to date, answer the following questions in one or more complete sentences.

1. What is the value of linking multiple computer systems for user access?

2. Why is it useless to consider what modern business would be like without computers?

3. What different methods would be used by managers and computer professionals in defining information requirements?

4. Why do operational managers need greater volumes of information than those at tactical and strategic levels?

5. Why are information systems organized on a bottom-up basis?

6. How is information developed to monitor the financial performance of a business unit?

7. What are information summaries and how do they help to carry out management by exception?

8. What kinds of internal and external information are needed at the strategic level?

9. Why is it important that an information system be able to keep track of individual data items?

10. Why has database software improved the usefulness of information for managers?

Projects

The purpose of the assignments below is to encourage you to increase your learning through outside reading or work assignments.

1. Prepare a personal budget that identifies your income and expenses on a monthly basis. List all sources of income and all of the expenses you expect. In doing this, determine which expense items are most important to you. Assign priorities to your expense items. Total income and expenses. Subtract expenses from income.

2. Monitor your actual income and expenses against the budget you develop. Report on how well you have done in planning for income and expenses.

CHAPTER 12

In What Ways Are Many Businesses Alike?

The Think Tank

When you finish reading this chapter and complete your work assignments, you should be able to answer the following questions.

❑ How do laws and government regulations lead to similarities in information needs and operations of businesses?

❑ How do standard principles of the accounting profession lead to similarities in financial information reporting?

❑ How do standard courses and requirements in college business schools contribute to similarities in business operations?

❑ How have common requirements for the processing of business applications on computers led to similarities within information systems of different companies?

❑ What are some common features of most business information systems?

DOING BUSINESS

"That's not like any income tax form I every saw," said Heidi. "I just read a whole book about taxes. I needed it too. This was the first year I filed a regular 1040 form with the Internal Revenue Service."

"This is a business tax return, IRS Form 1120, Sis," Hans told his older sister. "It's different from the 1040 form that you use to file a personal return. I didn't realize what we were getting into when we formed our house painting company as a Junior Achievement project."

"What's all this information in the middle pages of the report? They sure are nosey," Heidi commented.

Hans closed the tax return form. He put down his pencil, turned toward his sister and said: "Mr. Stein, our Junior Achievement adviser, explained the reason for all this. Income taxes on businesses are based on profits that result from operations. Profits are reported on income statements. Therefore, the government makes each company provide a complete accounting of its income and expenses. Part of the reason for forming a corporation under a Junior Achievement project is to learn about this kind of thing."

Businesses share *many challenges. All businesses within any community must conform to the same sets of laws, pay taxes, and report to governmental agencies. Many businesses also attempt to serve the same group of customers.*

Heidi noticed the papers that Hans had on his desk. "What are these reports?" she asked.

"That's the income statement for our business," Hans said. "We have to have a complete set of financial statements for each Junior Achievement project. That's also part of what we're supposed to learn. These reports are checked by our accounting teachers at school. Having proper reports in this way helps to protect our advisers and also our parents in case businesses get into trouble."

"That makes sense," Heidi said. "What I was wondering about is that the information on your income statement is exactly the same as your entries on this tax form. Why can't you just give your financial statements to the government instead of doing them over this way."

"If we used a computer," Hans explained, "the equipment would pick up the information and use it for our tax return. Managers of little, bitty companies like ours have to write it all out twice.

"It isn't all bad," Hans continued. "Once you have filed a Form 1120, you know a lot about financial reporting in business. I don't know if you've learned about this, but financial information reports by most businesses look alike. And you're looking at one of the reasons. Every corporation has to report the same type of information to the government. So, they might as well use the same formats for their own income statements. This means that, once you have prepared one of these corporate returns, you have learned the basics of working with financial statements. This experience will help us when we look for jobs in business."

MEANING

Many businesses look alike in some phases of their operations, and also in the way they report financial information. The narrative about the Junior Achievement project helps to explain why: All businesses are required to provide similar information to the government on tax returns and other reports.

This means that financial information systems and reports will be similar for many businesses. It means also that if you learn the standard principles of financial reporting, this knowledge will be useful in any business. Knowledge of standard reporting procedures can help you to find jobs and/or to advance your career.

Financial reporting is one of the ways in which operations at many companies are similar. Remember that all companies use information to model operations and status. For many reasons, some of which are covered in this chapter, financial reports are similar for most companies. Therefore, in learning about information systems, you are increasing your value to future employers.

HOW DOES THE GOVERNMENT ESTABLISH STANDARDS FOR BUSINESS REPORTING?

Taxation is a great standardizer. *Taxes,* of course, are ways in which businesses and private citizens pay for government services. To help with the processing of tax payments, government agencies have to establish forms and rules. These forms and rules apply to all companies or people subject to a given tax. The result is that businesses have to gather, process, and report information in a form that meets government tax rules.

Since all businesses and wage earners pay income taxes, the government forms tend to become standards. In turn, tax requirements mean that businesses tend to have similar systems for information reporting. There may be differences, of course. But the portions of information systems that develop information on income, expenses, and earnings are similar for most businesses.

How Have Income Taxes Led to Information System Standards?

The need to conform in tax reporting is unavoidable. Consider: The Internal Revenue Service receives more than 100 million tax returns each year. The money that accompanies these returns represents some 90 percent of the income for the Federal government. It would be impossible to deal with so many returns and account for the money without standard forms and procedures.

Just as the government benefits from standard forms, there also are some benefits for individual businesses. Forms like the portion of the 1120 return shown in Figure 12-1 require standard organization of information files. In turn, the fact that so many businesses have a common need creates a market for the computer software industry. Whole shelves full of financial reporting software products have been introduced. You can visit any computer store and see for yourself. There are literally hundreds of standard programs that can be used to process transactions, build information forms, and produce financial statements. There even are dozens of programs that will produce tax returns from business information files.

Many states also tax incomes of workers and businesses. In these situations, the state tax forms and rules are similar to those of the Federal government. Where state income taxes exist, therefore, they increase the need to follow standard information reporting methods.

Because of requirements such as tax forms and rules, markets have developed for information processing tools. Due to the number of people and companies that pay income taxes, these markets are large. Many businesses have been attracted to develop software products for use in information reporting. Competition has resulted. Competition, in turn, has led to comparatively low prices for software tools. The availability of software, in turn, has encouraged the sale of millions of personal computers.

Other taxes and reporting laws also have helped to encourage use of similar information handling and reporting techniques among businesses. Some of these other areas are described below.

How Do Payroll Taxes Cause Businesses to Standardize?

Some key standards in information systems originated with the introduction of payroll taxes. Until

Business Terms

tax
A payment to a government agency by a person or business as required by laws.

Form 1120

Department of the Treasury
Internal Revenue Service

U.S. Corporation Income Tax Return

For calendar year 1988 or tax year beginning _____, 1988, ending _____, 19 ___
▶ For Paperwork Reduction Act Notice, see page 1 of the instructions.

OMB No. 1545-0123

1988

Check if a—

A Consolidated return ☐

B Personal holding co. ☐

C Personal service corp.(as defined in Temp. Regs. sec. 1.441-4T—see instructions) ☐

Use IRS label. Otherwise, please print or type.

Name

Number and street (or P.O. box number if mail is not delivered to street address)

City or town, state, and ZIP code

D Employer identification number

E Date incorporated

F Total assets (See Specific Instructions.)

Dollars | Cents

$

G Check applicable boxes: (1) ☐ Initial return (2) ☐ Final return (3) ☐ Change in address

Income

1a Gross receipts or sales	b Less returns and allowances	c Bal ▶ 1c
2 Cost of goods sold and/or operations (Schedule A)		2
3 Gross profit (line 1c less line 2)		3
4 Dividends (Schedule C, line 19)		4
5 Interest		5
6 Gross rents		6
7 Gross royalties		7
8 Capital gain net income (attach separate Schedule D)		8
9 Net gain or (loss) from Form 4797, Part II, line 18 (attach Form 4797)		9
10 Other income (see instructions—attach schedule)		10
11 **Total** income—Add lines 3 through 10 and enter here ▶		11

Deductions (See Instructions for limitations on deductions.)

12 Compensation of officers (Schedule E)		12
13a Salaries and wages	b Less jobs credit	c Balance ▶ 13c
14 Repairs		14
15 Bad debts		15
16 Rents		16
17 Taxes		17
18 Interest		18
19 Contributions (**see instructions for 10% limitation**)		19
20 Depreciation (attach Form 4562)	20	
21 Less depreciation claimed in Schedule A and elsewhere on return	21a	21b
22 Depletion		22
23 Advertising		23
24 Pension, profit-sharing, etc., plans		24
25 Employee benefit programs		25
26 Other deductions (attach schedule)		26
27 **Total** deductions—Add lines 12 through 26 and enter here. ▶		27
28 Taxable income before net operating loss deduction and special deductions (line 11 less line 27)		28
29 **Less: a** Net operating loss deduction (see instructions)	29a	
b Special deductions (Schedule C, line 20)	29b	29c

Tax and Payments

30 Taxable income (line 28 less line 29c)		30
31 Total tax (Schedule J)		31
32 Payments: a 1987 overpayment credited to 1988	32a	
b 1988 estimated tax payments	32b	
c Less 1988 refund applied for on Form 4466	32c ( ) d Bal ▶	32d
e Tax deposited with Form 7004		32e
f Credit from regulated investment companies (attach Form 2439)		32f
g Credit for Federal tax on fuels (attach Form 4136)	32g	32h
33 Enter any **penalty** for underpayment of estimated tax—check ▶ ☐ if Form 2220 is attached		33
34 **Tax due**—If the total of lines 31 and 33 is larger than line 32h, enter amount owed		34
35 **Overpayment**—If line 32h is larger than the total of lines 31 and 33, enter amount overpaid		35
36 Enter amount of line 35 you want: **Credited to 1989 estimated tax** ▶ Refunded ▶		36

Please Sign Here

Under penalties of perjury, I declare that I have examined this return, including accompanying schedules and statements, and to the best of my knowledge and belief, it is true, correct, and complete. Declaration of preparer (other than taxpayer) is based on all information of which preparer has any knowledge.

▶ _____ | Date | ▶ _____
Signature of officer | | Title

Paid Preparer's Use Only

Preparer's signature ▶	Date	Check if self-employed ☐	Preparer's social security number
Firm's name (or yours if self-employed) and address ▶		E.I. No. ▶	
		ZIP code ▶	

Figure 12-1. *A source of similarities among businesses lies in the need to file uniform financial statements as part of the Form 1120 Corporation Income Tax Return.*

1935, workers were paid what they earned—exactly—with no deductions. Payrolls we calculated simply by multiplying hourly pay rates by number of hours worked. The process was simple. Businesses were not required to keep special records or prepare special reports for the government.

On January 1, 1936, Social Security laws went into effect. Employers had to calculate and withhold Social Security taxes from workers. Employers also had to set aside taxes on the payrolls they issued. It was necessary to keep track of these massive details, then pay the proper amounts to the government. Payroll processing became many times more complex than it had been. Large employers were forced to install special machines to process payrolls. Payroll processing became a major demand that led to the introduction of computers. Significantly, the first computer installed in a business organization in the United States was used to process payrolls.

Since 1936, all payroll processing and reporting have had to meet government standards and rules. The complexity of processing and the need for uniform methods increased as other deduction requirements were added. Companies now are required to withhold income taxes from employees and to pay those amounts to the government. Also, most states require that some form of insurance payments be made to protect workers from effects of on-the-job accidents. Today, payroll is one major way in which all companies are alike. All companies must keep payroll records according to government rules.

How Do Sales Taxes Affect Business Information Systems?

The majority of states generate at least some of their income through taxes on retail sales. In many states, necessities such as food are not taxed. However, for most products sold to consumers, the retailer has to collect a sales tax. Sales taxes are paid to state or city governments—or both.

The existence of sales taxes has led to special features for some business machines and special designs on business forms. For example, many cash registers have SALES TAX keys. The machines can be set to apply the tax amount collected in the state, such as six or seven percent. When the single key is pressed, the cash register multiplies the total for the sale by the correct percentage. The amount is added to the customer's total automatically. Also, the tax amount is saved and tallied within the cash register.

For transactions among businesses, most invoice forms now are designed with a space specifically for entry of sales taxes.

The point: Standard business practices in a major horizontal industry have been developed to deal with taxing practices in many states.

How Do Requirements of Other Government Agencies Affect Information Reporting?

A number of governmental agencies supervise operations and information reporting in specific industries. For companies within those industries, government activities require similarities in operations and in information systems. Just a few examples are described below:

- Securities dealers, also known as stock brokers, are regulated and monitored by the Securities and Exchange Commission (SEC). The SEC also oversees all offers of stocks and bonds sold to the public. This means that all securities dealers and all companies whose stocks are offered to the public must prepare special reports for the SEC. Also, the SEC has policing powers. The agency has an Enforcement Division that investigates any suspicious actions by securities dealers or companies. The Enforcement Division has a right to seek penalties from offenders or to bring accused parties to court on behalf of the government. To comply with the rules of the SEC, all publicly owned companies must submit uniform financial statements once a year. Securities dealers must report on their operations on a regular basis.

Sales taxes and other transaction reporting requirements make for high degrees of uniformity in business record keeping. Reporting regulations have contributed to the widespread use of computer terminals for recording point-of-sale transactions.

PHOTO BY LISA SCHWABER-BARZILAY

- Businesses whose vehicles use federal highways, such as trucking companies or organizations that ship their own products, must report to federal agencies. The reports must list the miles of travel over federal roads, often state by state. The purpose is to study usage of highways. For businesses, the effect is a need for uniform travel records.

- Airlines and companies that trade with foreign countries also must submit regular reports on use of airports and harbors, volumes of shipments, and other details. The effect, again, is uniform information reporting on operations.

- Production volumes must be reported to the government by companies in the mining, basic metals, and heavy manufacturing businesses. The government uses this information to report on the condition of the economy. The businesses involved can use the uniform information to form strategies and plans. From this information, each business can measure its position within its industry.

- Owners of some 50 million automobiles must register and license their vehicles in individual states. Also, to drive a car, it is necessary to take a driver's test that is controlled by an agency in each state.

- From the high school level upward, schools keep uniform records of student activities and grades. These records are designed for use by colleges considering applications of high school graduates. The records of school achievement also are useful to employers who are considering hiring former students. To meet these requirements, schools and colleges must follow standards and rules in keeping student records.

The point: The government is a force in the operation of businesses and in the lives of all citizens.

Review 12.1

1. In what ways does the content of the Form 1120 business income tax document help to create similarities among businesses?

2. How have payroll taxes led to similarities in information processing among businesses?

3. How have rules of the Securities and Exchange Commission contributed to similarities in the management of large corporations?

HOW DO STANDARD ACCOUNTING PRINCIPLES PRESENT COMMON REPORTING REQUIREMENTS?

Government regulations create a framework that requires uniform financial record keeping and reporting by many businesses. In addition, a number of laws require that businesses pay for policing themselves. The requirement, based on laws introduced during the 1930s, is that financial reports of many companies must be *audited.* An audit is an examination of a company's operations and information systems to verify accuracy and reliability.

Each audit must be "independent." This means that the work must be performed by outside people who have no connection with the audited company. All companies that sell securities to the public must have their records audited. Proof of the audit, in the form of a statement by the auditor, also must be provided by each public company.

Who Performs Financial Audits?

Each audit must be performed under the direction of a person who is licensed to provide this service. Most auditors are Certified Public Accountants (CPAs). To qualify as a CPA, a person must complete college courses in business and accounting. Other requirements include experience in performing audits. Finally, there is a difficult test given in all 50 states. An individual must pass this test to qualify as a CPA.

For each audited report, the CPA must provide a statement that describes the work done. The CPA also specifies that the reports meet the requirements of *Generally Accepted Accounting Principles (GAAP).* This is a published set of standards that cover the methods to be followed and the content to be included in preparing financial statements.

In effect, the laws qualify CPAs as specialized professionals for financial reporting. The principle is much the same as that used by the legal profession. Licensed attorneys are authorized to represent their clients. The attorneys function as officers of the courts in which they appear. In a similar way, CPAs function as independent representatives who oversee financial reporting. The financial reports prepared by companies are the responsibility of the officers of those companies. The CPA serves the company to determine that the reports meet the standards of Generally Accepted Accounting Principles.

What Are Financial Statements?

CPAs, as professionals, support the creation and regular updating of GAAP. The work is done by an independent group, the Financial Accounting Standards Board (FASB). The group reviews and amends GAAP as needed. According to GAAP, management of each reporting company must prepare a set of three financial statements that include the following documents:

- An *income statement*, as seen in Figure 12-2, shows the money received and expenses paid by a company. The final entry on an income statement, often called the *bottom line,* shows the profit (or loss) that has resulted from operations.

Business Terms

audit
An independent examination of a company's operations and information systems to verify accuracy and reliability.

Generally Accepted Accounting Principles (GAAP)
A published set of standards that cover the methods to be followed and the content to be included in preparing financial statements.

income statement
One element of a company's financial statements that shows money received and expenses paid.

bottom line
The final entry on an income statement that shows profit or loss for the period covered by the statement.

CONSOLIDATED STATEMENT OF INCOME
for the years ended December 31, 1987, 1986 and 1985

	1987	1986	1985
Net sales	$1,470,420,000	$712,260,000	$599,080,000
Cost of sales	(1,102,530,000)	(509,530,000)	(426,460,000)
Selling, general and administrative expenses	(160,070,000)	(97,700,000)	(86,190,000)
Special charge for energy-related operations	—	—	(49,000,000)
Equity in earnings of partially owned company	—	9,410,000	8,690,000
Operating profit	207,820,000	114,440,000	46,120,000
Interest expense, Masco Corporation	(14,640,000)	(55,520,000)	(52,280,000)
Other interest expense	(66,890,000)	(19,920,000)	(10,810,000)
Other income (expense), net	(28,740,000)	12,740,000	14,770,000
Income (loss) before income taxes, extraordinary item and cumulative effect of accounting change	97,550,000	51,740,000	(2,200,000)
Income taxes (credit)	52,320,000	19,350,000	(5,100,000)
Income before extraordinary item and cumulative effect of accounting change	45,230,000	32,390,000	2,900,000
Extraordinary income (charge) related to the early extinguishment of debt	5,390,000	(23,000,000)	—
Cumulative effect of change in accounting for income taxes	(6,320,000)	—	—
Net income	$ 44,300,000	$ 9,390,000	$ 2,900,000
Preferred stock dividends	$ 8,930,000	$ 1,880,000	—
Earnings available for common stock	$ 35,370,000	$ 7,510,000	$ 2,900,000
Earnings per common share:			
Before extraordinary item and cumulative effect of accounting change	$ .46	$ .41	$ .04
Extraordinary item	.07	(.31)	—
Cumulative effect of accounting change	(.08)	—	—
Net income	$ .45	$ .10	$ .04

The accompanying notes are an integral part of the consolidated financial statements.

Figure 12-2. *Uniform accounting principles lead to similarities in record keeping systems. One of the uniform reports issued by many businesses is the Statement of Income and Expenses, shown in this sample.*

- A *balance sheet* is a statement that shows the value of a business. The balance sheet lists the *assets,* or values of items owned by a business. Assets include cash and *accounts receivable* (amounts owed to the company). Other assets may consist of buildings, equipment, materials, and finished products ready for sale. The balance sheet also lists *liabilities,* or amounts owed by the business to vendors or lenders. Finally, there are entries that show the *net worth* or *shareholders' equity* in the business. In accounting terms, a business is worth the difference between its assets and liabilities. If a company is owned by a number of shareholders, the balance sheet also may show equity for each share of stock. A balance sheet is illustrated in Figure 12-3.

- A *statement of changes in condition* is designed to help users of financial information evaluate the progress of a company. This statement shows changes in assets and liabilities of the business for the current year, as compared with the previous year. Figure 12-4 presents a brief statement of changes in condition.

Financial statements may be prepared monthly and/or quarterly. They must be prepared at the end of each operating year. Together, the standard formats and content of financial statements are said to produce a "snapshot" that shows the condition of the company. Because most financial statements contain the same information items, these reports also help to compare performances of different companies. Certainly, the need for audits makes for similarities in the operating and financial reporting structures of businesses.

What About Companies that Don't Require Audits?

Many small companies do not require financial audits. However, most companies follow GAAP in preparation of financial reports anyway. The reason is simple: Public accountants prepare tax returns and financial statements for most businesses.

Even if a business does not have to report to the SEC, it is best to follow GAAP rules in preparing financial statements. This financial information will meet requirements for tax returns. Also, most businesses are required to file copies of financial statements and tax returns with banks and creditors. Managers at most banks and lenders prefer financial statements that follow the familiar format of GAAP.

So, even if financial statements are not audited, they often follow a uniform format. Thus, financial statements are one force that makes for similarity among operations and information systems in many companies.

Business Terms

balance sheet
A statement that shows the value of a business.

asset
An item of value owned by a business or person preparing a balance sheet.

account receivable
An amount owed to a business or person by a customer or debtor.

liability
An amount owed by a business or person preparing a balance sheet to a vendor or lender.

net worth
The value of a business or the total assets of a person, as reflected in one of the totals of a balance sheet.

shareholders' equity
The value of the shareholders' ownership interest in a business. *See also* net worth.

statement of changes in condition
One element of a set of financial statements that reflects changes in assets, liabilities, and equities since the previous reporting period.

CONSOLIDATED BALANCE SHEET
December 31, 1987 and 1986

ASSETS	1987	1986
Current assets:		
Cash and cash investments	$ 30,770,000	$ 59,070,000
Marketable securities	221,490,000	173,910,000
Receivables	205,530,000	169,700,000
Inventories	244,600,000	211,440,000
Prepaid expenses	26,190,000	24,050,000
Total current assets	728,580,000	638,170,000
Property and equipment	524,080,000	465,880,000
Excess of cost over net assets of acquired companies	437,440,000	294,410,000
Other assets	102,430,000	90,610,000
Total assets	$1,792,530,000	$1,489,070,000

LIABILITIES and SHAREHOLDERS' EQUITY

	1987	1986
Current liabilities:		
Accounts payable	$ 91,500,000	$ 79,710,000
Accrued liabilities	100,290,000	85,420,000
Current portion of long-term debt	12,040,000	12,930,000
Total current liabilities	203,830,000	178,060,000
Deferred income taxes and other	94,770,000	43,970,000
Long-term debt:		
Masco Corporation	166,000,000	256,000,000
Banks and others	933,230,000	675,510,000
Total liabilities	1,397,830,000	1,153,540,000
Shareholders' equity:		
Preferred stock, $1 par	—	880,000
Common stock, $1 par, outstanding – 90.1 million and 36.8 million shares	90,100,000	36,800,000
Paid-in capital	221,120,000	261,080,000
Retained earnings	69,580,000	32,930,000
Cumulative translation adjustments	13,900,000	3,840,000
Total shareholders' equity	394,700,000	335,530,000
Total liabilities and shareholders' equity	$1,792,530,000	$1,489,070,000

The accompanying notes are an integral part of the consolidated financial statements.

Figure 12-3. The value of a business is reflected in a Balance Sheet, which follows uniform reporting standards.

CONSOLIDATED STATEMENT OF CHANGES IN FINANCIAL POSITION
for the years ended December 31, 1987, 1986 and 1985

	1987	1986	1985
CASH PROVIDED BY (USED FOR):			
OPERATIONS:			
Income before extraordinary and accounting change items	**$ 45,230,000**	$ 32,390,000	$ 2,900,000
Depreciation and amortization	**73,230,000**	39,890,000	35,540,000
Equity earnings	**—**	(9,410,000)	(8,690,000)
Deferred taxes	**5,580,000**	9,900,000	(15,330,000)
Special charge	**—**	—	49,000,000
Total from earnings before extraordinary and accounting change items	**124,040,000**	72,770,000	63,420,000
(Increase) decrease in inventories	**(11,600,000)**	(8,620,000)	6,540,000
(Increase) decrease in receivables	**(12,060,000)**	14,710,000	(7,070,000)
(Decrease) in accounts payable and accrued liabilities	**(5,830,000)**	(10,220,000)	(1,520,000)
Total from operations before extraordinary and accounting change items	**94,550,000**	68,640,000	61,370,000
Cash provided by (used for) extraordinary and accounting change items	**5,390,000**	(41,400,000)	—
Total from operations	**99,940,000**	27,240,000	61,370,000
FINANCING:			
Long-term debt–Masco Corporation:			
Issuance	**130,000,000**	220,000,000	36,000,000
Retirement	**(220,000,000)**	(320,000,000)	—
Long-term debt–banks and others:			
Issuance	**702,450,000**	294,120,000	175,090,000
Retirement	**(485,760,000)**	(100,790,000)	(16,350,000)
Common stock issuance, principally upon conversion of preferred stock	**272,810,000**	—	—
Preferred stock issuance (conversion)	**(212,810,000)**	212,810,000	—
Repurchase of common shares	**(47,540,000)**	—	(36,000,000)
Other	**(7,650,000)**	(3,160,000)	—
Total financing	**131,500,000**	302,980,000	158,740,000
INVESTMENTS:			
Companies acquired, net of cash held	**(136,200,000)**	(158,250,000)	(113,010,000)
Capital expenditures	**(68,380,000)**	(56,200,000)	(38,490,000)
Other, net	**(7,580,000)**	(15,010,000)	(6,190,000)
Total investments	**(212,160,000)**	(229,460,000)	(157,690,000)
CASH AND MARKETABLE SECURITIES:			
Increase for the year	**19,280,000**	100,760,000	62,420,000
At January 1	**232,980,000**	132,220,000	69,800,000
At December 31	**$252,260,000**	$232,980,000	$132,220,000

The accompanying notes are an integral part of the consolidated financial statements.

Figure 12-4. *Business trends for individual companies are reflected in Statements of Changes. These statements show the increases or decreases in the assets and liabilities of a business.*

1. What are Generally Accepted Accounting Principles and what effect do they have on businesses?

2. What is a financial audit and who performs most audits?

3. What documents are included in a set of financial statements?

HOW DO MANAGERS HELP TO MAKE BUSINESSES LOOK ALIKE?

Management has become a recognized profession. It wasn't always this way. In the United States, most businesses have started small. The entrepreneurs who started businesses tended to be technicians or specialists rather than professional managers. They were mechanics, or engineers, or storekeepers. However, as businesses grew, specialists were needed to handle the jobs outside of invention or production. These were the jobs that needed to be done but often were outside the main interests of the "idea" people who started businesses. These positions involved planning, marketing, administration, and finance.

As demands for managers increased, colleges began to offer courses aimed at training future managers. As interest mounted, people began to write books that led to a professional discipline now called *management science*. Gradually, a body of knowledge was accumulated that serves as a basis for a management profession. Most working managers now share this body of knowledge and apply what has become standard information to the running of companies. To the extent that their managers share common knowledge and beliefs, companies can become similar. Companies managed by people who think alike can take on similar organization structures. They also can become similar in the way they operate.

What Are Some Advantages of Similar Management Styles?

The techniques that a manager believes in and uses are known as a *management style*. Through the years, styles of management have become well known and have developed their own followers. Management style is one of the ingredients of strategy. As you know, each strategy follows a pattern, or driving force. The basic beliefs of a company's chief executive establish management style. This style, in turn, helps to shape strategy.

An advantage of a defined and understood management style is that it provides guidelines that can help to build an organization. Managers and students of management tend to identify themselves with certain management styles. This means that there usually will be groups of trained people available to help run a business. The ability to find qualified people is vital in enabling a business to grow financially or to expand into new markets. Thus, similarity in management beliefs and styles can help companies to build organizations of like-minded people.

What Are Some Drawbacks of Similar Management Styles?

A firm set of beliefs about how companies should be run can become a drawback in some situations. Remember, all companies face change as a constant

Business Terms

management science
A discipline that studies the management of businesses and instructs students in the principles of business management.

management style
The approach or methodology followed by a manager in evaluating operations, reaching decisions, and establishing policies.

business condition. Change often requires creativity or innovation to resolve problems. If an organization is made up of people whose management styles are fixed, people may find it hard to adjust to major change.

For example, some large chains of retail stores actually failed and went out of business because their management styles became outdated. These stores had developed operating methods based on efficient systems for restocking stores. Information reporting techniques were developed that let a central office know exactly what customers were buying. Central office people found the best price and the least costly way of delivering products to stores. Procedures became so fixed that the stores could not keep up with changes in the economy and consumer tastes. At least three major retail chains that used similar management techniques failed during the 1960s and 1970s.

Following a proven management style can lead to a dead end as well as to success. Established knowledge and methods can be powerful tools. A challenge to managers lies in applying the right tools to each situation.

HOW DO COMPUTERS HELP TO CREATE SIMILAR METHODS AMONG BUSINESSES?

Laws, rules, and accounting regulations have established many common requirements in information processing and reporting. These common needs have formed a basis for the building of the computer industry. Business processing represents the largest single need for computers and standard software packages. Because of these common needs, manufacturers have developed computer devices designed specifically to meet business needs. A multibillion-dollar software industry has grown around the special needs of business processing and reporting.

The computer industry now is able to provide processing equipment for small businesses as well as large organizations. Small computers now cost less than former prices for electric typewriters. No matter what its size, any business can now find a computer and supporting software to meet its information needs. To use these hardware and software tools, a business selects the most practical tools. Then, the procedures and operations of the business are built around those tools.

Because computers and software packages are so practical, they have had the effect of promoting similar business operations. Consider a typical situation: A company develops a software package for transaction processing on microcomputers. The system is ideal for small businesses or for branch offices of larger businesses. Tens of thousands of copies of the program are installed in business offices. In each office, employees enter transaction data in response to identical displays on computer screens. Standard computing tools promote similarity of company operations.

WHAT DO BUSINESS SIMILARITIES MEAN TO YOUR FUTURE CAREER?

For a person planning a future career, similarities among businesses can be helpful. By understanding these similarities and the reasons for them, you can build an understanding of what future employers will expect. This understanding, in turn, can help you to plan your education so that you will be able to market yourself successfully as a job applicant.

Of course, there also are differences among industries and individual businesses. You also should be aware of these differences as you prepare yourself for entry into the work force. The chapter that follows reviews the ways in which businesses are different from one another.

Review 12.3

1. What is management science?

2. How has the discipline of management science contributed to similarities among companies?

3. How can knowledge about the similarities among companies be of value to a future job seeker?

Chapter Summary

❏ All businesses and workers must file income tax returns with the government.

❏ All businesses must process and report on payrolls according to government standards.

❏ Other government activities that lead to uniformity of business operations or information reporting include sales taxes, regulations by the Securities and Exchange Commission, highway use reports, vehicle licensing, and educational records.

❏ A body of rules, Generally Accepted Accounting Principles (GAAP), controls the way most companies process and report financial information.

❏ Companies that operate under SEC control must have audited financial statements.

❏ Financial statements that comply with SEC rules and GAAP include three separate documents: income statement, balance sheet, and statement of changes in financial condition.

❏ Many managers develop similar management styles as a result of their education and training.

Definitions

Write a complete sentence that defines each of the terms below.

tax	audit
income statement	bottom line
balance sheet	asset
liability	liability

Questions to Think About

Based on what you have learned to date, answer the following questions in one or more complete sentences.

1. How do personal and corporate income tax forms differ?

2. How do income tax laws and regulations lead to similarities in financial record keeping and reporting among business organizations?

3. In what ways have Social Security and other payroll deduction requirements led to uniformity in information handling and reporting among businesses?

4. How do sales taxes affect company operations?

5. What is meant by the statement that the SEC has enforcement powers?

6. Why do government agencies require such reports as high-use statistics from business organizations?

7. What are Generally Accepted Accounting Principles and what are their effect on business operations?

8. What is an audit and what is its purpose?

9. What documents are included in a set of financial statements and what information do they present?

10. How does the training received by managers lead to similarities in company operations?

11. How have computers helped to standardize some company operations?

Projects

The purpose of the assignments below is to encourage you to increase your learning through outside reading or work assignments.

1. From a local Post Office or IRS office, secure a copy of a Form 1120. From information in the financial statements used as illustrations in this chapter, complete the financial summary information required on a Form 1120.

2. In your library or in a computer store, find information on software packages that produce financial reports. Describe how one software package could be used to generate the financial statements illustrated in this chapter.

CHAPTER 13

How Are Businesses Different From One Another?

When you finish reading this chapter and complete your work assignments, you should be able to answer the following questions.

❑ What is the basic reason that each business is different from every other business?

❑ How can you identify the special, or unique, features that make a business different from others, even those in the same industry?

❑ How are differences in businesses included in and supported by the information systems of those businesses?

❑ Why is it important for you, as a future job seeker, to be able to identify the unique features of a business?

DOING BUSINESS

"I'm lost. Everything here is strange to me," Norm announced.

"So am I," replied Sid. "This is a surprise. This market belongs to the same chain as the one we shop at regularly. You'd think the stuff on the shelves would be in the same place. But it's all different."

Norm and Sid had been rooming together for just a few weeks. They had formed a habit of doing their "heavy" shopping for a week's supplies on Thursday evenings. Usually, they went to a supermarket near their apartment. On this Thursday, however, Norm had suggested that they stop on the way home from work rather than go out after dinner. There was a ball game that Norm wanted to

watch. He would miss part of the game if they had dinner first, then went shopping. Both Norm and Sid had expected the market near work to be just like the one near home. They purposely selected a store that was part of the same chain.

"I guess it must be that this market is larger," Norm said. "They have more room, so they spread things around differently. But there probably are other reasons. Why don't you tell me? You're the marketing type."

Norm was referring to the fact that Sid worked in the marketing department. Part of his job was to analyze competition for the company's products.

"You're partly right," said Sid. "Size is part of it. Supermarket chains rent space in shopping centers that are built by different developers. Each store is a little different from all the others.

Differences among businesses often exist in the way products or services are presented. For example, all supermarkets are expected to sell packaged groceries and other household products. Some chains attempt to enhance customer appeal through the way they handle special products, such as produce, meat, seafood, or dairy items.
COURTESY OF SAFEWAY STORES, INCORPORATED © 1988

Developers have to work with the land that's available.

"Just as important," Sid continued, "different neighborhoods support stores of different sizes. A neighborhood with a lot of young families needs more space than one where there are mostly adults who live in small apartments. A person who shops for a family fills up the grocery cart. It takes more food and different kinds of food to satisfy both adults and kids. By contrast, look at our cart. We're typical young adults. We buy frozen dinners and snacks."

"And ice cream," Norm cut in.

"Yes," Sid admitted, "and ice cream. That will probably stop in a few years. The way you eat, you're bound to put on weight."

Sid continued: "Every supermarket—actually, every business—adjusts to the buying patterns of its customers. It's called differentiation. We come to these markets because they have large selections of frozen foods that we enjoy. Other people select supermarkets because they like the fresh fruits and vegetables—or the meats.

"Also, each market sets up its food displays differently. In this market, peanuts and snacks are up front. They must sell a lot of this stuff. So they put their best selling products in the area with the highest customer traffic. In other stores, you'll find the front positions taken by soft drinks, or even pet food. I understand that, in the 1950s, baby food displays used to be big and prominent. The idea is that each business structures itself for its markets."

"You can see differences in the way different chains advertise on TV," Norm commented. "I guess that's the same thing. Some markets scream about low prices. Others talk about quality meats. Others say their produce is the best."

"It's exactly the same," Sid agreed. "Each business has to build its own identity with its customers. Businesses do this by establishing features that differentiate them from their competitors."

MEANING

Norm and Sid have encountered a basic characteristic of business. Each business is at least slightly different from every other business. Even different branches of the same business are different from one another.

One major reason is discussed in the narrative above: Each **business unit** develops services that are tailored to the needs of its own customers. A business unit is any facility or group that operates on its own. The unit delivers products or provides direct service to a group of customers. In the example, each store within a supermarket chain would be a separate business unit. Therefore, each store will be at least slightly different from every other store.

Another reason for differences: Each business or business unit is an organization that consists of a group of people. Each person and each group is different from every other group. People give the business in which they work unique features that make it different from every other business unit.

WHY ARE DIFFERENCES AMONG BUSINESSES IMPORTANT?

Differences—even small differences—are the basis for competition among businesses. As discussed in the previous chapter, many businesses are similar to one another. This is true particularly for businesses in the same industry that provide the same kinds of products and services. However, each business has to create some differences. It is the differences that attract customers to one business over another.

How About an Example of Business Differences?

As an excellent example, consider two businesses that you may know, McDonald's and Burger King. Both are part of the fast-food industry. The main item on the menu at both chains is the hamburger.

How do you introduce competitive differences into such a situation? A hamburger, after all is a four-ounce patty of chopped beef that is cooked, covered with sauce, and placed on a roll. Lettuce, tomato, or pickles may be piled on. But, no matter how it is treated, a hamburger on a bun bears a likeness to every other hamburger on a bun.

Differences in this competitive situation center on the potential for variations in customer taste. McDonald's seems to feel its customers prefer fast service and a clean place to eat. Employees are trained to keep each restaurant clean and neat. Procedures are set up to precook menu items to anticipate customer demands. There is no waiting for food to be cooked. Counterpeople simply remove precooked items from racks and deliver them immediately.

Burger King appeals to a different kind of customer. The burgers are cooked on grills that are likened to back yard barbecues. Each burger is prepared individually to customer order. The customers can decide if they want onions, sauce, lettuce, tomato, etc. Customers might have to wait a minute or two longer, but Burger King stresses that each customer can "have it your way."

How Can Similar Businesses Be Different From One Another?

In their similarities, both McDonald's and Burger King benefit from a general public taste for hamburgers and for quick meals. Both stress that they serve a quality product that includes beef patties and similar dressings. Also, both chains serve similar supporting items. It is expected that hamburger outlets will serve french fries. Both do. Also, both serve soft drinks and some varieties of hamburgers.

When businesses adopt similar features that fit them into an established industry, the process is known as *integration*. Integration is a basic part of a company's strategy. That is, a company identifies itself with a general market and industry. The strategy seeks to make the company part of that overall industry. The company is integrated into a known market. Integration, in turn, helps customers identify businesses with their product needs or tastes.

In addition to being part of an industry, a company has to have its own identity. The steps and features that separate a company from others in its industry are called *differentiation*. In the fast-food

All hamburgers are not exactly the same. Each major chain offers special features or services in its attempt to attract a market segment. Among the major competitors, McDonald's (right) features fast service through precooking and also provides playgrounds at some locations. Burger King (below, left) grills its burgers on charcoal. Jack-In-The-Box has added other sandwiches and "finger foods" to its menu.

PHOTOS BY BENEDICT KRUSE

industry, differentiation might lie in the way burgers are cooked. In supermarkets, differentiation might lie in the positions at which groceries are displayed. Claims about pricing and promises of fast service at checkout lines also represent attempts to differentiate companies.

Review 13.1

1. How is integration achieved?

2. What is differentiation and what is its purpose?

3. How do integration and differentiation help a company to attract customers?

Business Terms

business unit
Any facility or group that operates on its own.

integration
The elements of a company's strategy that identify it with a given industry or type of business, helping to identify the company's products or services with a given market.

differentiation
The selection or formulation of elements of a company's strategy that serve to determine products or services and markets, and that separate the company from others in its industry.

Integration is common in the automotive business. Manufacturers tend to introduce similar features on their cars. It even is common, as shown, for auto dealers to locate on the same streets. In this situation, competing dealers are across the street from each other. Other dealers are close by.

PHOTO BY BENEDICT KRUSE

WHY IS INTEGRATION IMPORTANT?

Every person wants to belong to some segment of society. The same is true for most businesses. Normal developments in society and the economy tend to group markets according to patterns of supply and demand. These patterns change continuously as companies innovate and find new ways to appeal to markets.

The trend is continuous: During the days of horse-drawn transportation, whole industries built up around harness making, carriage manufacturing, and animal feed. When the automobile was introduced, some of the carriage makers went into the auto-body businesses. Gradually, new industry lineups emerged. Today's personal transportation needs are met by auto manufacturers, car dealers, service stations, and repair shops.

The idea: Businesses integrate into industries that are formed around consumer needs. Companies integrate with established markets for recognition: The marketplace shows general expectations about the products and services it wants. Integration identifies a company as a potential supplier of certain categories of products or services.

How Does the Need for Integration Shape a Company's Overall Strategy?

Recall that strategy is based on a desire to serve identified markets with specific products or services. In effect, a company's marketing strategy addresses two questions:

* Where do we belong?

* How are we unique or different?

The first of these questions is resolved by identifying with a specific industry or market. Integration includes all actions and policies necessary to place the company in its market.

Innovation and emulation. The approach to integration depends on whether a company chooses to *innovate* or *emulate* within its markets. Innovate means to introduce new or different ideas, products, or services. A company that innovates develops a new product or service and builds its own markets.

To emulate means to act like, or imitate, something else. A company that emulates waits until a product has been introduced and a market has been formed. Then it emulates the products, services, or operations of the successful innovator.

Innovation often is linked to invention. Major innovations in business have been the electric light, telephone, automobile, airplane, and computer. It also is possible to innovate on a smaller scale. To illustrate, consider the skateboard and video games.

Think about video games. Pac Man was first. Atari introduced the product and built the new market. In a few years, video games grew to an industry with almost a billion dollars in annual sales. Very quickly, other companies emulated Atari. The general field of video games provided an identity. New companies entering the field integrated into this market identity. Several emulators also became successful. Each emulator, however, brought out its own characters or operating features to differentiate itself from others. Potential customers identified products by their special features. These features appealed to potential customers of different ages, interests, or skill levels.

In summary, innovative companies become successful by creating new products or services that establish or expand the business. Businesses that emulate become successful by concentrating on improving products or services or by competing with lower prices.

When an industry becomes established to a level that forms a market identity, it is said to be *mature*. Thus, computers were a new field in 1950 and are considered to be a mature industry today. Mature industries generally attract companies with strategies for emulation.

Review 13.2

1. What does a policy of innovation mean to a company's strategy?

2. How does a policy of emulation affect a company's strategy?

3. How do policies of innovation and emulation serve to differentiate companies?

HOW DOES DIFFERENTIATION WORK?

Recall that each company has a driving force. This is the element of strategy that guides selection of markets to be served and products or services to be delivered. A company's driving force also helps to establish the points that differentiate it from others in the same industry.

Consider an example: IBM has become the largest computer company in the world and one of the largest businesses in the United States. Sales now top $54 billion per year. The computer industry is a highly technical field. An entire new generation of computer products has been introduced every four to seven years. IBM rarely has had technical superiority in its field. Instead, it has become the largest and most successful company by building its driving force around customer service.

In part, the strategy of service came from IBM's founder, Thomas J. Watson, Sr. When Watson put the company together in 1914, selling was done by people who were known as "drummers." A drummer was a salesman of the day. He (women were not in the field yet) was a flashy dresser. The drummer had a smile to share and funny stories to tell. He patted people on the back. He sold himself first, then offered his product.

Business Terms

innovate
As part of a business strategy, a commitment to develop and introduce new, original products or services.

emulate
Within a business strategy, an approach that calls for waiting until new products or services are introduced and proven before entering the market.

mature
In regard to an industry, one that has become established and generally recognized in the marketplace.

Mass marketing of computers started with the IBM 1401 system, shown here. At a time when computers stressed bigness and power, IBM innovated with a relatively low-cost computer that could fit into medium-sized companies. More than ten thousand 1401 systems were sold, a record at the time.
PHOTO BY BENEDICT KRUSE

How Can Differentiation Reflect A Company's Market Commitment?

Watson decided to base IBM's marketing on its products and their capabilities. His idea of a salesperson was at odds with the business practices of the time. His salespeople were instructed to develop a quiet image, one that would not conflict with the product. IBM salespeople wore white shirts and dark suits. They spoke quietly and were instructed to ask questions that would get prospective customers talking about their problems.

The IBM concept was to sell solutions to problems. The salespeople studied markets and business needs in depth. They drew attention to customer problems and to their machines as solutions. Though this was contrary to the sales practices of the day, Watson's differentiation paid off. IBM built its initial market position with machines that captured and processed information through use of punched cards. These machines preceded introduction of computers. They solved information processing problems by capturing data items once, then reusing them without requiring further work.

When computers came out of the laboratories in the late 1940s, they were considered to be technical marvels. Another company, UNIVAC, introduced and sold the first computers. UNIVAC equipment was marketed on the basis of its ability to handle mathematical computations. IBM entered the computer age behind its competitor. Differentiation was important. So, the company stuck with its image as a solver of business problems. It brought out computers that were smaller and less powerful than those of its competitors. But, the IBM computers were designed to handle business information and to print reports at higher speeds than competitive systems. Very quickly, IBM dominated the computer market.

How Can Differentiation Help To Solve Business Problems?

The ability to "read" markets and meet needs played a major role in helping IBM to move quickly to a dominant position in the microcomputer field. In this area, IBM's market entry was so late that many people wondered whether the company would ever get into the field. Apple Computer introduced the

Small computers for small prices *proved to be an irresistible combination. Shortly after IBM introduced its Personal Computer, shown here, sales jumped to a rate of more than one million per month. It is estimated that more than 20 million personal computers are being used by businesses.*

PHOTO BY LIANE ENKELIS

first successful microcomputer in 1977. A microcomputer is a desktop computer that uses a tiny microchip as its processor. By 1981, hundreds of thousands of microcomputers had been sold.

Again, IBM did something different. With all of its other computers, IBM had been careful to design equipment that was different from its competitors. IBM made it as difficult as possible for other manufacturers to link their equipment to IBM devices. That approach worked for large computer systems. However, when it came to desktop equipment, IBM changed its strategy completely.

IBM executives studied the market and decided that the problem with small computers was that equipment of different companies was incompatible. Every company made equipment that was different from every other company's. This, in turn, held back the suppliers who wanted to develop software for desktop computers. IBM recognized that success for small computers depended upon the ability of users to purchase ready-to-use programs.

The strategy that resulted from this analysis represented a new approach for IBM. When IBM introduced its Personal Computer in 1981, it published

details of its equipment design and specifications. In particular, its operating principles were made known to the growing community of software suppliers. Also, IBM set up a large network of independent dealers for its personal computers. Previously, all sales had been handled only by IBM offices.

Within a matter of months, shipments of IBM Personal Computers reached a level of more than one million per month. For several years, IBM dominated the small computer field. Eventually, emulating companies produced cheaper copies and cut into IBM's market share. At that point, IBM took the lead in developing small computers that could be linked with large business systems. Under IBM's leadership, small computers were developed as executive workstations.

How Does Differentiation Differ From Innovation?

Differentiation efforts come from a company's driving force. In IBM's case, market service is the driving force. Other companies differentiate in different ways. Henry Ford differentiated his company from

Information systems like automatic teller machines make it possible to provide banking services with increased customer convenience. Originally, ATMs were innovative. Now, tens of thousands are in place.

PHOTO BY LISA SCHWABER-BARZILAY

the dozens of other competing manufacturers through innovation in production techniques. At the time, cars were being built one at a time in small workshops. Ford's idea was to build cars on an assembly line. The workers stationed along the line would perform one job each. Under Ford's innovation, unskilled workers could master individual jobs. As a result, Ford was able to build large numbers of quality cars for less money than his competitors.

Note that, in Ford's case, differentiation was through innovation. However, innovation is not the only way in which companies differentiate themselves from competitors. In the IBM examples cited, differentiation was through a proven market approach. Although IBM has been a major innovator in some areas, these examples show that differentiation does not require innovation.

The competition between McDonald's and Burger King illustrates differentiation without major innovation. McDonald's has adopted a strategy that features immediate service. Burger King's strategy is to grill its hamburgers to order.

One reason for stressing the difference is to make clear the nature of differentiation. Everybody differentiates. Comparatively few companies innovate.

Another point that should be made: Innovation does not lead automatically to success. Many products that are innovations fail. A classic example occurred when a company decided to pack frankfurters in round casings. The idea was that concession operators at ballparks and amusement parks could use the same buns for hamburgers and hot dogs. The innovation in this case was aimed at benefitting food concessions. The innovator had failed to consider the consuming public. People didn't take to round, flat hot dogs. The product disappeared.

The point: Integration helps companies to identify and fit into established markets. Differentiation helps companies to separate themselves from competitors. Differentiation is the way a company identifies itself to the specific customers it wants to serve.

HOW DO INFORMATION SYSTEMS SUPPORT DIFFERENTIATION?

Information systems model business operations. The policies and practices of differentiation should be part of the operations that are modeled. Therefore, the elements of strategy that make a company different from its competitors should be part of its information model. The database should have data items and/or records that represent the driving force of a business.

You probably have seen information tools that help to model the special features of a company's operations. Assume a company is market oriented. It differentiates by providing what its managers consider to be top-quality service within its industry. Within the information system, it is important to devise some way to monitor and measure customer reactions.

Many new products, and you may have seen some, come with warranty cards. The warranty card is sent in by the customer. To register for the warranty, the customer is asked to answer a number of questions. Usually, these questions deal with the reason for buying the product. Questions also may be included about where the product was purchased and the quality of service received.

In fact, warranty registration is not necessary. Customers could provide proof of warranty by saving their sales slips. The main reason for the registration card is to collect information on customer responses to the company and the product. The data items on the cards are entered into and processed by computers to review customer responses. If responses are neutral or unfavorable, adjustments can be made in customer services.

Say a company competes by offering lower prices than its competitors. If this is the case, the information system should be designed to monitor production costs closely. To sell at low prices, the company has to maintain low costs for materials and production.

In another situation, assume a company is in a seasonal business. Women's sportswear is a good example. The year is divided roughly into four 13-week selling season's. Retailers place orders for garments as much as three months before the beginning of a season. As the season approaches, consumer tastes are monitored. Orders may be modified. However, it is a general practice to begin each season with minimum inventories.

Nothing is known for sure until the garments are shown and selling begins. Then, sales are monitored closely, day by day. It takes a powerful information system to keep up with sales and to report on customer purchases within hours after the close of business each day. These reports, however, are the basis for reorders that make or break the selling season for the store. If orders are placed too late, the manufacturers may be out of stock. If the wrong garments are ordered, the store is stuck with them. Stores need information that measures trends on a timely and accurate basis.

The point: Information systems must be differentiated to match the strategy and driving force of each company.

WHY IS IT IMPORTANT FOR YOU TO BE AWARE OF DIFFERENTIATION?

When you apply for a job, an awareness of the driving force of the company may help to decide whether you are hired. First, you have to become aware of industry groupings and the need for differentiation. After that, a brief review of the company and its practices will help you to identify the special points that separate competitors. With this skill, you can guide your job search. And you can select and apply to the organizations with the policies and operations that you prefer. Get into the habit of asking yourself what markets are served by companies you encounter. Then, once you have identified industries, think about the things that seem to make each company different or special.

This kind of analysis can be valuable for each individual company that you encounter. In addition, you should become aware of general trends and expectations in the world of business as a whole. These considerations are covered in the chapter that follows.

Review 13.3

1. How does differentiation relate to a company's driving force?

2. Are innovation and differentiation connected directly?

3. How are a company's points of differentiation and its information system related?

Chapter Summary

❏ Each company is different from every other company. Differences center around the image the company wants to establish for its customers.

❏ The elements of a company's operations that make it part of an industry or market are known as integration.

❏ The elements that make a company different from others in its industry are known as differentiation.

❏ Integration establishes a company in the view of the marketplace as a provider of certain products or services. Integration brings a company into an established industry.

❏ To achieve integration, a company implements an overall strategy for the development of its products or services.

❏ Some companies are innovators. They develop and introduce products that are new or different.

❏ Other companies are emulators. They wait until a product or service is established in a marketplace, then they introduce similar items.

❏ Differentiation is achieved by implementing the driving force of a company. The driving force may be innovation. But it also may be emphasis on production or on customer service. Each company establishes its own unique identity.

❏ The practices and policies that establish differentiation should be modeled by a company's information system.

Definitions

Write a complete sentence that defines each of the terms below.

business unit	integration
differentiation	innovate
emulate	mature

Questions to Think About

Based on what you have learned to date, answer the following questions in one or more complete sentences.

1. Why are some business units within the same company different from others?

2. How do companies integrate themselves into a known industry?

3. How do companies differentiate themselves from others in the same industry?

4. How do integration and differentiation implement a company's strategy?

5. How does a policy of product innovation affect a company's strategy?

6. How does a policy of product emulation affect a company's strategy?

7. How does a company's information system support its strategies for integration or differentiation?

8. Why is it important that you understand the differences among companies?

Projects

The purpose of the assignments below is to encourage you to increase your learning through outside reading or work assignments.

1. From a newspaper or magazine, copy or clip advertisements for similar products from two or more competing companies. Analyze the advertisements. Report on the elements of integration and differentiation for the companies involved.

2. Visit two or more department stores in your area. Note the products offered, the store layouts, and the designs of displays. Pay particular attention to the way in which each store serves its customers. Report on the elements of integration and differentiation that you observe.

CHAPTER 14

Where Is Business Headed?

The Think Tank

When you finish reading this chapter and complete your work assignments, you should be able to answer the following questions.

❏ Why should you expect the rate of changes that affect your work and lifestyle to increase in the future?

❏ How will new technologies affect the future challenges and requirements you can expect as a worker?

❏ How will new technologies affect your lifestyle?

❏ Will the continuing development of industries and economies on a worldwide scale affect your own future opportunities and challenges?

❏ What future relationships can be expected between command and market economies?

DOING BUSINESS

"I've read about places like this," Irma said. "But it's hard to believe that people really went to all this trouble—and spent all this money."

"It does seem hard to believe now," Oscar agreed. "But the threat seemed real to a lot of people back in the fifties. To me, this kind of thing dramatizes the rate of change that we have lived with."

Oscar was an experienced architect. Irma was much younger, a student working as an apprentice in the firm that Oscar headed. They were surveying the site of a new high-rise construction project. Until recently, the site of the project had been occupied by large private homes. The new construction was to be a mix-use facility. There would be offices, shopping centers, and also a residential area—apartments.

As they checked over the land in preparation for detailed planning, Oscar and Irma came across an underground structure. Oscar explained that this was a survival shelter similar to many constructed during the 1950s. The shelter was a strong concrete structure that was completely underground. Supplies of food and water were still stored inside. There were beds, bathrooms, and a kitchen—complete underground living quarters.

"Today, people your age laugh at this sort of thing," Oscar commented. "That shows the kinds of changes we have lived through. In the 1950s, this world was a place of hostility. The United States and the Soviet Union were in an all-out arms race. The confrontations that were taking place were described as a Cold War. Many people really believed that the United States would come under nuclear attack. They built shelters like this in an honest belief that they were protecting their families.

"Time has shown," Oscar continued, "that people in all countries prefer living to dying. But this also shows something else: People always will try to predict the future. They will make plans and take actions to prepare for the future. Then, when you look back at the past, people's views of the future seem to be short sighted. Our greatest hopes and worst fears rarely happen."

"This is interesting," Irma said. "You have been a professional planner for many years. You've seen a lot of change. What do you think someone my age should expect in the future?"

Oscar didn't respond right away. He stared straight ahead and wrinkled his brow. Irma waited. She knew he took her question seriously and was thinking about an answer. "As you know, I've thought a lot about the future and about what life might be like 20 or 50 years from now. But the rate of change that we live with is so rapid that predictions are difficult. All anyone can say for sure is that the one thing you can count on is more change. And future changes will occur more rapidly than in the past. So, the only advice I can give is: Don't be surprised by anything that happens. Expect the unexpected and be ready to adjust."

MEANING

For most people, the future is where their worst fears and highest hopes exist. Depending on their concerns, people make **contingency plans**. A contingency plan is a set of preparations for an action that can be taken to deal with undesirable or unexpected developments. Individual people have different ideas about the realities that will occur in the future. The family that built a shelter designed to survive a nuclear bomb had one kind of future image. Their image apparently was dominated by fear—and by a desire to be prepared.

In other instances, families that spend everything they earn have great expectations for the future. They do not plan to encounter emergencies. A slogan for people of this type might be "the future will take care of itself."

Most people have a view of the future that is somewhere between these extremes. For people interested in the state of business, and possibly a career in business, a look to the future can be profitable. Remember: There is continuing change in your future. You are preparing yourself for jobs that may not now exist. Anticipation can be valuable.

Remember also that the future is not so far away that it can be ignored. The future starts for you tomorrow morning. As a popular song notes, the future "is only a day away." If it is your future you are dealing with, it pays to take some time to consider possibilities, to be prepared.

HOW WILL CHANGE AFFECT THE FUTURE?

For the future, even tomorrrow, there is only one continuing condition you can count on. That condition is *change*. Change has been called the only constant in today's world. Nothing is certain. The only thing you can be sure of is that changes will occur. To be on the safe side, you probably should count on change that occurs at an even faster rate than at present. Experience shows that the rate of change probably will continue to increase well into the future.

When you are predicting or planning for the future, change has a special meaning. *Change* is an external occurrence that requires a reaction. An occurrence is something that happens or develops. An external occurrence is an event that is beyond your control. Also, an external occurrence that produces a change that affects you requires your notice and a reaction. A reaction is required whether the situation is personal or whether an organization is involved.

Required reactions may be simple: You plan to wear a light summer outfit and the weather turns cold and rainy. You react by wearing something else. As a more complex example, suppose a company is

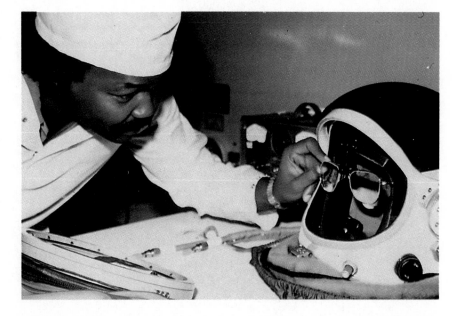

Focus on the future is highlighted By the work of this technician, who is fitting eyeglass lenses into an astronaut's helmet. Space exploration is certainly one of the frontiers of the future. Private sector organizations are moving into the space-exploration business.

COPYRIGHT FINLEY HOLIDAY FILMS

planning to build a new factory. Suddenly, interest rates increase and add many thousands of dollars to the cost. A decision is needed on whether to go ahead at higher costs or to cancel or delay the project.

What Is the Best Way to Handle Change?

Change requires a reaction. Actually, four basic responses are open when an external change occurs:

- **You can support the change.** If you do, you will work actively to carry out a change that affects you.

- **You can accept change.** If you do, you let change happen. But you don't work to support it.

- **You can resist change.** This means you don't accept the change as a good thing. Rather, you decide to work against letting the change happen.

- **You can ignore a change.** If you do, you simply act as though the change never happened. In most cases, the change will go on without you—and may leave you behind.

Though change is a constant, the reactions of people to occurrences of change vary. In the past, a major

problem faced by businesses has been resistance to change. People who have done their jobs the same way for many years become comfortable. They prefer not to change. In some situations, they oppose change—actively. This kind of reaction can cause tensions between those who oppose change and those who support it. Active resistance may delay change. However, changes will occur in your future. Count on it!

This is not to say that all changes are good. Neither are all changes unavoidable. Rather, changes require attention and reaction. Sometimes, reactions to change lead to discovery of a better solution to a problem. This is healthy, but blind resistance to change tends to be unhealthy.

Business Terms

contingency plan
A preparation for an action that can be taken to deal with undesirable or unexpected developments.

change
An external occurrence that requires a reaction.

Computers help to build computers in this robotics assembly line. Computer components are positioned in new computers automatically. Then the computerized robots test each new computer as it is being built.
COURTESY OF TEXAS INSTRUMENTS INCORPORATED

In the future, leadership in business and society will pass to a generation that has grown up in an atmosphere of change. Blind resistance should give way to constructive review. Different attitudes will encourage continuing change. In your planning, recognize that change will happen. Be flexible. Think before you react. Keep in mind that change is a source of opportunity. Look for the best solution as you consider each decision.

WHAT SPECIFIC CHANGES CAN BE EXPECTED?

In many ways, the future is an extension of the past and present. That is, trends or methods that exist today will be part of the future. Therefore, today's developments can help to predict future trends. A few of these trends and the probable developments they project include:

- **Factory production will use more automatic equipment.** Less human labor will be needed in manufacturing. A similar trend already has occurred in farming. At the time of American independence, 90 percent of the workers were

farmers. Today, the figure is about three percent. Automatic equipment made the difference.

- **Use of *robotics* will increase.** Robotics goes beyond simple automation. Automation deals with a single operation at a time. Robotics encompasses a series of operations that are carried out automatically by machines. Robots do jobs that used to require humans, even when the jobs had been automated. Already, some factories are fully automated. Products can be assembled, tested, and packaged—all with no people present. The role of people changes. People design and build production machines. After factories are set up, people are responsible for maintenance. However, actual production requires little or no human presence. To illustrate the new role of robotics and the reduced role for humans, consider: A number of robotic factories operate in darkness. This reduces costs and also cuts down on the need for heat or air conditioning.

- **Automation and robotics will affect your personal life** as well as your workplace. In the future, expect to use computers in your shopping, either in a store or from home. Expect more choices and more controls in your home entertainment. When you travel, expect eventually to ride on highways with automatic car control. The day may come when you drive your car onto a special lane and set it for automatic operation. An electronic system will take over steering, speed control, and safety monitoring.

- Despite automation in the workplace, **there will be a labor shortage in the very near future.** As the economy continues to expand, the demand for qualified people will exceed available supplies.

- **Workers will have to be better educated.** Also, workers will have to take part in continuing education and training programs. Continuing education will be a lifelong requirement.

- **The speed and comfort of travel should increase greatly.** Aircraft already are designed that will be able to travel from New York to Tokyo or from Los Angeles to London in about two hours. These planes will travel above the Earth's atmosphere. This will eliminate sonic booms on the ground. At altitudes above 100,000 feet, planes should be able to travel at speeds of more than 20,000 miles per hour.

- Faster travel and superior communication should lead to a **worldwide economy.** Companies will invest in and operate businesses around the world. When the entire world becomes a single market, opportunities for growth will be greater than anything that exists today.

Review 14.1

1. At what rate can you expect to encounter change in the future?

2. What are the differences between supporting and accepting change?

3. What are the differences between resisting and ignoring change?

4. What will increased use of robotics mean to the job market of the future?

HOW WILL TECHNOLOGY IMPACT THE FUTURE?

Developments like those described above will result from use of technologies that advance continuously. Also, entirely new technologies are expected to unfold and help to change the way people live and work. Some developments that can be expected are described below.

- **Electronics devices will become smaller and will produce more outputs for less money.** In particular, microchips will increase the memory capacities available in computers. Until 1986, the standard memory chip used in microcomputers had a capacity for 64,000 (64K) bits of data. By the end of 1988, shipments of megabit (one million bit) chips had begun. Experimental deliveries were under way for four-megabit chips. Projected future impact: Future computers will have memories that are many times greater than on current models. As a result, processing speeds and capacities will be far greater. Some of this extra memory will be used for new software applications that will make computers more useful. For example, laboratories are already at work on computers that will, some day, accept speech as input. The sounds will be processed to generate finished documents. Massive memories will be required to support this kind of application.

- **Future computers also will have increased internal processing speeds as** *superconductor*

Business Terms

robotics
The technology of automated manufacturing in which machines carry units of work automatically through multiple production processes.

superconductor
A device that carries electrical current with reduced resistance to achieve greater efficiency at higher speeds in the use of devices such as computers.

Communicating through light may develop into an important future technology. Fiber optic cables are made of strands of glass that carry sound and digital signals on waves of light. Future computer processors also may operate with light-carried signals.

COURTESY OF AT&T BELL LABORATORIES

components are introduced. Superconductivity is a major research area today. Tomorrow, superconductor products will provide faster computers and better energy sources. The principle of superconductivity has been known for some time. Laboratory experiments have established that, when metals are cooled to hundreds of degrees below zero, electrical resistance practically disappears. Electricity can flow faster and in greater volumes through superconductive carriers. In recent years, experiments have developed materials that are superconductive at

higher temperatures. Commercial superconductivity products are expected in the near future. Their availability will increase capacities of electric power systems, communications networks, and computers. Major new markets will develop around the power of superconductivity.

- **Light-based computing and communication systems** already have been introduced. As one example, the laser is being applied to a variety of applications. These include medicine, communication, and defense. As you probably know, laser beams are being used to record sound and images on compact disc devices. These are used presently for audio and video entertainment. Laser discs also are being used for information storage on many computers. In the future, laser devices will play a major role in information storage and retrieval. Also, fiber-optic systems are being used to carry telephone conversations and for delicate medical diagnosis. For example, a fiber-optic camera can help doctors to examine the internal organs of the human body. In the future, you can expect to encounter computers that process data in the form of light beams. Broadcasting and video display systems may use light beams or fiber-optics cables in place of radio waves and electron beams. Expected advantages will be greater speed and better quality.

- Expect a series of **improvements in methods of generating energy.** Experimental plants that develop electric power from the action of ocean tides already are in operation. In the future, the oceans and the immense movement of water that occurs with changing tides hold potential for great increases in power generation. Safer, less expensive atomic power plants already have been designed and may be built in the future. A new source of energy from the atom, the fusion reactor, is well along in development. Fusion draws power from a different kind of atomic function than present nuclear reactors. Current atomic engery sources come from the splitting of atoms. This leads to radiation and to radioactive wastes. The fusion process draws its power from a combining of elements. Hydrogen and oxygen atoms, which are plentiful, are combined. The byproducts are vast amounts of energy and pure water (or steam). The fusion process will be able to generate untold amounts of power. There also is potential for creating large quantities of liquid oxygen and liquid hydrogen. These have potential as clean-burning fuels that could replace gasoline. Liquid fuels are used to power the rocket engines of missiles and space vehicles.

- **Transportation speeds will increase,** both in the air and on the ground. In the air, development already is well along on an aerospace plane. This will be partly airplane, partly spacecraft. It will take off from conventional airports. Then, it will use rocket engines to climb rapidly out of the Earth's atmosphere. Travel across continents and oceans will be at the same level now used by orbiting space vehicles. On re-entry, the aircraft will become a passenger plane again. International flights to Europe or Asia will take two hours or less. On the surface, future trains or cars may operate without actually touching the ground. The vehicles could ride on cushions formed by magnetic fields or compressed air. They could operate automatically and with complete safety at speeds of hundreds of miles per hour. Vehicles of this type could relieve much of the traffic pressure in the busy population centers on the East and West Coasts.

- **Medicine and biology will continue to make major strides.** Among other developments, organ transplants will become regular occurrences. Also, scientists probably will develop artificial limbs and organs to replace parts of the human body. For hundreds of years, the human lifespan has grown continually longer. This trend should continue.

HOW WILL HUMAN RELATIONSHIPS CHANGE?

As this book goes to press, a major news development centers around the unemployment rate. Unemployment stood at close to 13 percent in 1980. By the end of 1988, it was just a little above five percent.

Even these encouraging percentages don't tell the whole story. In reality, there already are shortages of some kinds of workers. In the future, the balance will shift from the surplus of workers a few years ago to a major shortage. With more people working, the economy—and the personal standard of living of the American people—are bound to improve. The increasing numbers of workers will need more housing, manufactured products, and food.

By 1988, some 115 million people were at work in the United States. By 1995, the figure was expected to be approaching 130 million. These numbers represent a lot of opportunity. But there also are challenges involved. The number of jobs is one thing. Qualifications for holding those jobs are a different matter. The number of unskilled or semiskilled jobs available in the workplace has declined rapidly. This trend will continue. Jobholders of the future will require continually increasing skill levels in reading, writing, and mathematics.

What Knowledge and Skills Will Future Workers Require?

Consider a dramatic illustration of skill levels on new jobs: For many years, cities employed people with a job title such as "street sweeper." Literally, these people pushed brooms through the streets to keep them clean. Pushing a broom did not require skills in reading and writing. Today, however, streets are swept with complex machines. The drivers of these machines must be able to read operating manuals. They are skilled workers who have to operate and maintain complex equipment. Also, they have to be able to read work orders and write work completion reports.

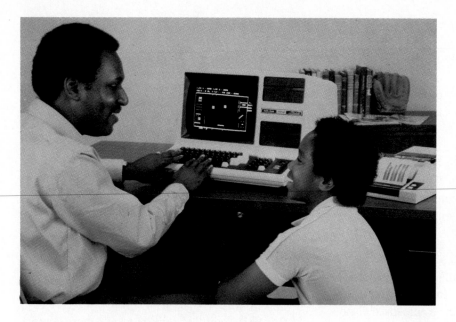

Future generations will benefit greatly from the power that computers can bring to education. Computers provide excellent instruction either in classrooms or at home.

COURTESY OF RADIO SHACK, A DIVISION OF TANDY CORPORATION

The point: In looking to the future, understand that **education pays.** A recent study indicated that people who earn high school diplomas can expect earnings far higher than dropouts. The survey concluded that a person with a high school diploma could expect lifetime earnings that were $500,000 greater than a person without a diploma.

Universal *literacy*—the ability to read—also will help to improve relationships among people. During this period of instant communications, information will be available to almost everyone—immediately and in great volumes. The ability to exchange information, in turn, will improve understanding among people. With understanding, the conflicts and tensions of society should be reduced.

The combination of computers and telecommunications networks will continue to promote a knowledge explosion. As knowledge levels increase, commerce also will grow. It no longer will be tolerable to have some nations that support a luxurious lifestyle while people are starving elsewhere. Knowledgeable people will show concern. The problems of shortages and poverty can be overcome if people and their leaders can be made to see the futility of conflict. As described below, it should become possible to solve conflicts even between opposing economic systems.

HOW WILL RELATIONSHIPS DEVELOP BETWEEN COMMAND AND MARKET ECONOMIES?

The world now supports two highly different economic systems. One is known as a *command economy*. The other is a *market economy*.

Under a command economic system, the government controls all sources of materials, production, and services. Command economies exist in communist and socialist countries. Government agencies decide what markets are served and what products are made available. There is no competition.

A market economy is one in which private businesses can produce what they want and can trade freely. Competition plays an important role in a market economy. In the United States, for example, it is against the law to enter into business arrangements that reduce competition. Market economies generally exist in democracies.

How Have Command and Market Economic Systems Been Modified?

Through the years, both types of economies have been modified by experience and necessity. In the United States, some monopolies are authorized by the government. Examples include telephone and energy utilities. Also, the government regulates some activities that use public resources. Thus, for example, broadcasters who use public airwaves are licensed and regulated by government agencies. The same is true for airlines that use the nation's airspace.

The largest command economy exists in the Soviet Union. There, the government has encouraged private enterprise on a limited scale. These moves recognize that motivation increases as people are able to benefit from their own activities. In both the Soviet Union and the People's Republic of China, private plots have been made available to farmers. The farmers can keep the money they receive for produce grown on these land parcels. In both countries, governments have recognized that the profit motive can help to increase productivity.

As understanding has increased among countries with differing economic systems, international commerce has grown. A global economy already seems to be developing. The mechanisms are in place to encourage investments and trade on a worldwide basis among different governments and economic systems.

One hopeful outcome for this process is global peace. The idea is that people are not anxious to bomb or destroy their own investments or sources of supply. Asian and European countries already have invested almost a trillion dollars in the United States. Conflict just wouldn't make sense under these circumstances.

This leads to possibly the brightest and most desirable of future business prospects. Business-people can develop an international economic climate that promotes and maintains world peace. There are no guarantees, of course. But, if you are going to hope for something for the future, this isn't a bad wish to have.

To date, this book has provided an overview of businesses, their transactions, organization structures, and relationships. With this information, you have some basis for thinking about your own future. One possibility, covered in the chapter that follows, is a career in business.

Review 14.2

1. What is superconductivity and what benefits are expected from its development?

2. How might superconductivity be used to support new methods of ground transportation in the future?

3. Why is it said that workers of the future will require more knowledge than in the past?

Business Terms

literacy
The ability to read.

command economy
An economy in which resources, production, and decisions about the products to be made and markets to be served are made by government agencies.

market economy
An economy in which private businesses are free to determine the resources they will use, the products they will make, and the markets they will serve.

Chapter Summary

❏ The one constant in your future is more change, at a more rapid rate.

❏ Options for dealing with change are: support, accept, resist, or ignore.

❏ In some ways, the future will see extensions of existing trends.

❏ Technological developments that are expected to impact business in the future include more powerful, smaller electronics devices; superconductivity, light-based computing and communication systems, new methods for generating energy, transportation breakthroughs in the air and on the ground, and improvements in medicine and health care.

❏ Human relationships will be changed because people will need more knowledge and better communication skills to hold jobs.

❏ A market economy promotes private enterprise and competition. A command economy is based on government ownership of the resources and production.

Definitions

Write a complete sentence that defines each of the terms below.

contingency plan	change
robotics	superconductor
command economy	market economy

Questions to Think About

Based on what you have learned to date, answer the following questions in one or more complete sentences.

1. What problems are encountered in predicting the future?

2. What are advantages of looking ahead to and being prepared for future developments?

3. How do you expect change to affect you, personally, in the future?

4. What is meant by an action that supports change?

5. How does accepting a change differ from supporting it?

6. What is meant by resistance to change?

7. How does ignoring a change differ from resisting it?

8. Why is the number of jobs expected to increase even though the percentage of the population employed in production work should decrease?

9. What is superconductivity and how is it expected to affect future computing and telecommunication systems?

10. What are command and market economies and how do they differ?

Projects

The purpose of the assignments below is to encourage you to increase your learning through outside reading or work assignments.

1. Through library research, gather information about the impact of regulation and/or deregulation of one industry in the United States. Possibilities include oil exploration, airlines, energy generation, and broadcasting. Describe how the developments you identify modify a market economy. Explain why controls exist. Give your opinion of how well the controls are working.

2. Watch a movie or television show about the future and prepare a report on how you think technology will affect your future lifestyle. Try to use examples from the movie or show to support your ideas.

3. From a newspaper, gather information on modifications to command economies in the Soviet Union and the People's Republic of China. Describe the changes and the reasons given for them. Explain how these developments modify the command economic structures in the two countries.

CHAPTER 15

Is a Career in Business for You?

When you finish reading this chapter and complete your work assignments, you should be able to answer the following questions.

❑ What are future job prospects for persons considering careers in business?

❑ What are your own main strengths and weaknesses?

❑ How do your strengths and weaknesses match up with the requirements and challenges of a business career?

❑ What are your career motivations, including income but considering other needs as well?

DOING BUSINESS

"It's been a good year," Stephanie said. "Considering the economy, you've done an excellent job in managing the farm, partner."

Kristofer laughed. "You seem to call me partner mostly at times when things have been good. But the truth is I couldn't keep running this place profitably without you, Steph."

Kristofer and Stephanie were brother and sister. They were raised on a farm that had been in the family for three generations. In college, Kristofer had studied agriculture. Farming was all he ever wanted. Stephanie had prepared for what turned out to be a highly successful business career. In college, she studied accounting and computer science. Though she was still considered young as business executives go, Stephanie was clearly successful. She was director of financial and information resources for a large company. When Kristofer took over the farm, their parents retired. He and Stephanie had agreed to be partners. Stephanie would study money and crop markets. They would meet every two or three months to discuss strategies and plans. Stephanie was the main source of information for plans on what to plant and how to use the land to best advantage. Kristofer actually ran the farm. The arrangement had kept them close. The brother and sister had mutual respect, as well as love, for each other.

After their business discussions were over, Kristofer asked a question that had been on his mind for some time: "Don't you miss farming,

Agriculture is probably the most mechanized industry in the country. Improvements are dramatized by historic methods (below) and modern techniques for planting cotton. Success in any area of agriculture today calls for high levels of business skills.

BOTH PHOTOS COURTESY OF THE
NATIONAL COTTON COUNCIL OF AMERICA

Steph? You certainly understand farming. You would have to be considered a first class agricultural business executive. Why do you stay in the city and stick to a career in business? It would be great if we could be in farming together."

Stephanie was quiet and thoughtful-for a moment. When she replied, she spoke slowly: "You know I share your feelings about farming, Kris. I also find it exciting to prepare the land and watch seeds grow into beautiful green fields. My appreciation may go even further than yours. I have learned a lot about what happens to crops after we ship them. We farmers support people and their lives. I have studied some of the figures about the number of jobs involved in handling crops. Literally millions of people are employed in running grain elevators, food processing plants, and food markets. I take satisfaction from these things.

"But I also take satisfaction from my life in business," Stephanie continued. "I see the same kinds of satisfactions in business. As a finance person, I worked recently with designers and engineers to bring out a new product line. Market acceptance has been great. Because I deal in information, I can see the results of these efforts. I know the new products are creating jobs. I know that consumers benefit from our work.

"For me, some business activities are extremely creative. For example, I recently worked with an architect who designed and supervised construction of a new office building for our company. The architect was all excited about the environment he was creating. At one point, I remarked that the average person looking at the building site would simply see a hole in the ground. The architect was seeing beauty—and a comfortable place for people to work."

Kristofer was quiet for a second. Then he replied: "At least I'm glad to see that your sense of values has not suffered. There's a tendency to see business as cold and inhuman. I guess any career can have individual satisfactions."

"Right," said Stephanie. "The person makes the job. You get out of a job what you bring to it."

MEANING

People are individual. They seek different kinds of jobs and careers. The satisfactions they realize from jobs also are individual. In the example, Kristofer has realized satisfactions from farming. Stephanie prefers her experience as a rising business executive. She helps Kristofer with planning and management for the family farm. But she seeks different challenges and satisfactions.

Stephanie has recognized one of the satisfactions that drive many business managers and executives. These people recognize that their efforts and their commitments create jobs for others. Also, the products that they develop or market meet needs or wants of other people.

WHAT ARE SOME RESULTS OF BUSINESS ACTIVITIES?

One important effect that Stephanie has recognized is that business promotes economic growth. In effect, one role of business is to create new wealth. The economy of a country is measured, among other ways, by its *Gross National Product (GNP)*. GNP is the total value of the goods and services produced by a society. Wealth, in turn, is a measure of what a job or a set of activities can buy. Measures of wealth include the average earnings of workers, the sizes of bank accounts, and the amount of property owned.

When a business introduces a new product or service successfully, jobs and cash flow result. Business activity helps to generate new wealth. Consider: In 1950, there was no computer industry. Today, the worldwide computer industry operates at a level of more than $1 trillion annually. Millions of people are employed. The world is wealthier because entrepreneurs introduced the computer, then promoted its success.

The point: People enter business careers to seek many different kinds of satisfactions. Earning money is one of those satisfactions, possibly the one you hear most about. But there are other reasons why people seek business careers. For many people, these other satisfactions are at least as important as money—possibly more important. The discussions that follow are designed to help you recognize and understand some features of business careers. Also, the discussions suggest some ways in which you can take stock of your own capabilities. The purpose is to help you decide if a career in business is for you.

WHY HAVE BUSINESS COURSES BECOME SO POPULAR IN COLLEGES?

During the late 1970s and through the 1980s, business has become a popular career choice for young people. One measure of this popularity: More college students choose business as their major course of study than any other field.

This is an indication that business careers are considered attractive. However, there has to be more

Business Terms
Gross National Product (GNP)
The total value of the goods and services produced by a society.

to a career choice than a willingness to follow a crowd. Each of the tens of thousands of business majors in the nation's colleges made an individual decision. Your choice also should be individual.

The point: The presentations that follow are not designed to "sell" you on a business career. Rather, the idea is to help you build a basis for individual choice. Some key reasons for the popularity of business as a college major include:

- Business has been expanding rapidly. Jobs have been available in every phase of business operations. These have included office jobs involving use of computers. Other growth areas have included marketing, administration, finance, and purchasing.

- Businesses have welcomed minority personnel and women into all jobs, at all levels.

- Business careers can provide rapid advancement opportunities. People can move ahead quickly if they perform well. These are known as "fast track" opportunities.

- Pay scales have been relatively high. Performance reviews and potential pay raises occur frequently, often every six months.

- Flexibility in hours and working conditions are available at many business organizations. Workers often prefer to vary hours to avoid traffic, to have time for college classes, or for other reasons. Many businesses cooperate in such programs.

- As in the example above, business careers offer many satisfactions other than money. These can include a feeling of accomplishment in seeing new products brought to market. It also can be satisfying to be part of a growing organization that creates new job opportunities.

Review 15.1

1. How do businesses create wealth?
2. What is the Gross National Product?
3. What is a "fast track" job?

WHAT ARE THE PROSPECTS FOR FUTURE BUSINESS CAREERS?

Persons who enter the workforce in 1990 and beyond can expect to find wide open opportunities awaiting them. This is true particularly in business-related fields.

In part, this situation results from the population patterns within the United States. Following World War II, the country went through what is now known as a baby boom. Between 1948 and 1964, the birth rate was highest in the nation's history. During the 1970s and through most of the 1980s, the baby boomers created a labor surplus. There were more people than jobs. By the end of the 1970s, unemployment reached levels of 13 percent.

Toward the end of the 1980s, demand had caught up with supplies of available labor. There were shortages of people in many key jobs. Overall, unemployment dropped to pre-baby boom levels.

Why Do Shortages Exist Today?

By the end of the 1980s, a new trend had taken shape. Business was expanding. New jobs were being created at an average rate of 1.3 million per year. But the supply of new workers was falling as the effects of the "baby bust," or lowered birth rates, affected the labor pool. For the future, a severe shortage of qualified workers promises a wide range of opportunities for **qualified** workers.

The word "qualified" is a key to opening the opportunities that are developing rapidly. Workers of the future will require continually expanding levels of knowledge and skills. A large proportion of the jobs that are being created result from new technologies and new methods. The workplace has changed dramatically during the years since World War II. Some of the effects of these changes are described next.

Computers set the type you read in newspapers, magazines, and books like this one. With the introduction of computers, typesetting speed has increased and costs have come down. The photo at right shows a Linotype machine that sets type in metal strips, or slugs. This was the standard typesetting tool for more than 70 years. Today, most type is set faster with greater accuracy on computers like the one in the photo below.

TOP PHOTO BY BENEDICT KRUSE; BOTTOM PHOTO COURTESY GRIFFIN PRINTING & LITHOGRAPHIC CO., INC.

Where Has the Impact of Technology Been Felt?

People often point to the computer as a force that has eliminated or changed many jobs. This is only partly the case. Many jobs that have been computerized involve people with relatively high skills, particularly skilled office workers and managers. The jobs that have been eliminated by computers have been replaced rapidly by jobs based on use of computers. Skilled workers have been retrainable. Skilled people have been able to move into more responsible and better paying jobs as they mastered computer-related skills.

Greater impacts from technology have affected jobs of unskilled or semi-skilled workers. As dramatic examples, consider just a few instances in which new technologies have displaced people with limited qualifications:

- The automatic cotton picker changed the face of farming in parts of the South. Cotton used to be farmed in relatively small plots. This was because of the time-consuming labor in picking one cotton boll at a time, by hand. When an automatic cotton picker became available, many farmers were displaced. The cotton picker and

other technological devices have been cited as causes for a mass migration from southern farms to northern cities during the 1950s and 1960s. It is estimated that this one population migration involved more than 10 million people.

- Mining of coal and other minerals used to be done largely with picks and shovels. Automatic machinery is faster and more productive. Many

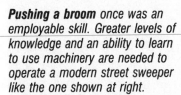

Pushing a broom once was an employable skill. Greater levels of knowledge and an ability to learn to use machinery are needed to operate a modern street sweeper like the one shown at right.

TOP PHOTO COURTESY OF ATHEY PRODUCTS CORPORATION; BOTTOM PHOTO COURTESY OF CARNEGIE LIBRARY OF PITTSBURGH

- Ships, rail cars, and trucks used to be loaded one package at a time, by hand. Complete unloading and reloading were needed each time a shipment was transferred. Transfers were needed from ships to rail cars, then from rail cars to trucks for local delivery. Today, much freight is loaded into containers that are carried as single units on ships, rail cars, or trucks. The manual labor of loading and unloading requires a fraction of the people who used to work at freight-handling jobs.

There are many other examples. But these situations illustrate the trend. The people who have been hit hardest are those with the lowest levels of knowledge and skills.

How About the Effects Of Foreign Competition?

Without technology in the workplace, the loss of jobs during the 1970s and early 1980s might have been even greater. This was a period of rapid growth for *newly industrialized countries (NICs),* particularly Asian nations. Growth of manufacturing industries in other countries has been dramatic. A number of

areas where mining is a major industry have become economically depressed.

- In the paper and lumber industries, it used to take hours to cut a single tree with hand saws operated by two men. The chain saw changed that. Now, a tree comes down in minutes. And one person does the job.

economic factors have been at work. In part, some of the countries involved suffered great damage during World War II or regional wars since then. When the wars were over, the governments of these countries took advantage of opportunities to build new, modern production facilities. These countries also had large labor pools. Salaries in some areas were as low as 10 percent of those in the United States.

American consumers have found foreign products tempting. Prices of many products have been lower than those for items made in the United States. At the same time, many American workers have resented the sales of foreign products in the United States. During the 1980s, international negotiations have attacked the trade problem. At this writing, many difficulties still exist. However, adjustments in the values of monies of a number of countries have helped. American manufacturers have increased their exports. Also, farm products from the United States have begun to enter new overseas markets.

Through all these developments, the United States has maintained the highest rate in the world for creating new jobs. Many of these opportunities are in business areas. These opportunities are varied. But the main chances center around knowledge and skills associated with information resources.

What Kinds of Workers Are in Demand?

Job opportunities reflect demands for products and services. In other words, the marketplace dictates the kinds of jobs that exist or will develop. Some opportunities that are growing or are expected to grow in the future are described below.

Services for an aging population.   As a simple example, consider the average age of the population of the United States. People, on average, are getting older. Every day, the population includes more people in the 65-plus age bracket.

This development will have an obvious impact on the job market. For one thing, older people need

more health-care services than others. Another requirement is that even healthy senior citizens need more care and services than younger people. For example, people whose children have grown and left home no longer are involved in family meals. These older citizens often eat more of their meals in restaurants than they used to. It figures, then, that health care and other services for the elderly represent large and growing job markets.

Information-related jobs.   As another example, consider the computer field. The main job responsibilities in this field include design, manufacture, software development, and customer service. Design and manufacturing are highly technical areas. These areas can benefit from the use of computers as working tools. There already are a number of plants that use computerized systems to manufacture computers. Job opportunities go way down in the production end of the business. Similarly, engineers and designers use computers to streamline efforts. Experts still are needed. But the areas of expansion lie in helping to make computers useful to people.

Under these conditions, there are major shortages of people who know how to put computers to work to deliver results for users. Systems analysts and system programmers are in short supply. This shortage will exist for many years to come. People in these jobs have background both in business and in computer applications. Their work involves analyzing problems to be solved and, in close coordination with users, developing computer-based solutions.

These same skills, incidentally, are in demand in every area of business operations. The skills are the ability to analyze situations, identify problems, and

Business Terms
newly industrialized countries (NICs) Countries that have had a relatively low state of industrial development but are advancing rapidly. Examples include South Korea, Singapore, and Hong Kong.

Career information on some 20,000 jobs is available in the Dictionary of Occupational Titles, a publication of the U.S. Bureau of Labor Statistics.

PHOTO BY LIANE ENKELIS

devise solutions. The end results are skills in decision making and planning. Individuals are most in demand if they have a wide range of skills in areas such as computer applications and knowledge of business functions.

Computer operations and information system management are related areas for which qualified people will be in high demand.

Jobs and company functions. Job openings vary with trends and cycles of the economy. For example, when economic conditions are bad, there is a tendency to cut staff jobs. More openings will exist in line positions. Reason: Staff jobs do not produce revenue. They become part of the *overhead*, or basic expense of doing business. When times are tight, managers concentrate on hiring people who can generate income for the company. This means, in turn, that more jobs will be available in operational areas than in tactical or strategic positions.

When the economy is expanding, personnel needs will change. When companies are growing, they often need employees in the areas of market support, planning, or other staff positions.

WHAT JOB OPPORTUNITIES CAN YOU IDENTIFY?

To help direct your planning or job-search efforts, you will need to identify specific opportunities that match your own qualifications. There are several places in which you can look for openings, and to which you can turn for specific information:

- For a general overview of the job situation, you might find it interesting to look through the *Dictionary of Occupational Titles (DOT)*. This is a large book (more than 1,300 pages) published by the Bureau of Labor Statistics of the U. S. Department of Labor. It lists and describes the work associated with some 20,000 job titles within more than 200 industries. The DOT also can be useful for a person who wants to get a general idea of what kinds of jobs exist. Browsing through this book is like shopping in a merchandise catalog. You can identify a range of possibilities to see which are interesting to you.

- The *Occupational Outlook Handbook (OOH)* is a detailed review of job trends and prospects. It is published every two years by the Bureau of

Labor Statistics. Where the DOT provides a broad, long-term overview, the OOH takes a closer look at specific industries that present promising, current job opportunities.

- The *Occupational Outlook Quarterly (OOQ)* is a magazine about the job market. It, too, is published by the Bureau of Labor Statistics. OOQ publishes articles that describe outstanding career opportunities. Because it is published every three months, OOQ has information that is more current than the OOH.

- Talk to your parents, other family members, and friends. People who work will have a close-up, practical view of the job situation. Their experiences and advice can be helpful. Local libraries also have books and other publications about careers and employment.

- Your counselor at school receives a constant stream of job and career information. These materials, and the services of experienced professionals, are available to you for the asking. Many counseling centers have computer-based career information systems. You can enter information about your interests and the computer will suggest career options that you should consider. Just visit the counseling office at any approved time and ask for help.

- Your daily and Sunday newspapers provide an opportunity for an immediate review of the job market. Review the "want ads" or "classified ads" in your local paper from time to time. Notice the titles of the jobs that are offered. Also notice the number of ads for each title, the job descriptions, and the salaries offered. A review of this type can be likened to "window shopping" before you make actual purchases.

- Employment agencies are organizations that specialize in identifying open jobs and finding prospective workers to fill them. Some agencies are private businesses. They charge fees either to the employer or the worker. Other agencies are operated by the government. Their services are provided without cost. In either case, the agency contacts employers to find job openings. Then job seekers are contacted and their qualifications are reviewed. The qualifications of job seekers are compared with the requirements for the job. When a match is found, the worker is referred to the employer for consideration.

- Information about some kinds of job openings is posted on bulletin boards. This is true for just about all *civil service* jobs. Civil service refers to positions with government agencies. Rules usually require that open jobs be announced to established employees and posted on bulletin boards for the general public. The idea is to encourage qualified workers to apply for all openings. You can find bulletin boards of this type at city hall, or at offices of state and federal agencies in your area.

- Personnel offices of individual companies in your area generally have information on available job openings. All you have to do is visit any company, ask for the personnel office, and inquire about opportunities.

Business Terms

overhead
Basic expense of doing business.

Dictionary of Occupational Titles (DOT)
A directory listing more than 200 industries and 20,000 job titles, published by the U. S. Bureau of Labor Statistics.

Occupational Outlook Handbook (OOH)
A detailed review of job trends and prospects, published by the U. S. Bureau of Labor Statistics.

Occupational Outlook Quarterly (OOQ)
A magazine that covers the job market, published by the U. S. Bureau of Labor Statistics.

civil service
Reference to a system for administration of programs of governmental employment.

Review 15.2

1. How will population trends in the United States affect your future job potential?

2. How can your family and friends help direct you toward future job opportunities?

3. How can your school counselor help to identify job and career opportunities?

HOW DO YOU DECIDE WHAT JOB IS RIGHT FOR YOU?

A good way to go about finding a job is to use a step-by-step process. The process starts by helping you to know yourself and to decide what kind of job would provide the greatest satisfaction.

What Steps Should You Follow To Identify the Right Career?

The steps to follow and the results you should expect are outlined below.

Start by knowing your self.   Your real *self* may be a stranger. Most people see themselves as they want to be or as they think they are. Usually, you will see yourself differently from the image viewed by others. Your view is *subjective*. This means that you color your image with personal ideas and beliefs. Others have an *objective* view. They see you as you are, without filtering images through your ideas about yourself.

Your self, or your *personality,* is shaped by your experiences and beliefs. As you mature, you are exposed to ideas and basic beliefs from family and friends. These beliefs form a *code of conduct,* or personal set of rules that guide you. Your code of conduct and your self determine the way you view others and the way you behave as a member of society.

Identify your personal strengths and weaknesses. Everyone has some likes and dislikes. The things you enjoy doing and do well are personal *strengths*. The things you don't like and don't do as well are personal *weaknesses*. The combination of your strengths and weaknesses guides your choices of activities and should play a part in the selection of a career.

For example, some people enjoy interacting with others, being sociable. Others would just as soon be alone most of the time. Some people are good with words; others have trouble expressing their ideas. Some people are good with numbers; for others, numbers don't figure. Some people are strong and enjoy sports or outdoor activities. Others have less strength and generally are more comfortable as spectators or in non-physical activities.

Develop a personal profile.   After you identify your main strengths and weaknesses, use this information to develop a picture of the ideal kinds of activities for you. This, in effect, is the perfect job that matches your abilities and enables you to use your strengths and avoid your weaknesses.

Match yourself to a job.   Use the information sources described above. Find the job description that presents the best match with the image you have created of yourself. If you don't find anything perfect, start to consider alternatives. Look for the closest match between you and a potential career.

Check out your findings.   Get more information. Visit companies that employ people in the jobs in which you are interested. Think seriously about whether each position that you consider will provide the satisfaction you seek. Be critical. Look for negatives. It is better to review and reject situations that won't work than to take jobs and find you are unhappy. A perfect match may not be available. But it is worthwhile to look for the best possible potential.

Prepare yourself.   Find out what it will take to succeed in your target career. Begin working, right away, to build the knowledge and skills that will be

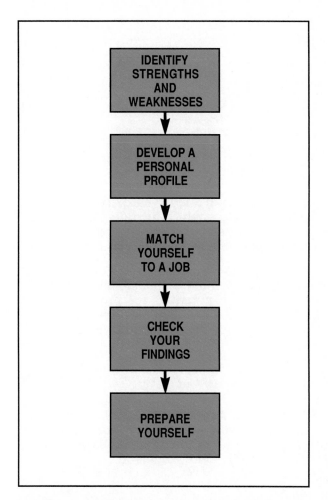

The career-selection process discussed on these pages is diagrammed in this illustration.

A first step in getting ready to apply for a job is to prepare a resume like the one shown in Figure 15-1. In a resume, you give basic information about yourself. This includes your name, address, and telephone number. You also state a job objective, as shown. A resume also should include a summary of your work experience (or qualifications if you are applying for your first job). Also included should be a summary of your education.

The resume, with a brief covering letter, can be sent to employers who prefer to be contacted by mail. Many jobs are offered in "blind" help wanted ads. A blind ad is one that gives a mailing address only and does not identify the company. To respond to ads of this type, you can send a resume with a brief letter identifying the ad to which you are responding. The letter also asks to be considered for the job.

Business Terms

self
A combination of elements that make up your personality and the image that you present to others.

subjective
A way of looking at yourself or at issues from your own viewpoint; your own view often does not match the image perceived by others.

objective
An external, or unbiased, view of a person or issue.

personality
The image you present to others, composed of and controlled by your appearance and your code of conduct.

code of conduct
A combination of beliefs and rules that a person follows in dealing with others.

strength
Something a person enjoys doing and does well.

weakness
Something a person does not enjoy doing and may not do well.

required for success. As part of your program, read about the field you have selected. Visit companies where you can observe people who are doing the kind of work you would like. Guide yourself toward success.

HOW DO YOU APPLY FOR A JOB?

To get a job, you sell yourself to a prospective employer. In other words, getting a job is a marketing task. First, you package yourself, then you present yourself to the marketplace.

RESUME

Katherine MacIntyre

PERSONAL INFORMATION

Address:	7246 E. Olive St. Chesterville, OR 86601	**Age:** **Height:** **Weight:**	17 5' 9" 128 lb.
Telephone:	(903) 555-0108	**SS #:**	981-33-4321

ABOUT MYSELF

I am in good health. I have excellent skills in writing and oral communication. I listen well and consider myself to be a patient person. I type 65 wpm and have experience with Multimate and WordPerfect word processing programs. My hobbies include horseback riding, hang gliding, and tennis. I attend plays whenever I can and have a strong interest in drama and interior design. I consider my interpersonal skills to be excellent.

JOB AND CAREER OBJECTIVES

I would like a position in data processing that provides as much responsibility as I am able to handle. If possible, the position should have a potential for professional growth. I plan to enroll in an evening program leading to a bachelor's degree in computer science and would welcome an opportunity to apply my increasing knowledge and skills at the same company where I start.

WORK HISTORY

Summer, 1988	L. K. Murphy, Automobile Survey Company Chesterville, OR 88602
Duties:	Data entry clerk. Learned procedures for encoding survey responses into a data processing system. Also worked with Lotus 1-2-3 for office administration reponsibilities. My immediate supervisor was Mr. Keith Anderson.
Summer, 1987	Bucket-O-Chicken Chesterville, OR 88601
Duties:	Counterperson and cook. I was responsible for many operating functions and enjoyed interacting with customers and employees. My immediate supervicor was Ms. Suzanne Bothell.

EDUCATION

Sept. 1985-present	Chesterville High. I will graduate in June as an academic major. I currently maintain an A average. I have been an aide in the school's computer lab. In this capacity, I assist students with assignments and projects.

REFERENCES

Ms. Stephanie Thurkettle, Counselor, Chesterville High, (903) 221-9440
Mr. Robert Thompson, Chesterville High Computer Lab, (903) 770-2683
Mr. Keith Anderson, L. K. Murphy, (903) 771-4409
Ms. Suzanne Bothell, Bucket-O-Chicken, Chesterville, (903) 223-5914

Figure 15-1. *A personal resume can be a valuable job-search tool. The resume gives personal information and professional qualifications about a job seeker.*

If you are to apply for the job in person, you can bring a copy of your resume with you. When you go to a company to apply for a job, you often will be asked to fill out an application. If you appear qualified, you probably will be asked to go through an *interview*. A job interview is a personal conference at which a prospective employer discusses your qualifications.

The better prepared you are for your job search, the more successful you are likely to be. So, it is a good idea to seek advice of teachers, family, and friends who have successful work experience. Remember that the task is to match yourself to the right job. Some 115 million jobs exist now. More are opening all the time. You can be confident that, if you really want to work, there will be a job for you. The challenge is to find the right one.

This chapter concludes a presentation designed to introduce you to business and to help you decide whether you are interested in a business career.

Regardless of what you decide, a logical next step, which may be available through use of this book, is to learn more about computers as business tools. Whatever career you choose, it is almost certain that you will encounter computers in your working situation. This is a good time to begin understanding computers and to build the skills needed to use computers as tools.

Review 15.3

1. What is your self?
2. What are strengths and weaknesses?
3. What is a personal profile?
4. What is a resume?

Business Terms

interview
A personal conference used for gathering information.

Chapter Summary

❑ In satisfying consumers and in creating jobs, business creates a level of wealth that supports a nation and its people.

❑ As evidence of the many job and career opportunities in business, business has become the most popular major among college students.

❑ There already are shortages of workers in many positions that require knowledge, skills, and the ability to learn. The number of openings and opportunities is expected to increase in the future.

❑ There are many sources of information about jobs. Included are government publications, counseling offices, employment agencies, and newspaper want ads.

❑ To select a career, you start by studying and learning about your self and the code of conduct that guides you. You identify your personal strengths and weaknesses and create a personal profile that identifies you for the benefit of a prospective employer. Then you match yourself to a job and prepare to go to work.

❑ An actual job search involves the preparation of a resume, visiting the offices of a target company, completing an application, and being interviewed.

Definitions

Write a complete sentence that defines each of the terms below.

overhead	civil service
subjective	objective
personality	strength
weakness	interview

Questions to Think About

Based on what you have learned to date, answer the following questions in one or more complete sentences.

1. What is wealth and how is wealth created?

2. Why does this chapter indicate that there will be shortages of qualified workers in the future?

3. Describe major changes in job structures within one industry—changes that have resulted from the impact of technologies other than computers.

4. What are newly industrialized countries and how has their development affected the economy of the United States?

5. What publications about the job market are available from the Bureau of Labor Statistics and how can these publications help you in the future?

6. What are your major strengths and weaknesses?

7. What are the major elements in your personal code of conduct?

8. Describe the activities that make up what you consider to be the ideal job.

Projects

The purpose of the assignments below is to encourage you to increase your learning through outside reading or work assignments.

1. From your work to date, prepare a report on whether you think a career in business is of interest to you. Explain what you do and do not like about the prospects of a business career. Explain the reasons for your choice. If you have decided you are not interested in a business career, identify potential careers that you think might be of interest.

2. Based on information in this book and on outside reading, prepare a report describing how you think technology will affect your future life. Identify the specific technologies you feel will be important to you and describe the changes or new developments that you anticipate.

II
Computer Applications in Business

The 15 chapters that follow cover the impact of computers on business. Note that these chapters are not about computers. Rather, the information presented is about business management and how managers depend on computers as vital tools. It is stressed that information is an essential asset for any modern business organization. The need for information has increased steadily through centuries of development by societies and their business organizations. Eventually, businesses became engulfed by what amounted to an "information avalanche." That is, so much information was generated that there was a threat that businesses would be swamped. The computer has functioned as a tool for accepting, organizing, and using information. Throughout the chapters that follow, emphasis is on business situations and needs. The computer is cast in the role of problem solver.

CHAPTER 16

What Is the Information Avalanche?

The Think Tank

A *think tank* is an organization that solves problems and answers questions. The Think Tank at the beginning of each chapter of this book presents questions for you to think about. When you finish reading this chapter and complete your work assignments, you should be able to answer the following questions:

❑ What are data and how are data related to information?

❑ How and why do data and information processing present special requirements as businesses grow larger?

❑ In business, what is meant by the term "information resources?"

❑ What is meant by the term "information avalanche" and why were computers chosen as the means of dealing with this avalanche?

DOING BUSINESS

"It's really an information machine," Greta explained. She was showing two new employees, Jose and Zelda, around the Food Monster store. "There's no way that a food chain like ours could operate today without this kind of system."

Jose and Zelda watched a checkout operation. The checker, Herman, simply picked up food items and passed them over a narrow window in the surface of the checkout counter. Each time a product crossed the window they noticed a brief flash of red light. Zelda asked about the light.

"The light is sensing information from product labels," Greta said. "Notice that there are rows of bars printed on the product labels. The cash register

actually is a small computer. The computer uses the light beam to read the product number that's coded in the bars on the labels. Then, the small computer at the checkstand sends the product number to a larger computer at the back of the store. That computer uses the number to search its electronic files for a description and price for each item."

"It sure is fast," noted Jose.

"It takes only a few hundredths of a second to find and deliver the information on each item sold," said Greta.

"Does the computer know the descriptions and prices for every item in the store?" asked Zelda.

"That's right," said Greta. "There are more than 50,000 product records in the computer. That's only the beginning. For each item we sell—and remember we have 14 checkstands—the computer keeps track of sales. Late tonight, a count of all products sold will be sent automatically from our computer to a computer at the central office. That computer knows how many units of each product we have in stock and how many have been ordered. From this information, the central office computer automatically makes up an order to replace the items we have sold."

"You mean the computer decides what this store sells?" Jose asked.

"Not exactly," Greta answered. "Computers don't decide. People do. Computers follow instructions. In this case, the people at the central office set up instructions that the computer follows. The decisions about when to order products and how many to order are made by people. The computer acts on information. There is no way that people, on their own, could handle so much information in such short times. The computer processes information on millions of transactions every day. The business that you see in operation today couldn't exist without computers. We'd be buried under an avalanche of information."

MEANING

Consider the scene in the supermarket. Until a few years ago, supermarkets recorded sales and developed customer totals on mechanical cash registers with rotating gears. The checkers had to press keys on the register to enter prices for each item sold. The registers were able to keep track of total purchases by each customer. Also, at the end of the day, the register could report totals for all sales. Some of these mechanical registers were able to maintain totals for a limited number of departments in the store. But there was no way of reporting sales for each of the tens of thousands of products in stock.

To decide what to order, employees had to walk through the store and examine the shelves. The number of units for each product had to be counted physically and recorded on large sheets that the people carried with them. These sheets were delivered to the central office. There, people had to check them out individually to decide what products to ship to each store. So many products were involved that it was impossible to check an entire store every day.

So much information was being created that store employees couldn't record it all or figure out what the information meant. Supermarket managers needed information to run their business. But, without computers, they were powerless to collect and handle all of the information their businesses were generating.

The computer has introduced the power to record details on hundreds of thousands of consumer purchases in each store, every day. Further, the computer has the power of *data reduction.* That is, the computer can combine information items so that people don't have to deal with the detail covering individual sales. Instead, the computer can figure out sales by product and by store. When products are needed to replace those that were sold, the computer reports this information. In other words, the computer analyzes information and gives it meaning. The computer deals with volumes of work that could build up to an *information avalanche.*

Just what is an information avalanche? One way to describe an information avalanche is to say that it results from too much of a good thing. In today's economy, information is a business necessity. Now, as you begin to learn about the role of computers in business, you are ready to think about *information overload.*

An information overload, or an information avalanche, occurs when a business generates too much information for its managers to absorb and understand. Managers make plans and operating decisions on the basis of information. A thorough understanding of information is essential to quality decision making.

The example at Food Monster is one version of an information avalanche and of the way computers deal with information overload. Other businesses face similar strains. Each business has its own, special problems. However, the majority of busi-

The information avalanche presents volumes of processing requirements. Major computer centers like the one shown have grown to handle growing workloads.

COURTESY TRW, INC.

ness information requirements can be met with a common-denominator tool—the computer.

WHAT IS INFORMATION MODELING AND HOW DOES IT HELP MANAGERS?

Taken together, the collected information about a supermarket or other business represents a *model* of its operations or condition. A model presents an image, or replica, of some object or operation. Some models look like the originals. An architectural model shows the appearance of a building. A model railroad puts real-looking trains on table-top tracks. Information models the business in terms of *transactions* and *status*.

Transactions, of course, are the buying and selling events basic to business operations. Status reflects the total impact of all transactions accumulated over time. The status of a business, in effect, is a snapshot of the information that represents the business at a given time. Status changes continually. But status must be known by managers as a basis for running the business.

Business Terms

data reduction
The combining of data items and information to reduce the volume of items delivered to users. Data reduction adds meaning and value to information for the people who use it.

information avalanche
A condition in which information is generated at rates faster than the ability of people to handle and deal with the total volume.

information overload
A condition in which people receive more information than they can use productively or interpret. *See also* information avalanche.

model
An image, or replica, of some object or operation. An information model represents the status of an organization through organized sets of information.

transaction
A basic act of doing business; an exchange of value between seller and buyer.

status
A condition that exists at a given point in time. An information model states the operating and financial condition of an organization.

An information model, then, provides a way of looking at and evaluating a business and its condition. Putting it simply, an information model is a kind of scoreboard that tells how a business is doing.

HOW DID THE INFORMATION AVALANCHE GET STARTED?

An information avalanche results from complexity. The bigger and more complicated a business becomes, the more information it generates. The point: Information overload is a comparatively modern development. Business has become so dependent on information that the current period is being called an information age. So-called information workers are said to make up a majority of the employed population. To succeed in almost any job, it will be necessary for today's students to know about and know how to use computers.

Things were not always this way. Collection of information was of little concern in earlier, simpler times. The need for information-processing machines grew gradually, keeping pace with the evolution of society. A brief look back at how people came to depend on information can help build your understanding of the needs and opportunities facing information workers.

WHAT INFORMATION WAS NEEDED WHEN AMERICA WAS A NATION OF FARMERS?

When America declared its independence, 90 percent of the people lived on farms. Each farm was an independent business. There were no income taxes and no reports to file with the government. The family bank might be a cookie jar or other container. Business decisions involved watching the weather and selecting the right time to plow, plant, and harvest. Experience played a major role in decisions. Natural forces took care of the rest.

Among businesses that supplied and served farmers, information needs also were simple—at least by today's standards. Businesses were small and individual. Each proprietor knew his or her customers personally. There were no fast-changing fads or styles to monitor. Also, businesses were small. It was common for a storekeeper who craved adventure simply to pack all the stock and move. When goods sold, new merchandise was ordered.

Information that was written down might consist of a book in which entries were made when credit was extended to a farmer. The merchant could be sure that the bill would be paid when crops were harvested.

An important point: As long as the owner of a business ran it personally, information recording and reporting needs were minimal.

HOW DID THE INDUSTRIAL AGE AFFECT THE NEED FOR INFORMATION?

The concentration of productivity in factories during the nineteenth century led to the building of business organizations. These growing organizations were absentee-owned and run by a new breed of professional managers. Business transactions involved large amounts of materials and goods. Credit became a factor in business record keeping. So did the role of banks and lenders and managers of money.

These developments created a need. Businesses had to be able to collect and distribute information quickly and accurately. To help picture the problem, consider what information processing was like through most of the nineteenth century.

All records were handwritten by a skilled group of men (women did not work in offices in those days). The recordkeepers were known as *scriveners*. They were highly trained individuals who delivered beautiful penmanship from quill pens that they hand-sharpened personally. Scriveners were artisans who couldn't be rushed. You could spot them the minute you walked into an office. They worked at high desks and sat on high stools. They wore green eyeshades

Manual processing of information in early twentieth-century offices became swamped as information volumes grew. Repetitive manual work simply couldn't keep up with growth in the volumes of information that were required.

COURTESY OF NATIONAL ARCHIVES

to cut the glare. They wore garters on their upper arms to pull back shirtsleeves so they could work freely. Then they wore covering garments over their sleeves so they wouldn't smear the ink as they worked.

The methods of scriveners simply couldn't keep up with growing needs to accumulate information on transactions and to report on the status of a business. Also, the growing volume of *correspondence*—letter writing—became far too great for the handwritten methods of scriveners.

During the last quarter of the nineteenth century, a number of new inventions attacked this problem—and conquered it temporarily. Key inventions included the adding machine, the cash register, the calculator, and the typewriter.

With the adding machine, people no longer had to sum columns of figures in their heads. Arithmetic had become a bottleneck in the processing of business paperwork. Adding machines and calculators broke down this obstacle.

The cash register changed the way consumers dealt with retailers. The problem for nineteenth-century retailers centered on how to control cash.

Stores used to have central "cages" at which cashiers handled money. When a consumer made a purchase, the salesperson wrote a ticket showing the amount. The customer went to the cashier's cage and paid. The slip, which was marked by the cashier to show the payment, was taken back to the salesperson and exchanged for the purchased items. The cash register made it possible to control the receipt of money at the point where sales took place. Stores could grow. Managers could get the information they needed to control operations.

The impact of the typewriter was particularly dramatic. Touch typists replaced scriveners. The machines produced more attractive correspondence in less time. Many scriveners clung stubbornly to

Business Terms

scrivener
A person trained to produce attractive handwritten documents.

correspondence
Communication carried out in written form.

their old ways. They refused to use machines to write letters. As one result, women were hired to run the new machines—the first large-scale employment of women in offices. The first female employees had job titles to match the machines they used. They were called typewriters.

Review 16.1

1. What is information overload?

2. What is an information model?

3. How did the growth of companies during the nineteenth century contribute to the need for improved methods for handling information?

WHEN WERE MODERN INFORMATION PROCESSING CONCEPTS INTRODUCED?

As business and government agencies grew larger, the *data processing* systems became overloaded. Data processing is the term for procedures that collect basic facts and figures for continuing use. *Data* are the basic facts that lead to development of information. Examples include prices and item numbers for groceries. Data items also might describe parts of your appearance. Typical data items might be 5 feet, three inches; 121 pounds; blonde hair, brown eyes, and other features. Together, the data items

about your features add up to a unit of information, your identification—Sara Hofstadter, Samuel K. Jones, Jaime Lopez, or other names.

When data are collected and combined, they are *transformed* into information. The processing that leads to transformation can include arithmetic operations or the combining of items. When data items are transformed, information results.

Information processing also is necessary. New meaning can be added by processing information. For example, 25 different names taken separately may have no connection or special meaning. However, if the 25 names are combined on a list, they could represent a class studying business computer applications.

Catching up in the numbers game. The more items of data and information that an organization must process, the bigger and more difficult the job becomes. This was the situation as the United States Bureau of Census prepared to count the country's population in 1890. A *census* is a collection of data about a population. A national census counts the people who live in a country and analyzes information about them.

By 1880, the population of the United States was 40 million. With the data collection and information processing methods available then, it took almost

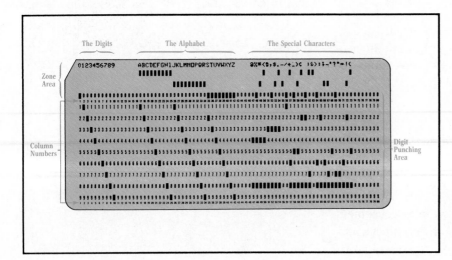

Figure 16-1. *The punched card made it possible to capture data records in a form that made them available for reuse. Reduction in the need to make multiple entries, coupled with the capacity for machine processing, increased information-handling capacities.*

eight years to compile and report data on the 1880 census. Thus, it was almost time to begin collecting data for the 1890 census before the reports on the 1880 census were complete. In 1890, the problem was worse. During the 1880s, the population of the United States had grown from 40 million to 50 million. But the job couldn't be put off. The law requires a census count every 10 years.

The problem was attacked by a young scientist named Dr. Herman Hollerith. Hollerith was hired especially for this job by the Bureau of Census. He identified the problem quickly: Too much time was spent in copying data from one reporting document to another. Also, because the work was done by hand, many errors occurred. Hollerith decided that the Census Bureau needed a method that made it necessary to record data only once. The idea was that, once the data were recorded, or *captured,* the items could be used over and over.

Hollerith's solution was the *punched card.* He devised machines that could punch holes in specific positions on cards. The numbers were coded in *columns* and *rows.* A column consisted of a series of data positions, or rows, that could represent the values 0 through 9. (Later, additional values were added so that the columns also could represent letters of the alphabet.) A punched card is reproduced in Figure 16-1.

Hollerith's inventions revolutionized data processing. The 1890 census count was completed in two-and-a-half years. Based on this success, Hollerith left the government and formed a company to produce and market his machines. His organization eventually became part of the International Business Machines Corporation (IBM).

Systems solve problems. As Hollerith began to market his machines commercially, his key idea remained constant: Capture data items once, then reuse them indefinitely. To develop information from data captured in cards, it was necessary to follow a series of steps performed on specialized machines. Some machines punched the holes in cards. Others sorted cards into sequence for processing. Some machines brought cards together from two different groups, or decks, in an operation known as *collating.* There also were machines that printed information from cards.

Business Terms

data processing
Term that describes the methods and procedures for collecting, processing, and retaining data for status reporting and future reference.

data
The basic facts that are processed and/or combined to generate information.

transform
To process data to generate meaningful information.

information processing
The handling and organization of information for access by or delivery to users. *See also* data processing.

census
A collection of data about a population.

capture
Within an information system, the act of encoding and/or recording data for continuing use.

punched card
A standard-sized card into which holes are punched to represent values of data. A method of recording and capturing data for future processing by machines and/or computers.

column
On a punched card, a vertical position that can be encoded to represent a data value.

row
On a punched card, a horizontal position that can be encoded through punching to represent the value of a column position.

collate
A process used with punched card machines or computers to match data items from two separate sets in a planned sequence.

Punched card methods *involved processing of data captured in cards through a series of machines. Punched card techniques thus led to introduction of information processing systems. A system is a series of steps followed in sequence to produce a planned result.*

COURTESY OF NATIONAL ARCHIVES

A series of steps that are followed in sequence to develop and report information became known as a *system*. This word has remained to become one of the main terms of the computer age. An *information system* may be carried on with handwritten methods, on punched card machines, or with computers. The concept is more important than the kind of equipment used: A system is a series of steps, followed in order, to reach a planned result. The systematic thinking necessary to design and operate punched card systems helped train people for use of computers.

For many years, Hollerith's punched card accounting machines were felt to be too expensive for all but the largest companies and government agencies. Then, history stepped in and created demands that made punched card accounting one of the world's fastest-growing industries. This growth resulted from two major developments: Social Security laws and World War II.

Social Security.   A major change in the data collection and information processing requirements for business occurred in 1936. On January 1, all employers had to start deducting one percent of the amount paid to each worker. The employer had to add another one percent to this amount and pay the total to the Social Security Administration.

Social Security laws have provided retirement and disability benefits to millions of workers. But data and information processing workloads of businesses were multiplied. Before Social Security, a worker's earnings could be figured simply by multiplying the number of hours worked by the hourly pay rate. The worker received the total amount. After Social Security, the company had to compute and withhold Social Security deductions for all employees. It also was necessary to set up information files for the total payments due to Social Security. This information processing job included computation of both deductions and employer contributions. Then, reports to the Social Security Administration had to show detailed information for each worker.

For medium- and large-sized companies, it became virtually impossible to handle this information processing with existing methods. Businesses needed a way to capture data items once, then reuse them to complete the entire payroll and government reporting job. Use of punched card accounting methods exploded as businesses tooled up for Social Security reporting.

As more businesses installed punched card equipment, more people were assigned to devise systems for their use. A major result of the expanding use of punched card accounting equipment was the emergence of *systems analysis* as a business specialty. People known as *systems analysts* studied information processing needs and devised step-by-step procedures to deliver needed results. As punched card systems gave way to use of computers, systems analysis emerged as a critical skill. Systems analysts became the people who put computers to work in business organizations.

World War II. A few years after the introduction of Social Security, business growth in the United States spurted. World War II broke out in Europe. America tooled up to become the world's arsenal, and also its most powerful industrial nation. In 1940, a buildup of the Armed Forces started with the introduction of a military draft.

During the war, some 10 million people were processed through the Armed Forces. These people had to be trained, assigned to jobs, and paid each month. One result was a bigger information-processing job than any organization in the world ever had handled before. The Armed Forces used as many punched card machines as were available. Business took everything that was left to help handle the growth of companies for wartime production. Also, information processing became increasingly complex for business as special taxes were passed to support the war effort.

Even with millions of punched card machines in use, the paperwork avalanche built up faster than information could be digested. The Armed Forces, other government agencies, and businesses all were looking for more powerful information processing tools. In addition, the scientists and engineers working on advanced weapons systems also needed more mathematical processing power for their work.

Several projects were launched to develop electrical and electronic calculators for use in weapons design and military planning. These efforts used some of the advanced electronics developments that had come out of military research. Included were the miniature parts used to create "walkie-talkie" radios for battlefield use. In addition, the electronics breakthroughs that led to the invention of radar contributed to development of new calculating machines.

The first practical electronic computers were ready for use just as World War II ended. The timing proved ideal. Consumers and business organizations had lived with shortages for years as resources were dedicated to the war effort. People were ready to buy anything that could be produced. Businesses were entering a period of explosive growth. The world was ready for the information processing capabilities of computers.

Business Terms

system
A sequence of steps followed in order to produce a planned result.

information system
A series of steps followed in sequence to deliver planned reports or to make information accessible to users. *See also* system.

systems analysis
A professional specialty for identifying and solving problems through the use of information, including the design of information systems.

systems analyst
A professional in systems analysis; a person who identifies information needs and develops systems to meet those needs. *See also* systems analysis.

Review 16.2

1. Why was the 1890 census a key event in the development of modern data processing?

2. What are the main differences between data and information?

3. What impact did Social Security legislation have on the need for companies to add data processing capacities?

4. What are some events or factors during the World War II era that led to development of computers?

WHAT HAVE COMPUTERS MEANT TO BUSINESS?

By 1948, developers were ready to begin shipping full-scale electronic computers for practical use. Early computers were seen as tools for scientific and engineering jobs—giant number processing factories. With this view in mind, early computers didn't even have printing devices to handle business documents. Computers would perform extensive calculations that resulted in brief answers that could be handled on simple typewriters.

However, people with imagination saw the possibility of using computers to stem the information avalanche faced by business. Fittingly, the first use of a computer was for calculation of census reports. The Bureau of Census ordered a large UNIVAC system for use in compiling information on the 1950 census. The place where punched card accounting made its debut also marked a milestone in the use of computers.

In 1951, the first computer, also a UNIVAC, was put to work processing business data. The computer was installed at the light bulb manufacturing plant of General Electric, in Lexington, Kentucky. The use of this system also was fitting from a historical viewpoint. The General Electric system was used initially for payroll processing. This was the same application that led to rapid growth of punched card accounting when Social Security deductions were enforced in 1936.

Some bad advice. At about the same time that the General Electric computer was being installed, a study was conducted to predict the worldwide market for computers. The study was commissioned by Thomas J. Watson, Sr., who was president of IBM at the time. The detailed survey estimated that the worldwide market would be satisfied with a total of 300 computers. This proved to be bad advice. At this writing, more than 20 million computers are in use in business organizations in the United States alone.

What Makes a Computer?

The term *computer* has become an everyday expression. For the purpose of your work in this book, however, you should have a specific definition. A computer is a set of connected devices that function together to process data and develop information. Other machines and methods can accomplish the same results. A computer functions in some special ways. To be a computer, a collection of equipment must have all of the following capabilities:

- A computer is electronic. Its computations are performed in circuits that have no moving parts. These computations include the arithmetic functions of addition, subtraction, multiplication, and division. Also, computers can compare two values and determine if one is equal to, less than, or greater than the other.

- A computer has the ability to store and follow sets of instructions called *programs*. These programs can be processed to completion independently, without the need for people to be involved.

- A computer has the ability to record processed data and/or information and to recall these items for continuing or future use.

- A computer must have some means of interacting with people.

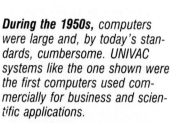

During the 1950s, computers were large and, by today's standards, cumbersome. UNIVAC systems like the one shown were the first computers used commercially for business and scientific applications.

COURTESY OF LAWRENCE LIVERMORE NATIONAL LABORATORY COMPUTER CENTER MUSEUM

The chapter that follows explains how computers operate and how they communicate with people and with one another. The remainder of this chapter concentrates on the development of computers and their role as business problem solvers.

What Developments Contributed To the Growth in Use of Computers?

The computers introduced in the early 1950s were gigantic. They included multiple devices that occupied complete rooms. The vacuum tubes that handled the electronic processing gave off so much heat that special air conditioning systems were needed.

The early computers were extensions of punched card processing techniques. The data items were captured into cards for entry into the computers. Results were punched into cards by different machines. Printing of reports was handled on the same kinds of punched card machines that had been in use since the 1930s.

Computers of the 1950s. Though they were crude by today's standards, early computers earned their

way as business data processing machines. Their value lay largely in the fact that they could process data from punched cards hundreds of times faster than the machines they replaced. There was so much work to be done that computers proved to be worth the major investments required to own them.

During the 1950s, four developments contributed to the acceptance and growth in use of computers:

- The *transistor* was invented in 1957. This device was a fraction of the size of the vacuum tubes it replaced. It also was more reliable and gave off

Business Terms

computer
A set of connected devices that function together to process data and develop information.

program
A set of instructions that controls the operation of a computer.

transistor
An electronic device that controls the flow of electricity or the storage of binary coded data.

Major expansions in capabilities and applications of computer systems came with the widespread use of tape drives (below) and the dominant position of IBM System/360 computers (left). Systems like the ones pictured dominated the data processing scene during the 1960s. Note, in photo at left, that punched card machines are still in evidence.

PHOTO AT LEFT COURTESY OF DATA PROCESSING MANAGEMENT ASSOCIATION; PHOTO BELOW COURTESY OF HUGHES AIRCRAFT COMPANY

less heat. Introduction of transistors made it possible to build computers that were smaller and yet far more powerful than units that used vacuum tubes.

- Electronic storage capabilities were added in the form of magnetic tape drives on which data and information could be recorded and reread for repeated processing. The dependence upon punched cards was reduced. As information files accumulated on tape, business managers began to realize that the major value of computers lay in the information they could accumulate and provide. Computer-generated information became a vital tool for managers with decision-making and planning responsibilities.

- *Programming languages* were developed. Earlier computers had to be programmed in *machine language,* symbols representing the on-off binary values of electrical circuits. The process was so detailed that few people were able to master the art of programming. Even for them, mistakes could be frequent and frustrating. Starting in 1956, a series of tools was developed that permitted people to write instructions in languages both people and computers could understand.

- High-speed printing devices were linked directly into computers. These increased the value of computers to business organizations because they could produce transaction documents and reports quickly and economically.

An important technological trend was started in the 1950s and has continued since then, throughout the years that have been called the "computer era." This trend is that computers have grown approximately 1,000 times more efficient and have been reduced to one-tenth their former size during each five to seven years.

These jumps in capacity and reductions in size have been referred to as *computer generations.* Four generations of computer equipment have been identified. The first consisted of computers built around vacuum tubes. The second generation featured transistors that were mounted on plastic-based *circuit boards.* A circuit board is a sheet of electrically resistant plastic to which current-carrying circuits are bonded. The circuit boards eliminated the need to string thousands of feet of wires inside a computer to establish connections for electronic parts. Third and fourth generations of computer equipment came later and are described as part of the discussion below.

Computers of the 1960s. During the early 1960s, scientists developed techniques for building transistors and other electronic parts on small, flat, glass-like surfaces. The devices, called *integrated circuits,* were much smaller and more powerful than groups of separate, or *discrete,* transistors. Use of integrated circuits marked the third generation of computers.

During the same time period, computer programs became much more sophisticated. The programs used to run computers and control the processing of data became known as *software.* Software was considered to be a companion for *hardware,* or computer equipment. A software breakthrough of the 1960s was the introduction of the *operating system.*

This was a series of programs that monitored and supervised operation of the computer itself. An operating system, also known as part of *system software,* controlled operation of hardware. Also, the operating system kept track of work that was entered into the computer for processing. That is, the system software called up the *application programs* that controlled individual jobs. The operating system also found and supplied data needed for processing.

Operating systems made computers more productive. Previously, people had to set up and load each job manually. This meant, literally, that computers were out of service most of the time while jobs

Business Terms

programming language
A set of instructions that can be understood by both people and computers.

machine language
A set of binary codes that represent the native language of a computer; machine language is written in strings of 0 and 1 values.

computer generation
A time frame in which technology produces a computer with processing capacities 1,000 times greater than previous models, usually four to seven years.

circuit board
A sheet of electrically resistant plastic to which current-carrying circuits are bonded.

integrated circuit
A device in which electrical circuits and electronic components, such as transistors, are created and positioned as part of a single manufacturing process.

discrete
Separate, distinct; in electronics, a reference to circuits built through use of a series of individual devices.

software
Reference to all of the programs that control operation of a computer.

hardware
Computer equipment, inclusively.

operating system
A series of programs that monitor and supervise operation of a computer.

system software
Reference to all of the programs that control operation of a computer.

application program
A set of instructions that controls processing of an individual user job.

Random access capabilities were made possible through disk storage. In turn, random access files made it possible to use computers in direct support of day-to-day business transactions. This proved a major factor in the expanded use of computers in business. The diagram below shows the layout for storage of information on disk tracks. Read/write devices can access individual records.

were being changed and started. With operating system software, the computer gained the ability to schedule its own work.

Operating system software could be developed partly because of the introduction of a major new piece of computer-support equipment during the 1960s. This was the *disk storage* device that made possible *random access* to stored programs and information.

Previously, computers had been limited to cards and magnetic tape for information storage. These are *sequential storage* techniques. With cards or tapes, information items were recorded in sequence, from the beginning of a file to the end. Each time a job was processed, its entire file had to be read and a new file had to be generated. This meant that computers could not be used for the processing of individual transactions as they occurred.

It simply was not feasible to have to set up and handle an entire set of files to process an individual transaction. Work for computers had to be set up in groups of documents and/or files for *batch processing.* This meant that companies still had to handle processing of actual transactions through some man-

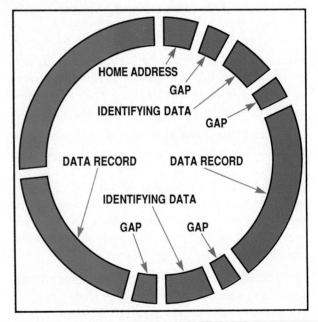

ual method. Computer processing was possible only after transactions were completed.

With disk files, it became possible to retrieve individual records from files and replace them after use. Individual transactions could be supported directly by random access disk files. The computer had become a tool for support of the mainstream operations of a business.

Another important development of the 1960s was the introduction of the *minicomputer.* The minicomputer, introduced during the mid-1960s, provided most of the capabilities of the large computers that preceded it. However, costs and space requirements were considerably lower. This meant that computers could be installed by companies too small to be able to afford previous models. Also, many minicomputers were installed in division or branch offices of large companies. With the advent of the minicomputer, the number of computers in use expanded rapidly.

Computers of the 1970s. During the 1970s, scientists and engineers kept crowding increasing numbers of transistors and other parts onto integrated circuits. This led to evolution of the *chip,* or *microchip.* A microchip is a device that can contain an entire computer processor or can store thousands of items of data. Use of microchips highlighted the fourth generation of computer equipment.

Another major event of the 1970s was the introduction of the *microcomputer,* or *personal computer.* The microcomputer got its name originally from the fact that its processor was built on a single microchip. Microcomputers represented a triumph for computer technology. Today's desk-top microcomputer has more power than the rooms full of computers used to control the space flights of the 1960s.

As the decade of the 1970s ended, the microcomputer was in its infancy.

Computers of the 1980s. During the 1980s, the computer became a universal tool. Today, computers can be found on millions of desk tops and in many thousands of homes. Microcomputers have become smaller and less costly throughout the decade. Shortly after IBM began making microcomputers in 1981, shipments climbed to a rate of about one million units per month. In 1988, it was estimated that some 20 million microcomputers were in use in business offices. Many millions of jobs require an ability to understand and use computers.

The 1980s also have seen growth at the large end of the computer family. Supercomputers have been introduced that provide the capacity to handle more than 80 million processing instructions each second. These computers are powering great advances in scientific research.

Business Terms

disk storage
Reference to a method of storing data on and retrieving data from a storage unit that contains one or more platters that accept magnetic encoding.

random access
Description of a storage method that makes it possible for a computer to record or read individual records without requiring processing of entire files to support each reference function.

sequential storage
Description of a storage method in which all records are recorded and read in a planned sequence, one after another. All records must be read and rewritten each time a sequential file is processed.

batch processing
A technique under which groups of transaction data items are grouped and processed together as a working unit.

minicomputer
A mid-sized computer that has most of the capacity of a large system at lower costs.

chip
A miniature device that can contain an entire computer processor or can store thousands of items of data.

microchip
See chip.

microcomputer
A self-sufficient computer that fits on a desktop and uses a microchip as its main processor.

personal computer
See microcomputer.

Large and small answers are being provided to meet information processing needs. At left is a Cray supercomputer. Cray systems can execute up to 80 million processing instructions per second. Big systems are made up of increasingly small parts, like the microchip below.

PHOTO AT LEFT COURTESY OF LAWRENCE LIVERMORE NATIONAL LABORATORY COMPUTER CENTER MUSEUM; PHOTO BELOW COURTESY OF IBM CORPORATION

Major software advances also have been made throughout the 1980s. Software moved beyond the boundaries of controlling computer equipment and monitoring the processing of applications. During the 1980s, computer use became information oriented. Computer systems moved into an area known as *information resource management (IRM).*

The IRM concept means that computers have gained the power to organize and use vast sets of information that represent company operations and status. Earlier, the major challenge in developing a computer system was to design and create programs to control files of information. That is, each application required its own, special files. Content of the files for one computer application could not be mixed with the files for other applications.

During the 1980s, new software made it possible to model, or represent, entire organizations in information files. These files could be treated as common property for multiple computer applications. With a collection of files known as a *database,* development of computer systems became easier. Computers became valuable as information management tools. Information could be treated as a resource in the same way as money, buildings, or materials.

The software programs that made information management concepts possible were known as *database management systems (DBMS).* DBMS software helped to introduce a fourth generation of programming languages. Most DBMS software packages include a *query language* capability. A query language is a set of commands that enables a computer user to instruct the system to find needed information and to prepare that information to meet user needs.

The instructions that make up a query language cause the computer to perform processing. This processing involves the same kinds of operations that used to require extensive sets of application programs. So-called *fourth generation languages (4GLs)* make it possible for a user to instruct the computer to perform desired processing. The information user can enter and control these commands personally, without having to wait for a program to be written.

This kind of capability is said to make computers *user friendly*. Computers really can be friendly for people who understand how they operate and how they can serve as tools. The chapter that follows introduces you to the capabilities of computers as tools. This is an important step toward making sure that computers will have a friendly place in your own future.

Review 16.3

1. What features and/or capabilities identify a computer?

2. What improvements did the transistor introduce as compared with the vacuum tube?

3. What is a chip, or microchip?

4. What is an operating system?

5. What is an application program?

6. When personal computers were introduced, what was their special feature?

Business Terms

information resource management (IRM)
A concept that treats information as an asset of a company and manages information assets for support of operations and management.

database
A collection of data that is organized and stored so that any application program can access individual data items at any location within the files.

database management systems (DBMS)
Software that assembles, monitors, and manages use of one or more databases.

query language
A set of commands that enables a computer user to instruct the system to find needed information and to prepare that information to meet user needs.

fourth generation languages (4GLs)
A set of commands that enable a user to prepare processing instructions that use information in a database; a 4GL makes it possible to develop applications without requiring the writing of traditional application programs.

user friendly
Reference to a computer system that is considered easy to use because of the software tools that are provided.

Chapter Summary

❑ The term ''information avalanche'' refers to a situation in which so much information is generated that people who need to use that information become swamped.

❑ A collection of information that represents the operating condition of an organization forms a model that can be used to study and manage that organization.

❑ As companies grew in size, the need for information and for information processing tools also expanded.

❑ Development of information begins with the collection of sets of raw facts and figures, known as data.

❑ When data items are processed, information results.

❑ Information is collected and processed to support planning and decision making.

❏ A major principle that helped deal with the information avalanche involves capturing data items initially in a reusable form. Then, the data can be used for further processing without repeating the capturing step. This principle was introduced with the invention of punched card accounting equipment.

❏ A major skill required to use punched card machines was the ability to establish step-by-step procedures for processing data and generating information. This work, known as systems analysis, was performed by a group of specialists known as systems analysts. Systems analysts played a key role in introducing and applying computers in business organizations.

❏ A computer is an electronic device that can follow stored programs. A computer also can store and retrieve data and information for continuing use. Processing capabilities include arithmetic and comparison functions.

❏ Initial computers were designed largely for scientific and engineering use. Business capabilities were added when it became apparent that managers needed advanced information processing tools.

❏ During the 1950s, major developments included introduction of the transistor, magnetic tape storage, programming languages, and high-speed printers.

❏ Major developments of the 1960s included operating system software, disk files, and minicomputers.

❏ During the 1970s, microchips and microcomputers were leading developments.

❏ The 1980s have seen progress at both ends of the computer equipment scale. Major developments have been supercomputers and microcomputers. Another major development has been the introduction of database software and fourth-generation application development languages.

Definitions

Write a complete sentence that defines each of the terms below.

information overload	data
data processing	transform
capture	system
information processing	systems analysis
computer	program
operating system	software
hardware	system software

Questions to Think About

Based on what you have learned to date about computers in business, answer the following questions in one or more complete sentences.

1. How does your report card model your achievements and status as a student?

2. Why were information requirements minimal during the early days of United States history?

3. How did the growth of companies affect the need for information by owners and managers?

4. How did the introduction of the typewriter change the staffing of business offices and the methods for producing correspondence?

5. What problem led to the development of punched card machines and what solution resulted?

6. What are data and information and what are the differences between them?

7. Who are systems analysts and what kind of work do they do?

8. What major events contributed to the widespread use of punched card machines and what problems were associated with these events?

9. How did events and developments during World War II contribute to the introduction of computers?

10. What features qualify a set of equipment to be called a computer?

Projects

The purpose of the assignments below is to encourage you to increase your learning through outside reading or work assignments.

1. Visit a medium- or large-sized computer center in your area. Gather information about the sizes and capacities of the equipment units in the installation. Compare the equipment at the computer center with the units that make up a typical microcomputer in your school's computer lab. How are the large computers different? How are they similar?

2. Through reading or through a visit to a computer center, find out how jobs are presented to large computer systems for processing. Then gather the same information about the handling of jobs on a microcomputer at your school. How are the methods different? How are they similar?

3. During the 1960s, the large computers that controlled space missions and major research projects had memories of appoximately 64,000 characters (64K) of information. Through reading, find out how this compares with the capacities of today's microcomputers. Describe the impact of technology on computer capacities over a period of a little more than two decades.

CHAPTER 17

How Do Computers Handle Information?

The Think Tank

When you finish reading this chapter and complete your work assignments, you should be able to answer the following questions.

❑ What is information retrieval?

❑ What is computer storage and why is this function so important to an information system?

❑ How are data and information organized for storage and retrieval by computers?

❑ What are files and databases and how are they related?

DOING BUSINESS

Darlene arrived by bus at the hospital at about 3:45 in the afternoon, shortly after school let out. She looked excited and followed the signs leading to the maternity wing. When Darlene saw a woman behind a counter in the waiting area, she felt too happy to keep quiet any longer.

"I'm an aunt!" she said to the woman. "My brother had a baby girl!"

The woman laughed. "You mean your sister-in-law had a baby girl, don't you? But, never mind, this is an exciting time for you," the woman replied, and then greeted Darlene. "I'm Lila, the administrator for the maternity ward," she said. "Unfortunately, you'll have to wait a few minutes. You can visit with your new niece and your sister-in-law at 4 o'clock."

Lila turned to a computer display unit on the counter. "What is your sister-in-law's last name?" she asked Darlene.

"Trenton. Why?"

Lila pressed a few keys on the keyboard and waited about three or four seconds. "Let's see what's on the screen," Lila said. "Sandy Trenton," she went on, "gave birth to Georgia Ann at 7:43 this morning. Georgia Ann weighed in at seven pounds, three ounces, has blue eyes and is in good health."

"Wow!" Darlene exclaimed. "You know more about Sandy's baby than I do."

Lila swiveled the screen of her computer display so that Darlene could see the information. Near the top of the screen was the heading BIRTH RECORD. The name GEORGIA ANN TRENTON was on the next line of the screen. Darlene then studied the other information items on the screen.

"This is really interesting," Darlene commented as she reviewed the display. "Is all of this stuff stored inside the computer in some way?" Darlene asked.

Healthy uses for computer capabilities have been developed in medical laboratories and in many other medical applications. In this photo, a computer is being used to analyze blood specimens.
COURTESY OF NATIONAL INSTITUTES OF HEALTH

"That's right," Lila replied. "Georgia Ann is only one of many thousands of babies who have been born at this hospital. I can instruct the computer to locate and display any of their birth records. And, for any given record, it only takes a few seconds.

"This is all so interesting to me," Darlene said. "Maybe I'll work in a hospital some day."

"Maybe you will," Lila laughed. "Right now, I have another piece of information that will interest you."

"What's that?" Darlene asked.

"It's 4 o'clock," Lila replied.

MEANING

Darlene is learning about the benefits of using computers to store information. For a hospital, newborn babies are a business activity. For other businesses, other kinds of information might be needed. The computer doesn't know the difference. People do. The computer will handle any information that people instruct it to, as long as standard letters, numbers, or symbols are used.

The basic mission of a hospital is to take care of people. People go to hospitals to have babies, to get well, or to receive other **health-care services.** But a hospital also has another role: It is a business, a service business. Health-care services represent business transactions. In turn, the patients of a hospital are its customers.

Health-care organizations generate extremely large volumes of information as they deliver services. Obviously, some method must exist for storing this information—and for finding it as needed.

Recall that computers are an excellent tool for managing information. This is true especially when high volumes of information threaten to overload users. Information should be an **asset** to users, not a burden. An asset, of course, is something that is owned and has value. Typical assets of a hospital would be money, buildings, medical equipment,

Business Terms
health-care service   Professional care that involves medical attention or care for persons who are ill.
asset   An item that is owned and has value.

and the talents of its staff. In addition, information about patients, diseases, and treatments is a vital asset. Also, the information that models the hospital as a business is essential. Any organization needs this kind of information to stay in business.

HOW ARE INFORMATION ASSETS USED?

Lila is said to be one of the *users* of the information system at the hospital. The ability to use stored information is important to Lila. Clearly, she qualifies as an information worker. She needs information to do her job.

As Lila demonstrated to Darlene, *retrieving* computer-stored information, such as selected birth records, is quick and simple. Retrieving includes the actions needed to find and display information in a usable form. The term *information retrieval* is another way to describe this process. In the story, Lila enters a brief command—the mother's last name. The computer does the rest. Only seconds after the request is made, a complete birth record is displayed.

Information retrieval may look easy. But that is only because the people who created the system understood Lila's needs. The system is designed specifically to follow commands from Lila and other information workers. The set of instructions followed to use a tool are known as *procedures.* It is necessary to follow procedures that apply to use of any computer. Procedures also are necessary for use of any business asset. This applies to cash, vehicles, land, or information. Each business will have procedures that protect all of its assets.

What Guides Planning For Information Retrieval?

In planning for storage and retrieval of information assets, users must think about the results they want to achieve. They need to understand what data will be put into the system and what information they want to get out.

As Lila has explained to Darlene, birth records alone may number in the thousands. In addition, hospital employees have to handle information for literally hundreds of other activities. For patients, examples include information about the person's condition, medical history, treatment history, medication taken, and diagnosis. Hospital employees also are responsible for requesting and processing payment for patient services. For staff members, administrators have to support activities that include the rounds of doctors, nurses, and other health-care specialists.

The point: Hospitals provide health-care services. But they run on information. Information is essential for medical treatment. Information storage and retrieval are central to the operations of hospitals or any other businesses. Remember that information models a business. Using the model properly helps people to do their jobs and to achieve the goals of their companies. Information resources also help people to solve problems and to make decisions.

To realize these benefits, information resources have to be managed. Today, if a company loses its information resources, it may be forced to go out of business. This has happened. A number of companies have had their computers destroyed by fire or flood. If the information developed by the computer is lost at the same time, the company may be unable to continue in business. Information stored in computers identifies customers, products, amounts owed to the business, and amounts owed to others. Without information resources, a company could not fill its orders, nor could it collect or pay bills. The only option, when disasters have destroyed information of many organizations, has been to go out of business.

HOW IS INFORMATION STORED BY COMPUTERS?

Computers are products of technology. Because they are complicated, they seem mysterious to many people. But that isn't the case at all. Computers consist of many parts, each of which performs simple operations. Complications result only because so

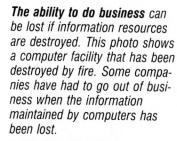
The ability to do business can be lost if information resources are destroyed. This photo shows a computer facility that has been destroyed by fire. Some companies have had to go out of business when the information maintained by computers has been lost.

COURTESY OF DATA PROCESSING MANAGEMENT ASSOCIATION

many simple things happen in extremely short periods of time. To understand computers, it is best to look to their basic simplicity.

The first thing to do is to get rid of the myths that often surround computers. A computer can perform so many simple tasks so quickly that it often appears to be thinking for itself. This is untrue. Computers don't think. They need people to create the sets of instructions, or programs, that direct their operations.

All computers, large and small, operate on a simple principle. That is, results are achieved either by directing or halting the flow of electrical current through circuits. A computer processor chip may have thousands of these circuits. At any given moment in the operation of a computer, some circuits are switched "on" while others are switched "off."

Think of what happens when you enter a darkened room at night. You throw a switch and there is light. The room is light or dark depending on whether the switch is on or off. In a computer, a circuit is connected or disconnected. That's all that can happen. Each circuit is on or off. Of course, there may be millions of circuits. But the basic structure is simple and uncomplicated.

When a computer handles data, it actually is altering the flow of current through its circuits. To illustrate, think about how a computer stores instructions to be followed and data to be processed. To support processing, each computer has a *main memory*. This unit also is called *primary storage*. Its

Business Terms

user, information
A person who requires information for job performance.

retrieve or **information retrieval**
In information processing, the reading or recalling of stored information.

procedure
A set of instructions followed to use a tool or device. In information processing, the instructions followed to process data and develop information.

main memory
A high-speed storage device that supports computer processing.

primary storage
See main memory.

function is to support processing by providing instructions and information.

The more main memory a computer has, the more efficiently it can operate. Therefore, modern computers, including microcomputers, will have hundreds of thousands, even millions, of circuits that store units of data. Main memory, in fact, refers to circuits of computer chips that store electronic signals. These "on" and "off" flows of current, in a sense, represent the "language" of a computer.

How Do Computers Code Information?

But how can this be? Think back to the light switch in the darkened room. When you turn the switch on, electric current flows to the bulb and the light goes on. When you turn the switch off, you cut the flow of electricity and the light goes off.

Now imagine trying to communicate by flipping several light switches on and off in different patterns. For instance, consider that you have six lamps, and six light switches to work with. To represent the "on" and "off" patterns of the switches, you assign each switch a number—either a 1 or a 0 *digit.* A digit is simply one of the 10 numbers from 0 through 9. You assign the digit 1 to a switch that is turned on. If a switch is turned off, you assign it a 0.

To develop a way to communicate with a friend by using the lamps, you could assign a separate on-and-off pattern for each letter of the alphabet and each digit. For instance, the letter "A" might be represented as 000000 (all lamps off); the letter "B" might be represented as 000001 (only the rightmost lamp is on); and the letter "C" could be coded as 000011 (the two rightmost lamps are on).

By changing the on-and-off combinations continually, you could spell out entire words. This, in turn, would allow you to create sentences and paragraphs. Of course, you could also represent numbers, like "345" or "12,160." The process would be painfully slow, but you could communicate with

someone who understands your "light" language, illustrated in Figure 17-1.

Think back to the developments covered in the previous chapter. A major breakthrough in the communication of information occurred with introduction of the Morse telegraph. This was nothing more than a series of on-off signals generated by pressing a simple key. At one point, this was the main method of long-distance communication throughout the world. The difference lies in speed. A human telegrapher could handle perhaps 200 on-off signals per minute. A computer can handle millions each second. The process is basic and simple. The power applied makes a great difference.

Sequences of on-off signals are, in essence, how a computer stores data and information. Current flows through some memory circuits but is kept from flowing through other circuits. An "on" circuit represents a 1 digit; an "off" circuit is a 0 digit. Memory circuits are turned on and off in different patterns to represent letters of the alphabet, numbers, and other characters.

Another term for a system that is based on only two parts or values is *binary.* (In the Latin language, "bi" means "two.") Electricity passes through a computer circuit at the same speed at which light travels—186,000 miles per second. For this reason, a computer can store or alter a binary digit representation within less than one-millionth of a second.

Review 17.1

1. What is information retrieval?

2. What is the purpose or function of computer memory?

3. Why is a computer called a "binary" device?

HOW ARE BINARY DIGITS USED TO ORGANIZE INFORMATION?

You know that computer memory represents letters, numbers, and other characters according to a *binary*

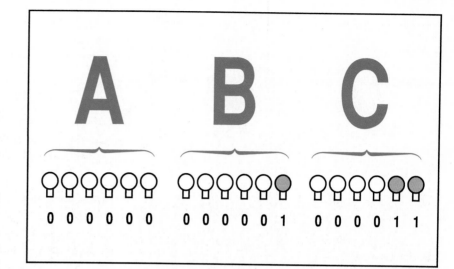

Figure 17-1. *Binary coding consists of a series of on-off conditions in electrical devices. A series of light bulbs sometimes is used to show how electrical signals can be controlled to represent information values.*

code. In computer terminology, each 1 or 0 digit is called a ***bit*** (for ***b**inary dig**it***). You certainly don't need to know how to read binary code to use computers. But you can benefit by understanding the basic binary principle of these machines. The reason: Bits are the building blocks for organizing and storing large volumes of information electronically. When a group of binary digits is combined to represent a character, the bits are said to represent a ***byte*** of data.

For instance, one widely used form of binary code uses seven digit positions to represent characters. In this coding system, the letter "A" represents one byte and is coded as 1000001; the letter "B" represents another byte and is coded as 1000010; and so on. This code is called ***ASCII*** (for ***American Standard Code for Information Interchange***). ASCII is used with most personal computers and some larger computers. ASCII also is the standard coding system for communicating information between different types of computers.

Another widely used coding scheme is called ***EBCDIC*** (for ***Extended Binary Coded Decimal Interchange Code***). The EBCDIC code uses eight digit positions, rather than seven. For this reason, EBCDIC can represent more characters than ASCII. EBCDIC is used chiefly for large, mainframe computers but also is used with some smaller computers.

Figure 17-2 shows the binary codes and the characters they represent for both ASCII and EBCDIC.

Business Terms

digit
A place value in a number system, such as 0 through 9 in the decimal system or 0 and 1 in the binary system.

binary
A number system with two values, 0 and 1.

binary code
A set of instructions based on the values 0 and 1.

bit
A binary digit with a value of 0 or 1.

byte
A set of bits that represent one unit in a character set processed by a computer; can be letters, numbers, or symbols.

ASCII (American Standard Code for Information Interchange)
A binary code set used in data communication and as the machine language for many microcomputers.

EBCDIC (Extended Binary Coded Decimal Interchange Code)
A binary coded machine language for large computers, particularly those made by IBM.

Character	Extended BCD Interchange Code (EBCDIC)	ASC II-7
0	1111 0000	011 0000
1	1111 0001	011 0001
2	1111 0010	011 0010
3	1111 0011	011 0011
4	1111 0100	011 0100
5	1111 0101	011 0101
6	1111 0110	011 0110
7	1111 0111	011 0111
8	1111 1000	011 1000
9	1111 1001	011 1001
A	1100 0001	100 0001
B	1100 0010	100 0010
C	1100 0011	100 0011
D	1100 0100	100 0100
E	1100 0101	100 0101
F	1100 0110	100 0110
G	1100 0111	100 0111
H	1100 1000	100 1000
I	1100 1001	100 1001
J	1101 0001	100 1010
K	1101 0010	100 1011
L	1101 0011	100 1100
M	1101 0100	100 1101
N	1101 0101	100 1110
O	1101 0110	100 1111
P	1101 0111	101 0000
Q	1101 1000	101 0001
R	1101 1001	101 0010
S	1110 0010	101 0011
T	1110 0011	101 0100
U	1110 0100	101 0101
V	1110 0101	101 0110
W	1110 0110	101 0111
X	1110 0111	101 1000
Y	1110 1000	101 1001
Z	1110 1001	101 1010

Figure 17-2. *Standard formats used to code data for computer processing are shown in this table.*

Again, it isn't necessary for you to learn binary code. Just keep in mind that, in general, one byte in memory is used to represent one character.

How Are Bits Used To Represent Data?

Just as bits can be grouped to represent different bytes (characters), so can bytes be combined to represent individual facts, or *data items*. For instance, your age represents a basic fact that describes you. In the story, the item "7 lbs., 3 oz." represents an important fact about Georgia Ann. The item "blue eyes" is another important data item.

When one or more characters of data are used to represent a single item or fact, they are said to be a *field* of data. A field is the same as a data item. Still another term used to describe a basic unit of data is *data element*. Regardless of the name used, a field is a single item of data that describes a person, place, event, object, or idea. The data elements, "7 lbs., 3 oz." and "blue eyes" are two items that describe Georgia Ann Trenton.

What Happens When Data Fields Are Combined?

Recall that a field of data, by itself, has little meaning, possibly none. The field "blue eyes," by itself, has no meaning because you have nothing with which to relate it. When "blue eyes" stands alone, you really can't tell what it means. When "blue eyes" is combined with several other facts, meaningful information results, as shown in Figure 17-3, a display that describes Georgia Ann.

The display in Figure 17-3, a collected list of fields, now represents information. Combining data elements has created meaning. Specifically, this collection of fields represents information that identifies Georgia Ann Trenton as a new person. In computer

Figure 17-3. Information records consist of a series of related data items about the same person, place, thing, event, or idea. In this case, the set of data items identifies a newborn baby.

```
                    BIRTH RECORD
                  CITY GENERAL HOSPITAL
                   STATE OF NEW YORK


PATIENT NAME:    Georgia Ann Trenton       DOB: 06/18/89    TOB: 0734
STREET:   455 Nasau Blvd.   CITY: Mineola  ST: NY           ZIP 13106

                    PHYSICAL INFORMATION
SEX:  F     EYES: Blue    WT. 7 lb. 3 oz.            BLOOD TYPE:  O


                        PARENTS
MOTHER:   Elena Listeck Trenton   AGE:  27    BLOOD TYPE:  O
FATHER:   Mark Randolph Trenton   AGE:  29    BLOOD TYPE:  A
```

terminology, a related collection of fields is called a *record*.

The first line in Figure 17-3 identifies the display as a BIRTH RECORD. The fields displayed on the screen represent a single birth record, for Georgia Ann Trenton. The individual fields develop a full picture, including her name, time and date of birth, address, color of eyes, and birth weight. Other fields provide her blood type, her parents' names, and the county in which she was born.

The point: Individual fields, which seem meaningless by themselves, become meaningful when they are related and grouped to form a record—an item of information.

Review 17.2

1. What is a bit?
2. What is a byte?
3. What is a data item?

HOW ARE INFORMATION RECORDS ORGANIZED FOR STORAGE AND USE?

Lila has explained to Darlene that the birth record for Georgia Ann is one of several thousand birth and

Business Terms

data item
One or more bytes used as a unit to represent a raw fact or figure that can be processed to generate information.

field
See data item.

data element
See data item.

record
A group of related data items that describes a person, place, thing, event, or idea.

other patient records in the hospital's computer. The appearance of each of these records is similar. That is, all records that describe patients of the hospital share the same types of fields, although the data elements in each record will be different.

For instance, the patient record for Harold J. Esteban would contain a field for his name, his date of birth, time of birth. Other fields would cover his birth weight if he was born in that hospital, his eye color, his blood type, and so on. The birth record for Judith Radke also would contain these fields. Of course, Harold J. Esteban and Judith Radke have different weights, different dates of birth, and other differences in data fields.

Even though the content of their records is not identical, the *format* of each record is the same. The term "format," in this case, means that each record contains the same basic field positions. Also, the number of bytes available in each field will be the same. This is true for each of thousands of records in the hospital's computer files. A computer needs this kind of uniform *structure* for data items and records. In this sense, structure describes the formats used for data items and records. That is, each record will have the same number of fields, the same field names, and the same number and type (numbers or letters) of bytes in each field.

When records with identical structures are grouped for use, they are said to form a *file*. A file is a collection of records with matching formats and related information. Files also share similar use patterns. This means that a program that can access any record in a file should be able to access all of the records. Also, the records in any given file contain information that meets similar user needs. Figure 17-4 diagrams the principles of data formats and structures.

Lila understands that all birth records make up a single file stored by the computer system. Knowledge of the file structure helps guide Lila in performing her job. To illustrate, imagine that Lila produces a daily report that lists the names and weights of babies born that day. This report would have to be submitted to county officials who record birth records. An example of a report that might result is shown in Figure 17-5.

The point: Organizing related records into files allows people to process and retrieve information quickly and in useful ways. Thus, the files stored by a business are at the heart of an information system. A company's files, taken together, model the business. In this sense, a model is a set of information that tells about the operations and status of a company. The information files describe the company's day-to-day business activities as well as its history. In turn, people rely on the content of files to perform their routine tasks, to solve problems, and to make important decisions.

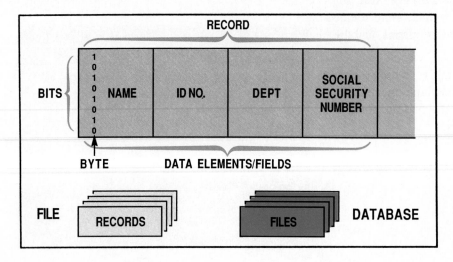

Figure 17-4. This diagram demonstrates the relationships used to form data structures, including bits, bytes, fields, records, files, and databases.

```
                    BIRTH REPORT
                CITY GENERAL HOSPITAL
                 STATE OF NEW YORK

      LAST NAME        FIRST NAME      MIDDLE NAME    LBS   OZ    S
      ADAMS            DAVID           ROBERT          7    5     M
      BILLINGS         THOMAS          ALFRED          8    2     M
      DENNING          CYNTHIA         ROSE            6    4     F
      FEIGN            JENNIFER        HELENE          6    8     F
      HOROWITZ         BENJAMIN        SAUL            8    7     M
      LAU              ROBIN           NMI             6    0     F
      NEWBERG          SUSAN           CHARLENE        5    11    F
      TRENTON          GEORGE          ANN             7    3     F
      ZYFFER           ARMAND          HENRY           7    8     M
```

Figure 17-5. *Files—and reports—are formed by grouping sets of related records. In this example, a computer-maintained file is used to generate a report on babies born in a hospital.*

WHAT HAPPENS WHEN MULTIPLE FILES HAVE TO BE SHARED?

An information system may store and process several files. It is not uncommon for a large business, such as a hospital, to have several hundred files. A birth file would be one, while a patient file might be another. An accounts receivable file would be another requirement. This file would contain records covering charges to patients for health-care services. The accounts receivable file would be used to process and mail *statements,* or bills, to patients who owe money to the hospital. Each patient represents a separate account record in every file.

For many businesses, it is helpful, even necessary, to relate information contained in different files. It also may be necessary to process existing files in different ways. For example, a hospital would combine information contained in separate files. Each birth record would be used to set up a new patient file. The patient file contains medical information for each patient who has been cared for in the hospital. Different departments of the hospital, such as X-ray and laboratories, would establish files on the treatments they provide.

Business Terms

format
The design or arrangement of a group of data items to form a record.

structure
A plan of organization for data items that results in a record format and in specifications for relationships among groups of records.

file
A collection of records with matching formats and related information.

statement
A document that tells a buyer an amount to be paid to a seller. Statements usually are issued after products are delivered or services are completed.

In running the hospital as a business, it often is necessary to find and combine information from different files. Until recently, use of files in this way—cross-referencing—was difficult or impossible. To meet the needs of users, software specialists known as *computer scientists* developed new information processing tools. Special system software products now make it commonplace to coordinate use of computer-stored files. These software products, and there are many available, are called "database management systems (DBMS)."

A database management system includes a set of programs that relates and processes information contained in multiple (separate) files. In turn, the collection of files that the DBMS processes is called a "database." Thus, all the information that Lila and other employees use is available as part of a single database. This database contains many files. However, under control of the DBMS software, it is possible to access records and fields from different files. This information then can be processed by separate programs to produce reports and other important information. Figure 17-6 is a diagram that shows how a DBMS controls access to multiple files.

To illustrate, a medical research project might call for identification of all patients who were treated for a specific disease or condition. The DBMS would provide commands that would direct the computer to search the diagnosis fields in patient records. The computer could produce a list of patients to be included in the research. Or, the computer could generate full treatment records for all patients. The information provided and the use of information resources is controlled by people—always.

A DBMS has many other advantages. These advantages, as well as the basic capabilities of a DBMS, are discussed in Chapter 22. For now, recognize that a database and DBMS programs provide a way to link different files. As you will see, this approach to file processing can be matched to the way a company does business.

WHERE ARE DATA AND INFORMATION STORED?

You know that data and information can be stored by a computer system over a long period of time. You know also that storage is through binary coding in structures that include bytes, fields, records, files, and databases.

During processing, data and program instructions are stored in memory. But memory is only a small part of computer hardware that is involved in storing and using information. The point of this chapter is that anyone interested in the role of computers in business should begin by understanding the value of information assets. That's where you are now. In the next chapter, you will be ready to look at the computer equipment that handles and stores data. This same equipment will accept input of data that you provide and also will deliver information according to your instructions.

Review 17.3

1. What is a record format?

2. What is a data structure?

3. What is a file?

4. What is a database?

5. What is a database management system?

Business Terms

computer scientist
A professional who designs software tools to facilitate use of computers.

Chapter Summary

❏ The main value of computers for people lies in the ability to store and retrieve information—in usable form.

❏ Information storage is through a series of electronic switches that can be set only in two positions, on and off. Data and information are represented in combinations of on and off patterns.

❏ Because it functions electrically, a computer is a two-state, or binary, device.

❏ A single on or off position in computer storage is called a bit, for binary digit.

❏ A group of bits that can be combined to represent a letter, number, or symbol is called a byte.

❏ One or more bytes can represent an item of data. The smallest unit of data maintained by computers is known as a data item, field, or element. A data element, by itself, has little or no meaning. Fields must be combined to create meaningful information.

❏ A group of fields that describes a person, place, event, object, or idea is a record.

❏ When multiple records with the same format are grouped, the result is a file. A file structure organizes information for storage and retrieval within computer systems.

❏ When information systems require access to multiple files, special software can be used to combine fields from these different files. The software is known as a database management system (DBMS). The collection of related files is called a database. A database models a company or a part of a company.

Definitions

Write a complete sentence that defines each of the terms below.

receive   procedure

main memory	digit
binary	bit
byte	field
record	file
database	DBMS

Questions to Think About

Based on what you have learned to date, answer the following questions in one or more complete sentences.

1. Why is the ability to store and retrieve information the most important benefit from use of computers in business?

2. In what way is computer-stored information a business asset?

3. Why is the coding system of computers referred to as binary?

4. What are bits of data and what is their function?

5. What are bytes and what do they do?

6. What is an item, field, or element of data and what does it contain?

7. What is a record and what does it contain?

8. What is a file and how is a file organized?

9. What is a database?

10. How does a database work and how is it used?

11. What is the meaning of the term, structure, in connection with data and information?

Projects

The purpose of the assignments below is to encourage you to increase your learning through outside reading or work assignments.

1. Determine what data items are needed to describe yourself as a student. List the main fields that would be included in your student record.

2. Develop a diagram for a file containing records for all the students in your class.

CHAPTER 18

What Is a Computer Information System?

The Think Tank

When you finish reading this chapter and complete your work assignments, you should be able to answer the following questions.

❏ What is a computer information system?

❏ What hardware devices are required for a computer information system and what is the role of each?

❏ How does a computer process data to deliver information?

❏ What roles do people play in developing and using a computer information system?

❏ Why are procedures important to the operation of a computer information system?

DOING BUSINESS

When Dan Turnkey's father came home from work, Dan was playing a popular game on his father's personal computer. Dan's father was becoming concerned. He was afraid that Dan's knowledge of computers began and ended with games.

"Dan," Mr. Turnkey asked during dinner, "how would you like to spend an afternoon at work with me? I thought I might give you a tour of our main computer information system in the building next door to the bank."

"All right!" Dan said.

The following afternoon, Dan met his father at the entrance to the bank's information systems building. As they entered the lobby, Dan's father told Dan he had to "sign in."

A guard at the entrance handed Dan a visitor's registration list. Dan wrote his name and the time he had arrived. The guard then handed Dan a badge to be pinned on his shirt. Next, he inserted a card into a strange-looking lock and pressed some buttons. The door buzzed and opened automatically. Dan looked amazed as he walked into a room full of computers.

"Seems like a lot of trouble to go to—just to protect a bunch of machinery," Dan commented.

"You've missed the point," Dan's father said. "Computer hardware can be replaced. We may be unable to replace the information generated by the computers."

During their tour of the computer center, Dan noticed a smaller room connected to the main room.

Protection of information resources *is a vital responsibility within the operation of computer information systems. This photo shows a controlled entrance to a computer facility. Employees insert their identification badges in an electronic lock. A computer identifies the badge and admits only those persons authorized to enter the facility.*

COURTESY OF LAWRENCE LIVERMORE
NATIONAL LABORATORY COMPUTER
CENTER MUSEUM

"This is our magnetic tape library," Dan's father said. "This room contains 'backup' tapes of all the information that our bank uses on a regular basis. A backup is simply a copy of a file or database. The room itself is fireproof and is locked when it isn't in use. The door and walls are capable of withstanding temperatures as high as 4,000 degrees Fahrenheit. In addition, we send copies of the files created today and yesterday to a warehouse in another city."

Dan looked puzzled. "You mean you keep one copy of files in the tape library and a separate copy in another city? Isn't that a waste of effort?"

Dan's father looked serious. "Not at all," Mr. Turnkey replied. "This information is as valuable to the bank as the money in the vault. Without the information, we couldn't do business. You see, Dan, computer games are fun, but they don't really have anything to do with the way computers are used in business."

"I guess not," Dan said. "Running and protecting this computer system isn't a game."

Dan's father smiled. "Now you're getting the point," he said.

MEANING

Dan's father was becoming concerned that Dan misunderstood the use and importance of computers in society. True, computers can be used to play games. However, computers serve valuable, serious purposes in society and in business. A computer, regardless of its size, is a tool and deserves to be respected and cared for.

The point: Information is an essential of business. Many safeguards—like those that Dan observed—are used chiefly to protect business information resources. Businesses need computers to deal with avalanches of information. Also, businesses depend on the information that results from supporting transactions and other processing.

WHAT IS A 'COMPUTER INFORMATION SYSTEM'?

A *computer information system (CIS)* consists of a group of resources that is used together to capture

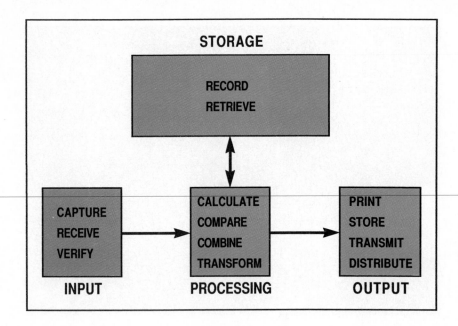

Figure 18-1. *Computer equipment performs four basic functions, identified in this diagram. Those functions are input, processing, output, and storage.*

data and generate information. The resources used to build a CIS include:

- Equipment
- Software
- People
- Procedures
- Facilities.

All five of these parts of a CIS should be integrated (combined) to form a working system. The sections below describe the importance and features of each of these parts of a CIS.

WHAT EQUIPMENT IS INCLUDED IN A CIS?

The term "equipment" refers to the devices, or hardware, used to set up and operate a CIS. Each unit of equipment is designed to perform a specific function:

- Input
- Processing

- Output
- Storage.

The first three of these functions are carried out in sequence. First, data items are entered into and captured within a computer. Next, processing changes the data into usable information. Then, information must be output so that it can be made available to people. This entire sequence of steps is supported by the ability to store information and make it available as needed. A diagram that outlines these steps, known as the ***information processing cycle***, is shown in Figure 18-1. The equipment units that can be used within a CIS are reviewed according to the functions they perform.

Which Devices Handle Input?

Input refers to the steps required to get data into a computer in usable form. As you know, a computer understands only electronic signals that are presented to circuits in binary form. That is, computer signals

Keyboards are the main devices used for input of data to computer systems. All keyboards have the same formats for entry of alphabetic and numeric information. Others may have special keys to control computer functions or special operations.

COURTESY OF MULTIMATE, AN ASHTON-TATE COMPANY

have to be input as streams of 1 and 0 bits. Computers understand and use binary code; people don't. People work with sets of letters and numbers. So, special input devices have been developed that convert data from a human-readable form into computer code. The main input units that you will encounter in your study of computers are identified and described below.

Keyboards.   The most widely used input device is the *keyboard.* A computer keyboard is similar to the keyboard of a typewriter. It has separate keys for letters of the alphabet, numbers, and special characters. Each key that is pressed sends a different electronic signal to the computer. In turn, each signal represents a different binary-coded character.

Most computer keyboards also contain a *numeric keypad.* This part of the keyboard allows people to enter numbers into the computer quickly. When keys are pressed, they usually are displayed on a screen called a *monitor.* A keyboard and monitor are part of virtually all microcomputers.

Mouse.   One of the jobs required to complete computer input is to select information, programs, or

Business Terms

computer information system (CIS)
A group of resources used together to capture data and generate information.

information processing cycle
The sequence of steps followed in processing data to develop information; the steps are input, processing, output, and storage.

input
The process followed to capture data in a computer in usable form.

keyboard
A set of keys that represent letters, numbers, and symbols that is used for computer input.

numeric keypad
The portion of a keyboard designed for high-speed input of numeric data.

monitor
A display device that presents information for user reference.

Use of a mouse *speeds the movement of a cursor and the selection of menu options provided by a computer.*

COURTESY OF RADIO SHACK, A DIVISION OF TANDY CORPORATION

up from counting or measuring devices. For example, many computers sense temperature readings and control heating or air conditioning systems. Other computers sense information about the condition of an automobile engine and identify repair requirements. In factories, computers accept inputs from production machinery. Also, some input devices have the ability to read text or special codes and enter information directly into the computer.

Computers also have the ability to read inputs at high speeds from storage devices like those described below. These include storage devices that record information on disk or tape units. Some computer systems still input information from punched cards.

The result is the same for each input method. Information is converted into codes that can be handled and stored in computer equipment.

services required. The most common method is through displays that react to keyboard entries. When a computer is turned on, a display called a ***menu*** is presented to the user on the monitor. The menu gets its name from the fact that it presents a list of choices. The user can select the program or service needed by entering numbers or letters through the keyboard.

As an alternative, some systems present ***icon*** menus and permit users to make choices through use of a ***mouse.*** An icon is a picture that represents a function or service that the computer can provide. A mouse is a small device that rolls around on the desktop alongside the computer. As the mouse is moved, an arrow on the display screen matches its movement. The mouse can be used to point to the icon for a needed service. Then a button on the mouse is pressed, or "clicked," and the selection is made. To illustrate the icon principle, a picture of a garbage can presents the option to discard an unwanted file.

Other input sources.   Computers also can accept input from a number of other sources. For example, signals from many machines, including cash registers, can be sensed and input directly into computers. In other instances, input signals can be picked

1. What are the main parts, or elements, of a computer information system?

2. What are the steps in the information processing cycle?

3. What is the main method for computer input?

4. What is a mouse and what does it do?

How Does a Computer Process Information?

Processing involves the activities that change, or ***transform,*** input data to produce information. The processing that a computer can perform is simple and limited. Simplicity is necessary because all processing is done by setting "on" or "off" switches on electric circuits.

The point: The things a computer does are simple and easy to understand. The power that a computer provides comes from doing simple jobs quickly and in large quantities. Computers in use today can process anywhere from 2 million to 80 million in-

Computer circuits are built onto tiny microchips that are assembled in groups and mounted on boards, as shown in this photo. Groups of chips form computer processors and memory units.

COURTESY OF DATA PROCESSING MANAGEMENT ASSOCIATION

A computer can direct its own processing according to the result of a comparison.

That is, the program uses the result of a comparison to determine what part of a program should be performed next. In this way, a computer can perform thousands, even millions, of operations on its own. To illustrate, a student grading program might compare an average earned by each student with a value stored in the computer. Suppose the computer stored the value 90. Each student record with a grade average of 90 or more would be assigned an A. Lower numbers would be used to check for and assign lesser grades.

structions in one second. Thus, computing power comes from the speed of electricity.

The simplicity of the operations performed is demonstrated by a single fact: All computer processing is limited to two operations:

- Comparison
- Arithmetic.

Comparison operations. During a *comparison* operation, the computer can compare two values to determine whether they are equal or unequal. If the two numbers are unequal, the computer can tell if one is larger or smaller than the other.

A computer can compare only two numbers at one time. For instance, a computer might be asked to compare the numbers 2 and 7. Consider that the computer program contains an instruction that guides the comparison. This instruction requests the computer to **return** the larger of the two numbers. Programmers use the term ''return'' to describe the way a computer handles the result of a comparison or arithmetic operation. In this case, the number 7 is greater than 2. The program then would return the number 7. This is an important computer feature.

Business Terms

menu
A list or display that presents a series of choices for selection by a computer user.

icon
A picture that represents a function or service that the computer can provide.

mouse
A small device that rolls around on the desktop alongside the computer as a tool for moving the cursor and selecting menu options.

processing
The activities, including calculations and comparisons, that change, or transform, input data to produce information.

transform
To alter, or change, data through processing to produce information.

comparison
A computer operation that matches values of two items to determine if they are equal or unequal and, if unequal, whether one is larger or smaller than the other.

return
The result delivered to a user by a computer following execution of a comparison operation.

This capability sets a computer apart from all other electronic devices. Consider a hand-held calculator: Say that you have just finished adding two numbers on your calculator. The window in the calculator displays the result. However, it's up to you to take the next step. You need to keep pressing keys and directing the calculator's operations—each step of the way.

With a computer, on the other hand, this wouldn't be necessary. Once a program designed by a person has been stored in a computer, the computer can proceed on its own. Long sequences of instructions can be followed automatically, until desired results are delivered.

Arithmetic operations. In the sections above, you read that a computer can compare only two numbers at a time. Computer arithmetic is just as simple. That is, computer arithmetic always takes place by adding two numbers at a time. The computer simply combines the binary codes in two different circuits.

By adding numbers in different ways, a computer can perform sophisticated math functions. For instance, consider that subtraction is negative addition. The two math operations below are the same, but are written differently:

$$5 - 2 = 3$$
$$5 + -2 = 3$$

The second operation is negative addition and represents the approach that a computer would use. Similarly, multiplication is repeated addition. Division, in turn, is repeated negative addition. By building upon this simple concept of addition, the computer can handle virtually any type of mathematical operation.

Processing equipment. Computer processing is done in a device, known as a *central processing unit (CPU)*. The CPU has two main parts—main memory and the *processor*. You already know about main memory from Chapter 17. Main memory consists of a series of microchips with the circuits that store data and program instructions temporarily.

The temporary nature of storage in memory is important. Information and instructions are held in main memory only briefly. First, items are brought into memory to await processing. Then, after processing, they are held only until they can be moved to a storage or output device. If information is to be held for a long time, it must be transferred out of memory. Also, memory is temporary because it is *volatile*. A volatile material evaporates easily. Thus, the term "volatile" means that the information in memory evaporates when the supply of electric power is interrupted. Accidental interruptions of electricity also wipe out memory.

The processor is the part of the CPU that makes comparisons, performs arithmetic, and directs the course of processing. In a personal computer, the processor is contained on a single microchip. That's how the microcomputer got its name: It uses a microchip as its processor. In larger computers, the processor might include several microchips. In any case, the processor of a computer has three major types of circuits:

- Arithmetic circuits
- Logic circuits
- Control circuits.

Arithmetic circuits perform the repeated addition operations involved in computer mathematics.

Logic circuits perform the comparison operations that help a computer guide the course of its operations.

Control circuits are used to direct computer processing. For instance, when a computer makes a comparison, the returned result is transferred to control circuits to be carried out. These circuits also handle the program instructions that direct computer processing. To do this, the control circuits also must control the writing and reading operations of main memory. Further, control circuits also direct the transmission functions involved in input, output, and storage devices. Figure 18-2 diagrams the relationships among CPU components.

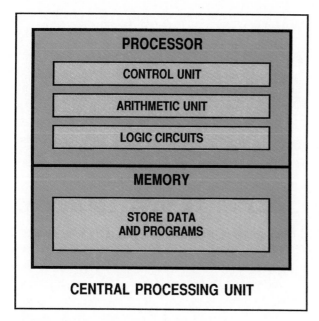

Figure 18-2. *A central processor includes circuits for control, arithmetic, logic, and memory.*

Review 18.2

1. What are the two basic processing functions that a computer can perform?

2. Which processing function does a computer use to direct the flow of processing?

3. How does a computer perform subtraction, multiplication, and division?

4. What are the parts of a central processing unit and what do they do?

5. Why is computer memory described as volatile?

How Are Outputs Generated?

To provide value to people, information must be delivered, or *output.* Output involves transmission of data items from the CPU to devices that will record, print, or store information. Also, outputs can involve transmission of signals between two or more computers or between computers and other equipment.

The output function encompasses distribution of information to users who require information to do their jobs. For distribution, it typically is necessary to display or print information in forms that are convenient for people.

Output devices include displays that can be viewed by people or printed documents that provide permanent records. Outputs also can be recorded on film in compact size. Some output devices draw pictures under computer control.

Business Terms

central processing unit (CPU)
The device within a computer that handles processing operations; consists of a processor and a main memory.

processor
The portion of a central processing unit that has circuits for execution of arithmetic, logic, and control functions.

volatile
Description of a property of computer memory; when power is turned off, memory is cleared of all stored information.

arithmetic circuit
An element within a CPU that performs repeated addition operations for mathematical calculations.

logic circuit
An element within a CPU that compares two values and directs the course of processing on the basis of results of the comparison.

control circuit
An element of a CPU that directs operation of computer hardware and the communication of information among devices that make up the computer.

output
The transmission of data items from a computer CPU to devices that record, print, or store information for reference and use by people.

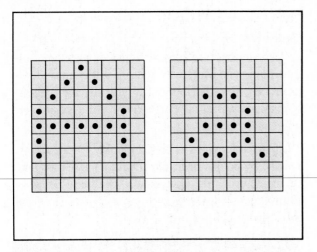

Figure 18-3. *Matrix printers form characters through a series of points within an imprint pattern, as illustrated.*

*A **daisy wheel** is used commonly to create letter-quality imprints.*

Output equipment. A monitor, described earlier, is an example of an output unit. When a computer processes data, the results are converted to characters that people can read. These conversions take place within special circuits that control the operations of the monitor. The characters then are displayed, or output, on the screen of the monitor.

A monitor displays only information that is stored in main memory. When a computer is turned off, the contents that are displayed on a monitor will disappear. For this reason, a monitor is used chiefly for temporary reference. When you input information or text, your keyboard entries are "mirrored" in a monitor display. Also, if you want to review information in computer files, you can enter instructions through the keyboard. The information you need is displayed on your monitor.

A more permanent form of output can be produced on **printers.** A printer produces a paper copy of the results of processing. Printed outputs also are called **hard copies.** Literally hundreds of different printers are available for use with computers. To understand printers, consider these four categories:

* Draft-quality printers
* Letter-quality printers

* High-speed printers
* Graphics.

A **draft-quality** printer uses a series of tiny wires to form characters. The wires strike an inked ribbon. The ink pattern then is transferred to paper. These units also are called **matrix printers** because the dotted patterns of the wires fall within a pattern known as a matrix. Figure 18-3 demonstrates how characters are formed through matrix patterns.

With a **letter-quality** printer, characters are pre-formed on a special **print element.** The principle is similar to the ball-type elements used on some typewriters. Letter-quality printers also transfer characters to paper by striking a ribbon. These can be cloth ribbons that are inked. Or they can be carbon-coated plastic. Because the characters are pre-formed, the print element of a letter quality printer produces high-quality outputs. By contrast, many draft quality printers print characters that are somewhat less easy to read. Both draft- and letter-quality devices are known as **character printers.** That is, they print just one character at a time. For higher volumes of output, a series of units with greater capacity can be used.

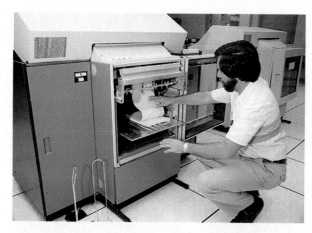

High-speed line printers are workhorses for computer documentation. Typical capacities are 2,000 lines per minute.

PHOTO BY ROBERT KOCH

Laser printers combine high quality and high speed in generating documents and reports. Costs also are relatively high.

PHOTO BY LISA SCHWABER-BARZILAY

One type of high-speed printer is the *line printer.* These devices get their name from the fact that an entire line of text is imprinted in a single operation. Line printers can output as many as 2,000 lines of text per minute, with up to 132 characters per line. By contrast, character printers have top speeds in the range of 200 characters per second, or perhaps 100 to 120 lines per minute.

High-speed outputs also can be achieved with *page printers,* also known as *laser printers*. These units form images on electrostatic drums like those used in xerographic copiers. The images are formed when a beam of high-intensity laser light scans the surface

Business Terms

printer
A computer output device that records information or images on paper for delivery to users.

hard copy
A printer output on paper, a document designed for delivery to users.

draft-quality printer
A character printer that produces text through imprints of dot-position patterns; finished documents are usable as drafts but are not of "letter quality."

matrix printer
See draft quality printer.

letter-quality printer
A character printer that produces high-quality outputs, usually at slower speeds than draft printers.

print element
The mechanism of a letter-quality printer that holds a pre-formed set of characters used in creating imprints.

character printer
An output device that imprints text one character at a time.

line printer
An output device that imprints a full line of type in a single operation; it generates documents at speeds of up to 2,000 lines per minute.

page printer
An output device that imprints a full page of text or images in a single operation. Functions through use of a laser beam that forms images on a xerographic drum.

laser printer
See page printer.

Computer graphics can add interest and meaning to outputs. The photo at left shows an integrated system that includes graphics input from a tablet, a computer display, and a color plotter for output. The photo below shows a color laser printer used for graphics output.

PHOTO AT LEFT COURTESY OF HEWLETT-PACKARD CO.; PHOTO BELOW COURTESY OF DIGITAL EQUIPMENT CORPORATION

of the drum under computer control. The light affects a magnetic field on the drum. A magnetic imaging material is attracted to the drum and transferred to paper. Different models of laser printers have output speeds ranging from eight pages to more than 7,000 pages per minute. These are full pages of text, each of which can contain as many as 56 lines of printed output.

In addition to processing character sets, computers also can create and process images. The technology is known as *computer graphics*. Simply, the computer divides an image area, such as a screen display, into many thousands of separate positions. Each position in a graphics area is a separate dot, or *pixel*. A pixel is a point on a display or printed output. Computer processing can establish color or black-and-white values for each pixel. The result is a drawing that consists of lines or shaded values. Outputs can be delivered on display screens, laser printers, or special devices called *plotters*. A plotter is a printer that drives a pen-like device called a *stylus* across the surface of a sheet of paper or film. The result is a picture that is drawn under control of a computer graphics program.

Many computers are equipped to transmit outputs over communication lines. These outputs are transmitted to other computers or to devices that process the computer-generated information. Computers serve as major communicators of information. Principles and methods of computer communication are covered in Chapter 26.

How Are Data and Information Stored for Long-Term Use?

Recall that main memory stores data and program instructions only temporarily. However, because infor-

Disk storage is the main method used for long-term storage of data. The drive shown uses multiple disk surfaces for high-capacity, random storage.

mation has become a business necessity, equipment is needed to store and retrieve computer-generated information. The term ''retrieve'' describes the overall process of finding and displaying or printing information held in computer files. Devices used to store information external to the computer processor are known as *secondary storage media.*

The term ''media'' is the plural form of ''medium.'' In this sense, a medium is a way to store and transmit information. Television and newspapers are two media that people use daily to store and/or transmit information. Secondary storage media used with computer systems provide another advantage. They store information in a form that computers can understand. Two widely used secondary storage media are *magnetic disk* and *magnetic tape.* In addition, a new technology that stores data through use of laser beams is coming into use.

Magnetic disk media.   Magnetic disks may be hard (rigid) or flexible. Flexible disks are also called *diskettes,* or *floppy disks.* In any case, the surface of a disk is magnetically sensitive. This means that the disk is coated with an iron-based material that can be magnetized or demagnetized. The principle is the

same as for audio or video tapes, except that diskettes are round platters that resemble phonograph records. Computer-coded information can be stored as a series of magnetized spots on circular *tracks* formed on a disk. The presence of a magnetic spot can indicate a 1 value; the absence of a magnetic spot can indicate a 0 value.

Business Terms

computer graphics
Reference to the ability of computers to generate image, as well as text, outputs.

pixel
A single point within an image-formation matrix generated by a computer.

plotter
An output device that generates drawn, graphic images.

stylus
A pen-like device that draws images on a computer plotter.

secondary storage media
Magnetically coated materials, such as disks or tapes, on which data are recorded for retrieval and continuing use.

magnetic disk
A storage medium that uses magnetically coated platters for the recording and storage of information.

magnetic tape
A storage medium that uses long strips of magnetically coated materials for the recording and storage of information.

diskette
Flexible magnetic storage medium used mostly with microcomputers.

floppy disk
See diskette.

track
A circular position on a magnetic disk that is used for the recording and storage of data.

Tape storage typically is used for programs and for backup and protection. Large numbers of reels can be involved.

These magnetic spots are written to or read from a disk by devices called *disk drives*. These drives use one or more metal arms that position *read/write heads* over the surface of a disk. The heads are responsible for recording or reading magnetic codes recorded on a disk.

Magnetic tape media.   Magnetic tape devices use the same magnetic principle as disk systems. That is, the tape is coated with magnetic material. A device called a *tape drive* contains read/write heads. As is the case with disk drives, the heads on a tape drive can record and read data to and from magnetic surfaces. Magnetic tapes are supplied in a number of ways, including reels, cassettes, or cartridges. Reels have to be threaded through drives and wound onto other reels. Cassettes and cartridges are self-contained. Tape reels are standard media for mass storage of backup files. A standard, 2,400-foot reel is inexpensive and can store up to 6,250 characters of data per inch. This means that many billions of characters of data can be stored—permanently and safely—on a single reel.

Laser disk devices.   Another method for storing data on disks is just coming into general use in the computer field. Under this method, a beam of laser light burns a series of coded entries onto the face of a plastic-coated disk. The codes can be read by a light beam that scans a surface on which recordings have been made. This technology handles storage of both data and images. Laser devices have extremely high capacities. Up to one billion characters of data can be recorded on one side of a laser disk. Initial versions of laser disks recorded data permanently. That is, once information was recorded, it could not be changed. Models being introduced at this writing have both read and write capabilities. Use of laser storage methods is expected to grow in the future.

Data access methods.   Magnetic disk and tape systems have different capabilities. With magnetic tape, records must be accessed in the same order, or sequence, in which they are recorded. It isn't possible to go immediately to a particular record stored in the middle of a reel of tape. The computer system must begin by reading the first record on tape and then continue in sequence.

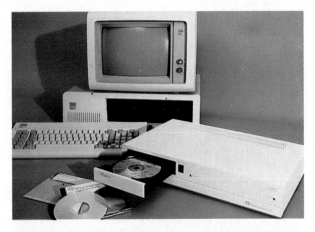

Laser disk storage provides high speeds and high capacities. Use of laser devices is expected to grow with introduction of read/write capabilities.

COURTESY OF REFERENCE TECHNOLOGY, INC.

widely. In fact, virtually all microcomputers used in business come with hard or floppy disk systems. Tape systems are used with microcomputers mostly as an efficient way to back up disk files.

Review 18.3

1. What are the differences—in method and performance—between character printers and line printers?

2. What is a laser printer and what are its main features?

3. What is sequential access?

4. What is direct access?

This approach to retrieval of records is called *sequential access*. Each time a tape is used, it must be processed completely by the computer—from beginning to end. Also, each time a tape is used, a new copy of its information must be written to a completely new tape. It is impossible to read and write data to the same tape. Generally, magnetic tape is used for jobs in which all or most of the records in a file are read each time. Magnetic tape also is used to make backups of files stored on disks.

Magnetic disks, on the other hand, support both sequential access and *direct access*. With direct access, it is possible to instruct the computer to go directly to a specific record. Each record stored on a disk has an *address,* or unique storage position. The operating system uses this address to position the read/write heads directly over a desired record.

Direct access is important for applications that require immediate access to a particular record or a group of records. Because disk systems have greater access capabilities than tape, they are used more

Business Terms

disk drive
A device that houses and uses magnetic disk media.

read/write head
A device that records and reads data on magnetically coated surfaces of magnetic tapes or disks.

tape drive
A device that houses and uses magnetic tape as a recording medium.

sequential access
An information retrieval pattern in which all records in a file must be read and processed in the order in which they are stored. Sequential access is essential to tape storage.

direct access
An information storage and retrieval technique under which records can be recorded and retrieved individually from any point within a file.

address
The unique storage position of a record retained on a magnetic disk device.

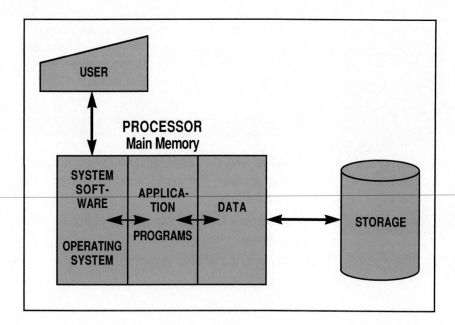

Figure 18-4. *Software represents the user within a computer system. As shown in this diagram, software provides direct interaction between user and the programs and data needed to process information.*

WHAT DOES SOFTWARE CONTRIBUTE TO A CIS?

Any computer needs two types of input before it can do anything—data and programs. Data are the raw facts and figures that a computer processes to deliver information. Programs are the sets of instructions that the computer follows to carry out processing. Two separate types of programs are required:

- Some programs control the operation of equipment.

- Others direct the processing of information for users.

All programs, taken together, are called *software.* Programs that control the operation of equipment are known as *system software.* Programs that direct the processing of information are called *application software.* The term *application* identifies any job that applies a computer to the processing of information. Applications are developed to meet the needs of information users.

What Is System Software?

System software programs are responsible for delivering hardware capabilities to users. One set of programs designed for this purpose is called the *operating system* of the computer. An operating system monitors and coordinates the operations of the hardware devices that make up a computer system. These devices might include a keyboard, monitor, disk drives, and a printer.

With a microcomputer, the most commonly used system software is called a *disk operating system (DOS).* For large computer systems, hundreds of different devices might be linked to the computer itself. The operating system for these big computers includes programs that manage the use of all of these devices. The operating system even manages the way the CPU processes application programs. Operating systems are written by people called *system programmers.*

What Are Application Programs?

An application is a set of related operations involved in performing a job. An application program contains the instructions for performing the operations to be carried out on computers.

For instance, a *word processor* is an application program that people use to process text. The word processor contains instructions for creating, editing, and printing documents. Other application programs are available for performing accounting tasks, for managing files, and so on. Application software is written by people called *application programmers.*

As a user of a computer information system, you will implement application programs. The reason: Application programs support business processing activities. You may have to know how to use such application packages as word processors, spreadsheets, and database management systems. These and other kinds of application software packages are described in later chapters.

HOW DO PEOPLE FIT INTO A CIS?

People are the reason any computer information system exists. The goal of any CIS is to deliver useful information to people. People also are responsible for monitoring and controlling the operations of a CIS.

For instance, in a large CIS installation, a single person often is responsible for making sure that a database management system satisfies users. This person is called a *database administrator.* Other CIS employees monitor the operations of hardware to make sure that the equipment is operating correctly. Programmers are another group of people who are important to a CIS. Perhaps most important, businesspeople themselves must participate in the development and operation of a CIS. Businesspeople are information users. They provide the guidance to help programmers and other system designers.

WHAT CONTRIBUTION IS MADE BY PROCEDURES?

All information systems, regardless of whether computers are involved, are guided by *procedures.* This

Business Terms

software
The complete set of programs that control computer operations.

system software
The set of programs that initiates, controls, and monitors operation of computer equipment.

application software
The programs that direct processing of user jobs.

application
A procedure, including programs, that applies a computer for a specific job or purpose.

operating system
A set of programs that monitor and coordinate the operations of the hardware devices that make up a computer system.

disk operating system (DOS)
An operating system package that is supplied on disk; DOS is the most widely used operating system for microcomputers.

system programmer
A programmer who specializes in writing system software.

word processor
An application program that sets up a computer for the processing of text.

application programmer
A person who prepares programs for the processing of user jobs.

database administrator
A person responsible for supporting use of and maintaining a DBMS.

procedure
The instructions and guidelines for operating an information system.

CIS facilities come in a wide range of sizes and capacities. The installation shown at left is a large, mainframe system. Below, CIS capacities are implemented on a desktop computer. All sizes and capacities have their place within the trillion-dollar annual computer industry.

PHOTO AT LEFT COURTESY OF COMPUTER SCIENCES CORPORATION; PHOTO BELOW COURTESY OF APPLE COMPUTER, INC.

term refers to all of the instructions and guidelines for operating the system. In a CIS, it is up to people to provide—and to follow—procedures.

Programs, because they are sets of instructions, provide procedures that apply to equipment. The procedures referred to here are those followed by people. Examples include instructions on how data items should be entered into a keyboard. Other procedures might cover the setup of secondary storage devices for an application or the types of forms to be used for outputs. In other words, procedures cover standards and instructions on how people and computers interact.

System procedures often are spelled out in *operations manuals* or *user manuals*. These manuals explain the capabilities of hardware devices and programs. They also provide instructions in the proper use of hardware and programs.

WHAT FACILITIES DOES A CIS NEED?

A *facility* is a place in which work is done. In a computer information system, facilities are the actual locations where hardware is installed. Also, facilities would include the workspace used by the people

involved in a CIS. CIS facilities may be a single room. Or, they may include dozens of offices and buildings all over the country. The size and *scope* of the facilities of a CIS depends on the scope of the business it supports. The term "scope" means range of activity or information content.

For instance, a computer information system might simply assist a business in processing its payroll or accounts receivable. In this case, the hardware might include only one or a few personal computers. In turn, the hardware and system operations might take place in a small office.

On the other hand, a large business might rely on its computer information system to handle processing at all levels of the business. The system might have to process hundreds of files and millions of records each day.

This kind of system probably would include a large computer and several smaller computers. The entire system might be linked to form a *network* between several buildings, or between locations in different cities. A network, then, is a way for people and their computers to communicate, even if they are in different places. The telephone system for your city or state is a type of network. A CIS network connects computers at different locations. In this way, people can use the combined power of network facilities to access information in many ways and many places.

CIS facilities can support a number of different sizes of computer system hardware, including the following:

- Personal computers (microcomputers)
- Minicomputers
- Mainframe computers
- Supercomputers.

Personal computers (microcomputers). All of the hardware for a *personal computer* is small enough to fit on a desktop. For this reason, these devices sometimes are called *desktop computers*. Of course, these units also are called microcomputers. A personal computer usually is operated by one person at a time and normally runs only one program at a time. Personal computers are used in homes, schools, and businesses. In business, a personal computer is often part of a *workstation*. A workstation is a place where a person performs most of his or her daily activities.

In a business today, a workstation for an employee often includes a personal computer system. This small computer might be linked with a larger computer to become part of a network. The personal computer handles routine processing activities for the employee. It also provides a way to access information stored in the files of the main computer for a business.

Minicomputers. A *minicomputer* is larger and more powerful than a microcomputer. Businesses often use a minicomputer to support a small network for a single department or branch office. The network typically includes several personal computers linked with the minicomputer. In many cases, the facilities for this type of network are located in one

Business Terms

operations manual
A published set of instructions for operating an information system.

user manual
See operations manual.

facility
A place in which work is done; in a CIS, an actual location where hardware is installed.

scope
In a CIS, a term that defines a range of activity or information content.

network
A group of computers and other devices linked through communication channels for access by multiple users from multiple points.

personal computer
A small computer, also called a "microcomputer," that uses a microchip as its processor.

desktop computer
See personal computer.

workstation
A place where a person performs most of his or her daily activities.

minicomputer
A full capability computer, larger and more powerful than a microcomputer, that performs most of the functions of a large, mainframe system but is smaller.

building. If so, the system is called a *local area network.* The processing power and storage capabilities of a minicomputer allow it to run several programs at one time.

Mainframe computers.   *Mainframe* computers are larger and more powerful than minicomputers. A mainframe computer provides the main source of computing power for medium- and large-size businesses. A mainframe computer can store hundreds of billions of bytes of information. This fact makes mainframe computers ideal for operating large databases that provide information for an entire business.

Supercomputers.   A *supercomputer* uses an ultra-high-capacity processor to expand the amount of computations that can be handled. Supercomputers usually are linked to mainframes or minicomputers that handle the functions of communicating with users and handling the work of input and output. This leaves the supercomputer to function as a high-production element of a total system. Supercomputers generally are used by very large businesses or large scientific organizations.

A mainframe or supercomputer can support a network that links several minicomputers and hundreds, even thousands, of personal computers. A large network also may support use of *dumb terminals.* A dumb terminal is a device with a keyboard and a display that does not have its own processing or storage capabilities. Instead, the terminal relies on the mainframe computer for its processing and storage.

When a personal computer workstation is linked into a network, it provides its own, local processing, storage, and printing capabilities. A personal computer used for interaction with a mainframe system may be called a *smart terminal,* or an *intelligent terminal.*

1. What is software?

2. What functions are performed by system software?

3. What functions are performed by application software?

4. What role do people play in a CIS?

5. What are procedures and what are their functions?

6. What are the size ranges of computers and how do computers of different sizes compare?

Business Terms

local area network (LAN)
Multiple computers and support devices linked, through communication lines, with all of the facilities located in the same building or in a single location.

mainframe
A large-scale computer with extensive processing and communication capabilities.

supercomputer
An ultra-high-capacity computer used to provide the productivity needed by large companies or scientific laboratories.

dumb terminal
A device with a keyboard and a display that does not have its own processing or storage capabilities.

smart terminal
An on-line workstation that has its own processing and storage capabilities.

intelligent terminal
See smart terminal.

Control over multiple computers that perform advanced research is centralized in a single control room at the Lawrence Livermore National Laboratory. The control consoles monitor and control both experimental equipment and a network of computers.

COURTESY OF LAWRENCE LIVERMORE NATIONAL LABORATORY COMPUTER CENTER MUSEUM

Chapter Summary

❏ A computer information system (CIS) accepts data as input and changes the raw data into meaningful information.

❏ A CIS requires a number of components that function in coordination. These include equipment, software, people, procedures, and facilities.

❏ A CIS uses a number of specialized equipment units. These perform the functions of input, processing, output, and storage.

❏ The main device used for input is a keyboard. Input also is completed with a device called a mouse. Some input is entered directly from machines that generate information or read printed text or code.

❏ All computer processing is accomplished through two functions, comparison and arithmetic.

❏ Comparison checks the value of two numbers and determines whether one is equal to, greater than, or less than the other. Then, the computer can adapt the course of processing to the results of comparisons.

❏ All computer arithmetic is performed through additions of two numbers. Subtraction is done by applying negative electrical values. Multiplication is repeated addition, division is repeated subtraction.

❏ Processing takes place in a device called a central processing unit (CPU). The CPU consists of a main memory and a processor. Memory retains information items and program instructions during processing. The processor performs arithmetic, logic, and control functions.

❏ Outputs present information in forms usable by people. The main output techniques are displays and printed documents. The computer also can produce images through use of graphics programs and output devices. Output also can be transmitted over communication lines to other computers or processing devices.

❏ A computer needs a method for retaining information entered into and generated by computers for long-term reference and use. Long-term retention is handled by secondary storage devices. The main storage methods record information magnetically on tape or disks. It also is possible to retain information on storage units that use laser technology.

❏ All of the programs needed to operate a computer are called software. There are two major categories of software, system software and application software.

❏ System software monitors and controls computer equipment.

❏ Application software directs processing of information for users.

❏ People play critical CIS roles as developers of systems and users of information.

❏ Procedures include the standards and instructions followed by the people who operate a CIS and use its information.

❏ Facilities are the working areas needed for both equipment and people.

❏ Computers come in a wide range of sizes and capabilities. The major breakdowns are personal computers, minicomputers, mainframe computers, and supercomputers.

Definitions

Write a complete sentence that defines each of the terms below.

computer information system (CIS)

comparison

central processing unit (CPU)

sequential access

system software

disk operating system (DOS)

microcomputer

local area network (LAN)

pixel

procedure

information processing cycle

processor

direct access

application software

database administrator

supercomputer

laser printer

secondary storage

Questions to Think About

Based on what you have learned to date, answer the following questions in one or more complete sentences.

1. What is a computer information system and what does it do?

2. What are the functions performed by individual units of computer equipment?

3. Describe at least three alternate ways of entering data into a computer?

4. What simple, basic processing functions does a computer perform?

5. How is the ability of a computer to compare two values used in processing operations?

6. How does a computer perform arithmetic?

7. What is the role of a computer's main memory?

8. What is secondary storage and which devices provide secondary storage support within a computer system?

9. What are the main output alternatives in a computer system and how do these methods present information to users?

10. What is system software and what does it do?

11. What are application programs and what do they do?

12. What are the main roles of people within a CIS?

13. Why are manual procedures needed within computer systems and what function do they serve?

14. How are computers classified and what are the main categories used to describe computer capabilities?

Projects

The purpose of the assignments below is to encourage you to increase your learning through outside reading or work assignments.

1. Visit a computer lab in your school or visit a business organization in your community that uses computers. Prepare a list of system software and application software programs that are used. For each system software program, describe briefly the services that are provided. For each of three application programs, describe input, processing, output, and storage elements.

2. Visit a computer lab at school or a computer-using business. Ask about the backup and protection measures applied for software and information resources. Describe the measures taken and explain the reasons given for the methods that are used.

CHAPTER 19

What Common Business Problems Do Computers Solve?

The Think Tank

When you finish reading this chapter and complete your work assignments, you should be able to answer the following questions.

❏ What is the difference between a transaction file and a master file?

❏ What is meant by the expression "updating a master file"?

❏ What is a word processing program and what processing capabilities does it provide?

❏ What is a database management system and what information management and processing capabilities does it provide?

❏ What is a spreadsheet program and what information reporting and processing capabilities does it provide?

DOING BUSINESS

As they left the grocery store, Thelma's father told her that he had to make one more stop. He wanted to stop by the bank to pick up some money for the weekend.

"But, Dad," Marcia said, "this is Saturday. The bank will be closed."

"It doesn't matter," her father responded. "I'll use the automatic teller machine."

When they arrived at the bank, Thelma's father walked toward a machine mounted near the entrance. When he saw how interested Thelma was, her father said: "That's right. I guess you've never seen me use this dandy little card. Why don't you watch?"

As they approached the machine, Thelma noticed a small video screen that displayed a message. The machine gave instructions to "INSERT YOUR ATM CARD IN SLOT AT RIGHT." Below the slot was a picture indicating how the card should be inserted. When the card was inserted, the machine displayed a message asking for a PERSONAL IDENTIFICATION NUMBER.

"It's called a PIN number," Thelma's father explained. He punched four keys on the keyboard below the display. The ATM responded by asking him to wait a moment. Then it flashed a display asking what kind of transaction was desired. The options included cash withdrawal, deposit, transfer between accounts, or a report on account balance. When Thelma's father indicated he wanted a withdrawal, the machine provided another display. This one asked how much he wanted.

Direct service to customers is provided by computer systems such as automatic teller machines (ATMs). With such devices, companies add to customer service capabilities. Costs are reduced because customers handle their own data entry.

PHOTO BY LISA SCHWABER-BARZILAY

Thelma's father told the machine he wanted $60. It displayed another WAIT message. Then, Thelma heard a clicking sound inside the machine. "It's counting out our money," her father explained. In a moment, there was another message asking that the money be removed. He opened a steel door and removed three $20 bills. Next, the machine ejected the plastic card and a printed ticket.

"This is my transaction receipt," Thelma's father said as he put the money in his wallet. "It's lucky this machine is here. We have a date to take your mother to dinner tonight for her birthday. And I was dead broke. Thanks to this machine, we can keep the family together for another weekend."

MEANING

Thelma has had the opportunity to see a computerized transaction processing system in action. Her father knew she was taking a course that involved work in a computer lab. He wanted her to have a close-up look at how computers and people interacted. Thelma's father was anxious to stress

one important thing about computer processing: People drive transaction processing systems. Computers are vital tools for businesspeople. However, computers themselves cannot drive business operations. Computer hardware and programs rely on people to make, process, and complete transactions.

Even more important, the purpose of computer systems in business is to solve problems for people. As shown below, the design and building of computer systems starts with identification of a problem involving information use. The design and building of the system ends when the problem is solved.

WHAT DOES A COMPUTER SYSTEM DO?

A computer system delivers needed results to information users. A starting point for the building of a system is to identify what information is needed. After that, the data items that can be processed to deliver the target information must be identified. The operational system, then, should solve an identified problem by transforming source data into useful information.

Where Does Input Come From?

Data items result whenever a transaction occurs. Of course, a transaction is any act of business and includes the buying or selling of goods and services. When you buy lunch at your school cafeteria, you participate in a transaction. Your school has products that will deal with your hunger—that is, items of food. The transaction is completed when you pay the cashier for the items that you buy.

This simple transaction requires that several data items be *captured,* or recorded. The cashier enters an identification and price for each item purchased. If you wish, the cashier will provide you with a *sales receipt.* This is a *source document,* or *transaction document.* It lists register entries to provide you with a printed record of the data items that go into the computer system.

Creating transaction files.   The register also stores data items covering your purchase within a computer system. These data items are used to create a *transaction file.* A transaction file is a group of records that describe individual transactions produced for a brief business period. The data items created for each sale typically make up a transaction record. Often, transaction records are accumulated for a single day or week. In some business situations, a transaction file may contain records that represent one hour of business, or even less time.

The point: Every computer information system must include procedures for recording data items that result from individual transactions. These data items form the building blocks used to create and process files, reports, and other information structures.

HOW DO YOU OPERATE A COMPUTER SYSTEM?

In general, five steps are involved in carrying out the procedures for operating a computer information system. This procedure is basic. It also is information oriented. That is, the procedure is aimed at collecting, organizing, and delivering information to meet user needs. The procedure involves creating and maintaining files that form the hub of any business computer application. The five steps are:

1. Capture transaction data
2. Create transaction files
3. Create master files
4. Update master files with current transaction data
5. Deliver information to people.

A diagram illustrating this process appears in Figure 19-1. Some computer professionals use different names to identify these basic system requirements. Others divide their efforts into more or fewer steps. Invariably, however, there will be common requirements. Recognition of a series of steps has, in turn, helped to ease the work of information system operations.

This series of steps recognizes that computers are tools for gathering, organizing, and using information. Information handling is the common requirement. Computer systems, big or small, all have this common requirement. Information is structured into records, then organized into files. The capturing of

Business Terms

capture
To record data.

sales receipt
A document prepared by the seller and given to the buyer as a record of a transaction.

source document
A hard-copy record used to provide input on a transaction to an information system.

transaction document
See sales receipt, source document.

transaction file
A group of records that describe individual transactions produced during a brief business period.

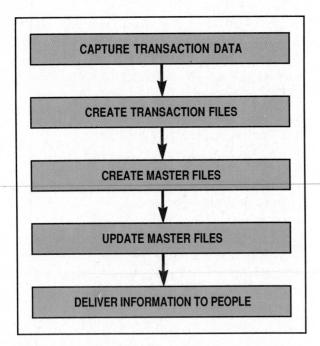

Figure 19-1. *This flowchart identifies and shows the sequence of steps involved in operation of most computer information systems.*

information, building of files, and use of files to satisfy information needs are, therefore, basic building blocks. With these requirements identified, computer professionals have developed standard tools. These tools can be applied to create and operate virtually any business information system. This means that knowledge of the basic system building blocks described below can be valuable to you. This knowledge may make it easy for you to understand and use information systems that you encounter in the workplace.

1. What is the starting point in the development of a computer system?

2. What is the relationship between transactions and data items for an information system?

3. What is a source document?

4. What procedure is followed to operate an information system and deliver outputs to users?

HOW ARE DATA ITEMS CAPTURED FOR USE IN A COMPUTER SYSTEM?

Data capture describes any technique for recording data—regardless of whether the items are in a format that can be input to a computer. You capture data when you take notes in class. Your notes, taken together, represent information that you can use to help recall what you have learned.

For a computer system, it makes sense to record data in a format that the computer can understand. Often, this is done by entering data through a keyboard or keypad of some kind. A computerized cash register is an example of this approach. The cash register contains a keypad with numbers and several special keys. By pressing keys in certain sequences, a cashier sends electronic signals to a main computer. The computer recognizes these signals as individual bits and bytes of data items. One code might signal the start of a new record. Other codes might identify a specific store or salesperson. Under control of a computer program, these data items can be organized to form a transaction record.

HOW ARE TRANSACTION FILES FORMED?

A transaction file, again, is a collection of records that describe transactions. The transactions are gathered over a relatively brief period, such as a day or week. At scheduled times, the transaction records are used to modify the master files that model the state of the business. This means that the useful life of transaction files is short. Although transaction files are saved for reference, their role in the system is over in a short time.

Transaction file example.   To illustrate, consider the sales transaction file for the VidView video rental store. At VidView, customers must become members before videocassette movies can be checked out. Each customer is assigned a customer number when he or she becomes a member. This number is shown on a membership card, which store clerks use to complete a rental transaction.

Each rental transaction is entered into a transaction sales file from the computerized register. Entry of data items is controlled by a *file creation program.* The program creates displays that require the clerk to enter one data item at a time, in a specific sequence. Entries at the register are transmitted to a main computer in the back of the store. Within a secondary storage device on the computer, the file creation program controls recording of transaction records. These are captured one after another, in the same sequence in which the transactions occur.

The rental transaction file contains five fields. The first field is the date of the transaction. The second field is the customer number. The third field is the number of videocassettes checked out, and the fourth field is the total rental cost. A fifth field is used to determine when the cassettes are returned. A diagram of the transaction record appears in Figure 19-2.

In this example, a transaction file might include all rentals for a single day. As indicated, these source records are recorded in the order in which they are entered. This ordering, based upon time of entry, is called *serial organization.* The transaction file creation program records only selected items into the transaction file. For example, it is not necessary to record the date of each transaction because the computer organizes the entire transaction file according to date. A partial listing of transaction records for the VidView system is displayed in Figure 19-3.

It would be difficult to store and keep track of daily transaction files for a long period. Imagine having to store and maintain all transaction files produced during a single year. This would mean keeping more than 300 separate files on hand. Instead, transaction files are used to create and *update* master files. As you will see, file updating involves adding recent transaction records to a long-term master file that models the business.

WHAT IS A MASTER FILE AND WHY ARE MASTER FILES IMPORTANT?

A *master file* is a group of records that represent, or model, a portion of a business. One master file accumulates transactions for a long period of time—a

---

Figure 19-2. *This is a data record layout for a VidView transaction.*

1.		DATE RENTED	CUSTOMER NUMBER	NUMBER RENTED	DATE RETURNED	
				RENTAL COST		

9 9 9 9 9 9 9 9 | 9 9 9 9 9 9 9 | 9 9 | 9 9 9 9 9 | 9 9 9 9 9 9 9 9 9 | 9 9 9
1 2 3 4 5 6 7 8 | 9 10 11 12 13 14 15 | 16 17 | 18 19 20 21 22 | 23 24 25 26 27 28 29 30 | 31 32 33

2.

9 9 9 9 9 9 9 9 9 9 9 9 9 9 9 9 9 9 9 9 9 9 9 9 9 9 9 9 9 9 9 9 9
1 2 3 4 5 6 7 8 9 10 11 12 13 14 15 16 17 18 19 20 21 22 23 24 25 26 27 28 29 30 31 32 33

Business Terms

data capture
Any technique for recording data for use in an information system.

file creation program
An application program used to develop transaction or master files, usually through entry of items in positions on display screens.

serial organization
Reference to a computer file in which records are entered chronologically, as data items are originated. Used to create transaction files.

update
An operation in which the content of a file is altered to reflect current transactions.

master file
A group of records that represent, or model, a portion of a business.

```
VidView Daily Sales Transaction Listing

DATE      CUST          NO.        DAILY       DATE
OUT       NO.           RENTED     CHARGE      RETURNED
=================================================
9/23/90   3488866        1          2.50
          3409872        1          2.50
          3497213        3          7.50
          3491304        2          5.00
          3428384        4         10.00
          3401103        2          5.00
          3491340        1          2.50      9/23/90
          3488221        3          7.50
```

Figure 19-3. *This display shows samples of transaction records that would be entered under the VidView system.*

month, year, or even longer. For instance, the daily transaction files of rentals at VidView are used to update a sales master file. Each record in this master file would contain a customer number, the monthly rental amount, and the yearly rental amount. As an information resource, this file models the sales status of the company.

How Do Master Files and Transaction Files Differ?

Recall that the transaction file in the example is created and organized in serial order. This ordering describes the *file organization* for transaction records. Records are entered into the file in the order that they occur. However, a master file typically is organized in some sequential order. This means that records follow a sequence of some kind. In a sequential file, each record has an assigned position. This position within the sequence is the basis for storing, finding, and using information.

Sequencing file records. For instance, the numbers 1, 2, 3, 4, and 5 are organized in *ascending*

sequence. The term ''ascending'' means that the numbers are arranged in order, from the lowest number to the highest number. By comparison, the numbers 4, 3, 2, 1 are said to be in *descending sequence.* That is, they are in order, from the largest number to the smallest number.

In the video store master file, records are organized in sequential order, according to the ascending sequence of customer numbers. This means that the first record in the store's master file is for customer 000001. The second record in the master file is for customer 000002, and so on through to customer 999999.

Record key. When a field is used in this way to determine the order of records, it is called a *record key.* The ordering of a master file in this way provides a way for programs to locate individual records for processing. In the example, the master file is sequential, meaning each record has a specific position. The transaction file, recall, is serial. This means records are stored in the order in which they are created.

Another chief difference between a transaction file and a master file lies in the uses for each file. A transaction file simply provides a temporary method for capturing information about business transactions. By contrast, a company's master files are the focus for most processing activities. A master file can be used to produce reports, mail customer statements, or analyze business trends. Many other applications are possible.

The point: Master files are storehouses of information. Businesspeople access selected information in master files to perform routine processing, and to solve problems and make decisions. In short, the master file is part of a model of its organization.

Review 19.2

1. Why are transactions recorded serially?
2. What is the organization plan for a sequential file?

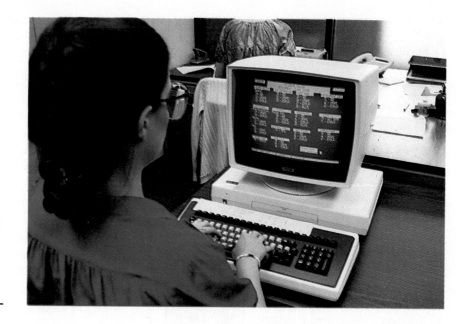

User references *are the key to usefulness of computer information systems. File references can be generated through entry of record keys or through selection of items to be reported.*

PHOTO BY LISA SCHWABER-BARZILAY

3. What are the differences between serial and sequential files?

4. What are ascending and descending sequences in file organization?

"Yearly Purchases" fields in the master file. With this information in master files, the computer can be instructed to search its master files for the current

HOW IS MASTER FILE UPDATING DONE AND WHY IS IT IMPORTANT?

In the VidView example, the transaction file stores rental records for one day. At the end of a business day, transaction records are ***posted*** to the master file. Posting includes transfer of information and transformation of master records to include new content. The posting of current transaction records keeps the VidView master files up-to-date. That is, the master file contains the most current information about videocassette rentals.

For this reason, the posting of current transaction records to master files is called file updating. For each tape, a master record shows a rental to a specific account number. The updating also shows a date of rental. For each customer, the idea is to add the daily rental sales amount to the "Monthly Purchases" and date. The system could list all records for the current

Business Terms

file organization
Reference to the method used to sequence records within a computer-maintained file.

ascending sequence
Arrangement of records within a file in order from the lowest value of a record key to the highest.

descending sequence
Arrangement of records within a file in order from the highest value of a record key to the lowest.

record key
The field within a record that identifies the record uniquely and can be used to identify and position the record within a file.

post
The entry of transaction data to update a master file. *See also* update.

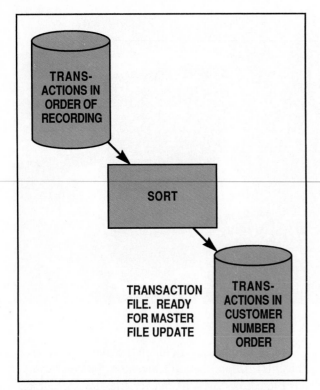

Figure 19-4. *This diagram shows the sorting process used to prepare transaction files for batch updating operations. The transaction records must be sorted into the same sequence as the records in the master file to be updated.*

date to show the tapes due for return. This is just one way in which the master files model the status of the business.

One approach to file updating is to begin by *sorting* all records into ascending, record-key order. In other words, a program will reorganize transaction records so that they are in customer-number order. Figure 19-4 is a diagram that shows the sorting process. The reason for doing so lies in the ordering of records in the master file. Recall that the master file already is in sequential order, by customer number. If transaction records are in this same order, the updating program can simply begin with the first record in the file. After all customer transactions for this first record have been updated, the program goes to the next record in the master file. Updating follows the master file sequence.

Must All Transaction Files Be Sorted Prior to Posting?

In the past, sorting transactions in this manner was a requirement. Master files were stored on magnetic tape, which is a sequential-access medium. That is, records on a reel of magnetic tape must be read, or accessed, in the same order in which they are entered. With magnetic tape, it is not possible to go directly to a particular record. Instead, the tape device begins by reading the first record stored on the tape reel. After this record has been read, the next record is located and read. This procedure continues until all records have been read or until processing has been completed. The problem can be seen in considering the diagram of a sequential-access tape file in Figure 19-5.

With the development of magnetic disks, access to stored records no longer was limited to sequential techniques. Instead, records could be stored in any order and then accessed directly. This approach to locating records is called direct access. This technique was made possible by the features of a disk drive. Recall that records are recorded in circular

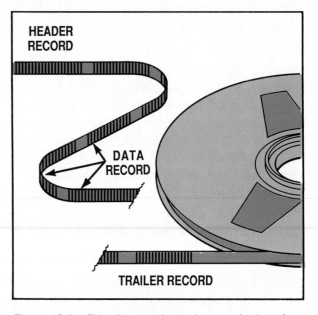

Figure 19-5. *This diagram shows the organization of records in ascending sequence according to record key.*

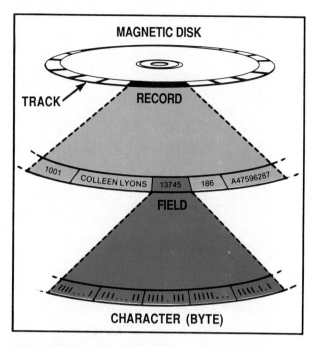

MAGNETIC DISK

TRACK

RECORD

1001 COLLEEN LYONS 13745 186 A47596287

FIELD

CHARACTER (BYTE)

Figure 19-6. *This diagram shows a method used to "address" records stored on disk according to track location.*

tracks around a disk platter. The read/write heads of a disk drive can go to any track position on a disk, at any time. Any individual record can be read, processed, and written back in place. It is not necessary to read complete files. To demonstrate, Figure 19-6 shows how disk files are set up. Each record has an address that is represented by its track position and its location on an individual track. This addressing system makes it possible to guide a read/write head to individual records.

How Does Direct Access Work?

Today, sequential access with disks is sensible only if all or most records in a file will be read. In the video store example, this is not the case, even though the master files are in ascending sequence by record key. On any given day, master file updating will involve only a fraction of all customers. For this reason, a direct access approach is used instead.

With this approach, each transaction record is read, in serial order. Then, the customer number in the transaction record is used to locate a master record directly. In other words, each customer number is a unique record key and indicates a separate disk address.

When a master record is identified, the total rental amount in the transaction record is added to two fields. These are the "Monthly Rental" and "Yearly Rental" items in the master file. The purpose for updating these fields is to keep them as current as possible. After all transaction records have been read, master file updating is considered complete.

In some businesses, the capabilities of direct access have led to a new method of updating files. Consider the information delivery requirements of an airline reservation system. To support customers' questions, ticket agents have to be able to access the most current flight information available. For this reason, these kinds of systems provide *on-line* transaction processing. Under this approach, transactions are written to a master file at the time they occur. The steps involved in creating, sorting, and posting transaction records in groups, or batches, is eliminated. In this way, employees can provide information about transactions on a minute-by-minute basis.

HOW IS INFORMATION DELIVERED TO PEOPLE?

The purpose of any computer system is to deliver information to people. In general, people get the information they need in two different ways:

- Scheduled reports
- On-line queries.

Business Terms
sort
To arrange records in sequence according to ascending or descending order.

```
                    VidView Daily Sales Transaction Listing
                             Week Ending 9/29/90
                          Print Date:   10/02/90                    Page  1

           DATE      CUST              NO.          DAILY        DATE
           OUT       NO.               RENTED       CHARGE       RETURNED
           =====================================================================

           9/23/90   3488866           1            2.50         9/25/90
                     3409872           1            2.50         9/24/90
                     3497213           3            7.50         9/26/90
                     3491304           2            5.00         9/25/90
                     3428384           4            10.00        9/26/90
                     3401448           2            5.00         9/24/90

                     3330277           4            10.00
                     3445678           2            5.00         9/29/90
                     3408340           1            2.50         9/30/90
                     3420056           2            5.00         10/02/90


                     TOTAL RENTALS COLLECTED:       845.00
                     NO. ACCOUNTS OUTSTANDING:      15
                ESTIMATED RENTALS OUTSTANDING:      90.00
                   TOTAL ESTIMATED WEEKLY SALES:    935.00
```

Reports can be generated as needed by management of a business. This report covers weekly sales at VidView. The blank area indicates that some detail items have been deleted. The report ends with a summary of business operations.

Scheduled Reports

A *scheduled report* is an output that has been designed for repeated delivery, on a regular basis. For instance, in the video store example, the manager might want a report that shows video sales figures for each month. In this case, a special program is designed to locate specific fields and records that will be on the report.

The program also *formats* the report by specifying the way each printed page is designed. A format is a design for the way in which information is organized and presented. The idea behind formatting a report is to produce an attractive, easy-to-read output. This typically involves organizing the content of a report into readable columns of information. Also, report formatting might involve calculating and printing totals for different columns.

On-line Queries

In some cases, businesspeople need immediate access to only one or a few records in a file. This kind of information access is called a *query.* Queries are processed through on-line access. The user enters a few commands that represent a request, or query, for information. These *query commands* are made up of English-like phrases that are easy to learn. In response to the query, the computer responds first by checking to be sure the user is authorized to see the information. Then, instructions are followed to find and present the information. On-line inquiry provides direct, immediate service. But displays themselves leave no permanent records. If a printed document is needed, reports must be generated. In many systems, users can instruct the computer to print special, hard-copy reports that contain information developed through queries.

On-line query *capabilities are used by many companies to take orders or to provide information in response to telephone calls.*

PHOTO BY LISA SCHWABER-BARZILAY

Review 19.3

1. How are transaction files prepared for master file updating through batch processing?

2. How is master file updating handled through direct access?

3. What options are available for delivery of output information to users?

WHAT TYPES OF APPLICATION PACKAGES DO BUSINESSES USE?

In the early years of computer systems, each business had to develop its own programs. This was a period when most computers were large mainframe systems. Application programming for these large computers was expensive and time consuming.

Over time, developments in computer hardware technology made it possible to build smaller, more powerful, and less expensive computers. As the use of computers increased, businesspeople discovered that many different businesses had similar processing requirements. For instance, all businesses create

transaction and master files. All businesses require reports. Also, many businesses follow similar procedures in processing customer accounts, payrolls, and other applications. Software development companies

Business Terms

on-line
Reference to the ability of a user to gain immediate access to a computer system from a terminal via a telecommunications link.

scheduled report
An output that uses a standard format and is delivered to users on a regular basis.

format
A design for the way in which information is organized and presented.

query
An operation in which a user makes a direct request for information from a computer.

query command
An instruction entered by a user as part of an information access request.

began to appear, which specialized in developing ap-plication programs that met the needs of several com-panies. An application program is a set of computer instructions that performs a specific job on behalf of computer users.

Today, the development of *application packages* is a multi-billion dollar business. An application package includes the programs that run the computer. In addition, the package contains a diskette or tape on which the program is recorded. Also included are instructions on how to use the program. Currently, it no longer is necessary for many businesses to de-velop computer application programs individually, from scratch. Instead, it is possible to purchase ready-to-use application programs from computer software companies.

Large numbers of application packages—for dozens of different jobs—are available for business use. Five of the most widely used types of applica-tion software packages are:

- Word processors
- Database management systems
- Spreadsheet programs
- Computer graphics
- Data communications.

HOW ARE WORD PROCESSORS USED?

The file processing example for VidView is said to implement *data processing* techniques. With data processing applications, it is possible to organize data into set patterns. For instance, each record in a file organized to hold data usually has an identical num-ber of fields. In turn, the content of each field among different records shares identical characteristics. Notice that each record in the VidView transaction file has the same number and type of fields. Data files, then, are useful for organizing large amounts of standard data items.

On the other hand, *word processing* or *text processing* programs handle *text files.* A text file contains content that is written in standard English. Text is unstructured in terms of storage requirements. There are no items or fields. Words are of different lengths. Sentences are composed of infinite combi-nations of words. Information is captured and stored in strings of letters, numbers, and symbols of un-predictable length. Word processing, or text process-ing, software consists of sets of programs that are designed to accept and handle unstructured files.

Consider what happens when you write a letter to a friend or relative. When you begin writing, you have no idea of the exact length of the letter. Also, it is not possible to organize information into set patterns, such as fields and records. For these reasons, you perform word processing, rather than data processing, to write your letter.

Before computers were used widely in business, most word processing was done with typewriters. Word processing applications include the writing of memos, letters, and other reports that have standard English-language content. Today, computer-driven word processing programs can be used to perform all of the tasks that can be handled with a typewriter. However, a computer-driven word processor offers several benefits that are not available with typewriters.

What Special Features Do Word Processing Programs Provide?

Word processing files and outputs are known as *documents*. Three basic types of processing can be performed on a document:

- Create a document
- Edit a document
- Print a document.

Create a document. This type of processing involves entering, or recording, text. When you write a letter on note paper, you are creating a document. You also are creating a document if you type a version, or *draft,* of the letter on a typewriter. A draft is a document that is not yet finished.

With a word processing program, creating a document is similar to the process used with a typewriter. That is, you enter words, punctuation, and other language elements through a keyboard. With a computer, text is displayed on the screen, rather than printed. Each time you touch a key, a character is added to your display.

A major difference occurs when you reach the end of a line of text. With a typewriter, you have to push a special key or operate a lever at the end of each line. This key or lever is called the *carrier return.* A carrier return causes the typewriter to begin a new line of text. Typically, a bell rings when you near the end of a line. This bell tells you that it is time to begin a new line.

A word processing program starts new lines automatically. You don't have to be concerned about forming lines, except at the beginning of a paragraph. Within a paragraph, the program uses a technique called *word wrap* to do this automatically. Word

Business Terms

application package
A tool for implementing a user application; includes programs and procedures.

data processing
A type of computer application that handles data items and records in fixed formats.

word processing
A computer application that processes unstructured strings of text.

text processing
See word processing.

text file
A file created to handle unstructured strings of characters without specific formats.

document
A group of data items or text prepared for presentation to a user.

draft
A preliminary version of a document that still needs work.

carrier return
A command that causes an electric typewriter to move to the first position on the next entry line. Also called "return."

word wrap
The ability of a word processing program to sense the end of an entry line and move automatically to the beginning of the next line.

wrap is a feature that senses the ends of lines and starts new lines automatically. The program detects when you have come to the end of a line. Then, it automatically positions, or "wraps," the next word that you type at the beginning of the following line. The word wrap process is illustrated in Figure 19-7. This illustration consists of two computer screens. In the first, text entry is nearing the end of a line. In the second, the final word on the line has been moved to the beginning of the next line.

Edit a document. When most people create a text document, they expect to make changes, called *revisions,* to the first version, or draft. These changes, or *edits,* are required to correct errors and to improve the wording. These improvements might include the addition or *deletion* (removal) of words, phrases, or entire pages. In some cases, it might be desirable to move sections of text from one location to another.

With a typewritten document, it generally is necessary to retype a page whenever a major edit is required. Even with minor changes, such as a single misspelled word, an erasure might look sloppy. For these reasons, each business letter generally is retyped four to seven times before it is mailed.

Word processing programs eliminate the need to retype entire documents. Changes are made to stored files rather than on paper. Words and phrases can be inserted or deleted easily. For an insertion, the program simply "pushes" existing text ahead of the inserted text. This feature is similar to the word wrap capability mentioned earlier. For a deletion, the program "closes up" the extra space that results when text is removed.

Other features that are common to professional word processors include the ability to move and copy sections of text from one location to another, as illustrated in Figure 19-8.

The point: With a word processor, you can make any number of changes to a document without affecting other portions of the text. The document always exists in main memory and/or on disk. After you have made all corrections and revisions, you can print an error-free document.

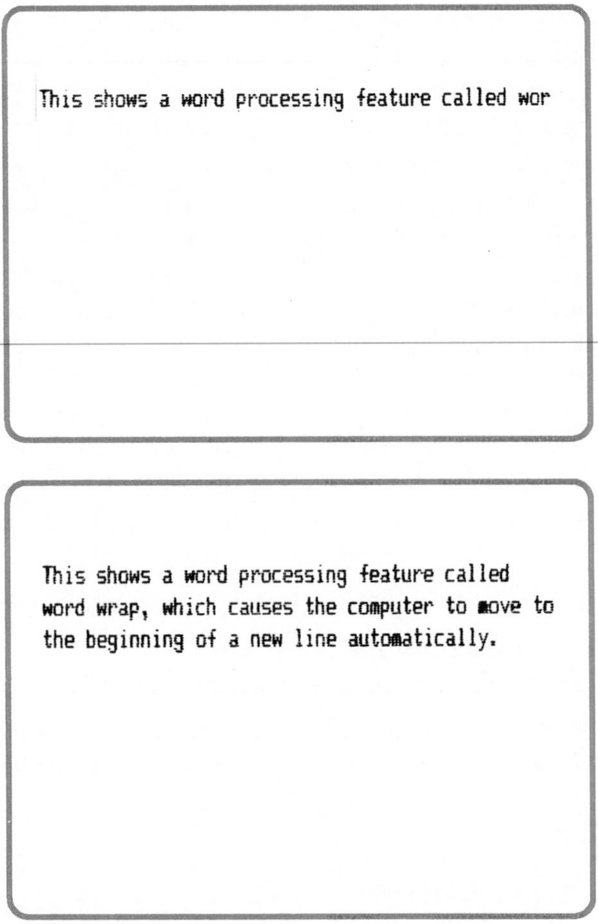

This shows a word processing feature called wor

This shows a word processing feature called word wrap, which causes the computer to move to the beginning of a new line automatically.

Figure 19-7. *Word wrap is an important feature of word processing programs. In the top display, a user entry is nearing the end of a line. In the bottom screen, the last word on the first line has been moved automatically as the user continues text entry.*

Print a document. A word processing program works in combination with the operating system to transmit text to a printer. Most word processing programs allow you to determine the format, or printed appearance, of a document. For instance, by entering a simple command, you can specify whether you want single-, double-, or triple-spacing between lines. You also can specify the width of margins and the maximum number of lines to be printed on a page. Other print capabilities include the ability to change the appearance of printed characters and to print multiple copies.

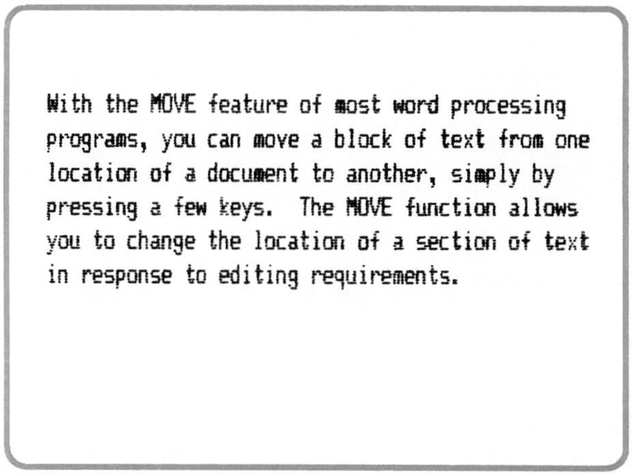

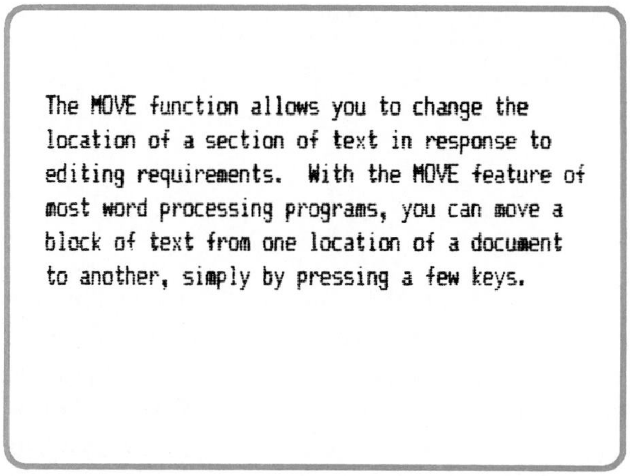

```
With the MOVE feature of most word processing
programs, you can move a block of text from one
location of a document to another, simply by
pressing a few keys.  The MOVE function allows
you to change the location of a section of text
in response to editing requirements.
```

```
The MOVE function allows you to change the
location of a section of text in response to
editing requirements.  With the MOVE feature of
most word processing programs, you can move a
block of text from one location of a document
to another, simply by pressing a few keys.
```

Figure 19-8. *The MOVE function is a powerful feature of most word processing application packages. The top screen shows text as entered. The bottom screen shows how a user has rearranged the order of sentences through use of the MOVE function.*

Word processing applications are described in greater depth in Chapter 21.

WHAT ARE DATABASE MANAGEMENT SYSTEMS AND HOW ARE THEY USED IN BUSINESSES?

A *database* is a collection of data files that can be controlled for coordinated use. Within a database, each data item can be accessed independently. Also, a database is a central information resource that can provide information support to multiple applications.

The software that provides these information management capabilities is called a *database management system (DBMS).* A DBMS is a set of programs that can store, and relate, or combine, data from multiple files.

Consider the VidView scenario introduced earlier. With database support, the sales portion of this system would include at least three master files. Transactions and file updating would be handled on-line. One file would be used to record and store sales transactions as they occur. A Sales (master) file would be used to store and process transactions on a long-term basis. A third file would keep track of videocassette inventories.

Other files also would be maintained by the VidView store. One file would be called the Customer Master file. This file contains names, customer numbers, addresses, and phone numbers for all members.

Under traditional file processing methods, each file would have to be stored and processed by separate programs. There would be no way to coordinate data easily between different files. Therefore,

Business Terms

revision
A change in a document. *See* edit.

edit
An operation in which an existing document is changed or revised.

deletion
An operation that removes text or data from a document.

database
A collection of data files that can be controlled for coordinated use and in which access is available to individual data items.

database management system (DBMS)
A set of programs that can store, and relate, or combine, data from multiple files.

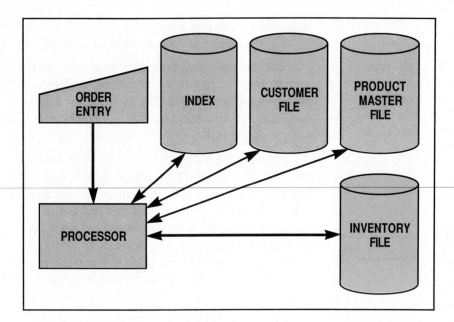

Figure 19-9. *This diagram demonstrates how database management software stores and retrieves information from a database. One file within the system serves as an index. The computer uses the index to find storage locations for the data items required to meet user needs.*

data items would have to be duplicated in multiple files. For example, customer name and address information or film titles would have to appear in two or more files.

With a database management system, data for all files are stored as a single collection. The need for duplication is eliminated because the DBMS permits access to any item or record. By eliminating duplication, the DBMS also reduces the need to update multiple copies of a record each time there is a change. In turn, a major potential for errors disappears. Suppose the same information is repeated in multiple files. If one copy of a record is not correct, an error exists and the information involved is unreliable.

Under a DBMS, each data item is recorded only once. The DBMS software then finds needed items by accessing multiple files. When a master record is changed, only one correction is needed to support all applications. For instance, the Inventory file might be processed along with the Customer Master file to notify customers who have overdue rentals. When a rental transaction occurs, the rented videocassettes

are marked in the Inventory file. At the end of each week, a report is produced that matches customer names and addresses with overdue rentals in the Inventory file. This report is used to call or mail overdue notices to customers. Programs available within the DBMS handle the details involved in relating and reporting on data in multiple files.

Figure 19-9 diagrams the way information from multiple files is handled by a DBMS. DBMS principles and applications are discussed further in Chapters 22 and 23.

WHAT ARE SPREADSHEET PROGRAMS AND HOW ARE THEY USED IN BUSINESS?

A *spreadsheet program* allows you to use a computer to perform financial planning and reporting applications. The program provides you with a screen that is divided into numbered rows and lettered columns. This screen is called an *electronic spreadsheet* display. The name comes from a time when financial

		1ST Q	2ND Q	3RD Q	4TH Q	TOTAL YR
1	VidView Quarterly Budget					
2						
3		1ST Q	2ND Q	3RD Q	4TH Q	TOTAL YR
4	INCOME ACCOUNTS					
5	Video Rentals	38550	39321	38550	39321	155742
6	Video Sales	12955	13473	12955	13473	52856
7						
8	TOTAL INCOME:	51505	52794	51505	52794	208598
9						
10	EXPENSE ACCOUNTS					
11	Equipment	9725	9822	9725	9822	39095
12	Rent	12000	12000	12000	12000	48000
13	Advertising	2020	2081	2020	2081	8201
14	Supplies	1275	1301	1275	1301	5151
15	Inventory	22150	22815	22150	22815	89929
16						
17	TOTAL EXPENSES:	47170	48018	47170	48018	190376
18						
19	PROFIT:	4335	4776	4335	4776	18223

Figure 19-10. *This electronic spreadsheet displays the budget figures developed for VidView.*

reports were created on wide sheets of paper called "spreadsheets." These spreadsheets were divided into rows and columns that could be used to enter financial data.

An electronic spreadsheet like the one in Figure 19-10 is similar to a paper spreadsheet. However, the electronic spreadsheet is developed by entering data on a display through a keyboard. The intersection of rows and columns creates blocks called *cells.* Under control of the program, you can enter numbers and other financial information into these cells.

The chief value of spreadsheets lies in making plans and decisions based upon financial information. One of the most common uses for a spreadsheet is to create *budgets.* A budget is a plan for receiving and spending money. All businesses require budgets to guide the use of *income,* or money received, and expenses.

Budgeting is a major burden for business managers. For this reason, spreadsheet software has become a widely used type of microcomputer application package. Managers could enter amounts into spreadsheet cells to reflect business income and expenses. Then, by entering *formulas,* the computer could calculate amounts in rows and columns to develop totals. A formula is simply a command that

instructs the spreadsheet program to perform calculations upon data stored in a group of cells.

When spreadsheets were prepared manually (on paper) managers found it to be a tedious, time-consuming chore. Whenever an error was identified or a change was made in a single cell, entire columns had to be recalculated and rewritten by hand. This led to sloppy erasures and time-consuming calculations.

With spreadsheet software, managers realized that they could make financial entries once and then get the computer to make calculations automatically. That is, the program handles all of the mathematical functions. The user simply enters values and formulas. Under this approach, it is possible to make corrections and recalculate spreadsheets in a matter of seconds. New spreadsheets could be printed or saved to disk at any time. These capabilities have helped to simplify hundreds of accounting and planning applications for businesspeople. Further discussions on spreadsheets and their uses appear in Chapter 24.

Business Terms

spreadsheet program
An application package that controls the creation of reports structured into fixed sets of columns and rows.

electronic spreadsheet
A software application package for preparation of spreadsheet reports.

cell
A data entry location in a spreadsheet.

budget
A plan for receiving and spending money.

income
Money received.

formula
An entry in a spreadsheet cell that controls computations.

WHAT ARE COMPUTER GRAPHICS AND HOW ARE GRAPHICS USED IN BUSINESS?

The term *graphic* identifies an image, or picture. *Computer graphics software* enables computers to generate images as well as text and data outputs.

The value of pictures is that they usually are easier to understand than pages of text or data. Thus, graphic outputs can improve communication and save user time. The time is saved by eliminating the need to study and analyze pages of text or data.

Computers can be equipped to produce graphics through use of special circuit boards and software packages. Examples of the uses and values of computer graphics are presented in Chapter 25.

HOW DO COMPUTERS COMMUNICATE?

Businesses run on information. To meet information needs, it often is necessary to transmit data from one computer to another. The volume of information shared among computers has been growing steadily. It has been predicted that, eventually, computers will become heavier users of telephone networks than people.

To communicate over communications circuits, computers need to format information into special codes. These codes match the binary format needs of the telecommunications industry, which are different from the machine languages of computers. The special devices that handle communication coding, along with supporting software, are described in Chapter 26.

Chapter 26 also covers another important capability for use of computers in business. The capability is known as *integration*. Special integrated software packages make it possible to bring together the information developed under the different kinds of software described above. For example, data produced under database or spreadsheet software may be needed within a text report. By themselves, the application programs described above are separate from one another. Special integrated application packages make it possible to mix text with data and graphics programs to improve communication and decision making in business.

This chapter describes some of the applications that computers can handle for business. In the next chapter, you have an opportunity to take a look at what it's like actually to work with a computer.

1. What are the values to business of packaged application programs?

2. What are the main differences between data and text files?

3. What kinds of documents are generated by word processing programs?

4. Why is it important that database management systems eliminate duplication of records in multiple files?

5. What kinds of documents are generated by electronic spreadsheet programs?

Business Terms

graphic
An image that conveys information.

computer graphics software
Sets of programs that enable a computer to generate images as well as text and data outputs.

integration
A software capability for including data and text from multiple application packages into coordinated outputs.

Chapter Summary

❑ Each business information system has a series of essential steps, or parts. These steps are the basis for maintaining systems and delivering information to users.

❑ The steps in each business system include data capture, transaction file creation, master file creation, master file update from transaction records, and delivery of information to users.

❑ Data capture involves entry of source data items into a computer or other storage file and recording of records for future use. Records generally are recorded in serial order.

❑ Master files contain information that models an organization. Master files generally are set up in sequential order. This means that each record has a fixed position that can be used as a basis for creating, storing, updating, and using the information.

❑ File sequencing generally is by numeric or alphabetic order. Ascending sequences proceed from the lowest to the highest order. Descending sequences start high and move to lower values.

❑ One way to update a master file is to sort transaction records into the same order as the records in the master file. The computer then accepts one transaction at a time. The corresponding master record is found and processed.

❑ If the master file is on a disk device, direct access can be used. Transaction records are accepted in any order. The master record is found individually. Master records are processed one at a time and rewritten to the file device.

❑ Information is delivered to users through scheduled reports or on-line queries. Scheduled reports have standard formats and are issued regularly. On-line queries can be entered directly by users at any time. Query commands are used to request the required information, which can be printed as a report or displayed on a screen.

❑ Five of the most common business applications processed on computers are word processing, database management, spreadsheet preparation, graphics, and data communications.

❑ Word processing programs provide the ability to create, edit, and print documents.

❑ A database management system (DBMS) provides the ability to coordinate use of multiple data files and to access individual data items. DBMS software makes it possible to support multiple applications from a single set of files. This eliminates the need to build and maintain files for individual applications.

❑ Electronic spreadsheet packages are tools that make it easier and more efficient to develop financial reports and forecasts. Entries are made into a display that has individual positions for each unit of information. Formulas can be entered that cause the computer to perform all totals and other computations automatically.

❑ Computer graphics applications make it possible to generate images through use of computers.

❑ Special hardware and software tools allow computers to communicate with one another over telecommunications links.

Definitions

Write a complete sentence that defines each of the terms below.

source document	data capture
serial organization	master file
ascending sequence	descending sequence
record key	query command
word wrap	cell
formula	computer graphics software

Questions to Think About

Based on what you have learned to date, answer the following questions in one or more complete sentences.

1. What is involved in the capturing of transaction data and why is this a basic requirement for many business information systems?

2. What are transaction files and what role do they play in business information systems?

3. What are master files and what role do they play in business information systems?

4. How are master files updated so that they reflect the current status of a business?

5. What techniques are used to deliver information to users and what purposes does each method serve?

6. What are serial files and what are typical uses for these files?

7. What are sequential files and what is their main value?

8. What are direct access files and how are they used?

9. How are word processing packages used in business?

10. What are database management systems and what purposes do they serve?

11. What are electronic spreadsheet packages and how are they used by managers?

Projects

The purpose of the assignments below is to encourage you to increase your learning through outside reading or work assignments.

1. Think of your school as a business that exists to educate students. Think of the activities performed by individual students and by the school organization. From your own knowledge, identify the transactions that take place and must be recorded. Then identify a series of master files that should be updated to reflect these transactions.

2. From information in this chapter and class discussions, identify one computer application that serves you regularly. The computer can be in an appliance at home, in your city, in stores where you shop, or in banks that you visit. Read about or ask about one application of a computer you have identified. Describe how transactions are processed on this system.

CHAPTER 20

What's It Like to Work at a Computer?

The Think Tank

When you finish reading this chapter and complete your work assignments, you should be able to answer the following questions.

❑ Why does the capacity of main memory help to determine the processing capabilities of a computer system?

❑ What is the difference between a near-letter-quality printer and a letter-quality printer?

❑ How does the use of a hard disk affect the capabilities of a personal computer system?

❑ Why is the COMMAND.COM program central to the disk operating system of a personal computer?

DOING BUSINESS

When Bob Gomez entered his office on Tuesday morning, he noticed something new. A personal computer system had been set up on his desk. The system included a monitor, a keyboard, and two disk drives. Bob noticed that a memo, written by Ryan Schalk, a young co-worker, had been taped to his monitor. He studied the body of the memo for a few moments:

Good morning, Bob. Your new personal computer system arrived late yesterday afternoon after you left. I took the liberty of setting it up for you. I tested the system to make sure all was in working order. I've also left the diskettes and user's manuals that you'll need to get started. If you have any problems, I'll be in at 9:30.

Bob looked at the computer hardware and felt a mixture of excitement and mild nervousness. He had been putting off buying a personal computer for several years. As Vice President of Communications for the bank, he knew that a desktop computer would be a valuable tool. But his constantly busy schedule had kept him from taking the time to learn how to use a personal computer.

Bob decided that he should begin his learning experience immediately. He was experienced at using the bank's mainframe computer system to review and process customer accounts. For this reason, he didn't believe that it would be necessary to review the user's manuals on his desk.

Bob noticed that one of the disks that Ryan had left was labeled "word processing system." Bob inserted the disk in one of the disk drives of his computer and turned the power switch on.

After a few moments, the computer responded with this message:

Non-system disk or system disk error. Press any key to continue.

Bob was annoyed. At that moment, Ryan walked into Bob's office and asked him how he liked his new computer.

"I don't," Bob replied. "Look at this message. Something's obviously wrong."

Ryan looked at the screen for a second. "That's easy to solve," he said. "You're trying to use an application program before you've loaded the operating system. All application software relies on an operating system. The operating system is your representative inside that black box. It gets the computer ready for you. Then it helps run your jobs. So you have to insert this disk first."

Ryan inserted the operating system disk in the disk drive and restarted the computer. He then removed the disk and replaced it with the word processing program disk. He pressed a few keys and waited. After about 10 seconds, a list of word processing operations appeared on the screen.

"Now you're ready to work," Ryan said.

"That's all that was wrong?" Bob asked. "It looks like learning to use a personal computer system is going to be easy, after all. Thanks, Ryan. I guess I just needed to understand some basic concepts before I began."

MEANING

Bob made two mistakes that are commonplace among first-time computer users. His first mistake was to ignore the hardware and software user's manuals. Bob believed he knew enough about computers to work without any help. User's manuals give step-by-step instructions for beginners as well as experienced users. By following these instructions, it is possible to develop confidence in the use of personal computer hardware and software.

By ignoring the user's manuals, Bob failed to learn about the importance of an operating system.

```
┌─────────────────────────────────────────┐
│  ┌───────────────────────────────────┐  │
│  │  M u l t i M a t e   A d v a n t a g e │  │
│  │          Version 3.50             │  │
│  └───────────────────────────────────┘  │
│                                          │
│     1) Edit an Old Document              │
│     2) Create a New Document             │
│                                          │
│     3) Print Document Utility            │
│     4) Printer Control Utilities         │
│     5) Merge Print Utility               │
│                                          │
│     6) Document Handling Utilities       │
│     7) Other Utilities                   │
│     8) Spell Check a Document            │
│     9) Return to DOS                     │
│                                          │
│        DESIRED FUNCTION: ■               │
│                                          │
│  Enter the number of the function; press RETURN │
│   Hold down Shift and press F1 for HELP menu    │
└─────────────────────────────────────────┘
```

Word processing functions are chosen from a menu provided by most application programs. This is an example of a menu for access to functions of the MultiMate program.

He tried to insert an application disk before the computer was ready to receive it. Recall that an operating system controls the use of hardware and supports all your application programs.

WHY IS THE OPERATING SYSTEM SO IMPORTANT?

Part of an operating system acts like the "traffic cop" for a computer. These system programs determine which devices should be used to perform specific processing tasks. They also assign different areas in main memory for the storage of program instructions and data. Further, the operating system directs the control unit of the computer in inputting and outputting program instructions and data.

For these and other reasons, the operating system of a computer must be *loaded* before any programs or data. A load operation reads software or files into memory to prepare a computer for use.

The following sections require you to use your imagination. The idea is to help you understand what it's like to begin working with a personal computer

Many managers handle their own computer processing through use of microcomputers and "user friendly" software packages.
COURTESY OF IBM CORPORATION

system in business. You are to imagine yourself as an entry-level employee who will use personal computers regularly in performing your duties. One of your first assignments will be to familiarize yourself with the capabilities of a personal computer operating system.

SCENARIO: COMPUTRENDS, INC.

You have recently been hired by CompuTrends, Inc., to manage customer accounts. CompuTrends, Inc. is a small company, with less than 10 full- and part-time employees. The company publishes a newsletter for businesspeople who use personal computers. The "CompuTrends" newsletter is designed to provide current information about personal computer hardware and software developments. Businesspeople apply this information in the use of their personal computer systems.

When you report to work on Monday morning, you are greeted by Christina Goodspeed, president and founder of CompuTrends. Christina has made it a point to participate personally in the *orientation* of all new employees. An orientation is an introduction

to the policies, procedures, and facilities of an organization. Christina feels that all members of the company function as a team. She believes that the success and reputation of the entire business are affected by the performance of each employee.

What Should You Know About Your Job?

Christina explains that the *circulation* of "CompuTrends" is about 6,000. In this case, the term

Business Terms

load
An operation that reads software or files into memory to prepare a computer for use.

orientation
A program that introduces new employees to the policies, procedures, and facilities of an organization.

circulation
The distribution and readership of a publication.

"circulation" refers to the number of people who purchase, or subscribe to, the newsletter.

"I realize that 6,000 readers might not seem like a lot," she says, "but our service is designed for businesspeople who demand the most up-to-date information about personal computers in business.

"The journalists on our staff are experts in the field of personal computing," Christina says with some pride. "They also are excellent communicators. They have the ability and resources to uncover major hardware and software developments taking place in the computer industry. In addition, they can communicate information so that it will be valuable to businesspeople.

"For this reason, we charge $150 a year for our monthly newsletter," Christina continues. "That's a small sum of money to pay for information that can aid a multi-million dollar corporation in improving business operations. Our subscribers, on the whole, are pleased with our information service. However, we at CompuTrends are continually working to improve the way we deliver service to our subscribers. That's where you come in," she says.

Job responsibilities.   "You will be responsible for handling accounts for half of our subscribers. Up to this point, Rebecca has been handling all subscription accounts." Christina then introduces you to Rebecca. "However, the number of subscriptions has grown by more than 2,000 in the past six months. The workload is more than Rebecca can handle alone. So, you will be handling the accounts for all subscribers whose last names begin with the letters 'L' through 'Z'. Rebecca will handle accounts for all customers whose last names begin with the letters 'A' through 'K'. For the rest of today, Rebecca will help you to orient yourself in your new job."

When Christina leaves your work area, Rebecca begins to explain the duties you will perform.

"You and I are the link between 'CompuTrends' and its subscribers," Rebecca says. "In a sense, we are the goodwill ambassadors of the business. It is our responsibility to seek new subscribers. It is also our job to try to get current readers to renew their subscriptions. But perhaps more important, we answer any questions or complaints that customers might have about 'CompuTrends' or their subscription account."

At this point, you ask Rebecca what type of software packages you will use to manage accounts.

"Good question," Rebecca says. "Each subscriber account is entered into a database under control of database management system software. We create separate files for general information about subscribers and for handling accounts payable. The accounts payable files contain information on the amounts to be collected from subscribers.

"We use a word processing package to develop subscription kits that we mail to potential and current subscribers. The word processing system also is used to write personal letters to subscribers in response to questions or complaints.

"Finally, we use a spreadsheet package to create short-term and long-range financial reports. You'll learn how to use these three application programs in the next few weeks. Right now, why don't I explain the features of the computer hardware you will be using."

Review 20.1

1. How does the size of main memory affect the efficiency of computer processing?

2. What is the role of an operating system?

3. What is meant by "loading" a program?

WHAT ARE THE PRIMARY AND SECONDARY STORAGE CAPABILITIES OF YOUR COMPUTER?

Rebecca guides you to the desk where you will be working. "This will be your computer system," Rebecca says, pointing to several pieces of computer hardware on your desktop. "Your system includes

Application preparation of a microcomputer is achieved by inserting a program diskette. Microcomputers are general-purpose devices. Loading software adapts a microcomputer to provide specific services required by users.

PHOTO BY LIANE ENKELIS

a monitor, a keyboard, one floppy disk drive, a hard disk, and a printer. The computer itself is called an IBM-PC compatible. That means that the computer will run any program that is designed for an IBM PC.''

You realize that the storage capabilities of a computer system are central to the ways in which information can be input, output, and processed. You ask Rebecca to begin by describing the main memory and secondary storage capabilities of your computer.

How Much Main Memory Is Available on Your Computer?

''Your computer contains 640K, or 640 thousand, bytes of main memory,'' Rebecca says. You tell Rebecca that you know main memory also is called *random access memory,* or *RAM.* ''That's right,'' she says. ''The computer uses RAM to load, or store, programs and data during processing. The phrase 'random access' means that memory locations are individually addressable. In other words, the operating system can set up memory locations that

can be identified by an address of some kind, such as a unique value. Individual fields and records then can be stored in memory and accessed at any time.''

''In other words,'' you say, ''the operating system controls my application programs. The operating system assigns data and program instructions to memory locations.''

''Exactly,'' Rebecca replies. ''It also is true that memory helps to determine the efficiency of your computer. The more memory you have, the greater the number of program instructions and data records that are available for processing. A bigger memory reduces the number of transfers that are needed between primary and secondary storage. As a result, the system runs faster. The computer you have came with about 512K of memory. We had it enlarged before it was installed.''

Business Terms

random access memory (RAM)
A device that permits access to any storage position.

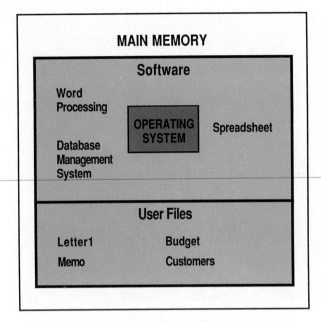

MAIN MEMORY

Software

Word
Processing

OPERATING
SYSTEM

Spreadsheet

Database
Management
System

User Files

Letter1   Budget

Memo   Customers

Main memory stores the programs and files needed to use a microcomputer. This diagram demonstrates that part of memory is used to store system and application programs. Other parts of memory store files to be processed by users.

"But you don't have to worry about the content of memory when you're using an application program. The software takes care of those kinds of details. The important thing to realize is that you have about 640 thousand characters available for the storage of data items and program instructions."

What Secondary Storage Capacities Do You Have?

Next, Rebecca explains the secondary storage features of your computer system. "As you can see," she says, "you have one floppy disk drive and one hard disk drive. A few years ago, all of our personal computers had two floppy disk drives. However, many of the programs in use today take up more storage space than is available on a single diskette. Also, it can become difficult to store and retrieve multiple files when only one disk drive is available for data.

"For instance, our database management system software comes on two diskettes. Each diskette can store about 360K bytes. When we used two floppy disk drives, we were constantly swapping the two program diskettes in and out of the 'A' disk drive. The reason is that one diskette contained programs to perform certain processing operations while other processing operations required the second diskette. It wasn't possible to put both diskettes in the drives together because the 'B' drive contained the data diskette.

"In turn," Rebecca continued, "our company grew. So did our files. Now, our files are too big to fit on a single data diskette. With more than 6,000 subscribers, we need almost two million bytes just to store files for the database management system. Spreadsheet and word processing files take up additional space. For these reasons, your computer includes a hard disk drive that can store about 30 *megabytes* of data and program instructions. A megabyte is about one million characters."

Roles of floppy and hard disks.   At this point, you ask a sensible question: "If you can store that much information on a hard disk, why do I even need a floppy disk drive?"

"A hard disk is non-removable," Rebecca says. "It is sealed and installed permanently inside the computer. You need the floppy disk drive for two chief reasons. First, whenever we purchase a new software package, it comes on one or more floppy diskettes. You need the floppy disk drive, then, to *install* the programs onto your hard disk. When you install a program, you set it up for use on your system.

"The second reason for using a floppy diskette drive is even more important. At the end of each business day, you will make *backup* copies of each file you create or modify."

"In other words," you say, "you want me to make a copy of each file by writing the data from the hard disk to a floppy diskette."

"That's right," Rebecca responds. "File backup activities are critical to our business. If, for any

Winchester disks are high-speed, sealed units that provide high capacities for data storage. Devices like the one in the photo can provide capacities for storage and retrieval of up to 85 million characters of data. Some Winchester drives have even higher capacities.

COURTESY OF BULL PERIPHERALS CORPO-RATION

reason, the information on the hard disk should be damaged or destroyed, a current copy of each file exists on a floppy disk. This includes program files. In this way, it is possible to recreate all files on the hard disk. And, believe me, the destruction of files is a very real threat.

"Since our company has been in business," Rebecca continued, "the content of my computer's hard disk has been damaged or destroyed four times. Thunderstorms, power surges, and other electrical disturbances can damage the content of a hard disk. In one case, an employee tripped near my computer and fell into my desk. The jolt was severe enough to cause the heads on my hard disk drive to strike the surface of the disk. Several of my files were destroyed. Fortunately, I had made backup copies of all my files. I was able to reconstruct the content of my hard disk in less than an hour."

What Other Peripheral Devices Are Attached to Your Computer?

Rebecca turns her attention to the remaining devices attached to your computer. "As you may know," she says, "the actual computer that processes your data and information is composed of electronic circuits. Many of these circuits are parts of microchips. Any other device that is connected to the computer is called a *peripheral.* Your floppy and hard disk drives are considered to be peripheral devices.

"The other three peripheral devices you need to know about are your monitor, keyboard, and printer," Rebecca says.

Business Terms

megabyte
Approximately one million characters.

install
To enter a program into memory for user access.

backup
A copy of a file or program created to protect against possible loss of or damage to the original.

peripheral
A connected device that supports operation of a computer.

Complete computer systems are set up on desktops in modern, electronic offices. Each worker in this photo has a microcomputer that includes capabilities for input, processing, storage on diskettes, and output through a display or printer.

COURTESY OF IBM CORPORATION

Monitor. "The monitor," Rebecca says, "has a screen used to display information visually. For instance, when you enter data through the keyboard, the characters usually are displayed on your monitor. Your monitor, as well as most personal computer monitors, can display 80 characters on each line. Also, the screen can show as many as 24 lines, from top to bottom. Your screen is called a *monochrome monitor.* This means that the screen displays data in one color only."

Keyboard. "Your keyboard," Rebecca says, "contains three sections. The rightmost section is the numeric keypad. This section is useful in entering numbers into spreadsheets and in performing other calculations. Also, these keys can be used to position the *cursor* on the screen. The cursor is a flashing shape that indicates the character position that you are currently using to enter and display data.

"The second, middle section contains the main keyboard that you use to enter numbers, letters of the alphabet, and other special characters. This portion of the keyboard is just like an electric typewriter.

"The third section of the keyboard is on the leftmost side. These are called *function keys,* and are labeled F1, F2, F3, and so on. On some keyboards, the function keys run along the top. In any case, you use these keys to enter instructions for special operations. The functions are different for each application package. For instance, when you press the F3 key with your word processing program, the line of text you are entering is centered on the screen. In general, a function key is used to activate a set of program instructions that complete a particular task."

Printer. "You and I have two different types of printers available to us," Rebecca says. "For most applications, you will use the dot-matrix printer that is currently linked with your computer. This printer can produce two different types of characters—*draft quality* and *near letter quality.* Usually, the phrase 'near letter quality' is abbreviated as *NLQ.*

"Your dot-matrix printer uses a set of pins, or wires, that create characters by striking a ribbon in different patterns. In draft-quality mode, the printer produces readable characters. However, these characters really aren't acceptable for submitting documents to people outside of the company. We use the draft-quality mode only for interoffice memos and other internal documents.

"For a more professional appearance, we use the NLQ mode with our word processing software. This mode is controlled simply by moving a switch on your printer. In NLQ mode, the pins create part of each character during one pass across a line of text. On the next pass, the pins create the remaining part of each character. Because the NLQ mode requires two passes across each line, this approach is much slower than the draft-quality mode. But it is important to have this improved appearance when we correspond with subscribers, advertisers, and other professional organizations. In these situations, we make a trade-off. That is, we sacrifice speed for quality of appearance.

"In certain cases, it helps to use the *letter-quality* printer to produce high-quality documents." Rebecca points to a printer located between the two desks. "With this printer, all characters are formed on a print element called a *daisy wheel*. Because each character is formed in metal or hard plastic, it looks extremely professional. We use the daisy wheel printer to produce advertising material, such as subscription packets. We mail these packets to potential subscribers as well as to clients whose subscriptions are up for renewal."

Review 20.2

1. Under what conditions is it almost a necessity to install a hard disk on a microcomputer?

2. What is meant by backing up files and data and software?

3. Why are backup files important for computer users?

4. What are the differences—in both performance and appearance—of outputs from draft-quality and letter-quality printers?

HOW DO YOU USE SYSTEM SOFTWARE?

At this point, Rebecca asks if you are ready to begin working with your computer system. You say that you are eager to get started. Rebecca says that the best way to begin is by familiarizing yourself with the computer's operating system.

"The operating system is called *DOS* by most personal computer users. The letters stand for *disk operating system*. When you purchase a computer, DOS comes on a single diskette. With a hard disk system, you have to install the operating system before you can begin to use the hard disk. Your machine already has DOS installed. However, I think it's important for you to know how to load as well

Business Terms

monochrome monitor
A computer display that presents images in one color only.

cursor
A blinking marker on the face of a display screen that identifies the point at which the next entry will be made.

function key
A key on a computer keyboard that calls up a function of an operating system or application program.

draft quality
Description of a printing capability that uses a matrix device to generate images of relatively low quality.

near letter quality (NLQ)
Description of a capability of some matrix printers to create imprints of improved quality through multiple impressions.

letter quality
Description of imprints that equal the quality of outputs from electric typewriters.

daisy wheel
A widely used imprint mechanism for letter quality printers.

disk operating system (DOS)
The operating system used with IBM PC and compatible computers.

as to use DOS. Let's begin by ignoring your hard disk. Consider that you have to load the operating system before you begin using any application programs. In other words, imagine that you're using your computer for the first time, without any software having been installed.''

NOTE: DOS is the operating system for IBM PC and compatible computers. These are the most popular personal computers. Other computers may use different operating systems. All operating systems have similar features and functions. If you are assigned to use a different make of computer, consult your user's manual for operating system instructions.

```
COMMAND   COM   26896   4-07-86    2:18p
CONFIG    SYS      39   1-01-80   12:07a
CONFIG    BAT      13   1-23-86    1:04p
ANSI      SYS    1852   3-25-86   11:40p
ASSIGN    COM    1509   3-25-86   10:37p
ATTRIB    EXE    7438   3-25-86   10:38p
BACKUP    EXE   21720   4-21-86    4:43p
CHKDSK    EXE    9296   3-25-86   11:00p
COMP      COM    2371   3-25-86   11:41p
DEBUG     EXE   15397   3-25-86   11:17p
DISKCOMP  COM    2352   3-25-86   11:43p
DISKCOPY  EXE   14336   6-19-86    4:13p
EDLIN     EXE    7122   3-25-86   11:29p
FDISK     COM    8025   5-27-86    3:10p
FIND      EXE    6403   3-25-86   11:36p
FORMAT    EXE   19968   6-03-86    4:06p
Strike a key when ready . . .
```

Figure 20-1.   *The DOS operating system includes a number of modules, which are listed in this screen display.*

How Do You Boot the Operating System?

''Your first task is to *boot* the operating system,'' Rebecca says. ''The word 'boot' is short for 'bootstrap.' When you turn a computer on, there are no programs in memory, no instructions to direct the equipment. The computer is designed to load the programs that are needed to control the system first. Then, other routines can be added. Starting from nothing this way and building gradually is called a bootstrap start.

''To begin, insert the DOS diskette into the 'A' drive and turn on your computer. On your system, the 'A' drive is the floppy diskette drive. For systems that have two floppy diskette drives, you would need to consult the manual.''

You do as Rebecca has instructed and insert a disk marked ''DOS 3.1'' and close the door of the disk drive. You then press the power switch and wait. After about 20 seconds, your machine responds with the following message:

MS-DOS version 3.10

© Copyright Microsoft Corp 1981, 1985

Enter Current Date:

''You can use the slash or dash character to enter a date,'' Rebecca says, ''just as you would use to write a date in your personal calendar.'' You enter the following:

7/21/89

The operating system responds with this message:

Enter Current Time:

''The time of day is not important to our applications,'' Rebecca says. ''You can bypass this entry simply by pressing the ENTER key.''

Drive selection.   You follow Rebecca's instruction by pressing the ENTER key. The computer responds by displaying a *prompt,* or a request for further instruction. In this case, the machine responds by displaying the following prompt:

A>

''This means that the computer is reading data from the 'A' drive, or the floppy disk drive,'' Rebecca tells you. ''The system is waiting for you to enter a processing command. Remember, though, that you are at the operating system level now. You haven't begun to use an application program. This is a good time to introduce yourself to some basic DOS functions.''

Displaying the directory. Rebecca then instructs you to enter the following command:

DIR

You do so, and the computer responds with the display shown in Figure 20-1.

"The letters 'DIR' are an abbreviation for 'Directory,' " Rebecca explains. "The directory is a list of files stored in a specified drive. In this case, your computer has listed all files on the 'A' drive of your system," Rebecca says. "Of course, the diskette in drive 'A' contains all of the files that are part of your disk operating system.

"Notice that the first file listed is called COMMAND.COM," Rebecca points out. "The COMMAND.COM file contains the operating system program instructions that direct the operations of the computer circuits as well as all attached peripheral devices. COMMAND.COM must be loaded into memory whenever you turn on your computer. This system program file directs the operations of all application programs that you will use."

Directory content. Rebecca then asks you to look at the way each file is displayed by the DIR command. "As you can see, the directory of the diskette in the 'A' drive lists four columns for each file. The first, leftmost column is the name of the file. For instance, the main program for the operating system is called COMMAND.

"The next column to the right lists the *extension* for each file. A file extension describes the general purpose for each file. For instance, the COMMAND file has the extension COM to indicate that the file contains a set of program commands. Other common extensions are EXE, DBF, and DOC. The extension EXE means that the file contains an application program that can be executed directly by the operating system. The extension DBF refers to a database file that contains information about business activity. The

extension DOC refers to a document, or text file that has been created by the word processing system.

"The third column shows the date that each file was last used. The fourth, rightmost column, shows the most recent time that a file was altered. At CompuTrends, we don't really need to know the time of each file change. However, the date for each file modification is important. The date helps us to recover a file from backup versions—in case the most recent version has been lost or damaged."

Rebecca then suggests that it is time to take a break. "After lunch," she says, "you'll have a chance to use the operating system a bit more. I'll also help you to become familiar with the use of our word processing software."

This chapter has provided a review of what it is like to encounter a personal computer in a business situation. As you continue into the next chapter, you will learn more about operating systems. You also will have a chance to learn about word processing applications in business.

Review 20.3

1. What does it mean to "boot" a computer?
2. What use is made of date and time entries that are made while the operating system is being loaded?
3. What is a file directory?
4. What is a file name extension?

Business Terms

boot
The action that turns a computer on and loads needed software to support its operation.

prompt
A message displayed by a computer that requests action by a user.

extension
A code appended to a file name to identify its purpose or function.

Chapter Summary

❑ Main memory, or primary storage, supports processing by making programs and data available as needed.

❑ The size of main memory can affect the efficiency of a computer. This is because larger memories can hold more programs and data, reducing the need to transfer data and programs from secondary storage.

❑ The operating system of a computer serves the user by controlling operation of hardware and access to application software.

❑ Secondary storage devices for microcomputers include diskettes and hard disks.

❑ Program and information files must be protected.

❑ Each personal computer requires at least three other attached devices, other than secondary storage units. These are a monitor, a keyboard, and a printer to produce outputs.

❑ A boot operation turns on the computer and loads system software. The idea is to make the computer ready for use.

❑ The current date and time can be entered each time the operating system is loaded.

❑ The DIR command causes the computer to list the content of the disk in the active drive.

Definitions

Write a complete sentence that defines each of the terms below.

load	RAM
megabyte	install
backup	peripheral
function key	draft quality
near letter quality	letter quality
DOS	boot
prompt	extension

Questions to Think About

Based on what you have learned to date, answer the following questions in one or more complete sentences.

1. What happens if you try to load an application program into a microcomputer before the operating system is loaded?

2. What is the role of an operating system?

3. What are the differences between floppy and hard disk drives?

4. How is the cursor positioned on a microcomputer screen?

5. What purposes are served by function keys on a microcomputer keyboard?

6. What purpose is served by completing time and date entries when you boot your operating system?

Projects

The purpose of the assignments below is to encourage you to increase your learning through outside reading or work assignments.

1. This chapter reviews the features of an operating system for IBM PC or compatible computers. Suppose you were assigned to use another make and model of computer, such as the Apple IIe. If this is the case in your school, find a manual in your computer center that describes the system software and booting methods for the Apple IIe or other make of computer. Identify the differences from the DOS system. Also, describe the booting procedure for this other system.

2. This chapter describes the function of the COMMAND.COM program of the disk operating system. There also is a listing of other programs within the DOS package. Select one other program on the DIR listing. By checking the manual or asking questions, gather information about and describe its purpose and functions.

CHAPTER 21

How Is a Computer Used For Word Processing?

The Think Tank

When you finish reading this chapter and complete your work assignments, you should be able to answer the following questions.

❑ How are application programs loaded and prepared for use?

❑ How do DOS utilities aid the COMMAND.COM file in processing application files?

❑ What are the chief differences between a typewriter and a computer-driven word processor?

❑ Why do different brands of word processors have many similar features?

DOING BUSINESS

Bob Gomez, a bank vice president, was frustrated initially when he tried to put his personal computer to work. Bob had tried to enter his word processing program first. Ryan Schalk, one of Bob's assistants helped by explaining that the operating system had to be loaded first. Then Ryan showed Bob how to load his word processing software. When this was done, the screen of Bob's computer displayed the main menu for the word processing package. The menu offered a series of options that included editing an existing document, creating a new document, printing a document, and others.

Bob reviewed the main menu on the screen. He knew that he wanted to begin by entering the text for a **memorandum.** A memorandum, or simply **memo,** is a document intended for internal communication within an organization. A memo is less for-mal than a letter, which usually is sent to someone outside the organization.

Menu choice 2 seemed like the processing option that Bob wanted at this point. The menu labeled choice 2 as "Create a New Document." Bob noticed this message near the bottom of the screen:

Enter the number of the function; press RETURN

Bob knew that the ENTER key on his keyboard was another name for the carrier "return" key used on electric typewriters. He reasoned, correctly, that the words ENTER and RETURN referred to the same key. He entered a 2 and pressed the key marked ENTER and was presented with a display that asked him to name a new document.

The message, or prompt, on the screen requested that Bob enter the name of the document that he wanted to create. Bob chose the name BOB'S MEMO, since it described the purpose of his document. He then pressed the ENTER key. The computer responded immediately with a disturbing message. The computer stated that Bob had made an **Invalid Entry.** This message meant that the word processing program was not capable of using Bob's file name.

Bob immediately called Ryan to ask for assistance. "It seems that nothing I do with this computer is correct," Bob complained when Ryan arrived. Ryan looked at Bob's computer screen.

"I see your problem," Ryan said. "This word processing program, like most application programs, doesn't accept the blank space character as part of a file name. Also, a file name can be up to eight characters long, no more. The reason has to do with the way file names are stored in memory. It isn't important for you to understand why the blank space character is not valid. Also, you don't have to worry about why file names are limited to eight characters. However, you do have to recognize the limitations and restrictions of each software package that you use. That means learning the basics first."

MEANING

Bob is finding out that computers are only as effective as the people who use them. Bob's computer does not operate by itself. For instance, the word processing program that Bob is using is said to be **interactive.** This term means that both the computer and the user participate in processing. The word processing program provides prompts and menus that Bob can use to direct processing. A prompt, remember, is a request to a user for some processing instruction. A menu is a list of choices. The computer does nothing until a human user responds to a prompt or makes a menu choice.

Although prompts and menus guide users, it is up to people to make selections and enter data accurately. As the interactive user of his computer system, Bob has to take charge. He has to understand the capabilities and limitations of each application program that he uses. This means that Bob has to

educate himself. With a strong understanding of computer hardware and software features, Bob can become a responsible and effective personal computer user.

SCENARIO: COMPUTRENDS, INC.

Recall from Chapter 20 that CompuTrends, Inc., publishes a newsletter for businesspeople who use personal computers. You have been hired recently to work with Rebecca to handle customer accounts processing. Before lunch, Rebecca introduced you to the COMMAND.COM program of the disk operating system. This program is at the heart of the operating system.

When you return from lunch, Rebecca is waiting to provide you with further instruction. "The COMMAND.COM program's chief role is to direct the flow of data and application program instructions," Rebecca reminds you. "The operating system also can perform a few file management operations. Later this afternoon, I'll show you how to use the COPY command to back up your files. Right now, how about learning to use the word processor?"

HOW DO YOU LOAD AN APPLICATION PROGRAM?

Rebecca explains that the word processing program you will use is called WordPerfect, a software package sold by the WordPerfect Corporation. She also mentions that the programs for WordPerfect have already been stored on your hard disk. However, to use this program, you first must load it by entering a few simple commands.

Loading a program means that the operating system creates a link with the application package. Then, all or part of the application program instructions are copied into main memory. At this point, your operating system turns over control of the computer to your application program.

Learning to interact with computers is an important skill for many managers. Today, many managers and executives generate their own text documents on microcomputers.

COURTESY OF HAYES MICROCOMPUTER PRODUCTS, INC.

As you sit at your keyboard, Rebecca begins to provide instructions. "When you turn on your computer in the morning, it will go through a warm-up and checkout routine," Rebecca tells you. This is handled by a part of the system software that is stored permanently on a microchip inside the computer. Programs that are stored permanently in this way often are called *firmware.*

What Is 'Firmware' and What Role Does It Play?

"In addition," Rebecca continues, "I have used a simple program that tells the firmware to load DOS automatically whenever the power is turned on. Recall that this is possible because the COMMAND.COM file is stored on your hard disk. You don't need to load DOS from a floppy diskette each morning. Your computer also will use its internal clock to store the date and time in memory when COMMAND.COM is loaded. Go ahead and turn on your computer now."

You do as Rebecca instructs and move the power switch to the ON position. The computer takes about

10 seconds to warm up and test its own circuits. Then, the screen displays the following prompt:

C>

"This prompt, like the '**A**' prompt you saw this morning, tells you what drive the operating system will use to read and write data," Rebecca says. "It's

Business Terms

memorandum, memo
A text document intended for internal communication within an organization.

interactive
An operational condition in which both the computer and the user participate in processing.

firmware
Program segments stored on read-only memory hardware devices for constant availability to the computer.

also important to know that a hard disk uses a *directory* system to organize stored data and application programs. A hard-disk directory, in effect, sets up a series of partitions that provide separate storage areas. Each application program is stored in a different directory. Right now, you are in the *main directory*. This directory simply tells the operating system the names and track locations for all other directories stored on the hard disk.''

```
┌──────────────────────────┐
│    WordPerfect           │
├──────────────────────────┤
│    Version 4.2           │
└──────────────────────────┘
```

(C)Copyright 1982,1983,1984,1985,1986
All Rights Reserved
WordPerfect Corporation
Orem, Utah USA

NOTE: The WP System is using C:

Are other copies of WordPerfect currently running? (Y/N)

Program loading for a word processing package begins with the display of a title screen. The screen shown serves as an introduction to use of the WordPerfect word processor.

How Do You Use Your Hard-Disk Directory?

''The WordPerfect directory is called WORDP. You have to enter a command that tells the operating system to change to this directory from the one with DOS.'' Rebecca then instructs you to enter the following:

CD WORDP

''The letters CD represent a basic operating system command and stand for the words 'Change Directory.' You enter this command, a blank space, and then the name of the *destination* directory. This term means that you are telling the computer where to go in its next operation. Remember, an interactive computer needs orders from you. In this case, your destination directory is called WORDP. Now press ENTER.''

You press the ENTER key, and the program responds instantly with a new prompt:

C: \ WORD >

How Do You Move an Application Program From Storage to Memory?

''Now you are ready to load your word processing program into memory,'' Rebecca says. ''Remember: At this point, the WordPerfect program exists only on the hard disk. You have to load the program into

memory before you can use it to process text. The command to load this program is simply **WP**. Enter that now, and then press the enter key.''

You enter the letters WP next to the prompt and press ENTER. After a few seconds, the title of the program is displayed on the screen, along with some other messages.

''This is the title and copyright screen,'' Rebecca says. The program also displays a message stating that WordPerfect currently is running in drive C.''

As you review the screen, you notice a puzzling instruction near the bottom of the display. ''The program asks me if other copies of WordPerfect currently are running. Why would I run two copies of a program at one time?''

Rebecca smiles and replies quickly. ''That message is designed for systems that are part of a network. A network is formed by linking several personal computers. Usually, one station in the network is more powerful than the others. Also, there can be a large storage device that maintains files that can be shared by all network stations. If you were on a network, you would answer 'Yes' to this prompt.

Coaching from co-workers can help a new user get started in the use of word processing or other packages. Each application requires the user to develop a "vocabulary" that involves mastery of a number of commands that direct the software.
COURTESY OF APPLE COMPUTERS, INC.

In doing so, you are notifying the operating system about other active versions of WordPerfect. This information prevents the operating system from becoming 'confused' as instructions and data are passed to and from the main computer."

You feel that you understand. "Obviously," you say, "I should enter an 'N' for 'No' at this prompt." Rebecca nods and you enter an "N" at the prompt. The computer responds with a screen that is blank, except for the bottom line. This line contains the following information:

Doc 1 Pg 1 Ln 1   Pos 10

"Your program loading operation is complete. You are ready to start word processing," Rebecca says. "The entry at the bottom of the screen is called the *status line.* The message Doc 1 is useful in case you are editing or printing more than one document at a time. The remaining three messages—Pg 1, Ln 1, and Pos 10—provide information about your location in the document. In this case, your cursor is on the first line of the first page. This is the position of the cursor when you begin creating a document.

"Also, the message 'Pos 10' tells you that the cursor is 10 positions to the right of the left margin. As you enter text, you'll notice that the page, line, and cursor position numbers will change. In other words, these numbers help you keep track of your

Business Terms

directory
A file that lists and describes the content of a secondary storage device.

main directory
A directory maintained by a hard disk that identifies the data directories stored on the device.

destination
The target for an access or search operation performed by a computer.

status line
A line at the top or bottom of the screen that identifies the file in use, the page number, and the position of the cursor.

place in a document. Now you're ready to begin entering text," Rebecca says.

1. What is the main directory on a hard disk?

2. How does interactive processing begin?

3. Where must an application program be stored before you begin to use it?

4. What is a status display and what does it tell the user?

HOW DO YOU ENTER TEXT WITH A WORD PROCESSOR?

Rebecca mentions that the keyboard of your computer works much like the keyboard of a typewriter. However, entered characters are displayed on the screen rather than printed on a sheet of paper. She asks you to enter text for a practice document. You begin by entering the line below:

```
Word processors are valuable tools used for
```

As you continue to watch the screen, you notice that part of your next word appears on the first line, like this:

```
Word processors are valuable tools used for cre
```

Then, it suddenly is moved to the left-hand margin of the second line:

```
Word processors are valuable tools used for
creating, editing,
```

You mention to Rebecca that this approach is different from the one you are used to following with a typewriter.

How Do You Format Text?

"That's right," Rebecca responds. "With a typewriter, you have to press a carrier return bar or key at the end of each line. The carrier return causes the paper to advance to the next line and moves the type ball to the left-hand margin.

"A word processing program handles this function automatically. It's called *word wrap.* This means a word that is too large to fit within the right-hand margin of a line is 'wrapped' to the next line. That is, the word processing system controls its line widths automatically from settings that are entered by users. You don't have to worry about that today. I have entered standard settings that we use on all company correspondence. So, the system is all set for you to get some practice with text entry.

"You don't actually enter lines of text. You just keep entering words, spaces, and punctuation marks until you come to the end of a paragraph. The only time you have to enter returns is at the ends of paragraphs. The computer doesn't record individual lines either. It just deals with strings of words. Line lengths are set up automatically when text is displayed or printed.

"Notice, too, that the program is set up for a double-spaced line. With WordPerfect, your document appears on the screen almost identical to the way it will appear when it is printed. That means that the program aligns your left margin 10 characters to the right of the edge of the screen. In turn, new lines are separated by a space to indicate double spacing. These features are part of the format, or appearance, of your document. I set these document format specifications when I installed WordPerfect on your hard disk. However, they can be changed at any time by entering a few simple commands.

"Why don't you go ahead and enter a paragraph or two of text?" Rebecca suggests. She explains that when you enter an incorrect character, you can press the Backspace key. This Backspace key erases any character that it passes over. This procedure is called

Entry of numbers into microcomputers can be speeded up through use of a numeric keypad like the one at the right of the keyboard in this photo.
COURTESY OF TELEVIDEO SYSTEMS, INC.

a *destructive backspace*. That is, when you backspace over a character, the letter, number, or other symbol is "destroyed," or erased. Then, simply enter the correct character and continue typing.

"When you're done, I can show you some of the document editing features of WordPerfect," Rebecca says.

HOW DO YOU EDIT TEXT?

After a few minutes of text entry, you are ready to show Rebecca your completed paragraph:

```
Word processors are valuable tools used for
creating, editing, and printing text.  With this
word processing package, you can edit text in
many ways, and as often as you like.  After you
have made any necessary changes, you can print a
final version--error free.
```

"Good," Rebecca says after she has reviewed your paragraph. "I see that you already understand the basic capabilities of word processing programs. Now I'll show you how to put your knowledge to work."

What Editing Functions Are Available?

Rebecca tells you that more than a dozen types of editing functions are available with most professional word processing packages. Some of the most widely used functions include:

- INSERT
- DELETE
- MOVE
- COPY
- SEARCH
- SEARCH/REPLACE
- SPELLCHECK

The INSERT function. The *INSERT* function provides the ability to add words, phrases, and sentences without destroying or altering the appearance of existing text. When you put your computer into INSERT mode, the program automatically adds

Business Terms

word wrap
The operation that automatically moves the text entry operation to the beginning of a new line when an end-of-line condition is sensed.

destructive backspace
An optional setting that causes a computer to erase the character to the left of the cursor each time the BACKSPACE key is depressed.

INSERT
An application software function that provides the ability to add words, phrases, and sentences without destroying or altering the appearance of existing text.

space to your document to allow room for the added characters.

To demonstrate, recall that you have just finished entering a paragraph in WordPerfect. The cursor on your screen is positioned after the end of your paragraph. This, of course, is where you stopped entering text. You want to insert text at the end of the first sentence. You use your ''up'' and ''right'' cursor arrow keys to move the cursor. You notice that these keys are on the numeric keypad, to the right of the main keyboard. By pressing the ''up'' arrow key three times, you are able to move the cursor to the middle of the second line:

```
Word processors are valuable tools used for
creating, editing, and printing text.  With this
```

Your cursor is now under the ''g'' in the word ''printing.'' You then hold down the ''right'' arrow key until the cursor is positioned under the ''W'' in the word ''With.'' Following instructions, you press the INSERT key and type in a new sentence as Rebecca dictates. As you add text, you notice that the text to the right and below your insertion is ''pushed'' forward:

```
Word processors are valuable tools used for
creating, editing, and printing text.  Many
other featuresWith this word processing package,
you can edit text in many ways, and as often as
```

You notice that the program wraps the existing text down to make room for the inserted words. When you finish, your paragraph looks like this:

```
Word processors are valuable tools used for
creating, editing, and printing text.  Many
other features are possible.  With this word
processing package, you can edit text in many
ways, and as often as you like.  After you have
made any necessary changes, you can print a
final version--error free.
```

Marking copy blocks for DELETE, MOVE, and COPY functions.   Rebecca then continues to explain procedures for the *DELETE, MOVE,* and *COPY* functions. With most word processors, text to be deleted, moved, or copied first must be *block marked.* A block refers to the portion of text that you want to delete, move, or copy. With block marking, you simply *highlight,* or label, the appropriate block. This must be done before the computer can follow your instructions for the delete, move, or copy operations.

As a demonstration, you are instructed to highlight the phrase ''word processing'' in the third sentence. You move the cursor until it is under the letter ''w'' in ''word.'' To begin highlighting, you press the ALT/F4 key combination. As you do, the phrase ''Block on'' flashes on the status line at the bottom of the screen. Next, you move the cursor to the blank space immediately following the word ''processing.'' At this point, the phrase ''word processing'' now appears brighter than the surrounding text. This completes the block marking procedure.

Now you are ready to delete this phrase. In WordPerfect, block deletions are made by using the *cut* operation. The word cut simply means you are going to remove, or cut, a marked block from your text.

Completing DELETE, MOVE, and COPY operations.   Rebecca tells you to press the CTRL/F4 key combination to begin the cut operation. The following choices appear near the bottom of the screen:

1 Cut Block; 2 Copy Block; 3 Append;
4 Cut/Copy Column;
5 Cut/Copy Rectangle: 0

This display provides the options you can use to process your highlighted block. In this case, you want to cut the phrase ''word processing.'' So you enter the number ''1''. As soon as you do, the phrase ''word processing'' disappears. The program automatically closes the space that this phrase occupied by pulling the existing text back.

Desktop computers have become standard office tools. American businesses now use about 20 million microcomputers.

The SEARCH and SEARCH/REPLACE functions. All commercial word processors have functions that enable you to search text files for special words or characters. The *SEARCH* operation is carried out at electronic speeds. Also, the computer is thorough in performing a search, more reliable than people who read text.

To illustrate, suppose you were working on the text for Chapter 20 of this book, which actually was written on a word processing system. You are not sure whether you have used the word DELETE correctly in every case. You want the word to be capitalized if it refers to a computer operation. However, if the same word is part of a general description, it should be in lowercase.

The MOVE and COPY commands work in a similar manner. You begin by highlighting the key words in the same way. Under WordPerfect, you go through a "cut" command just as you did for a deletion. The text that you cut is placed in a special area of memory. Then, if you want to do a MOVE or COPY operation, you place the cursor at the new location within the text where you want the block placed.

When you press CTRL/F4, the following choices appear on the status line:

Move 1 Sentence; 2 Paragraph; 3 Page;

Retrieve 4 Column; 5 Text; 6 Rectangle: 0

You want to move a sentence, so enter the number 1. When you enter this number, your first sentence reappears as the next to last sentence in your document. Your paragraph now looks like this:

```
With this package, you can edit text in many
ways, and as often as you like.  Many other
features are possible.  Word processors are
valuable tools used for creating, editing, and
printing text.  After you have made any
necessary changes, you can print a final
version--error free.
```

Business Terms

DELETE
An application software function used to remove text or data from a file.

MOVE
An application software function used to move text or data from one location in a file to another.

COPY
An application software function used to copy text or data in one portion of a file to another location while leaving the initial entries in place.

block mark
To identify a portion of a file as a target for a DELETE, MOVE, or COPY operation.

highlight
A technique used to block mark a segment of copy for further use.

cut
An operation that removes a segment of text from a display and places it in a special memory area. The cut text can be deleted, moved, or copied.

SEARCH
An application software function used to seek a specific set of characters within a text file.

You call upon the SEARCH function of your word processor. You key in the word: delete. Then you tell the computer to go ahead with its search. In seconds per page, the computer "reads" the text and matches each word with your search *target,* the word "delete." Note that, in most programs, the word will be found whether it is in upper- or lowercase in the text. You also can ask the system to search for specific letter patterns if you wish.

Under the procedure described, the computer will stop its search and place the cursor at each occurrence of the target word. Then you can examine the text and make any adjustments you wish.

It also is possible to replace a target word with a substitute term. You do this with a *SEARCH/ REPLACE* option that is available with virtually all commercial word processors. To illustrate, suppose you decide to change one of the terms in Chapter 20 of this book. In a first draft, you used the term "delimit" to describe the marking of text for DELETE, MOVE, or COPY operations. Delimit is a technical term that refers to setting boundaries around a target portion of text. You decide it will be easier to use the term "highlight."

With the SEARCH/REPLACE function your word processor asks first what is to be replaced. You enter the word: delimit. Next, you are asked for the replacement term and you enter: highlight. These entries program the computer to replace the word delimit with highlight. You can do this in either of two ways. One is a *global* replace operation. If you use this choice, the computer replaces your target word every time it is found. The operation is automatic.

The other choice is a *discretionary* replacement. Under this type of operation, the computer stops when it finds your target term and asks if you want to make the change. You can decide to do the replacement or to leave the text alone.

In the example situation, a discretionary operation probably will be best. The reason is that the computer doesn't have the judgment that you do. For

example, suppose the target word appears at the beginning of a sentence. It would have to be capitalized. However, the computer will not know this and, if you did not ask for a discretionary operation, it would make the replacement in lowercase.

There may be situations in which global replacement is best. For example, suppose you discovered that you had misspelled the word cursor. You have spelled it "curser" in several instances. You want to correct the error wherever it occurs. You are concerned, of course, about situations where the word comes at the beginning of a sentence. So, you instruct the computer to replace the string of letters "urser" with "ursor." The computer is a literal device that can deal with any set of instructions it is given.

The SPELLCHECK function.   As part of another option, most word processors can help you to check the spelling of the text you have entered. The *SPELLCHECK* function may have different names in different packages. But the idea is the same: The program includes an extensive dictionary. The text of your document is reviewed, word by word. Each word is checked against the dictionary. If the computer finds a matching word with the same spelling in its dictionary, it passes on to the next word.

If the computer does not find a matching word, it does one of two things. In some word processing packages, the computer will stop and place the cursor at the word that doesn't match. You can then change the word or tell the computer to proceed with its search. In other systems, the computer marks the word in some way that is easily recognizable. Then it continues its search.

Use of this feature will help you to check your work carefully and to find many of your errors. However, you have to realize that the computer has limits in the way it uses language. A spell checking program can overlook errors. It also can mark correct words as errors.

To illustrate, suppose you want to enter the word "tow." You key it incorrectly as "two." The com-

Keyboard editing is a fast, accurate, high-quality way to update the content of business documents. Only changes have to be made. The computer handles the work of printing new documents.

COURTESY OF HONEYWELL, INC.

puter recognizes two as an acceptable word and goes on.

Another problem is that most spell checking dictionaries look for only one version of a given word. If you use the plural of a noun or the past tense of a verb, the computer probably will flag an error even though the word is correct.

The point: There is no substitute for human language skills and for care in reading and checking your work.

Review 21.2

1. How is the word wrap feature of a word processing system different from a RETURN entry?

2. What happens when you ''cut'' a section of text from a document?

3. What are the differences between MOVE and COPY functions?

4. What are the differences between SEARCH and SEARCH/REPLACE functions?

5. What limitations should you be aware of when you use a spell checking function of a word processing program?

HOW DO YOU SAVE A FILE?

You tell Rebecca that the features of your new word processor should help make text entry and editing an easy process. ''That's the idea,'' she says. ''Now let me show you how to save your file. I also want to show you how to back up a file onto a floppy diskette.

''Remember,'' Rebecca points out, ''that your document exists only in main memory. You need to make a permanent copy by saving the document, or file, to the hard disk. You do this simply by pressing the F7 key. When you press this function key, the following message appears:

Save Document? (Y/N)

Business Terms

target
A set of characters that is the object of a SEARCH operation.

SEARCH/REPLACE
An application software function that looks for a set of characters within a text file and replaces the target characters with another set.

global
An option under a SEARCH/REPLACE function that acts upon all occurrences of a target set of characters within a file.

discretionary
An operation that is executed only upon specific instruction from a user.

SPELLCHECK
A function of word processing software that compares words within text with a stored dictionary and highlights any differences.

Safekeeping of storage media *is necessary to assure that information resources will be available when they are needed. The company in this photo keeps copies of diskettes in a fireproof safe file.*
PHOTO BY ROBERT KOCH

You enter the letter "Y" to indicate that you want to save the document to your hard disk. Another message then appears:

Document to be Saved:

"The program is asking you for a file name," Rebecca says. "You can use any eight characters, except for the blank space character." You enter the name TESTFILE and then press the ENTER key. The program displays a message indicating that TESTFILE is being saved to drive C of your computer system. After a few seconds, another prompt appears:

Exit WP? (Y/N)
(Cancel to return to document)

"Your editing session is over," Rebecca tells you, "so go ahead and enter a 'Y.'" When you enter a

"Y," the program returns you to the operating system. The C > operating system prompt appears on the screen.

HOW DO YOU COPY A DOCUMENT?

The COMMAND.COM program's chief role is to direct the flow of data and application program instructions. However, this program also can perform a few file management operations. You specify each operation by entering a command next to the C > prompt.

For instance the COPY command lets you copy the contents of a file from one disk to another. It's important to learn this command immediately because it plays a major role in protecting your files.

To illustrate, begin by copying the TESTFILE from your hard disk to the new floppy diskette. You enter the following command next to the C > prompt:

COPY TESTFILE A:

The word COPY tells the operating system that you want to copy a file. However, you need to provide three other pieces of identifying information.

First, you have to provide the operating system with the name of the file that you want to copy. The entry TESTFILE provides the name of the file.

Next, you have to tell the operating system where the file is to be copied. In this case, you want to copy the file to the disk in drive A. The "A:" part of the instruction provides this information, the destination of the file.

When you press ENTER, the lights on the floppy and hard disk drives flash briefly. Then, this message appears on the screen:

1 File(s) copied

This message advises you that the file copying operation has been performed successfully. If there had been any problems, the operating system would have *aborted,* or canceled, the copy operation. Whenever COMMAND.COM or another DOS utility aborts an operation, it displays a message describing the problem.

Now you have two identical, permanent copies of your file—one on the hard disk and the other on a floppy disk. Make sure to store the floppy diskette in a safe place. You might need to retrieve this backup copy if anything happens to your hard disk.

ARE ALL WORD PROCESSORS ALIKE?

Most professional word processing packages provide similar functions for processing text. For instance, virtually all word processing packages provide functions for moving, inserting, copying, and deleting blocks of text. However, the steps that you follow to carry out these functions may be different for each processing package. Also, other word processors might display menus, status lines, and text in different ways.

For instance, consider a technique used by a word processing package called MultiMate. The MultiMate word processor is sold by the Ashton-Tate Corportation. With MultiMate, the status line for a document is displayed along the top of the screen, rather than the bottom.

The appearance and use of the status line in MultiMate also differ from the approach used with WordPerfect. With MultiMate, all text is single-spaced on the screen. This approach allows users to view as much text as possible at one time. However, the status line might show that the document will be double- or triple-spaced when the text is printed. The status line in MultiMate also shows you where each *tab stop* is located. A tab stop indicates the position on a text line to which entries will move each time the TAB key is pressed.

The appearance of the status line is one of several differences between MultiMate, WordPerfect, and other word processors. However, these differences do not necessarily mean that different programs are difficult to learn. If you understand the basic functions available with a word processor, you can adapt easily. For instance, if you understand the principle behind block marking text, you can transfer this understanding from one program to another. Each word processor will use different key combinations for marking text blocks. Commands also will differ for moving, copying, and deleting text. However, the concepts are the same from one program to another.

The point: By understanding the basic features available with a type of application package, you can apply your knowledge to several different software products. It is relatively easy to learn new key combinations if you understand the functions that these keys control. This chapter has introduced the basic functions of word and text processing software. The same principles apply to other kinds of application packages. In the chapter that follows, you will deal with the basics of file and database management software.

Review 21.3

1. What happens when you enter a SAVE command?

2. What DOS functions can you use to make a backup copy of a file?

3. What do different word processing programs have in common?

Business Terms

abort
Cancellation of an operation that has been initiated or is in progress.

tab stop
A setting that causes the cursor to move to the selected position when the TAB key is depressed.

Chapter Summary

❑ An interactive computer is one that requires participation of both the user and the computer.

❑ To load an application package, the programs must be made available on disk.

❑ As text is entered, a word processing program maintains a display that identifies the document in work, as well as the page, line, and cursor position numbers.

❑ Entering text into a computer is similar to typing on a typewriter, except that the text is displayed on a screen.

❑ When you reach the end of a line on a word processing system, the word wrap feature is applied. This moves the word that goes beyond the end of any line to the beginning of the next line.

❑ To edit text you have entered, you have perhaps a dozen functions you can use.

❑ To save work you have done, you record a document you have entered into memory to a secondary storage device.

❑ To back up and protect your work, you prepare a copy of each document or file on a medium that can be removed from the computer. Diskettes are the most commonly used backup media. Copies of files should be stored in a safe place.

❑ Many word processing packages are available.

Definitions

Write a complete sentence that defines each of the terms below.

interactive	load
firmware	directory
destination	status line
word wrap	destructive backspace
block mark	cut
global	discretionary
abort	tab stop

Questions to Think About

Based on what you have learned to date, answer the following questions in one or more complete sentences.

1. What is interactive processing and what role does a human operator play in an interactive system?

2. What is firmware and what does it do?

3. How do operating system and application software packages interact?

4. Why is it necessary to load your application package into memory?

5. What is word wrap and what does this feature do for you?

6. What does the INSERT function do?

7. What is block marking and why is block marking necessary?

8. What is the DELETE function and how does it work?

9. What is the MOVE function and how does it work?

10. What is the COPY function and how does it work?

11. How do you save a file you have created?

12. What backup and protection measures should be applied to your computer files?

Projects

The purpose of the assignments below is to encourage you to increase your learning through outside reading or work assignments.

1. Review manuals or articles for two word processing programs. Compare the features of the two programs. Describe the one that seems best to you. Explain your reasons.

2. Visit an office in which personal computers are used. Find out what procedures are followed to back up and protect documents and files. Describe what you observe. Also describe the principles that are applied and what these mean to you.

CHAPTER 22

What Are Data Files and Databases?

When you finish reading this chapter and complete your work assignments, you should be able to answer the following questions.

❑ What are data files and what purposes do they serve?

❑ What is a database and how is a database different from a file?

❑ What is a database management system (DBMS) and what does it do?

❑ How does a database affect the development of business applications for computers?

❑ What is a data model and what kinds of data models are used for database management systems?

DOING BUSINESS

Saul Aguilar is a sales manager for a wholesale food distributor. This company sells food products in bulk, or large quantities, to restaurants and hotels. Saul recently came up with what he believed to be a great idea. He realized that certain customers regularly placed orders for amounts greater than $1,000. Most companies placed orders for much smaller amounts. Saul wanted to encourage customers to place larger orders. He wanted to do this by promising special, fast service on large orders.

Saul believed his company's computer system could help him to set up this service. He knew that customer orders were entered into the computer when they were received. For each order, the computer entered a new data item into the accounts receivable (A/R) file. Saul wanted to set up a system that searched the A/R file before deliveries were loaded each day. The computer would find orders for $1,000 or more. Then, it would search the files to find records for these customers. The computer would be instructed to set up these large orders to be delivered first each day.

Making this service known, Saul felt, would help his company to sell larger orders. Saul took his idea to Milton Jackson, the senior computer programmer for the company. "What I would like to do," Saul told Milton, "is to enter a request into the computer system at the start of each business day. In response, I would like the computer to produce a priority delivery report based upon data in the customer and A/R files. Can you design the program in a few days?"

"Sorry, Saul," Milton said. "It isn't that simple. Our system is designed to process each master file for a single set of application files. Combining the content of multiple files is possible, but not easy. The

Databases model *the status and operations of a business, including the inventories maintained in warehouses. Documents generated by computers guide warehouse and factory workers in producing, storing, and delivering a company's products.*
COURTESY OF SPACESAVER CORP.

report you want will require several hundred hours of programming and some redesign of file content. It will be expensive.''

"But I know that one of our competitors has this kind of capability,'' Saul protested.

"That's because their computer system uses a database management system to access and relate data from multiple files. We have a more traditional file processing system. I've been trying to convince top-level management to switch to a database management system approach for more than a year. But I haven't had much luck. They need to hear from managers like you—the people who have a need for information. If top-level managers recognize the potential for developing applications that can improve business performance, they might be willing to develop a DBMS.''

MEANING

Business situations and processing requirements change constantly. Saul recognizes this fact. He wants to use his company's computer system to improve service to customers. However, this company still uses single-application files. Milton and his staff originally had designed programs and set up files

for each application. It is difficult to combine the content of these files to meet changing needs.

To illustrate, look at the flow diagram in Figure 22-1. This illustrates the order processing system. Order information is entered directly into a computer that uses a series of programs to assemble order information and output order documents.

The system uses a series of master files separately. For example, the order-entry system can draw information from the customer master file. This information includes the name and address to which the order will be shipped. However, when it is necessary to change a record in the customer master file, this must be done separately. Another program is used to make additions or changes to the master file.

The same is true for the inventory file. The order processing program uses this file. But entries that cover receipt of new inventory must be processed separately. Thus, access to the accounts receivable file would, under this system, require a separate, special program.

Saul's request illustrates a problem. For Milton to satisfy Saul's processing request, it will be necessary to design complex new programs. Records in existing master files might have to be changed to

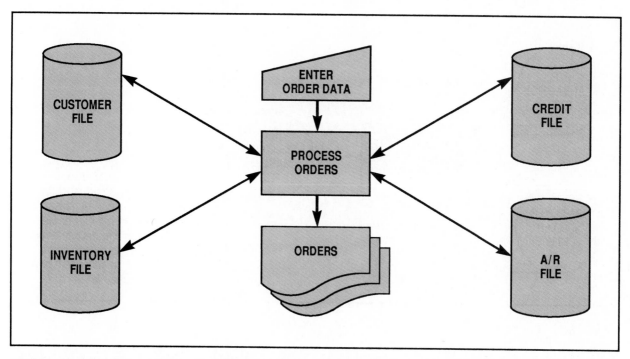

Figure 22-1. *This diagram demonstrates the way in which multiple files within a database maintained on disk drives are used to support a typical business application, generating orders.*

do the job he wants. This can be frustrating. The information Saul wants is in his computer. But the software used won't let him get at the records he needs. It is no wonder that Saul feels that it would be a good idea to set up a DBMS.

HOW DO SINGLE-APPLICATION FILES DIFFER FROM DATABASES?

In the early years of business computers, software development activities were major undertakings. Large companies frequently spent $2 million or more to develop individual applications.

During these years, main memory and secondary storage devices were expensive. Programmers recognized this limitation. In response, they developed programs that would use minimum amounts of memory and storage for each application.

One way to limit the use of primary and secondary storage involved designing separate files and programs for individual applications. In this way, data could be input and then stored *off-line*. This term refers to data files that are stored on media that are not mounted on drive devices. This means the data files are not currently available to a computer. Instead, they are stored on shelves or in cabinets. Before the data can be used, the media have to be taken to a computer and mounted for use.

Business Terms
off-line
Reference to data files that are stored on media not currently mounted on drive devices.

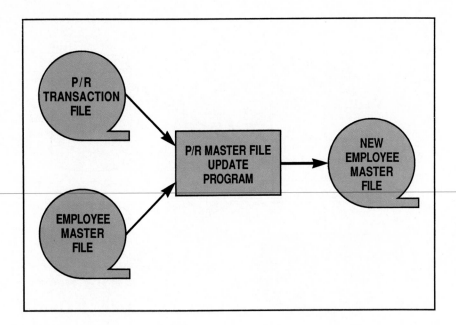

Figure 22-2. *This flowchart illustrates the use of tape files to process a payroll. A transaction file and a payroll master file, both sorted into the same record key order, are processed through a computer to generate a new payroll master file.*

How Are Tape Files Processed?

A good illustration can be seen in the processing of a typical payroll during the early 1960s. Employee master files were kept on tape reels. Throughout the week, payroll data items were captured as part of transaction files stored on separate tape reels. When it came time to process the payrolls, the transaction tapes were sorted into the same order as the master files.

Consider what happened in a tape sorting operation. One record from the transaction file was brought into memory. Then, a second record was brought in and compared with the first. The record with the lowest value (or highest, depending on the sort sequence) was written to a new tape. This operation was repeated a number of times before the transactions were in master file sequence. It may have been necessary to sort tens of thousands of records. But only two at a time occupied computer memory. Use of main memory was minimized.

The same was true when the master file was updated to reflect transactions. One transaction record at a time was brought into memory. It was matched

with one employee master record and processed. Then, a new employee master record was written to a new tape. Again, the demand on memory was small. To save memory through this approach, transaction records had to be saved and grouped before processing took place. The group of transactions used to update the master file formed a "batch." The updating method followed with tape processing techniques is known as "batch processing." The steps in a payroll batch system are illustrated in the flowchart in Figure 22-2.

How Is a Tape Library Built?

As explained earlier, each time a tape file is processed, a new file is created on an entirely separate reel of tape. The new tape becomes the master file. The previous master file and the transaction file used for updating become backups. The backup and master tapes are saved in a tape library. As indicated in the photo in Figure 22-3, tape libraries could become large and cumbersome in big companies. The main point, however, is that tapes in a library are not accessible to a computer. If the

Figure 22-3. *Large volumes of information are recorded in tape files. Many companies use tape reels to store backup copies of data files and also copies of system software and application programs.*

PHOTO BY LIANE ENKELIS

information is needed, a tape must be taken from the library and mounted on a secondary storage device. This takes time. If a company is using a computer that carries out tens of millions of instructions per second, even a few minutes represents a costly delay.

As the cost of disk storage has continued to drop through the years, user organizations have put increasing amounts of information into on-line files. These files, of course, are continually available for computer access. To ease the access—and to increase the value of information—database management software has been developed.

WHAT BENEFITS DOES A DBMS DELIVER?

With a database management system (DBMS), it is possible to store data for several files as a single collection, called the "database." Typically, an entire database is stored on random access disk files. This means that any records on the secondary storage devices can be accessed by the computer, in any order, at any time. In a large computer system, a database may contain several billion bytes of information.

How Does a Database Affect Development of Applications?

The DBMS software keeps track of the locations of individual data items, at all times. The DBMS also recognizes the format of each data item. In this way, new applications can be developed around existing files. Instead of having to build a file from scratch for each application, the database can be used. If additional data items are needed for a new application, they can be added easily to the database. The main idea is that it is not necessary to set up new files that contain existing data items. Any application can use any items within the database. One major advantage of a database approach, therefore, is that application development becomes easier and less expensive.

How Does a DBMS Affect Data Access for Users?

With a DBMS, it is possible for users to access data by posing simple *queries.* A query is a request for data. Query instructions are easy to learn. By entering a query command, a user can access selected data from a database within seconds. The built-in query language of a DBMS means that users can access data "on demand," without requiring a separate program. A sequence of queries can serve as an application program to set up a new information processing system.

For example, if Saul Aguilar's company had a database, he could get his report by entering a few query instructions. The DBMS would search the files and present his information in a printed list. Drivers could follow the listed information to provide priority service to the company's best customers.

Query languages and DBMS programs are discussed in greater depth in Chapter 23.

How Does a DBMS Help To Apply Data Security?

Another benefit of a DBMS involves *data security*. The term "data security" involves a set of protective measures that guard information against illegal or unauthorized use. Illegal use of data involves the commission of crimes. Criminals who gain access to computer files can make changes that lead to writing of checks or shipping of merchandise to people who are not entitled to them.

DBMS software contains capabilities for restricting data access to *authorized users* only. An authorized user is a person who has a need or a right to access and use stored information. For instance, the DBMS for a bank might allow tellers to view information about customer loans. However, the tellers would not be able to alter data about these loans.

The reason lies in the tellers' need to know. A customer might call to ask about the status of his or her loan. The teller should have the ability to access the loan record to answer the customer's request. However, the ability to change loan records should be limited. Most changes must be made by special programs that process transactions for customer payments. In addition, some types of changes may be made by loan officers of the bank.

This type of data security is called *read-only access*. The tellers can read information in loan records. However, the DBMS requires that a user enter a separate *access code* before the content of a record can be changed. In this case, only special programs or loan officers are able to use these access codes.

Another aspect of data security is physical protection for information files. A DBMS makes *physical security* possible through programs that back up files through duplicate entries and copying. Physical security simply means that the file media—disks and tapes—are protected against destruction. The backup copies of files can be stored in protected areas to guard against their destruction.

1. What are the advantages of a database over a system that uses separate files for individual applications?

2. What is a database query capability and what is its value?

3. How does availability of a database affect development of new user applications for information systems?

4. What is data security and how does a DBMS help to make it possible?

HOW DOES A DBMS MANAGE INFORMATION?

Finding and inserting data items into a database requires special techniques. The problem: A database consists of multiple files. Each file has multiple records. In turn, each record has multiple data items. It would not be efficient for a computer to read through a complete database to find individual items. Some method is needed to direct the computer to the data items that are needed.

One way to organize data items for DBMS access is by forming *tables*. A table typically is a set

NATIONAL FOOTBALL LEAGUE STANDINGS

National Conference

West	W	L	T	Pct.	PF	P A
New Orleans	9	3	0	.750	270	186
L. A. Rams	7	5	0	.583	300	232
San Francisco	7	5	0	.583	262	226
Atlanta	4	8	0	.333	208	260
East	**W**	**L**	**T**	**Pct.**	**PF**	**PA**
Philadelphia	7	5	0	.583	283	254
Phoenix	7	5	0	.583	282	274
N. Y. Giants	7	5	0	.583	253	246
Washington	6	6	0	.500	278	307
Dallas	2	11	0	.154	213	317

Figure 22-4. Examples of data tables can be found every day on the sports pages of your newspaper. Examples include league standings and boxscores for individual games.

of items arranged in set positions, usually columns and rows. A box score for a baseball game or the team standings for any sports league are examples of tables. The basic idea of a table is to organize data items into rows and columns. Figure 22-4 is a typical table showing team standings. The performance record of each team takes up a row in the table. That is, a row is a horizontal line that runs across the table. Each column takes up a vertical position in which performance data items are entered. For example, there are columns for games won, games lost, average, and other performance factors. These data item positions are columns that run vertically through the table.

You also have seen data tables if you have ever been to an airport. Many airlines provide large monitors, or screens, that display information about arriving and departing flights. For each flight, the screen shows a flight number, a scheduled arrival or departure time, a gate number, and a flight *status*. These four entries are considered to be separate data items, or fields. A field is a basic unit of data. The status field indicates whether the plane will be arriving or departing on time. If the plane is not expected to be on time, the status field displays the actual arrival time next to the scheduled arrival time.

Business Terms

query
A request for data to be processed by a DBMS.

data security
Protective measures that guard information against illegal or unauthorized use.

authorized user
A person who has a need or a right to access and use stored information.

read-only access
A DBMS protective measure that permits some users to access specified records but not to alter them.

access code
An identification that controls a user's access to data.

physical security
Measures that protect storage media and their information against destruction.

table
A set of items arranged in set positions, usually columns and rows.

status
In a database, an item that reflects current condition.

These four fields—flight number, scheduled time, gate number, and flight status—are arranged horizontally to form a single row. This row, then, represents a single flight record. Other flight records, or rows, are displayed below the first record.

In turn, each column displayed on the monitor represents the content of one kind of field, for several records. The left-hand column provides a list of flight numbers. The second column indicates the gate number at which the plane will arrive or depart. The third column displays a list of scheduled arrival or departure times. And the final column lists flight status information. Another term for this type of table is *array*. Array is a mathematical term. It is used by many computer professionals.

How Do Tables Help a DBMS To Access and Relate Data?

By using tables, a DBMS can keep track of data items in the same way that an airline locates flights. Each data item is represented in a table by the row and column at which it is located. The DBMS software then can access any position in the table by using this location. For instance, the record for Flight 276 might be located in the third row. The item for the flight number would be in the first column position of the third row.

Each flight number, of course, is unique. This uniqueness means that the DBMS can use the flight number as the *primary key* for each record. A primary key is a field that has a different, unique value for each record in a file. In a file of flight records, two or more flights might have identical scheduled arrival times. However, each flight number will be different in all records.

By assigning a unique primary key value to each record, the DBMS then can set up a separate table, called an *index*. The role of an index is to store primary key values and their locations within a table. To find a particular flight record, the DBMS simply searches the index of flight numbers. When the desired flight number is identified, the program uses

the location given in the index to go directly to the record. With this indexing structure in place, the DBMS also can look up any other field in a record.

How Do Tables Help a DBMS to Access Files?

Within a database that uses tables for information storage, all data items in all files are stored and identified by row and column positions. This arrangement allows the DBMS to find and combine rows, columns, and individual table entries from among different files.

In searching for needed data items, the DBMS uses primary and *secondary key* fields to locate data items. A secondary key can be any field in a record that adds information or meaning to the primary key. The content of a secondary field does not have to be unique. Information in secondary fields can be duplicated in multiple records, as long as each secondary field is linked to a unique primary field.

To illustrate, many records that describe automobiles can have identical information in the field for MAKE. Many cars have entries of Buick, Ford, Dodge, Toyota, or other names in this field. In each case, however, the secondary field appears with a unique primary field, such as license number. Thus, each secondary key is located through its relationship to a primary key.

Application example. To illustrate use of a database, consider the need for information on automobiles by law enforcement officers. When an officer is on patrol, information access can have life-or-death value. Say an officer chases a speeding car. It is imperative to know about the car before it is stopped and the officer approaches the driver.

To provide the needed information, many police cars now have computer terminals. The officers use these to query a database maintained in state offices. The officer simply gives the computer the license number of the car being followed. Within seconds, the terminal displays information on the status of the

Airline flight information *pro-*
vides a good example of the way
millions of people rely on data-
base systems regularly. Displays
are generated from database files
maintained by airlines and/or air-
port operations departments.
COURTESY OF CITY OF LOS ANGELES,
DEPARTMENT OF AIRPORTS

car. If the car is stolen or has been used in a crime, the officer can ask for assistance—and will be careful in approaching the vehicle.

In other situations, the officer can talk by radio with a dispatcher at police headquarters. The dispatcher enters the query to the vehicle database and relays the computer's response by radio.

The point: In this situation, the license number is a primary key. Several secondary keys may be important, such as the make, color, year, and owner of the car. In today's society, information is a vital tool. Computers and DBMS software are methods for using that tool.

Why Does a Database Have Multiple Files?

To support the law officer's information request, the computer had to carry out references to a number of separate files. These files function as part of a law enforcement database. To illustrate, state agencies will have a number of information files that deal with automobiles and criminal records. First, all vehicles are covered by records in the license files of a state

agency. Next, records describing stolen cars are registered in a "hot car file." A separate file may exist for vehicles used in crimes.

For all of these access operations, the license number is the record key. This information field must appear in each file with information about vehicles. Thus, the same record key might be in the state motor vehicle file, in the stolen car file, and in the file for vehicles used in crimes. In each file, there

Business Terms
array *See* table.
primary key A field that has a different, unique value for each record in a file.
index A table within a relational database that is used to locate data items in other files.
secondary key Any field in a record that adds information or meaning to the primary key; need not be unique.

may be different sets of secondary keys that provide additional information. The state vehicle file will have complete information on the vehicle and its owner. The stolen car file will have information on the date of the crime and the police agency that reported the crime. The file on cars used in crimes might have information on the nature of the crime, names of suspects, or other available data items.

It is not necessary to include all information in every file. Rather, the DBMS software can carry out *cross-reference* operations as needed. For example, a stolen car record might have license number and theft information only. When a computer shows a car as stolen, it will automatically search the state records and retrieve other key information. The officer sees a complete display because the computer can access multiple files quickly to deliver the needed information. This feature of a DBMS is called *controlled redundancy*. The word "redundancy" means repetition, or repeated occurrence. With controlled redundancy, a DBMS can minimize duplication of data items.

How Does Controlled Redundancy Aid a DBMS?

Use of controlled redundancy helps to save secondary storage space. This is because entries for secondary key items usually occur only once within a database. There is no need to repeat the entries because the DBMS can find any single item within a large database.

The reliability of information also is improved. In a single-application file, it used to be necessary to create a complete file to support each application. All needed items had to be included in files that supported each application. This led to a waste of file space because of the redundancies. Also, there were problems in keeping files up to date. Each time a master file record changed, updating was needed for each occurrence. Failure to update records led to erroneous files.

With a DBMS, a customer address typically exists in one file only. To record a new customer address, the correction is made to this one file. All programs that access the customer address then will retrieve the correct information.

Review 22.2

1. What is a data table?
2. How are records identified within a database?
3. How is a database search controlled?
4. What is "controlled redundancy" and why is it important?

WHAT TYPES OF DBMS ARE USED WITH COMPUTER INFORMATION SYSTEMS?

Sizes and processing requirements of businesses vary widely. Certainly, the processing capabilities required by a commercial airline are much different from those required by a law enforcement agency. To support different business needs, software companies have developed literally hundreds of DBMS programs. Each has its own set of capabilities and limitations. For instance, some programs limit the way in which records and files can be accessed. DBMS programs also vary in the speeds at which they store and access data.

Despite these differences, many database management systems share certain features. In general, these similarities involve the way in which the software organizes data for storage and access. In database terminology, a plan for organizing, storing, and accessing data is called a *logical model*. Virtually all DBMS packages fit within three categories of models:

- Relational
- Hierarchical
- Network.

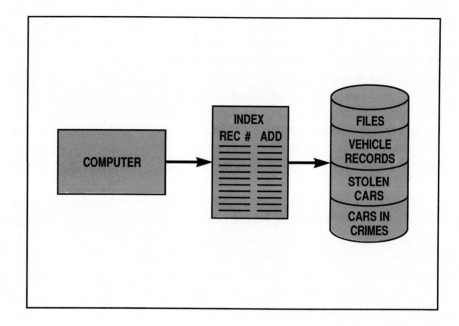

Figure 22-5. *A relational database stores multiple files on disk devices. Access to needed information is through an index maintained by the computer. The index identifies the file storage location for each record and data item within the system.*

What Is a Relational Database?

You already have been introduced to the *relational database* model. This type of database uses tables, or arrays, to "relate" data. Each of the multiple tables within a relational database is known as an *entity*. For instance, in the law enforcement example, vehicle licenses would be one entity. Stolen cars would be a second entity. Vehicles used in crimes might be a third entity. The idea is to identify each entity according to its chief purpose.

All data within each entity are organized into columns and rows. Each row, as has been explained, is considered to be a record. Each column contains all values for a single field. Taken together, the contents of all row and column positions are said to form a *relation*. In other words, a relation in database terminology is similar to a file in traditional processing.

DBMS software then creates the index files necessary to complete cross-references between tables. The linking of tables within a relational database is illustrated in Figure 22-5.

Relational database models are used widely with personal computers. In fact, most DBMS packages

Business Terms

cross-reference
Referral of access operations between tables in a relational database.

controlled redundancy
Principle of database organization that minimizes repetition of data items.

logical model
A plan for organizing, storing, and accessing data within a database.

relational database
A database that consists of a series of tables that can be used in coordination under DBMS software control.

entity
Name for a specific table within a relational database.

relation
A file within a relational database.

produced for microcomputers are based on a relational model. The relational model is easy to implement with limited memory and secondary storage space. Also, a relational database provides acceptable access speeds, as long as relations (files) are not too large. Because files stored by a personal computer are comparatively small, the relational model is ideal for small computers.

What Is a Hierarchical Database?

Business files can contain tens of thousands of records, often more. A relational database model cannot provide the processing efficiency required to support really large files. These businesses typically require the processing and storage capabilities of a mainframe computer. In this kind of high-volume processing environment, a *hierarchical database model* may be beneficial.

A hierarchical database is especially useful for companies with transaction patterns that are organized in a top-down manner. That is, the organization of information begins with a general, top level and proceeds through to more detailed, lower-level functions. This is the meaning of the word *hierarchy*. In a hierarchy, elements are linked to each other in a top-down manner.

To illustrate, think of the organization structure of a large business. Authority and responsibility for running the organization rest at the top. The chief executive, who also is chairman of the board of directors, has the top position. Beneath this level are a president and, next, a number of vice presidents. These executive-level people, in turn, direct the efforts of a number of department heads. Each department has personnel who follow the instructions of the department head. A company organization of this type is a hierarchy.

To apply the idea of a hierarchy to a database, consider the airline example given earlier. The topmost level of the flight information hierarchy consists of records for the cities to which the airline flies. The reason for this is that a hierarchical database models the way information is used. When an agent makes a reservation, the first information needed is the person's destination. Therefore, the top level of the database consists of destination cities.

The next, lower level is devoted to the next item of information needed to book a reservation. This is the city of origin. Therefore, the second level of a flight information hierarchy is used for origin points. Each destination is served by multiple origin points. Therefore, a single origin point will lead to multiple records at the second level of the hierarchy.

When this structure is diagrammed as in Figure 22-6, the shape of the illustration resembles a tree. Therefore, a hierarchical database also is called a *tree structure*. Below this level, records for individual flight numbers that link origin cities to destinations are given. At the bottom level of the tree are passenger rosters for each flight.

In a hierarchical database, each type of record, at every level, is called a *node*. In a flight information database, the top node would be destination city. Queries always begin with the top node, also called a *parent node*. An inquiry started with a destination parent node would lead to records for a corresponding origin point.

In a hierarchy, each lower-level node that is linked with a parent is called a *child node*. Inquiries to a database progress through a series of parent-child connections. A record on a given flight would be located in a child node that is linked to the origin city as a parent node. A series of parent-child relationships extends from top to bottom of a hierarchical database.

Because all references follow a fixed path between nodes, a hierarchical database does not need index tables like those in a relational database. The time required to look up record locations in an index also is eliminated. Therefore, the hierarchical model provides the fastest reference capability. Because of its speed, some very large databases with high levels of query transactions must use a hierarchical model. Users may lose some flexibility because they cannot

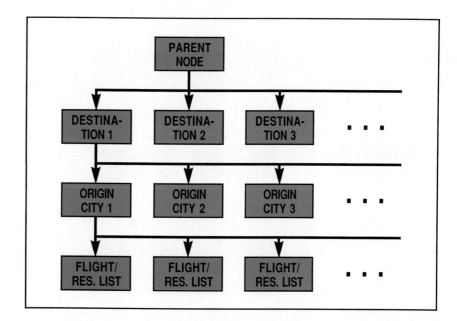

Figure 22-6. *This schematic diagram shows the organization and information access structure of a hierarchical database. Note that all inquiries enter at the top-most node and are processed through a top-down hierarchy.*

direct inquiries toward any record in the database as they can with an index. But, with a very large database, a hierarchical structure may be necessary.

What Is a Network Database Model?

Hierarchical databases represent the oldest technology among the three forms of logic models. Among large systems, the hierarchical model is the one used most widely. However, the fixed reference pattern of a hierarchical model presents problems to some users. For users who need more speed than is possible with a relational model and more flexibility than a hierarchical model, there is another answer. This is the *network model.*

The network model resembles a hierarchy in some ways. The records are organized into a series of nodes at different levels. Searches progress from one node to another. However, in a network model there is no single, top node at which queries begin. A query can begin at any level within the database. Therefore, a network permits bottom-up, as well as top-down, data searches. A diagram of a network model is shown in Figure 22-7.

Business Terms

hierarchical database model
A plan of organization that structures data items in a top-down manner for implementation under a hierarchical database.

hierarchy
An organization or set of data organized in a top-down manner.

tree structure
Description of a hierarchical data model.

node
A data storage location within a hierarchical or network data model.

parent node
A high-level storage location within a hierarchical or network data model.

child node
A low-level storage location within a hierarchical or network data model.

network model
A database structure in which nodes are linked directly to provide access in either upward or downward patterns; searches may begin at any level within the network structure.

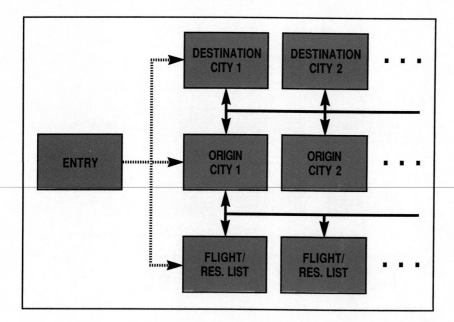

Figure 22-7. *This schematic diagram shows the organization and information access structure of a network database. The structure is similar to that of a hierarchical database. However, queries can enter the network at any level, rather than having to be processed in a top-down sequence.*

The main reasons that many computer systems exist are to collect information and to provide access for users. Database software is one of the main necessities of an information society like the one in which you live. Therefore, as a user of information, it can be valuable to understand how databases serve you. To help build this understanding, the chapter that follows describes how computers use databases to build and support application programs.

Review 22.3

1. What is a logical database model?

2. What is a relation and what is a relational database?

3. What is a hierarchy and what is a hierarchical database?

4. What is a network structure and what is a network database?

Chapter Summary

❏ A DBMS eliminates the problems that occur when information files are created especially for individual applications.

❏ A major problem with separate files is that existing files may not be available for new applications for user inquiries.

❏ A DBMS makes it possible for user applications or individuals who use query commands to find and relate data from multiple files.

❏ DBMS methods simplify and reduce costs of application development.

❏ DBMS programs implement data security measures by controlling access to stored information.

❏ One way to organize files within a database is through use of tables. Tables place information items in rows and columns. Positions within tables give each data item an individual location.

❏ Tables also can be used for indexing. An index table contains a record key and its location. The computer refers to the index first, then goes to the specified location to find the needed data.

❑ Databases follow a "controlled redundancy" principle in establishing file structures.

❑ Each database is structured to follow a logical model. The logical model is a plan for organizing, storing, and accessing data.

❑ Three types of logical models are used for databases: relational, hierarchical, and network.

❑ A relational model uses multiple tables for storage of data. Other tables index the content of data tables.

❑ A hierarchical model is built in a top-down structure. All access to data is through top-level records, or nodes. Access proceeds downward to multiple nodes at each lower level, following what is called a tree structure. Access is rapid. But users have only limited flexibility in searching for data.

❑ A network model uses directly linked nodes in its structure. In this respect, a network is similar to a hierarchy. However, searches within networks can begin at any level and can proceed either up or down.

Definitions

Write a complete sentence that defines each of the terms below.

off-line	query
data security	authorized user
read-only access	access code
table	index
secondary key	controlled redundancy

Questions to Think About

Based on what you have learned to date, answer the following questions in one or more complete sentences.

1. How is the use of information limited when a separate set of files supports each application?

2. What problems can be encountered when the same data record is present in multiple files?

3. How does a DBMS support access to multiple files within the same database?

4. What is a data table and how is it organized?

5. What is a data entity and what does it contain?

6. What is a relation and what structure does it use?

7. What is a relational database and what kind of data model does it use?

8. What is a hierarchical database and what kind of data model does it use?

9. What is a network database and what kind of data model does it use?

10. Describe the trade-offs of speed and flexibility among relational, hierarchical, and network models for databases.

Projects

The purpose of the assignments below is to encourage you to increase your learning through outside reading or work assignments.

1. On paper, develop a data table that could represent your class within a relational database. Fields should include an identification number (beginning with 101), last name, first name, birth date, and grade. The entity name for the file will be the course name, teacher name, and period (combined).

2. Assume you are assigned to develop a database that represents the student records for your school. Identify the file content that would be needed to respond to queries from students, teachers, and school administrators. Assume the database will cover a population of 2,000 current students and will contain records for 2,000 graduates. As databases go, this is relatively small. Explain the advantages and disadvantages of relational, hierarchical, and network databases for this application.

CHAPTER 23

How Are Computers Used For Database Applications?

The Think Tank

When you finish reading this chapter and complete your work assignments, you should be able to answer the following questions.

❑ What procedures are followed to develop an application that makes use of an existing database?

❑ How are new master files added to an existing database?

❑ How are data access operations performed through use of a query language?

❑ What is a host language and how does it relate to a database?

DOING BUSINESS

Leda Swann was new to the Fancy Fashions mail order company. However, she came to her job with more than 10 years of experience in the retail clothing industry. As a newly hired sales manager for Fancy Fashions, she was eager to put some of her knowledge to work. During her second week on the job, she approached Kitty Carson, a programmer for Fancy Fashions. Leda asked Kitty whether it would be possible to write a program that could combine data from two files and produce special reports. The application would use the Special Sales and Customer files.

"My idea," Leda told Kitty, "will be useful only if there is a need for it. What I would like to do is view a list of customers who have purchased clothing in small and extra small sizes. I'm thinking of putting a clothing catalog together designed exclusively for petite clients. But first I want to determine if there's

a market. I need to know if you can program our computer system to produce a report that lists these customers and their purchases."

Kitty was happy to give Leda some good news. "All of our files," Kitty told Leda, "are part of a database management system. With a DBMS, it usually isn't necessary to write a separate program just to view selected contents from multiple files. All you have to do is enter a query using the system's query language."

Kitty then walked over to her computer terminal and entered this query:

USE SPEC_SLS AND CUST_MAST

IN CUST_MAST DISPLAY ALL CUST_NAME AND ST_ADD–

FOR CUST_NO IN SPEC_SLS WITH SIZE = SM AND XSM

"These entries are part of the query language of the DBMS that we use," Kitty explained to Leda. "I've instructed the system to use the Special Sales and

Database applications *frequently involve data entry and file updating by users who work in factories or warehouses. Direct input from points where transactions take place helps to keep a database current and responsive to user needs.*

PHOTO BY LIANE ENKELIS

Customer Master files. From the Customer Master file, I want to display all names and addresses of customers who have made purchases in small and extra small sizes. The sizes are located in the Special Sales file. The DBMS uses the customer number field to cross-reference records and fields from the Customer Master and Special Sales files.''

Leda asked about the underscores in the file names and Kitty explained that the DBMS would not accept blank spaces in file names. The underscore is used to fill blank spaces within names of files, records, or fields.

Kitty then pressed the ENTER key on her machine. In less than 15 seconds, the computer responded with a display that listed the information Leda wanted.

"That's amazing," Leda said. "You'll have to teach me how to use this query language. I have dozens of ideas that I could test if only I had access to this kind of information."

"Of course," Kitty said. "That's what I'm here for. And that's what a query language is for. It's easy to use and quite powerful. You'll probably master it within a few weeks.''

MEANING

Leda has learned an important lesson on the power of a DBMS. Kitty has demonstrated to Leda that, with a DBMS, it is not always necessary to write a separate program to access information from files. All database management systems include a *query language* that allows users—even those with no experience—to access information. A query normally takes only a few seconds to enter. The response, in turn, can be displayed or printed a few seconds later. Information can be retrieved even if fields have to be cross-referenced and combined from two or more files.

Business Terms
query language A set of commands that can be used to access, update, or create files and records within a database.

HOW IS USE OF A DATABASE DIFFERENT FROM USE OF SINGLE-APPLICATION FILES?

The ability to process queries with such ease is a special advantage of database software. This capability is not present for files that support single applications.

The content of single application files is controlled by one, specific set of programs. The programs build the files and use their content. The only way to get at the content of a file is through its application program. Under this approach, files are designed and built to support production of planned, regular outputs. There is no provision for independent inquiry into files by users. If different or special data are needed from an application file, special programs have to be written. This is a slow, costly process.

By contrast, a database is an independent resource that is available to many applications or programs. Applications do not restrict the use of a database. In addition, program commands that can be used to build new applications are present within a DBMS. This means, in turn, that application programs become offshoots of a DBMS. By contrast, the development of applications through traditional methods takes the opposite approach. The greatest costs and efforts in systems development go toward creating and maintaining files—needs that are eliminated under a DBMS approach.

One way to describe this relationship is to say that a database is an independent, accessible collection of data. A traditional file is an offshoot of a specific program and may be useless except for support of that program.

HOW DO YOU CREATE A DATABASE?

Imagine a business that serves customers within a local area. A wholesale food distributorship might fit this description. We-Stock-It, a food wholesaler, has been formed recently by two brothers—Ralph and Ed Norton. The Nortons' business plan involves serving non-chain retail convenience stores. As the Nortons know, many of these stores often have only one to three employees working at any given time. This means store clerks have little time to stock shelves with newly delivered items. Often, deliveries remain in the storeroom for more than a day before an employee can take the time to stock items.

The Nortons' business approach, however, is to stock all items when they are delivered. In other words, Ralph, Ed, or another delivery driver will stock items at each convenience store—at no extra cost. In this way, store clerks are free to serve customers.

At present, We-Stock-It has 10 client companies. The Nortons realize that store owners often have offices that are at separate locations from the stores. To handle this situation, the Nortons want to begin building a database that contains two files: A customer master file and a store master file. The customer master file will contain names, addresses, and phone numbers for store owners. The store master file will contain the address and phone number at each store, along with the name of the manager or other contact person. The two files can be cross-referenced by using a customer number contained in every record within each file.

How Is the Customer Master File Created?

Ralph and Ed have purchased a database management system called dBXL, sold by WordTech Systems, Inc. The Nortons chose this product because it is *compatible* with another product called dBASE IV. The term "compatible" means that files and programs created with dBASE IV can be used with dBXL. The dBASE software series is the most widely used DBMS package for microcomputers. However, dBXL sells for less than one-third the cost of dBASE IV and meets all of the Nortons' needs.

Rapid file access to databases is a necessity of modern law enforcement. Vehicle dispatching and records about crimes and criminals are maintained in computer-maintained databases. Information must be made available to officers in cars in seconds.

By purchasing a dBASE compatible software package, the Nortons expect to achieve the benefits of both systems. Also, Ralph and Ed want to be able to *network,* or communicate electronically, with dBASE systems used by customers. The dBASE-compatibility of dBXL will make this possible.

Ralph has worked through the *tutorial* program provided with the dBXL package. A tutorial is a set of software and instructions that allows beginning users to "learn by doing." The tutorial guides the user through the development of an example database and the use of query language capabilities. Ralph also has studied the *User's Manual* that came with the software system. This manual contains instructions for using all of dBXL's features.

Ralph will begin by creating the customer master file. His first step, of course, is to turn on his computer. When the prompt appears, Ralph enters this command:

cd dbxl

Recall that "cd" stands for "change directory." Ralph has instructed the operating system to switch to the "dbxl" directory of the hard disk. He has stored the dBXL program files in this directory. Ralph then enters the following command:

dbxl

Business Terms

compatible
Usable on an interchangeable basis.

network
Reference to a group of computers and other devices connected through communication links for sharing of programs and information.

tutorial
A package of instructional materials that can include demonstration software and always includes user and reference manuals.

user's manual
A set of descriptions and instructions designed for guidance in use of a product or software package.

This command instructs the operating system to load the dBXL program into main memory for processing. After a few seconds, dBXL displays a title and copyright screen, along with this prompt:

XL[1]

This prompt tells Ralph that he is working with the dBXL system, rather than with DOS. Ralph then uses the CREATE command to create a file. He enters the following instruction, which requests dBXL to create a new file:

CREATE CUST_MAS

Ralph has chosen to call the customer master file "CUST_MAS." The underscore (_) character is used because file names in dBXL cannot contain any blank spaces.

In response to Ralph's instruction, dBXL responds with a screen display like the one shown in Figure 23-1.

Be aware that other DBMS software will have different procedures and commands. In some systems, menus and prompt screens may be provided to assist users in setting up files or searching for infor-

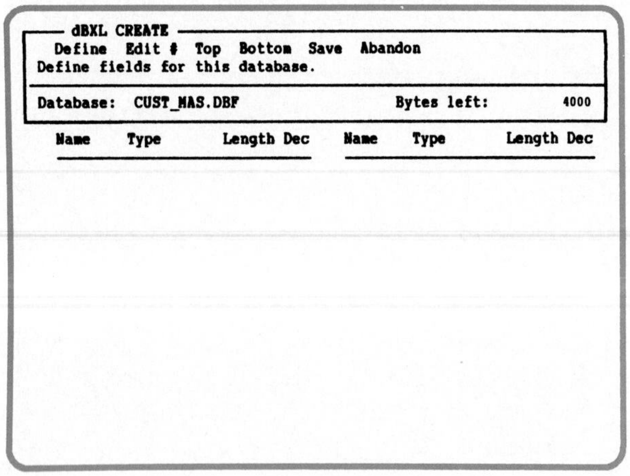

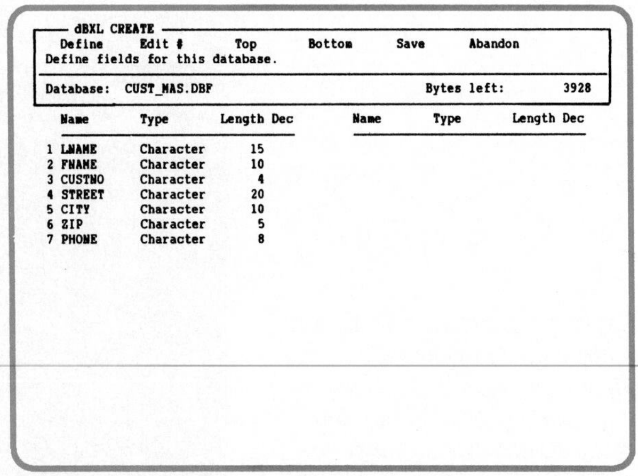

Figure 23-2. *Data item and record formats are defined by users through entries into displays like the one shown here for dBXL.*

mation. The examples given here may have to be adapted to procedures required by other DBMS programs.

Defining file content. The top of this screen displays a *menu bar*. This area contains a list of choices that can be selected during file creation activities. Ralph knows that he first must define all fields for each record in the master file. He presses the "D" key on the keyboard, which activates the **DEFINE** option from the menu bar.

The cursor now is positioned in the middle of the file creation screen, near the word "name." Ralph is ready to begin entering the field name, data type, and length for each field in the Customer master file. These entries will serve to define the format of records in the file. Ralph proceeds to enter name, address, and phone number field definitions. When he is finished, his screen displays the entries shown in Figure 23-2.

Notice that all fields have been given the data type "character." Ralph uses this data type even though the customer number, ZIP code, and phone number contain numeric data. Ralph knows that the "numeric" data type should be specified only for fields that will be used in performing calculations.

Figure 23-1. *Database file structures are defined by users through entries into displays like the one shown here. This display is generated by dBXL DBMS software.*

External information, including data items developed through library research, often is included in databases. This information can be valuable in supporting management planning and decision making.

COURTESY OF AMERICAN LIBRARY ASSOCIATION

Ralph next presses the ESC key to return to the file creation menu bar. He presses the "S" key on his keyboard. This causes the computer to activate the **SAVE** selection from the menu bar. The dBXL system then saves to disk all the definitions that Ralph has just entered. Next, the system provides Ralph with this prompt:

Append records now ? (Y/N):

Ralph is ready to enter data into the customer file and therefore enters a "Y" next to the prompt. The system responds with a display that asks for the following data entries:

Record No.	**1**
LNAME	
FNAME	
CUSTNO	
STREET	
CITY	
ZIP	
PHONE	

The system lists each field name for the first record to be entered. Ralph enters the content of fields for Hazel Axelrod, who represents the first record. When he finishes, the data entry screen contains the following fields:

Record No.	**1**
LNAME	**AXELROD**
FNAME	**HAZEL**
CUSTNO	**1054**
STREET	**212 S. ALABAMA**
CITY	**REXROTH**
ZIP	**57443**
PHONE	**555-1454**

Business Terms

menu bar
A list of choices available through a software package; usually displayed across the top line of a screen.

Ralph continues to enter data for the remaining nine records. When he has completed his data entry session, Ralph presses ESC. This causes dBXL to save the records to disk. The system prompt now includes the name of the active file:

XL [1] CUST_MAS >

Review 23.1

1. What is a query language?
2. How are query commands applied in place of special programs?
3. Why did the master file entries begin with the naming of a file?
4. Why is it necessary to identify numeric fields for the DBMS?

HOW DO YOU ACCESS DATA FROM A DATABASE?

One reason for using a database management system is to provide users with easy access to data stored in multiple files. When data items are defined within a database, the DBMS software automatically locates each stored item. This is done by creating a separate index file that notes the location of each record in every file.

A second important objective of a DBMS is efficient data access. A user should be able to retrieve data fields from multiple files through use of simple query commands.

For a database, most of the technical details involved in storing data are handled by the DBMS software. As you will see, it is important for users to plan the organization of stored data. These plans center on *logical* requirements. Under logical data organization, users define data items, records, and files in terms of their normal usage patterns. Users also establish primary and secondary key fields that can be used to relate data across two or more files. The technical details involved in storing and relating

data are taken care of automatically by the DBMS software.

The point: To build a database, logical storage requirements are specified by users. The physical techniques involved in storing data are handled by DBMS programs.

How Is the CUST_MAS File Accessed?

Ralph now is ready to view the file he has created. Next to the system prompt, he enters the command LIST. The dBXL system responds by displaying the records that Ralph has entered. A sample display is shown in Figure 23-3.

Notice, in Figure 23-3, that the phone number has been "wrapped around" to the left margin of the screen. The reason: The total number of characters in each record is greater than 80. The screen can show only 80 characters on each line. Ralph knows he can use the query feature of dBXL to list only those fields that are important. Ralph chooses to display all fields except for the first name of each customer. This field is not important to Ralph right

Figure 23-3. *Displays and reports like the one shown can be compiled by retrieving information from multiple files within a database. Note that the newly created records are too long to be displayed on individual lines.*

```
CREATE  :<C:>:                   :              :  : Caps

XL [1] CUST_MAS> LIST
REC# LNAMW      FNAME  CUST# STREET          CITY      ZIP
PHONE
1     AXELROD   HAZEL  1054  212 S. ALABAMA  REXROTH   57443
555-1454
2     PEPPER    HARVEL 1266  545 ADAMORE     NONENAD   57251
595-5935
3     MILAND    VELMA  7444  1266 ASHFORK    ARDWICK   57250
844-4790
4     VIXLEY    MARCUS 2005  277 S. HOWARD   BOWIE     57002
572-5925
5     PETTY     DOUG   2755  466 HAMNICH     LANGMERE  57025
533-7576
6     PORVAZY   JOHN   3958  BOX 215         MANVILLE  57205
593-1234
7     PORTER    HOMER  6776  955 STRATHMORE  ARDWICK   57250
844-2956

XL [1] CUST_MAS>
```

```
XL [1] CUST_MAS> LIST
REC# LNAMW    CUST# STREET          CITY      ZIP    PHONE
   1 AXELROD  1054  212 S. ALABAMA  REXROTH   57443  555-1454
   2 PEPPER   1266  545 ADAMORE     NONENAD   57251  595-5935
   3 MILAND   7444  1266 ASHFORK     ARDWICK   57250  844-4790
   4 VIXLEY   2005  277 S. HOWARD   BOWIE     57002  572-5925
   5 PETTY    2755  466 HAMWICH     LANGMERE  57025  533-7576
   6 PORVAZY  3958  BOX 215         MANVILLE  57205  593-1234
   7 PORTER   6776  955 STRATHMORE  ARDWICK   57250  844-2956
   8 ZIETRZAK 5022  4577 EDINBROUGH HOLBROOK  57004  466-4866
   9 NICELY   2001  4634 SOUTH FORK OXMOOR    57846  844-7575
  10 GRIER    7550  467 FOOTHILL    LANGMERE  57025  575-2499

XL [1] CUST_MAS>
```

Figure 23-4. *Adjusting the display instructions to a database enables the user to create a display in which each record is presented on a single line.*

```
XL [1] CUST_MAS> LIST
REC# LNAMW    CUST# STREET          CITY      ZIP    PHONE
   1 AXELROD  1054  212 S. ALABAMA  REXROTH   57443  555-1454
  10 GRIER    7550  467 FOOTHILL    LANGMERE  57025  575-2499
   3 MILAND   7444  1266 ASHFORK     ARDWICK   57250  844-4790
   9 NICELY   2001  4634 SOUTH FORK OXMOOR    57846  844-7575
   2 PEPPER   1266  545 ADAMORE     NONENAD   57251  595-5935
   5 PETTY    2755  466 HAMWICH     LANGMERE  57025  533-7576
   7 PORTER   6776  955 STRATHMORE  ARDWICK   57250  844-2956
   6 PORVAZY  3958  BOX 215         MANVILLE  57205  593-1234
   4 VIXLEY   2005  277 S. HOWARD   BOWIE     57002  572-5925
   8 ZIETRZAK 5022  4577 EDINBROUGH HOLBROOK  57004  466-4866

XL [1] CUST_MAS>
```

Figure 23-5. *On instructions from a user, DBMS software can sort records within a file into desired sequences. In this display, the records have been sequenced in alphabetic order.*

now. To view these fields, Ralph enters the following query:

LIST LNAME, CUSTNO, STREET, CITY, ZIP, PHONE

The dBXL system now displays only a single row of data for each record. The file displayed in response to Ralph's query is shown in Figure 23-4.

Ralph recognizes that the records in his file are in serial order. That is, they are displayed in the same order in which they were entered. Ralph prefers to have all records displayed in alphabetical order, by last name. To do this, Ralph enters the following INDEX command:

INDEX ON LNAME

This command tells the system to create a separate index file. Recall that this file contains the disk address for each record in the file. The index file also contains the last name for each customer, in alphabetical order. In other words, the last name is used as the record key that the index can use to locate

needed records. The *physical* order of records in the CUST_MAS file has not changed. The physical order is the sequence in which records are recorded on a disk storage unit. However, Ralph can view different logical orders for his file by creating separate indexes.

Ralph now wants to display the CUST_MAS file to check the alphabetic order of records. To do this, he simply re-enters the LIST command, along with the names of the fields he wants to view. The dBXL system responds by displaying the list in Figure 23-5.

Business Terms

logical organization
The arrangement of data within a database as seen from a user perspective.

physical organization
The arrangement of data on a storage device as viewed in terms of equipment requirements.

How Can a User Display Selected Records?

Ralph wants to check his knowledge of the access capabilities of dBXL. He decides to view only those records that contain the CITY called "ARDWICK." To do this, Ralph uses the SET FILTER command. This command "filters out" all records that do not meet the *search criteria* that Ralph provides. Search criteria are the values that the system uses to locate selected records. Ralph enters these commands:

SET FILTER TO CITY = "ARDWICK"

LIST LNAME, CITY, PHONE

The first command, SET FILTER TO, tells the system to filter out all records that do not contain the value "ARDWICK" in the CITY field. The second command, LIST, tells the system to display only the last name, city, and phone number for the desired records. The system responds to Ralph's query by providing the following display:

Record#	LNAME	CITY	PHONE
3	MILAND	ARDWICK	844-4790
7	PORTER	ARDWICK	844-2956

At this point, Ralph can create a second, store master file. With these two files in place, the Nortons will be able to cross-reference, or combine, data from both files. For instance, Ralph might want to produce a report that lists each customer name and phone number, along with the store name and address.

To produce this report, the system will use the customer number as a record key. This key field allows dBXL to cross-reference records with matching customer numbers, from both files. For Ralph's report, the system will access the customer name and phone number from the customer master file. The store name and address will be accessed from the store master file.

1. What information is contained in an index file for a relational database?
2. Why is it important for users to be able to search a database according to information content?

WHAT QUERY TECHNIQUES ARE AVAILABLE?

The examples above suggest an important concept: The users of a DBMS have to understand available techniques for locating and using stored information. A DBMS can't deliver benefits until users understand the power of the tools available to them. Different database management systems provide different sets of query commands. Remember, therefore, that the dBXL descriptions in this chapter are provided as illustrations. If you use other DBMS programs, you may have to learn different commands.

Virtually all database management systems offer two approaches for accessing data:

- Query languages
- Host languages.

How Is a Query Language Used?

Recall from Chapter 22 that a query language allows users to access selected records and fields "on demand." You already have seen how this query feature works in dBXL. When Ralph used the LIST and SET FILTER commands, he was entering queries.

From these examples, it is possible to see why query languages are such a powerful feature of a DBMS. The query commands are designed for people who have little or no knowledge about computer programs. In most cases, query commands are composed of English words and phrases (like LIST and SET FILTER).

Large volumes of reports and other documents can be generated rapidly from database systems. To keep up with document volumes, many large companies install high-speed laser printer systems like the one shown. Printers of this type can function at speeds of about 7,000 pages per hour. Documents can be organized into page sequences and stapled for distribution by the same printer.

COURTESY OF HUGHES AIRCRAFT COMPANY

A special advantage of a query language lies in the speed with which a user can get results. For instance, after Ralph entered a LIST query, the computer displayed the desired fields within three or four seconds.

Query languages do have some disadvantages, however. Chiefly, it is necessary to enter a separate query for each data access request. Recall that Ralph had to enter a separate LIST query each time he wanted to view the CUST_MAS file. For queries that are only one or two lines long, this is not a major problem. However, requests for data can become complex.

Suppose, for instance, that Ralph creates a third file that is designed to store and list customer orders each day. He calls this file DELVRIES (short for "deliveries"). Several times each day, Ralph wants to produce a delivery schedule that lists customer orders and addresses.

To provide this kind of access, the system must reference the STORE file to find the address for each store. Then, the customer number is used to cross-reference the DELVRIES file. From this file, the system accesses the day's ordered items and quantities, for each store. Ralph also wants records to be listed in ZIP-code order. This order allows We-

Stock-It to create a schedule that organizes deliveries by location.

This kind of complexity might require a query that contains 20 lines or more. It would be too time-consuming to enter this query each time Ralph wants to print a delivery schedule. Instead, Ralph should design a program to produce this report automatically.

What Is a Host Language And How Is It Used?

All database management systems are designed to interact with at least one *host language*. The host

Business Terms

search criteria
The values used to locate required records within a file or database.

host language
A language included within a DBMS that can be used to generate repeatable programs or routines involving use of the database.

Query languages can be used to develop information that meets user needs. In some instances, users may want information on a single item or order within a large facility like the one in the photo. Queries also can organize information to show the overall condition of a business or of individual functions.

PHOTO BY LIANE ENKELIS

language generally is one that can be used for traditional application development. Most computer centers employ programmers who are experienced in use of these standard languages. If a complex search is to be conducted as a basis for regular reports, programs often are written in the host language.

After a program has been designed and coded, it can be stored on disk. Then, the user simply calls the program into memory, where it is executed automatically. In other words, it is necessary to enter access requests one time only. From that point forward, the user simply instructs the computer to execute the instructions stored in the program.

For instance, Ralph can use the host programming language that is built into the dBXL system. With this language, he can design a program that will access desired records and fields and then print a delivery schedule.

Suppose that Ralph has designed and coded such a program. He calls the program DLV_SCH (for delivery schedule). To activate this program, Ralph enters this simple instruction:

DO DLV_SCH

The dBXL system then calls the DLV_SCH program into memory and executes the program instructions automatically. Instead of entering a 20-line query, Ralph needs only to enter a single line to produce the report he wants, automatically.

How Is a Host Language Used To Program Database Queries?

Programming is a skilled activity that requires creativity and knowledge about computer operations. Programmers have to be able to organize complex procedures into sets of individual steps that computers can follow.

Notice that this requirement makes no mention of programming languages. Programming is a problem-solving process. Programmers begin by breaking a problem into small, manageable units called *modules*. A module, in a sense, is a "subproblem" that falls within a more general problem.

The key to programming lies in identifying these subproblems, and then describing a logical solution for each subproblem, or module. This solution consists of individual program instructions. All of these modules, and all their instructions, fit together to solve the general programming problem.

The series of steps established by a programmer becomes a *program design.* The design, in turn, is used as the basis for coding instructions in a programming language. The finished program is converted to computer language for execution.

Programming is one of the important specialties of the computer field. The details of how to write programs in host languages are not covered in this book. Rather, this book is about use of computers and application software in business. Many people will be able to use computers effectively without ever having to learn computer programming. Other people will find that some knowledge of programming will be useful in their chosen careers.

For instance, Ralph is finding that it will be helpful for him to learn about the host language that is part of the dBXL software package. However, this does not necessarily mean that he will design programs for his business. Many companies hire programmers on a temporary basis to design computer programs for use with their database management systems. For Ralph and many other businesspeople, a sensible approach involves learning about the computer hardware and software they will be using. With this knowledge, they can make informed decisions.

The point: Computers, even though they are useful business tools, require people to determine how they will be used. As an informed DBMS user, for instance, Ralph will be able to determine his programming needs. DBMS packages are not the only tools that help users to gain control over computers. Another popular tool is spreadsheet software, covered in the chapter that follows.

Review 23.3

1. What methods are available for handling access to databases?

2. What are the limitations of query languages?

3. What are the requirements for preparation of query routines under host languages?

Business Terms

module
A portion of a program for which input, processing, and output elements can be designated.

program design
A step-by-step process that can be followed to define, design, and develop an application program.

Chapter Summary

❑ Database software provides tools for application development as well as for collecting and accessing data.

❑ To create a master file under DBMS control, the user establishes a file name first. Then, entries are made into a display that establishes formats for records to be stored and for all fields within the records.

❑ When data are entered, the system presents a display that identifies the data fields. The user enters data for each field in every record.

❑ To support access to data items, the DBMS is instructed to create an index of records to be used. The index contains only the record fields that will be used in data searches—plus an entry by the software that provides the disk address of the record.

❑ Query commands make it possible for users to select and combine records from multiple files. These records can be output in displays or reports. In addition, the records can be recorded in a working file used for special applications.

❑ Database access can be controlled through use of two different tools: query language and host language.

❑ Query languages limit access operations to one command at a time, entered manually by a user. Complex or high-volume access operations are handled better under control of host languages.

❑ A host language is a standard language used for full-scale application development. For volume or frequent jobs, it often is best to design and write database access programs in a host language.

Definitions

Write a complete sentence that defines each of the terms below.

compatible	network
tutorial	menu bar
search criteria	host language
module	program design

Questions to Think About

Based on what you have learned to date, answer the following questions in one or more complete sentences.

1. Why is it necessary to assign a name as a first step in creating a file?

2. Why is it necessary to establish a record structure for a file before data can be entered?

3. How are actual data entries related to the structure established for files and records?

4. Under what conditions are data fields designated as numeric or character?

5. What is the value of setting up a separate index within a database?

6. What is a logical organization for a data file?

7. What is a physical organization for a data file?

8. How are logical and physical files alike and different?

9. Why is a query language often inadequate for operations that are complex or that involve large volumes of data?

10. What is a host language and how is it used?

Projects

The purpose of the assignments below is to encourage you to increase your learning through outside reading or work assignments.

1. Turn to the index at the back of this book. Look up the term ''database.'' Count the number of references that have anything to do with the creation or use of database techniques. How would you go about finding these references if there were no index? Be prepared to describe the value of an index to the user of a database.

2. Look in two or more telephone directories. Be sure that at least one is a ''white pages'' directory that lists names alphabetically and that another is a business directory organized according to type of product or service provided. Describe at least three different relations that are formed to assist user access to information in the directories that you review.

CHAPTER 24

What Are Electronic Spreadsheets And How Are They Used?

The Think Tank

When you finish reading this chapter and complete your work assignments, you should be able to answer the following questions.

❑ How are spreadsheet programs different from database management systems?

❑ Why is a spreadsheet useful in making multiple calculations for a single application?

❑ How are spreadsheets used to support financial planning?

❑ What is a spreadsheet ''formula'' and how do formulas help to simplify accounting and financial planning activities?

❑ What basic types of graphics displays and reports can be generated from spreadsheets?

DOING BUSINESS

When Fred arrived home from school, the phone was ringing. It was his mother, in need of help. His mother had left some important business papers at home. She asked Fred if he would bring them to her office.

When Fred arrived at the real estate company where his mother worked, he found her seated in front of her personal computer.

''Oh, great!'' his mother exclaimed when she saw him. ''Thanks so much, Fred. I printed a spreadsheet yesterday at work. I wanted to study it at home and then use it today for some financial projections; but, I forgot to save the spreadsheet to disk yesterday evening. This printed version is the only existing copy.''

''What's a spreadsheet?'' Fred asked his mother. ''And what do you mean by 'projection?' ''

''I'm sorry,'' she said. ''I should have explained myself a little better. Take a look at the sheet of paper you brought.'' Fred reviewed the contents of the paper. He noticed that the title of the paper was PRO FORMA—SUMMER QUARTER. The remaining entries included groups of numbers organized into several rows and columns.

''A spreadsheet is a worksheet,'' Fred's mother said. ''I created this spreadsheet with a spreadsheet software program. The program allows me to enter different amounts into column and row positions. Each column represents income and expense amounts for the summer months of past and future years. I've entered actual amounts that represent sales and expenses for past summers. I'm trying to determine some ways to improve income during the

coming summer. I do this by altering a few income or expense amounts shown in the rows. Then I review the results and consider changes in business policy based upon those results.

"Each time I change an amount," Fred's mother said, "the computer recalculates totals for each column automatically."

"But that's cheating!" Fred protested. "At school, I have to use scratch paper to make and check arithmetic calculations."

Fred's mother smiled. "Your teachers want you to build your math skills. Businesspeople follow a different kind of math. Our time has value. Anything that can save time is a big plus in our arithmetic."

MEANING

Fred's mother is trying to stress that a computer can save businesspeople time and money in solving problems and analyzing situations. Her personal computer is a tool that saves her time on the job. By using her computer system, Fred's mother can spend more time thinking about her business and less time doing arithmetic.

To analyze a single business problem, Fred's

mother might have to perform dozens of separate calculations. If she relied on scratch paper, each spreadsheet could take more than an hour to create. If she made any errors, she might have to create a new spreadsheet. With an electronic spreadsheet, calculations are made automatically. Errors can be corrected within seconds. Spreadsheets allow businesspeople to develop financial calculations rapidly and effectively. The time Fred's mother saves by using spreadsheet software can be devoted to more creative planning and decision-making activities.

WHAT IS THE VALUE OF AN ELECTRONIC SPREADSHEET?

Chapter 19 includes an introduction to the features of and uses for spreadsheets. Recall that a spreadsheet program allows businesspeople to process information to support financial planning and reporting. A spreadsheet program generates a screen display with numbered rows and lettered columns. This screen is an "electronic spreadsheet" display. The name comes from a time when financial plans were written on worksheets. These were wide sheets of paper called "spreadsheets." Each paper spreadsheet was divided into rows and columns.

At that time, managers used paper spreadsheets to prepare handwritten reports. Obviously, this was tiring work. Each entry had to be written by hand. All calculations also had to be performed individually on desktop calculators. Then the manager had to check to be sure each entry was in the right space and was accurate. Errors had to be corrected by hand. If there were too many errors, the whole report had to be redone. Despite the trouble, spreadsheets have been necessary reporting and planning tools for many years. They are standard requirements for business management.

For this reason, spreadsheet software has proven to be one of the most popular categories of microcomputer application packages. With spreadsheet software, managers can make and correct entries through the keyboard into *cells.* Cells are the spaces at the intersections of rows and columns. These are the areas used to enter descriptions or numeric information. If calculations are needed, *formulas* are entered into cells and the computer does the arithmetic automatically. A formula is simply a command that instructs the spreadsheet program to calculate values from a group of identified cells.

What Kinds of Entries Do Spreadsheet Users Make?

In general, an electronic spreadsheet provides for three types of entries:

- Labels
- Values
- Formulas for mathematical operations.

Labels. Spreadsheet *labels* include the title of a spreadsheet as well as column and row headings. These headings are descriptions of the values that appear within cells.

Values. Spreadsheet *values* are the actual amounts that are entered. Each value is stored in a separate cell of the spreadsheet. Values can be quantities, dollars, or even dates.

Formulas for mathematical operations. Formulas for *mathematical operations* tell the spreadsheet system to make a calculation. Typically, a formula is used to calculate values taken from a *range,* or group, of cells. An arithmetic operation is used to add, subtract, multiply, or divide the values in two or more cells.

HOW DO SPREADSHEET PROGRAMS COMPARE WITH DATABASE MANAGEMENT SYSTEMS?

In Chapter 23, you became acquainted with data tables. One use for a table is as a file structure created and maintained within a relational database model. Keep the structure of a data table in mind. This will be helpful because a spreadsheet, basically, is a data table.

Business Terms

cell
A space at the intersection of a row and column, used for entry of values into a spreadsheet.

formula
A command that instructs the spreadsheet program to calculate values from a group of identified cells.

label
In a spreadsheet, an entry that can be the title of a spreadsheet or an identifier for a column or row.

value
A data item entered into a cell of a spreadsheet.

mathematical operation
See formula.

range
On a spreadsheet, a group of cells identified for a SUM operation.

Within a budget spreadsheet, for instance, all data are grouped into rows and columns. Each row would represent a different budget category, such as sales income or payroll expenses. Each column would list values for a single time period, such as a month or quarter. The column entries correspond with the category records in the rows.

Why Is There Different Software For Spreadsheets and Databases?

It makes sense, then, to consider how spreadsheets and database management systems are similar and different. If a database organizes data into rows and columns, you might wonder why a DBMS isn't used to create and store spreadsheets. On the other hand, why aren't spreadsheets used to store databases?

In fact, some businesspeople do use spreadsheet programs to create databases, and use their DBMS to design spreadsheets. However, this approach rarely works efficiently. The reason lies in the different applications for which spreadsheets and database management systems are designed.

Different needs.   The power of a DBMS lies partly in its ability to combine data from multiple files in response to user commands. In turn, the power of a spreadsheet lies in performing multiple calculations rapidly. When the two types of systems are combined, many of the basic features of each system have to be eliminated. The result is a product that sacrifices important processing capabilities for each application.

The point: Database management systems and spreadsheet packages share similar features in the way files are organized. These similarities are worth noting because they suggest that microcomputers can use row-and-column formats in a number of ways to process data. However, different types of business applications require different software packages. It doesn't make sense to use an 18-wheel truck to deliver a few cases of soft drinks to a convenience store. Similarly, it doesn't make sense to use an application package to perform processing tasks for which it is not designed.

1. What is a spreadsheet?
2. What is an electronic spreadsheet?
3. What is a cell?
4. What is a formula and what does it do?
5. What are spreadsheet labels?
6. What are spreadsheet values?
7. What is a range of cells?

HOW DOES A SPREADSHEET WORK?

Recall the We-Stock-It scenario presented in Chapter 23. Ralph Norton has used a DBMS package to create customer, store, and delivery files. Now, Ralph's brother, Ed, wants to use a popular spreadsheet package to create an operating budget for We-Stock-It. This package, called Lotus 1-2-3, is a product of Lotus Development Corporation.

Ed wants to begin by creating a two-year budget. This budget will serve as a financial plan for the company. As is true for any budget, the major categories to be developed are income and expense.

The income category will include all sources of income, or revenue, for the company. Thus, the income category will contain several subcategories, such as "Food Products," "Paper Products," and so on.

The expense category will show all amounts that must be paid out. Subcategories will include such items as "Cost of Goods Sold," "Rent," "Payroll," and "Utilities."

In the first year of operations, Ed expects that the company will make only a small profit. By the end of the second year, however, Ed hopes that the company will earn a profit that will promote future growth. This growth will allow Ralph and Ed to purchase new delivery vehicles, increase the number of

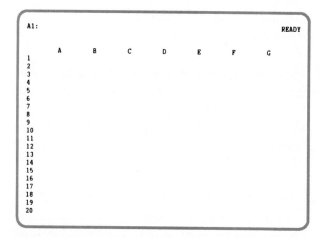

Figure 24-1. *This worksheet display generated by Lotus 1-2-3 is a starting point for development of an electronic spreadsheet.*

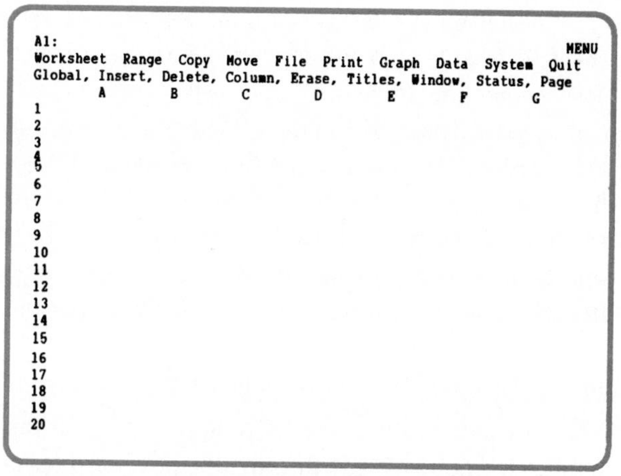

Figure 24-2. *A backslash entry causes the Lotus 1-2-3 program to generate a menu that guides a user in the creation of an electronic spreadsheet.*

employees, and so on. Ed will set up his electronic spreadsheet to reflect these budget expectations.

Getting started. In creating a database, Ralph's first task was to define the format for the customer master file. Ed's first spreadsheet file creation task is similar. That is, Ed must define the format and labels for rows and columns in his spreadsheet.

Ed begins by turning on his computer. He knows that the Lotus 1-2-3 programs and files are stored in a hard disk directory called LOTUS. When the C> prompt appears, Ed enters these commands:

CD LOTUS

123

The command on the first line tells the computer to switch to the LOTUS directory. The "123" entry tells the operating system to load the Lotus 1-2-3 system into memory for processing. After Ed enters 123, he watches as the Lotus screen with title and copyright information appears briefly. Then, this screen is replaced by the worksheet display shown in Figure 24-1.

Default settings. This blank worksheet contains the *default,* or standard, format settings for columns and rows. As Ed reviews these settings, he realizes that the default column widths won't work. These are set at nine characters per column. This is too narrow for Ed's purposes. He will be entering row labels into column A. Ed knows that several labels take up more than 20 character positions. Ed's first job will be to change the format for column A.

With Lotus 1-2-3, the main set of processing commands is contained on a *menu bar* above the worksheet. This menu of choices can be viewed by entering the backslash character (\). When Ed enters a backslash, the menu shown in Figure 24-2 appears.

Business Terms

default
A standard setting or value applied automatically by software; in a spreadsheet, the standard settings for column widths.

menu bar
A series of user options presented across a horizontal line of a screen display.

The leftmost command on the top line, **Worksheet,** is used to alter the appearance of a worksheet. The second line on the menu bar lists commands that can be performed within the ''Worksheet'' option. Ed enters a ''W'' to activate the ''Worksheet'' option. The options that previously appeared on the second line now are moved to the top line. These options include commands for making global changes that affect all format default settings. Other options can be used for inserting and deleting columns and rows, changing column formats, and so on.

Ed wants to select the ''Column'' option at this point. He enters a ''C'' through the keyboard to indicate this selection. A new menu bar appears that allows Ed to reset an existing column width, along with a few other column-formatting options. Ed enters an ''R'' to begin a reset operation. The following prompt appears in place of the menu bar:

A1: [W9]

Enter column width (1..240):

Changing defaults. The first line of this prompt tells Ed that the cursor in the worksheet currently is in Cell A1. This means that the column command will affect the ''A'' column. The entry [W9] means that the current width for this column is nine character positions. The second line of the prompt requests that Ed enter a column-width value between 1 and 240.

Ed enters the value 25 and presses the ENTER key. The spreadsheet automatically adjusts the width of Column A to 25 character positions. Ed next moves the cursor to Cell B1 and repeats the formatting operation for Column B. Ed resets the width for Column B to 12 characters and then repeats the procedure for Column C.

Entering labels. Ed now has completed his reformatting operations. He is ready to enter a title for his worksheet, along with column headings. Ed wants to call this worksheet ''Two-Year Budget.'' His first heading for Column A will be for INCOME entries. His heading for Column B will be YEAR 1 to indi-

cate that this column contains income and expense amounts for the first year. Column C will contain the heading YEAR 2.

Ed uses the cursor control keys (the arrows on the numeric keypad) to move the cursor to the cells that will contain headings. After he completes each title or heading entry, he presses the ENTER key. When Ed completes his entries, his worksheet display looks like the one in Figure 24-3. Notice how the widths of the A, B, and C columns have been widened in response to Ed's reformatting operations.

Ed's next task is to enter labels for each income and expense category, or row, along with labels for total income and total expenses. Ed also will include a label at the bottom of the worksheet to indicate the profit or loss amount. This amount results after total expenses have been subtracted from total income. Ed makes each entry in the appropriate cell position within Column A. When he is done, the worksheet display appears as shown in Figure 24-4.

Developing data entries. We-Stock-It has been in business for about three months. Ed has reviewed income and expense amounts for this quarterly period. He expects sales to increase by about five percent by the end of the year. Ed already has used a hand-held

---

Figure 24-3. *This display shows some initial entries into spreadsheet cells by a user. The cursor is moved to cell locations and entries are made through the keyboard.*

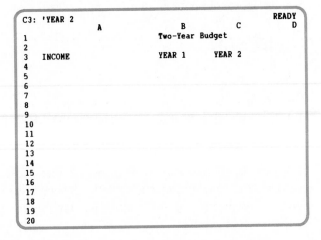

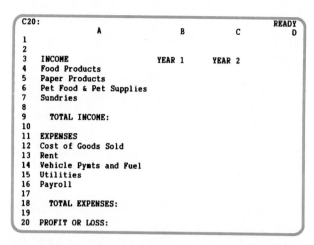

```
C20:                                        READY
                     A          B        C      D
1
2
3   INCOME                  YEAR 1     YEAR 2
4   Food Products
5   Paper Products
6   Pet Food & Pet Supplies
7   Sundries
8
9      TOTAL INCOME:
10
11  EXPENSES
12  Cost of Goods Sold
13  Rent
14  Vehicle Pymts and Fuel
15  Utilities
16  Payroll
17
18     TOTAL EXPENSES:
19
20  PROFIT OR LOSS:
```

Figure 24-4. *This display shows the spreadsheet under development with the labels positioned in column A.*

```
B18: @SUM(B12..B16)                         READY
                     A          B        C      D
1                            Two-Year Budget
2
3   INCOME                  YEAR 1     YEAR 2
4   Food Products        122,000.00
5   Paper Products        24,500.00
6   Pet Food & Pet Supplies 12,300.00
7   Sundries              48,000.00
8
9      TOTAL INCOME:     206,800.00
10
11  EXPENSES
12  Cost of Goods Sold    98,000.00
13  Rent                  28,000.00
14  Vehicle Pymts and Fuel 9,680.00
15  Utilities              5,200.00
16  Payroll               42,000.00
17
18     TOTAL EXPENSES:   182,880.00
19
20  PROFIT OR LOSS:
```

Figure 24-5. *In this display, the user has made value entries into column B of the spreadsheet. This covers the first year of a two-year budget.*

calculator to determine what these income amounts would be for the entire year.

Similarly, Ed has calculated expense amounts that he expects will have to be paid in the first full year of operation. Ed enters these budget amounts into the worksheet, within their appropriate cell positions. Of course, all income and expense entries for the first year will appear in Column B, under the heading YEAR 1.

Entering formulas. After Ed has entered amounts, he wants to enter formulas and operations that will cause the Lotus program to perform calculations automatically. Ed needs to perform three calculations in Column B. The first two calculations involve formulas. The first calculation will total all INCOME amounts. The second calculation will total all EXPENSE amounts. The third calculation will provide Ed with a profit or loss amount by subtracting expenses from income. If income is greater, there will be a profit. If expenses are greater, there will be a loss and a minus value will be entered at the bottom of the column.

As you can see from Figure 24-5, Ed enters income amounts in Cells B4 through B7. The TOTAL INCOME amount should be the sum of the values in these four cells. This total will be placed in Cell B9. Ed moves his cursor to Cell B9 and enters this formula:

@SUM(B4..B7)

The @ character tells the Lotus 1-2-3 program that Ed's entry is for a formula, rather than a label or a value. The SUM keyword tells the program that this formula will produce a sum (total) for a range of cells. The (B4..B7) entry provides the range to be summed—in this case, from Cell B4 through B7. When Ed presses the ENTER key, the TOTAL INCOME amount automatically is calculated and written to Cell B9.

Ed then moves the cursor to Cell B18 and repeats the basic SUM formula to determine the TOTAL EXPENSES amount. The formula in this instance is as follows:

@SUM(B12..B16)

When Ed executes this formula command, the sum for all expenses is calculated automatically and written to Cell B18. At this point, the worksheet appears as shown in Figure 24-5.

Determining profit or loss. Ed now is ready to determine the budgeted profit or loss amount for his first year. He moves his cursor to Cell B20, where this final total is to be written. He enters this mathematical operation:

+B9 − B18

In this case, the + sign tells Lotus 1-2-3 that a mathematical operation is to be performed. Ed wants the program to subtract the TOTAL EXPENSES amount (stored in Cell B18) from the TOTAL INCOME amount (stored in Cell B9). Next, Ed presses ENTER, and the program calculates and writes a profit amount in Cell B20.

Review 24.2

1. What are default settings in an electronic spreadsheet?

2. What is a menu bar?

3. How are column-width defaults reset?

4. How are labels applied to columns and rows?

HOW DO SPREADSHEET FEATURES HELP MANAGERS TO PREPARE PROJECTIONS?

At this point, Ed is ready to enter budget figures for the second year of operations. Earlier in the year, Ed and Ralph put together a *business plan* that included projections for the second year of operations. In this business plan, Ed and Ralph expect a 12 percent increase in second-year sales over the first year. They also anticipate a 12 percent increase in the cost of goods sold. In addition, they forecast a 2 percent increase in expenses to allow for inflation. Other projected expense category increases are:

Vehicle Payments and Fuel	15 Percent
Utilities	5 Percent
Payroll	10 Percent

How Are Percentage Figures Computed on Spreadsheets?

To calculate projections based upon percentages, some figures must already be in place on an electronic spreadsheet. In this situation, for example, Ed is setting his second-year figures as percentages of those for the first year. Thus, to determine his second-year sales of "Food Products," he would use the figure for YEAR 1.

Ed has to develop a formula that will reflect the predicted 12 percent increase. In this situation, Ed wants to take all of his sales for the first year and add 12 percent. To include all of the first-year sales, he multiplies that value by 1.00. To increase the value by 12 percent, this amount is added to the 1.00. So, to show an increase of 12 percent, Ed will multiply sales amounts for the first year by 1.12.

Ed moves his cursor to Cell C4 and enters this mathematical operation:

+B4*1.12

The "*" symbol is the operator that Lotus uses for multiplication operations. When Ed presses the ENTER key, the program automatically multiplies the value in B4 (122,000) by 1.12 and writes the product in Cell C4.

Ed repeats this procedure to show 12 percent increases for the remaining income categories. For instance, to calculate a 12 percent increase for Paper Products, Ed moves the cursor to Cell C5 and enters this formula:

+B5*1.12

Formula for column total. After Ed has calculated new, second-year amounts for all income categories, he is ready to specify a formula to calculate **TOTAL INCOME** for YEAR 2. Recall that the formula used to calculate **TOTAL INCOME** for YEAR 1 is

@SUM(B4..B7). Thus, the new formula for YEAR 2 will be as follows:

@SUM(C4..C7)

Developing expense increase formulas. Ed moves the cursor to Cell C9, enters the formula above, and presses the ENTER key. He now is ready to specify percentage increases for expense categories. Recall that the Cost of Goods Sold category will show a 12 percent increase, plus an additional two percent increase to account for inflation. One way to specify this operation is as follows:

(+B12*1.12)*1.02

The parentheses are not required for this operation. But, it is a good idea to include them whenever multiple operators are used to perform a calculation. The parentheses tell Lotus 1-2-3 the order in which separate operations are to be performed. In this case, as in standard mathematical procedure, the (+B12*1.12) part of the formula is calculated first. Then, that total is multiplied by 1.02.

Ed and Ralph expect their rental costs to remain stable (unchanged) throughout the second year of operations. To show this, Ed can copy the value from Cell B13 into Cell C13. Ed moves his cursor to Cell C13. He then enters this simple instruction:

+B13

This entry tells Lotus 1-2-3 that the current cell should contain the value stored in Cell B13. When Ed presses ENTER, the value from Cell B13 (28,000) is copied into Cell C13.

Ed and Ralph plan to purchase an additional truck during their second year of operation. For this reason, their business plan indicates that vehicle payments and fuel costs for the second year will increase by 15 percent. To show this increase, Ed moves the cursor to Cell C14 and enters this formula:

+B14*1.15

```
C20: [W12] +C9-C18                                    READY
        A                      B            C        D
  1                         Two-Year Budget
  2
  3    INCOME                 YEAR 1       YEAR 2
  4    Food Products         122,000.00   136,640.00
  5    Paper Products         24,500.00    27,440.00
  6    Pet Food & Pet Supplies 12,300.00   13,776.00
  7    Sundries               48,000.00    53,760.00
  8
  9      TOTAL INCOME:       206,800.00   231,616.00
 10
 11    EXPENSES
 12    Cost of Goods Sold     98,000.00   109,760.00
 13    Rent                   28,000.00    28,000.00
 14    Vehicle Pymts and Fuel  9,680.00    11,132.00
 15    Utilities               5,200.00     5,460.00
 16    Payroll                42,000.00    46,200.00
 17
 18      TOTAL EXPENSES:     182,880.00   200,552.00
 19
 20    PROFIT OR LOSS:        23,920.00    31,064.00
```

Figure 24-6. *This display shows a complete two-year budget as it would appear following entries under control of Lotus 1-2-3 software.*

Recall that the We-Stock-It business plan calls for a second-year increase of 5 percent for Utilities, and 10 percent for Payroll costs. These two calculations are left for you to specify in a Project presented at the end of this chapter. For now, assume that Ed has specified operations for these two amounts. His final Two-Year Budget will look like the one shown in Figure 24-6.

How Do You Save a Worksheet?

Ed is almost ready to print his budget. However, he first wants to save the completed worksheet to his hard disk. To do so, Ed must return to the menu bar. Recall that the menu bar is displayed by entering a backslash character. The menu bar now appears, as shown in Figure 24-7.

Business Terms

business plan
A set of projections covering future conditions of a business.

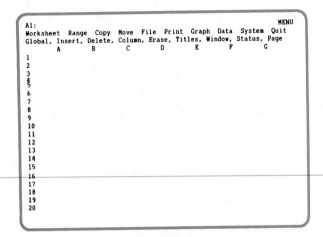

```
A1:                                                        MENU
Worksheet Range Copy Move File Print Graph Data System Quit
Global, Insert, Delete, Column, Erase, Titles, Window, Status, Page
        A        B        C        D       E       F        G
1
2
3
4
5
6
7
8
9
10
11
12
13
14
15
16
17
18
19
20
```

Figure 24-7. *To save a worksheet prepared under Lotus 1-2-3, the user begins by returning to the menu bar.*

A SAVE operation requires the use of the File option from the first menu bar. Ed enters an "F" to invoke this option. When he does so, a second menu bar appears. This set of options provides capabilities for retrieving a spreadsheet, saving an active spreadsheet, erasing an active spreadsheet, and so on. These are all activities that involve manipulation of a complete file. Ed enters an "S" to indicate that he wants to save the active file. The Lotus system prompts Ed for a file name:

**Name of file to save: C: \ Lotus **

This prompt indicates that the file name that Ed provides will be saved to drive C (the hard disk) within the currently active directory, "Lotus." Ed enters the name 2YRBGT and presses ENTER. The system saves the active worksheet under this new name, then returns Ed to the spreadsheet display.

How Is Spreadsheet Software Used To Perform 'What if...' Simulation?

Ed now can print his budget and then proceed to other spreadsheet activities. One possible use for his spreadsheet, at this point, is to create *pro forma* financial statements. A "pro forma" statement is a financial statement projected into the future. Normally, a financial statement shows the current status of a company. A "pro forma" statement presents future conditions on the basis of management projections.

Managers and business owners use the ability of computers to generate spreadsheets to preview the effects of decisions or plans. Managers ask "What if...?" questions about possible future developments. Then, spreadsheets are developed to show the situations that would result if these conditions happen. For instance, suppose Ed considers this question:

What if income for YEAR 2 increases by 5 percent, rather than 12 percent?

Ed wants to see what the profit or loss will be if growth for We-Stock-It is slower than expected. In this case, Ed can change all formulas for income categories to reflect a growth of 5 percent, rather than 12 percent. For the Cost of Goods Category, Ed would enter this formula in Cell C4:

+B4*1.05

He would enter similar formulas for other income categories. He also would change the Cost of Goods Sold formula to reflect the new projection:

(+B12*1.05)*1.02

Values for all other expense categories would remain the same. Under this approach, Ed needs to enter new formulas only. The Lotus 1-2-3 system then will perform recalculations automatically. The new spreadsheet display for this "What if...?" projection is shown in Figure 24-8. As you can see, the profit for We-Stock-It is small, less than for the previous year of operations.

```
C12: [W12] (+B12*1.05)*1.02                    READY
                          A              B         C        D
1                                 Two-Year Budget
2
3      INCOME                   YEAR 1     YEAR 2
4      Food Products          122,000.00  128,100.00
5      Paper Products          24,500.00   25,725.00
6      Pet Food & Pet Supplies 12,300.00   12,915.00
7      Sundries                48,000.00   50,400.00
8
9         TOTAL INCOME:       206,800.00  217,140.00
10
11     EXPENSES
12     Cost of Goods Sold      98,000.00  104,958.00
13     Rent                    28,000.00   28,000.00
14     Vehicle Pymts and Fuel   9,680.00   11,132.00
15     Utilities                5,200.00    5,460.00
16     Payroll                 42,000.00   46,200.00
17
18        TOTAL EXPENSES:     182,880.00  195,750.00
19
20     PROFIT OR LOSS:         23,920.00   21,390.00
```

Figure 24-8.   *This modified spreadsheet display could be used as a decision-making tool to complete "What if...?" simulations.*

```
C16: [W12] +B16*1.05                          READY
                          A              B         C        D
1                                 Two-Year Budget
2
3      INCOME                   YEAR 1     YEAR 2
4      Food Products          122,000.00  128,100.00
5      Paper Products          24,500.00   25,725.00
6      Pet Food & Pet Supplies 12,300.00   12,915.00
7      Sundries                48,000.00   50,400.00
8
9         TOTAL INCOME:       206,800.00  217,140.00
10
11     EXPENSES
12     Cost of Goods Sold      98,000.00  104,958.00
13     Rent                    28,000.00   28,000.00
14     Vehicle Pymts and Fuel   9,680.00    9,680.00
15     Utilities                5,200.00    5,460.00
16     Payroll                 42,000.00   44,100.00
17
18        TOTAL EXPENSES:     182,880.00  192,198.00
19
20     PROFIT OR LOSS:         23,920.00   24,942.00
```

Figure 24-9.   *This is a display of a modified budget based on adjustments to expense amounts.*

Testing alternatives.   In response, Ed might decide to increase profits by waiting to purchase a new delivery truck. He also might keep payroll costs to a minimum by waiting until the third year to hire new employees. To plan for this situation, Ed would copy the value in B14 into C14. He then would change the Payroll formula to show a 5 percent increase (to account for raises for current employees). Ed now can evaluate the anticipated profit under these new conditions. After making these two reductions in expenses, Ed views the new budget report, shown in Figure 24-9.

Keep in mind that Ed already has saved his two-year budget to disk. He can then alter the spreadsheet to reflect different changes in financial condition. Any new spreadsheets can be saved under different file names. In this way, Ed can make several projections that will help him plan for potential problems that may occur in the future.

The point: With electronic spreadsheet software, a manager can make new projections simply by altering values and formulas. The spreadsheet system performs all recalculations automatically. This approach enables managers to be ready for any future developments they can foresee.

Review 24.3

1.   What values must be established before projections can be calculated?

2.   What is the meaning of this entry: +B8*1.15?

3.   How is a SAVE operation carried out?

4.   What is a "pro forma" financial statement?

5.   How do managers use "What if...?" simulations?

HOW CAN SPREADSHEET SOFTWARE BE USED TO CREATE GRAPHICS?

Spreadsheet reports are tables of figures. The tables of numbers, by themselves, can be hard to understand. An information user must find corresponding

Business Terms

pro forma
In reference to financial statements, a document that projects the future results of business operations.

figures and develop his or her own analysis of what they mean. This takes time. Experience has shown that it can be easier and more efficient to represent important information in pictures.

For this reason, most commercial spreadsheet packages are designed to convert numeric values to images. These are known as *graphics* packages. A graphic, simply, is a picture. Computer graphics software uses values in spreadsheets to generate three major kinds of images:

- Pie charts
- Bar charts
- Line graphs.

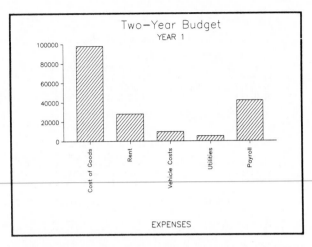

Figure 24-11. *This is an example of a bar chart generated by spreadsheet software.*

What Is a Pie Chart And How Is It Used?

A *pie chart* portrays values as portions of a whole value, represented as a "pie." Actually, the pie is a circle divided into different-sized slices. Each slice represents a percentage of an overall total. For instance, Ed might instruct the Lotus system to create

a pie chart for different income categories for YEAR 1. The system automatically would calculate the percentages of the overall total (206,800) that match each income category. A pie chart for this application is shown in Figure 24-10.

What Is a Bar Chart And How Is It Used?

A *bar chart* (also known as a *histogram*) is a graphic that compares values for two or more items. Values are shown through the comparative lengths of different lines (bars). Comparisons can be established quickly because bars of different lengths are presented alongside one another. Suppose, for example, that Ed wants to produce a bar chart that portrays values for YEAR 1 expense categories. Figure 24-11 shows how this bar chart would appear.

Figure 24-10. *This is an example of a pie chart generated by spreadsheet software.*

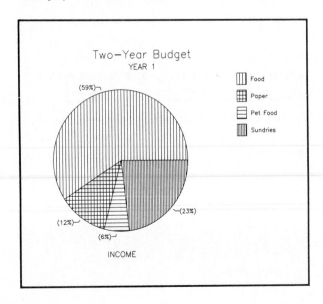

What Is a Line Graph And How Is It Used?

A *line graph* is designed to show *trends,* or changes in condition. The term "graph" means that values

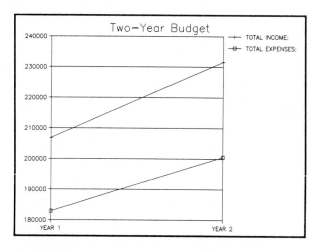

Figure 24-12. *This is an example of a line graph, or trend line output, generated by spreadsheet software.*

are presented on a series of evenly spaced lines called a *grid.* The spacing of the lines represents values. For example, the horizontal lines on a grid might represent values, such as business volumes. The vertical lines might represent time, such as months or years. Values are marked as points on a grid. Lines are then drawn between the points to show the rise and fall of values for different time spans. In this way, line graphs show value changes over time.

As an example, consider that Ed wants to produce a line graph that shows TOTAL INCOME and TOTAL EXPENSES for both years. The TOTAL INCOME amounts would be represented by two connected line segments. The TOTAL EXPENSES amounts also would be represented by two connected line segments. With a graphic of this type, Ed could tell, at a glance, the relationships between income and expenses. If expenses are rising faster than income, the lines on the graph will not be parallel. If the relationships between income and expense remain the same, the lines will be parallel. Ed's line graph is shown in Figure 24-12.

As you review Figures 24-10 through 24-12, notice how easy it is to detect business patterns from the graphic images. This is the value of graphics displays. These kinds of "pictures" allow managers to view the performance of a business "at a glance." It isn't necessary to study details that accumulate on a spreadsheet. A bar chart, pie chart, or line graph can provide meaning after only a few seconds of careful study. These results can be delivered because computers can be set up to process and output images as well as text and data. The techniques for processing graphics are covered in the chapter that follows.

Review 24.4

1. What is a pie chart and what does it show?
2. What is a bar chart and what does it show?
3. What is a line graph and what does it show?

Business Terms

graphic
A pictorial presentation of information.

pie chart
A graphic image that portrays a total value and shows the percentage relationships of its parts.

bar chart
A graphic that compares values for two or more items presented through lines of different lengths.

histogram
See bar chart.

line graph
A graphic that portrays trends by connecting value points on a grid with straight lines.

trend
A change that develops over time.

grid
A series of equally spaced horizontal and vertical lines placed over a display area.

Chapter Summary

❑ Spreadsheets are basic management tools used to report financial results and produce financial plans. Spreadsheets have been used for many years. Before computers were available, spreadsheets were prepared manually. Computers have become a better way to do a necessary job.

❑ Users make three kinds of entries to create electronic spreadsheets: labels, values, and formulas for mathematical operations.

❑ The basic structure for a spreadsheet is a table. In this respect, a spreadsheet is similar to a file in a relational database. Different software packages are used for databases and spreadsheets because of differences in user requirements.

❑ When an electronic spreadsheet package is loaded, a blank spreadsheet with default settings for column widths appears on the screen.

❑ If the default settings are not acceptable, the user completes a series of entries that change column formats.

❑ When the format is satisfactory, the user enters labels.

❑ The next step is to enter data into cells where specific figures are needed. Where the content of a cell will be completed, a formula is entered into the cell. The formula gives the specific cells or range of cells from which data will be used. In addition, symbols are entered to identify the arithmetic operations to be performed.

❑ Spreadsheet software enables managers to develop financial plans with ease.

❑ Projections are made for changes in future conditions as compared with current or past results.

❑ Formulas are developed that apply mathematical operations to values in cells that show current or past status.

❑ The software carries out the operations and inserts the computed values in place of the formulas.

❑ The process can be repeated as often as necessary to forecast results of alternative developments or economic conditions. Use of spreadsheet software in this way is known as "What if...?" simulation.

❑ Most spreadsheet packages are able to convert numeric values to images through graphics outputs. Three major forms of graphics generated by spreadsheet software include pie charts, bar charts, and line graphs.

❑ A pie chart is circular. Its image represents a comparison of the values of parts to a whole. For example, expenses can be represented on a pie chart as "slices" of a circle.

❑ A bar chart represents and compares multiple values as lengths of a series of lines, or bars.

❑ A line graph represents comparative values as points on a grid. These points are connected by lines that represent up or down trends in values or business activities.

Definitions

Write a complete sentence that defines each of the terms below.

cell	formula
label	value
range	default
menu bar	graphic
pie chart	bar chart
line graph	grid

Questions to Think About

Based on what you have learned to date, answer the following questions in one or more complete sentences.

1. What is a spreadsheet and what does it show?

2. Why are spreadsheets used for financial forecasts rather than database software?

3. What contributions have microcomputers and spreadsheet software made to the ability of managers to prepare spreadsheets?

4. What are spreadsheet labels and what do they do?

5. How are known values entered into electronic spreadsheets?

6. How are computations handled under spreadsheet software?

7. Describe the procedures for "What if...?" simulation.

8. What is a pie chart and what does it show?

9. What is a bar chart and what does it show?

10. What is a line graph and what does it show?

Projects

The purpose of the assignments below is to encourage you to increase your learning through outside reading or work assignments.

1. Develop the formulas to be used in the We-Stock-It spreadsheet to show increases for Utilities and Payroll. Use the spreadsheet in Figure 24-5 as your basis. Develop formulas that will allow for a 5 percent increase in Utilities and a 10 percent increase in Payroll.

2. By hand, draw a pie chart that shows the relationships of the Income items in Figure 24-8.

3. By hand, draw a bar chart that shows the relationships of the Expense items in Figure 24-8.

CHAPTER 25

How Do Computers Prepare Graphics and Publications?

The Think Tank

When you finish reading this chapter and complete your work assignments, you should be able to answer the following questions.

❑ How do graphics outputs meet the problem-solving and planning needs of businesspeople?

❑ How do graphics displays differ from text displays?

❑ What is a pixel and how are these elements generated and represented by computer systems?

❑ What are bit mapping and vector graphics techniques and what are the differences between them?

❑ What basic devices are available for input, display, and output of graphics?

DOING BUSINESS

Mauricette had just finished preparing for an oral presentation due for her geography class on Friday. As part of her presentation, Mauricette wanted to provide a special map that students could refer to during her lecture. She needed to make 35 copies of this map, one for each student in her class.

When Mauricette entered the copy and printing center, she noticed that all of the employees were busy performing tasks. As Mauricette waited at the counter to be served, she noticed an employee seated at a microcomputer. This employee seemed to be typing text into the computer. However, Mauricette also noted that the screen on the employee's computer also displayed two drawings. The employee, a "typesetter," noticed Mauricette watching him work. He stood up, approached the counter, and introduced himself as Martin. He asked Mauricette if he could help.

Mauricette explained her copy needs. Then, she asked Martin what he was doing on his computer.

"I'm preparing an annual report for the stockholders of a locally based corporation," Martin replied. "Several employees are busy preparing this report."

Mauricette asked about the display she had observed. "Oh, that," Martin responded, "I'm entering text for the report. Our staff artists have created several illustrations for the annual report. I'm using a 'desktop publishing program' to combine text and illustrations on each page of the report. This job is called 'page makeup.'

"Normally," Martin continued, "graphic artists paste sections of type, or text, onto boards that

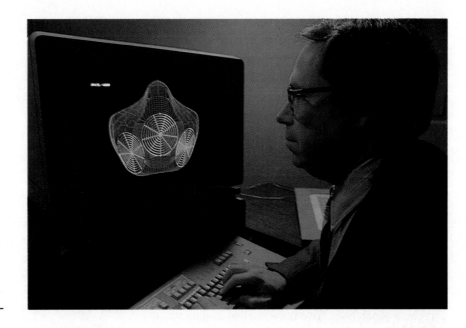

Computer graphics *capabilities enable engineers to design and analyze products before they are used. The technique is known as computer-aided design.*
COURTESY OF HARTMAN SYSTEMS
© HENLEY & SAVAGE

represent pages to be printed. Then, graphics— such as drawings and diagrams—are pasted into spaces between type. This process takes a great deal of time. With desktop publishing software, it is possible to create both graphics and text elements on the computer. Then, we can combine graphics and text electronically. In this way, we can perform paste-up tasks on the computer. We eliminate much of the work normally involved in manual production of publications.''

"In other words," Mauricette said, "you eliminate some of the work that graphic artists used to perform by hand."

"That's right," Martin said. "The graphics capabilities of computers help us to develop publications entirely by computer. Several manual operations usually performed by graphic artists are eliminated."

MEANING

This scenario describes an important, growing capability of microcomputers, ***desktop publishing.*** Desktop publishing evolved from electronic publishing methods that have been in use since the late 1970s. Thousands of newspapers and magazines now are produced with the aid of large computers. Computers are able to set type and prepare illustrations. Then, the type and illustrations can be assembled into finished pages. Recently, similar capabilities have been developed for microcomputers. Desktop publishing uses microcomputers.

For the preparation of illustrations and publications on microcomputers, special tools are needed—both hardware and software. Hardware includes a series of special devices that are attached to microcomputers. Then, special software is needed to control the operation of the hardware.

The previous chapter describes ways in which computers generate graphics from spreadsheets. It also is possible for computers to accept graphics inputs directly from users. The full computing cycle—including input, processing, output, and storage—can be applied to graphics, just as is done for information.

Business Terms

desktop publishing
Techniques for design and development of publications through use of microcomputers; capabilities include typesetting, preparation of line illustrations, and page makeup.

HOW DO COMPUTER GRAPHICS CAPABILITIES HELP TO MEET BUSINESS MANAGEMENT NEEDS?

You already know how spreadsheet software can generate graphics that make it easier to understand the meaning of financial information. The same benefits apply to other business needs. Businesspeople need to communicate. They communicate with one another, their customers, and their suppliers. The ability to add graphics to information exchanges adds interest and aids understanding.

Some of these needs are met by spreadsheet software. Many other graphics capabilities are provided through use of tools that enable people to take direct control of graphics processing. In business, computer graphics capabilities have been applied in four major areas:

- Presentation graphics
- Reports and other standard documents
- Publications
- Product design and development.

These applications and the techniques for implementing them are covered in the remainder of this chapter.

How Are Graphics Used for Presentations?

A presentation is a personal method for imparting information. An individual speaks before a group, much as a teacher talks to a class. One purpose of a presentation is to enable a speaker and members of an audience to communicate directly. People can offer suggestions to one another or ask questions. The purpose is to share ideas. To help make the ideas clear, *presentation graphics* aids often are used. The term ''presentation graphics'' takes in any pictorial materials used at meetings or other gatherings.

Graphics aids used at meetings include slides, video images, and printed notes or illustrations. These visual images make the information easier to understand. Also, use of graphics helps to hold audience attention. Graphics aids have been used at business meetings for many years. Computer tools make presentation graphics easier to prepare and less costly.

How Do Graphics 'Dress Up' Reports and Other Documents?

As you know, businesses generate millions of pages of communication documents through use of word processing software. Words certainly are valuable tools for communication. But page after page of only words can create a dull appearance. Also, just as with spoken presentations, pictures can promote understanding.

For this reason, software companies now are offering word processing, spreadsheet, and database packages that are compatible with each other. With these programs, it is possible to *import* spreadsheet graphics or data tables into text documents. In addition, a number of word processing programs make it possible to include graphics outputs developed by users directly into text documents.

As an example, many engineering reports now include bar graphs and line graphs that describe performance of new products. Also, computer-produced drawings of the products can be included. To help clarify information content, many budget and financial reports include pie charts.

How Are Publications Produced With Desktop Publishing Tools?

Businesses also create many documents that require a polished, or professional, appearance that goes beyond normal word processing capabilities. Examples include product description sheets and catalogs. These publications sell products. Their appearance and quality represent the company that makes the

Presentation and instruction applications represent important uses for computer graphics capabilities.

COURTESY OF TELEVIDEO SYSTEMS, INC.

products. Other types of publications include manuals on use of products or services. Many companies produce newsletters that provide information to customers and employees.

Until recently, companies had to go to great expense to produce professional looking publications. One approach was to install typesetting equipment and hire a staff of artists. Another was to buy professional services from outside organizations. With desktop publishing techniques, however, professional-quality publications can be created within the company. The work can be done by people with only minimal training. As a result, quality work can be produced at greatly reduced costs.

How Do Computer Graphics Fit Into Product Design?

At an early stage in the process of *product design,* it is necessary to prepare pictures of the item under development. This work used to be done by skilled engineers and drafters. The drawings took a long time to prepare. Changes—and changes always were required—took more time.

Computers were applied to the preparation of drawings and to actual manufacturing operations during the 1960s and 1970s. During the 1980s, these capabilities were adapted to microcomputers. Applications for computer-supported drafting and manufacturing operations are described in Chapter 27.

Business Terms

presentation graphics
Pictorial materials used at meetings or other gatherings.

import
In computer operations, a reference to the ability to find materials prepared under another software package and access them for inclusion in outputs for an active program.

product design
The activities connected with creation of a new product prior to manufacturing and marketing.

Review 25.1

1. What are the main differences between graphics generated by spreadsheet software and images produced directly by users?

2. What are presentations and how do computer graphics fit into presentations?

3. What is the value of including computer-generated graphics in word processing documents or publications?

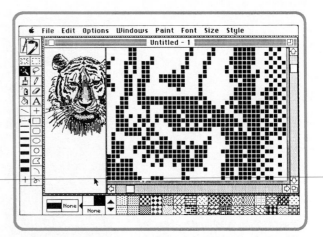

Bit-mapped graphics techniques are used to develop detailed illustrations that include tone values.

HOW DOES A COMPUTER DO GRAPHICS PROCESSING?

Up to this point, the computer applications you have encountered deal chiefly with text and numerical data. Entries are through keyboards and are displayed on screens. Under procedures for text or data operations, users simply type in the entries to be processed. The computer system does the rest. For instance, with text and data, individual bytes are stored and displayed within row and column positions.

On a typical personal computer screen, 80 character, or column, positions are available on each line. In turn, 24 rows are available for typed entries on computer-generated displays. The operating system interprets each pressed key as a unique code. Each code represents a different alphabetic, numeric, or special character.

With graphics, input and processing are handled differently. A graphics image is formed by dividing the screen into thousands of individual row and column positions. These positions are called *picture elements,* or simply *pixels.* Each pixel represents a tiny spot on the computer screen. Each pixel can be addressed, or located, by using a set of binary codes that indicate the pixel's horizontal and vertical positions. This approach to forming images is called *bit mapping.* That is, each pixel position is treated as a separate data item. Under this approach, pixels can be highlighted in patterns to represent almost any image a user needs.

There are many more pixels on a screen than characters of text. A pixel is a single, minute point. On your TV screen, for example, there are more than 25,000 pixel positions. By contrast, a typical character display with 80 columns and 24 rows has a maximum of 1,920 positions. There may be 10 or 12 pixel positions for each character position. Clearly, a different method is needed to identify and present information in a pixel pattern than is used for text outputs.

Character displays are generated by your computer's operating system. The software contains instructions that create images for letters, numbers, and symbols. This means only a specific number of images, each with a specific pattern, can be generated.

By contrast, each graphics image must be made up from scratch. Your computer needs different equipment to do this job. If your computer is equipped to handle graphics, a special circuit card must be included in its processor. This *graphics card,* in effect, is a *co-processor,* or a device that works alongside the processor. It handles data and generates outputs. In addition, as described below, a number of special devices are needed for graphics input and output.

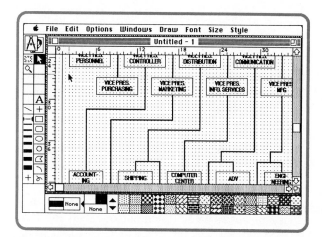

Vector graphics methods generate line drawings that can include type. Major applications include development of charts like this one.

WHAT TECHNIQUES ARE USED FOR GRAPHICS PROCESSING?

Two general methods are available to create graphics:

- Direct bit mapping
- Vector graphics.

What Is Direct Bit Mapping?

Direct bit mapping means that user-controlled software can examine, review, and even modify the pixel content of an image. Pixel images are created with *paint software* or through electronic input devices.

Paint software permits a user to create images by drawing on input devices. The resulting images have "tone values." That is, parts of the images are represented by shades of gray rather than by just solid lines. These shades are created through electronic mixtures of solid and blank pixels. The tones that may be used are provided on a menu presented by the software. For paint programs, these tone menus are called *palettes*. A palette is a work surface on which an artist mixes colors to be used in a painting.

Bit-mapped images also can be input through devices known as *scanners*. A scanner senses tone values with a beam of light that passes over the surface of the image. The sensed values are translated to pixel codes that are stored within the computer.

As another option, input can be accepted from video cameras or from other electronic devices.

Regardless of the input technique, the result is an image formed by assigning black, white, or color

Business Terms

picture element
See pixel.

pixel
A point within a display or output that plays a role in forming a picture; tens of thousands of pixels are needed to form a one-page image.

bit mapping
Formation of an image through control of black, white, or color values of individual pixels.

graphics card
A circuit board placed in the computer processor to control the creation and output of graphic images.

co-processor
A processing device that augments the main processor of a computer; a graphics card that forms images is a typical co-processor.

direct bit mapping
Pixel image creation under direct user control. *See also* bit mapping.

paint software
Computer graphics technique that enables the user to produce bit-mapped graphics with tone or color values.

palette
In computer graphics, a menu that offers choices of tone or color values for user application.

scanner
An input device that can read and enter bit-mapped values for graphic processing.

values to individual pixels. The user can control the content of a bit-mapped image with tools provided by paint software. With these tools, a user can highlight or erase the content of individual pixels. The equipment used for this purpose is described later in this chapter.

The point: Pixel images are composed of tiny points of black, white, or color values. Tens of thousands of these points make up a single image display or printed page. Pixel graphics are highly detailed. Computer systems that process pixel graphics require extra-large memory and storage capacities.

How Are Vector Graphics Created?

A *vector* is a mathematical term used to define a line segment that has direction. To illustrate this concept, take a sheet of paper and make a dot anywhere on the sheet. Now, draw a line that connects the lower lefthand corner of the paper with this dot. You can tell the relative direction of this line segment by comparing it with either edge of the paper.

Now draw three or four dots at random on the paper. Connect these dots to the lower lefthand corner of the paper. Label each of the lines you have drawn with the letters B1, B2, B3, and so on. Then draw new line segments to connect your dots (B1, B2, and so on). This is the approach used with vector graphics. That is, several directed line segments are used to guide, or plot, the creation of new lines. Because vector graphics techniques generate lines, the results are known as *line art.* There are no tone values in line art, as there are in bit-mapped graphics.

When hundreds or thousands of vectors are generated, it is possible to guide the creation of arcs, circles, and wave forms. *Vector graphics* is a mathematical technique used to draw lines and shapes. *Drawing programs* provide capabilities for producing vector graphics images on microcomputers.

Common uses of vector graphics in business are for charts and diagrams. Also, the graphics generated by spreadsheet software—pie charts, bar charts, and line graphs—are produced through vector graphics methods.

Engineers frequently use vector graphics techniques to make drawings of products and devices. These principles are part of a computer graphics technique called computer-aided design (CAD), discussed in Chapter 27.

Other applications for vector graphics include medical technology. For instance, special computer-driven machines have been developed to monitor patient heart rates. These heart rates are shown as lines and curves on a printed output called an "electrocardiogram (ECG)." The ECG images are defined by a series of vectors.

Review 25.2

1. What is a pixel?

2. What is bit mapping and how are bit-mapped images formed?

3. What are vector graphics techniques and how are vector graphics images formed?

4. What are the differences between images formed through bit mapping and vector graphics techniques?

HOW DO USERS CONTROL GRAPHICS PROCESSING?

Just as text and data can be input, processed, output, and stored, so can graphics. However, special techniques and equipment are used for graphics applications.

How Are Graphics Input And Processing Handled?

With graphics techniques, input and processing steps often take place together. For instance, special input devices often are used to make conversions between electronic signals and picture forms. Even though in-

Graphics and publishing input are achieved through use of both a keyboard and a mouse.

puts result, the needed conversions represent processing activities. To illustrate, a user can draw a picture on a metal surface and generate an image on the display screen. To produce this result, input and processing have to be handled together. Some of the special devices used for graphics input are described below.

Keyboard. The keyboard cannot easily be used to draw images. (Some systems permit use of the cursor control keys to develop images. But these methods are not of professional caliber.) However, most graphics software packages accept special function commands from the keyboard. Examples include the saving of files, printing, and others.

Mouse. A *mouse* is a device that enables a user to move the screen cursor in any direction, at high speeds. One important use of the mouse is to select function options provided on menus. Another is to point to and select image and text elements for processing. In some situations, the mouse can be used for drawing.

The mouse is housed in a small, low case that is moved along the surface of a desktop pad. Most mouse devices include a small, rolling ball that senses movement. This movement is translated to shift the location of the cursor. Some devices operate electronically. A beam of light senses positions on a grid

Business Terms

vector
A mathematical term used to define a line segment that has direction.

line art
An illustration composed entirely of lines, with no tonal values; can be created under vector graphics software.

vector graphics
A mathematical technique used to draw lines and shapes.

drawing program
A software tool that provides capabilities for producing vector graphics images on microcomputers.

mouse
A device that enables a user to move the screen cursor rapidly in any direction and to make menu selections by clicking a switch.

built into the mouse pad. Results are the same as with a rolling ball. Usually, the user makes choices from displays on the screen by "clicking" a button on top of the mouse when the cursor is in the proper position.

Graphics tablet. A *graphics tablet,* sometimes called a *touch tablet,* provides capabilities for direct drawing of images. Also, with some software, the tablet can be used to select processing functions. For these applications, the tablet is marked to indicate selection positions. The effect is the same as moving the cursor to a menu selection position with a mouse.

For graphics input, a graphics tablet is used this way: The tablet—a flat, *touch-sensitive,* rectangular pad—is placed near the computer. The user then presses a pen or other writing instrument against the surface of the tablet. The position where the pad is pressed then is translated by the software. The cursor is moved to a position on the screen that matches the point at which the tablet is touched. At each point where the tablet is touched, a pixel is highlighted. If the user draws on the tablet, corresponding lines are displayed on the screen.

Light pen. A *light pen* can sense a point of light placed on a display screen under software control. When the light-sensitive pen is activated, the point of light can be moved across the face of the screen to draw images.

Use of a light pen typically begins by entering an instruction that illuminates all pixels on a screen. Then, the user makes contact between the light pen and one pixel position. This contact then can be moved along the face of the screen. As the point of light moves, a black line is traced. The result typically is a black drawing on a green or orange background.

Scanners. In some cases, people want to input drawings that already have been completed on paper. For instance, suppose an architect has drawn plans for a house. He or she then wants to input these

plans into a computer system for further work and modification.

For these kinds of applications, a scanner usually is an efficient graphic input device. A scanner can transfer images such as drawings from paper to computer-stored files. Then, the drawing can be displayed and changed through use of graphics software.

How Are Graphics Output?

The display of input graphics is one method used to output drawings, charts, and other pictorial designs. Recall from an earlier chapter that a computer monitor often is considered to be a combination input/output device. However, computer monitors provide only a temporary, limited method for viewing outputs. Other output methods are covered in the discussions that follow.

Plotters. Permanent, hard-copy graphics outputs can be created with devices called *plotters.* A plotter actually "draws" outputs onto sheets of paper. A plotter draws with a pen-like device called a *stylus.* The stylus is driven by an electrical unit. As it moves, the stylus traces a pattern to match the pixel patterns stored in vector graphics files. The result is a drawing similar to those developed manually by engineering drafters.

Printers. Laser and dot matrix printers can provide hard-copy outputs of graphics images. On laser printers, a light beam traces the same image that appears on a computer screen onto a xerographic drum. Laser printers can create images on sheets of acetate. These outputs can be used as "overhead transparencies." That is, they can be used on special projectors that process images from clear acetate masters.

Paper copies of the images are reproduced. Some programs also make it possible to generate graphics outputs on dot-matrix printers. Dots are imprinted to form the image.

Hard-copy graphics outputs can be developed with plotters like the one shown in this photo. Many plotters, with a wide range of prices, are available.
COURTESY OF HEWLETT-PACKARD COMPANY

Cameras and projectors. Graphics outputs can be captured on color slides by devices that photograph pixel or vector images. The slides then are used as presentation graphics at meetings or training sessions. It also is possible to attach a device that projects the computer's VDT image onto a large screen. Sometimes, this method is referred to as an "electronic slide projector."

How Are Graphics Stored?

Each pixel has an assigned position on the screen. This position is used as a basis for storing graphics information in computer files. For each pixel used to form an image, a location code and a value are stored in memory and on magnetic media. Each image generally is stored in a separate file.

Graphics files are more complicated to store than text or data. Individual software packages often use storage methods that are different from all other graphics programs. Thus, it may be impossible to transfer graphics files among different software packages.

Business Terms

graphics tablet
Device that provides capabilities for direct input of images drawn on a touch-sensitive surface.

touch tablet
See graphics tablet.

touch-sensitive
Refers to the ability to sense and transmit information based on points at which a surface is touched by a sharp instrument.

light pen
A graphics input device that can sense a point of light placed on a display screen under software control.

plotter
A graphics printer that creates images with computer-driven drawing instruments.

stylus
The drawing instrument on a plotter.

Review 25.3

1. Why is it necessary to combine some input and processing operations under computer graphics programs?

2. What is a mouse and how is it used?

3. What is a graphics tablet and how is it used?

4. How do plotters produce graphics outputs?

HOW ARE BUSINESS REQUIREMENTS MET THROUGH COMPUTER GRAPHICS?

At the beginning of this chapter, some key business applications for computer graphics are identified. These include presentation graphics, documentation, desktop publishing, and product design. Many of these requirements can be met through use of drawing software packages. Some vector graphics outputs can be used to satisfy all of these applications. Therefore, the discussion that follows describes use of drawing software to produce a business graphics output. Desktop publishing can make use of vector graphics outputs. In addition, desktop publishing has some special application dimensions. These also are discussed in the section that follows.

How Do You Draw Pictures With Vector Graphics Tools?

One business requirement that can be met easily with computer graphics methods is the development of an organization chart. An organization chart is a diagram that defines the positions in a company and illustrates the relationships among those positions. A typical organization chart includes a series of labeled boxes. These boxes identify positions within the organization and show how they are related to one another. The accompanying series of illustrations are prints from computer screens on which an organization chart is developed.

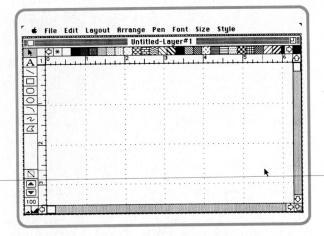

Figure 25-1. *This is a graphically oriented menu that provides access to a popular drawing program.*

Figure 25-1 shows a screen display for a popular drawing software package. Note the menu along the left side of the screen. This presents a number of options for line thicknesses and shapes that can be selected. To start the development of the organization chart, the user selects the rectangular shape. A rectangle is positioned on the screen as shown in Figure 25-2.

Figure 25-2. *This display demonstrates a starting point for development of an organization chart. The user begins by positioning a rectangle on the screen.*

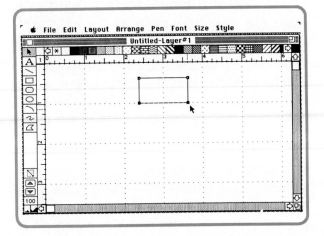

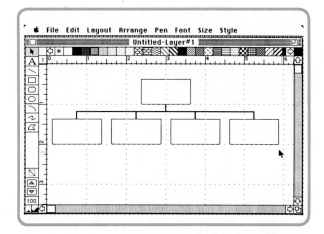

Figure 25-3. *By repeating the rectangle shape and positioning connecting lines, the user builds the structure for an organization chart.*

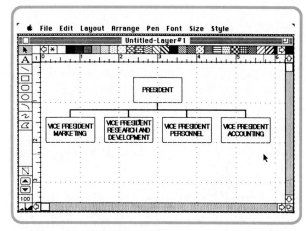

Figure 25-4. *This display shows an organization chart with type in place to identify all the positions. Arrowheads will be added later.*

A special feature of the drawing software is used to create the rest of the boxes needed for the organization chart. The user simply selects the existing box with the mouse. This causes the system to create a duplicate rectangle that overlaps the first box. Then, the mouse is used to move the second box to its desired location. After that, additional boxes are copied and positioned as necessary. When the boxes are in place, the software is used to position lines that connect them. An organization chart with a series of boxes and lines in place is shown in Figure 25-3.

To finish the organization chart, the capability of the system to mix type and graphics is used. The user simply moves the cursor to each box and enters job titles through the keyboard. The result is the finished chart shown in Figure 25-4.

A graphics image of the type shown in Figure 25-4 can be used to create masters for projection. The same image can be printed on paper and distributed. Also, the image can be included in a message produced on a word processor for distribution within an organization. Similar capabilities for creating and positioning images are keys to desktop publishing systems, discussed next.

How Are Publications Created With Desktop Publishing Tools?

Many books, newsletters, newspapers, and magazines use type and illustrations prepared through desktop publishing techniques.

The manuscript for a publication is written on a microcomputer. Word processing software is used to originate the manuscript and to make any needed editing changes. If necessary, the manuscript is transferred to a desktop publishing system through a communications link. The desktop publishing computer sets the text into type. A computer display of typeset text is shown in Figure 25-5.

It also is possible to use software packages to assemble complete book pages on desktop systems. Figure 25-6 shows a reproduction of a screen on which a full book page has been assembled.

Experience has shown that desktop publishing techniques can reduce costs by between 25 and 40 percent as compared with traditional methods.

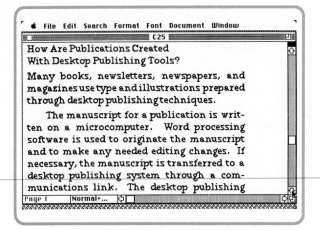

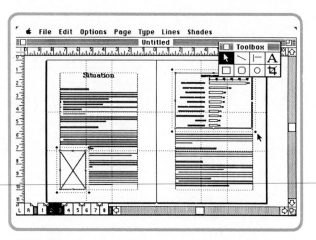

Figure 25-5. *Desktop computers can do a professional-looking job of setting type for publications.*

Figure 25-6. *This display shows part of a composed book page created with the aid of desktop publishing software.*

HOW ARE COLOR GRAPHICS PRODUCED?

For special presentations, such as sales meetings, it can be effective to use full-color graphics presentations. Computer systems can simplify the creation of these kinds of graphics outputs. Many computers can process and display full-color images. This is done through electronic circuits that output three separate signals within the display tube. These signals create coordinated images of red, green, and blue. The process is similar to the one you view on a home TV screen. The major difference is that the computer, rather than a broadcast station, generates signals.

For presentation graphics, full-color displays can be photographed. Slides are created that can be projected at meetings or other presentations. In addition, color drawings can be created on plotters that drive sets of multi-colored pens. Some laser printers also have color capabilities.

For presentations and other special situations, color graphics can help to improve the appearance and quality of computer graphics outputs.

Among the applications described in this chapter is the ability to include graphics in documents generated on word processing systems. In the chapter that follows, additional, valuable methods for integrating information from multiple applications are covered.

Review 25.4

1. How do graphics software tools make it possible to create drawings or diagrams without requiring that the user draw any images?

2. What is desktop publishing and what outputs can be generated?

3. How are color slides created from desktop computers?

Chapter Summary

❑ In addition to developing graphics through use of spreadsheet software, it is possible for a user to generate graphics directly through use of special hardware and software tools.

❑ Graphics applications in business include presentations, business documents, publications, and product design.

❑ Presentation graphics support and help communicate information that is carried out through personal lectures or demonstrations, usually at meetings.

❑ Documents generated by word processing systems can include graphics "imported" from other software packages.

❑ Publications produced by companies include product information sheets, catalogs, and newsletters. Desktop publishing methods make it possible to control these operations internally and to realize large savings.

❑ Graphics processing capabilities can be used to create drawings of new products and to control operation of machines that manufacture those products.

❑ Computers form images by using tiny points on screens or documents. These are known as picture elements, or pixels.

❑ Image formation is through either of two methods, bit mapping or vector graphics.

❑ Bit mapping assigns light, dark, or color values to many thousands of points on computer screens or printouts. Bit-mapped inputs are entered through use of "paint" software or by electronic scanning. Paint software enables users to change values of pixels that form an image.

❑ Vector graphics use mathematical values to form lines, curves, and other shapes. Images created with vector graphics software are formed from solid lines.

❑ Computer graphics systems require special capabilities for handling input, processing, output, and storage.

❑ Input and processing generally are performed together. This is because processing is necessary to form images entered through input devices. Input devices include the keyboard, mouse, graphics tablet, light pen, and scanner.

❑ Output methods include displays and the drawing of images through use of computer-driven plotters.

❑ Storage is based on location and value codes for active pixels. Different storage methods may be used by individual programs.

❑ Drawing software provides sets of shapes and lines that can be used to create vector graphics, or line drawings. Complete illustrations can be created by the computer under control of a user who enters instructions with a mouse.

❑ Entire publications can be created through use of microcomputers set up for desktop publishing software. The computers can accept word processing inputs and set type. The systems can assemble type and illustrations into finished pages ready for publication.

❑ Computers can generate images in color. These can be used as presentation graphics in business situations. Color outputs can be transferred to slides or can be printed by plotters or laser printers.

Definitions

Write a complete sentence that defines each of the terms below.

desktop publishing	presentation graphics
import	pixel
bit mapping	graphics card
vector graphics	graphics tablet

Questions to Think About

Based on what you have learned to date, answer the following questions in one or more complete sentences.

1. What are presentation graphics and what is their purpose?

2. How can graphics be used to enhance the value of reports and other business documents?

3. What is a graphics card and what does it do?

4. What is a mouse and how is it used?

5. What is a pixel and what role does it play in computer graphics?

6. What is bit mapping and what results does it deliver?

7. What are vector graphics and what role do they play in computer graphics?

8. What is a graphics tablet and how is it used?

9. What is desktop publishing and what results are delivered?

Projects

The purpose of the assignments below is to encourage you to increase your learning through outside reading or work assignments.

1. Describe three incidents in which you have experienced use of presentation graphics for instruction or for the sharing of information. Did the graphics help you to understand the message being presented? Did the graphics make the presentation more interesting? Think of what the experiences would have been like without the graphics. Then report on whether and how the graphics affected you.

2. Find a magazine article that describes an actual case in which a business has used desktop publishing methods. Describe both benefits realized and problems encountered. Report on what you feel to be the place of desktop publishing techniques in the future of business organizations.

3. If you have a desktop publishing system available, use drawing software to create an organization chart for your school.

CHAPTER 26

How Are Data Communications And Integrated Systems Used?

The Think Tank

When you finish reading this chapter and complete your work assignments, you should be able to answer the following questions.

❑ What is a data communications network?

❑ What is a modem and how does it work?

❑ What is distributed processing and how does this concept relate to data communications networks?

❑ What is a job stream and how does a job stream affect applications processed by computers?

❑ How do integrated software packages aid in processing separate applications within a job stream?

DOING BUSINESS

Joe Lane almost bumped into Carl Kunasek as he rounded the corner. "Carl!" Joe exclaimed, "I was just coming to talk to you." Joe was employed as an operations manager for his company's accounts receivable department. Carl was a specialist in computer systems development. They walked back to Carl's office. At Carl's invitation, Joe explained what he had in mind.

"Our new Atlanta branch has taken off like a missile," Joe said. "Sales are almost 100 percent ahead of forecast."

"That doesn't sound like a problem to me," Carl commented.

"Actually," Joe said, "our problem is with our prosperity. Things are going better than anybody dreamed they would. Now we are worried about cash flow. We're spending a lot of money to ship products into that area. But, because of distances, collections are running slower than we'd like."

Carl cut in. "Are we still waiting to get shipping orders in the mail before we bill customers?" he asked.

"You hit it," Joe replied. "But that's only part of the problem. We're losing five to nine days between waiting for shipping orders and getting bills to our Atlanta customers. Then we lose another four to six days waiting for our money to get here in the mail.

"Zelda Childs, our Atlanta manager, has come up with suggestions that makes sense," Joe said. "That's why I'm here."

"I've been expecting you," Carl confided. "Zelda called me for some technical information before she made her proposal to you. As you know,

I've been trying for some time to get the company to put in a data link from here to Atlanta. So, your visit is good news. Go ahead, please.''

"Zelda wants to connect her microcomputers in Atlanta directly to our mainframe computer here. Right now, she's using the microcomputer to write orders. After shipment, we get hard copies of the orders and a diskette. We do the input in the accounts receivable department and issue invoices. That job puts us under pressure because the bills are already late by the time we get them mailed.

"If the microcomputers in Atlanta could talk to our mainframe," Joe continued, "the bills could be delivered out of Atlanta. Now, here's the rest of it. Zelda has found a bank in Atlanta that will give us a lock box service. Customer payments would be addressed to our Atlanta office. But they would be picked up by the bank in Atlanta and deposited to our account there. All told, this should give us money in the bank two weeks sooner."

"Does that give you any problems?" Carl asked. "Do you need to receive the checks here?"

"The paper checks don't matter," Joe answered. "My job is to help make the cash available to the company as soon as possible. If we set up the data link you want, we can deal with a bank in Atlanta just as easily as the one on the ground floor of this building. The bank would make up the deposit records for all our checks and send them to our computer each day. The bank would charge for the service. But it wouldn't cost any more than if we processed the paperwork here. Also, we can write checks on the Atlanta bank to meet some of our expenses. Or, if we prefer, we can arrange to transfer money from the Atlanta bank to our local bank. We could do this by computer, so our money would be available immediately."

"You know it will take some time to set all this up," Carl explained. "You're asking us to do more than just send signals across telephone lines. We have to be able to integrate our system with the bank's. We have to find out what it will take for us to be able to accept their deposit records into our accounts receivable files. And, while we are at it, we have to figure out how to integrate our microcom-

puters in Atlanta with our central mainframe. These things can be done, but they take time.''

"The sooner the better," Joe concluded.

MEANING

Joe seems to recognize the value of data communications. He has pointed out that a data communications link could bring his office and one in a distant city close together. Distance doesn't have to be an obstacle in an age of computers and electronics. The availability of information matters. Management is based on information.

Carl also pointed out that there are technical considerations. It is exciting to Joe to be able to use information from the bank's system. He also sees no problem in having a microcomputer in Atlanta tied to the company's mainframe computer. However, as Carl pointed out, technical bridges exist and have to be crossed. Special equipment and software are needed to permit computers to talk to one another. Also, special software is needed to allow computers to share files that are created through use of different software. This chapter discusses the problems that have to be overcome before data can be communicated and systems can be integrated.

WHAT IS THE VALUE OF DATA COMMUNICATION IN BUSINESS?

A business runs on information that is structured to model its status and operations. As a business spreads out into wide geographic areas, challenges for gathering and organizing information can grow. Gaps develop as managers are expected to know about and control operations that may be thousands of miles away.

As businesses spread out, their information systems must keep pace. **Data communications** links are necessary to exchange information over distances. Data communications is the ability to transmit and receive digital, computer-compatible information via telecommunication links. In general, the term ''data

Data communications networks have become worldwide in scope with the introduction of satellite transmission capabilities. Transmissions are sent and received from "dishes" like this one and are bounced off communication satellites that orbit at more than 20 miles above the Earth.
COURTESY OF AT&T

communications" describes transmissions that go from one point to another.

It also has become necessary for many organizations to set up systems under which multiple locations can transmit and receive data. These capabilities are known as a *network,* or *data communications network.*

The value of networking is that managers of a company doing business on a nationwide or worldwide scale can have access to current information. The main duties of managers—planning, organizing, and controlling—are carried out through use of information. With data communications networks, information needed for planning, organizing, and controlling can be placed at the fingertips of managers anywhere.

How Do Networks Serve Managers?

A data communications network is set up to support information collection and distribution in patterns that match a company's operations. In some instances, small branch offices may use networks for access to large, central computers. The branch office sends information to the main office. The branch also draws

on the power of a central computer. It's something like turning on a light switch and drawing power from generators that may be hundreds of miles away. Electricity is delivered through networks of power lines. Computing power is delivered through networks of communication lines.

Business Terms

data communications
The ability to transmit and receive digital, computer-compatible information via telecommunication links.

network
A communication link within which multiple stations can transmit and receive messages.

data communications network
A network dedicated to the exchange of information in digital format. *See also* network.

distributed processing
A technique under which a company puts its computing power at the points where it transacts business and uses information.

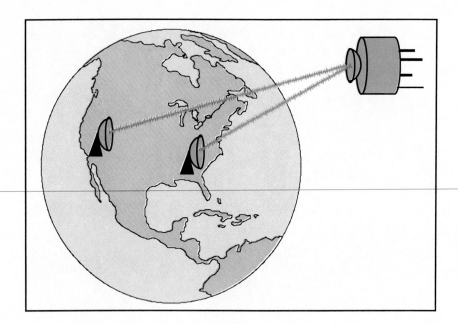

This illustration demonstrates the method and scope of satellite communications links that handle data transmissions at ultra-high speeds.

The example of the branch office connected to a central office computer is just one kind of network service. Large companies may have large computers in multiple locations. Communications links enable these computers to share processing workloads for the entire company. For example, one company with international operations has large computers in the Southwest, the Midwest, and Europe. A network connects these computer centers as though they were in the same building. A job entered for processing in the Southwest may be run in Europe. Results of processing are shared in any location served by the company.

When processing takes place at multiple locations and information can be shared throughout a company, the system provides *distributed processing*. This term means that a company puts its computing power at the points where it transacts business and uses information.

HOW DO COMPUTERS COMMUNICATE?

All data communications systems must use a *carrier* of some kind to transmit data from one location to another. A carrier is a connection, or link, over which signals are transmitted from an origin to a destination. The major communications network used to transmit data between computers is the public telephone system. In the simplest form of data communications, a telephone connection is established. This is done the same way as when you call a friend on the telephone. Once the connection is made, special devices are used to enable computers to talk to one another.

Telecommunications networks use many types of carriers. Originally, all signals were carried by cables with many strands of copper wire. These multi-strand wire carriers are *coaxial* cables. Sound is carried in waves that are formed by converting sound to electrical signals. At the receiving end of a telephone connection, the electrical signals are converted back to sound. Over the carrier, the sound moves in waves of electrical current known as *analog* signals. An analog signal is one in which information is represented by varying amounts of electrical current.

Telecommunications circuits also use radio waves and light waves. Radio-wave transmission generally is done through *microwave* systems. A microwave signal uses special wave forms that deliver high-quality signals. Microwave circuits can be set up through use of special towers that relay signals every 90 miles or so. Microwave signals also can be beamed up to satellites, then back to earth at a distant point.

Telecommunications signals also can be transmitted over strands of glass that carry light. This is the *fiber optics* method. Instead of electrical signals, bursts of light are used to represent information. Light also can be used to carry signals on *laser* beams. A laser is a powerful beam of light that can be carried through the air or by special, guiding tubes.

Review 26.1

1. What is data communications?

2. What is a network?

3. What is meant by distributed processing?

4. What is an analog signal and how were analog signals used before the introduction of computers?

HOW ARE DIGITAL SIGNALS CARRIED ON ANALOG CIRCUITS?

Regardless of the type of carrier used, the telephone system was designed originally to carry analog signals. Computers, however, use a different signalling method. Computers are *digital* devices. Computer signals are carried in stop-start patterns through bursts of energy that represent binary bits.

Information users recognized that computers had to talk to one another. Telecommunications technicians had to develop a method to communicate digital signals over analog circuits. To illustrate, Figure 26-1 presents diagrams that show the wave forms of analog and digital signals.

Role of the modem. To carry digital signals over analog circuits, a signal converter is needed. At the sending end, digital computer signals need to be converted to analog form. Then, at the receiving end, the signals have to be changed back into digital form that computers can understand. Special devices, called *modems,* were developed to do this job.

Modem is short for the functions performed: *MOdulate* and *DEModulate.* Modulation is the for-

Business Terms

carrier
A connection, or link, over which signals are transmitted from an origin to a destination.

coaxial
A telecommunication cable that contains multiple strands of wire and can establish many carrier links.

analog
A signal in which information is represented by varying amounts of electrical current.

microwave
A radio-type carrier that uses special wave forms that deliver high-quality signals.

fiber optics
A communications carrier that transmits messages as bursts of light which are used to represent information.

laser
A powerful beam of light that can transmit messages through the air or through special, guiding tubes.

digital
Reference to codes and signals based on stop-start transmission rather than on varying amounts of electrical current.

modem
A device that converts computer signals to telecommunications code for transmission, and reverses the process to receive transmitted signals for computer processing.

modulate
The formation and transmission of special analog signals. *See also* modem.

demodulate
A method for removing the analog formats and converting signals back to their original form. *See also* modem.

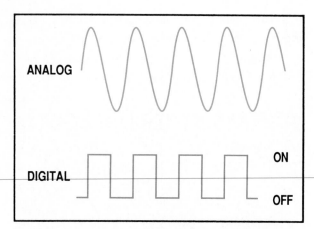

Figure 26-1. *These diagrams represent the forms of analog (top) and digital communications transmission signals.*

mation and transmission of special analog signals. Demodulation is a method for removing the analog formats and converting signals back to their original form.

When data stored by a computer are ready for transmission, they are input to the modem. There, they are converted to a series of analog waves that carry digital information. On the receiving end, the analog waves are input to a second modem. This

modem converts the analog waves back into digital signals. These digital signals then can be input to the receiving computer.

Types of modems. The most widely used modem is called a ***direct-connect*** modem. This name refers to the ability to plug the modem directly into a standard telephone jack. Two types of direct-connect modems are in common use today: external and internal.

An ***external direct-connect modem*** looks like a rectangular-shaped box about the size of a thick, paperback book. One end of the modem plugs into a telephone jack. The other is connected to a special ***communications port,*** or plug, in the back of a computer. An external modem is shown in Figure 26-2.

An ***internal direct-connect modem*** is built on a computer circuit board. It can be installed directly into the hardware circuits of a computer. An internal modem is shown in Figure 26-3.

How Are Digital Signals Coded for Transmission?

In addition to converting analog and digital signals, modems do a second job: They convert digital signals

Figure 26-2. *This photo shows an external modem in use. The modem is the small device placed on top of the book at the front of this scene.*
COURTESY OF HAYES MICROCOMPUTER PRODUCTS, INC.

Figure 26-3. *This photo shows an internal modem being inspected. The modem is built on a circuit board that is placed within a computer.*

COURTESY OF HAYES MICROCOMPUTER PRODUCTS, INC., PHOTO BY TIM OLIVE

Character	ASC II-7	Character	ASC II-7
0	011 0000	I	100 1001
1	011 0001	J	100 1010
2	011 0010	K	100 1011
3	011 0011	L	100 1100
4	011 0100	M	100 1101
5	011 0101	N	100 1110
6	011 0110	O	100 1111
7	011 0111	P	101 0000
8	011 1000	Q	101 0001
9	011 1001	R	101 0010
		S	101 0011
A	100 0001	T	101 0100
B	100 0010	U	101 0101
C	100 0011	V	101 0110
D	100 0100	W	101 0111
E	100 0101	X	101 1000
F	100 0110	Y	101 1001
G	100 0111	Z	101 1010
H	100 1000		

Figure 26-4. *ASCII code, presented here for your review, is the standard language of data communications.*

to code formats that are standard for the telecommunications industry. For many years, the communications industry has had a standard digital coding system. This system evolved from the Morse code used by telegraphers. Morse code was used originally to transmit signals for teletypewriters, machines that sent typewritten messages.

When computers were developed, little or no thought was given to data communications needs. Technicians developed their own coding systems for internal use in computers. These are the byte patterns used to process and store data within computers. Many internal computer coding systems are not the same as the standard telecommunications format. The telecommunications coding system is the *American Standard Code for Information Interchange (ASCII)*. The formats for ASCII characters are illustrated in Figure 26-4.

Many microcomputers and many software packages for microcomputers use ASCII formats. However, many large computer systems use other formats. So, code conversions are essential parts of

Business Terms

direct-connect modem
A communication processor that can be connected directly into a standard telephone jack. *See also* modem.

external direct-connect modem
A modem that can be plugged into a telephone jack but is external to the computer it supports. *See also* direct-connect modem.

communications port
A plug receptacle on a computer frame into which communications devices can be connected.

internal direct-connect modem
A modem that can be plugged into a telephone jack that is built onto a circuit board and can be plugged into a computer. *See also* direct-connect modem.

American Standard Code for Information Interchange (ASCII)
A digital code used for telecommunications transmissions and as the machine language of many microcomputers.

data communications operations. These conversions are part of the processing that takes place within modem circuits.

How Are Computers Linked for Communication?

Modems and telecommunications circuits are the basic tools for data communications. These tools are used to link computers under two general approaches:

- Point-to-point transmission
- Data communications networks.

Point-to-point transmission. *Point-to-point transmission* links one computer to another. The computers talk to each other the way you talk on a telephone. In many instances, the connections are created by dialing a telephone. Internal modems have software that can dial automatically. Figure 26-5 is a display screen for a typical communication package. Entries in this screen direct the originating computer to set up a connection with the receiving computer.

Data communications networks. In a network, multiple computers are linked so that they can communicate with one another as necessary. That is, one computer user should be able to connect to any other computer within a network. A number of techniques have been developed to link computers into networks. Two of the most commonly used are the *ring network* and the *star network*. Figures 26-6 and 26-7 show diagrams of ring and star networks.

The computers linked into a network are called *nodes.* This is the same term as an information point in some database models. The principle is similar. A node is a point to which computer and information storage capabilities have been distributed.

In a ring network, nodes are connected in a continuous path, usually represented as a circle. All mes-

```
===DIALING DIRECTORY  1 ===   Modem dialing command = ATDT
                  Long distance service +# =
                                    -# =
      Name                  Phone #   Comm Param  Echo Mesg Strip Pace
1-leykis                    944-6397  1200-E-7-1    Y    Y    N    N
2-asu                       965-7001  1200-E-7-1    Y    Y    N    N
3-asu                       965-7002  1200-E-7-1    Y    Y    N    N
4-asu                       965-7003  1200-E-7-1    N    N    1    N
5-Crossroads                941-2005  1200-E-7-1    N    N    N    N
6-Broadcast BBS            1934-4999  1200-E-7-1    N    N    N    N
7------------------------   - --- --- ----  300-E-7-1   N    N    N    N
8------------------------   - --- --- ----  300-E-7-1   N    N    N    N
9------------------------   - --- --- ----  300-E-7-1   N    N    N    N
10-----------------------   - --- --- ----  300-E-7-1   N    N    N    N
11-----------------------   - --- --- ----  300-E-7-1   N    N    N    N
12-----------------------   - --- --- ----  300-E-7-1   N    N    N    N

Dial entry #:            # or...     Enter: R to revise or add to directory
                                            M for manual dialing
                                            F / B to page through directory
                                            X to exit to terminal
                         # For long distance service, precede entry # with +/-
```

Figure 26-5. *A modem user activates transmission or receipt of data through entries in a display like this.*

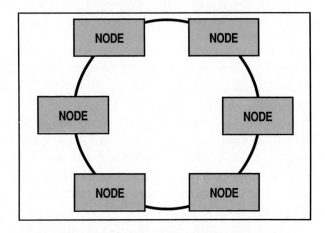

Figure 26-6. *The diagram above shows a ring network.*
Figure 26-7. *The diagram below shows a star network.*

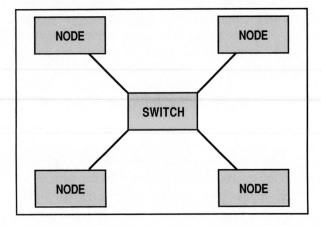

sages are transmitted through the entire network and are picked up by the nodes to which they are directed. All nodes have to be operative for the network to function. If one node breaks down, the entire network may be interrupted.

A star network has a hub to which all nodes are connected directly. The hub acts as a controller, or *switch*. All messages are directed through the hub to the receiving node.

A special category of business communication link is the *local area network (LAN)*. This is a network set up within a single office or building. The idea of a LAN is to enable co-workers to share information and workloads. A LAN can follow any configuration, or pattern—ring, star, or other. Local area networks usually include a number of microcomputers.

Many LANs permit users to enter data to or access data from large, mainframe computers. The technique for entering data from a microcomputer to a mainframe is known as *uploading*. When information is transmitted from a mainframe to a microcomputer, this is known as *downloading*.

Common applications for LANs also include *electronic mail* and *calendaring* services. Electronic mail means simply that any network user can address a message to any other user. The network stores messages in areas, known as ''electronic mailboxes,'' that are set up for each user. The user can call for waiting messages at any time. Calendaring is a system in which each user can enter information on appointments or meetings. If a manager wants to call a meeting, the calendars of participants can be checked. If the needed time is available, it can be reserved.

The data communications techniques discussed above make it possible for a company, regardless of its size, to meet its information needs. No matter how large or spread out operations are, information can be timely and reliable.

Business Terms

point-to-point transmission
A type of data communication that links only two points for the sending and receiving of digital data.

ring network
A multiple-station data communications link in which transmissions move through all nodes in the system.

star network
A multiple-station data communications link in which all transmissions are through a central computer that serves as a hub, or switch, for the transfer of messages.

node
In data communications, a sending-receiving station within a network.

switch
A central computer within a data communications network that accepts all transmissions and transmits messages to their proper destinations.

local area network (LAN)
A data communications link that serves multiple users within a single office or building.

uploading
An operation in which information is transmitted on a LAN from a microcomputer to a central minicomputer or mainframe.

downloading
An operation in which information is transmitted on a LAN from a central minicomputer or mainframe to a microcomputer.

electronic mail
An operation in which messages are transmitted on a network from origin to destination points, with interim storage in ''electronic mailbox'' files as necessary.

calendaring
A service on a LAN in which the computer keeps track of appointments and schedules of multiple users and can, in some systems, block time for multiple persons for meetings or events.

Data communications techniques represent just one way of bringing together, or "integrating," information about a company. To meet total information needs, other types of *integration* also are necessary. The kinds of information required to operate a modern company are developed under a large number of separate application programs. In the past, it has been difficult to integrate information from separate programs. However, new software tools, described in the remainder of this chapter, are helping companies to gain new information and management flexibility.

1. What type of signals are processed and generated by computers?

2. What is a modem and what does it do?

3. What is a ring network?

4. What is a star network?

HOW ARE APPLICATIONS SET UP?

Programmers design an application package to meet a set of related processing needs. For instance, word processors provide users with the ability to create, edit, and print text documents.

By contrast, a spreadsheet package typically focuses on financial reporting. A programmer who designs a spreadsheet package will face design problems that differ greatly from those of a word processor. With a spreadsheet, data fields have to be defined, or structured, carefully. With a word processor, emphasis is on creation, manipulation, and storage of unstructured text.

Basic differences also exist between spreadsheet and DBMS packages. The power of a spreadsheet program lies in its ability to make multiple calculations efficiently. The power of a DBMS package lies in its ability to store and relate massive amounts of data.

The point: Separate applications require separate treatments.

How Do Applications Relate to Business Organization Structures?

A business is organized into related sets of operating functions. These organizational units, in turn, have different missions, or jobs. Often, organizational needs are met by creating separate departments. In a medium-sized business, the company might be organized into a dozen or more departments. Employees at different positions should function as teammates.

As is true for any team, many business functions overlap between departments. For instance, sales of products create needs to manufacture new supplies. Yet, sales transactions may use entirely different files and programs from manufacturing control systems.

The point: Separate applications, even though they require separate treatment, often require an interchange, or integration, of information.

It is relatively easy for people to handle overlapping functions. People adapt easily. However, application software packages do not possess this kind of intelligence. Application programs and their files focus on specific business operations. Normally, application packages are independent of one another. A file created by a spreadsheet package, for instance, usually will not fit into a report created by a word processing package.

The independence of application programs often creates problems for businesspeople. Programs tend to be isolated from one another. But business operations tend to be related. The need, then, is to find ways to relate information to match the business operations and management needs.

Business operations tend to flow together in *job streams.* A job stream is a set of transactions that follow in sequence. The steps within a job stream help

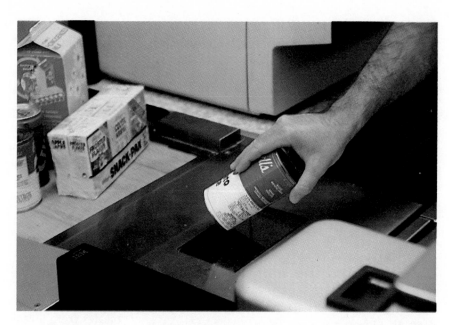

Input for data communication *begins with the capture of source data. In many applications, such as a supermarket checkout counter, input is automated through use of computerized devices.*

to meet the results that a business wants to achieve. Information processing also takes place in job streams. Usually, the information streams match the way work is done in a business. However, information systems need to break work down into programs for computer processing. These limitations on program scope tend to create barriers to the flow of information within a business. These barriers are being eliminated by special software tools that permit integration of information from different applications.

WHAT FORM DOES A JOB STREAM TAKE?

Within a business job stream, information flows from one department to another. Along the way, transformations, or changes, take place and files or databases are updated. As an example, the following is one typical job stream:

- Order entry
- Invoicing
- Accounts receivable
- Inventory (shipping/receiving)
- Purchasing and accounts payable
- General ledger.

This stream involves applications that process transactions between a business and its customers. Other job streams also are typical within businesses. For instance, another job stream would trace transactions that occur between employees and their employer. Applications within this stream would include payroll processing, evaluation of production costs, and preparation of tax reports.

What Data Transformations Stem From Customer Transactions?

When a customer places an order, an order entry clerk might check the customer's credit status within

Business Terms

integration
The ability to combine information and/or graphics from multiple applications into unified displays or printouts.

job stream
A set of related transactions that follow in sequence.

accounts receivable files. The clerk also might check inventory files to determine whether the desired items are currently in stock, or available for delivery.

The accounts receivable job stream.   If the order is approved, an invoice is written. Copies of this invoice are sent to the accounts receivable department and shipping/receiving department. At the same time, invoice items are used to update the accounts receivable and inventory files. These files are used to monitor collections from customers and levels of inventories.

Thus, basic order information is transformed to change status information. Processing creates information on amounts due from customers. Also, by changing the inventory figures, the system helps to determine when new goods should be purchased or manufactured.

The inventory job stream.   The shipping/receiving department uses the invoice data to assemble and ship ordered items. If problems in inventory levels are noted when goods are assembled and shipped, corrections can be entered into computer files. The ability to update in this way is necessary to deal with errors in the handling of goods. For example, if the wrong goods are shipped to the customer, records for inventory items will be wrong. The items shipped by mistake will show lower levels than the computer records. At the same time, the items that were not shipped will have higher levels.

At the end of each day, the computer system might output an *open-to-buy* report. This is an exception report that lists inventory items that currently are low in stock. Purchasing specialists can make entries into the computer that result in output of *requisition* forms. A requisition is a purchasing request. Requisitions are sent to the departments that use or sell the low-stock products. If the responsible manager wants to reorder, the requisition is signed and returned to the purchasing department.

When a requisition is approved, the purchasing department prepares a *purchase order*. This docu-

ment is a formal order for goods, and is sent directly to suppliers.

Accounts payable job stream.   When a company places an order with a seller, it becomes a customer. Customers, of course, are required to pay for ordered and delivered products and services. For this reason, all businesses have an accounts payable function. Accounts payable acts from documents or computer entries made in the receiving department when ordered goods arrive. Of necessity, then, inventory, purchasing, and accounts payable applications are linked closely within a continuous job stream.

Financial reporting job stream.   Finally, financial reports are prepared periodically to describe the status of the company. These reports include summaries from all transaction files, including income and expense items. Information for financial reports is developed under *general ledger* software. General ledger is an accounting term. All income and expense items for a company usually are accumulated in sets of independent files, called *ledgers*. The general ledger, then, is a summary of the contents of all financial files, or ledgers.

What Software Tools Help to Integrate Information Files?

To support its normal business operations, a company needs to integrate information resources. If files are set up separately for each application, problems can result. To assure integration of and access to information, many companies use database management techniques. Database files, in turn, are indexed and coordinated to model the operations of the company and the kinds of access needed.

Integrated databases were implemented first on large computers. For microcomputers, the ability to integrate information between applications was not available for many years. The problem: Microcomputers are a new development. Software companies brought out simple products first. Applications were individual and separate. So were the files they

Documentation is vital for implementation of data communications applications. The package in this photo includes full documentation along with either an external or an internal modem.
COURTESY OF HAYES MICROCOMPUTER PRODUCTS, INC.

created. Gradually, microcomputer users found they too needed to be able to integrate information from files that supported multiple applications. Over time, this demand has been met through development of software that permits integration of files from multiple applications.

Review 26.3

1. In what ways is information integration required among departments or functions of a typical business organization?

2. How did the practice of creating files for single applications fail to meet information needs of many businesses?

3. How do database techniques meet needs to exchange information among applications and files?

HOW CAN DATA FROM APPLICATION SOFTWARE PACKAGES BE INTEGRATED?

Special software has been developed for processing job streams with personal computers. These are special tools that make it possible to integrate process-

ing and reference to the same information for multiple applications. These tools are known as *integrated software* packages. Integrated software is

Business Terms

open-to-buy report
An exception report that lists inventory items with stocks that are below established reorder levels.

requisition
A purchasing request form.

purchase order
A formal order for goods that is sent directly to a supplier.

general ledger
A set of files that contains data on the financial condition of a company.

ledger
A file that contains information on a single account that relates to the financial condition of a company. *See also* general ledger.

integrated software
A special set of programs that provides access to multiple, separate application packages.

made of special programs that provide access to multiple, separate application packages.

One way in which multiple applications can be integrated is through a technique known as *windowing*. Windowing gets its name from the fact that the microcomputer display screen is subdivided into a series of panels. Each panel presents a menu or information from a different software package. The user can move immediately to the capabilities of the different packages.

In some instances, integrated packages contain multiple applications and can interchange information among them. For instance, one popular integrated package, called Symphony, combines a word processing program, spreadsheet system, and DBMS. Under this approach, files from spreadsheet or database programs can be incorporated into text developed under a word processor.

Integrated software is ideal for many small businesses. Virtually any business application can be processed by a computer under control of one of the available application programs. Then, through use of windowing software, data produced by one application can be combined with data produced by other programs. Integrated packages like Symphony also include data communications programs that allow for the exchange of information on telecommunication networks.

Another kind of integrated package is designed specifically for a set of business applications—that is, for a particular job stream. Under this approach, a separate program is used for each application within the job stream. However, all programs define data under a common format. Thus, data can be transferred from one file to another automatically, for use

by a different program. A typical integrated package organized in this manner provides separate programs for order entry and invoicing, accounts receivable, accounts payable, inventory control, and general ledger. These packages also typically include data communications software that allow for the creation of networks.

Systems that integrate data to support business operations have become realities. Through networking techniques and integrated software, managers now can arrange to make any needed information available. The three chapters that follow carry the ideas of information use forward by discussing applications in key industries. Chapter 27 covers the use of computers in manufacturing companies.

Review 26.4

1. Why was integration of information a problem on early microcomputers?

2. How does windowing software make integration of microcomputer files possible?

3. What are the advantages of software packages that include word processing, spreadsheet, and database applications?

Business Terms

windowing
A technique for integrating information from multiple applications; access is provided through sets of overlapping displays that establish access windows.

Chapter Summary

❑ Data communications involves transmission of information between computers.

❑ A network is a system that links multiple computers for interchange of information.

❑ A plan that places computing power and information resources at points where a company does business is known as distributed processing.

❑ Most data communications signals are transmitted over telecommunications networks. These communication links were designed initially for

❏ electrical transmission, or analog signalling. Analog signals use continuous waves.

❏ Computers are designed for digital signals that follow start-stop patterns.

❏ Connections between computers and communications carriers are formed by modems. These are devices that convert digital signals to analog forms—and back again to digital formats. Modems also format messages into the standard coding of the telecommunications industry, ASCII.

❏ Data communications can be transmitted from point to point or on networks that permit multiple nodes to address one another.

❏ A ring network links all nodes in a continuous chain. Each message is routed through every node.

❏ A star network connects all nodes to a single hub, or switch. All messages go through the switch, which routes them to the assigned destinations.

❏ Computer applications have been developed to support individual functions of a business.

❏ A typical business does not exist as a series of unconnected parts. A business carries out a series of connected functions that form a job stream.

❏ Information processing also fits naturally into a series of job streams that follow the normal operations of a business. Computer applications tend to be related to normal transaction patterns of the organization.

❏ Access to information across departmental and functional lines of a company has been made possible by database management techniques.

❏ When microcomputers were introduced, capabilities were limited to processing and file management for individual applications.

❏ To meet demands for integration of information from multiple files, special software has been developed.

❏ One method for integrating data from different microcomputer applications is to use special software that can make the necessary translations.

❏ Another method for integrating application information is to use software that has word processing, spreadsheet, and database capabilities in a single package.

Definitions

Write a complete sentence that defines each of the terms below.

data communications	network
distributed processing	carrier
coaxial	analog
microwave	fiber optics
laser	digital
modem	ring network
star network	local area network
upload	download

Questions to Think About

Based on what you have learned to date, answer the following questions in one or more complete sentences.

1. What is data communications and what are data communications networks?

2. What is distributed processing and how does it work?

3. What are analog signals and what do they do?

4. What are digital signals and how do they differ from analog signals?

5. What is a modem and what functions does a modem perform?

6. What are ring and star networks and what are the operating differences between them?

7. What are network nodes and what do they do?

8. What is a job stream and how do job streams affect the need for computer processing and information support?

9. Why is it important for microcomputer users to be able to access files from mutiple applications?

10. How does integrated software for microcomputers work?

Projects

The purpose of the assignments below is to encourage you to increase your learning through outside reading or work assignments.

1. Read an article about a windowing or other integrated software package. Assume you are a microcomputer operator for a medium-sized company. A department head in the company asks you to describe how information from a spreadsheet package can be included within the body of a report being prepared on a word processing package. Write a memo or prepare an oral presentation that describes how this job can be done.

2. Read an article about database or bulletin board services available to microcomputer users through data communications. Describe the services that are available and explain how you would set up a microcomputer to use these services.

Windowing software *divides a display screen into segments that show the status of multiple application packages and files. This software tool makes it possible to communicate data content among multiple software packages and applications. Windowing software can be valuable for the building of composite files to be communicated.*
COURTESY OF DIGITAL RESEARCH

CHAPTER 27

How Are Computers Used in a Manufacturing Business?

When you finish reading this chapter and complete your work assignments, you should be able to answer the following questions.

❑ What special problems or situations concern managers in manufacturing businesses?

❑ What are the transaction processing requirements of a manufacturing company?

❑ What is job status reporting and why is it critical for manufacturing managers?

❑ How do special software tools help managers with shop loading and other planning requirements for a manufacturing company?

❑ How are computers used in product design and for automated manufacturing operations?

DOING BUSINESS

"Why do you want me in the program?" Rocco's question showed how puzzled he was. "I know we've known each other a long time. I appreciate the offer. But I won't do you much good. I wouldn't know a computer if I fell over one."

Rocco had been addressing Sean Kelly, a long-time friend. Rocco and Sean had completed high school together almost 25 years earlier. They had taken factory jobs together at the auto plant that was the main industry in town. Sean had applied for and received a work-study scholarship offered by the company. After college, he had moved up rapidly. He was now a division head. Rocco had decided against going to college. He had needed the money he could make through full-time work. Through hard

work, Rocco also had done well. He was a shift supervisor in the plant.

Rocco was surprised when he was called to Sean's office in the middle of a working day. He was even more surprised when he was asked to enroll, at full pay, in a computer training school that the company was going to run.

"I mean it," Rocco continued. "I do appreciate the offer. You'll never know how much. I value your friendship. But I can tell you that computers scare the daylights out of me. You need some of the younger workers for this program. They grew up with computers. They can run rings around me when it comes to learning new tricks."

"Listen carefully, Rocco," Sean said. "And believe what I'm telling you. I'm not kidding. Friendship had nothing to do with my decision. I need you in that class. You know our business better than anyone on the factory floor. I don't have to tell you what business we're in. We make cars. And those cars have to be driven a long way after they leave our factories.

"This company needs car people building our products. We don't need hotshot computer operators who know nothing about what makes a car go together and stay together. The company is much better off teaching car people about computers than trying to teach a bunch of computer freaks how to make cars. Computers are tools. You understand tools. We'll do whatever it takes to get car people to learn computers. When you succeed, it will be an example to the other experienced people we want to attract into this program.

"So," Sean continued, "don't make any mistakes about what's going on here. I'm not doing you any favors. I'm asking you to do me a favor. Computers are revolutionizing the manufacturing business. We need experienced manufacturing people to help keep the revolution from getting out of hand."

MEANING

Sean was right on several points. First, computers are revolutionizing the manufacturing industry. He also was right in pointing out that computers don't make products. People do. Computers are outstanding tools. But computers don't have the understanding and judgment of people. Human experience cannot be replaced by computers. Instead, experienced people should learn how to master computers.

Another factor is the continuing importance of manufacturing to the United States economy and to American society. To illustrate, one of the key economic indicators reported by the federal government is based on manufacturing. The statistic is the percentage of manufacturing capacity that is used each month. This shows that manufacturing performance, or productivity, is a key indicator of how well the economy is doing.

Manufacturing industries are major employers of people and are major factors in the economy.

Profitable manufacturing plants offer steady employment and contribute to the wealth of their communities. The money spent by manufacturing companies supports other businesses that sell to the companies and their employees.

In manufacturing, computers have assumed an essential role. Therefore, people who hold or want jobs in manufacturing must become comfortable with computers as co-workers. As is true in other industries, computers are general-purpose tools for manufacturers. That is, computers have the ability to handle input, processing, output, and storage. Computers don't know what the information they generate means. Rather, it is up to people to devise the ideas and the programs that adapt computers as tools for specific jobs.

HOW DO COMPUTERS FIT INTO A MANUFACTURING BUSINESS?

In most businesses, computers serve primarily as information tools. Information resources are developed to model the status of the company. Information models deal largely with transactions and financial condition. In manufacturing, all of the information-related functions also apply. However, in manufacturing, the role of computers also is **physical.** That is, computers operate machines and produce products. They do this through use of information. But, there is a big difference.

> **In information applications, computers deliver outputs to people who take the necessary actions. In some manufacturing applications, computers take actions directly. They operate the machines that produce end products.**

The point: In manufacturing, computers are production machinery. Computer users must be qualified both as production specialists and as sophisticated computer users.

The presentations that follow cover the full scope of the value of computers in manufacturing com-

Computers are part of production processes for many modern manufacturing plants. This photo shows use of an advanced process under which a computer-controlled laser device cuts delicate, precise metal parts.
COURTESY OF SPECTRA PHYSICS

panies. Physical, or direct, manufacturing applications are reviewed first. This is done because the principles used are new to this book. Later, the special needs of manufacturing companies for information system applications are covered.

HOW ARE DESIGN AND TOOLING OPERATIONS AIDED BY COMPUTERS?

Computers came into existence as mathematical tools. The first computers were created during World War II. The intent was to use them for military applications. Examples include computation of artillery ranges and anti-aircraft targeting. Later, computers were used as design tools as jet aircraft were developed.

During the early years, however, the results of design calculations were limited to numeric outputs. That is, scientists and engineers had numeric values that they had to interpret. The actual drawings and manufacturing operations were carried out by hand.

During the early 1960s, computers gained limited graphics capabilities. Graphics processing presented some special challenges. The main problem centered around the massive amounts of data required. This requirement was demonstrated in the discussions about graphics in Chapter 25. To illustrate, a typical page of text or statistical tables requires some 1,700 to 2,000 bytes of storage. By contrast, a display showing a picture of an auto or airplane might require a minimum of 35,000 to 40,000 bytes.

In addition to the massive storage required for graphics data, image-processing computers also needed special software. Graphics programs were far more complex than those that processed information in character formats. This meant, in turn, that powerful processors were needed. The first graphics programs for engineering and manufacturing work were introduced during the early 1960s. At the time, the applications required all of the capacity of the largest computers available.

What Kind of Equipment Is Used?

As computers became smaller and more powerful, graphics processing for manufacturing jobs became more practical. However, manufacturing applications are beyond the capabilities of most personal computers. Today, manufacturing jobs are being handled on computers known as scientific or engineering workstations. These, typically, are supermicrocomputers with memories in the range of four megabytes. Secondary storage usually starts at 300 megabytes and often becomes much larger. Also, these systems usually have large display screens so that images may be shown in detail.

In most situations, these workstations are part of a network. Each workstation is connected to a central facility that includes a supercomputer. The supercomputer, in turn, will have a powerful processor and billions of bytes of secondary storage.

to be designed and laid out. Typically, it is five to seven years between the beginning of design and actual production.

Computers reduce the design process to a matter of months. Further, many thousands of working hours are saved because computers generate the needed drawings and documents. Models and prototypes can be created on machines controlled by the computers. The same databases with design information are used to operate production machinery. When the product is ready for production, a series of computer-controlled robots are put to work. The most important result: Finished products move to market in as little as one-quarter of the time required under traditional methods.

Where's the Payoff?

Obviously, it requires major savings in time and large increases in manufacturing output to cover costs of such systems. To understand why manufacturing businesses invest so heavily in computers, consider what is involved in a mass-production operation.

Producing a product such as an automobile or an airplane occupies workforces of tens of thousands. Design of a new product can take two or three years under traditional methods. Many designs have to be created and tried. For each, it is necessary to calculate such factors as weight, amount of material, stress on metal parts, wind resistance, power requirements, and so on.

When designs are complete, scale models are built. The models are reviewed for design appearance and often are tested in wind tunnels to preview performance. When the models perform acceptably, full scale models are built. These are called *prototypes*. Even after prototypes are accepted, long-term work still has to be done. *Tooling* has to be built to adapt manufacturing equipment to generate parts. Tooling includes the fixtures that hold parts during production, drills, molds, and patterns that guide and control manufacturing. In addition, assembly lines have

Review 27.1

1. What are the special applications of computers in manufacturing?

2. Why do manufacturing computers need massive memories?

3. Why is use of computers in manufacturing profitable?

WHAT KINDS OF MANUFACTURING OPERATIONS ARE CONTROLLED?

Direct support of manufacturing is available through a number of computerized applications, including the following:

- Computer-assisted design (CAD)
- Computer-assisted manufacturing (CAM)
- Computer-integrated manufacturing (CIM)
- Robotics.

All four of these techniques use the ability of computers to create, process, and output graphics data.

Computers can design computers with the aid of CAD software. Under the application shown here, a computer is used to design circuits for advanced computing and communications devices.

COURTESY OF NORTHERN TELECOM, LTD.

What Is Computer-Assisted Design and How Does It Work?

Use of ***computer-assisted design (CAD)*** software also is known as "electronic drafting." The user can cause the computer to display images of a product under development. Techniques include the ability to start with hand-drawn designs that are traced on drawing tablets. The traced images are recorded as pixel positions and the lines appear on the computer screen.

Another method is to process drawings through a scanner. The scanner senses the light and dark values of the drawing and generates a pixel image within the computer system.

Still another technique is to use a light-pen and draw directly on the computer screen. This method, like scanning, is described in Chapter 25. Light pens can be used either to create original drawings or to modify drawings that are displayed.

Modern CAD software enables a designer to examine a displayed image from any angle. For example, if an auto design is drawn from a side view, the computer develops information on all dimensions. The designer then can instruct the computer

to show the same image from the front, rear, or at different angles.

CAD programs also can ***simulate*** operating conditions for designed products. Simulation imitates actual operating conditions. For example, CAD routines can be used to simulate the effects of wind on

Business Terms

prototype
A full-scale, operational model of a planned product.

tooling
The accessories needed to manufacture a product, including the fixtures that hold parts during production, drills, molds, and patterns that guide and control manufacturing.

computer-assisted design (CAD)
Techniques for the application of computers for development of design drawings and mathematical testing for new products.

simulate
Use of a computer to imitate conditions for product use and to test a product before it is manufactured.

an airplane. The computer image can show the effect of stress on the wings. As values are entered by designers, the CAD image will show the conditions under which failures might take place. In effect, a new plane can be "flown" in the computer before any actual construction takes place. The result of CAD operations is a designed product. The designers are ready to build models or prototypes with the aid of other software tools.

What Results Are Delivered by Computer-Assisted Manufacturing?

Data generated under CAD procedures can be used by *computer-assisted manufacturing (CAM)* programs. CAM systems include data communication links among computers and manufacturing machinery. The computers can transmit operating instructions to the production machines. Sensors on the production equipment, in turn, can transmit status information back to the computer.

The exchange of instructions and information takes place in *real time.* Real-time computer responses are completed within the time frame of the transaction being supported. The service is provided by an interactive computer. That is, a person or machine enters an instruction and the computer responds.

The *response time* is the elapsed time between entry of an instruction and completion of the operation. A real-time response is one in which the reaction is complete within the normal time needed to complete a transaction. For a customer buying an airplane ticket or making a bank deposit, two to five seconds would be a real-time response. For an on-line manufacturing operation, a two-second delay could destroy the product. Response times have to be within a few hundredths of a second.

Under CAM software, the specifications developed by CAD programs are translated to the shapes of parts to be made. For example, the computer can operate large machines that bend sheets of

steel into fenders or body parts. Engine blocks can be machined and drilled automatically.

All these operations can be carried out without the great expense involved in making special tooling. CAM systems use *electronic tooling.* The term "electronic tooling" means that signals from computers control production machines. The need for complex physical tooling is reduced or eliminated. The finished parts can be ready in less time than with regular manufacturing. Considerable time and money can be saved in the building of models and prototypes. In some situations, CAM methods can be adapted to mass-production runs. Examples include the cutting of lengths of sheet metal for manufacturing operations, automatic welding to join parts, or the control of sewing machines to produce garments.

What Kind of Production Is Handled Under Computer-Integrated Manufacturing Systems?

The term *computer-integrated manufacturing (CIM)* usually is used to highlight advances from CAM methods. In general, CIM controls the same kinds of operations as CAM, only CIM systems do more.

Typically, CAM programs control machine tools through *numerical control* techniques. Numerical control is a method that controls metalworking through a system of numbered positions. Numerical values are used to locate the functions to be performed. One value is for the X dimension of a workpiece that is being processed. This is the width of the workpiece. The Y dimension represents the length of the workpiece. The Z dimension describes the depth to which holes are to be drilled or other metal-removing operations are to be applied.

Under CAM programs, the computer guides a machine tool after a workpiece has been positioned. CIM carries automatic manufacturing capabilities further. Under CIM programs, multiple devices are controlled. With these, it is possible to perform a

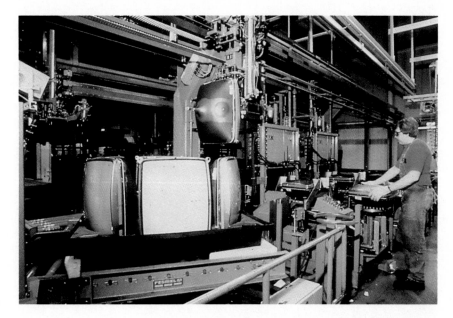

Assembly operations can be monitored and controlled with the aid of computer systems. This photo shows a facility in which TV sets are being assembled with the aid of equipment that handles parts and also checks the quality of assembled units.

COURTESY OF RCA

sequence of operations. Several computers might be involved in a CIM system. The workpiece would be carried from one machine to another on automatic conveyors. The workpieces also would be positioned automatically for the completion of each operation.

Under one CIM operation now in use, an engine block is carried to more than a dozen work stations. Processing starts with a bare metal block. When the process is complete, the block has more than 100 different holes. Further, each hole has been inspected electronically. Any blocks that do not meet specifications are pushed aside as rejects.

To support these operations, the computer carries out some of the same basic functions as in an information system. A database contains information on the measurements of the products to be processed and on the operations to be performed. The machine tools have both driving and sensing mechanisms. When tools are being positioned for work, the computer sends signals to the machines. As work is done, the sensors report on their positions and other factors, such as temperature. When work is complete, instructions from the computer tell the machines to stop what they are doing. Then, instructions are transmitted to start the next production operation.

Business Terms

computer-assisted manufacturing (CAM)
Techniques that enable computers to use CAD files and other specifications to control operation of manufacturing devices.

real time
A description of a computer response time. A real-time response is completed within the normal cycle of the transaction being processed. Real time can vary with the nature and urgency of individual transactions.

response time
The elapsed time between entry of an instruction into a computer and completion of the operation.

electronic tooling
The software and instructions that control manufacturing processes.

computer-integrated manufacturing (CIM)
Computer-controlled operations that extend to multiple manufacturing functions.

numerical control
A method that controls metalworking through a system of numbered positions and execution of standard operations.

Robotics techniques *make it possible to assemble parts of auto bodies and to weld the parts together, all automatically.*
COURTESY OF MCDONNELL DOUGLAS CORP., ST. LOUIS

What Is Robotics and What New Dimensions Does It Provide?

The techniques described above generally automate and control traditional production and conveyor-type equipment through use of computers. For example, a CAM program performs basically the same operations as a trained factory worker. The tools used are similar. The difference is that the computer operates the controls that position workpieces and apply tools. Under CIM, additional tools can be used and conveyors can move workpieces between work stations.

Robotics is a technology under which entire manufacturing operations can be controlled through use of computers. To illustrate, consider a plant that assembles small computers automatically. The facility has a series of assembly stations that do individual jobs. Work starts with a metal frame. At different stations, individual parts are placed within the frame and tested. When the process is finished, the last computerized station packs the finished computer into a box and seals the box ready for delivery.

Another example is the assembly of automotive bodies. Robotic equipment picks up parts and welds them together to form bodies. Then roof panels are picked up and joined with the bodies. Further down the line, the bodies are rustproofed and painted—all automatically.

In many offices, mail is delivered by robots programmed to travel through entire routes on their own. The robots have electronic sensors to prevent collisons with furniture or people. The major advance of robotics lies in the ability of machines to function largely on their own.

In all these applications, computers play special roles that meet needs of manufacturing companies. In addition, as discussed below, manufacturers also need information systems. These information systems take on special dimensions to support the kinds of plans and decisions required of managers in this field.

Review 27.2

1. What is CAD and what are its capabilities?

2. What is CAM and how does it work?

3. What is CIM and what are its special features?

4. What is robotics and what are its special capabilities?

WHAT SPECIAL TRANSACTION PROCESSING AND MANAGEMENT INFORMATION NEEDS MUST BE MET?

Any information system will model the organization that uses it. Therefore, a good place to start an understanding of an information system is to learn about the business. Each information system must deal with the nature and special needs of the using business. In other words, the job is to find out what is to be modeled.

What Is the Transaction Pattern of a Manufacturer?

The basic transactions in manufacturing are orders and shipments. A customer places an order for products. The company ships the products. In some cases, the products are made to order. In others, the products are manufactured in advance and stocked in *finished goods inventory*. A good is a manufactured product. A finished good is a product that has been made and is ready for delivery. Inventory, or course, is a stock of goods held for future use. Manufacturing companies also have inventories of raw materials, parts, subassemblies (partly completed products), and tools.

To process orders, a company's sales representatives need reliable information. Remember, transactions depend on information that models the status of the company. In the old days, information on product status was obtained by walking through the factory or storage areas. Today, this information is maintained in a computer database. Transactions are based on this information.

To accept an order, a salesperson at a computer terminal needs a number of records. The first transaction reference usually is to a customer record. Once the customer identification (and credit status) is established, the transaction requires product information. Product inventory files indicate the items on hand, quantities, prices, and discounts. Other infor-

mation might show the warehouse location in which the item is stored.

A manufacturer also might need some special items. For example, if a product is in work in the factory, the order information might be noted in a product master file. This would guide a user to a "work-in-process" file that indicates current status in the factory. From this information, the salesperson can tell the customer when delivery is expected. The operating procedures and supporting files for a manufacturing system, therefore, might include the following.

Order entry.   A salesperson enters information on the customer and products required. This operation may use separate files on customers, credit status, inventories, and work in process. The output is an order to ship products to the customer.

The order is sent to the factory or warehouse, where it will be filled. After the products are shipped, delivery information can be entered in different ways. Under one method, shipping department employees may enter the information from terminals in their area. Another method would be to mark shipping information on a copy of the order. This document then would be sent to the sales department, where shipping information would be entered. This entry becomes the basis for billing the customer.

Billing.   The order information is recalled from storage and displayed on a screen. Changes or additions are made according to shipping information. When the information is correct, the records are

---

Business Terms

robotics
A technology under which entire manufacturing operations can be controlled through use of computers.

finished goods inventory
A supply of products for which manufacturing has been completed and which are ready for delivery.

Work in process in this computer assembly plant is controlled by computer-produced documentation and operated with the aid of computer-assisted manufacturing techniques.

COURTESY OF APPLE COMPUTER, INC.

released and used to issue an invoice to the customer. At the same time, the computer records the amount owed on an *accounts receivable* file. An account receivable, simply, is any amount owed that should be collected in the future.

Accounts receivable.   The accounts receivable file is set up according to invoices and dates invoices are issued. When a customer pays a bill, a notation is made on a computer terminal. As one result, the paid item is deleted from the accounts receivable file. Also, an entry is made in an income file to indicate that the money was received.

Shop loading.   Information from the order file is used for a *shop loading* application. Shop loading means that jobs are scheduled for production. The master file that controls this application contains information on manufacturing operations. For each product, the file has information on how long it will take to produce parts. For each work station in the factory, there are entries on setup time and time to make each part.

Order information is processed against the file. The computer determines the amount of time required at each work station for every ordered product. This information, in turn, is added to a master file that shows the *backlog* at each work station. A backlog is the amount of work planned for each production station. Shop loading information lets managers know where a factory stands in completing scheduled work.

Work in process.   The shop loading information becomes the basis for monitoring status of jobs that are in work. Each time an operation is finished, the job is taken off the shop loading file. The shop loading file is set up according to factory work stations. A *work-in-process file* contains the same information—organized according to individual jobs. By checking a work-in-process file, a manager can tell where each job is and how soon it should be ready for delivery.

Payroll.   Payroll processing often is the basis for updating the work-in-process file. Each time a job is completed, information is entered into the computer system. These entries serve as the basis for changes to the work-in-process file. Of course, these entries also are accumulated as a basis for paying workers. Under one system, workers are paid according to the number of pieces of work they complete. If this is the case, the work-in-process entries become the basis for worker earnings.

Finished goods inventory. When jobs are finished, product information is entered into a master file that keeps track of finished goods. Salespeople use this file as the basis for ordering shipments to customers.

Job costing. All materials and payroll entries into the computer are entered into a job cost file. This file accumulates information on all expenses for each manufacturing order that is completed. The information then is accumulated according to product. As a result, managers know exactly what it costs to build every item. This cost information, then, becomes the basis for setting prices at which products are sold to customers.

As in any other business, information sources begin with sales transactions. This transaction information updates a series of files that reflect the status of the company. Information becomes a tool for scheduling use of manufacturing machinery. Also, order information helps managers to determine how many workers are needed and at what production stations. Finally, job cost information helps managers to determine whether their business is running profitably.

These discussions have covered the special opportunities and needs of manufacturing businesses. The idea is to demonstrate that the general principles of information use that you have learned can be adapted to the needs of any industry. The chapter that

follows provides a similar review about the use of information systems in distribution organizations.

Review 27.3

1. What is the basis of information system and management reporting applications in a manufacturing company?

2. What processing must be complete before an order is shipped from a manufacturing company?

3. What is shop loading and what is the value of this application?

4. How do computers help manufacturing companies to determine the costs of the products that they make and ship?

Business Terms

account receivable
An amount that is owed to a company in payment for a product or service that has been delivered.

shop loading
Procedures for planning and scheduling work to be performed in a manufacturing plant.

backlog
Work that is pending completion or orders for which goods are pending shipment.

work-in-process file
A set of records covering work that is in process in a manufacturing plant.

Chapter Summary

❏ Computers play special roles in manufacturing because, rather than being limited to furnishing information, they can operate production machines.

❏ Computer-aided design and other manufacturing applications use graphic image processing techniques like those described in Chapter 25.

❏ Computers used for product design and manufacturing usually have to be large systems. Millions of bytes of memory and billions of bytes of storage capacity generally are required.

❏ A major payoff for computerized methods lies in the savings of time and money realized by shortening the design cycle for new products and from the ability to use computers to drive production machinery.

❏ Applications that involve computers directly in manufacturing include computer-assisted design (CAD), computer-assisted manufacturing (CAM), computer-integrated manufacturing (CIM), and robotics.

❏ CAD uses graphics and engineering programs to develop images of new products and to test them mathematically before they are built.

❏ CAM uses files developed under CAD and through special inputs to operate machines that build the computer-designed products.

❏ CIM expands on CAM by controlling a series of operations rather than operating one machine at a time.

❏ Robotics controls complete manufacturing sequences without human aid. Robots pick up and position parts for manufacturing operations that can be carried out automatically. Entire products can be assembled, processed, and packaged without human assistance.

❏ Information system applications are used to model and control the business aspects of a manufacturing operation.

❏ The transaction stream in a manufacturing business begins with order entry. Processing then proceeds through filling the order, shipping, invoicing, and accounts receivable.

❏ Specialized uses of information files in manufacturing organizations include shop loading, monitoring work in progress, payroll cost reporting, finished goods inventory, and job costing.

Definitions

Write a complete sentence that defines each of the terms below.

robotics	CAD
real-response time	prototype
simulate	CIM
CAM	

Questions to Think About

Based on what you have learned to date, answer the following questions in one or more complete sentences.

1. What special role do computers play in manufacturing organizations?

2. What kinds and sizes of computers are needed for manufacturing applications?

3. What is computer-assisted design and what results does this application produce?

4. What results are produced under a computer-assisted manufacturing operation?

5. How are computer-assisted design and computer-assisted manufacturing operations related?

6. What is computer-integrated manufacturing and what is the scope of this application?

7. What is robotics and what are its special features?

8. Where does the transaction chain start for a manufacturing organization and what information is generated by transactions?

Projects

The purpose of the assignments below is to encourage you to increase your learning through outside reading or work assignments.

1. In a newspaper or magazine, read a major article about any manufacturing company. The article should give some information about production, growth, or earnings of the company. Note the figures that are given and describe how this information might have been produced by a computer system.

2. If possible, visit a company that uses computers in its manufacturing operations. Ask the people who work at the company what changes have resulted from the introduction of computers. Try to identify the costs and benefits that have resulted from the use of computers. On the basis of this information, state whether computers are paying for themselves and, if so, how.

CHAPTER 28

How Are Computers Used in a Distribution Business?

The Think Tank

When you finish reading this chapter and complete your work assignments, you should be able to answer the following questions.

❑ What special planning and operational challenges are faced by managers in distribution companies?

❑ What computer applications are unique to distribution companies?

❑ What special transaction processing applications are needed by distribution companies?

❑ What features should be present in an information model of a distribution business?

DOING BUSINESS

"This truck is a special tool," Noreen explained to Hector. Noreen had made her regular daily stop at the distribution center where Hector worked. She was a route driver for United Parcel Service (UPS), the biggest private package distribution service in the country. While Noreen was picking up a cart full of packages, Hector examined her truck.

"I was going to tell you that you left the engine running when you went into the building," Hector said.

"We leave them running all day," Noreen explained. "With as many stops as we make, the batteries would die if we killed the engine each time. Also, the engine is a small diesel. It takes less fuel to leave it running than to stop and start it again.

"As I said," Noreen continued, "this truck is a special tool. Notice that the inside is high enough for me to stand up. There are racks on both sides of the truck. And there's a plastic skylight. It provides enough light so I can read the packages. The truck is really a distribution center on wheels. When I leave our garage in the morning, all of the packages that I have to deliver are in these racks.

"It's done with computers. The computers give me a list that shows all my stops. I just keep looking at the list and going to one address after the other. The packages I need are in the racks. They are arranged in the same order as my stops. We make all our deliveries in the morning. Then we start our pickups, usually in the afternoon.

"We follow a set pickup route. We check every regular customer, every day. We pick up all packages that are ready to go. By afternoon when we

Product delivery is an essential function. All companies that make or handle products must make provisions for distribution. This photo shows a large printing plant operating its fleet of trucks to deliver products to customers. In addition, the company is involved in distribution as a consignee for paper, ink, and other supplies.

COURTESY OF GRIFFIN PRINTING & LITHOGRAPHIC CO., INC.

make pickups, the racks in the trucks are empty. We stack the parcels we pick up in the empty spaces in the rack, like I've just finished doing. Now I've got to run. I still have a lot of stops to make.''

Hector admired the way Noreen got rolling with no wasted motion. She strapped herself into the one seat in the truck, put it into gear, looked around, and was off. Hector took just a moment to think about his talk with Noreen as he watched her truck turn onto the highway. He knew that thousands of drivers like Noreen delivered millions of packages to locations all over the country every day. He knew the packages he had just seen loaded would be sorted at a number of distribution centers. Hector realized that these distribution centers employed tens of thousands of people.

Hector knew each package would ride on a series of trucks and airplanes. Some would be delivered to points thousands of miles away the next morning. The main thing that amazed Hector was that, with each delivery, a customer would be asked to sign a computer-printed list. Even with millions of packages to move every day, each shipment could be traced individually.

Quickly, Hector returned to work. Items for the next day's shipments already were piling up around his work station.

MEANING

Hector had learned an important lesson in economics. A major portion of all the money you spend for products represents distribution costs. For the typical product, the costs of materials and manufacturing usually is between one-eighth and one-quarter of the selling price. Much of the rest of your money goes for expenses of distribution, advertising, and marketing. Whatever is left over is profit. In many instances, it costs more to distribute a product than to make it.

In total, hundreds of billions of dollars are spent every year on the distribution of products. Part of the economic growth of the United States results from continuing improvements in distribution capabilities. It now is possible to ship a package from any point in the United States to any other point—overnight. Factories on the East Coast can provide next-day service to West Coast customers.

Overall, the distribution business is huge. Tens of millions of individual packages are delivered every day. Hundreds of ships are dispatched and unloaded at U.S. ports. And many thousands of freight cars and trucks move across country. Each freight car contains perhaps 100,000 pounds of materials and products. And each truck trailer may contain 40,000 pounds.

WHAT SERVICES ARE PROVIDED BY DISTRIBUTION COMPANIES?

The transporting of goods is only a part of the distribution business. Distributors also maintain facilities, called *terminals,* in which packages and materials are transferred between vehicles. For example, the packages from Hector's company are picked up by a small "route" truck designed for in-city use.

This route truck unloads each evening at a terminal. There, information on the packages is recorded into computerized files. At the same time, the packages themselves are sorted into other vehicles. Some packages may go into containers that will be carried by planes or ships. Others will go into large trucks to be driven to distant cities. When these trucks, planes, and ships reach their destinations, the packages are sorted again. At the destination end, the packages go back into route trucks for final delivery.

The distribution industry also stores some products in *distribution centers* or *warehouses.* A distribution center receives bulk shipments and distributes products to local destinations. A warehouse is a facility that specializes in storage of goods. In a warehouse, most receipts and shipments are for large batches of goods.

The idea: Products are shipped in bulk, and inexpensively, to regional centers. Individual packages then are shipped from the distribution centers. This kind of service can be especially important for *imports,* foreign products brought into this country. The U. S. government collects special taxes, called *tariffs,* on imported products.

One method of collecting tariffs is to demand that money be paid as products are taken from ships or airplanes. This procedure can tie up a lot of money for the manufacturer. Another method is to call upon specialized distributors. These companies operate facilities called *bonded warehouses.* The bonded warehouses are permitted to accept and hold imported products until they are sold. Tariffs are collected as part of the service of shipping the products to customers in the United States.

The point: Distribution is an essential service for all people. Every product you eat or use had to be transported for your benefit. Distribution, like other major businesses, is dependent upon information. The distribution system upon which you and the entire economy depend could not exist without computer support.

HOW DO COMPUTERS FIT INTO A DISTRIBUTION BUSINESS?

In the distribution industry, just as in every other business, transactions are based on information. People do business on the basis of information. For example, if a department store needs four dozen sweaters, it places an order with a supplier. The supplier indicates that delivery will be made in three weeks. The department store can continue to serve customers because it has five weeks' supply on hand.

Business Terms

terminal
A distribution facility in which packages and materials are transferred between vehicles.

distribution center
A facility that receives bulk shipments and distributes products to local destinations.

warehouse
A facility that specializes in storage of goods for local delivery.

import
Receipt of products made in a foreign country into a destination country.

tariff
A tax on imported products.

bonded warehouse
A facility that receives and holds imported goods and is permitted to collect tariffs when the goods are shipped to final destinations.

The supplier makes the delivery commitment on the basis of information. In some instances, the information indicates that the products are being made in the factory. From the information, the salesperson knows when the products will be ready for shipment.

Other kinds of information also may be used. For example, the supplier may have information that indicates the needed sweaters are on a ship. The ship is due to dock in San Francisco in 10 days. The supplier uses this information to make delivery commitments. Arrangements can be made to deliver the ordered products right from the dock to the customers. In effect, the ship that is carrying the goods is a floating warehouse. The company avoids the cost of storing and reshipping the goods later on.

What Operations Are Involved In the Distribution Process?

The series of distribution steps from completion of manufacturing through delivery of products to customers is known as a channel. A typical *distribution channel* includes the steps and distribution procedures described below.

In-plant storage. Most products, particularly those that are mass produced, are held at the factory after production. This holding operation usually is necessary because factories tend to turn out products in large quantities. Typically, the factory cannot ship all of the production immediately as it is completed.

However, attempts usually are made to put products into distribution as soon as possible. Where delivery can be completed immediately, storage and handling costs are eliminated. The potential problem: It costs money every time a product is moved or stored. The fewer the handling operations, the lower the overall cost.

Direct shipment. Whenever possible, manufacturers try to ship products directly from the factories where they are made to customers. For example, auto manufacturers in the U. S. prefer to ship cars directly from factories to dealers who will sell them. However, interim use of terminals and transfers sometimes is necessary. As an example, consider the situation of an automobile factory in the Midwest. Within distances of perhaps 500 miles, it is possible to ship cars on special trucks. The cars go directly from the factory to the dealers who will sell them. This means there is only one handling and one trip from factory to customer. However, direct shipment is not always possible.

En-route transfer terminals. To deliver cars from a Midwest auto factory to points more than 500 miles away, another method may be used. Suppose, for example, the cars are moving from Detroit to Los Angeles—more than 2,000 miles. It usually is more efficient to ship entire trainloads of cars to the Los Angeles area. In Los Angeles, a storage area is needed to *break* the shipment. Breaking a shipment means simply that a large shipment is received and held temporarily in a transfer terminal. Then, smaller shipments are dispatched to local customers from stocks created by large shipments. In the case of a trainload of cars, trucks would deliver them to local dealers. Deliveries would include six or seven cars at a time.

This kind of handling is necessary for products imported from other countries. Typically, large quantities are received from ships. These may include truckload-size shipments in large containers. Typically, the containers are taken to special terminals where they are unloaded and held temporarily. Then, smaller quantities are sent to local stores or other customers. Companies that provide this kind of service are called *distributors* or *forwarders*. A distributor's services are part of a continuous trip. The forwarder provides a facility to transfer and re-route products.

Warehousing. Some industries generate products that must be stored after they are produced and brought to market gradually. For example, consider food products that are packed in cans or jars. Crops are harvested at specific times, generally in early fall. At that point, a food processor buys a full year's sup-

Space saving can be an important operating factor for distribution companies. The storage equipment in this photo moves from side to side. Space is provided for only one aisle that people use to access stored items. The rest of the space can be devoted solidly to storage of products. This arrangement makes it possible to store maximum amounts of goods in minimum amounts of space.

PHOTO BY LIANE ENKELIS

ply of the fresh fruits or vegetables. Then, the crop must be processed and packaged quickly, often within a few weeks. This means that, each fall, a food processor has a full year's supply of a product such as canned tomatoes or catsup. The answer: Store the product in warehouses for delivery as orders are received.

Another example involves imported goods. These items generally are shipped in large quantities to minimize shipping costs. Then they are stored in warehouses awaiting orders. The need for warehousing applies to any industry in which products are made or shipped in large quantities.

In addition, some industries have special warehousing needs. These are based upon the nature of the products. A good example is frozen foods. Most frozen food processors use services of specialized shipping companies and warehouses. The foods are shipped in refrigerated trucks or rail cars. They are received and stored in large refrigerated warehouses. Because of the danger of spoilage, there are many frozen food warehouses. These are located close to the markets where frozen foods are used in quantities. The idea: Keep the trip from warehouse to the retail store or restaurant as short as possible.

Warehousing, like other areas of distribution, requires special kinds of operational and informational support from computers. Each of the types of distribution described above presents its own special needs. Some of the computerized solutions that meet these needs are described below.

Business Terms

distribution channel
A series of steps followed in transporting and delivering products from point of manufacture to final destination.

break
In shipping, a service that receives bulk shipments and selects items for local delivery.

distributor
A company that provides sales and delivery services as part of the normal routine of delivering products to customers.

forwarder
A specialized shipper that routes bulk shipments; a forwarder acts as a middleman between shippers and freight carriers.

1. How do the costs of distribution affect the production and marketing of products?

2. Why do manufacturers attempt to deliver products directly from factories to customers?

3. How do distribution companies use information?

HOW DO COMPUTERS SUPPORT DISTRIBUTION OPERATIONS?

As is true in all major industries, distributors have developed a number of special, operations-support computer applications. These applications are separate from and in addition to the use of computers as general information tools. Some special applications for distribution companies include:

• Materials handling

• Vehicle dispatching

• Container loading and unloading

• Automated rail yard operation

• Warehouse location planning.

How Do Computers Provide Support For Materials Handling Operations?

The term *materials handling* describes any method used to move products or materials. Materials handling needs occur in manufacturing operations as well as in distribution. A manufacturing assembly line is a materials handling system. In distribution, materials handling begins when products are completed in a factory and carries through to delivery to customers.

For many years, the handling of materials has been automated through use of *conveyors.* A conveyor is a system that carries people or products from point to point. You probably have been served by conveyors. Examples include escalators used in stores and office buildings. Also, the "moving sidewalks" in many airports are conveyor systems. Distribution organizations use conveyors to carry products from storage points to trucks or rail cars for loading. Also, conveyors are used regularly in terminals where packages are moved from one vehicle to another. The idea: It is more efficient to use machinery to carry packages and materials than to require people to do the work.

A simple conveyor that carries packages to waiting trucks generally does not require computer support. Computers have made major contributions by making possible the *automated warehouse.* An automated warehouse is a facility in which packages are transported, stored, retrieved, and delivered automatically.

For example, some large supermarket chains use automated warehouses to control distribution. In these operations, goods are ordered and received in standard *pallet* loads. A pallet is a platform, usually made of wood, on which boxes of products are stacked. Supermarkets with automated warehouses establish standards for the loading of pallets by suppliers. These are based on the usual number of boxes of a product that are shipped to stores.

When goods are received at a warehouse, they are placed on computer-controlled conveyors. Operators identify the products and enter codes into the computer system. The conveyor then receives instructions from the computer about where the product is to be stored. The pallet is routed through a series of conveyors to the identified location. Then, the system automatically places the pallet on a rack. It is held there until the computer issues a message that causes the system to pick it up. Then, the conveyor loads the pallet automatically onto a truck for delivery to a store.

To support this kind of operation, the computer uses a database that models the warehouse. Each storage location is represented by an information record. When the record storage position is blank, the computer is free to route products there. As pallets are placed in rack positions, the computer updates its database to show the product and location.

When orders from stores are entered, the computer finds the needed products. The pallets then are

Packages with coded markings identify themselves for computers as they move through the distribution process. This photo shows use of a reading device that senses markings on products stored in warehouses. This capability reduces the work of keeping track of inventories or of identifying products to be selected for shipment.

COURTESY OF L.X.E., INC.

picked up automatically and carried by conveyor right into the outbound trucks.

The devices that pick up and transfer packages or materials automatically also are computer controlled. These are robots. They use sensors and controls similar to those described in the discussions of manufacturing in the previous chapter.

trucks to their pickup and delivery points in the shortest distance and shortest time.

To do this, several distribution organizations have developed databases that control routing and dispatching of vehicles. Addresses of customers are coded to correspond with points on a map. Coding also considers one-way streets, construction projects,

How Do Computers Control Dispatching of Vehicles?

The programs that control automated warehouses have a special capability. In addition to keeping track of locations, computers must be able to figure out routes. That is, the computer must instruct a complex network of conveyors. The instructions tell the equipment how to get to each location in the warehouse.

Similar computer applications are used to control delivery of products in vehicles. Recall that UPS and other package services have routes that are followed in sequence by their drivers. It is important that managers of distribution organizations be able to route their vehicles efficiently. The idea: Get the

Business Terms

materials handling
Any method used to move products or materials.

conveyor
A system that carries people or products from point to point.

automated warehouse
A facility in which packages are transported, stored, retrieved, and delivered automatically—under computer control.

pallet
A platform, usually made of wood, on which boxes of products are stacked.

and other traffic factors. Routes are mapped to cover the entire service area most efficiently.

Other types of route delivery companies accept pickup calls over the telephone. These organizations generally are in radio contact with their trucks. Location information is entered into computers as pickups are scheduled. From this information, the computer can find the truck that is closest to the location of the pickup.

Similar systems are being used to dispatch police and fire vehicles to handle emergencies. A special capability has been added for some firefighting systems: As trucks travel to answer an alarm, the computer turns all the lights to green along their route.

The point: Controlling the movement of a fleet of trucks is a complex job. Computers are able to apply their power to keep track of locations of customers and vehicles. Managers make better use of their equipment and provide better service.

How Do Computers Support Use of Containerization?

Containerization is a method under which metal structures the size of truck trailers are shipped as units. Most container shipments travel by ship for some part of their journey.

Typically, a shipment originates when a container mounted on a special trailer is towed to a factory. The container is loaded in the same way as an ordinary truck trailer. The container is towed to a shipping dock, where the container is lifted from the trailer. The work is done by a large crane that lifts loads of 40,000 pounds or more with ease. A crane is a device that lifts and moves objects or materials. The crane moves the containers to a position on the deck of a special freighter.

When the freighter arrives at a destination port, the container is lifted onto another trailer—or onto a railroad car. The container then is transported to a warehouse or to its customer destination. The idea: The goods being shipped are handled once for load-

ing and once for unloading. Containerization eliminates two to four loading or unloading operations that are necessary if individual boxes are shipped.

Computers help to deliver the operating speeds necessary to make containerization work. A freighter earns money for its owners when it is at sea carrying cargo. When a freighter is tied up in port for loading or unloading, it costs the owners between $2,000 and $5,000 per day. To move containers quickly, instant information access is necessary. As each container is unloaded, it is identified to a computer system. Crane operators receive immediate instructions on how to direct the container to its destination. All paperwork, including computation and payment of tariffs to customs officials, is supported by the same computer system.

Customers also can be advised immediately about the status of shipments. This can be valuable. Remember, customers often sell products while they are in shipboard containers. Arrival of ordered products represents a vital transaction. Computers can be programmed to make this kind of information available to customers immediately.

How Do Computers Operate Railroad Freight Yards?

Railroad freight yards are transfer points. Shipments arrive in freight cars, also called "box cars" because they are shaped like large containers. As indicated earlier, each car might carry up to 80,000 or 100,000 pounds of products or materials.

Freight trains travel between yards in distant cities. A train is assembled, or "made up," in a freight yard and dispatched along tracks that link it to an assigned destination. Individual trains may transport between 80 and 200 loaded cars. At the destination yard, the trains of cars are "broken." This means the cars are separated and rerouted. Some cars will be sent out in other trains. Others will be unloaded in terminals within the yards. Still others will be sent on private tracks directly to warehouses or manufacturing plants.

Containerization makes it possible to ship goods around the world without having to load and unload shipments at transfer points. In this photo, containers received in Tacoma, WA, by ship are loaded onto railroad cars that will carry them directly to their destinations. Huge materials handling devices are needed. Also, computer systems are needed to monitor and direct shipment of the large numbers of containers carried by special ships.

COURTESY OF PORT OF TACOMA, PHOTO BY ROD KOON

Operation of a freight yard is a complex, tense job. Trains enter a yard from the main tracks, or lines. The engines are detached and the cars are pushed over a high point at the entrance to the yard. This is known as the "hump." At the top of the hump, cars are detached from their trains and permitted to roll into the yard. The yard contains a large number of side-by-side tracks. A series of switches must be set to direct the car to a specific track. On the individual tracks, new trains are being formed. These new trains will move the cars to the next freight yard.

This is a critical job. There is no turning back once a car is joined to a train. If a car gets attached to the wrong train, it will be pulled to the wrong destination. Until computers were programmed to manage yard operations, each switch, on every track, had to be set by hand. The people doing the switching had lists to work from. Because of the need for accuracy, the operation had to be slow enough to permit people to keep up.

Today, the switches are set automatically under computer control. In some yards, codes are read from the sides of cars by a TV camera. In others, an operator enters the car number as it approaches the hump. The computer uses a database that includes records for each car on every train. The database also includes information on outbound trains being made up in the yard. From the identification of the car, the track switches are set. Each car is guided automatically to its outbound train. With computerized systems, railroads provide better service, faster, and at lower cost.

How Do Computers Help Find Locations for Warehouses?

The location of a distribution point can have a great effect upon the quality of service provided to customers. A decision about the location of any given warehouse involves a number of trade-offs. Ideally, each warehouse should be as close as possible to as

---

Business Terms

containerization
A method under which metal structures the size of truck trailers are shipped as units.

many customers as possible. However, warehouses often must be located in areas zoned for commercial use. Zoning laws are passed by local governments. They control the uses that can be made of land. Often, retail and business structures must be built in different areas from commercial buildings, such as warehouses. Costs for land and buildings also can be important.

Computer programs called *decision support systems (DSS)* can help managers find the best locations for distribution centers. A decision support system is a database-oriented set of programs. The DSS enables the manager to model the outcomes of several alternatives for each decision. As you know, a database models current operations of a company. A DSS enables managers to predict outcomes of different solutions to problems. The outcomes present pictures of future situations. Managers can compare, identify the best choice, and make decisions that provide the best solutions for their problems. This technique is reviewed in Chapter 25, where use of spreadsheets for "What if...?" simulation is discussed.

As in any industry, distribution companies face special problems. Where the problems lend themselves to computerized solutions, special systems have been developed. In addition, distribution companies also have information system problems that are similar to those faced by all companies. The computerized information handling procedures used by distribution companies are described below.

Review 28.2

1. How do computers control operation of automated warehouses?

2. How are computers used to manage truck delivery and pickup operations?

3. How have computers helped to make containerization of shipments possible?

4. What role do computers play in automated rail yards?

WHAT SPECIAL TRANSACTION PROCESSING AND MANAGEMENT INFORMATION NEEDS MUST BE MET?

Distribution is a service business. Transactions support the basic unit of service that is provided. Distribution includes the shipment of goods and frequently includes other services, such as warehousing. To provide these services, distribution companies use a number of information-related computer applications. Some of these are described below.

What Source Documents Are Generated?

Warehousing services can involve accepting goods, holding items for future shipment, or actual shipment. Any one of these transactions generates source documents that provide the basis for the building of information records, files, and databases.

A typical source document is a *freight bill.* This is an invoice that meets the specifications of the transportation industry. For shipments by air, the same basic document sometimes is called an *air bill.* Information on a freight bill includes identification of the *shipper,* the *consignee,* and descriptions of articles shipped. The shipper is the company or person that originates a shipment. The consignee is the company or person to whom the shipment is addressed.

The description of articles shipped is important because it determines the cost of the service. The government has established a series of rates, or charges, for shipments. These are based on *commodity codes,* or product classifications, of the items. To illustrate, products that are breakable are more expensive to ship than those that are less subject to damage. The same is true for perishable products that are subject to spoilage.

From these entries, specialized office workers *rate* and *route* the shipments. Rating involves use of computers and/or special tables to establish charges. Routing is done by *dispatchers.* These are people who are trained to figure the best way to get a ship-

Delivery of shipments to customers is the payoff for distribution operations. To keep up with business growth and demands for service, a number of companies, such as Federal Express, provide overnight delivery to any point in the United States from any other point in the country.

PHOTO BY BENEDICT KRUSE

ment to its consignee. Both rating and routing operations now can be supported by computer systems.

What Special Information Services Are Necessary?

Distribution company managers must be able to locate shipments while they are en route. The ability to provide information on delivery status to customers is a major point of competition among distribution companies. This means it is important for information on each shipment to be available within the company's computer system. Initial data entries typically are made when the shipment is received for dispatching. From then on, the shipment record should be updated each time the goods are moved—until delivery is made.

Maintenance costs. Maintenance and repair of vehicles are important management concerns in the distribution industry. Consider that each truck and trailer "rig" rides on more than $10,000 worth of tires. The transmission of a large truck has up to 18 forward gears. Costs of keeping trucks rolling represent a major expense.

Business Terms

decision support system (DSS)
A database-oriented set of programs that enables a manager to model the outcomes of several alternatives for each decision.

freight bill
An invoice that meets the specifications of the transportation industry.

air bill
An invoice for airborne shipments.

shipper
The company or person that originates a shipment.

consignee
The company or person to whom a shipment is addressed.

commodity code
A classification of a product that serves as a basis for determining its shipping costs.

rate
To determine the basis for shipping charges.

route
To establish the path of travel for a shipment.

dispatcher
A person who directs the routing of shipments.

The consequences of maintenance failures are even higher. It can cost thousands of dollars to have a truck break down on the road. If it happens too frequently, the company can lose business.

To monitor maintenance costs, computer systems generally are set up to accumulate labor and parts costs for each vehicle. When maintenance is done on any vehicle, the payroll cost is added to the maintenance record for that vehicle. The same is true when parts are used for vehicle maintenance.

Keeping records in this way enables managers to evaluate performance of vehicles and people. The records show which make and model of vehicle has the lowest (or highest) maintenance costs. Also, the records enable managers to trace breakdowns of vehicles to specific mechanics or drivers.

Highway usage information.   Operators of commercial vehicles generally are taxed for the use of highways. Distribution companies must submit reports to state and federal agencies on miles traveled by each vehicle, in most states. The records must be accurate. Highway taxes can run to thousands of dollars per year for each vehicle. Penalties for submitting wrong information are severe.

Records are developed by processing information from dispatch tickets. For each route followed by a truck, information is generated on the number of miles covered, state by state. The computer maintains the mileage files as part of the system that tracks shipment status.

The distribution industry is vital to the economy of the country, and to the delivery of products required by its businesses and citizens. Distribution operations have grown to a scale that would make it impossible to meet today's demands without computers. In this respect, distribution has much in common with other industries. The next chapter illustrates this principle with discussions of computer applications in retailing and service businesses.

Review 28.3

1. What is a freight bill and how is it used?

2. Why is the ability to keep track of shipments a major point of competition among distribution companies?

3. How do computers help shipping companies keep track of maintenance costs?

Chapter Summary

❑ Costs of distribution represent a major portion of the prices consumers pay for the products they buy.

❑ The steps followed from completion of manufacture of a product through to delivery to consumers is called a distribution channel.

❑ Operations and services involved in distribution include in-plant storage following manufacture, direct delivery from factories, en-route transfers, and warehousing.

❑ Computers are used for a number of applications that are special to distribution companies. These include materials handling, vehicle dispatching,

container loading and unloading, automated rail yards, and warehouse location planning.

❑ Materials handling applications include the control of systems that use multiple conveyors to carry goods through warehouses or distribution centers.

❑ Computers plan delivery routes and dispatch vehicles through use of a database that simulates locations and traffic conditions.

❑ Container unloading is a volume operation that must be carried out under tight schedules. Computers identify containers and issue instructions for their handling.

❑ In automated rail yards, computers identify cars and set the switches that direct them into outbound trains or to local delivery tracks.

❏ Warehouse location planning can be aided by computerized decision support systems. These systems enable managers to consider all the aspects of a given location and to choose the best alternative.

❏ The chief source documents for distribution transactions are freight bills or orders for storing goods in warehouses. Shipping and warehouse charges are based on the type of goods handled.

❏ Transaction documents are the basis for setting up computer files that keep track of shipments.

❏ Distribution companies have special needs to keep track of maintenance costs and highway mileage.

5. How do computers help to dispatch and set up routes for vehicles?

6. What is containerization and how do computers help to support the ability to ship in containers?

7. How do computers help to operate rail freight yards?

8. How do decision support systems help distribution managers?

9. What is a freight bill and what information does it contain?

10. How do transportation companies use computers to keep track of vehicle maintenance costs?

Definitions

Write a complete sentence that defines each of the terms below.

terminal	distribution center
warehouse	import
tariff	conveyor
freight bill	commodity code

Questions to Think About

Based on what you have learned to date, answer the following questions in one or more complete sentences.

1. Why is it said that the cost of distributing a product may be higher than manufacturing costs?

2. What is a distribution terminal and what services are performed at terminals?

3. What is a warehouse and what is its purpose?

4. Why do manufacturers prefer to be able to ship products directly from factories to customers?

Projects

The purpose of the assignments below is to encourage you to increase your learning through outside reading or work assignments.

1. Find a newspaper or magazine article on containerization. From the information you read, describe the changes in distribution services and costs that have been made possible by containerization. Analyze the information you find. Give your opinion on the major benefits and potential problems that have resulted from containerization.

2. Three major transportation systems are part of the distribution network in the United States. These methods of shipment are truck, rail, and air. Read about these transportation systems in magazine articles or in an encyclopedia. From your readings, report on the types of shipments for which each method presents advantages. Also, report on the disadvantages of each shipping method.

CHAPTER 29

How Are Computers Used in Retailing and Service Businesses?

When you finish reading this chapter and complete your work assignments, you should be able to answer the following questions.

❑ What special planning and operational challenges are faced by managers in retailing and service companies?

❑ What applications are processed that are unique to retailing and service organizations?

❑ What special transaction processing applications are needed by retailers?

❑ What features should be present in an information model of a retailing or service business?

DOING BUSINESS

As the salesperson rang up her purchase, Noel looked surprised. Her older brother, Jerry, nudged her, a signal to keep quiet. After some serious shopping, Jerry had helped Noel to pick a glove of her own. She had tried out for Little League with her brother's glove. When she made the team, the family decided she should have a glove of her own. Jerry was elected to help her pick a fielder's mitt.

The shopping had taken some time. Noel had insisted on looking at every glove in the store. She tried most of them. Eventually, she narrowed the selection to a few she liked best. Jerry advised that they buy one of the more expensive gloves. He believed it was worth some extra money. The glove that Noel and Jerry selected had a large trap, the webbing between the thumb and first finger. It would do a better job than the others of enabling Noel to stop and hold onto the ball.

It was agreed that the glove was worth the price on the tag, $24.95. Noel brought the glove to the cashier. The salesperson passed the tag on the glove through a reader attached to the register. As the sale was being rung up, Noel took $30 from her purse. When the amount of the sale was displayed on the screen, it was $17.95. With tax, the register showed a total cost of $19.03.

That's when the surprised look came to Noel's face. A split second later, Jerry nudged her, indicating that she should say nothing.

"That's a good price for the mitt," he said. "You'll get away by paying under $20, just what you hoped."

Ella, the salesperson, had spotted Noel's look and Jerry's reaction. Her supervisor had alerted her to expect this kind of response. Ella was ready: "You picked the right day to shop at our store," she told her customers. "We've just started a manager's sale this morning. The manager picks a series of

Heavy customer traffic is one of the challenges faced by retailing companies that are part of the service sector of the economy. Large retailers could not have grown to their present size without the aid of computerized transaction processing.

COURTESY OF THE KROGER CO.

surprise items for the sale. The amounts are changed in the computer. When customers buy the reduced-price items, they get the better price automatically.

"Now," Ella continued, "is there anything else you need? Bring me anything you want and we'll see if the computer discounts it for you."

"I see how it works," Jerry remarked. "We saw the sale signs all over the place. That's one reason we came to this store. We picked this glove because it's the best we found. The discount makes the deal even better."

Jerry and Noel looked at each other. "Can we look at those T-shirts we didn't think I could afford?" Noel asked.

MEANING

For Noel and Jerry, the ability to alter prices with simple computer entries provided a pleasant surprise. For the store, the computer made it easier to stage a sale. It was unnecessary to change the price tags on thousands of items. The sale could be carried out with signs announcing that merchandise was being discounted.

This capability is valuable because retailing and other service businesses are *labor intensive.* This means that it takes a lot of people to run a retail or service business. It also means that the costs of labor form a large part of the total expenses of a retail or service organization. Using computers to save time and the cost of labor reduces expenses in retail and service businesses.

WHAT IS THE SERVICE SECTOR?

Retailing is part of what is known as the *service sector* of the economy. The service sector includes all private companies that deliver services and also all

Business Terms

labor intensive
Description of a business in which payroll represents the major expense.

service sector
The portion of the economy that includes all private companies that deliver services and also all government agencies.

government agencies. Service organizations now represent the majority of the total economy. Also, the majority of jobs now are in service occupations.

In some instances, there are no products involved in the delivery of services. For example, when you go to a doctor or dentist, you pay for knowledge, advice, and treatment. You are not buying products—with the exception of medication or fillings in your teeth.

Some service businesses do deliver products. Retailers are one example. Restaurants are another. You receive food. But most of the payments you make go for the services involved in delivering food to you.

Computer applications in retailing and service organizations are important to you. One reason is that you are a consumer of services who can benefit from an understanding of what you buy. Another reason is that service organizations are major employers. Knowledge about service operations may help in your job and career planning.

What Kinds of Businesses Form the Service Sector?

The principles and applications covered in this chapter apply to almost all service organizations. As examples, the following are just a few services that you use and that might provide future employment.

Retailing. *Retailing,* as you know, involves sale of products to consumers. Retailers fit into a number of subindustries. Included are food, fashion, discount, and department stores. There also are retailers who handle gasoline, automotive parts, and many others. Most of these retailing specialty areas have their own associations. Most have special problems and needs.

However, there also are common requirements for dealing with customers, handling cash, and processing credit card purchases. Computers have come to play special roles for retailers. Computers now process many millions of retail transactions. Information systems also help to control inventories of items displayed and the purchasing of new supplies. Modern retail stores could not operate without computers.

Professions. The term *profession* takes in most fields that require advanced education or licenses. Examples include medical doctors, dentists, attorneys, and accountants. Professional organizations sell services. Generally, there are no products involved. In the professions, the value sold is the time of the people involved. Therefore, a common need met by computers is to account for time spent and services provided. These services are the transactions of professional organizations. Computers provide special capabilities in capturing information on these specialized transactions. Computers become tools for issuing invoices and monitoring cash flow.

Health care. The *health care industry* represents a vital and growing portion of the economy. The main health-care facilities are hospitals. Also included are hospitals and *extended care* facilities. Extended care refers to places where people with illnesses can receive nursing care and rest. The term "extended care" comes from the fact that many people are sent to these facilities after a hospital stay. The idea is that they don't need the "acute care" provided by hospitals. However, people still need services that will help them to regain their health.

A special need for computers in the health-care field stems from the way bills are paid. Most patients now have some form of insurance coverage. It would be impossible to keep up with the record keeping required by insurance plans without computers.

Hospitality. The *hospitality industry* takes in all businesses that provide food and accommodations. Included are fast-food outlets, restaurants, hotels, motels, trailer parks, and campsites.

A common problem of hospitality management is the *volatility* of the items sold. Volatility describes the process of rapid evaporation. Gasoline left in the air is volatile. The same idea can apply to a hotel room that is not used or food that is not eaten.

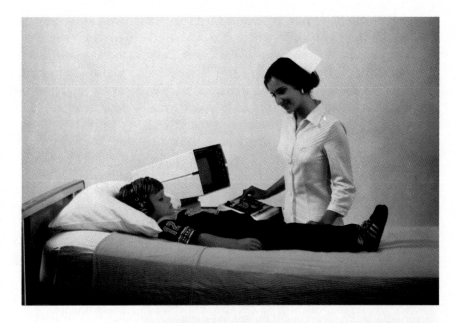

Health-care services organizations have faced continually increasing demands. Computers have played important roles with such applications as patient diagnosis, shown in this photo. In addition, computers assist with operation of x-ray and laboratory equipment, laboratory procedures, and administrative record keeping.

COURTESY OF TRACOR, INC.

The potential income from those items disappears quickly. Each empty hotel room represents lost income.

Therefore, the hotel industry has been a leader in the development of computerized reservation systems. You already know that some types of restaurants use computers for transaction processing. Inventory control and staffing also are important.

Passenger transportation. Transportation of goods, as you know, is part of the distribution industry. Passenger transportation also is an important service area. This field takes in the rapid transit systems in large cities, including subways, buses, and street cars. Also included are taxis and special services, such as transportation to and from airports. Intercity transportation also is part of this category. Intercity passenger service now is dominated by airlines. However, trains and buses still provide intercity service.

Computers play major roles in all of these fields. In particular, airlines pioneered and are major users of computerized reservation systems. Other applications include route planning and vehicle dispatching.

Business Terms

retailing
The industry that specializes in selling goods to consumers.

profession
A field with qualification requirements that can include advanced degrees and special licenses.

health care industry
The industry that cares for persons with illnesses. Includes hospitals and "extended care facilities" such as nursing homes.

extended care
A reference to long-term care that usually is provided following discharge from a hospital after major surgery or a serious illness.

hospitality industry
The industry that takes in all businesses that provide food and lodging accommodations.

volatility
Description of an item with a short life, subject to rapid evaporation. The term usually is used to describe chemicals such as gasoline that evaporate rapidly. Also can refer to a product with a short life, such as an uneaten meal or an unoccupied hotel room.

Government. Taken together, all agencies of government form a major portion of the service sector of the economy. Government agencies generally are regarded as the *public sector.* This term refers to the fact that the government serves the people. Services provided by businesses are called the *private sector.* This reflects the fact that ownership of businesses is by individuals, or private citizens.

Government services are vast. The combination of federal, state, and local governments spends hundreds of billions of dollars of public money every year. The system of checks and balances for government operations requires careful accounting. Computers are used in every phase of government, including control over all income and expenses. Special government services have pioneered some areas of computer use. As described later in this chapter, these include education and law enforcement.

Finance and insurance. The handling of money, particularly by businesses, is a major service area. Business transactions could not be conducted efficiently without the ability to write and exchange checks. Banks now process more than 40 billion checks a year. This volume of work could not be handled without computers. In addition, computers now are making it possible for businesses and government agencies to transfer funds directly between computers. The service is known as *electronic funds transfer.* As the name suggests, computers are instructed to take money out of one account and put it into another. Paperwork is eliminated.

The insurance business is considered to be related to the finance industry because of the vast amounts of money that are handled. Insurance companies accept payments from individuals and businesses. Portions of this money must be set aside to pay benefits if death, fire, flood, accident, or other insured situation occurs. The money accumulated by insurance companies becomes a major force in the economy. Insurance companies provide investment services, loans for construction of buildings, and many other financial services.

Another part of the finance industry is the *brokerage* field. This industry segment consists of brokers who deal in securities such as stocks and bonds. Billions of dollars of transactions are processed by brokers every day. Trading on major stock exchanges often involves exchange of 200 million or more shares of stock in a single day.

Housing management. Housing construction is a major industry on its own. Existing homes and apartments represent a major need for services. These services are separate from the construction business. Included are the repair and upkeep of homes and apartments. In addition, the services connected with finding places to live represent a major industry. This involves sale of existing private homes and rental of existing apartments. Computerized networks now are in use that list housing units that are available for sale or rental.

Convenience services. This category takes in the many needs and demands for which people are willing to spend money. The range of businesses in this field covers businesses as different as laundry and cleaning, barber and beauty shops, TV repair, and dog grooming. Most of these are small businesses. Computers are not a major factor. However, small, inexpensive computers are proving valuable for some businesses.

Review 29.1

1. What is meant by the term ''public sector''?

2. What is meant by the term ''private sector''?

3. Why is payroll a vital computer application in the service sector?

4. Why are hotel rooms considered to be ''volatile'' assets?

WHAT SPECIAL COMPUTER APPLICATIONS DO RETAIL AND SERVICE ORGANIZATIONS USE?

The selling of services is personal. An employee of the service organization is in direct contact with a

Securities trading volumes have multiplied in recent years. Computers have made it possible for the New York Stock Exchange to keep up with transactions involving 200 million or more shares in a single day. This photo shows the headquarters of a large stock-quotation service. The company operates a computer network that supports on-line quotation references by companies or individuals who trade in securities.

COURTESY OF KNIGHT-RIDDER NEWSPAPERS, INC.; PHOTO BY PAUL BARTON

customer. If service is not satisfactory or if necessary products are not available, an immediate loss occurs. Lost business is never recovered fully, even if a customer does return later. The personal nature of services leads to requirements for a number of specialized computer applications.

What Operations Do Retailers and Service Organizations Perform?

The special computer applications that support retail and service operations are based on the kinds of transactions that take place. In some situations, a transaction is completed through a single contact between employee and customer. In other situations, customers require future services. Followup is necessary. Regardless of the type of contact involved, all service operations experience large volumes of contacts between employees and customers. Because of the size of some service organizations, computers now play important roles in supporting delivery of services, as described below.

Consumer sales. When retail employees sell products to customers, *point-of-sale transaction*

recording takes place. That is, source documents are prepared and exchanges of value occur as part of each sale. For many years, the cash register was the main processing tool for point-of-sale transactions. The cash register was designed to control the financial portion of transactions. That is, income data items were entered and recorded in a cash register.

Business Terms

public sector
Portion of the economy that includes all government agencies.

private sector
Portion of the economy that consists of privately owned businesses.

electronic funds transfer
Use of computers to complete banking transactions, including the transfer of funds.

brokerage
A company that deals in securities.

point-of-sale transaction recording
Method for recording source data as an integral part of transaction processing.

This provided a basis for making sure the store received all of the cash paid by its customers. But there was no information on specific items sold or of inventory levels. Also, with traditional cash registers, credit sales had to be handled separately, by hand.

The point-of-sale computer terminal has brought new levels of management and control to retailing. Much more information on sales can be processed during transactions because retail terminals can read information from product tags. This means that computer systems can record information on products sold as well as on money received.

With product information included in transactions, inventory and purchasing operations can be managed more efficiently. As each transaction is entered, the computer files reflect sales and inventory status. Some computer files accumulate information on sales by product. Other files show the current inventories of products.

Inventories and purchasing operations can be managed on an exception basis. That is, managers can concentrate on the items that the computer identifies as needing attention. Items for which the status is normal need no management attention. The computer lets managers know when stocks are low enough to consider reordering. Under some systems, purchase orders for new stocks are issued automatically by computers. Modern retailers could not handle today's sales volumes without computerized point-of-sale and merchandise control applications.

Food Sales.   Fast-food restaurants depend on special point-of-sale systems to keep up with customer volumes. A typical fast-food terminal has special keys that represent menu items. When counterpersons press these keys, the computer completes entries for descriptions and prices of the items. If food is being cooked to order, the same information is delivered to the kitchen. If food is pre-cooked, the counterperson delivers purchased items directly to customers.

The computer also accumulates information on sales. This information is used, in turn, to schedule deliveries of replacements for food items and supplies that were used. Also, figures are developed that show sales for each hour. This information is used to set staffing levels. Employee work schedules are tailored to the business volume expected in each restaurant.

Even in full-service restaurants, computers are used to provide better speed and accuracy in computing customer food checks. Under some systems, servers can enter customer orders directly from the restaurant floor. The servers use terminals that permit entry of menu items. The orders are printed in the kitchen and on customer checks. The server still has to go to the kitchen to pick up orders. However, this system eliminates one trip to the kitchen to turn in orders. The automatic development of totals for customer checks also saves time and assures accuracy. The computer system also keeps track of sales for each menu item. This helps in menu planning and in the ordering of supplies to meet customer demands.

Accommodations and travel.   Reservation systems are vital to hospitality and passenger travel companies. In a typical transaction, a customer calls an airline, hotel, or travel agent. Dates are provided and reservations are arranged for airline seats, hotel rooms, and rental cars. The reservation service provides peace of mind for the traveler, who feels assured that needed services will be available.

Reservation records also can prepare the hospitality companies for completion of transactions. For airlines, the reservation record becomes the basis for issuing tickets and boarding passes. For hotels, the reservation record can be used to set aside rooms for guests. Also, the computer can generate check-in cards that save time in dealing with incoming guests.

Computer systems are tools that help to make possible today's giant airlines and hotel chains. In the accommodations field, success is measured by percentage of occupancy. This is the number of rooms or seats actually filled, as compared with the total number available. Before computers were introduced, airlines and hotel chains relied on handwritten reservation records. Because of the need to have seats or rooms available to honor reservations,

Education is a vital part of the service sector—and also a vital service to the nation. Computers are finding increasing educational roles as instructional aids.
COURTESY OF APPLE COMPUTER, INC.

airlines and hotels limited the reservations they took. Typically, about 10 percent of rooms or seats were not booked in advance. This allowed for a margin needed to meet commitments. The reason: Manual records could not be updated quickly enough to assure that reservations could be honored. With computerized systems, the companies can sell every room or seat. Occupancy rates and income are greater.

Education.   Since government provides so many diverse services, application areas for different agencies are covered separately. More than 50 million Americans are enrolled in schools or colleges. Each student is assigned to one or more classes. From the seventh grade upward, each student takes a number of separate courses. This represents a difference from elementary grades, in which most students remain in a single classroom all day.

All these activities have to be planned and scheduled. In effect, educational institutions have scheduling needs that resemble the reservation requirements of accommodations companies. Therefore, registration and class scheduling are major applications in education.

Registration operations are part of a larger requirement for the keeping of student records. As

work is completed, each student's achievements become part of a permanent record. This record, in turn, can be the basis for future educational program assignments and/or job qualifications. So, records must be accurate and must be accessible for reference. Most school systems and colleges now maintain student records on computerized databases.

In addition, computers are being used increasingly within learning systems. In this role, computers display test questions or information for students who work at terminals. The student reviews the material, then answers questions displayed by the computer. Responses to the questions help computers to track the progress of students. Instructional use of computers in this way is known as *computer-assisted instruction (CAI)*. With CAI techniques, students can progress individually, according to their own capabilities. Computers show great potential for helping to relieve the overload in the educational system.

Business Terms
computer-assisted instruction (CAI) An application under which a computer presents information to a student and monitors the learning that takes place.

In addition, of course, computers represent job potentials. Many millions of workers now function as computer professionals or information users. Education systems are expected to graduate students with computer-related knowledge and skills.

Law enforcement. Law enforcement can be a dangerous business. Accurate information can, literally, make a life-or-death difference. Consider what happens when an officer stops a car for speeding or other violation. Before computers were available, every officer who made a traffic stop was at risk. The officer is relatively unprotected as he or she approaches a car. A number of officers have been injured and killed in such situations. Today, officers have access to information that has saved many lives.

As indicated in Chapter 22, some police departments have computer terminals directly in their patrol cars. In other departments, officers are in radio contact with dispatchers who work at computer terminals. From these terminals, the officers enter the license number of an offending vehicle.

In seconds, displays are generated that indicate whether the car has been involved in a crime or is stolen. The display also indicates whether the owner of the car is wanted or has outstanding traffic violations. In other words, if the situation is dangerous, the officers are warned. Additional officers can be called to the scene if necessary.

Law enforcement depends upon reliable information. Computers help make the work of police officers safer and more efficient.

Judiciary. The courts interpret and enforce laws. Courts also face tremendous backlogs. In most states and cities, there are more cases to be tried than there are courts to hear them. To help establish a perspective on their workloads, many courts use computerized *docketing* systems. A docket is a schedule of cases to be heard. Cases are scheduled and monitored in much the same way as is done in the shop loading application described in Chapter 27. A computer can't try a case. But computers do help to schedule cases and to get the best results from facilities that are available.

In addition, many judges and attorneys are using computers for legal research. Computers are being used to find or base decisions on points of law. A number of agencies have built computer files that contain the texts of state and federal laws. Researchers can enter a series of key words that establish a "profile" for legal conditions. These profiles then are compared with complete texts of existing laws. The computer identifies laws that might apply to a given case. Attorneys take over from there. Computers do a complete job of searching legal texts. This kind of thorough search was not possible when people had to read through multiple volumes of legal texts.

Legislative. Legislators are in the business of generating and publishing text documents. Every law starts as a draft that is presented to lawmakers. Just about every law goes through a review and amendment process that leads to changes in text. After laws are passed, they must be published and distributed. Management of the drafting process and the publication of new laws is handled by word processing and computerized publishing applications. The word processing systems capture the texts of bills as they are introduced. Amendments are handled through online text editing. Then, when a law is passed, computerized tools handle typesetting and preparation for publication.

In addition, proposed laws require research. Legislators must know if the new law changes or eliminates any existing laws. If so, specific references are necessary in the new laws. Therefore, legislators use computers for legal search operations in the same way as is described above for judiciary applications.

Real estate sales and management. There are tens of millions of housing units in the United States. Millions of these units are sold or rented each year. Much of this activity is serviced by real estate agents. These are service organizations that bring sellers and buyers (or owners and renters) together.

Governmental agencies use computers for every aspect of their operations. This photo shows a computerized voting system in use in the legislature at the New York State capitol in Albany.

PHOTO BY BENEDICT KRUSE

The agents *list,* or contract to handle, individual housing units. The information then must be distributed to potential customers and to other agents. In most areas, real estate agencies belong to a *multiple listing* association. The association establishes a computer reference network and publishes information about listed properties. The listings are used by agents to bring customers and properties together.

Today, many families relocate to different parts of the country as workers change jobs. In response to demands, a number of chains of real estate agencies have been formed. These organizations and the multiple listing associations use computer applications that are similar to reservation systems. Without computer support, services on this scale would be difficult, perhaps impossible, to provide.

Real estate also attracts many investors. These people own properties that are managed by specialized agencies. The agencies keep track of income and maintenance expenses. Reports are issued regularly to property owners. Bills must be paid when maintenance is needed. Profits must be delivered to owners. Computerized information systems have made this kind of service possible on a large scale. As a result, large sums of money have been attracted for real estate investment. In turn, many housing units are built and maintained because of the availability of such computer applications.

Automated service.   Costs of labor are a challenge for all service organizations. Some industries are using computers to improve service and reduce costs. Two key examples are applications in banking and gasoline retailing.

Banks provide convenience through self-service. This is done by installing automatic teller machines (ATMs). An ATM is a computer terminal that enables customers to process their own transactions.

Business Terms

docketing
The scheduling of cases for trial in courts.

list
Action by a real estate agent that records the availability of a property for sale or rent.

multiple listing
A service that distributes information to real estate agents about property listings.

Customers receive plastic cards that are coded to permit use of ATMs. Each customer also is assigned a *personal identification number (PIN).* Each PIN is set up by the computer and delivered to the customer in a sealed envelope. Even bank operations personnel do not have access to these numbers. With the card and the PIN, a customer can handle banking transactions directly at ATMs. Money is stored in the machine and is counted out for depositors who process their own transactions. Deposits also can be handled automatically.

Many gasoline retailers have converted from full service to self-service stations. Typically, the cost of gasoline is 20 to 40 cents per gallon higher for full service. For the retailer, labor costs are much lower in a self-service station. A single cashier can operate a station with as many as 15 or 20 pumps. Computers and data communications links are vital to self-service operations.

To make a purchase at a typical station, the customer goes to the cashier first. The customer pays cash in advance or leaves a credit card that will be charged for the purchase. The cashier has controls that unlock the pump for the customer. If the customer has prepaid, the amount of gas to be pumped can be set by the cashier. Under some systems, the entire station is tied to a central computer. Credit card sales tickets are printed automatically.

Some gasoline stations are using terminals that accept ATM cards. Under these systems, the customer doesn't even have to deal with a cashier. The terminal accepts the ATM card and requests the customer's pin number. The amount of the purchase is charged directly to the customer's bank account. The charge appears on the customer's bank statement.

The point: In some industries, computers are playing a role in the actual delivery of services.

Review 29.2

1. How does transaction information from point-of-sale terminals assist in the management of retail organizations?

2. How does transaction information from point-of-sale terminals help in deciding how much staff is needed at a fast-food restaurant?

3. What is computer-assisted instruction? How does it work and what are its potential benefits?

4. How do computers contribute to the passage of new laws?

5. What kinds of automated services are being provided and what purpose do they serve?

WHAT USE IS MADE OF STANDARD TRANSACTION PROCESSING SYSTEMS?

Retailing and other service businesses share some operating and management requirements with companies in other fields. Some of these general applications are identified and described below.

Payroll. Because these industries are labor intensive, computerized payroll processing is a common requirement. The majority of service workers are paid on an hourly basis. That is, basic pay is computed by multiplying the number of hours worked by pay rate. Many software packages are available for payrolls of this type.

In retailing, another standard approach is used by many stores: At least part of the pay of sales personnel is on a *commission* basis. Commission systems pay employees a percentage of the value of the items they sell. Often, employees receive a low rate of hourly pay, with commissions on sales added. Standard software packages also are available for this kind of payroll.

Regardless of the way employee pay is computed, it is important that payroll expense be monitored. Payroll is the major expense item for almost all service industries. Managers have to plan for and budget payroll expenses with care. Then, actual payroll figures have to be compared with sales or other income. The financial health of service organizations depends on how well employees perform and how well costs are related to earnings.

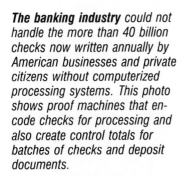

The banking industry could not handle the more than 40 billion checks now written annually by American businesses and private citizens without computerized processing systems. This photo shows proof machines that encode checks for processing and also create control totals for batches of checks and deposit documents.

PHOTO BY LISA SCHWABER-BARZILAY

Accounts receivable. Most companies have to collect bills to produce income. An account receivable is an amount owed as an exchange for the delivery of products or services. Credit sales are common in retailing and service industries. Also common is the use of computers for accounts receivable processing. Some service organizations collect their receivables through standard processing methods. That is, each invoice is processed as an item due for payment. When payment is received, an entry is made that eliminates the receivable item.

Many retailers sell merchandise under credit card plans. These transactions are handled like bank deposits. The credit card sales slips signed by customers are deposited in banks. The procedure is similar to deposit of checks. The bank charges a fee for most items. But the money is credited immediately to the store's account.

Management applications. Retail and service organizations also use computer-generated information to establish plans and to monitor operations. Planning is a primary responsibility of top managers in any company. Future plans are based partly on historic information about business trends. A company's information system provides a model of the status of the company. Managers use this information to carry out their basic responsibilities: plan, organize, and control. Plans include all efforts aimed at building or guiding a business for the future. Organizations are structured to carry out plans. Control is applied by using information systems to compare results with plans. Adjustments in current operations are based on the content of information produced by computers.

In summary, computers have become essential business and management tools—in just about every industry. The time has come in which the majority of jobs require knowledge about how computers work. According to projections, the numbers of computers and computer terminals in use soon will equal the

Business Terms

personal identification number (PIN).
A user entry that permits access to computer files; used with automatic teller machines.

commission
A method of payment based on results produced, such as sales volume.

number of cars on the road. In the near future, it will become as important for people to learn to use computers as it presently is to be able to drive a car. The chapter that follows covers some developments and expectations that relate to the future of computers—and their impact on careers.

1. What is a commission payroll?
2. What advantage do retailers get from selling under bank credit card plans?

Chapter Summary

❑ The service sector of the economy includes all government agencies and private businesses that deliver services, rather than just products. Some service organizations deliver products as part of a service. Included are retailers and restaurants.

❑ Computers play important roles in service organizations because business is labor intensive. This means that payroll processing and the control of labor costs are important.

❑ The service sector has many parts, including retailing, professions, health care, hospitality, passenger transportation, government, finance, housing management, and convenience services.

❑ A number of special devices and systems have been designed to provide computer support for retailing and other service businesses.

❑ In retailing, transactions are processed at point-of-sale terminals that record both cash and merchandise identification. As a result, the computer can assist in managing inventory and in purchasing of merchandise.

❑ Special point-of-sale devices also are used in fast-food restaurants. Service restaurants also are installing computers that help in handling of orders and the preparation of checks.

❑ Reservation systems have made a big difference for accommodations and travel organizations. Organizations in this field could not have grown to present sizes without support from computerized reservation and management systems.

❑ In education, computers provide both record keeping and instructional support.

❑ Law enforcement applications include on-line availability of information about crimes and criminals. Also, computers are used for the dispatching of police and fire vehicles.

❑ Legislators use computers to draft new laws and to research the texts of existing laws.

❑ Real estate sales and rentals are conducted through computerized listings that resemble hotel reservation systems.

❑ Automated services are being offered to consumers in banking and gasoline retailing fields. Customers operate computer terminals with help from plastic cards that permit access to computer networks.

❑ Retail and service organizations use some of the same computer applications as many other businesses.

❑ Standard applications that play a role in retailing and service organization management include payroll, billing, accounts receivable, and decision support systems.

Definitions

Write a complete sentence that defines each of the terms below.

labor intensive	service sector
retailing	profession
health care	extended care
volatility	public sector

private sector

electronic funds transfer

brokerage

list

Questions to Think About

Based on what you have learned to date, answer the following questions in one or more complete sentences.

1. What is the service sector of the economy and what does it include?

2. Is it possible for products to be handled by service organizations? If so, how?

3. How are computers used to help process retailing transactions?

4. What kinds of businesses are included in the hospitality industry?

5. What are some of the main uses for computers in education?

6. Why are computers important tools for members of legislatures?

7. Why is reservation processing a key application for hotels and airlines?

8. How is the work of law enforcement made safer and more efficient through use of computers?

9. How are computers delivering services directly to customers of service organizations?

10. Why is payroll processing so critical for service organizations?

Projects

The purpose of the assignments below is to encourage you to increase your learning through outside reading or work assignments.

1. Find a magazine article or information in a book that describes the service sector of the economy. Prepare a report that gives information on the size of the service sector, the number of jobs in the service sector, and the employment trends for the service sector as compared with the economy as a whole.

2. Visit at least two service businesses that use computers. Examples can include supermarkets, department stores, banks, hospitals, or gas stations with computer-controlled pumps. Describe and compare the procedures followed for use of computers in two of these businesses.

CHAPTER 30

Is There a Computer in Your Future?

The Think Tank

When you finish reading this chapter and complete your work assignments, you should be able to answer the following questions.

❏ How knowledgeable will you have to become about computers?

❏ How will computers affect you in your future experience as a student?

❏ What new developments in computer technology can you expect to encounter in your working career?

❏ How will computers affect jobs in which you may be interested?

DOING BUSINESS

Helen interrupted her father. "But, Dad, you're home. You're talking about a meeting with Mr. Salinas. When you meet with him, you usually have to go to Chicago. You're usually away overnight."

Her father laughed. "The world is changing, Helen. We now hold meetings at which all managers can work right from their own offices. We do it through our computer system. It really has a lot of advantages."

"As far as I'm concerned," Helen's mother said, "the biggest advantage is that we have you home in the evening. With this kind of meeting, we can be a normal family."

Helen was fascinated. "How does it work?" she asked.

Her father finished a mouthful and spoke as the family continued with dinner. "All of our offices have been linked into a central computer for some time. Until now, we've used the system mostly to gather information on transactions and to produce status reports. Now, we have a new kind of software that supports meetings for people at different locations. It's called **computer conferencing.** The type of software we use is called **groupware.** It means a group of people can coordinate their work through a central computer."

"But what's it like?" Helen asked. "What do you do?"

"The computer sets up the meeting. At a certain time, the terminals of all the people who are to attend are connected. The computer asks everyone to check in. If anyone is missing, someone else in the office is contacted and told to get hold of that person.

"Once everybody is in place, the **coordinator**

Teleconferencing has become a standard product offered by communications companies, as shown in this photo of a sales exhibit. New groupware software enhances the value of conferencing networks. With groupware, people at multiple locations can contribute to a conference session and can share information or ideas contributed by other participants.

PHOTO BY LIANE ENKELIS

asks for comments on solutions to problems or questions we are covering.''

"Who's the coordinator?" Helen cut in.

Her father smiled. "This has really grabbed your imagination," he said. "The coordinator is the person who sets up and runs a meeting. He or she also may be called a *facilitator.* The idea is that somebody has to sort things out and keep the meeting on track.

"The thing that surprises me," Helen's father continued, "is how quickly these meetings go. It takes a lot less time than when people get together for personal discussions. The reason is that people talking to each other have to take turns. Everyone has to have a chance to say something. Only one person at a time can speak. The computer system has the effect of letting everybody talk at once."

Helen's mother cut in again. "It sounds horrible."

"That's the point," Helen's father said. "It doesn't sound at all. We all use keyboards. I enter my comments on my own computer. The system picks up the comments of all participants and displays them so we can share our views. The coordinator combines comments that are the same and arranges all of the entries in a logical order. Then,

we can all make new recommendations. Pretty soon, we have decided on what action to take. When our business is complete, the coordinator enters a command and the computer ends the meeting.

"This is a whole new way to use computers," he explained. "Until now, computers have been tools. In effect, the computers were off to one side

Business Terms

computer conferencing
A technique for holding meetings among persons who share computer access. *See also* groupware.

groupware
Software that supports concurrent entries of ideas and suggestions from multiple points by persons taking part in a computer conference. *See also* computer conferencing.

coordinator
Person who oversees the conduct of a computer conference and assists participants.

facilitator
See coordinator.

of the business. We used computers and their information for certain purposes. When we needed them, we threw switches and they were there. That's not the way it's going to be in the future. Computers are right in the middle of things. They are a central part of the company, and of the environment in which we work.''

"Working through your computer could be a great idea," Helen said. "You're on your own. You don't have to sit around looking at those stuffy old executives."

MEANING

Helen's father described the importance of a trend that is changing the way people and computers work together. The computer is becoming part of the process of communication and exchange of ideas.

This kind of trend has happened before. As an example, think about the telephone. This is a machine that has become a natural part of interactions among people. Yet, there was a time when offices were served by single telephones hung on a wall. Telephone conversations were not part of the mainstream of human activities.

When computers were introduced, they replaced such devices as punched card accounting machines. Early computers often were referred to as "back room" systems. They were considered to be production machinery. Computer centers were figurework factories. Computers were outside the main activities of managers in the same way as manufacturing plants.

The change has been gradual. First, managers recognized the value of information. Computers were used to accumulate files and databases. Reports were generated that helped to focus management attention on potential problems.

Gradually, the technologies of computing and telecommunications were merged. Many telephone systems now use digital signal systems that are compatible with computer coding. Sound recordings also use digital techniques. As a result, communication and recording quality is improved greatly. As an example, think about the quality of

recordings on compact discs. These are digital. Their quality is much better than older systems.

In effect, the computer has become a personal instrument, an extension of the telephone as a communication device. Now, computers can make it possible for busy people to share ideas and workloads. Interaction between people takes less time and is more efficient. Helen's father had experienced a meeting at which people were in different offices, some in different cities. As he described it, people didn't have to wait around listening to one another. The computer enables everybody to contribute at once. People get more done in less time when computers become an active part of the work environment.

WHAT NEW TECHNOLOGIES WILL CHANGE COMPUTERS?

As indicated above, digital telecommunications is one of the technologies that has made computers more valuable. Information can be transmitted faster and at lower costs because new technologies add efficiency. In effect, telecommunications and computing have become part of a unified technology. As a result, both communications and computer systems have become more valuable. Some of the specific developments that are advancing the unified computer/communications industry are described below.

Microelectronics.   The microcomputer, the supercomputer, and many other breakthroughs owe their existence to the microchip. Personal computers, for example, use microchips both as processors and for memory. Microchips are the devices that have made computers more powerful and less costly.

Progress has been rapid in increasing the power of microchips. To illustrate, the integrated circuits introduced to the computer field in the mid-1960s had memory capacities of 16 bits per chip. The chips used on the first microcomputers in the late 1970s had 64,000 bits per chip. By the mid-1980s, memory chips with capacities of 256,000 bits had become standard.

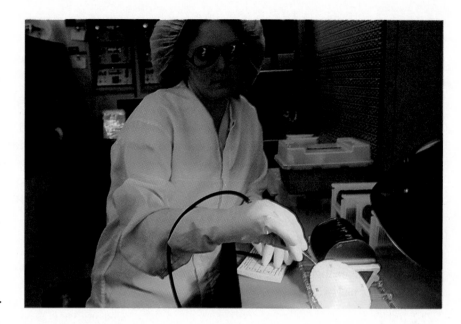

Circuit technology can be counted on to deliver smaller computer components that provide continually greater processing power. As a result, users can expect faster devices, greater memory, and lower costs in comparison with capacities.

PHOTO BY LIANE ENKELIS

In the near future, capacities of four megabits per chip are expected. As discussed below, increased amounts of low-cost memory hold the key to applications of the future. One dramatic example will be the ability of computers to transcribe and print text directly from dictated voice input.

Computer processors also are built from microchips. Engineers have continually increased the number of circuits on and the power of processor chips. To illustrate, the microcomputers of the late 1970s processed eight-bit instructions. This meant that only one byte of data could be accepted in each instruction. By 1981, the standard moved to 16-bit instructions. By the late 1980s, processors that handled 32-bit instructions were becoming commonplace. In the near future, 64-bit processor chips should be standard.

Meaning: Computers will become ever more powerful. Costs in relation to power will become continually smaller.

Special-purpose computers. The great majority of computers introduced between 1960 and 1988 had general-purpose hardware. This meant that the equip-ment itself was not designed for specific applications. Application capabilities came from the software that was used. As you know, for example, simple insertion of new diskettes changes the capabilities of microcomputers. The same equipment, with different diskettes, can be a word processor, a database system, or a spreadsheet processor.

Things weren't always this way. During the 1950s, computer hardware was designed to perform a certain type of processing. Some computers were designed for use by scientists, engineers, and mathematicians. Others were intended for business applications. With the introduction of high-speed microchips, computers were powerful enough to be adapted to virtually any use.

During the 1980s, the picture has changed again. Computer scientists and engineers have identified needs that make it attractive to increase speeds of computers used for scientific applications. Accordingly, new processors have been designed that introduce special-purpose hardware. One example is a database processor. This is used as a peripheral to a general-purpose computer. System software delegates processing of all database operations to the special processor. The processor has a set of instructions that speed the handling and finding of data items.

Another example is the *reduced instruction set computer (RISC)*. As its name implies, a RISC has fewer commands in its instruction set than a general-purpose computer. With fewer commands to execute, a RISC operates much faster. This increased speed can be valuable to engineers or scientists. RISC systems are used to monitor scientific experiments or to control robotic devices.

Special-purpose hardware seems to be a trend. In the future, users may not have to rely entirely on software to support new applications. If an application is important enough, engineers may develop special computer hardware.

Parallel processing. Another development that is increasing the power of computers is the *parallel processor*. A parallel processor is a computing device that will execute more than one instruction at a time. The parallel processor will have multiple processing chips and will be able to execute a number of instructions at the same time.

From the very beginning of the computer age through the mid-1980s, all computers were designed to execute one instruction at a time. The standard design was known as the "von Neumann processor." This processor was named after John von Neumann, a mathematician and computer pioneer. During the 1940s, von Neumann proposed the approach that led to CPU designs like those discussed in Chapters 17 and 18. That is, a processor works with a control unit and a memory. The control unit prepares instructions for execution. The memory stores program instructions and data. The computer itself performs one processing function at a time.

For many years, technicians improved computers by shortening processing cycles. Most computers in use today have execution times of less than one-millionth of a second. Eventually, demands for computing power grew to levels that exceeded the capacities of single-processor systems. To get still more

power, designers came up with ideas for computers that would have multiple processors.

Multiple-processor systems currently are being designed and introduced. System software analyzes programs and assigns instructions to processors with special capabilities. Parallel processing relies heavily on the increased memory that is being made available by advanced microchips, as described above. As a result, computers now being introduced can execute multiple instructions at the same time. The expected result: still more computing power in the future.

Voice recognition. Increased memory capacities also hold the key to future systems that will permit people and computers to communicate through speech. That is, people will be able to dictate words. Computers will process speech as an input. The speech will be transcribed into text that is displayed for human editing and revision.

By the late 1980s, a number of systems already were in use that permitted voice input to computers. However, the number of words that computers could process was limited. In one application, personnel in warehouses were able to dictate the locations at which pallets of goods were to be stored. With existing memory and processor capabilities, computer vocabularies were limited to a few dozen words or numbers.

In the future, it is expected that computers will be able to understand almost any normal human speech. Vocabularies will run into tens of thousands of words. Word and text processing will become much faster and more convenient. This application, when it happens, also will lead to a change in office work. Secretaries and word processing specialists will become key people. They will have to review texts transcribed from spoken input. Computers will not generate perfect text. People will have to make adjustments in text to account for different spellings or uses of words. As this application evolves, language skills will become ever more valuable for workers of the future.

Computers that talk to people already are in use. This photo shows a telephone station in a bank lobby that customers can use to learn the balances in their accounts. Use of audio inputs and outputs for computer systems can be expected to increase in the future.

PHOTO BY LIANE ENKELIS

almost any Touch-Tone telephone can become a computer terminal.

Computer systems already are recording telephone messages and reading them back to users.

Another application under development would input texts of books into computer files. The books could then be "read" to blind persons through audio output techniques.

Superconductivity. A computer is a series of interconnected electronic devices. This means that computers operate by directing and controlling the flow of electrons through conductors. Electrons, of course, are tiny parts of atoms. Atoms, in turn, are the basic structures that combine to form the Earth and its atmosphere. Electrons are parts of atoms that can be released and can flow to other atoms. Electron flows produce electricity. Computing devices harness the abilities of devices that control the flow of electrons. These devices use electricity to perform calculations or to store information.

A problem with electronic devices is that the flow of electrons encounters resistance. Masses of material block the free flow of electrons. Force must be applied to cause electrons to flow. As electrons overcome resistance, two things happen. One, the flow of current is slowed slightly. This reduces the speed at which computers operate. Two, heat is generated by the friction between electrons and their conductors. This leads to a need for extensive cooling systems to support computers.

Audio output. In addition to understanding spoken input, computers of the future will be able to generate spoken output. This already is a major application. Most of the messages you hear from the telephone company are computer-generated. In addition, some business applications already use spoken responses as outputs. For example, some banks have a service that permits customers to inquire about account balances. The computer gives the balance with a spoken response. Through approaches of this type,

Business Terms

reduced instruction set computer (RISC)
A computer with a command set that is smaller than that of a general-purpose computer. The reduced instruction set makes possible greater processing speeds.

parallel processor
A computing device with multiple microprocessors that make it possible to execute more than one instruction at a time.

Technology is dealing with this problem by developing techniques for *superconductivity.* Superconductors are materials that present lower resistance to electron flows. Superconductivity virtually eliminates the problems of resistance and heat generation.

Initially, it was discovered that conductors lose their resistance at supercold temperatures. Superconductivity was achieved at temperatures approaching minus 280 degrees Fahrenheit. These temperatures could not be maintained for commercial products. A series of experiments has led to superconductivity at higher temperatures. It is expected that future computers will contain superconductive components. As these developments occur, computers will become faster and more efficient.

Light-based techniques.   Another approach toward building computers that eliminate problems of resistance and heat is the use of light. Already, light-based methods have had a major impact on telecommunications. Messages now are being transmitted through *laser* beams and *fiber-optic* cables. A laser is a beam of intense light that is transmitted through air or special tubes. Lasers transmit energy and also can be used to carry sound and digital signals. Fiber-optic techniques also transmit signals through use of light. However, the signals are carried on fine strands of special glass.

An advantage of light over electron carriers is that the problems of resistance and heat are eliminated. Electron beams travel through air at the same speed as light—186,000 miles per second. However, the resistance of solid carriers causes friction-related problems for electronic systems.

Following the success of light-based carriers in telecommunications, experiments have begun to use light for computing. In the future, it is expected that powerful computers will operate with beams of light. Light-based components will replace some of the devices that now use electronics. It is hoped that these methods will contribute to continuing increases in performance and reductions in costs for computers.

Satellite communications.   Satellites have become standard vehicles for transmission of broadcast, telephone, and data communications signals. Use of satellites should continue to expand for many years to come.

Review 30.1

1. How does the length of an instruction word handled by a computer affect its productivity?

2. How does a reduced instruction set affect the operation of a computer?

3. What is superconductivity and how does it affect the operation of computing devices?

4. What are the potential advantages of computers that can accept spoken input from people?

HOW WILL TECHNOLOGY CHANGE THE WAY COMPUTERS ARE USED?

For an example of the full impact of computers in the future, think of the automobile. Thirty years after cars were introduced, vehicles themselves still were crude and noisy, at least by today's standards. Roads were rough—and there weren't enough of them. Gradually, the United States became a society on wheels. The automobile shaped society around the freedom of movement that it provided.

In the future, the computer will become more than a toy or a tool. It will become a source of convenience, control, and knowledge that will change the way people think, work, and play. The main impacts of technology that have affected computers since the 1950s should continue into the future:

• Computers will be smaller in size.

• Capabilities will be more powerful.

• Costs will continue to drop in relation to productivity.

Satellite communications *capabilities should increase at a rapid pace in the future. This photo shows a team of scientists and engineers preparing a satellite for launching.*
COURTESY OF TRW, INC.

Aside from the continuation of these established trends, some new developments are anticipated. These are identified and described below.

Computers will become better communication tools. As described above, computing and telecommunications technologies have drawn closer. The two fields have shared a number of breakthroughs. Light-sensitive signaling, mentioned above, is one of these developments. In addition, satellite communication systems have become standard channels for the telecommunications and computing industries. Today, it is possible to use computers as though they were specialized telephones.

One result will be the ability of computers to tie together workstations, processors, and databases throughout an organization. Increasingly, transaction processing operations will have direct impacts on computer files and on exception reporting for management. Rather than having to inquire about status or wait for reports, managers will be advised immediately as problems develop. Also, computers will transmit output signals directly to automatic equipment. This already is being done in automatic

manufacturing operations. In the future, these technologies will increase in capabilities and decrease in cost.

Networking capabilities will grow. The potential value of interactive networks has been obvious for some time. Only costs have blocked widespread use. The cost of communication links to support local and long distance networks was comparatively high for many years. These costs are coming down, thanks largely to the use of computer technology in the communications industry. Also, long-distance telecommunications has become more competitive as a result

Business Terms

superconductivity
A condition in which resistance and heat generation of electrical conductors is virtually eliminated.

laser
A beam of intense light that is transmitted through air or special tubes; lasers can carry sound and digital signals.

of court actions that have eliminated a monopoly in this industry.

The time is approaching when it will be less costly to transmit correspondence over computer networks than to mail a letter. As these developments become realities, computers will become tools for instant communication and information access. Most of the guesswork can be eliminated from management as information access capabilities increase.

HOW WILL COMPUTERS CHANGE THE WORKPLACE?

The computer already has brought great changes to the workplace. Millions of Americans have had to make adjustments. The kinds of work they do and the way in which they work already have changed. As computers gain power, there will be more changes ahead. Some of these trends and expectations are described below.

Electronic mail and voice mail. Communication will be more immediate as computers replace carriers for delivery of imprinted messages. One application that is becoming popular is known as *electronic mail*. This means that a person with a message to deliver can enter it into a computer or terminal. The message can be addressed to one person or to an entire group. A central computer accepts and transmits the messages, which are stored in file devices that serve as "electronic mailboxes." Individuals can enter queries at their terminals that cause mail to be displayed. As necessary, hard copies can be printed for further action.

Voice mail is a similar service, except that it operates through telephones. If a person is away from the office, the telephone can be answered by a computer. The caller can record a message through a digital recording system. The person called can ask for messages. These are read by the computer through high-quality recordings.

Both electronic mail and voice mail permit the person receiving messages to control his or her own time. For example, certain times of the day can be set aside for picking up and answering text or voice messages. However, the immediacy of electronic mail systems can cause pressures. If messages are delivered sooner, executives will expect faster responses.

The point: Workers of the future will have post offices and message services right at their fingertips. Communication will be faster and more efficient.

Groupware. Most middle- and top-level managers spend the majority of their time at meetings. This is costly. Also, as described at the beginning of this chapter, meetings often require out-of-town travel. This can disrupt the plans of individuals.

With groupware, computer storage can replace a meeting room. People can get together at a specific time and share their ideas. Under this plan, the computer is advised of the meeting time and given the names of participants. The computer sends notices to the individuals involved. At the appointed time, all the authorized terminals are linked to the system.

The computer can display topics to be covered and can accept comments or suggestions from multiple stations. A coordinator or facilitator can sort out the inputs quickly and can direct the combined efforts of participants. The results can be more effective than if people are sitting in the same room. For one thing, most of the people at a meeting have to sit quietly and listen most of the time. In an in-person meeting, only one person can contribute at a time. With groupware, everybody can enter suggestions at once. Then, the inputs can be organized and everybody can react at once. Meetings take less time, cost less, and accomplish more.

Decision support and expert systems. The terms *decision support system* and *expert system* describe software tools designed to help managers.

A decision support system enables managers to review databases and to assemble information to support decision making. Management decisions, typically, are aimed at meeting needs or solving problems. To reach decisions, managers begin by

Security *and other government services will benefit increasingly from use of computers. This photo shows a U.S. Customs agent screening arrivals from foreign travel. Computers can assist agents in checking passport validity and tracking activities of travelers.*

COURTESY UNITED STATES CUSTOMS SERVICE

defining their purposes. Then, they identify a series of alternative solutions that might meet the need or solve the problem.

With decision support systems, managers can bring together information that models each alternative solution. The manager assumes that each alternative, in turn, is carried out. The information assembled shows the results for each alternative. The alternative that produces the best potential results becomes the decision choice. DSS software, then, enables managers to carry out advanced "What if...?" simulations.

Expert systems use special software that, in effect, enables a computer to evaluate and recommend alternatives. Expert systems use a technique known as *logic programming.* A user prepares a series of statements that relate conditions and results for decision situations. The user then enters an inquiry that causes the computer to compare a sequence of conditions and results. The computer comes up with an answer that represents a solution to be considered by the human expert.

To illustrate, some of the most dramatic applications of expert systems to date have been for medical diagnosis. A doctor enters a statement that describes patient symptoms. The computer searches

Business Terms

fiber-optic
Description of carriers that transmit communication signals over fine strands of special glass.

electronic mail
A system for delivering message documents over computer networks.

voice mail
A system for storing and delivering spoken telephone messages through use of computers.

decision support system
An application that permits use of database software to help managers evaluate and select decision alternatives.

expert system
A system that uses a computer to imitate human decision making processes to help establish courses of action.

logic programming
The mathematical principles that provide the basis for development of expert system software. The computer matches a set of conditions presented by a user with a series of statements stored in the computer.

a series of information items and tries to match the patient's symptoms with those for a disease or illness. The computer may ask for more information if a possible match is found. After processing, the computer lists possible conditions that the doctor should consider in treating the patient.

In business, expert systems have been used to capture the thought patterns that have been developed by human experts. Applications have included selection of equipment for manufacturing plants and the steps to take in containing oil spills.

Altered work patterns. The times and places where work is done may be changed as a result of computer capabilities. Today, work patterns typically require direct interaction between people. To interact with one another, people have to be in the same places, at the same times. As a result, it is typical for office workers to have to be in the same place, during the same business hours.

In the future, work may be exchanged through computers as well as with other persons. Office workers will gain flexibility. It no longer will be necessary for everyone to be in the same office at the same hours. Another factor will be that skilled workers will be in short supply. It may be easier to hire and hold skilled people if a business can offer some job flexibility. Some alternatives to standard work days already are being considered. These include *flex time, satellite offices,* and offices at home.

Flex time, in effect, allows employees to set their own work hours. People can choose work schedules that avoid traffic. They also can accommodate needs of families. Workers who qualify for flex time typically are able to receive and deliver their assignments through computers. The co-workers who set up and receive the results of their work interact through computers. This approach is being encouraged in large, congested cities where attempts are being made to reduce the rush-hour crush.

Satellite offices are designed to bring work closer to prospective employees. Typically, a company with a downtown headquarters will open a series of small offices in outlying or surburban areas. These are easier to reach for many employees. Also, rents tend to be lower in outlying areas. Both employees and companies benefit from the ability to set up satellite facilities that are linked with headquarters through computer networks.

For some people, computer networks can extend the workplace right into their homes. Usually, this arrangement applies to managers and/or executives with heavy travel schedules. Whenever possible, many of these people prefer to work at home instead of traveling to offices. Home workstations permit them to receive electronic and voice mail. They can respond and generate new instructions to co-workers from home computers. For high-level executives, elimination of commute times can save money and increase efficiency. So far, this arrangement seems best for managers who already have working space at home.

Product development cycles. For manufacturers, new products **are** the company. Products are what customers see in the marketplace. Products are the things for which customers spend money. Many people contribute ideas for and participate in the development of products. In the past, this has meant that many sets of drawings and models had to be developed before a product could go into production. In part, managers were cautious because a large investment was needed to prepare tooling and begin production. These requirements, in turn, meant that product development took a long time.

It used to require an average of seven years of lead time to introduce a new automobile. Today, the process can be completed in two years. In the future, the cycle may be shortened even further. The difference lies in the fact that computers can be used to develop pictures of new products. Computers also can perform calculations that serve to test new products before they are built. When designs are complete, computers can drive machines that build the products. The "electronic tooling" capabilities of computers save considerable amounts of time and expense.

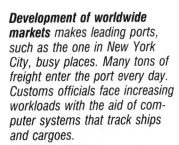

Development of worldwide markets makes leading ports, such as the one in New York City, busy places. Many tons of freight enter the port every day. Customs officials face increasing workloads with the aid of computer systems that track ships and cargoes.

COURTESY UNITED STATES CUSTOMS SERVICE

Consumers benefit because they have more choices and better prices. Manufacturers benefit because the cost and time required to bring a product to market have been reduced.

Worldwide markets.   Advances in transportation and distribution have served to expand markets beyond individual countries. Today, it is possible to think of the whole world as a single marketplace. Worldwide production and distribution have increased competition and lowered the prices of products and services. International markets are supported by worldwide computer communication networks.

Ownership of businesses also has crossed national boundaries. Some people are concerned about loss of control over part of their country's economy. This is a real concern that should be monitored. On the other hand, there appear to be benefits as well. Lower prices and improved quality through competition are among the benefits. In addition, cross-boundary business activities can help to promote world peace. The idea: People with business interests in another country will not be anxious to destroy their assets in a war.

Organizations and jobs.   According to experts, you are now living in an "information society." This is an environment in which most workers rely on information to perform their jobs. Also, information has come to be considered as a necessary ingredient within the lifestyles of average citizens.

The impact on business of massive information systems already has been dramatic. Businesses used to be organized in multiple levels of management. The main responsibilities of people positioned between operational workers and top managers was the handling and organizing of information. As the accumulation and organization of information has been

Business Terms
flex time
A plan that enables employees to vary work hours and schedules.
satellite office
An outlying office that is closer than downtown facilities to the homes of many workers; set up to shorten commute times and locate offices in areas with lower rents.

taken over by computers, many middle-level jobs have been eliminated. Observers refer to this development as a "flattening" of organization charts. That is, organization charts show fewer levels of authority between operating and top management levels.

As a result, many people have found the nature of their work changing. People who formerly occupied administrative, or "staff," jobs have been moved into other positions. Growing organizations have needed their help in positions involving direct service to customers in growing markets. Though jobs have been eliminated, there continues to be a shortage of people qualified to hold administrative or management positions.

Review 30.2

1. What is flex time, how does it work, and what are its potential advantages?

2. What is electronic mail, how does it work, and what are its potential advantages?

3. How do computers help to shorten product development times?

4. Why are businesses "flattening" their organization charts as a result of computer applications?

WHAT COMPUTER-RELATED ISSUES CAN AFFECT YOUR WORK AND YOUR FUTURE?

The computer, to put it mildly, has had a major impact on society and on the workplace. Inevitably, some questions or conflicts have developed in key areas. Some of the issues that might affect your own future as a worker include:

- Privacy
- Security
- Copyright.

What Do You Need to Know About Information Privacy?

Every citizen has a right to privacy. This is assured by the Fourth Amendment in the Bill of Rights that is part of the Constitution of the United States. Your rights include protection against misuse or illegal use of private information about you.

The potential problem: From the time you are born, computers gather and store information about you. Some of this information is routinely available for public reference. For example the record of your birth is part of open public documentation. The same is true if you buy a car or a house. These are public records.

However, some of the data items about you that have found their way into computers may be private. These items may relate to your experiences in school, at work, or as a borrower. Information about your health also may be involved.

Both you and the professionals who design and operate computers have responsibilities related to your rights of privacy. Computer systems must be designed so that private information is delivered to authorized persons only. DBMS software has been designed to apply this level of protection. Codes within database index files identify authorized information users. The computer should be programmed to permit information access by authorized people only.

You have the authority to permit access to information about you. This is a responsibility about which you should be aware. You should know when you are assigning the right to access information about you. And you should know who has this right. The most usual way of permitting access to information about you is to sign a permission document. Example: When you apply for a loan, the application you sign gives the lender the right to conduct credit checks about you. This means the lender can seek information from credit reporting and other organizations about your status. When you apply for a job, some employers ask for permission to check your

Data in vast amounts *is collected in on-line computer files. On one hand, disk storage has made data files and records more accessible to users. On the other hand, the ability to store and use data presents challenges. An important challenge lies in protecting the rights of privacy for people about whom personal information is accumulated on computers.*

COURTESY OF COMPUTER SCIENCES CORPORATION

work history. Your job application may assign these rights. Your educational history normally will have to be provided to any college to which you apply.

The other major reason for permitting access to private information occurs in cases involving safety or health. For example, if you are in an accident, the people treating you have a need to know about your blood type and any allergies you may have. If you commit a crime, law enforcement officers have a right to information on your background.

If your rights are violated, you have a right to protection through law enforcement agencies and the courts. That is, if anyone gives out information without your authorization, this is an illegal act. You have both rights and responsibilities for management of information about you. When you give away some of these rights, you should be aware of the consequences.

What Do You Need to Know About Information Security?

As an information user or as a future computer professional, you should be aware of the need to pro-

tect information resources. Two general types of security measures apply to information in computer files:

- Physical security
- Access controls.

Physical security. A computer center, including all its equipment and storage media, must be protected against loss. Loss can be accidental or purposeful. For example, computer centers sometimes are damaged or destroyed by flood, fire, earthquake, or tornado. Protection against this kind of loss is provided through *recovery* and *restart* programs.

Business Terms
recovery
Reference to a plan for protecting information resources for use in restoring service if a computer center or its files are destroyed.
restart
A set of procedures used to restore services of a computer center following an interruption.

Protection for information resources *is a major concern in companies that depend upon computer systems. The large bank in which this photo was taken protects information resources by providing a large, fireproof vault for storage of vital media.*

PHOTO BY LIANE ENKELIS

As part of a recovery program, copies of data media are stored at a location that is distant from the computer center. Special storage facilities are available from commercial companies. Backup copies are files sent to these facilities on a regular basis. If the original files are destroyed, the backups are used to create new working files.

Restart programs are sets of procedures that are followed to restore service if a computer center has been damaged or destroyed. Companies usually make arrangements to rent computer time from other organizations. These backup computers are used with the backup files to restore service.

Another aspect of physical security includes locked doors that permit only authorized people into computer centers. Within the computer center itself, fire alarms and controls over the use of media should be enforced strictly.

Access controls.   Access controls include measures that restrict unauthorized users from receiving information. As described above, part of this need relates to the privacy of individuals. In addition, information on company operations can be the basis for crimes that involve thefts of money or property.

Access controls include restrictions of user access to certain terminals. Sometimes, user terminals have key-operated locks that can restrict access to information.

Software controls can be applied through use of password systems. Users receive entry codes that are processed through an index that identifies their rights of information access. Users are responsible for protecting the secrecy of these codes. Also, confidential information should be used only when it is necessary to do this as part of job responsibilities.

What Do You Need to Know About Copyright Protection?

A *copyright* is a right assigned by the U. S. Copyright Office. A copyright protects its owner against copying, duplication, or sale of protected products. Most publications—such as newspapers, magazines, and your schoolbooks—are covered by copyright protection. So are most of the software packages that you may use in your computer lab or work assignments.

Except under specific circumstances and for special purposes, it is illegal to make copies of copyrighted materials, even for your personal use. The reason: The people who own the copyright usually are in business to sell the materials involved. Illegal copying takes away the income of companies that have created publications or software.

It may seem natural to make a xerographic copy from a book or to copy a diskette with software you would like to own. You should be aware that such actions are crimes and are subject to punishments that can be serious. Computers are valuable assets to their users and to society as a whole. These assets should be protected to assure that full benefits are realized from these valuable tools.

The future of computers promises to create a workplace with increasing numbers of challenges, opportunities, and responsibilities. For workers who are prepared to accept and meet these challenges, satisfying and rewarding jobs can be expected.

Review 30.3

1. Under what conditions can information about you be released without your permission?
2. What is a recovery program for information resources?
3. What is a restart program for a computer center?
4. What is a copyright and what does it mean to you?

Business Terms

copyright
A protection assigned to an idea or created product by the U. S. government. Copyrighted materials cannot be copied without permission from the copyright owner.

Chapter Summary

❑ The computing and telecommunications industries are merging their development through use of the same technologies, which are based on digital signaling.

❑ One technological development that is forecast for the computer/communications field is smaller, more powerful microelectronics devices. Microchips of the near future are expected to deliver four or eight megabytes of memory capability. Processors with 32-bit word lengths are already in production. Units that handle 64-bit words are expected soon.

❑ Special-purpose computers are expected to play increasing roles. Included are special database processors and reduced instruction set computers (RISCs).

❑ Increased productivity for computers is expected to come through designs that use parallel processors, rather than a single processor for each computer.

❑ A major new application probably will make it possible for computers to understand and to generate text from spoken input, and also to generate spoken outputs.

❑ Superconductors are expected in the near future. These carriers will reduce the friction that comes from electron flow. The results should be faster devices that give off less heat.

❑ Increased use of light-based techniques is expected. At present, growing use is being made of laser and fiber-optics technologies. In the future, actual computing may be done with light-sensitive devices.

❏ Use of satellites for communication should continue to expand.

❏ As new technologies are adopted, computers can be expected to become smaller, more powerful, and less costly in comparison with performances available.

❏ In particular, computers will contribute to improved communication through such developments as networks, electronic mail, voice mail, electronic meetings, decision support systems, and expert systems.

❏ Computers also may alter work patterns. Developments that are being discussed include flex time, satellite offices, and offices at home.

❏ Product development times will be shortened through use of computer capabilities.

❏ Computers will play a role in the building and operation of a marketplace that expands and becomes worldwide in scope.

❏ Business organization structures will become smaller as computers take over information handling tasks that used to be done by middle managers.

❏ You have rights to privacy of personal information. These rights extend to information stored in computers. In the normal course of your activities, you will be asked to give up this right in specific situations. You should be aware of the consequences of your actions. Also, if information about you is released without your permission, a crime has been committed against you.

❏ Computer professionals are responsible for both physical and access security measures. These responsibilities extend to the computer facility, its equipment, and its information resources.

❏ Most of the published materials and software diskettes you handle are protected by copyright laws. Copying these materials, even for personal use, may be a crime.

Definitions

Write a complete sentence that defines each of the terms below.

groupware	RISC
parallel processor	superconductor
electronic mail	voice mail
decision support system	flex time
recovery	copyright

Questions to Think About

Based on what you have learned to date, answer the following questions in one or more complete sentences.

1. What is an electronic meeting and what purpose does it serve?

2. What is groupware and how is it used?

3. What technological developments have brought the telecommunications and computer industries closer together?

4. What is a RISC and what does it do?

5. What is parallel processing and what are its potential advantages?

6. What are voice recognition systems and what are they expected to do for business?

7. How is use of light-sensitive devices expected to impact future computers?

8. What is electronic mail and what benefits are expected from its use?

9. What is a decision support system and how is it used?

10. What is an expert system and what benefits are expected from this new software?

Projects

The purpose of the assignments below is to encourage you to increase your learning through outside reading or work assignments.

1. One of the developments predicted for the computer industry is the so-called ''laptop'' computer. This is a full-capacity microcomputer in a package that weighs perhaps 10 or 12 pounds. The computer is contained in a small case and can be battery-operated. Laptop computers can be used on airplanes, at home, or in hotel rooms. Find one or more articles on laptop computers. Report on the value of these computers and the applications they are expected to handle. Prepare a prediction on what impact you feel laptop computers will have in the future.

2. Read at least one article on computer-integrated manufacturing or robotics. Prepare to report on why many people who work in factories now are called ''information workers.''

A Short Course in Keyboarding

INTRODUCTION

The lessons in this section are designed to help you learn to operate the keyboard of a microcomputer. Keyboarding skill has become a requirement for most jobs—whether they be in manufacturing, service, or government organizations. Anyone going on to college will certainly find that keyboarding is a valuable skill.

You will learn the "touch method" for keyboarding. This means you should be able to make keyboard entries without looking at the keys. This skill is built through practice. So, you will need to repeat each lesson several times. Then, to develop proficiency—speed and accuracy—you will have to continue practicing after you have completed all the lessons.

Before you begin, you should become acquainted with the microcomputer you are going to use. If possible, look at the manual for the equipment. The microcomputer should be turned on and set up for keyboarding with a word processing program. It should also be set for a 60-character line width. You may do this yourself or the microcromputer may be set up and ready for you to begin work. Follow whatever instructions you are given for getting started.

Look at the diagram and place your fingers on the keys as shown. The fingers of your left hand should be on **a s d f**. The fingers of your right hand should be on **j k l ;**. This is the **HOME** position for your fingers. Notice that your right thumb should be on the long **SPACE** bar.

When you use a microcomputer, you do not need to press down or hit the keys with any force. Just tap or touch the keys lightly and quickly and the letters will appear on your screen. With your fingers on the **HOME** keys, as shown in the diagram, tap each letter lightly to make it appear on the screen. This will give you a feel for your particular keyboard. As you key, or enter, each letter, you will notice a blinking line or marker where your next letter is to appear. This marker is called the "cursor" and indicates where your entries will appear on the screen. It also helps you to know where you are in text you have entered and may be correcting or changing.

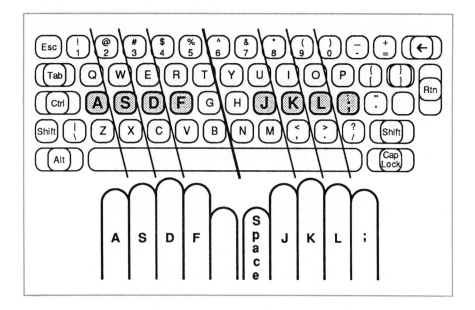

When you get to the end of a line of text in an exercise, your micro-computer will automatically move your next entry to the next line. This is called "word wrap." You do not do anything to make this happen. The word wrap feature helps to add speed to keyboarding skills. You need to tap the RETURN key only when you are entering a space between lines or paragraphs.

You are now ready to start your first keyboarding lesson. In preparation, ask for instruction on how to clear your microcomputer screen. The idea is to erase any practice keystrokes you have entered. Once the screen is clear, move on to Lesson 1.

Lesson 1

Be sure you are sitting comfortably and your fingers are on the **HOME** keys as shown in the diagram. Try not to look at the keyboard as you type. Wherever there is a space between letters or words, you are to tap the space bar with your thumb.

Do the exercise at least three times. Do not rush the first time. Try to be as accurate as possible. You are learning the keys. Gradually, your fingers will automatically tap the correct keys. Start slowly, concentrating on the correct keystrokes. Try to increase your speed a bit each time you repeat the exercise, but not so much that you make errors. If possible, repeat the exercise until you can do it without errors and without glancing at the keyboard.

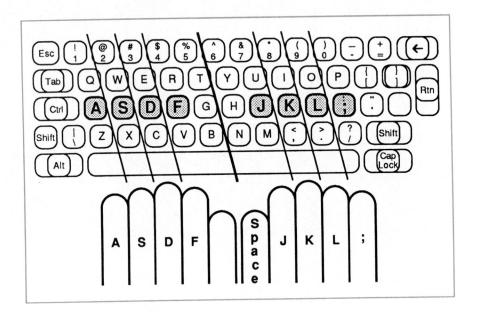

```
a a s as sa a s d asd dsa a s d f asdf fdsa ad af fa da dads
sad sass ad fad fads add adds sad fad sad dad adds fads sass
j j k jk kj j k l jkl lkj j k l ; jkl; ;lkj jl j; ;j k; ;k ;
ja aj ka ak la all lad lass ask flask lads ja fad lads flask
dad adds all fads; lad asks lass; jak falls; lass asks lads;
dad dads sad lad fall falls jak jaks ask flask aj adds sass;
ad sal salad fad fads all fall falls ask flask ja jak flask;
all sal salad fall falls sass; as a lad asks lass; jak falls
sal adds a salad; a lass asks dad; jak asks dad; adds a lass
all dads fall; as a fad; lass adds a salad; lass asks a dad;
```

Lesson 2

In this exercise:

- Reach with the first finger of your left hand to the **g**.
- With the first finger of your right hand, reach the **h**.
- Reach up to the **e** with the second finger of your left hand.
- Use the second finger of your right hand to reach up to the **i**.

After each reach, bring your fingers back quickly to the **HOME** keys. Do this exercise at least three times.

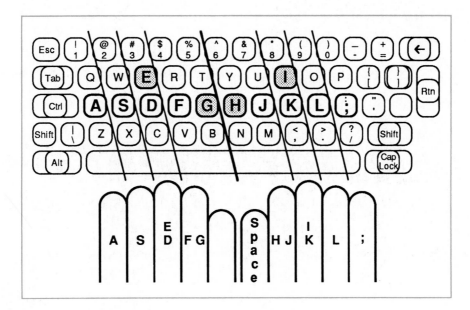

```
asdf f g gf gfdsa asdfg gas sag ;lkj j h hj hjkl; ;lkjh hall
lass glass lad glad gas gall hall shall ash sash flash gash;
alf half gaff hag gag had; jak had half a glass; gags salads
asd d e de ed deed see seed fee feed egg eel heel heed heeds
jell jade jake keel led lead head lease egg geese leak flake
edge hedge ledge sledge age self flesh hash dash shell shelf
;lk k i ki ik kiss kid did skid disk aids said is sis if fig
gig ill kill sill dill fill gill jill hill ail fail jail hid
hide side lied died dial deal seal heal lid glide slide hail
feel file isle aisle leg gale jigs siege kisses hisses flies
```

Lesson 3

In this exercise:

- Reach up with the first finger of your left hand to the **r**.

- Reach up with the third fingers of your left hand to the **w**.

- Use the third finger of your right hand to reach up to the **o**.

Remember, after each reach you should bring your fingers back quickly to the **HOME** keys. Do this exercise at least three times.

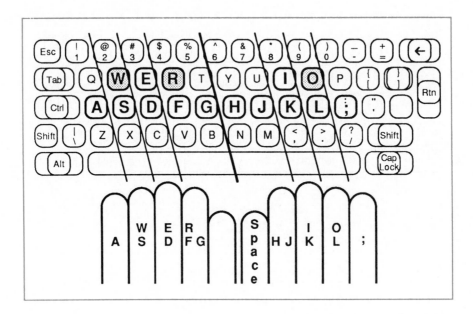

```
as sass sad fad fade gas has jade ask lad lid lied slide if;
life isle aisle jail glide glides kids dish dishes fishes is
as s w wa sw swiss wisk swill will wisk wiles while wide wig
was wag wall wage we well weeks wed weak jaw saw law dew few
asdf f r fr rf rid risk ride rile rise rifle rag ark lark re
reel reed reef err her here dead deer dear ear rear fear are
raw wiggle wriggle weak wreak freak was where were wear fire
jkl l o lo ol old loss load loaf lode log low door wore sore
how jog hog hook shook look or for floor fool shore oar soar
owe lower shower lord ford word sword doer fewer oil soil of
```

Lesson 4

In this exercise:

- Reach up with the first finger of your right hand to the **u**.
- Reach up with the fourth (little) finger of your left hand to the **q**.
- Reach up with the fourth (little) finger of your right hand to the **p**.

Remember, after each reach you should bring your fingers back quickly to the **HOME** keys. Do this exercise at least three times.

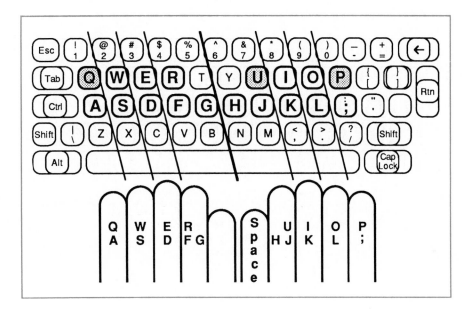

as sad fads fade feed see sees ease seal lease eel keel eke;
sake lake jade jaw jewel jerk her here hair rare gas lag leg
age edge girl swirl wag wiggle were where ware wade wail wig
so do does foes doll foil soil hole golf joke woke soak oars
;lkj j u ju uj judge judges grudges suds duds rude full gull
dull hull skulls sulk hulk rough dough fluff world hurl dues
fdsa a q aq qu aqu aqua aquire quaffs queer quell squ squeal
square squawk squeak squashed squish squid squirrel required
jkl; ; p pa pap paper pass pad page gape leap peal keep peek
poke spoke spook pier pike pill pile wrap equip ripe sleeps;

Lesson 5

In this exercise:

- Reach up to the right with the first finger of your left hand to the **t**.
- Reach up to the left with the first finger of your right hand to the **y**.
- With the fourth (little) finger of your left hand, reach down to the **z**.

Remember, after each reach you should bring your fingers back quickly to the **HOME** keys. Do this exercise at least three times.

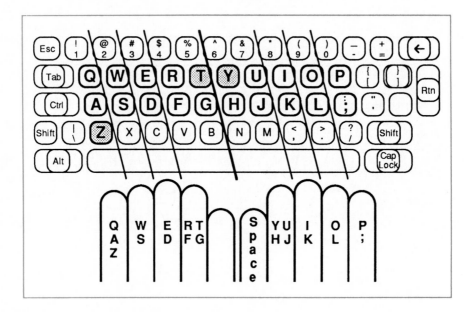

```
proud people applauded; queer squashed squids; while we walk
would we wiggle; girls giggle; we are sure of all our grades
asdf f r f t ft tf to too tool toot top pot toll lot jot tot
rot tore togs tall tag trip true tree tee teepee tea teak at
the there their frill thrill free tree three two twill twist
;lkj j u j y jy yj jet yet jar year yard say day ray way pay
gray trays hay they jay lay play fully joyful joyfully truly
fdsa a z az za zap zoo zip zipper zig zigzag zero zest zippy
lazy people prefer soft sofas; fresh as a daisy; tough quiz;
quiet for the hospital; the prize was a surprise; try harder
```

Lesson 6

In this exercise:

- Reach down to the right with the second finger of your left hand to the **c**.
- Reach down with the first finger of your right hand slightly to the left for the **n**.
- Reach down with the first finger of your right hand slightly to the right for the **m**.

Remember, after each reach you should bring your fingers back quickly to the **HOME** keys. Do this exercise at least three times.

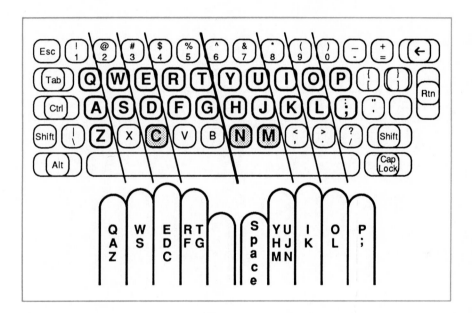

```
proud papas speak highly of their kids; they applaud loudly;
they sat quietly while we rehearsed; do they always eat here
just zip it up for her; we thought; your father told us that
asd d c dc cd dull cull luck pluck plucky cop copy luck lick
flick flicker cook cool cup coy cut cot tea teach reach each
cat cash case cast car cargo carry caw jack lack act factual
;lkj j m jm mj jar mar jam ram cram teem team cream merge me
map mark madly mask masque fame family jump grime crime time
;lkj j m j n jn mn nj me men mend mean ma nag nasty near nor
more snore snuff nip snip normal north land handle candle no
```

Lesson 7

In this exercise:

- Reach down to the right with the third finger of your left hand to the **x**.

- Reach down with the first finger of your left hand slightly to the right for the **v**.

- Also with the first finger of your left hand, reach down and further to the right for the **b**.

Remember, after each reach you should bring your fingers back quickly to the **HOME** keys. Do this exercise at least three times.

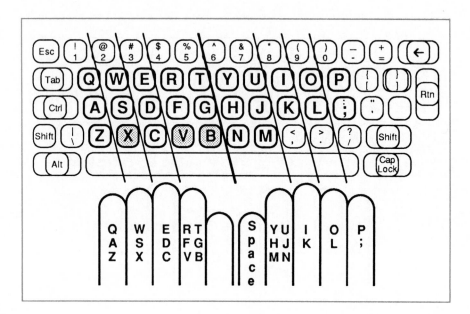

```
the hungry children ran quickly home across the empty fields
where were you when they needed you; men and women came here
sincerely yours; cordially yours; remember me to your family
as s x sx xs as sax sex exhale exhaust exit exam examination
asdf f v fv vf for void off offer over oven love clover cove
cover civic life live livid vivid rivers drivers strive jive
asdf f fv f b fv vb fb bv bf full bull fill bill fox vox box
boil burn burning by buy boy bring brought bad baskets brisk
back backwards bisquit buzzing bump thumb tremble thimble my
read ancient myths; buzzing bees; blueberry pie and icecream
```

Lesson 8

Congratulations! You have learned all of the letters and should be able to key them without having to look at the keyboard. You now need to learn how to capitalize the letters and add some punctuation.

To capitalize a letter, you use the shift keys. There are two shift keys—one on each side of the keyboard. Look at the diagram above and note where they are located. Now, find the shift keys on your keyboard. To capitalize a letter, you need to hold the opposite shift key down with the fourth (little) finger of the other hand. For example, to capitalize **j**, press down on the shift key with the fourth finger of your left hand. This will produce **J**. Remember, however, to keep your other fingers on their **HOME** keys.

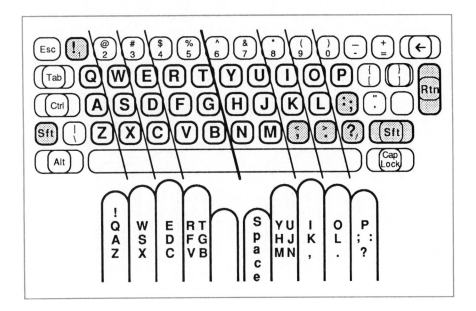

Look at the diagram. Now, find the punctuation marks on your keyboard. The colon (:) is produced by using the shift key with the semicolon (;). For the period (.) and the comma (,), reach down from the **l** and **k** keys without shifting. For the question mark (?), you need to shift as you reach down from the **;** key. The exclamation point (!) requires a long reach with your left fourth finger while holding the shift key with your right little finger. Practice these marks until you feel confident you know where they are without looking at your keyboard. Proficiency comes with practice.

Do the following exercise at least three times. Notice where there are two spaces after periods, question marks, and exclamation points. Note, also, that you are to add a line space after both the first and second group of five lines. You will need to tap the return key twice: once for the end of the paragraph, and once for the space between the groups or paragraphs.

You will notice that the last group of entries—one sentence—contains all of the letters of the alphabet. This one sentence can be used as an easy drill to help you develop accuracy. Repeat it until you can key the entire sentence quickly without errors. Then use the sentence as a warm-up exercise as you practice to gain keyboard proficiency.

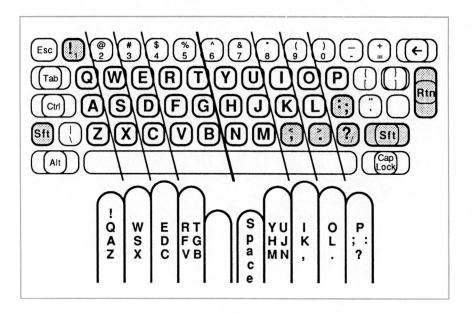

all Alan bet Betty car Carl dell Della edge Edward free Fred
gray Grace help Helen iron Irene janitor Janice keen Kenneth
laud Laurence man Manny nice Nicholas old Oliver pat Patrick
quinine Quincy rob Roberta step Stephanie the Thelma use Una
vivid Vivian wends Wendy exact Xavier yet Yetta zany Zachary

l . l. k , k, ; : ? ! ., ;:?! !,.?:; Run! Why? Wow! When?
His name is Fritz. Stanley and Beverly live in Alabama now.
May I go with you to the zoo? When will you finish the job?
Stop! Fire! Walk! Hurry up! Is he crazy about the candy?
Congratulations! You can now type sentences and paragraphs.

The quick brown fox jumped over the lazy sleeping dog.

Lesson 9

This exercise will give you practice in keying sentences and paragraphs. At this point you should know your keyboard. You should not have to look at the keys to enter letters or characters. The rest is up to you. Do the following exercise at least three times.

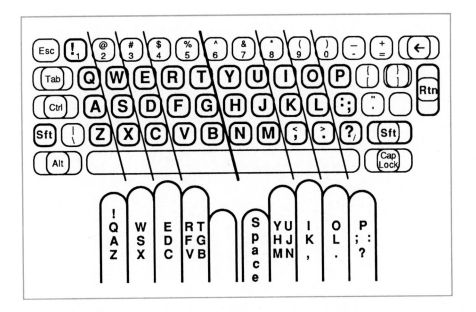

You should always sit in a comfortable position whenever you are working at a microcomputer. Where should you place the material you are copying? You should place it where you can see it easily. A copy stand can be helpful. You can adjust it quite quickly. It will hold standard size papers. Have you ever used a copy stand? Make sure you have good light.

You now know how to key, or enter, text on a microcomputer. You are on your way to becoming a word processor. You will gradually build up your speed and accuracy. You also will need to learn about your microcomputer and about the word processing program you are using. As a word processor, you will have to insert or delete words in text already entered. This means knowing how to use the various function keys.

Lesson 10

This exercise is intended only to acquaint you with the number keys in the top row of the keyboard. To gain proficiency, you will need to practice these keystrokes on your own. Locate the keys on the diagram and note the fingers that are to be used for each number. Then, find the numbers on your keyboard. Reach for each key with the correct finger, one at a time. Remember, always bring your fingers back to the **HOME** keys.

Do each section of this exercise at least three times; then do the entire exercise three times. Remember to leave an extra space between sections.

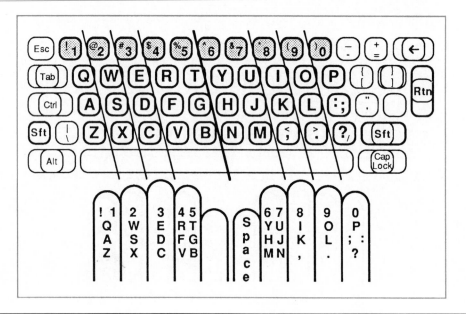

```
al s2 d3 f4 f5 r5 r4 e3 w2 q1 j6 j7 k8 19 ;0 p0 o9 i8 u7 u6
13 24 56 57 79 80 09 98 87 76 54 43 53 32 31 14 15 07 60 96
769; 897; 906; 806; 541; 314; 10:29 12:45 11:52 12:38 10:56

Azuza, California; Bethlehem, Pennsylvania; Canton, Ohio;
Denver, Colorado; Eaton, New Jersey; Fort Wright, Kentucky;

General Ulysses S. Grant was President of the United States
from 1869 to 1877.  He was a general in the Union Army when
Abraham Lincoln was President.  Did you study the Civil War
in school?  General Robert E. Lee led the Confederate Army.
The Civil War ended when General Lee surrendered to General
Grant at Appomattox Courthouse, Virginia, in the year 1865.
Every U. S. citizen should be acquainted with this history.
```

When you have completed this lesson, you will see that there are still characters that have not been covered. Only the basic keyboard characters are covered in these lessons. It is necessary to develop accuracy and speed in keying these characters first. Then, on your own you can increase your skills by learning and practicing the reaches for other characters.

Using Microcomputer Software

THE ROLE OF SOFTWARE IN BUSINESS

Many businesspeople purchase and use professional application programs to perform routine business jobs. These programs, called *software packages,* or *application software,* are written by professional programmers. The applications are designed to meet common needs shared by many businesses.

This textbook explains that application software packages are used widely in three areas of business:

- Word processing
- Database management
- Spreadsheet processing.

YOUR LEARNING OPPORTUNITIES

The exercises that follow can aid you in developing skills with these three types of software packages. For each exercise, explanations are given for use on two alternative systems. One is for an IBM-PC and compatibles package called STARTware. The second is for AppleWorks software that runs on Apple II series computers.

If you are using an IBM or compatible computer, begin each lesson at the STARTware PROCE-DURES heading. If you are using an Apple II series computer, begin each lesson at the AppleWorks PROCEDURES heading.

Organization of Lessons

The first lesson introduces you to the *operating system* for your computer. The operating system, recall, directs the operations of hardware devices as well as application programs. You should understand a few features of your operating system before you begin to work with professional applications.

Three lessons each are provided for word processing, database management, and spreadsheet processing. These exercises allow you to create and modify the types of files that businesspeople use frequently.

Finally, two lessons are included to demonstrate the *integrated software* features of some professional application packages. An integrated software package combines the capabilities of two or more different types of application packages, such as word processing and spreadsheet applications. In fact, you will be given an opportunity to learn how to integrate, or combine, a spreadsheet within an existing document created with a word processing program. Both STARTware and Appleworks are integrated packages that combine word processing, spreadsheet, and database management capabilities within a single system.

Lesson 1

Using an Operating System

INTRODUCTION

This lesson introduces you to the operating system of your computer. You use the operating system to view the content of a disk, to make backup copies of files, and to perform other file handling operations.

STARTware PROCEDURES

The STARTware software package is designed for use on IBM personal computers or *compatibles.* An "IBM-compatible" is simply a computer that can run programs designed for IBM units.

IBM personal computers use an operating system called PC-DOS (for Personal Computer-Disk Operating System). Virtually all IBM-compatible computers use an operating system called MS-DOS. The "MS" portion of the label stands for MicroSoft, the company that designed and sells this operating system. In other words, MS-DOS stands for Micro-Soft-Disk Operating System. PC-DOS and MS-DOS are virtually identical, and have identical command structures and features. For this reason, these lessons refer to the operating system simply as "DOS."

Lesson 1 guides you through the use of the date, time, and DIR entries available with DOS. For this lesson, you will need a DOS disk and a STARTware disk. *Read each step carefully before you begin following the instructions described in the step.*

1. Place your DOS disk in the floppy disk drive of your computer system. If your system has two floppy disk drives, place the disk in either the top slot or the left-hand slot. This is known as Drive A. The second slot is for Drive B. To insert the disk correctly, the label on the disk should be facing up and should be closest to you, rather than to the computer. Close the drive door handle to activate the read/write heads of the disk drive.

2. Turn on the power switch to your computer. If your computer system includes a separate switch for your screen, or monitor, turn this switch on also.

3. After about 20 to 30 seconds, your computer should display this *prompt,* or request for additional instruction. (The prompt displayed on your screen should be similar, although not identical to the one below):

Current date is Tue 1-01-90

Enter new date

The operating system is asking you to enter a date that can be used to track information about files that you create and use during your session. Enter today's date, with month first, day second, and year third. Separate each part of the date with a hyphen character (-). Use the backspace key (shown on your keyboard with a left-pointing arrow) to back up if you need to correct mistakes. When you are finished, press the RETURN key.

4. Your computer now should prompt you for the current time:

Current time is 4:12:40.40

Enter new time

You can enter time specifications to within one one-hundredth of a second of accuracy. Such accuracy can be useful to programmers and scientists. However, you will only need to enter a time accurate to within the current minute. Enter the current time by entering the hour first, then a colon (:), followed by the minute. For instance, if it is currently half-past nine o'clock, enter the following:

9:30

Press the RETURN key when you are finished.

5. The operating system now should display the following prompt:

A >

The letter "A" tells you that the operating system will look for data and programs on the A disk drive. The " > " sign is called a *prompt symbol.* Whenever you see this symbol preceded by a letter (such as A, B, or C), you are working directly with your computer's operating system. By contrast, other prompts that you will use control functions of application programs, rather than operating system functions.

At this point, enter the following command:

DIR

Now press the RETURN key on your computer and watch the screen. (NOTE: Your computer keyboard might show a key that says ENTER or simply contains an arrow with a stem on the right side. This key is the same as the RETURN key on other computer keyboards.)

6. The command you have entered, DIR, stands for DIRectory. A *directory,* in this case, is a listing of the contents of a disk. A separate row of information is provided for each file stored on the disk. Your DOS disk directory should look something like the accompanying illustration.

```
COMMAND  COM   26896   4-07-86    2:18p
CONFIG   SYS      39    1-01-80   12:07a
CONFIG   BAT      13    1-23-86    1:04p
ANSI     SYS    1852    3-25-86   11:40p
ASSIGN   COM    1509    3-25-86   10:37p
ATTRIB   EXE    7438    3-25-86   10:38p
BACKUP   EXE   21720    4-21-86    4:43p
CHKDSK   EXE    9296    3-25-86   11:00p
COMP     COM    2371    3-25-86   11:41p
DEBUG    EXE   15397    3-25-86   11:17p
DISKCOMP COM    2352    3-25-86   11:43p
DISKCOPY EXE   14336    6-19-86    4:13p
EDLIN    EXE    7122    3-25-86   11:29p
FDISK    COM    8025    5-27-86    3:10p
FIND     EXE    6403    3-25-86   11:36p
FORMAT   EXE   19968    6-03-86    4:06p
Strike a key when ready . . .
```

The DOS directory. *Individual disks may list different program modules.*

You can see that five columns are listed. The first, left-most column is the name of each file stored on the DOS disk. The second column is the *file extension.* This three-letter code indicates the basic use for the file. For instance, COMMAND.COM tells you that the COMMAND file has a COM extension. This indicates that the file contains commands that can be executed as program instructions.

Another example: The ANSI.SYS file indicates that the file, ANSI, is used exclusively by the operating system for internal file management purposes. Other commonly used extensions include BAS (for BASIC program), TXT (for text file or word processing file), and PRG (for application program file).

The third column lists the number of bytes, or characters, that are required to store the file on the disk and in main memory.

The fourth column shows the date on which the file was either created or last altered. In turn, the fifth, right-most, column shows the time at which the file was created or last altered. These entries can be important in tracking creation and updating information about files used by application programs.

7. You now have completed Lesson 1. Remove the DOS disk from the disk drive and return it to its protective sleeve. Turn off your computer system and wait for further instructions from your teacher.

AppleWorks PROCEDURES

The AppleWorks software package is published and sold by a company called Claris Corporation. AppleWorks is designed for use on Apple II computers. Apple II computers contain a basic operating system called AppleSoft, which is stored on firmware. In other words, AppleSoft is part of the hardware of your computer.

To run many application programs, AppleSoft needs to be linked with a more powerful *disk operating system (DOS).* This term simply means that the operating system is stored on a floppy disk and must be loaded into main memory after the computer has been turned on.

The AppleWorks software package uses a disk operating system called ProDOS. The ProDOS programs that you must use with AppleWorks are loaded into memory when you use the AppleWorks startup disk.

Lesson 1 guides you through the procedures you will follow each time you start the AppleWorks program. You also will learn how to use the ProDOS LIST function (available within AppleWorks) to view the files stored on a disk. For this and later lessons, you will need two disks:

* The AppleWorks startup disk
* The AppleWorks program disk.

The steps to follow for Lesson 1 are provided below. *Be sure to read each step carefully before you begin following the instructions described in the step.*

1. Place your AppleWorks startup disk in the floppy disk drive of your computer system. If your system has two floppy disk drives, place the disk in the drive marked drive 1. (If you are not sure which drive is drive 1, ask your teacher for assistance.) To insert the disk correctly, the label on the disk should be facing up and should be closest to you, rather than to the computer. Close the drive door handle to activate the read/write heads of the disk drive.

2. Turn on the computer's power switch. If your computer system includes a separate switch for your screen, or monitor, turn this switch on.

3. After about 20 to 30 seconds, your computer loads the ProDOS programs it will need to run AppleWorks. After the computer has finished reading the startup disk, it will display a copyright screen briefly. Then a title screen will appear. At the bottom of this screen, a prompt asks you to insert the AppleWorks disk (the program disk).

When you see this prompt, open the disk drive door and remove the startup disk. Return the startup disk to its protective sleeve. Then, insert the AppleWorks disk in drive 1 and close the drive door. Press the RETURN key to continue.

4. The operating system next will ask you to enter a date. This date can be used to track information about files that you create and use. Enter today's date, with month first, day second, and year third. Separate each part of the date with a slash character. For instance, if the date is January 8, 1989, enter:

01/08/89

Use the backspace key (shown on your keyboard with a left-pointing arrow) to back up if you need to correct mistakes. When you are finished, press the RETURN key. The AppleWorks main menu now should appear on your screen.

5. The main menu that you now should see on your screen is the starting point for using any of AppleWorks' application programs and other features. At this point, it is a good idea to understand the technique used to view information about all files stored on a disk. To view file names and other information, begin by selecting option 5, "Other Activities," from the main menu.

AppleWorks now provides a menu of options that allow you to use ProDOS to manipulate files in a number of ways. In this case, you want to list the names of files stored on the disk drive currently in use (drive 1).

6. So, enter a 2 to select Option 2, then press RETURN twice. Your computer now displays a list of all files stored on the startup disk in drive 1. Take a few moments to study this list.

You can see that five columns are listed. The first, left-most column is the name of each file stored on the AppleWorks disk. The second column shows the type of file for each file name. In this case, most—if not all—files on your AppleWorks disks should be program files.

The third column provides the number of bytes, or characters, that are required to store the file on the disk and in main memory. This number is rounded to the nearest thousand. For instance, a program file that takes up to 4,076 characters of memory will have a size of 4K. The *K* stands for *kilobytes,* or one thousand characters.

The fourth column shows the date on which the file was either created or last altered. In turn, the fifth, right-most column shows the time at which the file was created or last altered. You will see entries for this column only if your Apple computer contains an internal clock.

7. You now have completed Lesson 1. Remove the AppleWorks disk from the disk drive and return it to its protective sleeve. Turn off your computer system and wait for further instructions from your teacher.

Lesson 2

Using a Word Processor: Creating a Text File

INTRODUCTION

For this lesson, you will create a brief file of text. This lesson provides an opportunity for you to learn about keys for *navigating,* or moving through, a text document. You also will gain practice in using a computer keyboard to enter text.

STARTware PROCEDURES

1. Your computer system should be turned off when you begin this lesson. With your system turned off, insert your DOS disk in the A drive. Then, turn on the power switch of your computer (as well as the monitor switch, if this applies to your system).

When the date prompt appears on the screen, bypass it by pressing the RETURN key on your keyboard. You will not need to enter the date or

time for this lesson. When the time prompt appears, press RETURN again to cause the A> prompt to appear.

2. The A> prompt now should be displayed on your screen. You are ready to *boot* your STARTware system. A boot procedure means that you are activating a program by entering a command to load the program into main memory.

Remove your DOS disk and return it to its protective sleeve. Then place the STARTware disk in the A drive. To boot STARTware, enter the command START next to the A> prompt. Now press RETURN and wait a few seconds.

3. Your computer should display the STARTware *main menu.* A main menu is a list of basic processing choices from which you can make a selection. The STARTware main menu that you should be viewing is shown in an accompanying illustration.

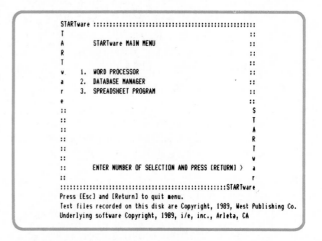

The STARTware Main Menu provides a choice of functions.

As you can see, three choices are available to you. Notice the message, or prompt, near the bottom of the screen:

ENTER NUMBER OF SELECTION AND PRESS [RETURN] >

To select the word processing program, you enter a 1. To select the database manager, enter a 2. Finally, to select the spreadsheet program, enter a 3.

For this lesson, you need to select the word processor. Enter the number 1 and then press RETURN.

4. STARTware now displays the word processor main menu. This menu, shown in the accompanying illustration, provides the basic word processing choices you can choose to edit, create, delete, print, and format, a text file.

```
STARTware: WP ::::::::::::::::::::::::::::::::::::::::::::
T                                                    ::
A                                                    ::
R       WORD PROCESSOR MAIN MENU                     ::
T                                                    ::
v                                                    ::
a    1.  REVIEW/EDIT AN EXISTING FILE                ::
r    2.  CREATE A NEW FILE                           ::
e    3.  DELETE A FILE                               ::
::   4.  PRINT A FILE                                S
::   5.  FORMAT/FUNCTION MENU                        T
::   6.  PROTECT/UNPROTECT A FILE                    A
::                                                   R
::                                                   T
::                                                   v
::        ENTER NUMBER OF SELECTION AND PRESS RETURN > a
::                                                   r
:::::::::::::::::::::::::::::::::::::::::::::::STARTware
Press [Esc] and [Return] to quit menu.
```

The STARTware Word Processor Main Menu provides a choice of word processing functions.

5. To begin your word processing learning program, you will create a new file and then enter text. The content of the file you will create and enter is shown next. Review this text carefully before you continue. In other words, Step 5 asks you to *read* the text you will enter. Do not make any entries until you have read the following paragraphs. Then continue to Step 6.

Word processing programs used with computer systems offer many features not available with electronic typewriters. For instance, a word processor allows you to enter text continuously.

With most electronic typewriters, you must press a special key, called a carrier return, whenever you reach the end of a line of text. This carrier return causes the print element to move to the left margin of a new line.

A word processor eliminates the need for pressing a carrier return key. Computers use a feature called "word wrap." This word wrap feature refers to the capability of a word processing program to detect the right margin of a line of text. When this limit is reached, the program automatically moves a word that will not fit within the right margin to the left margin of a new line.

6. To indicate that you want to enter text, you need to make a selection from the word processor main menu currently displayed on your computer screen. You want to create a new file. As you can see from the main menu, this is entry 2. Enter the number 2 and then press RETURN to continue.

7. The screen that appears is called CREATE A NEW FILE. The prompt near the bottom of this screen requests a *file name*. This name will be used by the operating system as well as the STARTware system to locate your file in main memory and on disk. Enter the name WPINTRO. Press the RETURN key when you are done.

8. The STARTware system now displays a screen that contains a *status* line and a *format* line. The top line, the status line, provides the name of the file you have created, and indicates the page, line, and column position of your *cursor*. The cursor is the blinking line or block character that indicates the position at which your next keystroke will be displayed.

The format line of STARTware shows the width of each text line, indicated by a series of dashes, as well as *tab stops.* A tab stop represents the position to which the cursor will move when the TAB key is pressed. The TAB key is shown on most keyboards by a set of arrows, one of which points to the left, and one of which points to the right.

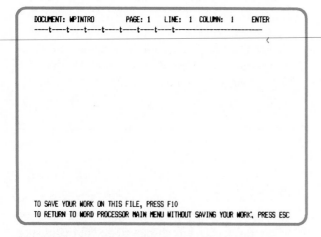

```
DOCUMENT: WPINTRO          PAGE: 1  LINE:  1  COLUMN:  1        ENTER
---t---t---t---t---t---t---t------------------------------
                                                           <
```

```
TO SAVE YOUR WORK ON THIS FILE, PRESS F10
TO RETURN TO WORD PROCESSOR MAIN MENU WITHOUT SAVING YOUR WORK, PRESS ESC
```

The STARTware status line identifies line width, tab positions, file name, and cursor position.

9. Now enter the text for WPINTRO, provided earlier. *Do not* correct any mistakes that you make. You will have an opportunity to correct mistakes in the next lesson. When you have finished with text entry, continue with Step 10.
10. When you have completed text entry, press the F10 function key located either on the left side or top of your keyboard. This key saves the new WPINTRO document to the STARTware disk. The screen that appears next asks you to enter the name of the file to be saved. Recall that you have already provided a file name, WPINTRO, for your text. To keep this file name, simply press RETURN. The STARTware system then will save your entered text under the WPINTRO name.
11. You now have completed Lesson 2. Remove your STARTware disk from the A drive and

return it to its sleeve. Turn off your computer system and wait for further instructions from your teacher.

AppleWorks PROCEDURES

1. Your computer system should be turned off when you begin this lesson. The following lessons assume that your computer system has two floppy disk drives. If you have only one disk drive, you will have to use this drive for both your program and data disks. Simply follow instructions that appear on the screen to change disks at the appropriate times.

 With your system turned off, insert your AppleWorks startup disk in drive 1. Place a blank, *formatted* data disk in drive 2. If you are not sure whether your data disk has been formatted, ask your teacher for assistance before you continue. You cannot store files permanently unless your data disk has been formatted. When you are ready to continue, go on to Step 2.

2. Turn on the power switch of your computer (as well as the monitor switch, if this applies to your system).

 When the prompt for AppleWorks appears, replace the startup disk in drive 1 with the AppleWorks program disk. Press RETURN to continue.

3. When the date prompt appears, bypass it by pressing the RETURN key on your keyboard. You will not need to enter the date for these lessons. The AppleWorks main menu now should appear on your screen. A main menu is a list of basic processing choices from which you can make a selection. The AppleWorks main menu that you should be viewing is shown in an accompanying illustration.

 As you can see, six choices are available to you. Notice the message, or prompt, near the bottom of the screen.

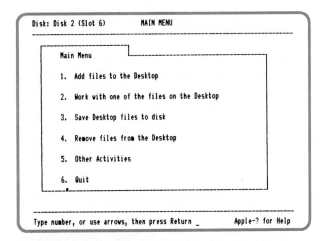

The AppleWorks Main Menu *presents a choice of six functions.*

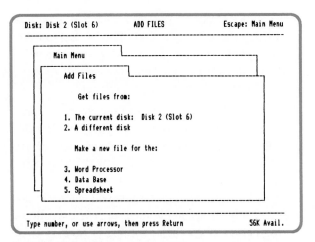

The AppleWorks Files Menu *provides for file access and/or creation.*

Type number, or use arrows, then press Return

To create a file or to move a file from disk into memory, you would enter a 1. This command adds a file to the Desktop. In AppleWorks, the Desktop means main memory. By selecting option 1, you tell AppleWorks that you want to add (and work on) a new file within main memory.

Option 2 offers you the ability to work with a file currently within the Desktop. In other words, by entering a 2, you can work on a file currently stored in main memory.

Study the other available main menu options briefly before you continue with Step 4.

4. At this point, you want to create, or add, a file into memory (the Desktop). Select option 1 and press RETURN. AppleWorks now displays the Add Files menu, shown in an accompanying illustration. This menu offers options for selecting an existing file or for setting up a new file. For this lesson, you want to create a new file for the word processor. As you can see from the display, this is option 3 from the Add Files menu. Enter a 3 now and press RETURN to continue.

5. AppleWorks now displays a word processor menu. This menu, shown in an accompanying il-

lustration, provides the basic word processing choices you can select to work with text (word processed) files. To add a file, AppleWorks needs to know whether you want to add a file from "scratch" or from a file built with a different program or operating system. In this case, you want to build a file from scratch. Select option 1.

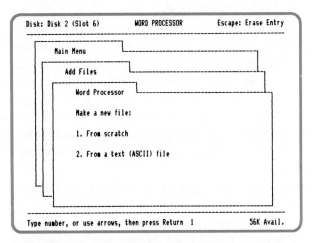

The Appleworks Word Processor Menu *enables users to retrieve or create text files.*

You now need to specify a name for your new file. For this lesson, use the file name WPINTRO. Enter this file name now and then press RETURN to continue. AppleWorks now creates space in main memory (the desktop) for storage of your new word processor file. However, keep in mind that this file will not exist on disk until you save it to disk later.

6. To begin your word processing learning program, you will enter text into your new WPINTRO file. The content of the file you will create and enter is shown next. Review this text carefully before you continue. In other words, Step 6 asks you to *read* the text you will enter. Do not make any entries until you have read the following paragraphs. Then continue to Step 7.

Word processing programs used with computer systems offer many features not available with electronic typewriters. For instance, a word processor allows you to enter text continuously. With most electronic typewriters, you must press a special key, called a carrier return, whenever you reach the end of a line of text. This carrier return causes the print element to move to the left margin of a new line.

A word processor eliminates the need for pressing a carrier return key. Computers use a feature called "word wrap." This word wrap feature refers to the capability of a word processing program to detect the right margin of a line of text. When this limit is reached, the program automatically moves a word that will not fit within the right margin to the left margin of a new line.

---

7. AppleWorks now displays a screen that contains a *status* line and two *format* lines. The top line, the status line, provides the name of the file you have created. It also indicates the current *mode* in which you are working. You are currently in REVIEW/ADD/CHANGE mode. That is, you can look through the content of a document (REVIEW), make new entries into a document

(ADD), and alter the existing content of a document (CHANGE).

The first format line, near the top of the screen, is located below the status line. This line shows the maximum line width allowed for a word processor document, indicated by a series of dashes, as well as *tab stops*. A tab stop represents the position to which the cursor will be moved when the TAB key is pressed. The TAB key is shown on most keyboards by a set of arrows, one of which points to the left, and one of which points to the right.

The second format line is shown near the bottom of the screen. Entries on this line indicate the line and column position of your *cursor*. The cursor is the blinking line or block character that indicates the position at which your next keystroke will be displayed.

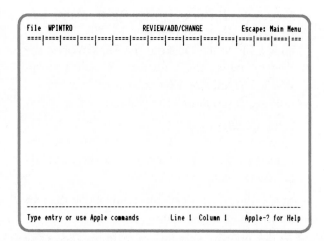

```
File  WPINTRO              REVIEW/ADD/CHANGE            Escape: Main Menu
====|====|====|====|====|====|====|====|====|====|====|====|====|====|===




















-------------------------------------------------------------------
Type entry or use Apple commands        Line 1  Column 1     Apple-? for Help
```

AppleWorks text entry *is done through screens like this one.*

---

8. Now enter the text for WPINTRO, provided earlier. **Do not** correct any mistakes that you make. You will have an opportunity to correct mistakes in the next lesson. When you have finished with text entry, continue with Step 9.

9. When you have completed text entry, press the ESC key. This key returns you to the Apple-

Works main menu. At this point, your WP-INTRO file exists only in main memory. If you turn off your computer now, all of your work will be lost. Of course, you don't want this to happen. Instead, you want to save your new file to disk.

Notice that option 3 on the main menu is labeled "Save Desktop files to disk." This is the option that you want to select now. Enter a 3 and press RETURN.

10. AppleWorks now asks you for the names of files that you want to save from the Desktop (memory) to disk. Select the name WPINTRO, which should be the only file currently in memory. Press RETURN to activate the save option. Now press 1 and RETURN to save the file on the current disk.

11. You now have completed Lesson 2. Remove your disks from the drives and return them to their protective sleeves. Turn off your computer system and wait for further instructions from your teacher.

Lesson 3

Using a Word Processor: Editing a Text File

INTRODUCTION

This lesson offers you some practice in using basic editing features of the STARTware or AppleWorks word processing program. These features allow you to insert, delete, and alter selected characters.

STARTware PROCEDURES

1. Make sure your computer system is turned off. Remove your DOS disk from its protective sleeve and place it in the A drive of your computer. Turn on your computer system.

2. When the date prompt appears, bypass it by pressing RETURN. Also bypass the time prompt by pressing RETURN. At this point, DOS should display the A > prompt.

3. Remove the DOS disk and return it to its sleeve. Insert your STARTware disk in the A drive. Enter the following next to the A > prompt:

wp

This command tells STARTware to bypass the system's main menu and instead display the word processor main menu. When this menu appears, enter the number 1 to indicate that you want to edit an existing file. The accompanying RE-VIEW/EDIT AN EXISTING FILE menu should appear on your screen.

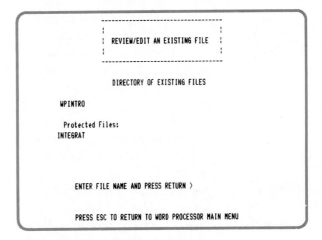

```
---------------------------------------
:                                     :
:    REVIEW/EDIT AN EXISTING FILE     :
:                                     :
---------------------------------------


         DIRECTORY OF EXISTING FILES


   WPINTRO

     Protected Files:
   INTEGRAT




        ENTER FILE NAME AND PRESS RETURN >


    PRESS ESC TO RETURN TO WORD PROCESSOR MAIN MENU
```

A STARTware directory is presented as the beginning point for an edit operation.

4. Enter the name of the file that you created in Lesson 2, WPINTRO. Press RETURN when you are ready to continue. The STARTware system will display the text that you entered previously. This file may contain several text entry errors that you have made. Such mistakes are a natural process in learning about and practicing use of a program. In this lesson, you will have an opportunity to correct your mistakes as well as to perform some *edits,* or changes, provided in later steps.

STARTware provides four *cursor movement* keys that you can use to position the cursor in your document. The cursor movement keys are shown as arrows on the numeric keypad of your keyboard. Take a moment to practice using these keys to "navigate" through your document.

5. STARTware provides six additional keys that are used exclusively to navigate through a document or to edit text. These keys and their related functions are described in an accompanying table.

STARTware
WORD PROCESSING FUNCTION KEYS

KEY	DESCRIPTION
Backspace	Moves cursor one space left and erases one character.
Del	The delete key erases one character each time it is pressed.
PgUp	Moves cursor to and displays screen that is one position higher in the document than the one shown.
PgDn	Moves cursor to and displays screen that is one position lower in the document than the one shown.
Home	Moves cursor to top left of a screen display.
End	Moves cursor to bottom right of a screen display.

Experiment with these keys for a few moments. When you feel that you understand what they do for you, use them to make any corrections that are required for your document. After you have corrected all errors you have made earlier, continue with Step 6.

6. Now make the following changes, or edits, to the WPINTRO document:

A. In the first sentence, change the word "offer" to "provide."

B. In the third sentence, delete the last two words, "of text."

C. In the second sentence of the second paragraph, insert the phrase "time-saving" before the word "feature."

D. In the final sentence of the document, insert "to the next line" after the word "moves."

E. In the final sentence, insert a period after "right margin," and delete all remaining words in this sentence.

When you have made these edits, save the document under the name EDIT1. If you are unsure how to save a document, refer to the steps in Lesson 2. If you need additional help, ask your teacher for assistance.

7. You have now completed Lesson 3. Remove your STARTware disk from the disk drive and return it to its protective sleeve. Turn off your computer system and wait for further instructions from your teacher.

AppleWorks PROCEDURES

1. Make sure your computer system is turned off. Remove your AppleWorks startup disk from its protective sleeve and place it in drive 1 of your computer.

   Place your data disk, the one on which you recorded the WPINTRO file, in drive 2.

   Turn on your computer system. When you are prompted to do so, replace the startup disk in drive 1 with the AppleWorks program disk and press RETURN to continue.

2. When the date prompt appears, bypass it by pressing RETURN. Follow instructions by removing the startup disk and replacing it with the AppleWorks disk. Press RETURN to continue.

   When the AppleWorks main menu appears, select option 1—"Add files to the Desktop." Press RETURN to continue.

3. At the "Add Files" menu, select option 1 to input a file from the current disk. Use the cursor keys (the Up Arrow and Down Arrow keys) to move the highlight to WPINTRO. When the highlight is on WPINTRO, press RETURN.

4. AppleWorks will display the text that you entered previously. This file may contain several text entry errors that you have made. Such mistakes are a natural part of learning about and practicing use of a program. In this lesson, you will have an opportunity to correct your mistakes as well as to perform some *edits,* or changes, provided in later steps.

   AppleWorks provides four *cursor movement* keys that you can use to position the cursor in your document. The cursor movement keys are shown as arrows on the numeric keypad of your keyboard. Take a moment to practice using these keys to navigate through your document.

5. AppleWorks provides one additional key, Delete, that can be used to navigate through a document or to edit text. When you press the Delete key, it deletes one character—the one to the *left* of the cursor. For this reason, the Delete key is sometimes called a *destructive backspace.*

   Try using the Delete key as you make needed corrections to your document. After you have corrected all errors you made earlier, continue with Step 6.

6. Now make the following changes, or edits, to the WPINTRO document:

   A. In the first sentence, change the word "offer" to "provide."

   B. In the third sentence, delete the last two words, "of text."

   C. In the second sentence of the second paragraph, insert the phrase "time-saving" before the word "feature."

   D. In the final sentence of the document, insert "to the next line" after the word "moves."

   E. In the final sentence, insert a period after "right margin," and delete all remaining words in this sentence.

7. When you have made these edits, you can save the document under the name EDIT1. To do this, return to the main menu by pressing ESC. From the main menu, choose the "Save Desktop files to disk" option and press RETURN. Select the file named WPINTRO by pressing RETURN.

   AppleWorks will ask you whether you want to save the file to the current disk. Answer "Yes" by selecting 1, then press RETURN. AppleWorks now provides you with options for replacing the current WPINTRO file with the edited version, or for saving the edits to a new file. In this case, you want to leave WPINTRO intact and create a new file called EDIT1.

   Select the option to "Save with a different name." Press RETURN to carry out this action. AppleWorks now asks you to provide the name for your file. Enter the following:

   EDIT1

   Press Apple-Y to delete remaining characters from the file name. This is an important command. Whenever you press Apple-Y, whether you are in a menu or a document, AppleWorks will delete all remaining characters from the cursor to the end of the current line. Press RETURN to create this new file. AppleWorks now has saved your edited file to disk and created a permanent copy that you can use later. The original WPINTRO file also is kept on your disk, since you instructed AppleWorks not to replace this file with the edited version.

8. You have now completed Lesson 3. If you are not already at the main menu, press ESC to call this menu. At the main menu, select option 6 to Quit. When AppleWorks asks if you are sure you want to quit, highlight the word "Yes" and press RETURN. Remove your disks from the disk drives and return them to their protective sleeves. Turn off your computer system and wait for further instructions from your teacher.

Using a Word Processor: Advanced Editing

INTRODUCTION

In Lesson 4, you will practice techniques for using the *block editing* capabilities of STARTware or AppleWorks. The term "block editing" refers to capabilities for moving, copying, inserting, or deleting large sections of text. Each section of text to be moved, copied, inserted, or deleted is called a "block."

STARTware PROCEDURES

With STARTware, you perform block editing operations with three basic steps. First, you mark the block of text to be moved, copied, or deleted. (For a block insertion, the block insert command marks the starting point for text to be inserted.)

Second, you specify the type of operation you want to perform—a move, copy, or deletion. (For a block insertion, you simply specify the ending point for inserted text.)

Third, you mark the ending point for the marked block and, for a move or copy operation, the location to which the marked block should be moved or copied.

The following steps guide you through the use of block editing features for deleting, moving, and inserting sections of text.

1. Make sure your computer system is turned off. Remove your DOS disk from its protective sleeve and place it in the A drive of your computer. Turn on your computer system.

2. When the date prompt appears, bypass it by pressing RETURN. Also bypass the time prompt by pressing RETURN. At this point, DOS should display the A> prompt.

3. Remove the DOS disk and return it to its sleeve. Insert your STARTware disk in the A drive. Enter the following next to the A> prompt:

wp

4. Select the REVIEW/EDIT AN EXISTING FILE option from the word processor main menu and press the RETURN key.

When the REVIEW/EDIT AN EXISTING FILE screen appears, enter the file name EDIT1 and press RETURN to continue.

5. You now are ready to use the block delete function of STARTware. Recall that, for the previous lesson, you deleted one character at a time through use of the DEL key. At this point, you will use a technique for rapid deletion of an entire section of text at a time.

To demonstrate block deletion, you will remove the final sentence of the first paragraph. Move the cursor to the first character of the sentence (the "T" in "This").

6. The block marking function is specified by the F5 key positioned on the left side or along the top of your keyboard. Press this key now. You have marked the starting point for your block editing operation.

7. You want to delete the final sentence of the first paragraph. So, you need to mark the end point for the text you want to delete. To do so, move the cursor to the period that ends this sentence.

8. To specify that you want to delete a block of text, press the F7 key. STARTware reserves this key to specify a block delete operation. You now have deleted this sentence from the current document.

9. Your next block editing task is to move the first sentence of the second paragraph. For this operation, you will move the sentence to the position following the second sentence of the paragraph. In other words, you want to move the first sentence after the currently displayed phrase, "word wrap."

To begin, move the cursor under the first character of the first sentence (the "A"). You now want to mark a block of text to be moved. To do so, press the block marking key, F5.

10. Now move the cursor to the space immediately before the second sentence of the paragraph— that is, the space before the "C" in "Computers." You want to include the blank spaces in your move, since they are part of the first sentence. Press F7 to delete the marked block from your document.

    Actually, the deleted text is not destroyed. Instead, it is stored in a special area of memory. By using the MOVE function key, described next, you can move the deleted text to a new position in the document.

11. To complete your move operation, you first must position the cursor at the location where you want the moved text to begin. For this operation, you want to place the marked sentence after the second sentence. So, move the cursor to the space immediately before the first letter of the third sentence (the "T" in "This").

    Now press the MOVE key, F8. The move operation will be completed within a fraction of a second. Notice the new position of the moved text.

12. The final block editing feature to be performed for this lesson involves inserting a section of text. When you moved the sentence in the steps described above, you might have noticed that some of the meaning of the paragraph has been lost. The second and third sentences of the second paragraph now read:

    Computers use a feature called "word wrap." A word processor eliminates the need for pressing a carrier return.

13. You can improve the meaning of the second sentence by inserting the phrase "In other words," at the beginning. So, the second sentence should read as follows:

In other words, a word processor eliminates the need for pressing a carriage return.

To perform a block insertion, move the cursor to the location where you want to begin inserting text. In this case, move the cursor to the first character of the new second sentence (the "A"). Now press the INS key located on the numeric keypad of the computer.

This key causes the word processing program to move existing text to the right as you key in new text. Your entries push the existing text over to make room for the new keystrokes. Enter the following now:

In other words,

Be sure to include a space after the comma. This space will separate the comma from the text that follows. Now press INS again. The ability to make new entries within existing text stops. Any new keystrokes will replace existing text. To complete your editing operation, change the uppercase "A" in the third sentence to a lowercase "a" character.

When you have finished, save your document under the file name EDIT2.

14. Congratulations. You now have completed the word processing section of this Appendix. Remove the STARTware disk from the A drive and return it to its protective sleeve. Turn off your computer system and await further instructions from your teacher.

AppleWorks PROCEDURES

With AppleWorks, you perform block editing operations with three basic steps. First, you mark the block of text to be moved, copied, or deleted. (For a block insertion, you simply enter new text in front of existing text. AppleWorks "pushes" the existing text forward, without deleting it.)

Second, you specify the type of operation you want to perform—a move, copy, or deletion.

Third, you mark the ending point for the marked block and, for a move or copy operation, the location to which the marked block should be moved or copied.

The following steps for this lesson guide you through the use of block editing features for deleting, moving, and inserting sections of text.

1. Make sure your computer system is turned off. Remove your AppleWorks startup disk from its protective sleeve and place it in drive 1. Place your AppleWorks data disk in drive 2. Turn on your computer system. When the computer prompts you to do so, remove the startup disk from drive 1 and replace it with the AppleWorks program disk. Press RETURN to continue.

2. When the date prompt appears, bypass it by pressing RETURN. Follow instructions by removing the startup disk and replacing it with the AppleWorks disk. Press RETURN to continue.

   When the AppleWorks main menu appears, select option 1—"Add files to the Desktop." Press RETURN to continue.

3. At the "Add Files" menu, select option 1 to input a file from the current disk. Use the cursor keys (the Up Arrow and Down Arrow keys) to move the highlight to EDIT1. When the highlight is on EDIT1, press RETURN. The text for the document you edited in Lesson 2 now appears on the screen.

4. You now are ready to use the block delete function of AppleWorks. Recall that, for the previous lesson, you deleted one character at a time through use of the Delete key. At this point, you will use a technique for rapidly deleting an entire section of text at a time.

   To demonstrate block deletion, you will remove the final sentence of the first paragraph. Move the cursor to the first character of the sentence (the "T" in "This").

5. The block marking function is specified with the Apple key near the bottom-left part on your key-board. This key looks like an apple with a small bite taken from it. To mark text for deletion, you enter the Apple-D key combination. That is, while holding down the Apple key, press D. Press this key combination now. You have marked the starting point for your block editing operation.

6. You want to delete the final sentence of the first paragraph. So, you need to mark the end point for the text you want to delete. To do so, move the cursor to the period that ends this sentence.

7. To delete the marked text, simply press RETURN. The sentence now is removed. In this way, your document looks as though the deleted sentence never existed.

8. Your next block editing task is to move the first sentence of the second paragraph. For this operation, you will move the sentence to the position following the second sentence of the paragraph. In other words, you want to move the first sentence after the currently displayed phrase, "word wrap."

   To begin, move the cursor under the first character of the first sentence (the "A"). You now want to mark a block of text to be moved. To do so, press the Apple-M key combination. That is, while holding down the Apple key, press M. This is the move command.

9. AppleWorks now asks you where you want to move the text. Use the first option, "Within document," since you want to keep the text within the EDIT1 document.

   Next, AppleWorks asks you to mark the ending point of the text to be moved. Move the cursor to the space immediately before the second sentence of the paragraph—that is, the space before the "C" in "Computers." You want to include the blank spaces in your move, since they are part of the first sentence. Press RETURN to continue on to the next step.

10. To complete your move operation, you first must position the cursor at the location where you

want the moved text to begin. For this operation, you want to place the marked sentence after the second sentence. So, move the cursor to the space immediately before the first letter of the third sentence (the "T" in "This").

Now press RETURN. The move operation will be completed within a fraction of a second. Notice the new position of the moved text.

11. The final block editing feature to be performed for this lesson involves inserting a section of text. When you moved the sentence in the steps described above, you might have noticed that some of the meaning of the paragraph has been lost. The second and third sentences of the second paragraph now read:

Computers use a feature called "word wrap." A word processor eliminates the need for pressing a carrier return.

12. You can improve the meaning of the second sentence by inserting the phrase "In other words," at the beginning. So, the second sentence should read as follows:

In other words, a word processor eliminates the need for pressing a carriage return.

To perform a block insertion, move the cursor to the location where you want to begin inserting text. In this case, move the cursor to the first character of the new second sentence (the "A"). Enter the following now:

In other words,

Be sure to include a space after the comma. This space will separate the comma from the text that follows. Also change the Capital "A" to a small, or lowercase, "a." Notice that, as you enter characters, the existing text is pushed forward. This feature illustrates one benefit of the word wrap capability of AppleWorks. That is, AppleWorks automatically repositions text for you by wrapping text forward as you make new entries.

When you have finished, save your document under the file name EDIT2. After the document has been saved, make sure you return to the main menu and use option 6 to Quit the program.

13. Congratulations. You now have completed the word processing section of this Appendix. Remove your disks from the disk drives and return them to their protective sleeves. Turn off your computer system and await further instructions from your teacher.

Lesson 5

Using a Database Management System: Creating a Database

INTRODUCTION

A *database management system (DBMS)* is a set of programs that allows users to create and process multiple files, for multiple applications. In Lessons 5 through 7, you will learn how to create, modify, and process database files.

Recall the description of the HOTCAR file in the chapter of this book that deals with database applications. It is explained that law enforcement agencies create and process files that can be used to record and track information about stolen vehicles. In the following lessons, you will be given an opportunity to see how these files are created, maintained, and used by police departments.

STARTware PROCEDURES

1. Begin this lesson with your computer system turned off. Insert your DOS disk in the A drive of your computer and press RETURN. Bypass the date and time prompts by pressing RETURN when each of these prompts appears.

2. When the A > prompt appears on your screen, enter the following command to load the STARTware database management system:

db

STARTware recognizes both uppercase (capital) and lowercase (small) letters. So you can enter either uppercase or lowercase letters when you specify commands in STARTware. Press RETURN when you are ready to continue.

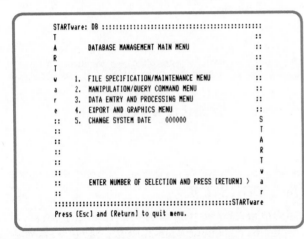

```
STARTware: DB ::::::::::::::::::::::::::::::::::::::::::
T                                                   ::
A        DATABASE MANAGEMENT MAIN MENU              ::
R                                                   ::
T                                                   ::
w    1.  FILE SPECIFICATION/MAINTENANCE MENU        ::
a    2.  MANIPULATION/QUERY COMMAND MENU            ::
r    3.  DATA ENTRY AND PROCESSING MENU             ::
e    4.  EXPORT AND GRAPHICS MENU                   ::
::   5.  CHANGE SYSTEM DATE    000000               S
::                                                  T
::                                                  A
::                                                  R
::                                                  T
::                                                  w
::       ENTER NUMBER OF SELECTION AND PRESS [RETURN] >  a
::                                                  r
:::::::::::::::::::::::::::::::::::::::::::::::STARTware
Press [Esc] and [Return] to quit menu.
```

The STARTware Database Management Main Menu is a gateway to submenus that make specific functions available.

3. The DATABASE MANAGEMENT MAIN MENU now appears on the screen. A replica of this menu is presented in an accompanying illustration. In creating the HOTCAR file for the STARTware DBMS, you must begin by setting the *attributes* of the file. In a relational database, a file attribute is a characteristic that describes a data item within a file. In STARTware, you can think of an attribute as the name for a column of data.

For each field name that you use, you must display attributes for data type, field width, number of decimals (for numeric fields only), and whether the field is a record key (used to organize and locate records).

STARTware also provides an attribute specification used to determine whether a defined field should be *cross referenced* with other database files. You will not use this cross referencing option in this Appendix.

For the HOTCAR file, you will specify attributes for the following nine fields:

LIC#   This is the license number for each reported stolen vehicle. LIC# will have a field width of eight characters.

ST   This is the state in which the vehicle is registered; the field width will be two characters.

YR   The YR attribute specifies the model year of the vehicle; the field width will be two characters.

MAKE   The MAKE is the manufacturer of a vehicle, such as Ford, Buick, or Honda. The MAKE field will have a width of five characters.

MODEL   This field describes attributes for the vehicle model, such as Corolla, 280Z, Bronco, Mustang, and so on. The MODEL width will be 10 characters.

COLOR   This field indicates the color of a stolen vehicle and will have a width of five characters.

BODY   The BODY is the type of body of the stolen vehicle, such as sedan, truck, motorcycle, convertible, wagon, hatchback, and so on. The BODY field will have a maximum width of four characters.

REGOWN   This is the name of the registered owner of a reported stolen vehicle. Of course, a person's full name can have many letters. For this reason, REGOWN will have a width of 20 characters.

LASTSEEN The final field for each record in the HOTCAR file specifies the date on which a stolen vehicle was reported, or "last seen." The LASTSEEN date will be eight characters, to provide month number, day number, and year—with the remaining two characters reserved for a slash (/) to separate each part of the date.

4. You now are ready to create and specify attributes for the HOTCAR file. Begin by selecting the FILE SPECIFICATION/MAINTENANCE MENU option from the DATABASE MANAGEMENT MAIN MENU. To make this selection, enter a 1 at the prompt and press RETURN.

5. The CREATE AND MAINTAIN FILE SPECIFICATIONS menu now appears on the screen. The first menu option, FILE SPECIFICATION AND MODIFICATION, will allow you to specify attributes for a new file. Select this option now by pressing 1 and then RETURN.

6. The "Maintain File Specification" screen that now appears prompts you for a file name. At this point, you want to create a new file. Enter the following name at the prompt, then press RETURN.

HOTCAR

Again, you can use either uppercase or lowercase characters to enter the file name.

7. The program will search its existing database directory to see if HOTCAR currently exists. Since it does not yet exist, the system will display a "not found" message, and then will proceed to create a new database file.

After the STARTware system has allocated space on disk and in memory for HOTCAR, it will display the "Setting File Attributes" screen. This screen allows you to specify the attributes for the HOTCAR file. These attributes, again, are described in Step 3 above. The "Type" for

all fields in the HOTCAR file should be "C" (for Character.) The other two type options, "N" (for numeric) and "L" (for logical), do not apply to these lessons.

Use the descriptions in Step 3, along with the instructions shown on the current screen, to enter attributes for the HOTCAR file. Your entries should look like those shown on the accompanying screen illustration. If your entries differ from this screen, use the cursor and INS/DEL keys to make corrections before you continue to Step 8.

```
        -------------------------------------
        |        Setting File Attributes        :File: HOTCAR.DB
        -------------------------------------
   Field      Type   Width  Dec's  Key  Cross Reference
   Name       C/N/L  1-20   0-4    Y/N

 1 LIC#        C       8            Y
 2 ST          C       2            N
 3 YR          C       2            N
 4 MAKE        C       5            N
 5 MODEL       C      10            N
 6 COLOR       C       5            N
 7 BODY        C       4            N
 8 REGOWN      C      20            Y
 9 LASTSEEN    C      15            N
10

   ESC to create file and return to Database Main Menu
   UP/DOWN/RIGHT cursor keys to modify entries
   Press RETURN after data entries
   INS/DEL to insert/delete whole lines
```

The STARTware attributes prompt screen *is used to establish record formats.*

8. When you are certain that your attribute specifications match those in the illustrated screen, press ESC. This command causes the STARTware DBMS to write the HOTCAR file specifications to disk.

9. The CREATE AND MAINTAIN FILE SPECIFICATIONS screen should reappear on your monitor. At this point, you are finished with this lesson. You have defined and created a database file to store records for HOTCAR. Remove your STARTware disk from the drive and return it to its protective sleeve. Turn off your computer system and wait for further instructions from your teacher.

AppleWorks PROCEDURES

1. Your computer system should be turned off when you begin this lesson. With your system turned off, insert your AppleWorks startup disk in drive 1. Insert your AppleWorks data disk in drive 2. Next, turn on the power switch of your computer (as well as the monitor switch, if this applies to your system).

   When the prompt appears on the screen, replace the startup disk with the AppleWorks program disk. Press RETURN to continue.

2. When the date prompt appears, bypass it by pressing the RETURN key. As you learned from the word processing lessons earlier, the Apple-Works main menu (now displayed) offers you six choices. At this point, you want to create, or add, a file into the desktop—just as you did in Lesson 2. Select option 1 and press RETURN.

3. AppleWorks now displays the Add Files menu. Recall that this menu offers options for selecting an existing file or for setting up a new file. For this lesson, you want to create a new file for the database system. As you can see from the display, this is option 5 from the Add Files menu. Also notice that AppleWorks uses a two-word spelling, "Data Base." This is simply another way to spell database.

   Enter a 5 now and press RETURN to continue.

4. AppleWorks now needs to know whether you want to add a file from "scratch" or from a file built with a different program or operating system. In this case, you want to build a database file from scratch. Select option 1.

   You now need to specify a name for your new file. For this lesson, use the file name HOTCAR. Enter this file name now and then press RETURN to continue.

5. AppleWorks displays the "Change Name/Category" screen, shown in the accompanying illustration. In creating the HOTCAR file for the AppleWorks DBMS, you must begin by setting

the *attributes* of the file. In a relational database, a file attribute is a characteristic that describes a data item within a file. In AppleWorks, you can think of an attribute as a category. Each category that you create is the name for a column of data.

```
File: HOTCAR           CHANGE NAME/CATEGORY         Escape: Review/Add/Change


Category names
===============================================================================
Category 1
                                    |   Options:
                                    |
                                    |   Change category name
                                    |   Up arrow   Go to filename
                                    |   Down arrow Go to next category
                                    |   Apple-I    Insert new category
                                    |
                                    |
          ----------------------------------------------------------
Type entry or use Apple commands                             55K Avail.
```

The AppleWorks Change Name/Category screen is used to identify a database file on which to work.

For the HOTCAR file, you will specify columns, or category names, for the following nine types of fields:

LIC#   This is the license number for each reported stolen vehicle.

ST   This is the state in which the vehicle is registered.

YR   The YR attribute specifies the model year of the vehicle.

MAKE   The MAKE is the manufacturer of a vehicle, such as Ford, Buick, or Honda.

MODEL   This field describes attributes for the vehicle model, such as Corolla, 280Z, Bronco, Mustang, and so on.

COLOR   This field indicates the color of a stolen vehicle.

BODY   The BODY is the type of body of the stolen vehicle, such as sedan, truck, motorcycle, convertible, wagon, hatchback, and so on.

REGOWN This is the name of the registered owner of a reported stolen vehicle.

LS DATE The final field for each record in the HOTCAR file specifies the date on which a stolen vehicle was reported, or "last seen."

The LS DATE name is used for a reason. Whenever AppleWorks finds the word DATE in a category name, it automatically puts data into a date format. This format is a three-letter month, such as (Apr), a two-digit day (07), and a two-digit year (89). For instance, imagine that you make these entries into the LS DATE column:

April 7th, 1989

4/7/89

4-07-89

AppleWorks automatically will convert these three entries into this format:

Apr 07 89

So, you can enter a date in any commonly used format and AppleWorks will automatically convert your entry into its own date format. However, this works only if the word "date" appears in the category name.

6. You now are ready to enter the nine category names shown above. Begin by typing the name of your first category:

LIC#

Remember to press Apple-Y to remove extra characters from the line. Press RETURN to save the category name. Now enter the second category name:

ST

You will notice that the category name area on the screen still contains two characters (C#) left over from the previously entered name. To remove these letters, press Apple-Y. That is, hold down the Apple key, then press Y. Press RETURN to save the second category name.

Continue these procedures to enter the remaining seven categories. Remember to press Apple-Y whenever you need to delete extra letters from a category name. Also, you can use the delete key to correct any errors you make in a category name.

When you have finished entering all category names, continue to Step 7.

7. At this point, you can practice entering a few records into the HOTCAR database. To close the "Change Name/Category" screen, press ESC.

Next, press the space bar to display the INSERT NEW RECORDS screen, shown in the accompanying illustration. This screen contains a status line that you will use later. For now, notice that the screen contains the names of each category, or field, that you specified in the previous steps. Also, above the double-dashed line, you can see the entry "Record 1 of 1." This tells you that you currently are inserting a record into the first position of a new file. This entry will change as you insert new records.

```
 FILE: HOTCAR              INSERT NEW RECORDS    Escape: Review/Add/Change



 Record 1 of 1
 ==================================================================================
 LIC#: -
 ST: -
 YR: -
 MAKE: -
 MODEL: -
 COLOR: -
 BODY: -
 REGISTERED OWNER: -
 LS DATE: -


 --------------------------------------------------------------------------
 Type entry or use Apple commands                                56K Avail.
```

The AppleWorks Insert New Records screen is used to define a record format.

For this lesson, you will enter the following three records into the HOTCAR database. Each row represents a single record. Each column represents a category, or group of fields for a single category name:

LIC#	ST	YR	MAKE	MODEL	COLOR	BODY	REGISTERED OWNER	LS DATE
YBB 123	AZ	82	HONDA	CRX500	BLACK	MC	VOSS KENNETH A	Oct 10 90
ABX 511	NM	84	DODGE	OMNI	BLUE	2DR	LAMERS ROSE	Oct 30 90
TB 5979	OH	88	FORD	ESCORT	BEIGE	SDAN	BURGETT LINDA S	Oct 30 90

You are ready to enter the nine fields for the first record—the one with the license number YBB 123. Enter this license number now. Use the backspace key to correct any mistakes that you make. Press RETURN when you have finished. The cursor now will be positioned next to the second field name, ST. You can make this field entry now. That is, enter the state name AZ for the first record, then press RETURN.

8. Continue entering the remaining seven fields for the first record. When you press RETURN after entering the DATE, AppleWorks will display a new blank INSERT NEW RECORDS screen. Notice that you now are working on "Record 2 of 2." In other words, you are working on the second record of a database that currently has two records.

Use this blank screen to enter fields for the second record shown above. Continue data entry procedures until you have entered all fields for all three records.

9. AppleWorks now should display a blank screen for entering a fourth record. However, you are finished with this data entry session. So, simply press ESC twice to return to the main menu.

It is time to save your newly created HOTCAR database file. To do so, select the "Save Desktop files to disk" option. That is, enter a 3 and press RETURN.

AppleWorks now lists the files currently stored in memory. In this case, only one file—HOTCAR—is shown on the list. To choose this file, simply press RETURN.

Apple now asks you whether you want to save the file on the current disk or on some other disk.

Enter the number 1 and press RETURN. Make sure to return to the main menu and quit the program (option 6).

10. You now have completed Lesson 5. Remove your AppleWorks program and data disks from the disk drives and return them to their protective sleeves. Turn off your computer and wait for further instructions from your teacher.

Lesson 6

Using a Database Management System: Adding Records to a Database

INTRODUCTION

In Lesson 6, you will display records in the current database and add a few records. A database file that uses the specifications you created in Lesson 5 has been created for you. This file demonstrates the appearance of records created using the HOTCAR attributes.

STARTware PROCEDURES

1. Begin with your computer system turned off. Insert your DOS disk and turn on your computer. Bypass the date and time prompts by pressing RETURN when each prompt appears. At the A> prompt, enter the following to load the STARTware database management system into memory:

db

2. When the DATABASE MANAGEMENT MAIN MENU appears, select the DATA ENTRY AND PROCESSING MENU. In other words, enter a 3 to indicate that you want to work with an existing database file. Press RETURN to activate your selection.

```
STARTware: DB ::::::::::::::::::::::::::::::::::::::::::::
T                                                      ::
A          DATA ENTRY AND PROCESSING MENU              ::
R                                                      ::
T     1.  ENTER RECORDS TO AN EXISTING FILE            ::
w     2.  MAINTAIN INDIVIDUAL RECORDS IN AN EXISTING FILE ::
a     3.  VALIDATE/EDIT TRANSACTION FILE               ::
r     4.  POST TRANSACTION FILE TO UPDATE MASTER FILE  ::
e     5.  REGISTER A TRANSACTION FILE                  ::
::    6.  PRINT A FILE                                  S
::    7.  ZERO/BLANK/INITIALIZE A COLUMN IN A FILE      T
::    8.  TRANSFER/PURGE A TRANSACTION FILE             A
::    9.  DISPLAY A FILE                                R
::                                                      T
::                                                      w
::        ENTER NUMBER OF SELECTION AND PRESS [RETURN] > a
::                                                      r
::::::::::::::::::::::::::::::::::::::::::::::::::STARTware
Press [Esc] and [Return] to quit menu.
```

The STARTware Data Entry and Processing Menu presents options for input and/or processing functions.

```
000000    DISPLAY OF FILE HOTCAR2.DB
 1 EBZ 842  AZ 86 HONDA CIVIC      GOLD  WGN BAUMAN CHRISTINA G  10/25/90
 2 BBY 176  AZ 82 TOYOT COROLLA    BLUE  HTCH PRONK RONALD R     10/27/90
 3 TTY 925  AZ 86 FORD  BRONCO     BEIGE TRUK WEISKAMP KEITH J   10/28/90
 4 MY JEEP  AZ 87 SUZUK SAMURAI    BLACK JEEP SCHALK ROBERT AND  10/29/90
 5 WHY 845  CA 87 OLDS  CUTLASS    WHITE SDAN KRUSE BETTIJUNE    10/27/90
 ‡‡‡NO MORE RECORDS‡‡‡



                    UP/DOWN (U/D/ESC) ?)
```

This STARTware display shows the contents of the HOTCAR2 file.

3. The DATA ENTRY AND PROCESSING MENU now appears on your screen. Take a moment to review the selections made available with this menu. You may not understand some of these options, although it can help to be familiar with these data entry selections. You may use them in later computer application work.

To assist you in using the STARTware DBMS, a file already has been created that contains a few example records. These records follow the attribute specifications you defined in the previous lesson. The file is called HOTCAR2.

Begin by selecting 9, DISPLAY A FILE, from the current menu and press RETURN to display the selected screen. At the prompt, enter the following file name and press RETURN.

HOTCAR2

4. Five records are displayed for this file, as shown in the accompanying illustration. Study the content of these records. Pay special attention to the way in which entries fit within the attributes that you specified in the previous lesson.

Your job at this point is to add records to the existing HOTCAR2 file. To do so, press ESC to return to the DATA ENTRY AND PROCESSING MENU.

5. You now want to add records to the HOTCAR2 database file. Selection 1, ENTER RECORDS TO AN EXISTING FILE, provides this capability. So, enter a 1 now, and press RETURN to activate your selection.

6. STARTware now prompts you for a file name. In other words, STARTware needs to know the name of the file in which you want to enter records. Enter the following file name and then press RETURN.

HOTCAR2

7. STARTware now displays the "ENTERing Data Records" screen. This display shows the attributes for each field, so that you can make sure your entries fit within the defined attributes. For this practice session, you will add three records to the existing database. The content of each record is shown below. Study these records before you continue. Also study the screen instructions for entering records.

LIC#	ST	YR	MAKE	MODEL	COLOR	BODY	REGOWN	LASTSEEN
YBB 123	AZ	82	HONDA	CRX500	BLACK	MC	VOSS KENNETH A	10/30/90
ABX 511	NM	84	DODGE	OMNI	BLUE	2DR	LAMERS ROSE	10/30/90
TB 5979	OH	88	FORD	ESCORT	BEIGE	SDAN	BURGETT LINDA S	10/30/90

8. Enter the above three records into the HOTCAR2 database file. Use the keys described on the screen to make any necessary corrections. When you are ready to continue, press ESC to store your entries onto your STARTware disk.

9. You now have completed Lesson 6. Remove your STARTware disk from the drive and return it to its protective sleeve. Turn off your computer system and wait for further instructions from your teacher.

```
File: HOTCAR              REVIEW/ADD/CHANGE          Escape: Main Menu

Selection: All records


LIC#            ST            YR            MAKE
=========================================================================
YBB 123         AZ            82            HONDA
ABX 511         NM            84            DODGE
TB 5979         OH            88            FORD
-               -             -             -




-------------------------------------------------------------------------
Type entry or use Apple commands                          Apple-? for Help
```

This AppleWorks multiple-record layout screen has the ability to list content of several records within a display.

AppleWorks PROCEDURES

In Lesson 6, you will display records in the HOT-CAR database, add a few new records, and change the content of an existing record.

1. Follow the startup procedures described in Lesson 5. When you reach the "Add files" screen, select option 1. This option tells AppleWorks to load an existing file from disk into memory (the desktop).

   AppleWorks now lists the files currently stored on the disk in drive 1. Use the Down Arrow cursor to highlight the HOTCAR database file. When this file name is highlighted, press RETURN.

2. The HOTCAR file now is displayed in *multiple-record layout,* shown below. This term means that AppleWorks lists several records on a single screen. With the multiple-record layout, AppleWorks will display as many fields and records as can fit on a screen. Each record is displayed across a single row. Fields, or categories, are displayed in columns. Take a moment to study the multiple-record layout for the HOTCAR file you created in Lesson 5. Your display should be the same as the accompanying illustration.

3. The next step is to add three new records to the HOTCAR file. However, you cannot add records to the end of a file when the multiple-record layout is currently in use. Instead, you need to switch to the *single-record layout.* This layout looks a lot like the one you used to enter records in Lesson 5.

   To switch to single-record layout, begin by moving the cursor to the last record in the HOT-CAR file. This is the third record in the file. Now enter the "zoom" command by pressing Apple-Z. That is, hold down the Apple key, then press Z.

4. AppleWorks now "zooms in" on the single-record layout for record number 3. To indicate that you want to go past this record, press the Apple-Down Arrow key combination. The program now asks you if you want to insert new records. Select "Yes" by pressing RETURN.

5. Now add the following three records into the HOTCAR database. Follow the same data entry procedures that you used in Lesson 5. After you have entered all fields for these records, go on to Step 5.

   NOTE: Make sure to press RETURN after you enter the LS DATE field in each record. If you fail to do so, AppleWorks will not store the dates that you enter.

Here are the records to be entered now:

LIC#	ST	YR	MAKE	MODEL	COLOR	BODY	REGISTERED OWNER	LS DATE
EBZ 842	AZ	86	HONDA	CIVIC	GOLD	WGN	BAUMAN CHRISTINA G	10/25/90
BBY 176	AZ	82	TOYOT	COROLLA	BLUE	HTCH	PRONK RONALD R	10/27/90
WHY 845	CA	87	OLDS	CUTLASS	WHITE	SDAN	KRUSE BETTIJUNE	10/2790

When you are finished, zoom back to the multiple-record layout by pressing Apple-Z. AppleWorks now displays six records, including the three that you have just entered.

6. The next step is to make a few changes to existing records. If you have made any mistakes in entering records, you can make these corrections also.

   To begin, use the Up Arrow key to go to the first record (the one with license number YBB 123). The model for this entry is incorrect. It now reads "CRX 500." However, it should read "CX 500."

   To make the change, zoom to single-record display. Then move the cursor to the "X" in "CRX 500." Now press the Del key to remove the letter "R."

7. Another change is necessary. In the second record (with license number ABX 511), the first name of the registered owner is misspelled. The name currently reads "ROSE." However, it should read "ROSS." To make this change, move the cursor down until "Record 2 of 6" is displayed. Now move the cursor past the "E" in "ROSE." Now enter an "S" to correct the spelling error. Notice, however, that the "E" was not deleted. Instead, it was pushed forward. To remove this letter, press the Apple-Y key combination.

   You now can see how simple it is to make corrections to existing records. If you made any additional errors when you entered records, correct them now. When you are certain that your HOTCAR file is correct, continue to Step 8.

8. You now are ready to save your new file. Press ESC to return to the AppleWorks main menu.

Select the "Save desktop files to disk" option by pressing a 3 and then RETURN.

At the current screen, select option 1 to save the file on the current disk.

The next prompt asks you whether you want to save your file with the existing name HOTCAR or with some new name. In this case, you should keep the contents of the HOTCAR file you created in Lesson 5. So, select option 2 to save your work to a new file. When AppleWorks prompts for a file name, enter this name:

HOTCAR2

Use Apple-Y to delete extra characters in the name, then press RETURN to save your work to disk.

9. Follow procedures that you have learned earlier to quit the AppleWorks program. You now have completed Lesson 6. Remove your AppleWorks disks from the disk drives and return them to their protective sleeves. Turn off your computer and wait for further instructions from your teacher.

Lesson 7

Using a Database Management System: Manipulating Multiple Files

INTRODUCTION

One of the chief values of a database management system lies in the ability to create, modify, and process multiple files. In this lesson, you will see how STARTware can use two or more files within a single database.

Consider that the Arizona state police department that uses the HOTCAR2 file created in Lesson 6 wants to produce a report that lists out-of-state stolen vehicles. This report will be used to notify other states about vehicles registered by their agencies that have been stolen in Arizona.

For this lesson, you will create an out-of-state hot car file called OSHOTCAR. This file will contain information only on stolen vehicles registered in states other than Arizona. This allows the police department to create a report that lists out-of-state stolen vehicles. Your job will be to create this new file for the period ending October 30, 1990.

STARTware PROCEDURES

1. Make sure your computer is turned off before you begin. Boot DOS and bypass the date and time prompts by pressing RETURN at each prompt. Load the STARTware DBMS by entering the following command at the A > prompt:

   db

   Press ENTER to display the DATABASE MANAGEMENT MAIN MENU.

2. At this point, you want to copy the HOTCAR2 file into a new file that can be modified. You will name this file OSHOTCAR (for "Out-of-state Hot Car"). The copy option is provided on the DATABASE MANIPULATION/QUERY COMMAND MENU. So select 2 from the main menu and press RETURN.

```
STARTware: DB ::::::::::::::::::::::::::::::::::::::::::::::::::
T                                                     ::
A          DATABASE MANIPULATION/QUERY MENU           ::
R                                                     ::
T    1.  SORT                                          ::
v    2.  SELECT                                        ::
a    3.  PROJECT                                       ::
r    4.  COMPUTE                                       ::
e    5.  JOIN                                          ::
::   6.  DELETE                                        S
::   7.  COPY                                          T
::   8.  UNION                                         A
::   9.  DISPLAY                                       R
::                                                    'T
::                                                     v
::      ENTER NUMBER OF SELECTION AND PRESS [RETURN] > a
::                                                     r
::::::::::::::::::::::::::::::::::::::::::::::::::STARTware
Press [Esc] and [Return] to quit menu.
```

This STARTware display provides a choice of available manipulation and query commands.

3. Notice that the displayed menu provides several options for changing or manipulating the contents of existing database files. You want to copy an existing file into a new file. So, select the COPY option by pressing 7 and then RETURN.

   The STARTware system responds by asking you for the name of the file to be copied. Enter the name HOTCAR2 and press RETURN.

   The system now asks for the new file name for the copied file. Recall that this file will be called OSHOTCAR. So, enter this file name now, then press RETURN. STARTware continues by creating a duplicate file under the new name OSHOTCAR.

4. Now that you have created a working file, you can make changes to it without affecting the content of your original, HOTCAR2, file. The idea here is to *select* only those records that have out-of-state license plates.

   From the DATABASE MANIPULATION/ QUERY MENU, press 2 (for the SELECT option) and then RETURN. This causes the STARTware database to select only those records that meet *criteria* that you specify. The term "criteria" refers to field values that must be tested to determine which records will be contained in the SELECTed file.

5. The SELECT option begins by prompting you for the field number to be used in defining your selections. In this case, you want to use Field 2, ST. The reason: You want to base your selection on state fields that are not equal to AZ (Arizona). So, enter a 2 next to the prompt and press RETURN.

   The system now prompts you for a *relationship* to a *comparison value* that you will specify next. For this application, your comparison value will be "AZ" to compare the ST field of records to determine whether they are greater or less than (not equal to) "AZ."

   The relationship is defined by the following operators:

> for greater than the comparison value

< for less than the comparison value

> = for greater than or equal to the comparison value

< = for less than or equal to the comparison value

= for equal to the comparison value

< > for less than or greater than the comparison value

You want to select all records that are less than or greater than the comparison value (AZ). Enter the following next to the prompt, then press RETURN:

< >

6. STARTware responds by prompting you for the comparison value. Enter the following value:

AZ

Your SPECIFYING SELECTION screen should now look like the one in the accompanying illustration. If it does not, press ESC to exit the SELECT and try again. If your screen matches the one shown, press RETURN to carry out the SELECT operation.

```
          ------------------------------
          :     SPECIFYING SELECTION    :
          ------------------------------
 FIELD  /Field  /Data/Field/No. of/
 NUMBER / Name  /Type/Width/Decim./

    1     LIC#    C    8    0
    2     ST      C    2    0
    3     YR      C    2    0
    4     MAKE    C    5    0
    5     MODEL   C   10    0
    6     COLOR   C    5    0
    7     BODY    C    4    0
    8     REGOWN  C   20    0
    9     LASTSEEN C  15    0
    ESC to cancel the SELECT

    ENTER FIELD NUMBER FOR SELECT >2
    ENTER RELATIONSHIP : >,<,>=,<=,=,<> <>
    ENTER COMPARISON VALUE : AZ
```

*This **STARTware screen** is used to enter search parameters for file access operations.*

This step completes the SELECT operation. STARTware removes from the OSHOTCAR file all records that **do not** match the selected criteria. In other words, this file should now contain only those records that have out-of-state license plates.

To check this, select the DISPLAY option from the DATABASE MANIPULATION/QUERY MENU. That is, select 9 and press RETURN.

7. STARTware now should display three records. These records, shown in the accompanying display, reflect the entire content of the OSHOTCAR file:

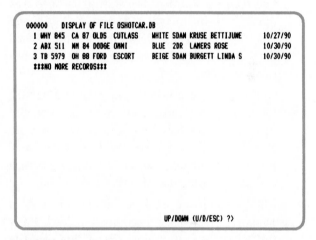

```
000000    DISPLAY OF FILE OSHOTCAR.DB
 1 WHY 845  CA 87 OLDS  CUTLASS    WHITE SDAN KRUSE BETTIJUNE    10/27/90
 2 ABI 511  NM 84 DODGE OMNI       BLUE  2DR  LANERS ROSE        10/30/90
 3 TB 5979  OH 88 FORD  ESCORT     BEIGE SDAN BURGETT LINDA S    10/30/90
‡‡‡NO MORE RECORDS‡‡‡





                        UP/DOWN (U/D/ESC) ?>
```

STARTware lists all records that meet criteria in response to a search operation.

8. If your display matches the one shown in the accompanying illustration, you have successfully completed the database management lessons for this Appendix. Continue on to Step 9.

If your display differs from the one shown in the accompanying illustration, review Steps 3 through 6 of this lesson to determine the problem. First, try to identify and correct your processing errors on your own. If you feel that you need help, ask your teacher for assistance. When you have created the OSHOTCAR file correctly, continue on to Step 9.

9. Congratulations. You have completed the database management portion of this Appendix. The STARTware system automatically saved your OSHOTCAR file to disk when it was created. So, you can remove the STARTware disk now and return it to its protective sleeve. Turn off your computer system and wait for further instructions from your teacher.

AppleWorks PROCEDURES

1. Make sure your computer is turned off before you begin. Follow the startup procedures described in Lessons 5 and 6. Add the HOTCAR2 database file to the desktop. When the contents of this file are on your screen, continue to Step 2.

2. At this point, you want to copy the HOTCAR2 file into a new file that can be modified. You will name this file OSHOTCAR (for "Out-of-State Hot Car"). To begin, you need to create a new file that has the same structure (category names and other formats) as the HOTCAR2 file.

   The first step is to rename the file currently in memory. The rename function is Apple-N. Press this key combination now. Enter this new file name next to the prompt:

   HOTCAR3

   Press RETURN to save this name. Then Press ESC to return to your database display. Keep in mind that you have changed the name of the file in memory only. The HOTCAR2 file that you created in the previous lesson still is stored safely on disk. In a moment, you will see why this renaming feature is important.

3. Now you need to insert an empty record that will serve as a basis for adding records later. Zoom to single-record display. Make sure your cursor is positioned at the top of your database file (at the start of the first record). Now press Apple-I to insert an empty record here.

4. You now are ready to *initialize* this file by deleting all records except the empty one that you just created. File initializing clears the contents of a file and prepares it for a new set of processing activities.

   To begin the initialization operation. Zoom back to multiple-record display. Place your cursor on the second record (which was the first record before you inserted the empty one). Press the Apple-D key combination to specify a delete operation. Now press the Apple-9 combination. This command tells AppleWorks to highlight all material from the starting point to the end of the file. Now press RETURN. Your HOTCAR3 database is initialized and ready for further processing.

5. Press ESC to return to the main menu. Now use the add files option to add the HOTCAR2 file to the desktop. (Remember, the file you added at the start of this lesson now is called OSHOTCAR). Your complete HOTCAR2 file should be displayed before you continue to Step 6.

6. The idea here is to *select* only those records that have out-of-state license plates. Then you will copy these records into your OSHOTCAR file.

   To make a selection in AppleWorks, you have to specify the criteria, or *rules* that the computer will use to find only the records that you want. In this case, you want AppleWorks to select only those records that do not have an AZ in the ST field.

   Press Apple-R to set the selection rules. You now should see a list of category names, with a number provided for each category. Notice that ST is category 2. To select this category, enter a 2 and press RETURN.

7. AppleWorks now displays a set of *relationships* that you can use to determine which ST records to select. These relationships are shown in an accompanying illustration. For this lesson, you want to select all records with an ST field that is not equal to AZ. As you can see, the "is not

equal to'' relationship is number 4 on the menu. Enter a 4 now and press RETURN.

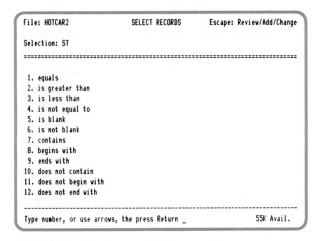

AppleWorks relational operators *are presented on this screen.*

AppleWorks now needs some comparison information. In particular, the program needs to know which value in the state file to use in making its comparison. So far, you have told AppleWorks to use the ST category to make an ''is not equal to'' comparison. In a sense, AppleWorks now needs to know ''is not equal to *what*?''

To provide this comparison information, enter the following next to the prompt:

AZ

Press RETURN to store this information. Apple-Works now knows that it should select all records with a ST value that is not equal to AZ. The program next gives you the opportunity to include more comparison information. Since you are through entering comparison information, press ESC. AppleWorks now makes the selection, then displays these records for you.

8. At this point, you are ready to copy the selected records into the OSHOTCAR file. You will use AppleWorks' *clipboard* function to do this. The clipboard is an area in memory that AppleWorks sets aside to store data temporarily that will be moved or copied in some way.

Position the cursor on the first record currently being displayed. Now press the Apple-C command to tell AppleWorks that you want to copy records somewhere. When AppleWorks asks you whether you want to copy to the current document to the clipboard or to other options, choose the ''to the clipboard'' option and press RETURN. Now press the down arrow key to highlight all three records for copying. Press RETURN to store them in the clipboard area of memory.

9. Now press Apple-Q to select the file to which the records will be copied. Highlight OSHOTCAR, if this file is not already highlighted. Press RETURN. Zoom to the multiple-record display. AppleWorks now should display the empty record of the initialized OSHOTCAR file. This is where you want to copy the out-of-state records.

Press Apple-C to continue the copy operation. Now select the ''From clipboard'' option to tell AppleWorks you want to copy records that are currently stored in the clipboard area of memory. AppleWorks now displays your new OSHOT-CAR file, with only the out-of-state records shown.

10. Now follow the steps you learned in Lessons 5 and 6 to save your OSHOTCAR file to disk. Keep the name OSHOTCAR when you perform the save operation. When you are finished, return to the main menu and quit the program. Finally, remove your AppleWorks program and data disks from their drives and return them to their protective sleeves.

Congratulations. You have completed the database management section of this Appendix. Turn off your computer and wait for further instructions from your teacher.

Lesson 8

Using a Spreadsheet Package: Creating a Spreadsheet

INTRODUCTION

Lesson 8 introduces you to some basic features of electronic spreadsheet packages. An electronic spreadsheet allows you to record, calculate, and modify financial information efficiently. A built-in ability to create *formulas* helps you to make calculations and modifications rapidly. With built-in formulas, managers can make several spreadsheets that show projections about business activity under different conditions. You will see how these formulas can be used in a later lesson.

For this lesson, you will begin to familiarize yourself with the STARTware or AppleWorks spreadsheet system. Think back to the VidView videocassette rental store discussed in Chapter 19. The manager for this store wants to analyze the projected budget for the coming year by comparing it with the budget for the previous year. This type of projection is called a *pro forma* report. It will be your job to create and specify labels and formulas for this spreadsheet.

STARTware PROCEDURES

1. Begin this lesson with your computer turned off. Remove your DOS disk from its sleeve and place it in the A disk drive. Turn on your computer system and wait for the date prompt. Bypass both the date and time prompts by pressing RETURN twice. The operating system now should display the A > prompt.

2. Remove your DOS disk from the drive and return it to its protective sleeve. Place your STARTware disk in the A drive. To load the spreadsheet portion of STARTware, enter the following command next to the A > prompt.

   ss

3. Your system now should display a blank STARTware spreadsheet screen that matches the one in an accompanying illustration. Study this display for a few moments. Focus your attention on the top two lines shown on the screen. The top line displays the *status* of the spreadsheet program, including the name of the spreadsheet currently in use.

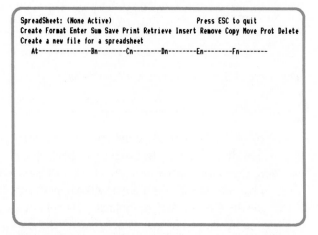

```
SpreadSheet: (None Active)                    Press ESC to quit
Create Format Enter Sum Save Print Retrieve Insert Remove Copy Move Prot Delete
Create a new file for a spreadsheet
    At--------------Bn--------Cn--------Dn--------En--------Fn--------
```

STARTware spreadsheet construction *begins from this screen display.*

When you are working within the spreadsheet, the status line also will display the *row* number and *column* letter position of the cursor. The combination of a row number and column letter defines a data entry area called a *cell*. In other words, a cell is the block created by the intersection of a row and column. You will enter labels, values, and formulas into these cells. You will see how cells are used to enter data in Lesson 9.

Notice that the status line indicates that no spreadsheet is active, or open, at present. You will create a new spreadsheet in a moment.

The second line of the spreadsheet display is called a *menu bar.* This type of menu lists processing choices horizontally, or along a row.

Briefly study the spreadsheet processing options available to you. Notice that a *tutor line* below the menu bar describes the menu option currently being highlighted. You can move through the menu bar by using the left and right Arrow keys shown on the numeric keypad. Take about 30 seconds to experiment with these keys. Note how the message on the tutor line changes as you move the cursor.

4. To begin, you normally must create a new spreadsheet. This activity instructs the program to set aside space on the STARTware disk for storing your work. For this lesson, a file name has been created for you. You can retrieve this empty spreadsheet file by highlighting the "Retrieve" option from the menu bar. Do this now. Highlight "Retrieve" and then press RETURN.

5. STARTware displays a new screen called RETRIEVE A NEW SPREADSHEET FILE, reproduced in an accompanying illustration. Read the contents of this screen before you continue. The display contains a *directory* of existing spreadsheet files. To retrieve an existing spreadsheet, you must enter a file name. Notice that the directory contains a file named VVPROFOR. This name is an abbreviation for

```
  ----------------------------------
  |  RETRIEVE A SPREADSHEET FILE   |
  ----------------------------------

          DIRECTORY OF EXISTING FILES

  VVPROFOR
    Protected Files:
    VVPRO3




          ENTER FILE NAME AND PRESS RETURN >

        PRESS ESC TO RETURN TO SPREADSHEET COMMAND LINE
```

This STARTware screen *enables a user to retrieve a spreadsheet file.*

"VidView *Pro forma.*" You will retrieve VVPROFOR for this lesson.

The following prompt for a file name is shown near the bottom of the screen:

**ENTER FILE NAME AND
PRESS RETURN >**

On many computers, the RETURN key is labeled ENTER. Whenever you see the instruction "PRESS RETURN" on the screen, use either the RETURN or ENTER key on your keyboard.

Enter the following name next to the prompt:

vvprofor

6. STARTware searches its directory for this file and then provides you with the main spreadsheet display. However, notice that the status line now indicates that the spreadsheet VVPROFOR is currently active, or open.

Take a look at the top line in the spreadsheet area of the display. This line contains sets of letters, such as "At," "Bn," and "Cn," as well as a set of dashed lines between each set of letters. The first letter in each set provides the column position. The second letter, along with the dashed line, specifies the *data type* and *width* for each column.

Data types include *numeric* for numbers and *text* for columns that will contain labels only. In other words, the column marked with the set of letters "At" indicates that this is column A, and will store data that have type "text." Column A has a text data type because it will be used to store labels that describe the content of other columns.

To begin creating labels, highlight the "Enter" option on the menu bar and press RETURN. The "Enter" option lets you exit the menu bar and enter the spreadsheet work area.

7. You now can move through the spreadsheet in two basic ways. First, you can move the *cell pointer* by pressing the RETURN key. The cell pointer is a bar that indicates the cell in which you currently are working. Notice that the cell

pointer currently is in column A, row 1—that is, cell A1.

Practice moving through cells by pressing the RETURN key a few times. You can move backwards through cells by pressing the key combination SHIFT-Tab. Try pressing this key combination a few times. When you are done, press the Home key on the numeric keypad. This key returns you to cell A1, the first cell position of your spreadsheet.

The second method for moving through the spreadsheet is through use of the cursor control keys—the arrow keys on the numeric keypad of your keyboard. The left and right arrow keys allow you to move one character position at a time through a single cell. The Up and Down Arrow keys allow you to move to higher or lower rows of the spreadsheet. Practice using these keys now. When you feel comfortable with your ability to navigate through a spreadsheet screen, press ESC.

8. The ESC key returns you to the menu bar of your spreadsheet. At this point, you have completed your work for Lesson 8. In the next lesson, you will create labels for your *pro forma* report.

9. Note that the status line currently displays the message "Press ESC to quit." You are ready to end your current work session. So, press ESC now. If you have made any text entries in the VVPROFOR spreadsheet, STARTware will ask you if you want to save these changes. If you see this prompt now, select "NO" and press RETURN. If you have not made any entries in the spreadsheet, STARTware will return you to the main menu. Remove the STARTware disk from the drive and return it to its protective sleeve. Turn off your computer system and await further instructions from your teacher.

AppleWorks PROCEDURES

1. Your computer system should be turned off when you begin this lesson. With your system turned off, insert your AppleWorks startup disk in drive 1, and your data disk in drive 2. Then, turn on the power switch of your computer (as well as the monitor switch, if this applies to your system).

When the prompt appears on the screen, replace the startup disk with the AppleWorks program disk. Press RETURN to continue.

2. When the date prompt appears, bypass it by pressing the RETURN key on your keyboard. You will not need to enter the date for these lessons. The AppleWorks main menu now should appear on your screen.

3. At this point, you want to create, or add, a file into memory (the desktop). Select option 1 and press RETURN. AppleWorks now displays the Add Files menu. For this lesson, you want to create a new file for the spreadsheet program. As you can see from the display, this is option 5 from the Add Files menu. Enter a 5 now and press RETURN to continue.

4. AppleWorks now displays the spreadsheet "make a new file" screen. To add a file, AppleWorks needs to know whether you want to add a file from "scratch" or from a file built with a different program or operating system. In this case, you want to build a file from scratch. Select option 1.

You now need to specify a name for your new file. For this lesson, you will be creating a spreadsheet that you can use for practice only. So enter the name PRACTICE now and press RETURN to continue.

5. AppleWorks now displays a blank spreadsheet screen, as illustrated. This screen includes four lines of information—two at the top and two at the bottom. The top line is called a *status line* and includes the name of the spreadsheet file currently in use. This line also tells you that the spreadsheet program is in REVIEW/ADD/CHANGE mode. In this mode, you can look through a spreadsheet file (REVIEW), add information to the spreadsheet (ADD), and make

changes to the content of the spreadsheet (CHANGE).

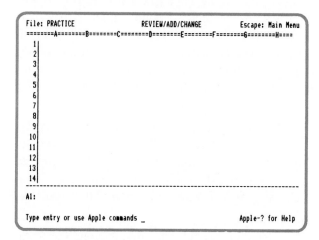

```
File: PRACTICE              REVIEW/ADD/CHANGE          Escape: Main Menu
=======A=======B=======C=======D=======E=======F=======G=======H====
    1|
    2|
    3|
    4|
    5|
    6|
    7|
    8|
    9|
   10|
   11|
   12|
   13|
   14|
_____
A1:

Type entry or use Apple commands _              Apple-? for Help
```

This AppleWorks screen is set up for spreadsheet entries for the PRACTICE file.

The second line near the top of the screen is called the *format line.* This line provides letters that name each column. In AppleWorks, a column name (letter) is centered over its column. The dotted lines between column letters indicate the width, in characters, of each column. Also notice that, along the left side of the spreadsheet, a set of numbers runs from top to bottom. These numbers identify the rows of the spreadsheet.

Now take a look at the two lines near the bottom of the screen. The first line is called the *cell indicator.* With a spreadsheet, a *cell* refers to a rectangular data entry area formed by the intersection of a column and row. The bottom line is called a *tutor line* that provides instruction to guide you through spreadsheet operations.

6. You now can move through the spreadsheet by using the arrow keys to manipulate the *cell highlighter.* The cell highlighter is a bar that indicates the cell in which you currently are working. Notice that the cell pointer currently is in column A, row 1—that is, cell A1. Practice moving

through cells by pressing the four arrow keys. When you feel comfortable about your ability to use the arrow keys to move through cells, continue to Step 7.

7. To enter data into a cell, you begin by positioning the highlight cursor, or simply highlight, on the cell that you want. Then, you enter data. However, your entries will appear in the cell indicator line, not the cell itself. AppleWorks places data in the cell only after you move the Left Arrow or Right Arrow key.

When you use one of these keys during data entry, you are telling AppleWorks that you want to store your entry in the currently highlighted cell and move on to the next cell. You can also store data in a cell by pressing RETURN. When you press RETURN, AppleWorks stores your data but does not move to a new cell. So, you must use the arrow keys to move between cells.

Also, you can make corrections during data entry by pressing the Delete key. Each time you press Delete, AppleWorks will backspace and erase one character shown on the cell indicator line.

8. Practice using the cell indicator line to enter data. Don't worry about ruining the appearance of your PRACTICE file. You can exit the spreadsheet without saving your work. When you feel comfortable that you understand, in general, how the cursor highlight and the cursor indicator are used, continue to Step 9.

9. Press ESC now to return to the main menu. There is no need to save the spreadsheet, since you were only experimenting. Select option 6 and Quit the program without saving your PRACTICE file. At this point, you have completed your work for Lesson 8. In the next lesson, you will create labels for your income analysis spreadsheet.

Remove the AppleWorks program and data disks from their drives and return them to their protective sleeves. Turn off your computer system and wait for further instructions from your teacher.

Lesson 9

Using a Spreadsheet Package: Labeling a Spreadsheet

INTRODUCTION

In this lesson, you will enter labels that describe the contents of your spreadsheet. Labels include *title lines, column headings,* and *row headings.* A title line names your spreadsheet. Ideally, a title line should tell about the purpose of your spreadsheet—that is, the reason you have created the spreadsheet. A column heading describes the content of a column of data. A row heading describes the content of a row of data.

STARTware PROCEDURES

1. Begin this lesson with your computer off. Use your DOS disk to boot DOS and to arrive at the A > prompt. Then load the STARTware spreadsheet. If you are not sure how to perform these activities, refer to Steps 1 through 3 of Lesson 8.

2. The blank spreadsheet display should be showing on your screen. You need to retrieve your *pro forma* spreadsheet file, VVPROFOR. To do so, highlight the "Retrieve" selection from the menu bar and press RETURN.

3. When the RETRIEVE A SPREADSHEET FILE screen appears, enter the name of your spreadsheet file. That is, enter the following:

VVPROFOR

You may use either uppercase (capital) or lowercase (small) letters when you enter the file name. STARTware accepts both sets of characters. Press RETURN when you are ready to continue. STARTware will load the specified spreadsheet into memory and then will return you to the spreadsheet display screen and menu bar.

4. To begin making entries in the VVPROFOR

spreadsheet, highlight the "Enter" option from the menu bar and press RETURN.

5. The title of the spreadsheet will begin in row 1. Notice that the cell pointer now is located in column A of row 1. This is called cell A1 and is the *home* position, or starting point, of the spreadsheet. Press RETURN once to place the cell pointer in cell B1. This is where you begin entering the title line for the spreadsheet.

Before you begin to make entries, recognize this important feature of STARTware: When you have finished entering data into each cell, you must press RETURN to store your work. Otherwise, STARTware will ignore what you have done.

Also, you cannot enter data beyond the maximum width of a cell. For instance, cell B1 has a maximum width of 10 characters. (To check this, count characters in the format line, beginning with the letter "B" and ending with the final dash character before the letter "C." So, if you want to create a title line that fills more than one cell, you must press RETURN after you have filled each cell. For example, imagine that you want to enter this title:

My Practice Spreadsheet

This entry requires 23 character positions. If you are entering this title into cells that have a width of 10 characters each, three cells will be required to hold the title. Thus, when you enter the tenth character—the second "c" in "Practice"—you must press RETURN to store your work and to go on to the next cell. In turn, when you reach the twentieth character, the "h" in "Spreadsheet," you must press RETURN again. When you finish entering the word "Spreadsheet," you have to press RETURN a third time to save your work in this third cell.

You are ready to check your knowledge of these features. Beginning at the first character position in cell B1, enter the following title:

VidView Pro Forma

When you have finished, the cell pointer should be positioned in cell D1. If your entry looks like the one in the accompanying illustration, go on to Step 6. If you need to correct any errors, do so now and then continue to Step 6.

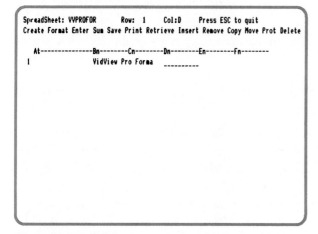

The spreadsheet title has been included in this START-ware display.

6. The remaining labels to be entered are for column and row headings. The pro forma statement will include two basic types of accounts: income and expense.

For each account, you will enter the budgeted amount for the previous year. Then, you will enter the projected amount for each account—for next year's budget. Finally, you want STARTware to calculate the difference between these two amounts—for each account. This is done by subtracting the budgeted amount for the previous year from the projected amount for the new year. The result will be stored in a separate column. Managers can use these amounts to study the increase or decrease in an amount for the projected year.

The manager of VidView also wants you to calculate the total income for the previous budget and for the projected budget. Similarly, you are to calculate total expenses for the previous budget and for the projected budget. These totals then will be used to calculate the profit (or loss) for each year. The profit is calculated by subtracting total expenses from total income.

The manager of VidView has given you a handwritten spreadsheet format that shows the column and row labels that you are to use. This format, shown in the accompanying illustration, also indicates the cells you are to use in entering labels.

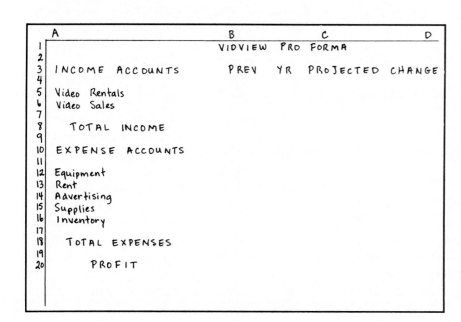

This handwritten spreadsheet provides input to the STARTware file for the VidView pro forma statement.

7. Enter all labels shown on the handwritten spreadsheet form. Your entries should appear in the cell positions indicated on the form. Also, be sure to store your work in memory by pressing RETURN after you have completed each cell entry. This step should take about 10 minutes to complete. When you have entered all labels correctly, continue to Step 8.

8. You now have a formatted and labeled spreadsheet display that can be saved to your STARTware disk. A spreadsheet that has been formatted and labeled, but contains no data, is called a *template*. A template is useful because you can store it as a separate file, then retrieve it as often as necessary to create different spreadsheets that share the same format and labels.

   You are ready to save your template. Press ESC to return to the menu bar.

9. Highlight the "Save" selection from the menu bar and press RETURN. For this lesson, you will save your spreadsheet template under a different name. At the prompt for a file name, enter the following:

   VVTEMPLA

   This name, of course, is short for "VidView Template." Once your template has been saved, it can be used or modified repeatedly to create new budgets and pro forma reports.

   Press RETURN to save your template under the name VVTEMPLA.

10. You have completed Lesson 9. In the next lesson, you will practice entering values and formulas into your spreadsheet. Remove your STARTware disk from the drive and return it to its protective sleeve. Turn off your computer system and wait for further instructions from your teacher.

AppleWorks PROCEDURES

1. Follow the startup procedures described in Lesson 8 to start AppleWorks. Use the Add Files option to add a new spreadsheet file called VVINCOME. The managers of VidView want you to use this file to enter past and projected income information about the VidView store. Later, the "income analysis" file that you create will be expanded into a complete *pro forma* statement.

   If you are unsure about the steps to follow in making a new file, review Steps 1 through 5 in Lesson 8. When your screen shows a blank spreadsheet, with the file name VVINCOME in the status line, continue to Step 2 of this lesson.

2. The sales manager for VidView has prepared a handwritten format that you can follow in entering spreadsheet labels. This format, shown in an accompanying illustration, includes the title, column, and row headings.

   Notice that the title of the spreadsheet will begin in cell A1. (Notice that the cell pointer now is located in column A of row 1. This is called cell A1 and is the *home* position, or starting point, of the spreadsheet. This is where you begin entering the title line for the spreadsheet.)

   Before you begin to make entries, recognize this important feature of AppleWorks: When you are making labels, the program allows you to enter letters continuously across two or more cells. AppleWorks knows that you are entering a label whenever you begin data entry with a letter of the alphabet, rather than a number or some other character. When you fill up a cell with characters, AppleWorks automatically moves the cell highlight to the next cell position. You simply continue entry of your label until you are finished.

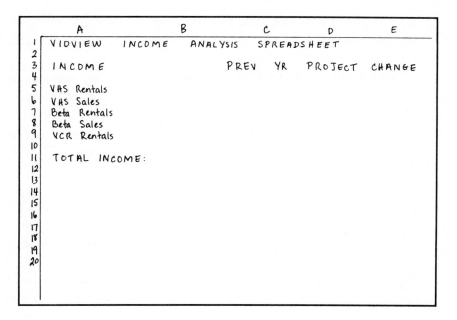

Input for the AppleWorks spreadsheet to be used for VidView income analysis is presented in this handwritten worksheet.

You are ready to check your knowledge of some AppleWorks spreadsheet features. Enter the following title now:

VidView Income Analysis Spreadsheet

Use the Delete key to correct any errors before you continue. When you are finished with this title, you can continue by entering column headings. To do so, position the cell highlight in cell A3.

3. Four labels are needed to describe the column headings. These headings will be placed in cells A3, C3, D3, and E3. Use the handwritten spreadsheet format, shown above, to enter these column headings now. Continue with Step 4 after you are certain your entries are correct.

4. The next step in creating the spreadsheet format is to include row labels. Notice from the handwritten form that five labels are needed for the five income accounts—VHS Rentals, VHS Sales, Beta Rentals, Beta Sales, and VCR Rentals. These row labels are to be placed in cells A5 through A9. A sixth label will be used to show the total income for all five accounts, for each

analysis category (Previous Year, Projected, and Change).

Enter these row labels now. Your labeled spreadsheet should look like the one in the accompanying illustration. When you are certain that your entries are correct, continue with Step 5.

```
File: VVINCOME              REVIEW/ADD/CHANGE         Escape: Main Menu
=======A=======B=======C=======D=======E=======F=======G=======H====
 1 VidView Income Analysis Spreadsheet
 2
 3 INCOME          PREV YR PROJECT  CHANGE
 4
 5 VHS Rentals
 6 VHS Sales
 7 Beta Rentals
 8 Beta Sales
 9 VCR Rentals
10
11 TOTAL INCOME:
12
13
14
------------------------------------------------------------------
A1:

Type entry or use Apple commands _          Apple-? for Help
```

The AppleWorks spreadsheet for the VidView income analysis application is shown on this screen.

5. You now have a formatted and labeled spreadsheet display that can be saved to disk. A spreadsheet that has been formatted and labeled, but contains no data, is called a *template.* A template is useful because you can store it as a separate file, then retrieve it as often as necessary to create different spreadsheets that share the same format and labels.

6. You are ready to save your template. Press ESC to return to the main menu. Select option 3, "Save Desktop files to disk." That is, enter a 3 and press RETURN. Next, specify that you want to save the VVINCOME file, which is the only file currently stored in the desktop. Next, tell AppleWorks that you want to save this file to the current disk drive. Finally, tell AppleWorks that you want to save the file under a new name, VVTEMPLATE. Return to the main menu and quit the program.

You have completed Lesson 9. Remove your AppleWorks program and data disks from the drives and return them to their protective sleeves. Turn off your computer and wait for further instructions from your teacher.

Using a Spreadsheet: Entering Formulas and Making Calculations

INTRODUCTION

With an electronic spreadsheet, it isn't necessary to use a calculator or adding machine to compute totals. In a sense, an electronic spreadsheet provides a built-in calculator that performs these operations automatically. However, it is up to you to enter formulas that the program can follow in making calculations. In this lesson, you will practice using some of the spreadsheet formulas available with STARTware or AppleWorks.

STARTware PROCEDURES

1. Begin with your computer turned off. Boot DOS, then load the STARTware spreadsheet program. Retrieve the spreadsheet template file that you saved in Lesson 9. When the labeled spreadsheet display appears on your screen, continue to Step 2.

2. Select "Enter" from the menu bar to enter the worksheet area of your spreadsheet. Before you begin entering formulas, practice entering a few numbers into cells. For this lesson, do not use commas within numbers. Also, don't worry about aligning, or positioning numbers correctly under each other. STARTware will do this for you automatically when it makes calculations.

Use the table below to enter income amounts for the previous year and for the projected year:

	PREVIOUS YEAR	PROJECTED YEAR
Video Rentals	200595	220955
Video Sales	64350	76650

3. When you have completed entering the four income values, your spreadsheet should look like the one in the accompanying illustration.

```
SpreadSheet: VVTEMPLA                           Press ESC to quit
Create Format Enter Sum Save Print Retrieve Insert Remove Copy Move Prot Delete
Retrieve a spreadsheet previously Saved in a disk file
 1                    VidView Pro Forma
 2
 3 INCOME ACCOUNTS  PREV. YR. PROJECTED CHANGE
 4
 5 VHS Rentals      200595    220955
 6 VHS Sales         64350     76650
 7
 8    TOTAL INCOME
 9
10 EXPENSE ACCOUNTS
11
12 Equipment
13 Rent
14 Advertising
15 Supplies
16
17    TOTAL EXPENSES
18
19    PROFIT
```

This STARTware spreadsheet contains initial entries for the VidView pro forma statement.

If your spreadsheet matches the one shown, press ESC to return to the menu bar. If your spreadsheet differs from the one shown, make the necessary corrections. Then, press ESC to return to the menu bar. Save your work into a new file called VVPRO2 (for VidView Pro Forma Version 2). To save a file, highlight "Save" and press RETURN. At the file name prompt, enter the name VVPRO2 and press RETURN.

4. Entering numbers into a spreadsheet is a fairly routine task—although an important one. The power of a spreadsheet lies in its ability to apply calculations with these numbers through the use of formulas. For this lesson, a special spreadsheet file, labeled VVPRO3, has been prepared for you. Retrieve this file now. Your screen should show the display in the accompanying illustration.

```
SpreadSheet: VVPRO3        Row: 20    Col:E      Press ESC to quit
Create Format Enter Sum Save Print Retrieve Insert Remove Copy Move Prot Delete
 1                   VidView Pro Forma
 2
 3 INCOME ACCOUNTS  PREV. YR. PROJECTED CHANGE
 4
 5 Video Rentals    200595    220955   C5-B5
 6 Video Sales      64350     76650
 7
 8    TOTAL INCOME  B5+B6
 9
10 EXPENSE ACCOUNTS
11
12 Equipment        37689     35500
13 Rent             48000     48000
14 Advertising      8050      12000
15 Supplies         4855      4500
16 Inventory        88600     100000
17
18    TOTAL EXPENSES B12@B16
19
20    PROFIT        B8-B18
```

This STARTware screen presents the VidView pro forma statement with a series of entries completed.

Notice that many of the spreadsheet entries have been created for you. Most of these entries represent data values, or numbers, for income or expense accounts. However, four example formulas also have been entered. Take a moment to locate these formulas on your screen. When you have identified their cell positions, continue to Step 5.

5. Your job for the remaining part of this lesson involves entering the missing formulas and then calculating the spreadsheet. To understand the use of formulas, study the four that have been entered already. These formulas appear in cells B8, D5, B18, and B20.

The formula in cell B8 reads as follows:

B5+B6

This simple instruction tells the computer to add the values stored in cells B5 and B6. These two cells, of course, contain the "Video Rentals" and "Video Sales" income amounts for the previous year. By adding the values in these cells, the spreadsheet will provide the total income amount for the previous year.

After the spreadsheet has been calculated, the result will appear in cell B8 and will replace the formula that appears there now.

The formula in cell D5, shown below, requests the program to calculate across a row, rather than down a column.

C5−B5

Notice that this formula is located in the CHANGE column. By subtracting the previously budgeted amount (stored in cell B5) from the projected amount (stored in cell C5), the program will indicate the difference between the two years. This difference, or change, will allow managers to examine budget expectations.

The third formula, shown below, is located in cell B18:

B12@B16

This instruction tells the computer to add a *range* of numbers, rather than just two numbers. The @ symbol tells the software that all cell values between and including the specified cells will be added to produce a total. In other words, STARTware will sum the amounts stored in cells B12, B13, B14, B15, and B16.

By using the @ symbol to specify a range of values to be summed, you can avoid entering lengthy formulas. In this case, the formula B12@B16 replaces the lengthier formula B12+B13+B14+B15+B16.

The fourth formula, shown in cell B20, calculates the profit that was earned for the previous year. This formula is as follows:

B8−B18

That is, the total expense amount (which will be calculated and stored in cell B18) is subtracted from the total income amount (which will be calculated and stored in cell B8). The calculated result, of course, will be placed in cell B20.

6. You now should be ready to enter the remaining formulas. Twelve formulas are needed for the following cells:

1. D6	7. D15
2. C8	8. D16
3. D8	9. C18
4. D12	10. D18
5. D13	11. C20
6. D14	12. D20

It is up to you to determine the formulas that should be entered in these cells. Refer to the descriptions of the four example formulas for guidance. Also, you may enter the formulas in any order; however, it is recommended that you follow the order provided in the numbered list above. When you feel that you have entered all formulas correctly, continue to Step 7.

7. Now you are ready to have STARTware calculate your spreadsheet automatically. The procedure is simple. Press ESC to return to the menu bar. Select the "Sum" option from the menu and press RETURN. Your computer may take 30 seconds or more to make all calculations. The final spreadsheet should be identical to the one illustrated.

If your calculated spreadsheet contains different values from the ones shown below, or if STARTware displayed an error message, you have made one or more incorrect entries. Try to find and correct these errors on your own. When

```
SpreadSheet: VVPRO3                          Press ESC to quit

 1                VidView Pro Forma
 2
 3 INCOME ACCOUNTS  PREV. YR. PROJECTED CHANGE
 4
 5 Video Rentals    200595    220955    20360
 6 Video Sales       64350     76650    12300
 7
 8   TOTAL INCOME   264945    297605    32660
 9
10 EXPENSE ACCOUNTS
11
12 Equipment         37689     35500    -2189
13 Rent              48000     48000        0
14 Advertising        8050     12000     3950
15 Supplies           4855      4500     -355
16 Inventory         88600    100000    11400
17
18   TOTAL EXPENSES 187194    200000    12806
19
20     PROFIT        77751     97605    19854
```

The final STARTware entries *for the VidView pro forma statement have been included in this display.*

you have made all corrections, use the "Sum" command again to recalculate your spreadsheet. If you still are having difficulty achieving the correct results, ask your teacher for assistance.

8. When you have calculated your spreadsheet and achieved correct results, save your work into a new file named VVPRO4.

9. Congratulations. You have completed the spreadsheet portion of this Appendix. Remove your STARTware disk from the computer and return it to its sleeve. Turn off your computer system and wait for further instructions from your teacher.

AppleWorks PROCEDURES

1. Begin with your computer turned off. Follow the startup and Add Files procedures that you have already learned to load AppleWorks and the VVTEMPLATE file into memory. (Remember, files are added to the desktop portion of main memory.) When the spreadsheet that you created in Lesson 9 appears on the screen, continue to Step 2.

2. Before you begin entering formulas, you will practice by entering a few numbers into cells.

For this lesson, do not use commas within numbers. Also, don't worry about aligning, or positioning numbers correctly under each other. AppleWorks will do this for you automatically.

Use the table below to enter income amounts into the previous-year column of the spreadsheet:

	PREVIOUS YEAR
VHS Rentals	200595
VHS Sales	24350
Beta Rentals	87585
Beta Sales	12225
VCR Rentals	8060

3. After you have entered the five income values, your spreadsheet should look like the one in the accompanying illustration.

```
File: VVTEMPLATE            REVIEW/ADD/CHANGE        Escape: Main Menu
=======A========B========C========D========E========F========G========H====
 1|VidView Income Analysis Spreadsheet
 2|
 3|INCOME          PREV YR  PROJECT  CHANGE
 4|
 5|VHS Rentals      200595
 6|VHS Sales         24350
 7|Beta Rentals      87585
 8|Beta Sales        12225
 9|VCR Rentals        8060
10|
11|TOTAL INCOME:
12|
13|
14|
15|
16|
-----------------------------------------------------------------
A1:

Type entry or use Apple commands _            Apple-? for Help
```

This AppleWorks spreadsheet *screen shows initial entries for the VidView income analysis application.*

If your spreadsheet matches the one shown, you are ready to continue on to Step 4. If your spreadsheet differs from the one shown, make the necessary corrections. You can change cell values in AppleWorks by re-entering them or by using the *edit* function.

To use the edit function, move the highlight to the cell that you want to edit. Next, enter the editing command, Apple-U. AppleWorks now places the content of the cell in the cell indicator area so that you can make changes.

At this point, you can use the Arrow keys to move back and forth within this cell entry. If you need to delete a number, simply move the cursor until it is on the number to the right of the one you want to delete. Then press the Delete key. To insert a number, place the cursor on the number that will follow the inserted character. Now enter the number that you want to insert. Press RETURN after you finish editing the cell. You also can use the editing function to correct any errors in your labels. When your spreadsheet is correct, continue to Step 4.

4. Entering numbers into a spreadsheet is a fairly routine task—although an important one. The power of a spreadsheet lies in its ability to apply calculations to these numbers through the use of formulas. Your job for the remaining part of this lesson involves entering formulas into the spreadsheet.

To understand the use of formulas, consider that the manager of VidView wants to see what the income amounts would be if each income category earned five percent more this year than in the previous year. A simple formula can be used to make this projection.

Move the highlight cursor to cell D5. As you can see, this is where the projected amount will be placed for the "VHS Rentals" income category. Now enter the following formula:

+C5*1.05

In this formula, the "+C5" tells AppleWorks that it will be performing an arithmetic operation on the value in cell C5. You need to enter the "+" sign first so that AppleWorks knows you are entering a formula, rather than a label. If you had entered a "C" first, AppleWorks would think that you want to enter a label, since the first character would be a letter of the alphabet.

The *asterisk* (*) character tells AppleWorks to perform a multiplication operation. The asterisk works just like the multiplication operator ($\times$) that you use with a hand-held calculator.

The 1.05 tells AppleWorks to multiply the value in cell C5 by 1.05. This will cause the program to increase the value in C5 by five percent and to place the product (the result) in cell D5.

If you haven't already done so, move the Right Arrow cursor now. AppleWorks performs the multiplication operation, then places the new value automatically in Cell D5.

5. Now move the highlight cursor to cell E5, if it isn't there already. The formula to be entered in this cell, shown below, requests the program to calculate across a row, rather than down a column:

+D5−C5

Notice that this formula is located in the CHANGE column. By subtracting the previously budgeted amount (stored in cell C5) from the projected amount (calculated and stored in cell D5), the program will indicate the difference between the values for the two years. This difference, or change, will allow managers to examine budget expectations.

Enter this formula now and press the Left Arrow or Right Arrow cursor key to cause AppleWorks to calculate and store the result in cell E5.

6. The third formula to be entered, shown below, is located in cell C11:

@SUM(C5...C9)

This instruction tells the computer to add a *range* of numbers, rather than just two numbers. In this case, the formula tells AppleWorks to sum, or add, all values stored in cells C5 through C9.

The @ symbol tells AppleWorks a special function will be performed. The SUM notation means that a SUM function will be performed on a range of cells. Finally, the range of cells must be specified. The cell range information must be placed within parentheses. The three *ellipses,* or dots, tell AppleWorks to sum all cell values between the two that are specified. In other words, AppleWorks will sum the amounts stored in cells C5, C6, C7, C8, and C9.

By using the SUM function to specify a range of values to be added, you can avoid entering lengthy formulas. In this case, the formula @SUM(C5...C9) replaces the lengthier formula C5+C6+C7+C8+C9.

7. Move the highlight cursor to cell C11 now. Enter the SUM formula shown above. Press the Left Arrow or Right Arrow key to cause AppleWorks to calculate and store the product. Your spreadsheet now should look like the one in the accompanying illustration.

```
File: VVTEMPLATE              REVIEW/ADD/CHANGE          Escape: Main Menu
=======A========B========C========D========E========F========G========H====
 1|VidView Income Analysis Spreadsheet
 2|
 3|INCOME          PREV YR  PROJECT  CHANGE
 4|
 5|VHS Rentals      200595   210625   10030
 6|VHS Sales         24350
 7|Beta Rentals      87585
 8|Beta Sales        12225
 9|VCR Rentals        8060
10|
11|TOTAL INCOME:    332815
12|
13|
14|
------------------------------------------------------------------
C11: (Value) @SUM(C5...C9)

Type entry or use Apple commands _              Apple-? for Help
```

The VidView spreadsheet *to be used for income analysis is nearing completion in this AppleWorks screen display.*

8. The three formulas are the only ones that you need to enter by hand. AppleWorks can enter the others for you automatically through use of the *relative copy* function.

The relative copy function tells AppleWorks to use an already entered formula, then copy the same formula to a new cell. However, the copied formula will be a little different from the original formula. With the relative copy function, AppleWorks copies the formula, but changes the cell values in the formula to reflect the new cell position.

For example, recall that the formula to multiply the previous year's VHS Sales by five percent is stored in cell D5. This formula is +C5*1.05. Also recall that VidView managers want all income categories to be increased by five percent. So, similar formulas need to be entered into cells D6, D7, D8, and D9. The easiest way to enter these formulas is through use of the relative copy function.

9. To see how this function works, move the highlight cursor to cell D5. Now enter the copy command, Apple-C, to tell AppleWorks that you want to copy something. The program now asks you how you want to perform the copy. Simply press RETURN to select "Within the worksheet."

Now the program asks you what you want to copy. You want to copy only the formula stored in cell D5, which already is highlighted. So, press RETURN to specify this formula.

Now move the highlight cursor down to cell D6 and then press RETURN. AppleWorks asks you whether you want to copy the same formula as the one in cell D5 or a relative formula. You want to copy a relative formula. In fact, you want to copy a relative formula four times—for cells D6, D7, D8, and D9. To specify this *repeated relative copy,* press R four times. Notice that, each time you press R, the program copies a relative formula and moves down one cell.

Your spreadsheet now should look like the accompanying example.

10. To complete your spreadsheet, you need to make relative copies of the other two formulas that you have entered. Begin by moving the cursor to cell E5, where the formula D5−C5 is located. You want to make a relative copy of this formula in cells E6, E7, E8, and E9. This will cause AppleWorks to calculate the CHANGE in income amounts between the previous year and the projected year—for all income categories.

With the highlight cursor in cell E5, press Apple-C to start the copy function. At the prompt, tell AppleWorks that you want to copy within the

```
File: VVTEMPLATE              REVIEW/ADD/CHANGE        Escape: Main Menu
=======A=======B=======C=======D=======E=======F=======G=======H===
 1|VidView Income Analysis Spreadsheet
 2|
 3|INCOME            PREV YR  PROJECT  CHANGE
 4|
 5|VHS Rentals        200595   210625   10030
 6|VHS Sales           24350    25567
 7|Beta Rentals        87585    91964
 8|Beta Sales          12225    12836
 9|VCR Rentals          8060     8463
10|
11|TOTAL INCOME:      332815
12|
13|
14|
-----------------------------------------------------------------------
D9: (Value) +C9*1.05

Use cursor moves to highlight Source, then press Return _   Apple-? for Help
```

AppleWorks formula entry is demonstrated in this screen display.

worksheet. When AppleWorks asks you what to copy, press RETURN to specify the formula in the current cell, E5.

Next, move the cursor to the new cell location, cell E6. Press RETURN to tell AppleWorks that this is where you want the copy to begin. When the prompt appears, tell the program that you want to make four relative copies. Do this by pressing R four times. AppleWorks automatically makes relative copies of the formula and places the products in cells E6 through E9.

11. You have one formula remaining to be copied. This, of course, is the formula shown in cell C11—@SUM(C5...C9). You need to make one relative copy of this formula for cell D11. Use the relative copy procedures that you learned in Steps 9 and 10 to make this copy now. Your spreadsheet should now be complete.

12. You now are ready to save this file to disk. However, you don't want to save the completed spreadsheet over the template you made in Lesson 9. Instead, you should save your completed spreadsheet under a new name.

Follow procedures that you learned in Lesson 9 to save the spreadsheet under the new name,

VVINCOME2. If you are unsure how to do this, refer to Step 6 in Lesson 9.

13. Congratulations. You have completed the spreadsheet portion of this Appendix. Remove your AppleWorks disks from the computer and return them to their protective sleeves. Turn off your computer system and wait for further instruction from your teacher.

Lesson 11

Using Integrated Software: Combining Multiple Application Files

INTRODUCTION

The STARTware and AppleWorks software packages are integrated systems. As you know by now, an integrated package allows users to combine information files that have been created under different types of application programs.

For instance, the VidView management might want to prepare a report to investors. This report is to contain information that describes to owners the financial status of the business. Much of the report can be written through use of a word processing program. However, financial information—such as budget amounts shown on a ''pro forma'' spreadsheet—are created under control of a spreadsheet program.

With separate application programs, it is difficult to combine text from a word processing program with spreadsheet data into a single document. However, this type of application is ideal for an integrated package. Such packages can move, or *export,* a spreadsheet or database display into a text report. Some packages, such as AppleWorks, even allow users to combine spreadsheet and database files. (Remember, both spreadsheet and database programs make use of column-and-row, or table, formats to process and store data).

In this lesson, you will practice integrating files created under separate application programs.

STARTware PROCEDURES

The management of VidView has prepared a *Report to Investors* through use of the STARTware word processing program. This report describes the progress made by the VidView store during its first year. Management also makes projections about the profit potential for VidView in the coming year.

To emphasize these financial points, managers have instructed you to integrate the VVPRO3 *Pro Forma* spreadsheet into the report. This spreadsheet, of course, will allow investors to review financial results and projections.

1. Make sure your computer is turned off before you begin. Boot DOS and bypass the date and time prompts by pressing RETURN at each prompt. Load the STARTware spreadsheet by entering the following command at the A> prompt:

   ss

   Follow the procedures you learned earlier to retrieve the VVPRO3 spreadsheet file. You need to SUM the spreadsheet so that the imported file will contain values, rather than formulas. The summed spreadsheet should be displayed on your screen before you continue to Step 2.

2. At this point, you want to copy the VVPRO3 spreadsheet into the *Report to Investors.* This report currently is stored in a word processing file called INTEGRAT.

   To begin, make sure the cursor highlight is in the menu bar area of the spreadsheet screen. Move the highlight to the ''Output'' option. Notice the tutor line that now appears on the third line of the menu area:

   Print spreadsheet as displayed; graphics; export

   You can perform three activities within this menu option. First, you can print the VVPRO3 spreadsheet through use of a printer. Second, you can create a graphics representation of the spreadsheet. You will implement this option later. The third option, called *export,* refers to the ability of STARTware to move, or export, a spreadsheet into a text document. This is the option that you will be using next.

Press RETURN to activate the "Output" option. The OUTPUT MENU, shown in an accompanying illustration, now appears.

```
STARTware: SS ::::::::::::::::::::::::::::::::::::::::::::::::
T                                                        ::
A                                                        ::
R            OUTPUT MENU                                 ::
T                                                        ::
w                                                        ::
a    1.  PRINT ACTIVE SPREADSHEET AS DISPLAYED           ::
r    2.  EXPORT DISPLAYED SPREADSHEET TO WORD PROCESSOR  ::
e    3.  DISPLAY BAR CHART                               ::
::   4.  EXPORT BAR CHART TO WORD PROCESSOR              S
::                                                       T
::                                                       A
::                                                       R
::                                                       T
::                                                       w
::           ENTER NUMBER OF SELECTION AND PRESS RETURN > a
::                                                       r
:::::::::::::::::::::::::::::::::::::::::::::::::::::STARTware
Press [Esc] and [Return] to quit menu.
```

This STARTware output menu activates preparation of documents with content developed under multiple applications.

3. Notice that the displayed menu provides four options for outputting the currently active spreadsheet. At this point, you are ready to export the displayed spreadsheet to a word processor file. To do this, enter the number 2 and press RETURN.

4. The STARTware system responds by asking you for the name of the word processor file in which the spreadsheet is to be inserted. Enter the following file name and press RETURN:

SSINT

5. Now press ESC and RETURN to return to the spreadsheet menu. Press ESC again to exit to the main menu. Now, press 1 to select the word processor, then RETURN. Retrieve the word processor file named INTEGRAT.

Notice that the tutor line near the bottom of the screen indicates that the F9 key is used to import

a file into a word processing document. Press F9 now. STARTware next prompts you for the name of the document to be imported. Enter the name SSINT and press RETURN.

STARTware next loads the SSINT file into a buffer area of memory in preparation for the import operation. Press RETURN twice to return to your word processor document. STARTware now expects you to position the cursor at the point where the spreadsheet is to be inserted. Move the cursor to the line beneath this sentence:

The following Pro Forma spreadsheet shows the income and expense account results for the previous year, as well as the results we expect to achieve in the coming year:

6. Press RETURN once or twice to create space between the end of the text and the start of the spreadsheet to be imported. You are ready to complete the import operation. As the tutor line at the bottom of the screen shows, the F8 key is used to move the block stored in the buffer into the document. Press F8 now. STARTware will insert the SSINT spreadsheet at the location you have specified.

7. Now review the new document. Insert any RETURN characters that you feel are necessary to enhance the appearance of the spreadsheet within your document.

Then, follow the steps you learned earlier to save the new word processor file under the name INVREP (for Investors' Report).

8. Remove the STARTware disk now and return it to its protective sleeve. Turn off your computer system and wait for further instruction from your teacher.

AppleWorks PROCEDURES

For this exercise, you want to illustrate the integration feature of AppleWorks. Specifically, you will move an existing spreadsheet into an existing word processor file.

1. Make sure your computer is turned off before you begin. Follow the startup procedures described in earlier lessons. Add the VVIN-COME2 spreadsheet file and the EDIT2 word processor file to the desktop. Now, follow the procedures you learned earlier to display the EDIT2 document on your screen. When this document is displayed, continue with Step 2.

2. At this point, you want to prepare your text document for the integration of a spreadsheet display. Move the cursor to the end of the EDIT2 document. Begin a new paragraph that contains the following text:

   With AppleWorks, it also is possible to "import," or integrate, a spreadsheet into a text document. For instance, the following spreadsheet was integrated into this document through use of the import feature of AppleWorks

3. Now ESC to the main menu. Follow the instructions you learned earlier to display the VVINCOME2 spreadsheet on your display screen. At this point, you are ready to import the spreadsheet into your EDIT2 document.

   To begin, you need to create a report format, so that AppleWorks knows how much of the current spreadsheet is to be transferred.

   Press Apple-P to specify that you want to print a report. At the next prompt, select "All" to specify that the report is to include all entries in the spreadsheet. Press RETURN. A third prompt will appear, asking where the report should be printed. Select "The clipboard," and press RETURN. Your spreadsheet report now is in the clipboard area of memory.

4. Now ESC to the main menu. Call up the word processor document EDIT2 so that this document is displayed on your screen.

   Position the cursor at the end of the document (on the line following the last line that you just entered). This is where the imported spreadsheet will appear.

5. Now press Apple-M to specify that you want to begin a move operation. At the prompt, select "From clipboard," since this is where the spreadsheet to be imported currently resides in memory. AppleWorks now transfers, or imports, the spreadsheet into your EDIT2 document.

6. You now are ready to save your new word processor document. However, do not write over the current EDIT2 document. Instead, follow the instructions you learned earlier to save the current EDIT2 document to disk, using the new file name, "INTEGRATE".

7. When you are finished, return to the main menu and quit the program. Finally, remove your AppleWorks program and data disks from their drives and return them to their protective sleeves.

Lesson 12
Using Integrated Software: Advanced Features

INTRODUCTION

Lesson 11 introduced you to some basic integration features of STARTware and AppleWorks. In this lesson, you will learn how to use additional integration features to combine files. For STARTware, you will learn how to create and integrate a bar chart into a text document. For AppleWorks, you will learn how to format a database so that selected fields can be integrated into a text document.

STARTware PROCEDURES

1. Begin this lesson with your computer turned off. Follow the procedures you learned earlier to load DOS, then load the spreadsheet portion of STARTware. Finally, retrieve the VVPRO3 spreadsheet that you used in the previous exercise. This spreadsheet should be displayed on your screen before you continue to Step 2.

2. For this lesson, you will enhance the ***Report to Investors*** by including a ***bar chart*** that portrays spreadsheet content. Recall that a bar chart portrays values through use of bars of varying lengths. STARTware includes a graphics capability for creating bar charts and integrating them within text documents.

   To begin, make sure the cursor is in the menu bar area of the spreadsheet screen. Move the highlight to the ''Output'' option and press RETURN.

3. STARTware now displays the OUTPUT MENU that you learned about in Lesson 11. Notice that this menu includes two graphics options:

   3. DISPLAY BAR CHART

   4. EXPORT BAR CHART TO WORD PROCESSOR

   As these options suggest, you can create a bar chart that describes an existing spreadsheet. You also can export, or move, a bar chart to a file created with the word processor program of STARTware.

   For this lesson, you will create a bar chart from the VVPRO3 spreadsheet and move the created chart to the ***Report to Investors***. Recall that this report is stored in the INVREP word processor file.

   From the OUTPUT MENU, select option 3, DISPLAY BAR CHART. The BAR CHART SPECIFICATION screen now appears. This screen is shown in an accompanying illustration.

4. Three prompts are supplied. The first prompt requests the letter of the column to use for applying bar chart labels. In other words, the program wants to know how to label each graphed bar so that it can be identified by users. In most cases, you will specify column ''A,'' since this column contains labels for values shown on the spreadsheet.

   Press RETURN to leave the default column, ''A,'' as the label column.

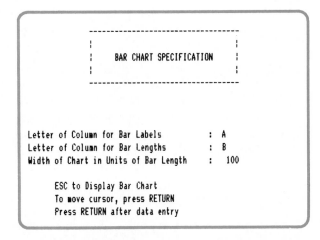

Bar chart specifications *are entered through use of this STARTware display.*

The second prompt asks you which column is to be used to begin creating bars for amounts. In most cases, this will be column ''B.'' So press RETURN to leave column ''B'' as the default, or standard entry.

The third prompt requests that you enter the maximum bar length. This number establishes the maximum value that STARTware will use to create bar lengths for different spreadsheet categories. The highest value in the current spreadsheet is a TOTAL INCOME amount, 297605. To accommodate this number, as well as smaller values, enter the number 300000 next to the prompt. Press RETURN to store the value.

5. Now press ESC to display the bar chart that you have specified. With this chart in place, you are ready to export it into the INVREP word processor file.

   Your job now is to transfer the bar chart you have created into the INVREP text file. From the OUTPUT MENU, select option 4, EXPORT BAR CHART TO WORD PROCESSOR, and press RETURN.

6. STARTware now prompts you for the name of the file to which the bar chart is to be stored.

Enter the name BAR and press RETURN. At this point, you must enter the word processor portion of STARTware. Follow the procedures you learned earlier to return to the WORD PROCESSOR MAIN MENU, then retrieve the file INVREP. You now are ready to import the created bar chart into your word processing document. Press F9 to specify that you want to perform an import operation. At the next prompt, enter the file name BAR to specify that you want to import this document. Press RETURN to continue.

In response to the next prompt, move the cursor to the starting point for the bar chart—the line that follows this section of text:

The contents of the spreadsheet shown above can be highlighted through use of the bar chart shown below

7. Press F8 to activate the export operation. Your INVREP file now should contain both the VVPRO3 spreadsheet and the bar chart.

8. Save the final report to disk with the name FIN-REP (for Final Report). Remove your START-ware disk from the computer and return it to its sleeve. Turn off your computer system and wait for further instruction from your teacher.

AppleWorks PROCEDURES

1. Make sure your computer is turned off before you begin. Follow the startup procedures described in earlier lessons. Add the OSHOT-CAR database file and the EDIT3 word processor file to the desktop. Now, follow the procedures you learned earlier to display the EDIT3 document on your screen. When this document is displayed, continue with Step 2.

2. At this point, you want to prepare your text document for the integration of a database display. Move the cursor to the end of the EDIT3 docu-

ment. Begin a new paragraph that contains the following text:

An additional file integration capability of AppleWorks lies in the importing of a database file into a text document. For instance, the following database was integrated into this document through use of the import feature of AppleWorks

3. Now ESC to the main menu. Follow the instructions you learned earlier to display the OSHOTCAR2 database file on your display screen. At this point, you are ready to import the database file into your EDIT3 document.

To begin, you need to create a report format, so that AppleWorks knows how much of the current database file is to be transferred. It is not possible to transfer all fields of each database record into the text file. The reason: Each database record takes more than 80 characters. However, each line of text in the EDIT3 file allows a maximum of 65 characters per line. So, you first must remove database fields that are not necessary to the report you want to produce. In other words, each database record should take up no more than 65 characters per line after it has been transferred to the EDIT3 text document.

4. Press Apple-P to specify that you want to print a report. At the next prompt, select ''Create a new tables format.'' AppleWorks now asks you to enter a name for your report format. Enter the name OSREPORT and press RETURN.

The next screen displays several report formatting options that you can use to determine how your database file should appear. For this exercise, it is important only to delete unnecessary columns from the database.

To print a meaningful version of the OSHOT-CAR database, you should include the fields LIC#, ST, REGISTERED OWNER, and LS DATE. All other fields are to be deleted from this report. To make these deletions, you simply move the cursor to the column that contains fields to be deleted. Then, press Apple-D to delete the column from the report. Do this now. Delete the YR, MAKE, MODEL, COLOR, and BODY columns.

5. Now ESC to the REPORT MENU. Enter Apple-P to specify that you are ready to print a report. AppleWorks next asks where you want to print the report. Enter a 3 to specify that you want to send the report to the clipboard for the word processor. Press the space bar to continue.

6. To switch to the word processor document, EDIT3, press Apple-Q and select the EDIT3 file. Move the cursor to the spot where you want the database report to be inserted, or imported. Press Apple-C to specify a copy operation. At the prompt, select "From the clipboard" to indicate that you want to copy the contents in the clipboard into the current word processing document. Your EDIT3 document now should contain the database entries.

7. Save this word processing file under the name INTEGRAT. Follow the procedures you learned earlier to quit AppleWorks. Remove the disks from the drives and return them to their sleeves. Turn your system off and wait for further instruction from your teacher.

Computer-Related Careers

THE COMPUTER IN YOUR FUTURE

Whatever career you choose, it is virtually certain that one or more computers will become part of your regular living and working routine. Past experience can help preview the kind of relationships that are developed between people and computers. Consider some other technologies that have blended into your environment:

- The telephone was a strange technology at one time. Placing telephone calls used to be a special occupation. A caller picked up the phone and waited for an operator. It took a specialist to make connections between callers. Then, as demands for services grew, telephones acquired dials and became universal. There's no question that the telephone is part of your life. The computer is in the process of assuming a similar role.

- The automobile is a high-tech device that millions of people have mastered. Society has adjusted by constructing millions of miles of roads. The training and practice involved in getting a driver's license are far greater than requirements for taking hold of a computer. If you feel comfortable about your ability to drive a car, you also can be confident that you can deal with the computers in your future.

- A generation ago, the TV set was a novelty. Today, 90 million American homes have television. TV uses many of the same basic technologies as computers. If you are comfortable in front of a TV set, consider the computer as a different and better source of information—and possibly entertainment.

As with other technologies, people and computers can interact at different levels. Your future relationships with computers will depend on your own career choices. Some of the ways in which you can expect to encounter computers are reviewed below. The presentations that follow start with careers that involve only casual contact with computers—information users. The discussion then covers careers involving hands-on use of computers. Finally, there are brief descriptions of some of the jobs performed by people who are involved with computers full time—computer professionals.

INFORMATION USERS

In business applications, computers operate largely as information-generating machines. Businesses run on information. Information was needed long before computers were available. If a company had no computers at all, its managers and employees still would need information—or they couldn't do their jobs.

The connection between managers and computers lies in information. A computer is a tool that can process and deliver almost any information that people describe. The first challenge faced by managers and information users is to understand their own information needs. Then, they must know enough about the capabilities of computers and of computer professionals to understand how their information is developed.

These are two separate elements. First, there is an understanding of what information is needed. Second, there is a basic knowledge about computer systems and how information is developed. With these two elements of knowledge, a user is ready to deal with computer professionals.

This is the basic, computer-related challenge for businesspeople who need information: They must know their needs and know the sources of data required to develop the information they require. Then, users must be able to communicate with the computer professionals who can cause computers to meet the needs they have defined.

COMPUTER EQUIPMENT USERS

People classified as "information users" usually didn't work directly on or with computers. They received documents, reports, or displays developed by people who designed systems and operated computers. For many years, only specially trained professionals actually came into direct contact with computers. Since the introduction of microcomputers, however, this situation has changed.

It is possible today to use a computer regularly, even though you are not a technician. In this capacity, the computer becomes a tool for performing a job. You have to understand your job and the contribution of your computer toward meeting your responsibilities. In effect, the computer is a tool at work in the same way as a car is a tool for getting to work.

At this level of computer-related careers, workers use prepared software and interactive computers. That is, workers need specific results or requirements from their computers. Computers are programmed to provide specific services. The workers are interested in doing their jobs. Any changes or new systems that may be required are described in terms of basic business operations. Equipment users solve their problems by buying and installing software tools and, if necessary, hardware attachments to support them.

At this level, computer-related careers can be developed without any technical or software expertise. A computer keyboard and a video display are the points of focus. This level of user doesn't have to know what's inside the "black box" that contains computer electronics. The situation is the same as the driver who doesn't have to be an expert about the equipment under the hood of a car.

COMPUTER PROFESSIONALS

Computers are the basis for a worldwide industry with business volumes of more than $1,000,000,000,000 (one trillion dollars) a year. Tens of millions of people are needed to design, build, install, and operate computer systems. The nature of the work these people do changes rapidly as new technologies are introduced. Also, changes result from the rapid rate at which people find new uses for their computers.

The review that follows describes some general categories of jobs held by computer professionals. The jobs identified and the descriptions that follow do not represent a complete review. The purpose is to give you an idea of the opportunities that may be available.

MANAGING THE INFORMATION FUNCTION

Information Resources Manager is just one term used to identify the top computer professional in a company. Alternate titles may be Director of Information Services or Director of Computer Operations. Regardless of title, most large organizations have recognized that computers are important enough to require appointment of a top-level manager to oversee their use.

The idea behind creating this job: Every business has some key assets necessary to its continued existence. Control of these assets, because of their importance, generally is assigned to a top-level

Millions of jobs have opened up for persons trained in the development of information systems and the use of computers. Some opportunities exist in large computer installations like this one. Many others involve work with smaller computers or jobs available to knowledgeable computer users.

COURTESY OF MCDONNELL DOUGLAS CORP., ST. LOUIS

manager. Information resources have reached the level of importance that requires appointment of a senior executive for their management. The role of the Information Resources Manager is similar to that of a Treasurer, who is responsible for management of a company's money and other financial resources.

The Information Resources Manager must be a special person. He or she must have experience and skills in business. In a large company, the information resources function may employ hundreds of people. Information resources budgets may run into tens of millions of dollars. Because of the numbers of people and amounts of money involved, the top information executive must be a talented manager. At the same time, the person must have a technical background that makes it possible to deal with computer professionals. The information resources manager must be able to review and evaluate plans and programs that involve advanced hardware and software.

For all people interested in computer-related careers, the very fact that this job exists can be important. If companies recognize the need for a top-level manager, this means, in turn, that the function itself is seen as vital. This situation can help the career prospects of everyone who wants to work with computers.

Computer Systems

Within the information resources function, the "Systems Group" is responsible for analyzing needs and developing information tools. People in the systems function have both communications and technical responsibilities. The systems function provides services for design and development of computer systems for managers and other information users.

For example, if a manager wants to install a microcomputer system to prepare spreadsheets, the systems group would help select the best hardware and software for the job. Then, systems people would provide the instructions necessary to help the user develop desired results. In addition, the systems personnel would play a quality-assurance role. They would make sure that the manager's data could fit into overall company systems. They also would make the manager aware of databases or other resources that might be helpful.

To meet major information needs, the systems group might undertake multi-year projects that involve spending millions of dollars. Systems of this type might affect the operations of the entire company.

Some of the key career opportunities within the systems function are described below.

Director of Systems Development. The *Director of Systems Development* is a tactical-level manager. This individual reports to the Information Resources Manager. The job itself can be likened to that of a marketing or service manager for a large company. The customer base for systems services consists of all managers and other employees of the company. The units of service are useful information. Responsibilities of the systems staff are to respond to customer requests or to suggest improvements through introduction of new methods.

The systems function has special communications responsibilities. Systems professionals must be able to identify user needs and describe them in ways that make it possible for technicians to deliver desired results.

The Director of Systems Development also needs the general management skills necessary to plan, organize, and control the staff that delivers these services.

Systems Analyst. A *systems analyst* requires multiple skills. The systems analyst has to be a businessperson who can understand management problems. With this knowledge, the systems analyst helps managers to identify and solve general business problems. Then, the systems analyst needs enough technical background to apply computers to problem solutions. The systems analyst uses his or her technical knowledge to guide computer professionals in the development and operation of systems.

Programmer/analyst. A *programmer/analyst* does both systems analysis work and programming. This position is most likely to exist in relatively small computer installations. The idea: The company's computer operations may be too small to support a separate systems analysis staff. The same people must function both as problem solvers and programmers.

Programmer. A *programmer* is an expert in developing sets of instructions that guide computer processing. Usually, a programmer receives a set of specifications prepared by a systems analyst. These specifications describe solutions in terms of the results that users expect. The programmer must design the sequence of computer operations that will meet the specifications. Then, specific instructions must be written in a programming language. The programmer also has quality-control responsibilities. All program segments must be tested and proven before they are released for work on user applications.

Computer Operations

Computer operations is a major function within the IRM area. This group is responsible for maintaining facilities, operating computer equipment, and providing direct service to users.

Director of operations. The *director of operations* is the top manager in charge of running the computer facility. This individual assumes the same responsibilities within the IRM area as does the director of manufacturing for the company as a whole. That is, this person is both a production manager and a technician capable of overseeing use of millions of dollars worth of computer equipment. This individual is responsible to the IRM director and to users for the input, processing, output, and storage of information. Responsibilities also call for the delivery of specified reports or on-line access.

Data control personnel. The *data control group* is the service point within a computer center. People within this group accept source documents from users. They establish schedules for processing and delivery of batch jobs. For companies that support on-line computer access, members of this group

As the number of computers continues to increase, many opportunities are opening for technical support personnel. Technical services personnel maintain and repair computers. Other persons in the technical services function specialize in system software.

COURTESY OF HEWLETT-PACKARD CO.

handle complaints, training requirements, or special services required by users. In effect, the data control function is the point at which incoming work is received, distributed, and scheduled.

Console operators. The *console* is the hub position from which a large computer system is operated. *Console operators* must be highly experienced personnel. They oversee the scheduling of jobs to be run on computers. They have the critical task of scheduling and monitoring reruns for the jobs that are not completed on a first attempt. There are many reasons for failure to complete a scheduled computer operation. As many as 25 percent of all jobs have to be rerun. Console operators also deal with error messages generated by computer software.

Peripheral operators. The job of *peripheral operator* often is held by entry-level personnel who are just starting their careers in the computer field. Peripherals, of course, are devices that are linked to the central processor. Included are tape drives, disk drives, and printers. Peripheral operators receive needed tapes or disks from the data library and

"hang" them on the proper drives. They also load the necessary paper or forms into printers. Setting up and monitoring operation of peripherals is necessary for the execution of batch jobs.

Data entry operators. The *data entry* section in a computer facility is responsible for receiving source documents from users and capturing data. Specific jobs include the entry of data into terminals or recording devices. Data entry personnel also are responsible for verifying the accuracy of captured data. Operators must be proficient in touch keyboarding. Training in use of specific data entry equipment usually is provided on the job.

Technical Services

Computers apply technology. Users of large computers need a group of professionals who oversee the technical functions required to install computers and keep them operating. The *technical services* function includes specialists in both hardware and software.

Director of technical services. The *director of technical services* is the manager in charge of computer equipment and system software. This person requires an extensive technical background and also must have the management skills necessary to oversee a staff, make recommendations about purchases of hardware and software, and schedule the maintenance functions needed to keep a computer center in operation.

Software support specialist. A *software support specialist* usually is responsible for monitoring use of system software and for utilization of processing capacity. Major operating systems are revised frequently, often several times a year. Each revised version should be reviewed and recommendations should be made on whether to change over from the present operation system to a new one. Large computer systems may support three or more versions of operating system software. Each version must be reviewed to determine whether its use requires modification of application programs. Installation of a new operating system is a serious undertaking. Also, technical specialists must monitor usage levels for computer processors. At appropriate times, recommendations must be made about when to add additional storage devices, more main memory, or to move to a larger processor.

Database administrator. A *database administrator* is responsible for monitoring the information resources maintained by a computer system. Periodically, it may be necessary to reorganize the information content of a database. This need occurs when users continually add new records to an existing database. Ultimately, the files become so large that access times begin to rise and the system loses efficiency. DBMS maintenance is a highly technical and vitally important job.

Technical support personnel. Computer equipment must be inspected, cleaned, and repaired periodically. Some companies employ technicians who monitor and maintain equipment. Others contract for maintenance services from outside organizations.

Regardless of the source of these services, specialized technicians are needed to keep computers in service.

Information Media

The information stored on disk and tape media are vital assets. These information files are the reason that computer facilities exist. Because these media are so important, special measures are followed to protect them against loss or unauthorized use. Assigning responsibility for media, usually as an independent function, is a protective measure in itself. The principle is known as ''separation of duties.'' The idea: computer operators and some systems personnel have access to equipment that could be used to alter or misuse data files. This is why control over access to media is placed under an independent person. The people responsible for storing information media generally do not have access to equipment that can process or change stored records.

Data librarian. The data librarian is the person in charge of maintaining media files. In a large installation, tens of thousands of tapes and disk packs may be in use. Each must be labeled and filed carefully. As media are needed to run applications, the librarian prepares the media for pickup by computer operators. After jobs are run, the new and old versions of the media must be returned to the library. The librarian is responsible for keeping several versions of media files for backup and protection. Responsibilities extend to the shipment of backup files to remote sites for protection.

The people who hold the positions described above make up a team that is responsible for providing, maintaining, and protecting the information assets of an organization. Their responsibilities form a continuous job stream. At the same time, there are checks and balances among the positions that serve to protect information assets without which a company might not be able to operate.

Making Decisions and Solving Problems

COMPUTERS AND THE NEED FOR HUMAN DECISIONS

Computers have become essential business tools. As tools, computers are expensive. They present special challenges related to their purchase and application. In many instances, the required decisions involve commitments of millions of dollars and many person-years of labor.

To illustrate, the following are some of the types of decisions that responsible users and computer professionals are required to make:

- If a new system or software package is being installed, does it have to integrate with others? If so, how? Severe problems can develop if different computer users purchase and install incompatible software. For example, there have been situations in which managers purchased microcomputer software to assist in planning and budgeting. Problems developed when it was learned that managers could not use the financial and budgeting information within the company's central computer system. Also, the budgets developed by individual managers were not usable within the companywide system. Care in planning and decision making can avoid this kind of problem.

- When a new business application is developed, it will require information files. For each new application or package, managers should find out whether the new system can use existing files or databases. If not, why not? If new files are needed, will they be compatible with and enhance existing data resources?

- What is a new application program or software package worth to a company? What benefits will it deliver? Will the value of the benefits be greater than the expense of creating the system? Can the new job be run comfortably on existing equipment or will the company face major expenses for upgrading equipment and system software?

- What problems or special needs can be expected when it comes time to implement a new system? Is the organization ready? What is the best way to make the changeover?

- What training will computer users need? Are prospective users ready for the new system and do they really want it? Is change being forced upon unwilling people? What can be done to assure user participation?

ANTICIPATING AND AVOIDING COMPUTER-RELATED PROBLEMS

In any activity as complex as a computer system, problems are inevitable. The trick is to expect that problems will develop. Procedures should be adopted that help people to look ahead. Identify problems. Then avoid or solve the problems.

The notes that follow outline a series of steps that provide a proven procedure for identifying and avoiding problems. The same steps can be followed to troubleshoot problems that come up unexpectedly.

1. **Identify the problem or need.**
   - What is the problem or need?
   - What change is to be made?
   - What are the desired results?

2. **Identify alternatives.**
   - What options or alternatives are available to achieve the desired results?
   - For each option: Suppose this alternative was implemented. What adverse (bad) consequences could develop? Are the adverse consequences bad enough to disqualify this option? If so, the alternative should be discarded.
   - For alternatives that pass the adverse consequences test: What are the benefits or positive consequences for each alternative?
   - Do the benefits outweigh the costs and potential problems that have been identified?

3. **Select a course of action.**
   - Which alternative will deliver the greatest benefits?
   - Which alternative should be chosen?

4. **Make a commitment.**
   - What are the requirements to implement the decision?
   - What schedules are feasible?

5. **Manage change.**
   - What steps must be completed to implement the decision that has been committed?
   - What information has to be collected and reviewed, at what points in time, to monitor implementation of the new system?

- What reviews should be performed after implementation?

APPLYING THE PROCESS

One reason that a decision making/problem solving process is needed is that situations involving computers rarely are as simple or easy as they may seem. People tend to search for solutions before they have identified problems fully.

To illustrate, consider the case of Nate Jumper, an insurance agent in a branch office of Casualty Coverage, Inc. Nate has been successful in telephone followup of inquiries to ads placed in magazines and on television by the home office.

Nate works from his home, on his own. He quickly develops a reputation of being a hard worker and a self-starter. One day, when he visits his company's regional office, Nate springs a new idea on his supervisor, Sally Sage. Nate has seen TV and newspaper ads for a microcomputer sale. He thinks he can get a system that will enable him to computerize coverage of his sales territory. He can buy a full computer system, complete with printer, for about $900. With his own system, Nate feels he can write sales letters, prepare his reports to the regional office, and maybe even prepare proposals for his prospective customers.

Sally values Nate's ambition and recognizes that his idea is basically good. But she also recognizes some of the problems involved. Instead of describing the problems in response to Nate's request, she arranges for Nate to meet with Yuko Suzuki, a systems analyst for the company. Sally feels that Yuko can help Nate to build his understanding of information systems as a whole and the value of computers.

Addressing the Problem or Need

When Yuko and Nate meet, she begins the work session by asking him to identify his problem or need.

"It's simple," Nate says, "I want to produce my own automatically typed letters."

"Letters aren't a problem or need," Yuko pointed out. "What is it that you want to do with the letters?"

Nate smiled. "That's a good question. I see your point. You want me to define results."

After a few minutes of discussion, Yuko and Nate agreed on a statement that described Nate's need: "Develop one or more techniques to increase sales in my sales territory."

"The use of a computer is an alternative for meeting your objective," Yuko said. "It is a possible solution, not a beginning goal."

Identifying Alternatives

"Now you have the computer at the point where it belongs," Yuko explained. "It is one alternative for solving your problem."

At this point, Nate produced the newspaper ad for the computer he had proposed. Yuko smiled. "You're jumping for solutions again, Nate," she said. "A computer is clearly one of the alternatives you should consider. But you are ahead of yourself in looking at a specific computer so early in your study."

Yuko described the need to consider adverse consequences of decision alternatives. Just by examining the newspaper ad, she was able to explain that the computer that had interested him wasn't suitable for his job. Yuko explained that the advertised computer came with a draft-quality printer. This was not acceptable for writing letters to the company's customers. Yuko also advised that the company had a number of services that could help agents in the field. There were disks that contained sample letters for agents to use. There also were services for developing mailing lists within agent territories.

"The idea of using a computer is basically a good one," Yuko explained. "That's why Sally wanted me to work with you. The solution you proposed has too many adverse consequences. It is not workable in your situation. But it does seem worthwhile for us to take time to look at some realistic alternatives."

Yuko and Nate then reviewed the features of a microcomputer that would help Nate to increase his sales. The requirements included features that would enable Nate's computer to fit in with the company's overall resources. When they were through detailing the features that Nate's computer would need, Yuko came up with a cost estimate of about $3,200. The company had identified three different makes of computer that were suitable for agent use. Also, an additional investment of about $1,100 was needed for software.

"Which one should I buy?" Nate asked eagerly.

"That's the wrong question again," Yuko said. "We need to figure out what benefits you and the company might realize from an investment of $4,300 for a computer and software."

"I hadn't thought about spending $3,200," Nate admitted.

"But Sally thought about it," Yuko said. "She told me to work with you to figure out the potential return that would result if you had your own computer. If we can show that it really would be best for you and the company, Sally will authorize me to buy a computer and software and help you set it up."

Yuko then explained that she would have to look over company records about Nate's sales history. She also would look up market information about his sales territory. The idea: Find out if use of a computer could pay for itself by increasing earnings for both Nate and the company.

Yuko explained that they had gone as far as they could for the moment. Before carrying the study further, they had to know what results could be expected from purpose and use of a computer and software.

"If it's profitable, we'll go ahead with the computer," Yuko said. "If a computer isn't the answer, we'll find another way to help you. The point is that we now are focused on the subject. It's not about using a computer. It's about covering your sales territory more effectively. If it is too expensive to buy a computer for your personal use, we may be able to provide letter-writing and other promotional services from the home office. This is a good start. We have a clear target.''

Glossary

A

abort Cancellation of an operation that has been initiated or is in progress.

absentee owner A person who invests in, but does not operate, a business.

access code An identification that controls a user's access to data.

account receivable An amount that is owed to a company in payment for a product or service that has been delivered.

address The unique storage position of a record retained on a magnetic disk device.

agrarian Related to farming.

air bill An invoice for airborne shipments.

American Standard Code for Information Interchange (ASCII) A digital code used for telecommunications transmissions and as the machine language of many microcomputers.

analog A signal in which information is represented by varying amounts of electrical current.

application A procedure, including programs, that applies a computer for a specific job or purpose.

application package A tool for implementing a user application; includes programs and procedures.

application program A set of instructions that controls processing of an individual user job.

application programmer A person who prepares programs for the processing of user jobs.

application software The programs that direct processing of user jobs.

arithmetic circuit An element within a CPU that processes electric current to perform calculations.

array *See* table.

ascending sequence Arrangement of records within a file in order from the lowest value of a record key to the highest.

ASCII (American Standard Code for Information Interchange) A binary code set used in data communication and as the machine language for many microcomputers.

asset An item of value owned by a business or person, including buildings, equipment, and money.

association A organization of companies and/or people with common interests.

audit An independent examination of a company's operations and information systems to verify accuracy and reliability.

authority The right, or power, to take actions to meet responsibilities.

authorized user A person who has a need or a right to access and use stored information.

automated warehouse A facility in which packages are transported, stored, retrieved, and delivered automatically —under computer control.

B

backlog Work that is pending completion or orders for which goods are pending shipment.

backorder An order for an item that is not in stock, recorded so that delivery can be made as soon as goods are available.

backup A copy of a file or program created to protect against possible loss of or damage to the original.

balance sheet A statement that shows the value of a business.

bar chart A graphic that compares values for two or more items presented through lines of different lengths.

barter A transaction based on the exchange of goods or services of equal value.

batch processing A technique under which groups of transaction data items are grouped and processed together as a working unit.

bill *See* invoice.

binary A number system with two values, 0 and 1.

binary code A set of instructions based on the values 0 and 1.

bit A binary digit with a value of 0 or 1.

bit mapping Formation of an image through control of black, white, or color values of individual pixels.

block mark To identify a portion of a file as a target for a DELETE, MOVE, or COPY operation.

board of directors The group whose members oversee planning for and operation of a company; the board delegates responsibilities for company operations to top managers.

bonded warehouse A facility that receives and holds imported goods and is permitted to collect tariffs when the goods are shipped to final destinations.

bonus Payments made to managers, and possibly other employees, on the basis of operating results delivered by a business.

boot The action that turns a computer on and loads needed software to support its operation.

bottom line The final entry on an income statement that shows profit or loss for the period covered by the statement.

break In shipping, a service that receives bulk shipments and selects items for local delivery.

brokerage A company that deals in securities.

budget A plan for receiving and spending money.

business A person or an organization that sells products or services to other organizations or to individual people.

business plan A set of projections covering future conditions of a business.

business unit Any facility or group that operates on its own.

byte A set of bits that represents one unit in a character set processed by a computer; can be letters, numbers, or symbols.

C

calendaring A service on a LAN in which the computer keeps track of appointments and schedules of multiple users and can, in some systems, block time for multiple persons for meetings or events.

capture Within an information system, the act of encoding and/or recording data for continuing use. *See also*, data capture.

carrier A connection, or link, over which signals are transmitted from an origin to a destination. Also, a company that transports people or goods by rail, ship, airplane, truck, bus, or automobile.

carrier return A command that causes an electric typewriter to move to the first position on the next entry line. Also called "return."

carrying charge A service fee related to a credit purchase.

cell A space at the intersection of a row and column, used for entry of values into a spreadsheet.

census A collection of data about a population.

central processing unit (CPU) The device within a computer that handles processing operations; consists of a processor and a main memory.

chain of command A term that describes the top-down structure of authority and responsibility within an organization.

chairman of the board The person elected by a board of directors to carry out its instructions in the operation of a company.

change An external occurrence that requires a reaction.

character printer An output device that imprints text one character at a time.

chief executive officer The highest executive in a company; often serves as chairman of the board of directors.

chief operating officer The person responsible for operations of a company; usually the president.

child node A low-level storage location within a hierarchical or network data model.

chip A miniature device that can contain an entire computer processor or can store thousands of items of data.

circuit board A sheet of electrically resistant plastic to which current-carrying circuits are bonded.

circular flow of money Description of the way money spent by a business circulates through the economy of the community in which the business is located.

circulation The distribution and readership of a publication.

civil service Reference to a system for administration of programs of governmental employment.

coaxial A telecommunication cable that contains multiple strands of wire and can establish many carrier links.

code of conduct A combination of beliefs and rules that a person follows in dealing with others.

collate A process used with punched card machines or computers to match data items from two separate sets in a planned sequence.

column On a punched card, a vertical position that can be encoded to represent a data value.

command economy An economy in which resources, production, and decisions about the productions to be made and markets to be served are made by government agencies.

commission A plan under which people are paid a percentage of the value of products they sell.

commitment In business planning, a firm agreement among planners that their goals can be achieved.

commodity code A classification of a product that serves as a basis for determining its shipping costs.

communications port A plug receptacle on a computer frame into which communications devices can be connected.

comparison A computer operation that matches values of two items to determine if they are equal or unequal and, if unequal, whether one is larger or smaller than the other.

compatible Usable on an interchangeable basis.

competition A situation in which two or more people or organizations attempt to supply products or services to the same consumers.

computer A set of connected devices that function together to process data and develop information.

computer-assisted design (CAD) Techniques for application of computers for development of design drawings and mathematical testing for new products.

computer-assisted instruction (CAI) An application under which a computer presents information to a student and monitors the learning that takes place.

computer-assisted manufacturing (CAM) Techniques that enable computers to use CAD files and other specifications to control operation of manufacturing devices.

computer conferencing Technique for holding meetings among persons who share computer access. *See also* groupware.

computer generation A time frame in which technology produces a computer with processing capacities 1,000 times greater than previous models, usually four to seven years.

computer graphics Reference to the ability of computers to generate images, as well as text outputs.

computer graphics software Sets of programs that enable a computer to generate images as well as text and data outputs.

computer information system (CIS) A group of resources used together to capture data and generate information.

computer-integrated manufacturing (CIM) Computer-controlled operations that extend to multiple manufacturing functions.

computer scientist A professional who designs software tools to facilitate use of computers.

computer terminal A device that communicates with a computer.

conglomerate A company that controls a number of smaller companies and tends to judge results on the basis of financial returns.

consignee The company or person to whom a shipment is addressed.

consolidate To combine information for ease of use.

constant Unchanging, steady.

consumer A person or organization that buys products or services from a business.

consumer co-op A cooperative owned by its customers.

containerization A method under which metal structures the size of truck trailers are shipped as units.

contingency plan A preparation for an action that can be taken to deal with undesirable or unexpected developments.

control circuit An element of a CPU that directs operation of computer hardware and the communication of information among devices that make up the computer.

controlled redundancy Principle of database organization that minimizes repetition of data items.

converter In the textile field, a company that produces thread or cloth from raw materials.

conveyor A system that carries people or products from point to point.

cooperative (co-op) A form of business organization that is owned by its customers or suppliers.

coordinator Person who oversees the conduct of a computer conference and assists participants.

co-processor A processing device that augments the main processor of a computer; a graphics card that forms images is a typical co-processor.

COPY An application software function used to copy text or data in one portion of a file to another location while leaving the initial entries in place.

copyright A protection assigned to an idea or created product by the U.S. or other governments. Copyrighted materials cannot be copied without permission.

corporate shield The legal protection against liability afforded to owners or employees of a corporation, which is legally responsible for acts of its owners or managers.

corporation An organization in which the functions of ownership and management are separated, with ownership represented by stock certificates.

correspondence Communication carried out in written form.

cost The price paid to secure a product or service.

credit A sales plan in which the buyer is given an extended time to pay for purchased items.

credit limit The greatest amount a customer is allowed to owe.

crop management A management specialty in the agriculture industry; involves decision making about the use of land and other resources.

cross-reference Referral of access operations between tables in a relational database.

cursor A blinking marker on the face of a display screen that identifies the point at which the next entry will be made.

customer A person or organization that purchases goods or services.

custom report A printout output that contains information requested specifically by a user.

cut An operation that removes a segment of text from a display and places it in a special memory area. The cut text can be deleted, moved, or copied.

D

daisy wheel A widely used imprint mechanism for letter quality printers.

data The basic facts that are processed and/or combined to generate information.

data capture Any technique for recording data for use in an information system.

data communications The ability to transmit and receive digital, computer-compatible information via telecommunication links.

data communications network A network dedicated to the exchange of information in digital format. *See also* network.

data element *See* data item.

data item One or more bytes used as a unit to represent a raw fact or figure that can be processed to generate information.

data processing Term that describes the methods and procedures for collecting, processing, and retaining data for status reporting and future reference.

data reduction The combining of data items and information to reduce the volume of items delivered to users. Data reduction adds meaning and value to information for the people who use it.

data security Protective measures that guard information against illegal or unauthorized use.

data structure A design for the organization and storage of data items within a database.

database A collection of data that is organized and stored so that any application program can access individual data items at any location within the files.

database administrator A person responsible for supporting use of and maintaining a DBMS.

database management systems (DBMS) Software that assembles, monitors, and manages use of one or more databases.

decision support system (DSS) A database-oriented set of programs that enables a manager to model the outcomes of several alternatives for each decision.

default A standard setting or value applied automatically by software; in a spreadsheet, the standard settings for column widths.

delegate To assign responsibility to another person.

DELETE An application software command used to remove text or data from a file.

deletion An operation that removes text or data from a document.

demand The total amount of a product or service that consumers are willing to buy.

demodulate A method for removing the analog formats and converting signals back to their original form. *See also* modem.

department A part of an organization that performs a single, special job.

descending sequence Arrangement of records within a file in order from the highest value of a record key to the lowest.

desktop computer *See* personal computer.

desktop publishing Techniques for design and development of publications through use of microcomputers; capabilities include typesetting, preparation of line illustrations, and page makeup.

destination The target for an access or search operation performed by a computer.

destructive backspace An optional setting that causes a computer to erase the character to the left of the cursor each time the BACKSPACE key is depressed.

detail In the information field, a reference to information source items that are generated in great quantities and cannot be analyzed without special processing.

Dictionary of Occupational Titles (DOT) A directory listing more than 200 industries and 20,000 job titles, published by the U.S. Bureau of Labor Statistics of the U.S. Department of Labor.

differentiation The selection or formulation of elements of a company's strategy that serve to determine products or services and markets, and that separate the company from others in its industry.

digit A place value in a number system.

digital Reference to codes and signals based on stop-start transmission rather than on varying amounts of electrical current.

direct access An information storage and retrieval technique under which records can be recorded and retrieved individually from any point within a file.

direct bit mapping Pixel image creation under direct user control. *See also* bit mapping.

direct-connect modem A communication processor that can be connected directly into a standard telephone jack. *See also* modem.

direct-mail sales A technique for offering products or services through the mail.

director A member of a board of directors.

directory A file that lists and describes the content of a secondary storage device.

discipline A group of professional firms that provides similar services to the same market.

discrete Separate, distinct; in electronics, a reference to circuits built through use of a series of individual devices.

discretionary An operation that is executed only upon specific instruction from a user.

disk drive A device that houses and uses magnetic disk media.

disk operating system (DOS) An operating system package that is supplied on disk; DOS is the most widely used operating system for microcomputers.

disk storage Reference to a method of storing data on and retrieving data from a storage unit that contains one or more platters that accept magnetic encoding.

diskette Flexible magnetic storage medium used mostly with microcomputers.

dispatcher A person who directs the routing of shipments.

distributed processing A technique under which a company puts its computing power at the points where it transacts business and uses information.

distribution center A facility that receives bulk shipments and distributes products to local destinations.

distribution channel A series of steps followed in transporting and delivering products from point of manufacture to final destination.

distributor A company that provides sales and delivery services as part of the normal routine of delivering products to customers.

dividend Corporate profits distributed to shareholders.

docketing The scheduling of cases for trial in courts.

document A group of data items or text prepared for presentation to a user.

documented Completion of a transaction through the recording of information, often on a special business form.

downloading An operation in which information is transmitted on a LAN from a central minicomputer or mainframe to a microcomputer.

draft A preliminary version of a document that still needs work.

draft quality Description of a printing capability that uses a matrix device to generate images of relatively low quality.

draft quality printer A character printer that produces text through imprints of dot-position patterns; finished documents are usable as drafts but are not of "letter quality."

drawing program A software tool that provides capabilities for producing vector graphics images on microcomputers.

driving force The element of strategy that is most important in determining the products or services developed and the markets served.

dumb terminal A device with a keyboard and a display that does not have its own processing or storage capabilities.

dynamic In a state of constant change.

E

EBCDIC (Extended Binary Coded Decimal Interchange Code) A binary coded machine language for large computers, particularly those made by IBM.

economies of scale The savings or efficiencies that can be realized in purchases or production as volumes increase.

economy All buying and selling activities, or exchanges of value, within a region or country.

edit An operation in which an existing document is changed or revised.

effectiveness A measure of results, or values produced.

efficiency A measure of how well a job or function is performed.

electronic funds transfer Use of computers to complete banking transactions, including the transfer of funds.

electronic mail An operation in which messages are transmitted on a network from original to destination points, with interim storage in "electronic mailbox" files as necessary.

electronic spreadsheet A software application package for preparation of spreadsheet reports.

electronic tooling The software and instructions that control manufacturing processes.

emulate Within a business strategy, an approach that calls for waiting until new products or services are introduced and proven before entering the market.

engineer A person who applies technology to design and build products.

entity Name for a specific table within a relational database.

entrepreneur A person who innovates and takes risks in business.

exception An information item that identifies a condition that is outside the normal limits set by managers.

exchange of value The basis for a transaction; the seller and buyer each receive satisfactory value to cover a purchase.

expectation Something you think will happen in the future.

expense In business, the total cost of operations or for delivery of a good or service sold to a customer.

expert system A system that uses a computer to imitate human decision making processes to help establish courses of action.

exploration In the petroleum industry, the function of searching for oil deposits and drilling wells.

extended care A reference to long-term care that usually is provided following discharge from a hospital after major surgery or a serious illness.

extension A code appended to a file name to identify its purpose or function.

external direct-connect modem A modem that can be plugged into a telephone jack but is external to the computer it supports. *See also* direct-connect modem.

extrovert A person who is "outgoing" and enjoys the company of others.

F

facilitator *See* coordinator.

facility A place in which work is done; in a CIS, an actual location where hardware is installed.

feedback Information that compares actual results with plans.

fiber optic A communications carrier that transmits messages as bursts of light which are used to represent information.

fictitious name A name taken as an identity of a business.

fictitious person The legal status of a corporation; a corporation has an identity of its own and the same responsibilities as any citizen.

field *See* data item.

file A collection of records with matching formats and related information.

file creation program An application program used to develop transaction or master files, usually through entry of items in positions on display screens.

file organization Reference to the method used to sequence records within a computer-maintained file.

finished goods inventory A supply of products for which manufacturing has been completed and are ready for delivery.

firmware Program segments stored on read-only memory hardware devices for constant availability to the computer.

fixed asset Facilities, equipment, inventories, or other items that have value but are not easily converted to cash.

fixed costs The regular, recurring expenses of the business.

flex time A plan that enables employees to vary work hours and schedules.

floppy disk *See* diskette.

formal strategy A stated strategy developed through a special effort by managers.

format The design or arrangement of a group of data items to form a record.

formula A command that instructs the spreadsheet program to calculate values from a group of identified cells.

forwarder A specialized shipper that routes bulk shipments; a forwarder acts as a middleman between shippers and freight carriers.

fourth generation language (4GL) A set of commands that enables a user to prepare processing instructions that use information in a database; a 4GL makes it possible to develop applications without requiring the writing of traditional application programs.

franchise A right, or assignment, that permits one business to use the name of another.

freight bill An invoice that meets the specifications of the transportation industry.

function A required business operation or responsibility that is assigned to a specific person or department.

function key A key on a computer keyboard that calls up a function of an operating system or application program.

G

general ledger A set of files that contains data on the financial condition of a company.

general partner The partner who undertakes management duties and is responsible for the operation of a limited partnership.

Generally Accepted Accounting Principles (GAAP) A published set of standards that cover the methods to be followed and the content to be included in preparing financial statements.

global An option under a SEARCH/REPLACE function that acts upon all occurrences of a target set of characters within a file.

glossary A set of definitions of terms used in a publication such as a textbook.

goals In business, targets, or plans, to be achieved by an organization.

good *See* product.

graphic A pictorial presentation of information.

graphics card A circuit board placed in the computer processor to control the creation and output of graphic images.

graphics tablet Device that provides capabilities for direct input of images drawn on a touch-sensitive surface.

grid A series of equally spaced horizontal and vertical lines placed over a display area.

Gross National Product (GNP) The total value of the goods and services produced by a nation.

groupware Software that supports concurrent entries of ideas and suggestions from multiple points by persons taking part in a computer conference. *See also* computer conferencing.

H

hard copy *See* printout.

hardware Computer equipment, inclusively.

health care The industry that cares for persons with illnesses. Includes hospitals and ''extended care facilities'' such as nursing homes.

health care provider A person or organization that provides medical services, including patient care.

hierarchical database model A plan of organization that structures data items in a top-down manner for implementation under a hierarchical database.

hierarchy An organization or set of data organized in a top-down manner.

hierarchy chart A diagram that represents a set of top-down relationships, such as an organization chart.

highlight A technique used to block mark a segment of copy for further use.

histogram *See* bar chart.

hospitality industry The industry that takes in all businesses that provide food and lodging accommodations.

horizontal industry A group of companies that provides similar services that can be used by companies in diverse fields.

host language A language included within a DBMS that can be used to generate repeatable programs or routines involving use of the database.

human resources Name of the business function responsible for recruiting, hiring, and training personnel.

I

icon A picture that represents a function or service that the computer can provide.

image In business, the way an organization is seen by its employees, its customers, and others.

imitation A type of strategy that waits until products are introduced and proven, then develops copies.

import In computer operations, a reference to the ability to find materials prepared under another software package and access them for inclusion in outputs for an active program. Also, the receipt of products made in a foreign country into a destination country.

income The money received from selling products or services, or from other sources.

income statement One element of a company's financial statements that shows money received and expenses paid.

index A table within a relational database that is used to locate data items in other files.

Industrial Revolution Period of rapid development of manufacturing and introduction of work-performing machinery.

industry A group of companies that provides similar products or services to the same market.

informal strategy A strategy that develops without planning, through the beliefs and actions of managers.

information age Name given to the current period, in which most people work with and depend on information.

information avalanche A condition in which information is generated at rates faster than the ability of people to handle and deal with the total volume.

information custody An assigned responsibility to maintain and protect data resources to assure their continued accessibility by users.

information overload A condition in which people receive more information than they can use productively or interpret. *See also* information avalanche.

information owner User who generates information or for whom information resources are created and maintained. Information is said to belong to its users.

information processing The handling and organization of information for access by or delivery to users. *See also* data processing.

information processing (IPOS) cycle A sequence of operations followed in processing or transforming data into information; consists of the basic steps of input, processing, output, and storage.

information resource management (IRM) A concept that treats information as an asset of a company and manages information assets for support of operations and management.

information society A condition in which most workers in an area deal with information on their jobs.

information system A series of steps followed in sequence to deliver planned reports or to make information accessible to users. *See also* system.

information worker A person who creates or requires information on the job.

infrastructure All of the support capabilities required by a region.

innovate As part of a business strategy, a commitment to develop and introduce new, original products or services.

innovation A type of strategy that stresses development of new or different products or services.

input The process followed to capture data in a computer in usable form.

INSERT An application software function that provides the ability to add words, phrases, and sentences without destroying or altering the appearance of existing text.

inside sales Transactions that take place at the stores, offices, or factories of selling companies.

install To enter a program into memory for user access.

installment A time payment against a credit purchase.

insurance policy A document that describes the risk protection to be provided to an insured person or organization.

integrated circuit A device in which electrical circuits and electronic components such as transistors are created and positioned as part of a single manufacturing process.

integrated software A special set of programs that provides access to multiple, separate application packages.

integration The elements of a company's strategy that identify it with a given industry or type of business, helping to identify the company's products or services with a given market. Also, a software capability for including data and text from multiple application packages into coordinated outputs.

intelligent terminal *See* smart terminal.

interactive An operational condition in which both the computer and the user participate in processing.

interchangeable part A part of a product that will fit any device of the same make and model.

interest A charge (or payment) for the use of money.

intermediate-range plans Plans intended for implementation in time frames such as one to four years.

internal direct-connect modem A modem that can be plugged into a telephone jack that is built onto a circuit board and can be plugged into a computer. *See also* direct-connect modem.

interview A personal conference used for gathering information.

introvert A person who tends to be quiet and who generally prefers to avoid meeting or working with strangers.

inventory Items that are being held in storage for sale or use in a manufacturing operation.

inventory level The number of units of a given stock item in inventory at any given moment.

invoice A document that records information on a sales transaction.

J

job stream A set of related transactions that follow in sequence.

joint venture An organization formed by two or more persons or businesses to do just one job or to operate in a special, limited area.

K

keyboard   A set of keys that represent letters, numbers, and symbols that is used for computer input.

L

label   In a spreadsheet, an entry that can be the title of a spreadsheet or an identifier for a column or row.

labor intensive   Description of a business in which payroll represents the major expense.

laser   A beam of intense light that is transmitted through air or special tubes; lasers can carry sound and digital signals.

laser printer   *See* page printer.

law of supply and demand   A set of principles indicating that prices and supplies of products or services adjust to the willingness of consumers to pay for them.

ledger   A file that contains information on a single account that relates to the financial condition of a company. *See also* general ledger.

letter quality   Descriptions of imprints that equal the quality of outputs from electric typewriters.

letter-quality printer   A character printer that produces high-quality outputs, usually at slower speeds than draft printers.

liability   Legal responsibility for individual or business actions. Also, an amount owed by a business or person preparing a balance sheet to a vendor or lender.

light pen   A graphics input device that can sense a point of light placed on a display screen under software control.

limited partner   An investor in a partnership who is not active in management and assumes only limited, defined responsibilities to the organization.

limited partnership   A form of organization that assigns limited roles and responsibilities to some partners and gives other partners the right to run the organization.

line art   An illustration composed entirely of lines, with no tonal values; can be created under vector graphics software.

line function   A person, department, or group that holds direct responsibility for producing products or delivering services to customers.

line graph   A graphic that portrays trends by connecting value points on a grid with straight lines.

line printer   An output device that imprints a full line of type in a single operation; generates documents at speeds of up to 2,000 lines per minute.

liquid asset   Cash or items that can be converted easily to cash.

list   Action by a real estate agent that records the availability of a property for sale or rent.

literacy   The ability to read.

load   An operation that reads software or files into memory to prepare a computer for use.

local area network (LAN)   Multiple computers and support devices linked through communication lines, with all of the facilities located in the same building or in a single location.

logic circuit   An element within a CPU that compares two values and directs the course of processing on the basis of results of the comparison.

logic programming   The mathematical principles that provide the basis for development of expert system software. The computer matches a set of conditions presented by a user with a series of statements stored in the computer.

logical model   A plan for organizing, storing, and accessing data within a database.

logical organization   The arrangement of data within a database as seen from a user perspective.

long-range plans   Plans intended for implementation over extended time periods, such as five to seven years.

luxury   A product or service purchased for enjoyment rather than for necessity.

M

machine language   A set of binary codes that represent the native language of a computer; machine language is written in strings of 0 and 1 values.

magnetic disk   A storage medium that uses magnetically coated platters for the recording and storage of information.

magnetic tape   A storage medium that uses long strips of magnetically coated materials for the recording and storage of information.

main directory   A directory maintained by a hard disk that identifies the data directories stored on the device.

main memory   A high-speed storage device that supports computer processing.

mainframe   A large-scale computer with extensive processing and communication capabilities.

management by exception (MBE)   A system in which information identifies and directs management attention to problems.

management information system (MIS)   A system that provides information designed to support management analysis and decision making. An MIS is created by summarizing transaction information and applying management-by-exception principles.

management science A discipline that studies the management of businesses and instructs students in the principles of business management.

management style The approach or methodology followed by a manager in evaluating operations, reaching decisions, and establishing policies.

manager A person responsible for operation of and/or decision making about a business.

manufacture To put together from a series of parts.

manufacturing function The operating unit or department that makes a company's products.

market All of the demand by all of the consumers who might need or want a given product or service.

market economy An economy in which private businesses are free to determine the resources they will use, the products they will make, and the markets they will serve.

market segment A portion of a market that can be identified separately as a target for business transactions.

marketing *See* sales.

markup The difference between the cost and selling price of an item.

master file A group of records that represent, or model, a portion of a business.

materials handling Any method used to move products or materials.

mathematical operation *See* formula.

matrix printer *See* draft quality printer.

mature In regard to an industry, one that has become established and generally recognized in the marketplace.

medium of exchange One of the values exchanged during a transaction; money is the most common medium of exchange.

megabyte Approximately one million characters.

member Term for an owner-participant in a cooperative.

memorandum, memo A text document intended for internal communication within an organization.

menu A list or display of choices that presents a series of choices for selection by a computer user.

menu bar A series of user options presented across a horizontal bar of a screen display.

microchip *See* chip.

microcomputer A self-sufficient computer that fits on a desktop and uses a microchip as its main processor.

microwave A radio-type carrier that uses special wave forms that deliver high quality signals.

minicomputer A mid-sized computer that has most of the capacity of a large system at lower costs.

model An image, or replica, of some object or operation. An information model represents the status of an organization through organized sets of information.

modem A device that converts computer signals to telecommunications code for transmission, and reverses the process to receive transmitted signals for computer processing.

modulate The formation and transmission of special analog signals. *See also* modem.

module A portion of a program for which input, processing, and output elements can be designated.

monitor A display device that presents information for user reference.

monochrome monitor A computer display that presents images in one color only.

monopoly A condition in which one company controls business in one industry to a degree that lessens or eliminates competition.

mouse A small device that rolls around on the tabletop alongside the computer as a tool for moving the cursor and selecting menu options.

MOVE An application software function used to move text or data from one location in a file to another.

multiple listing A service that distributes information to real estate agents about property listings.

N

near letter quality Description of a capability of some matrix printers to create imprints of improved quality through multiple impressions.

need Necessity required by consumers.

net worth The value of a business or the total assets of a person, as reflected in one of the totals of a balance sheet.

network A group of computers and other devices linked through communication channels for access by multiple users from multiple points.

network model A database structure in which nodes are linked directly to provide access in either upward or downward patterns; searches may begin at any level within the network structure.

newly industrialized countries (NICs) Countries that have had a relatively low state of industrial development but are advancing rapidly. Examples include South Korea, Singapore, and Hong Kong.

node A data storage location within a hierarchical or

network data model. In data communications, a sending-receiving station within a network.

non-liquid asset *See* fixed asset.

numeric keypad The portion of a keyboard designed for high-speed input of numeric data.

numerical control A method that controls metalworking through a system of numbered positions and execution of standard operations.

O

objective An external, or unbiased, view of a person or issue.

Occupational Outlook Handbook (OOH) A detailed review of job trends and prospects, published by the U. S. Bureau of Labor Statistics.

Occupational Outlook Quarterly (OOQ) A magazine that covers the job market, published by the U. S. Bureau of Labor Statistics.

off-line Reference to data files that are stored on media that are not currently mounted on drive devices.

on-line Reference to the ability of a user to gain immediate access to a computer system from a terminal via a telecommunications link.

open-to-buy report An exception report that lists inventory items with stocks that are below established reorder levels.

operating system A set of programs that monitor and coordinate the operations of the hardware devices that make up a computer system.

operational plan A plan that covers the short range, the current year.

operations manual A published set of instructions for operating an information system.

organization In business, a combination of the people, places at which they work, equipment they use, and the instructions they follow.

organization chart A diagram that shows a company's organization structure.

organization plan A set of assignments that identifies the jobs that have to be done and shows how those jobs relate to one another.

organization structure A document or understanding that positions departments within an organization.

orientation A program that introduces new employees to the policies, procedures, and facilities of an organization.

output The transmission of data items from a computer CPU to devices that record, print, or store information for reference and use by people.

outside sales Transactions conducted in the customer's place of business by a sales representative who travels to deliver products or services.

overhead Basic expense of doing business.

P

page printer An output device that imprints a full page of text or images in a single operation. Functions through use of a laser beam that forms images on a xerographic drum.

paint software Computer graphics technique that enables the user to produce bit-mapped graphics with tone or color values.

palette In computer graphics, a menu that offers choices of tone or color values for user application.

pallet A platform, usually made of wood, on which boxes of products are stacked.

parallel processor A computing device with multiple microprocessors that make it possible to execute more than one instruction at a time.

parameter A boundary or limit; an information value that is used as a checkpoint for reporting items as exceptions.

parent node A high-level storage location within a hierarchical or network data model.

partnership A business owned by two or more persons who may, but need not, be involved in management.

partnership agreement A legal contract that presents terms for formation and operation of a partnership.

peripheral A connected device that supports operation of a computer.

personal computer A small computer, also called a microcomputer, that uses a microchip as its processor.

personal identification number (PIN). A user entry that permits access to computer files; used with automatic teller machines.

personality The image you present to others, composed of and controlled by your appearance and your code of conduct.

physical organization The arrangement of data on a storage device as viewed in terms of equipment requirements.

physical security Measures that protect storage media and their information against destruction.

picture element *See* pixel.

pie chart A graphic image that portrays a total value and shows the percentage relationships of its parts.

pixel A point within a display or output that plays a role in forming a picture; tens of thousands of pixels are needed to form a one-page image.

plan Projections for future conditions and steps to be taken in the future to deal with expected situations.

plotter A graphics printer that creates images with computer-driven drawing instruments.

point-of-sale transaction recording Method for recording source data as an integral part of transaction processing.

point-to-point transmission A type of data communication that links only two points for the sending and receiving of digital data.

post The entry of transaction data to update a master file. *See also* update.

prediction A forecast covering future developments.

prefabrication Techniques for building sections of structures in factories for erection on building sites.

presentation graphics Pictorial materials used at meetings or other gatherings.

president The person responsible for operations of a company; the president is responsible to the chairperson and to the board of directors.

primary key A field that has a different, unique value for each record in a file.

primary storage *See* main memory.

print element The mechanism of a letter-quality printer that holds a pre-formed set of characters used in creating imprints.

printer A computer output device that records information or images on paper for delivery to users.

printout A computer output printed on paper.

private sector Portion of the economy that consists of privately owned businesses.

pro forma In reference to financial statements, a document that projects the future results of business operations.

pro forma financial statement A set of information that predicts income, expense, and profits of an organization for a future time period.

procedure A set of instructions followed to use a tool or device. In information processing, the instructions followed to process data and develop information.

procedures manual A document that presents instructions for job performance.

processing Operations within a computer that handle and/or transform data, including calculations, comparisons, or combinations among data elements.

processor The portion of a central processing unit that

has circuits for execution of arithmetic, logic, and control functions.

producer co-op A cooperative owned by its suppliers.

product A physical object that can be used by people.

product design The activities connected with creation of a new product prior to manufacturing and marketing.

profession A field with qualification requirements that can include advanced degrees and special licenses.

professional corporation A special form of business organization available to professional persons.

profit The money earned by a business; the difference between income and expenses.

program A set of instructions that controls the operation of a computer.

program design A step-by-step process that can be followed to define, design, and develop an application program.

programming language A set of instructions that can be understood both by people and computers.

prompt A message displayed by a computer that requests action by a user.

proprietorship A business that is owned and operated by an individual.

prototype A full-scale, operational model of a planned product.

provider *See* supplier.

public sector Portion of the economy that includes all government agencies.

punched card A standard-sized card into which holes are punched to represent values of data. A method of recording and capturing data for future processing by machines and/or computers.

purchase order A formal order for goods that is sent directly to a supplier.

Q

query An operation in which a user makes a direct request for information from a computer.

query command An instruction entered by a user as part of an information access query.

query language A set of commands that enables a computer user to instruct the system to find needed information and to prepare that information to meet user needs.

R

random access Description of a storage method that makes it possible for a computer to record or read individual records, without requiring processing of entire files to support each reference function.

random access memory (RAM) A device that permits access to any storage position. *See also* direct access.

range On a spreadsheet, a group of cells identified for a SUM operation.

rate To determine the basis for shipping charges.

read-only access A DBMS protective measure that permits some users to access specified records but not to alter them.

read/write head A device that records and reads data on magnetically coated surfaces of magnetic tapes or disks.

real time A description of a computer response time. A real-time response is completed within the normal cycle of the transaction being processed. Real time can vary with the nature and urgency of individual transactions.

receipt A document that records delivery of money or goods.

record A group of related data items that describes a person, place, thing, event, or idea.

record key The field within a record that identifies the record uniquely and can be used to identify and position the record within a file.

recording The entry of transaction information on a business or into a computer for inclusion in the company's information processing and/or accounting systems.

recovery A plan for re-creating and making available data resources that are destroyed through use or accidental event.

reduced instruction set computer (RISC) A computer with a command set that is smaller than that of a general-purpose computer. The reduced instruction set makes possible greater processing speeds.

redundancy In a database, the duplicated use of the same data item in multiple files.

refiner A company that inputs crude oil and produces finished petroleum products, such as gasoline or lubricating oil.

regulatory agency A government agency that monitors compliance with laws that control delivery of services, profits, and prices in specific industries.

relation A file within a relational database.

relational database A database that consists of a series of tables that can be used in coordination under DBMS software control.

reorder level The inventory level at which new supplies of an item are ordered.

report to To be responsible to or to work for a person.

requisition A purchasing request form.

resources In business, the money to be made available and facilities to be developed for the operation of a company.

response time The elapsed time between entry of and instruction into a computer and completion of the operation.

responsibility An assigned job that a person is required to complete.

restart A set of procedures used to restore services of a computer center following an interruption.

retail Description of an operation that sells products directly to consumers.

retailing The industry that specializes in selling goods to consumers.

retrieve In information processing, the reading or recall of stored information.

return The result delivered to a user by a computer following execution of a comparison operation.

return on investment (ROI) Earnings that result from the money and other resources put into a company; usually stated as a percentage.

revenue The money received by a business.

revision *See* edit.

ring network A multiple-station data communications link in which transmissions move through all nodes in the system.

robotics A technology under which entire manufacturing operations can be controlled through use of computers.

route To establish the path of travel for a shipment.

row On a punched card, a horizontal position that can be encoded through punching to represent the value of a column position.

rule of 80-20 A principle governing the value of information: 20 percent of the information items have 80 percent of the value, and 80 percent of the items have 20 percent of the value.

S

safety stock Extra supply of an inventory item to protect against running out.

sales The function of a business that is responsible for completing transactions with customers.

sales receipt A document prepared by the seller and given to the buyer as a record of a transaction.

satellite office An outlying office that is closer than downtown facilities to the homes of many workers; set up to shorten commute times and locate offices in areas with lower rents.

scanner   An input device that can read and enter bit-mapped values for graphic processing.

scheduled report   A printout with specified information content that is printed at regular intervals.

scope   In a CIS, a term that defines a range of activity or information content.

scrivener   A person trained to produce attractive hand-written documents.

SEARCH   An application software function used to seek a specific set of characters within a text file.

search criteria   The values used to locate required records within a file or database.

SEARCH/REPLACE   An application software function that searches for a set of characters within a text file and replaces the target characters with another set.

secondary key   Any field in a record that adds information or meaning to the primary key; need not be unique.

secondary storage media   Magnetically coated materials, such as disks or tapes, on which data are recorded for retrieval and continuing use.

segment   A basic part of a business that requires special skill or experience.

self   A combination of elements that make up your personality and the image that you present to others.

selling price   The value of a product or service on which the seller and buyer agree.

sequential access   An information retrieval pattern in which all records in a file must be read and processed in the order in which they are stored. Sequential access is essential to tape storage.

sequential storage   Description of a storage method in which all records are recorded and read in a planned sequence, one after another. All records must be read and rewritten each time a sequential file is processed.

serial organization   Reference to a computer file in which records are entered chronologically, as data items are originated. Used to create transaction files.

service   An act performed by a *supplier* that has value to a customer.

service sector   The portion of the economy that includes all private companies that deliver services and also all government agencies.

shareholders' equity   The value of the shareholders' ownership interest in a business. *See also* net worth.

shipper   The company or person that originates a shipment.

shop loading   Procedures for planning and scheduling work to be performed in a manufacturing plant.

short-range plans   Plans to be followed during a current operating time frame, such as one year.

shortage   A condition in which demand for a product or service exceeds supply.

silent partner   A part owner of a partnership business who is not active in management.

simulate   Use of a computer to imitate conditions for product use and to test a product before it is manufactured.

smart terminal   An on-line workstation that has its own processing and storage capabilities.

software   Reference to all of the programs that control operation of a computer.

sole proprietorship   *See* proprietorship.

sort   To arrange records in sequence according to ascending or descending order.

source   A position or person from which information originates.

source document   A hard-copy record used to provide input on a transaction to an information system.

SPELLCHECK   A function of word processing software that compares words within text with a stored dictionary and highlights any differences.

spreadsheet   A form or report with multiple columns for entry of financial information.

spreadsheet program   An application package that controls the creation of reports structured into fixed sets of columns and rows.

staff job   A position that is not directly involved in producing products or serving customers; provides support to line personnel.

star network   A multiple-station data communications link in which all transmissions are through a central computer that serves as a hub, or switch, for the transfer of messages.

statement   A document that tells a buyer an amount to be paid to a seller. Statements usually are issued after products are delivered or services are completed.

statement of changes in condition   One element of a set of financial statements that reflects changes in assets, liabilities, and equities since the previous reporting period.

status   A condition that exists at a given point in time. An information model states the operating and financial condition of an organization.

status line   A line at the top or bottom of the screen that identifies the file in use, the page number, and the position of the cursor.

stockholder   A person who holds a certificate that represents ownership of a company.

strategic plan   A plan that foresees the condition of a company in the long-range future, perhaps five to seven years.

strategy   A set of guidelines that establishes the identity, or image, of a company.

strength   Something a person enjoys doing and does well.

structure   A plan of organization for data items that results in a record format and in specifications for relationships among groups of records.

stylus   A pen-like device that draws images on a computer plotter.

subjective   A way of looking at yourself or at issues from your own viewpoint; your own view often does not match the image perceived by others.

subsystem   A set of procedures that fits within a larger system.

summarize   To develop totals for multiple information items to derive meaning from large volumes of data items.

summary   A total or recap that reduces the volume of information items and helps managers to analyze conditions or situations.

supercomputer   An ultra-high-capacity computer used to provide the productivity needed by large companies or scientific laboratories.

superconductivity   A condition in which resistance and heat generation of electrical conductors is virtually eliminated.

superconductor   A device that carries electrical current with reduced resistance to achieve greater efficiency at higher speeds from use of devices such as computers.

supplier   A business or person that delivers a product or service to a customer.

supply   The total amount of a product or service that is available.

switch   A central computer within a data communications network that accepts all transmissions and transmits messages to their proper destinations.

synthetic   Imitation or artificial; in the textile industry, description of fibers made from chemical compounds.

system   A set of related parts that function together to produce a planned result.

system programmer   A programmer who specializes in writing system software.

system software   The set of programs that initiates, controls, and monitors operation of computer equipment.

systems analysis   A professional specialty for identifying and solving problems through the use of information, including the design of information systems.

systems analyst   A professional in systems analysis; a person who identifies information needs and develops systems to meet those needs. *See also* systems analysis.

T

table   A set of items arranged in set positions, usually columns and rows.

tab stop   A setting that causes the cursor to move to the selected position when the TAB key is depressed.

tactical plan   A plan that deals with the intermediate time frame, one to four years.

tally   The operation that develops totals for a group or list of data items.

tape drive   A device that houses and uses magnetic tape as a recording medium.

target   A set of characters that is the object of a SEARCH operation.

tariff   A tax on imported products.

tax   A payment to a government agency by a person or business as required by laws.

telephone sales   Transactions in which the buyer calls the seller or the seller calls the buyer to offer products.

terminal   A distribution facility in which packages and materials are transferred between vehicles.

text file   A file created to handle unstructured strings of characters without specific formats.

text processing   *See* word processing.

tooling   The accessories needed to manufacture a product, including the fixtures that hold parts during production, drills, molds, and patterns that guide and control manufacturing.

top-down planning structure   A system under which plans originate at the highest level in an organization, then are carried forward by managers at lower levels.

touch sensitive   Refers to the ability to sense and transmit information based on points at which a surface is touched by a sharp instrument.

touch tablet   *See* graphics tablet.

track   A circular position on a magnetic disk that is used for the recording and storage of data.

transaction   A basic act of doing business; usually involves delivery of goods or services in exchange for something of equal value.

transaction document   *See* sales receipt, source document.

transaction file   A group of records that describe individual transactions produced during a brief business period.

transform   To change or add to data items to generate information; transformation occurs when data items are combined or when new items are created through computation.

transistor   An electronic device that controls the flow of electricity or the storage of binary coded data.

tree structure   Description of a hierarchical data model.

turnover   In terms of human resources, the rate at which employees quit their jobs. Also, in terms of inventory, the time period in which a given number of items should be sold. Turnover also is measured in terms of the number of ''turns'' per year of a store's total stock.

tutorial   A package of instructional materials that can include demonstration software and always includes user and reference manuals.

U

update   An operation in which the content of a file is altered to reflect current transactions.

uploading   An operation in which information is transmitted on a LAN from a microcomputer to a central minicomputer or mainframe.

user friendly   Reference to a computer system that is considered easy to use because of the software tools that are provided.

user, information   A person who requires information for job performance.

user's manual   A set of descriptions and instructions designed for guidance in use of a product or software package.

V

value   A data item entered into a cell of a spreadsheet.

variance   A difference between a planned and an actual result.

vector   A mathematical term used to define a line segment that has direction.

vector graphics   A mathematical technique used to draw lines and shapes.

vertical industry   A group of companies that use the same raw materials or resources to serve a select, specialized group of customers.

vertical integration   A company that performs several functions in connection with developing and marketing products.

vice president   A person who reports to the president and is responsible for oversight of a portion of a company's operations.

voice mail   A system for storing and delivering spoken telephone messages through use of computers.

volatile   Description of a property of computer memory; when power is turned off, memory is cleared of all stored information.

volatility   Description of an item with a short life, subject to rapid evaporation. The term usually is used to describe chemicals such as gasoline that evaporate rapidly. Also can refer to a product with a short life, such as an uneaten meal or an unoccupied hotel room.

W

want   A product or service a person likes to have but does not actually need.

warehouse   A building that stores and handles goods.

WATS (Wide Area Telephone Service)   A plan that permits extended, sometimes unlimited, telephone calling privileges under special, volume-discount fees.

weakness   Something a person does not enjoy doing and may not do well.

wealth   Money, facilities, and other resources used to create jobs and produce incomes for employees and owners.

wholesale   Sales transactions conducted with companies or people who are not consumers, but are purchasing and stocking products for sale to consumers.

windowing   A technique for integrating information from multiple applications; access is provided through sets of overlapping displays that establish access windows.

word processing   A computer application that processes unstructured strings of text.

word processor   An application program that sets up a computer for processing of text.

word wrap   The ability of a word processing program to sense the end of an entry line and move automatically to the beginning of the next line.

work-in-process file   A set of records covering work that is in process in a manufacturing plant.

workstation   A workstation is a place where a person performs most of his or her daily activities.

Index